Countries, Peoples & Cultures

Central & South America

Countries, Peoples & Cultures

Central & South America

First Edition

Volume 1

Editor

Michael Shally-Jensen, PhD

SALEM PRESS
A Division of EBSCO Information Services, Inc.
Ipswich, Massachusetts

Publisher's Cataloging-In-Publication Data
(Prepared by The Donohue Group, Inc.)

Central & South America / editor, Michael Shally-Jensen, PhD. – First
  edition.

   pages: illustrations; cm. – (Countries, peoples & cultures ; v. 1)

  Includes bibliographical references and index.
  ISBN: 978-1-61925-800-6 (set)
  ISBN: 978-1-61925-788-7 (v. 1)

   1. Central America – History. 2. Central America – Economic conditions. 3. Central America – Social life and customs. 4. South America – History. 5. South America – Economic conditions. 6. South America – Social life and customs. I. Shally-Jensen, Michael. II. Title: Central and South America

F1408.C46 2015
972.8

First Printing
PRINTED IN CANADA

Contents

Publisher's Note

Countries, Peoples & Cultures: Central & South America is the first volume of a new 9-volume series from Salem Press. *Countries, Peoples & Cultures* offers valuable insight into the social, cultural, economic, historical and religious practices and beliefs of nearly every country around the globe.

Each 20-page country profile includes colorful maps—one highlighting world location and one with major cities and natural landmarks—and country flag, and 10 categories of information: General Information; Environment & Geography; Customs & Courtesies; Lifestyle; Cultural History; Culture; Society; Social Development; Government; and Economy. Each profile also includes full color photographs, valuable tables of information including fun "Do You Know?" facts, and a comprehensive Bibliography.

Each country profile combines must-have statistics, such as population, language, size, climate, and currency, with the flavor and feel of the land. You'll read about favorite foods, arts & entertainment, youth culture, women's rights, health care, and tourism, for a comprehensive picture of the country, its people, and their culture.

Appendix One: World Governments, focuses on 21 types of governments found around the world today, from Commonwealth and Communism to Treaty System and Failed State. Each government profile includes its Guiding Premise, Structure, Citizen's Role, and modern-day examples.

Appendix Two: World Religions, focuses on 10 of the world's major religions from African religious traditions to Sikhism. Each religion profile includes number of adherents, basic tenets, major figures and holy sites, and major rites and celebrations.

Countries, Peoples & Cultures will be published in 9 volumes throughout the year, as follows: *Central & South America; Central & Southeast Asia; Western Europe; Eastern Europe; Middle East & North Africa; East & Southern Africa; West & Central Africa; North America & the Caribbean;* and *East Asia & the Pacific.*

Introduction

Central and South America are two regions that, along with North America, form that great band of continental landmasses known as the Americas or, alternatively, the New World. The two regions have long been important to the United States (and, earlier, to the American colonies) and today play a central role in the global economy.

Central America consists of seven nations: Belize, Costa Rica, El Salvador, Guatemala, Honduras, Nicaragua, and Panama. The region is mountainous in the interior and includes several active volcanoes; earthquakes are fairly frequent. Along the coasts there are extensive lowlands and humid swamps. The climate is largely tropical, although cooler in higher elevations. The chief commercial crops are coffee, cacao, and bananas, but much else is exported besides. More than two-thirds of the population is of mixed European (primarily Spanish) and indigenous descent, the vast majority of them Roman Catholic. Many, however, blend their Catholicism with traditional folk religion. Spanish is the majority language, with pockets of indigenous languages. Central America suffers from chronic economic and political problems, owing, in part, to the legacy of a landowning system that divides the populous into wealthy elites and poor masses. Despite such problems, the region is culturally rich.

The original inhabitants were indigenous peoples. Among them were the Maya, who developed a great civilization between AD 250 and 900. The Spanish arrived in the early 16th century and ruled for the next 300 years. In the 17th century the English arrived, settling what became British Honduras (later, Belize). By 1821 Spanish rule had come to an end, and shortly thereafter (1823) the United Provinces of Central America (Costa Rica, El Salvador, Guatemala, Honduras, and Nicaragua) were formed. (Panama remained part of Colombia, and British Honduras did not join the federation.)

A constitution was adopted in 1824 but remained operative only until 1838, when the federation broke up. A series of cooperation agreements were drawn up, in 1923, at a Washington, DC, conference on Central America. Some forty years later (1960) the region moved toward economic integration under the Central American Common Market, which today is part of the broader Central American Integration System (an organization for regional cooperation). Meanwhile, from the 1950s through the 1980s numerous military coups and counter-coups occurred within the individual countries, some of them assisted by the United States. That legacy persists today, even as the governments and the citizens of the various Central American nations work to leave that violent past behind them.

South America, by comparison, is much larger and more diverse as a region, even while its constituent nations share many commonalities among them and the region, as a whole, is culturally and historically linked to Central America. South America is marked geographically by the presence of the Andes Mountains, which extend along a north-south axis through much of the western half of the continent, paralleling the Pacific coast. The highest point on the Andes chain is Mount Aconcagua (22,837 ft; 6,961 m) in Argentina; indeed, Aconcagua is the highest mountain outside of Asia. The Andes widen in Bolivia and Peru, in the north-central region, forming multiple ranges and a high plateau—the altiplano—that gave birth to the great civilization of the Incas. South America also has great expanses of lowlands, including the tropical plains running along the Orinoco and Amazon rivers. The Amazon region itself represents the world's largest rain forest area and is host to a vast array of wildlife and numerous indigenous peoples. Other notable plains regions include Paraguay's Gran Chaco and Argentina's Pampas, both known for their drier conditions, fertile areas, and cattle raising traditions. Much of South America lies within the tropics, yet because of variable elevations and the sheer extent of the landmass, significant temperate, arid, and cold zones exist as well.

The countries comprising South America are Argentina, Bolivia, Brazil, Chile, Colombia, Ecuador, Falkland Islands, Guyana, Paraguay, Peru, Suriname, Uruguay, and Venezuela. (French Guiana is a country-sized overseas department of France.) Many of these countries are rich in industrial metals (iron, copper, tin), and some (e.g., Venezuela) have significant oil deposits. Commercial crops include bananas, citrus fruits, sugar, and coffee; corn, wheat, and rice are also grown. Power is supplied in most of the populated regions by hydroelectric works. South America has one of the fastest growing populations in the world, and that population is increasingly urbanized. The most populous South American nation by far is Brazil, which occupies about a third of the continental landmass and holds about half of the continent's people. Sao Paulo not only is Brazil's largest city but is also the largest city in the Americas (population 11.9 million; 20.3 million in the metro area), surpassing Mexico City and New York City. Other major South American cities include Buenos Aires (Argentina), Río de Janeiro (Brazil), Lima (Peru), Santiago de Chile (Chile), and Bogatá (Columbia).

The four major ethnic groups inhabiting South America are the Iberians, or the Spanish and Portuguese who arrived as explorers and conquerors in the 16th century; the Amerindians, or indigenous peoples; the Africans who were brought in as slave labor between the late 17th and 19th centuries; and the various European, South Asian, and other populations that arrived more recently. The majority of South Americans are Roman Catholic and Spanish-speaking, but in Brazil the principal language is Portuguese. Other religions include Evangelical Protestantism and indigenous and folk religions. Other languages include English (Guyana; the Falklands), Dutch (Suriname), French (French Guiana), and hundreds of indigenous languages.

Sizeable populations of descendants of German, Italian, and French immigrants live in Argentina, Chile, and elsewhere. As in Central America, a great gap between the rich and the poor exists throughout much of South America. Most of the countries rely on the free-market system, with Chile regarded as a leader in this regard; but, in general, there is a mix of partially centralized and private-enterprise economies. Venezuela has a largely socialist economy.

The Inca Empire was still quite strong when the Spanish arrived in the mid-1500s and quickly destroyed it. Owing to competition between Spain and Portugal for the acquisition of new lands, under the Treaty of Tordesillas (1494) the continent was divided between the two powers, with Portugal given license to conquer what is today Brazil and Spain given license to do the same in the rest of the region. As a result, the native peoples were decimated. Most of those who survived were reduced to serfdom, even while a blending of European and indigenous bloodlines occurred throughout the earlier era and into the modern one (producing the so-called Mestizo). By the early 1800s the European powers had lost their dominance, as the countries of the region began to gain independence and to adopt a republican form of governance. Continuing socioeconomic inequalities led to a number of revolutions and counter-revolutions, and various border disputes produced wars between neighboring nations. After World War II, all of the South American nations joined the United Nations, and most of them (save Guyana) joined the Organization of American States, a sociopolitical union. The Latin American Free Trade Association was established in 1960. Today, South America still struggles to emerge from its colonial past even as it has made great strides to advance toward a new and different future.

Culturally, Central and South America are linked together under the umbrella term Latin America. Since independence in the 1800s, art and culture in the region have developed along national lines as well as regional, or pan–Latin American lines. There has been and continues to be significant cultural interaction in Latin America, more so than many other multinational regions of comparable size. This is owing to the common historical roots of the various nations and the dominance of Spanish and the closely related Portuguese language and culture in most of the region. The area's colonial origins favored the intermixture and assimilation of peoples and local cultures. Especially in Brazil, a sort of "racial democracy" developed, even while ethnic distinctions continued to be made. Thus, Latin America, in the modern era, represents a cultural synthesis, a synthesis that is played out in the arts, popular music, folklore, social traditions, and intellectual life. The growth of the mass media in recent decades, including radio, television, motion pictures, and the Internet has only speeded the process of cultural cross-fertilization within the region. Yet each country, each locality, can point to its particular cultural traditions and unique customs to set it apart from the others and mark it as a unique nation within the Latin American community. This combination of distinctiveness and interrelatedness is largely what the present volume seeks to explore, doing so on a country-by-country basis.

Michael Shally-Jensen, PhD

Bibliography

Booth, John A., Christine J. Wade, and Thomas W. Walker. *Understanding Central America: Global Forces, Rebellion, and Change,* 6th ed. Boulder, CO: Westview Press, 2015.

Hillman, Richard A. and Thomas J. D'Agostino, eds. *Understanding Contemporary Latin America,* 4th ed. Boulder, CO: Lynne Rienner Publishers, 2011.

Jackiewicz, Edward L. and Fernando J. Bosco, eds. *Placing Latin America: Contemporary Themes in Geography,* 2d ed. Lanham, MD: Rowman & Littlefield, 2012.

King, John, ed. *The Cambridge Companion to Modern Latin American Culture.* New York: Cambridge University Press, 2004.

Sullivan, Lawrence E., ed. *Native Religions and Cultures of Central and South America.* New York: Continuum, 2002.

Williamson, Edwin. *The Penguin History of Latin America.* New York: Penguin, 2010.

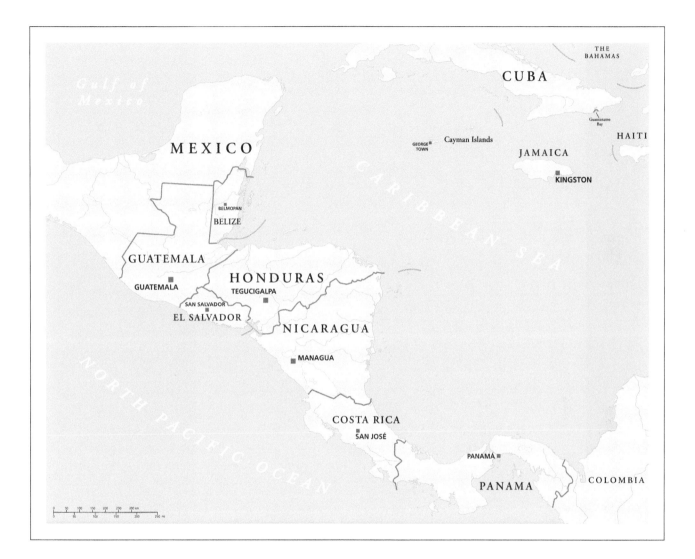

CENTRAL AMERICA

Fishing port in Haulover Creek Canal in Belize City, Belize/Stock photo © bilgehan yilmaz

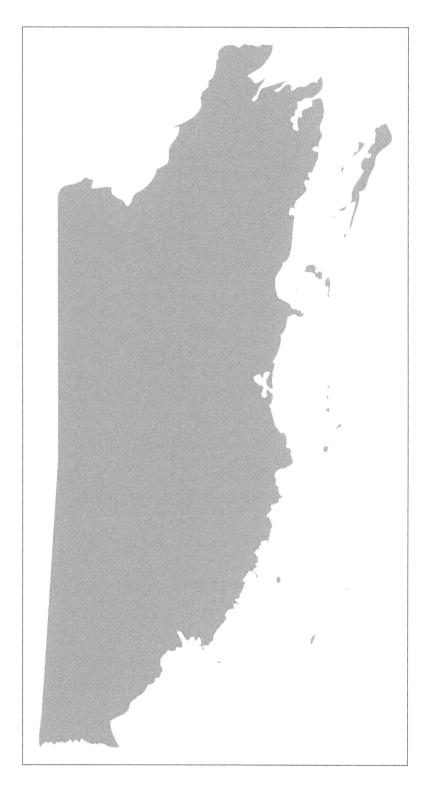

BELIZE

Introduction

Belize is the second smallest country in Central America. Bordered by the Caribbean Sea to the east, Mexico to the north, and Guatemala to the west and south, the country is an independent member of the British Commonwealth. Before 1973 it was known as British Honduras. The country gained independence in 1981.

Comprised of sub-tropical mountainous jungle and swampland, Belize is relatively undeveloped. In recent decades, Belize has become one of the premier eco-tourism destinations in the world, and is visited by over a million tourists each year.

GENERAL INFORMATION

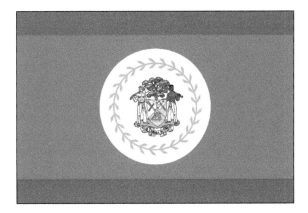

Official Language: English
Population: 340,844 (2014 estimate)
Currency: Belizean dollar
Coins: The Belizean dollar is subdivided into 100 cents. Coins are available in denominations of 1, 5, 10, 25, and 50 cents, and one dollar.
Land Area: 22,806 square kilometers (8,805 square miles)
Water Area: 160 square kilometers (61 square miles)
National Motto: "Sub Umbra Florero" (Latin, "Under the Shade I Flourish")
National Anthem: "Land of the Free"
Capital: Belmopan
Time Zone: GMT -6

Flag Description: The flag of Belize is blue with narrow bands of red across its top and bottom. In the flag's center is a white circle on which a coat of arms is featured. The coat of arms is surrounded by a garland of green mahogany leaves. The colors red and blue represent the country's two major political parties: the PDP and the UDP.

Population

Approximately 50 percent of the population of Belize is Mestizo, which is a mixture of Spanish and Maya Indian ancestry. Mestizos speak Spanish and live in the interior of the country. Creoles (African-European) comprise 25 percent of the population and live in the central coastal region. Mayan Indians, who also live in the interior of the country, comprise 11 percent of the population, and the Garifuna, who are a mixture of African and Caribbean, comprise six percent. The Garifuna were once called Black Caribs.

Principal Cities by Population (2014 estimate):

- Belize City (60,184)
- San Ignacio (20,027)
- Belmopan (18,326)
- San Pedro (15,484)
- Orange Walk (13,692)
- Corozal (11,427)

About four percent of the population is Caucasian, the remaining four percent is classified as "Other."

Small populations of East Indians, Arabs, Africans, Chinese, Americans, and Europeans also live in Belize. In addition, there is a sizeable population of Mennonites who are of German/Dutch origin and speak a German dialect.

Belize is the least densely populated country in Central America. It has only a handful of sizable towns. The largest is Belize City with a population of just over 60,000. This main port city was initially the capital of the country until a hurricane destroyed the area in 1961. Afterwards, the capital was moved further inland, to Belmopan.

As of 2011, approximately 45 percent of the country's total population lived in urban areas.

Languages
The official language is English. However, Spanish is also prevalent and has been used more widely since independence. Spanish, in fact, has become a mandatory part of many school curriculums and many Belizeans value bilingualism. Most Belizeans also speak a Creole dialect. Some segments of the population also speak Mayan and Garifuna.

Native People & Ethnic Groups
There are more than a dozen Mayan ruins within Belize. However, the Maya origin of Belize has been complicated for centuries by the colonial influences of the Spanish and British.

Belize was a center of Maya civilization between 300 BCE and 1000 CE. (The peak of the Maya civilization occurred between 250 and 900 CE.) The first European visitors to the area were Spanish explorers, who arrived during the 16th century. However, their efforts to convert the native Mayans to Christianity were unsuccessful, and Spain failed to settle the region. In the mid-17th century, Britain had more success exploiting the area's logging resources. In 1862, British Honduras became an official colony of the crown. The British used the country primarily for sugar cane harvesting fueled by slave labor.

The Mestizo (Spanish-Mayan) now represent close to 50 percent of the population of Belize, as well as Latino refugees and immigrants from nearby countries.

Religions
The majority of the population is Christian. Nearly 40 percent of the people are Roman Catholic, 34 percent are Protestant, 14 percent are non-Christian, and the remainder, indicated no religious preference, on the 2010 census.

Climate
Belize's hot and humid climate is subtropical. The Caribbean trade winds that moderate the subtropical temperatures along the coast do little for the interior of the country, where the capital of Belmopan reaches highs of over 37.7° Celsius (100° Fahrenheit) in the summer. The rainy season lasts from May to November, and the dry season lasts from February to May. Rainfall varies greatly, averaging 1,295 millimeters in the north (51 inches) and 4,445 millimeters (175 inches) in the south. These totals are also affected by autumn trade winds from the north, which bring drier air.

Hurricanes strike Belize regularly between June and November. The country is also prone to coastal flooding in south. Belmopan serves as an important hurricane refuge site for coastal communities.

ENVIRONMENT & GEOGRAPHY

Topography
The northern section of the country is mostly limestone lowlands and swamp. The topography in the south is almost the exact opposite, comprised of mountain ranges such as the Maya

Mountains. The country's highest point is at Doyle's Delight (1160 meters/3,805 feet).

In the north, the Hondo and New rivers flow into Chetumal Bay and drain the northern lowlands. The Hondo River also forms the country's northern border with Mexico. The Belize River flows through the center of the country. Belize City is located on this river.

There are several coral reefs, called cays, off the coast of Belize. The Belize Barrier Reef is the longest in the Western Hemisphere.

Plants & Animals

In addition to the numerous deciduous and hardwood trees, there are also mangrove trees located near the coastline, and pine trees, palmettos, and savannah grassland in the south coastal plain.

Animals commonly found in Belize include deer, crocodiles, manatees, pumas, and jaguars. The tapir, also known as the "mountain cow," is the national animal of Belize. It is not actually a cow, but is related to the rhinoceros and the horse. Weighing up to 270 kilograms (600 pounds), it is the largest land mammal in Central America.

The Cockscomb Basin Wildlife Sanctuary, opened in 1986, has the world's most concentrated population of jaguars. It covers 1,024 square kilometers (395 square miles) of land near Victoria Peak.

CUSTOMS & COURTESIES

Greetings

Over 75 percent of Belizeans speak a form of English creole or "kriol." Though most of the words are recognizable to English speakers, there is a distinct difference in pronunciation. A typical greeting is "Weh di go aan?" ("How are you?" or "Hello"), which is the commonly used phonetic translation of the kriol phrase. The phrase "Gud maanin" ("Good morning"), is often used before noon. In most Belizean schools, the use of Belizean kriol is discouraged. However, there has been a recent movement to protect kriol as a legitimate language.

Belize also has a significant number of Spanish speaking communities. Individuals in the Spanish and Mayan communities may use Spanish greetings such as "Buenos días" ("Good morning"), "Buenas tardes" ("Good afternoon"), and "Buenas noches" ("Good evening"). The simplified greeting "Buenas" ("Good") may be used in informal circumstances.

In general, visitors often classify Belizeans as a friendly and outgoing people. Even minor acquaintances will stop to greet each other in passing. Though simple, verbal greetings are most common. Friends usually shake hands while close friends may embrace or pat each other on the arms, shoulders, or back. Women may kiss each other on the cheek as a form of greeting, but this is usually reserved for close friends. Within the traditional Maya communities of Belize, interactions between men and women are discouraged and physical contact is typically rare.

Gestures & Etiquette

In formal conversation, Belizeans will use titles in addition to surnames, but generally first names are used among acquaintances and friends. In comparison to some Central American cultures, Belizeans engage in less physical contact during conversation. However, Belizeans do not observe any strict rules regarding personal space and often stand close to one another when interacting. Eye contact is avoided in social situations except among close friends, a behavior that is most likely inherited from the British. In addition, it is considered rude to ignore even minor acquaintances in passing.

When hailing or beckoning a person, Belizeans tend to wave the entire hand up and down rather than relying on the movement of the fingers. As in many Central American cultures, Belizeans tend to use a wide variety of facial gestures to communicate. Wrinkling the nose, for example, is a gesture meaning "I don't understand."

Eating/Meals

Most Belizeans eat three meals a day. A light breakfast early in the morning is typical, with the most common component of the morning meal consisting of beans, either red or black, which may be accompanied by eggs, fried meat, and fruit. Coffee and fruit juice are also commonly served with the morning meal.

The midday meal, usually served between noon and 2 pm, is typically the largest meal of the day. Meat and wild game are common in Belizean cuisine, as are certain varieties of seafood, especially in coastal areas. Many Belizeans may set aside between one and two hours for the midday meal and a short rest period before returning to work. The evening meal is often less substantial than the midday meal, though many of the dishes are similar. In rural communities, families may serve leftovers from the afternoon meal in the evening.

Beer and liquor are commonly served with both the afternoon and evening meals. While many Belizeans drink casually with meals, there is no social stigma associated with refusing an alcoholic drink at mealtime.

LIFESTYLE

Family
Belizeans tend to live in close proximity to extended family, including aunts, uncles, and grandparents. Children generally remain in their parents' homes until marriage, and thereafter may choose to stay close to their parents. It is not uncommon for several generations to live in the same town or village and for older generations to take a significant role in childrearing while both parents work outside the home.

Family planning has been on the rise in Belize since the 1980s. The nation's largest reproductive education, planning, and information agency is the Belize Family Life Association (BFLA), which operates six centers around the country. These centers provide pregnancy tests and health screenings for children and mothers, in addition to a variety of other services. Abortion is legal in Belize but only under certain circumstances, including protecting the life of the mother, and is not allowed in the case of rape or by request. Additionally, sociological studies from the latter half of the 20th century found that the rate of illegitimacy among children is higher in Belize than most other Central American countries. The proportion of males who leave Belize to find work is a contributing factor to rate of unwed motherhood.

Housing
Because Belize has a relatively small population in relation to the amount of available land, home ownership is fairly common among the middle class. Most Belizean homes are constructed of a combination of wood and concrete. Bricks are not manufactured in large quantities, and are therefore expensive and rare. Some poor, rural families live in basic houses made from stone or plaster with thatched roofing and dirt floors.

Vast majorities of Belizean homes are built with zinc or aluminum roofing material, and only wealthy families can afford tile or slate. In coastal cities and towns, flooding is a major problem, and many homes are built on stilts to protect the interior of the home from floodwaters. Erosion is a more difficult problem for families who own property on the coast, as unstable soil can lead to the necessity for frequent home repairs.

In urban areas, home and apartment rental is more common. In an effort to promote housing for low-income individuals, the Belizean government has initiated programs to sponsor rental and leasing fees and to provide mortgage and repayment assistance. Belize also has a significant problem with homelessness, resulting in the establishment of informal settlements or shantytowns, and further initiatives are required to provide low-cost housing options for poor citizens.

Food
Belizean food is a blend of Caribbean, Mexican, and African influences, along with culinary traditions borrowed from the English and Spanish during the country's colonial period. An abundance of tropical ingredients, such as coconuts and plantains, has also contributed to the development of a unique local cuisine. Rice, beans and

locally grown vegetables are traditional staples, and are served with most meals. In fact, whether served as an accompaniment or as a main dish, rice and legumes (beans) typically form the backbone of Belizean cuisine. These are commonly eaten with beef, chicken, pork, and fish. There are varieties of Belizean dishes that call for red beans cooked with meat, such as oxtail or ham, and then mixed with rice.

A common dish served in Belize, often as an appetizer, is the conch fritter. The basic recipe involves cooking strips of conch, a type of mollusk common in the coastal waters around Belize, in balls of dough with peppers and onions. Conch fritters are common at restaurants and are one example of the extensive use of seafood in Belizean cuisine. A typical breakfast dish, called fry jacks, consists of deep fried dough served with beans or butter and jam. Similar to the Mexican sopapilla, the fry jack may also be served dusted with sugar, or with sweet honey. Some restaurants serve savory fry jacks with meat and cheese.

An unusual dish served in Belize is gibnut stew, which is made from the flesh of the paca, a rodent slightly larger than a rabbit that is a common food item in Central and South America. The stew is made with a variety of vegetables and generally flavored with salt, pepper, and sometimes a hot salsa or pepper sauce. Gibnut stew is a traditional Garifuna dish and is similar to a number of dishes served by other Caribbean tribes. Another common Garifuna dish is hudut, a stew made from seafood served in coconut milk and usually accompanied by plantains. Restaurants in Belize often serve gourmet versions of traditional dishes such as hudut and gibnut stew.

Life's Milestones

Rites of passage in Belizean society typically differ according to ethnic affiliation. The Garifuna, for example, are predominantly Catholic and follow the major Catholic traditions, including baptism, communion, and marriage rites. The Maya and Mestizos follow traditions similar to those of Catholic populations in Mexico or other Central American countries. In Maya culture, a girl's 15th birthday, or quinceañera as it is often called in some Latin American countries, is usually accompanied by a large, festive celebration that marks the young woman's transition to adolescence or maturity.

In Belizean society in general, marriage is the traditional mark of the transition to adulthood. Most Belizeans continue to live with their parents until they are married, and home ownership generally follows marriage. In contemporary Belizean society, many young women, and men, choose not to be married, but live together nonetheless in common law unions.

In Garifuna tradition, parents choose godparents for their children shortly after birth. This custom often coincides with baptism. In general, godparents play an important role in Belizean culture by forming links between unrelated families. For example, godparents often donate to the dowries of newly married couples, may sometimes aid in child rearing, and also participate in family celebrations. Additionally, birthdays and holidays are times for family gatherings in Belize, and are often accompanied by feasts with music and dancing.

CULTURAL HISTORY

Art

Most Belizean artists, whether working in paint, sculpture or other media, typically use Belize's natural resources as the inspiration and primary subject of their work. Paintings and sculptures of flora and fauna are common in the Belizean art scene, both as commercial, fine and folk art.

During Belize's colonial period, art representing Caribbean and Mayan culture was largely discouraged and repressed by colonial authorities. They feared that unification of the artistic community could fuel a revolutionary movement. A revivalist movement began in the 1960s and led to a resurgence of interest in the history of Belizean cultural development. Painter and musician Pen Cayetano (1954-), in particular, is recognized as one of the most respected and successful native painters. One of his key goals as an artist is to preserve the culture of Garifuna people. As such, many of Germany-based Cayetano's artworks have themes derived from Garifuna folklore and oral history.

One artistic tradition closely linked to African slaves is the craft of traditional wooden sculpture. Working primarily with hard woods like ziricote, a red-brown exotic wood, traditional woodcarvers produced abstract sculptures, animal figures, and detailed realistic sculptures. Belizean Mayans also have a vibrant sculptural tradition and there are several contemporary artists carrying on this work. Among these, the Garcia Sisters in the city of San Antonio have gained the most widespread attention, and their sculptures, largely created from native black slate, are in high demand.

Architecture

Belize is home to a wide variety of architectural styles resulting from its ancient, colonial, and post-colonial periods. Ancient Mayan ruins are located throughout the country. Two famous Mayan ruins are Altun Ha (located north of Belize City) and Cahal Pech (located in San Ignacio). Some Mayan structures, such as temples, have been restored and are present-day tourist attractions.

Traditional tropical architecture in the form of raised wooden huts is common in Belize. These huts, which are a common form of residence in the country, usually include two verandas and two bedrooms, as well as a kitchen.

Colonial architecture can be seen today in Belize City, particularly in the Southern Foreshore and Fort George regions of the city. Churches such as Sacred Heart Church in San Ignacio and Our Lady of Mount Carmel in Benue Viejo are also examples of Spanish colonial influence. The Old City Jail, built in 1857 (then called Her Majesty's Prison), became, in the early 21st century, the location of the Museum of Belize.

Drama

Theater arrived in Belize alongside its Spanish and British colonizers. Contemporary native playwrights of Belize include George Gabb (1928-) and John Alexander Watler. Their works often touch on social and political issues, such as post-colonialism and racism, and their role in modern-day Belizean society.

Music

The geographic location of Belize—on the Caribbean coast of Central America between Mexico and Guatemala—has played a major role in forming the nation's culture. Belize was colonized by the Spanish in the 16th and 17th centuries, resulting in a hybrid Mayan and Spanish heritage. After the arrival of the British, Belize became a haven for pirates and privateers. Additionally, thousands of Africans were brought to Belize as slave labor for the agricultural industry. As a result, Belize is home to a "creole" culture, which includes elements of Caribbean, African, and European tradition. Though little is known about Belizean music before the arrival of Europeans, the native music of Belize is characterized by its multicultural origins.

The Garifuna, a population of mixed Mayan, Mexican, and Central American heritage, have played a significant role in the development of Belizean art and music. Garifuna musical traditions are at the core of traditional and contemporary Belizean music. Among these forms is "punta," a genre that is similar to Latin music, but unique in its rhythmic and melodic patterns. While considered a traditional form of music, punta has remained popular with Belizean youth. A number of modern variations have been created, including punta fusion or punta rock. The latter, which features fast rhythms and electric instruments, is widely considered Belize's national music.

Punta fusion first became popular in the 1970s and is recognized by the use of electronic percussion and other non-traditional instrumentation, generally blended with more common types of instruments. The development of punta fusion is linked to the work of Delvin "Pen" Cayetano (1954–), who is recognized as a pioneer in Garifuna music. Modern artist Andy Palacio (1960–2008), who was one of Belize's most popular musicians, was a leading punta artist also known for his efforts to research and develop traditional Garifuna music styles.

Another native form of music that has persisted to modern times is "brukdown," a musical style that combines a number of dissimilar European traditions with African rhythms. Similar to American jazz, bluegrass, and zydeco (a style of American folk music), brukdown places emphasis on improvisation and creativity. Belizean Wilfred Peters (1930–2010), a popular brukdown artist, toured internationally with his brukdown orchestra and helped introduce Belizean music to the rest of the world. He is often referred to as the "King of Brukdown," and is regarded as a national icon.

Literature

Belize has not produced a library of work that can be seen as constituting a native literary tradition. One of the difficulties in establishing a native literary movement is that many of the Caribbean, Native Central American, and African cultures that were absorbed into Belizean culture had oral rather than written traditions. The earliest writings of note were religious texts produced by British monks and religious scholars during the colonial period. In the modern era, some Belizean writers have attempted to commit the oral histories and legends of the Garifuna and Maya to written form. These stories, collections of fables and poetry, are the first evidence of an emerging literary tradition.

Zelma "Zee" Edgell (1940–), an associate professor at Kent State University, is the most famous Belizean writer to publish on an international scope. Her first novel, *Beka Lamb* (1982), provides a fictionalized account of the nationalist movement in Belize when it was under British rule and known as British Honduras. Another modern writer who has achieved national and international acclaim is Evan X. Hyde (1947–), a journalist and short story writer whose work is

rife with political and social commentary. Hyde and Edgell have contributed to collections of Belizean fiction and non-fiction, and are active in promoting native literature to an international audience.

CULTURE

Arts & Entertainment

Unlike other countries with a mix of diverse ethnic groups, there is no history of animosity between the different ethnicities in Belize. Instead, the different cultures have combined to form a vibrant local arts and entertainment culture. Belize's multicultural nature, for example, has created an interesting amalgam of North American, Latin, and Caribbean music. "Punta rock" mixes reggae and soca with hip-hop and salsa. "Brukdown" is a sort of street percussion that uses bottles, cans, garbage bins, and other objects as instruments.

Though many Belizean towns and cities boast large artistic communities, art education is rare, and few resources are typically used in the promotion of local art and culture. The fine arts community is largely concentrated in Belize City, which contains a small but vibrant gallery district. Government funding is available for artists whose work is seen as helping to preserve Mayan or Carib culture. In addition, there are several galleries in the Cayo District specializing in Maya art.

The National Institute for Culture and History (NICH) in Belmopan, established in 2003 as part of the Ministry of Culture and Tourism, is the organization responsible for supporting arts education and development. The four departments under the NICH include the Institute for the Creative Arts, Institute of Archaeology, Institute of Social and Cultural Research, and the Houses of Culture. Through their Houses of Culture program, the Belizean government promotes concerts and other promotional activities designed to promote native art, music, and other cultural heritage.

Cultural Sites & Landmarks

Belize City is the nation's largest city and primary port. As the former capital, it is home to numerous cultural sites and landmarks (the government relocated the national capital to the city of Belmopan

Belizean coral reef

in 1970, after a hurricane ravaged Belize City in 1961). The Fort George Lighthouse, which is located off the coast of Belize City at the entrance to Belize Harbor, is perhaps the city's most recognizable landmarks. The lighthouse was part of an 18th-century French fort, separated from the city by a small creek. Near the lighthouse sits the Baron Bliss Memorial, a building created under a fund donated by Baron Henry Edward Ernest Victor Bliss (1869–1926), a wealthy British baron largely considered Belize's national benefactor (he left most of his fortune to the country upon his death).

Belize City is also home to the oldest Anglican church in Central America, St. John's Cathedral, which itself is also the oldest building in Belize. Built in the early 1800s from bricks made of the ballast from visiting ships, the cathedral retains much of its original structure, though it has been renovated to repair weathering damage. The Museum of Belize, opened in 2002, is built on the site of one of the country's first colonial prisons. The prison was built in 1857, and parts of the original structure remain intact. In addition, the National Museum contains exhibits on archeology, culture, and natural history. The city is also known for its colonial style architecture.

Belize is also famous for its pre-Columbian history. The Maya were once spread out across Belize, flourishing in the country until 900 CE, when the civilization began to mysteriously decline. In fact, Belize is home to over 600 sites related to the Mayans, including the oldest known Mayan site. Many of Belize's best-known Mayan archeological sites are located in the Cayo District, which surrounds Belize City. Xunantunich (Maya for "old white woman") and Caracol are two of the most famous Mayan sites in Belize. Both sites contain remnants of stone architecture from the Mesoamerica's Classic period (250–900 CE). Though most of Belize's archeological sites have been documented and studied by archaeologists, only the most significant, such as Xunantunich and Caracol, are protected by the government as part of the nation's cultural heritage.

The Belizean coast contains the largest coral reef system in the Western Hemisphere. The entire barrier reef system is preserved under government law and, in 1996, was designated as a World Heritage Site by the United National Educational, Scientific and Cultural Organization (UNESCO). Along with numerous aquatic habitats—representing a breeding habitat for thousands of fish, invertebrates, and aquatic reptile species—the reef system zone also contains mangrove forests, coastal lagoons, and estuaries. Additionally, Belize's ocean habitat has made the country a popular destination for ocean explorers and scuba divers.

Libraries & Museums

The Museum of Belize, located in Belize City in a former colonial prison, serves as the national museum, opened in 2002. It features an extensive collection relating to the Mayan civilization. Other museums of significance in the country include the Maritime Museum, also located in Belize City, and which focuses on the fishing and boating building heritage of the country.

Belize's national library is also located in Belize City. The Belize National Library Service and Information System (BNLSIS), which oversees the public library network, consists of 39 service-points nationwide.

Holidays

In addition to the traditional Christian holidays, Belizeans celebrate Independence Day (September 21), Baron Bliss Day (March 9), Commonwealth Day (May 24), St. George's Cay Day (September 10), Garifuna Day (November 19), and Boxing Day (December 26).

Youth Culture

Music and dance plays a major role in Belizean youth culture. Dance clubs are enormously popular with teenagers and college students, and form a central component of the nation's recreational options. Dance clubs often play electronic music, with punta fusion and brukdown which is also popular. In recent years, hip-hop culture and funk fusion music have become increasingly popular among young Belizeans, and an underground music scene has developed in Belize City. In addition, young people in cities, where imported films, programming, literature, and music are more common, have more recreational options available to them.

Sports are popular for young Belizeans, with fútbol (soccer) being the most popular sport in the country. In addition, the government supports the establishment of youth sports clubs as a way of helping Belizean youth to avoid drug use and criminal activities and to develop healthy social networks. Belize Youth Soccer is the largest organization supporting instruction and soccer competitions for Belizean youth. Belize also has a number of scouting organizations attracting children, pre-teens, and adolescents to camps across the country. Similar to scouting organizations in the U.S.—such as the Boy Scouts of America—Belizean scout organizations conduct team-building activities, encourage community involvement, and allow for safe social interaction while learning about the society and ecology. The largest scouting organization in the country is the Scout Association of Belize, which was established in 1988.

SOCIETY

Transportation

Public buses are the most affordable option for transportation. There are bus lines that serve all of the major metropolitan areas and extended routes that service rural areas. Though the bus system is fairly extensive and widespread, many locations are only accessible by hiking a short distance from the nearest stop. Belizean transport companies commonly use decommissioned passenger buses and/or school buses imported from the United States.

Many types of vehicles are used as taxis in Belize; their green license plates can identify all legitimate taxis. Taxis never include meters and passengers need to negotiate price in advance, typically before entering the taxi. Most taxi companies are headquartered in urban areas but will usually travel a considerable distance from their central location. Booking private transport can be the most convenient way to reach remote destinations, but is usually more expensive than traveling by public bus.

Traffic moves on the right-hand side of the road.

Transportation Infrastructure

Belize has an estimated 2,872 kilometers (1,785 miles) of roads, but only 488 kilometers (303 miles) are paved. There are a number of small airports in Belize offering affordable city-to-city transport. The country's only international airport is located in Belize City and offers connecting flights to a variety of international locations. For travel along the coast, many choose to use boat and ferry transport. Boat travel is affordable and runs on a frequent schedule, thereby providing an excellent option for alternative travel.

Media & Communications

There are no daily newspapers in Belize and the most frequent publications are available on a weekly or monthly schedule. In addition, many Belizean publications are financed and, to some extent, controlled by political parties. All local newspapers are published in English but there are several imported, Spanish-language publications available, especially in the Cayo district, which boasts a large population of Mayans. While political influence is widespread in the publishing industry, the government does not censor content and allows criticism of official policy through the news media.

The largest print publications in the country are published from Belize City, and include *Belize Times* and *The Guardian*, both of which are published weekly, and *Amandala*, which is published biweekly. The *Belize Times* is widely regarded as an instrument of the People's United Party (PUP) of Belize, and often publishes articles in support of party policies. *The Guardian* newspaper is the main competitor of the *Belize Times* and supports the rival United Democratic Party (UDP). *Amandala* is a private newspaper with less political influence than the other major news sources. It is considered the largest circulation newspaper in the country.

Belize had no television coverage until the 1970s, and there were few local broadcast options until the 1980s when the Belize Broadcasting Authority was formed to regulate the industry. Cable television became available in the mid-1990s. By 2008, cable coverage was common in cities and Internet service had also become well established, though still relatively expensive. In addition, as of 2010, an estimated 19 percent of the population was considered as Internet users.

Belize also has a number of public and private radio stations, most of which are headquartered in Belize City and Belmopan. Some radio stations are closely aligned with major political parties, influencing their broadcast choices. The government decided to privatize the broadcast industry in the 1990s and this has led to an explosion in media options. The nation's largest radio station, Love FM, is a private station that broadcasts commercial and talks radio programs, and is funded by commercial income.

Standard of Living

Belize ranked 84th out of 187 countries on the 2013 United Nations Human Development Index, which compiles quality of life and standard of living indicators.

Water Consumption

Belize has significant reserves of groundwater and surface water. Approximately 70 percent of water used in urban areas is from groundwater sources. In 2012, 94 percent of the country's urban population and 387 percent of its rural population had access to sanitation facilities. In 2012, it was estimated that 99 percent of the country's population had access to improved water sources.

Education

In Belize, there is free, compulsory schooling for children ages six to 14. In the late 1990s, there were 280 primary schools and 30 secondary schools throughout the country. Most schools are run by churches, while the rest are run by the government.

Although only a small portion of the population receives higher education, Belize has a variety of post-secondary schools. These include the University College of Belize, and the School of Continuing Education, which is maintained by the University of the West Indies. There are also several technical and vocational schools, including the two-year Belize Teachers College and the Belize Technical College.

The average literacy rate in Belize is 77 percent—76 percent for men and 77 percent for women).

Women's Rights

Generally, women's rights in Belize have not been a matter of national concern. The penal code prohibits rape and domestic penalties, and recommends strict punishment. In addition, there is no distinction made between spousal rape and other types of rape, and all cases carry penalties between eight years–to–life imprisonment. However, monitoring agencies have found that authorities are less likely to investigate and penalize spousal rape.

Domestic violence remains the most significant problem, despite substantial penalties imposed under the penal code. Furthermore, social mores often prevent women from bringing cases of abuse to the authorities. Statistical analyses indicate that reports of domestic abuse are becoming more common, which is attributed to a greater willingness to report crimes rather than an increase in incidence. While prostitution is legal in Belize, it is illegal to operate a brothel or to solicit prostitution. Though prohibitions against organized prostitution are intended to protect women from exploitation, some critics believe that the penal code also prevents sex workers from operating in a safe and secure manner.

Belize has a number of laws aimed at promoting gender equality and preventing discrimination. However, monitoring agencies regularly report that women have fewer employment opportunities and are less frequently offered chances for advancement. Additionally, reviews of major corporations indicate that women hold fewer management positions.

Health Care

Medical care in Belize has improved in recent years, due in part to increased government funding for child care and hospitals. There have also been improvements in sanitation and water supply. The government also established a social security program during the 1980s. The infant mortality rate is 20 deaths for every 1,000 live births. The life expectancy at birth is 67 years for males and 70 years for females (2014 estimates).

However, there is a shortage of doctors, particularly in the rural areas. The country has a network of seven district hospitals, as well as the Belize School of Nursing. Most specialists, however, are trained abroad at the University of the West Indies or in Mexico, Guatemala, or Costa Rica.

GOVERNMENT

Structure

Belize has a parliamentary democracy and is part of the British Commonwealth. Its head of state is Queen Elizabeth II of England, who is represented in the country by a governor-general. However, this role is primarily ceremonial. The head of the executive branch is the prime minister, who is appointed by the majority legislative party. Since 2008, this has been Dean Oliver Barrow.

The legislative branch is a bicameral National Assembly. There is a 12-member Senate, the members of which are appointed by the governor-general, on the advice of several government, and non-governmental, groups. The 31 members of the House of Representatives are elected by popular vote and serve five-year terms. There is universal suffrage for citizens eighteen and older.

Since gaining its independence, Belize has been involved in a border dispute with Guatemala, which still lays claim to the southern half of Belize. The dispute has its origins in the initial dispute between the Spanish and British over control of the region. Spain allowed the British to settle the land in the 16th century. A century later, after a war between the two colonial powers, the British took control of the region and declared it a colony.

Belize's move toward independence began in the 1950s, but was delayed because of Guatemala's claim to the territory. When Belize declared its independence in 1981, Guatemala refused to recognize it as a country. Consequently, British troops remained in Belize to protect its border. Guatemala finally recognized the sovereign country in 1991. In 1994, Britain removed its troops, though border protection remains the country's single largest military concern.

Political Parties

Political parties in Belize include the People's National Party (PNP); the People's United Party (PUP); the National Alliance for Belizean Rights (NABR); the National Reform Party (NRP); and the United Democratic Party (UDP).

In the 2012 House of Representatives election, the United Democratic Party won 17 seats and the People's United Party won 14 seats.

Local Government

Local government in Belize comprises two city councils, seven town councils, and 193 community and rural village councils. Belmopan is governed locally by its own unitary city council. Local elections were held in March 2009.

Judicial System

The Supreme Court is the highest court in Belize; it comprises three members, one of whom is named Chief Justice by the country's governor-general (who consults with the prime minister, as well as the leader of the opposition). Other courts include the Court of Appeal and the Privy Council.

Taxation

The highest income tax rate in Belize is 45 percent, and the top corporate tax rate is 25 percent. Other taxes levied include a stamp duty tax and a goods and services tax (GST).

Armed Forces

The Belize Defense Force (BDF) is the armed forces of Belize. Consisting mostly of ground forces, they primarily serve a defensive function. Military service is voluntary, but the government has a conscription policy in place should the number of military volunteers ever dip too low. However, military volunteers often exceed the number of available openings.

Foreign Policy

Belize maintains cooperative relations with its neighbor countries and is an active member of the international community. Among other international groups, Belize is a member of the UN, the Organization of American States (OAS), and the Caribbean Community (CARICOM). In terms of trade, the US is the country's strongest trading partner, and has the largest population of Belizeans living outside the country. In 2014, the US donated more about 1.2 million (USD) to the Belizean government for economic and development initiatives. In the 21st century, Belize and the US have also cooperated to create agreements aimed at combating the transport of illicit drugs and weapons. In addition, Belize is also one of the few nations to maintain diplomatic relations with the Republic of China (ROC), or Taiwan, instead of the People's Republic of China.

The most significant transnational issue for Belize is an ongoing territorial dispute with Guatemala. The dispute predates Belizean independence, which occurred in 1981, and involves the disposition of territories established in an 1859 British-Guatemalan treaty. The Guatemalan government feels that the 1859 treaty is void because Britain failed to meet with certain economic assistance programs promised in the treaty. Since 2000, Belizean and Guatemalan officials have attempted to negotiate the issue with mediation by the OAS. After several months of failure in organizing negotiations, the OAS recommended that Belize and Guatemala, take their dispute to the International Court of Justice (ICJ).

Human Rights Profile

International human rights law insists that states respect civil and political rights, and also promote an individual's economic, social and cultural rights. The United Nations (UN) Universal Declaration of Human Rights (UDHR) is recognized as the standard for international human rights. Its authors sought the counsel of the world's great thinkers, philosophers, and religious leaders, and were careful to create a document that reflects the core values shared by every world culture. (To read this document or view the articles relating to cultural human rights, visit: www.udhr.org/UDHR/default.htm.)

In general, human rights monitoring agencies have been satisfied that the Belizean government provides for the welfare of its citizens and, through its penal code, protects its citizens from unlawful prosecution and abuse. However, in 2000, Amnesty International (AI) reached out to the Belizean government to increase efforts to protect citizens from physical abuse by local police, in violation of Article 5 of the UDHR. While police abuse has remained a primary concern for monitoring agencies, the Belizean government states that incidents of abuse are isolated and not indicative of a national trend.

AI also called attention to conditions within the country's only prison, Hattieville Central Prison, where prisoners live in conditions below international standards for the treatment of inmates. Several monitoring agencies have reached the conclusion that the nation's prison system is below international standards. Currently, the Belizean government also allows capital punishment, or the death penalty, for certain classes of crime, which is in opposition to some monitoring agencies that believe the death penalty is a violation of basic human rights. However, the Belizean government defends the death penalty as an effective method to deter crime and an appropriate punishment for criminals who commit serious human rights violations.

In addition, media monitoring agencies have found that Belize supports a wide variety of media. Media outlets, both print and broadcast, were able to air programming without interference from the government. Nonetheless, the government retains the option to review any media with political content, and to prevent the publication or broadcast of libelous or defamatory content. The government rarely exercises this right, however, and regularly allows the publication of material critical of government policy.

ECONOMY

Overview of the Economy

As of 2013, the gross national product (GNP) of Belize was $3.083 billion USD. Belize has experienced continued growth in the early 21st century, attributed in part to the rise in tourism, the recent discovery of oil, and an emphasis on manufacturing, as well as fiscal reform. However, the country continues to be plagued with a trade deficit, foreign debt, poverty, and a high unemployment rate. The government has been trying to reduce poverty with the help of international donors.

Belize has implemented several initiatives to expand their manufacturing industries. The discovery of oil, in 2006, has allowed Belize to compete in the petroleum world market, as well as to supply some of the country's energy needs. In 2013, Belize exported $633 million USD in total exports, but the country continues to run a trade deficit.

The federal government, which is based in Belmopan, is the city's largest employer. So far, Belmopan has played a small role in the economic arena, especially when compared to Belize City, a vibrant port with well-established industries and tourist attractions. The development of Belmopan did boost the construction industry, and the city is beginning to expand on the services it now offers (banking, hotels, retail stores, restaurants).

Industry

Manufacturing makes up the smallest portion (about one-eighth) of Belize's economy, however, adding in petroleum production, industrial activities now exceed the value of agricultural production. Aside from sawmills and furniture factories associated with the country's timber industry, there are plants that produce clothing, fertilizer, and food. The country also produces cigarettes and gum. Belize also has a thriving black market.

Labor

In 2013, the unemployment rate was estimated to be just over 15 percent. The labor force numbers approximately 120,500.

Energy/Power/Natural Resources

Belize's natural resources include forested land, hydropower, oil, and fish from the nearby Gulf of Guinea.

Fishing

The fishing industry is a significant component of the Belizean economy. The industry meets the needs of domestic consumption and exports fish products to the United States and other trading partners. Overfishing and illegal fishing are problems in Belize and have negatively affected species such as conch, lobster, snapper, and grouper.

Forestry

Nearly half of the country's area consists of undeveloped, arable land, much of which is forested. These trees are among Belize's chief natural resources. Deciduous trees are found in the northern part of the country, while the south is dominated by tropical hardwoods. These include oak, palm, and pine trees, as well as cedar, rosewood, and mahogany, which is the national tree. Timber exports, however, have decreased in importance since the 1960s, but several sawmills still operate in Belize. The wood is often used for utility poles and for making furniture.

Mining/Metals

The mining industry of Belize is relatively small. Commonly mined materials include clay, sand, and gravel, all of which are used in the country's construction industry. Other less-commonly mined materials include marble, limestone, and gold.

Agriculture

About a quarter of the population is employed in agriculture. Sugar cane is the largest cash crop of Belize, and is exported to Europe and the United States along with chicle, which is used in chewing gum. Because of its reliance on sugar cane, Belize's economy often fluctuates according to the world market price of sugar.

Animal Husbandry

Common domesticated animals include pigs, cattle, goats, sheep, poultry, and horses. In 2006, there were over 80,000 head of cattle, 13,000 pigs, and almost 10,000 sheep. There are approximately 10 major processing and slaughtering facilities in Belize.

Tourism

In the 1980s, service industries, fueled by tourism, raced past agriculture as the most important sector of Belize's economy. Almost half of Belizean employees are connected to the tourist business in some way.

Tourists visit Belize for its scuba diving and fishing, as well as its large barrier reef. There has also been an increase in ecotourism in the central region of the country.

Micah Issitt, Barrett Hathcock,
Sally Driscoll

DO YOU KNOW?

- There are differing explanations of the origin of the Belize's name. Some believe that the name comes from the Spanish pronunciation of "Wallace." It is believed that Scottish buccaneer Peter Wallace began a settlement near the Belize River in the 17th century. Alternate sources of the name are the Mayan words "belix ("muddy water") and "belikin" ("land facing the sea").

- The Belize Barrier Reef is the second largest barrier reef system in the world.

- The scenic highway that connects the coastal city of Dangriga with Belmopan as it winds through the Maya Mountains is called the Hummingbird Highway.

Bibliography

Bethell, Leslie. *Central America Since Independence.* Cambridge, UK: Cambridge University Press, 1991.

Booth, John A., Christine J. Wade and Thomas W. Walker. *Understanding Central America: Global Forces, Rebellion and Change.* Jackson, TN: Westview Press, 2006.

Bridgewater, Samuel. *A Natural History of Belize: Inside the Maya Forest.* (Corrie Herring Hooks Series) Austin: University of Texas Press, 2012.

Brignoli, Hector-Perez. *A Brief History of Central America.* Berkeley, CA: University of California Press, 1989.

Campbell, Mavis C. *Becoming Belize: A History of an Outpost of Empire Searching for Identity, 1528-1823.* Kingston, Jamaica: University of West Indies Press, 2011.

Chandler, Gary and Robert Reid. *Central America on a Shoestring.* Oakland, CA: Lonely Planet Press, 2004.

Coates, Anthony G. and Olga F. Linares. *Central America: A Natural and Cultural History.* New Haven, CT: Yale University Press, 1999.

Counihan, Carole and Penny Van Esterik. *Food and Culture: A Reader.* New York: Routledge Publishing, 2007.

Curtis, Dawn and Amber Dobrzensky. *The Rough Guide to Central America on a Budget.* 3rd ed, New York: Rough Guides, 2013.

Eltringham, Peter. *The Rough Guide to Belize*, 6th ed. New York: Rough Guides, 2014.

Eltringham, Peter. *The Rough Guide to Central America.* 3rd ed. New York: Rough Guides, 2004.

Fodor's Central America, 3rd ed. New York: Fodor's Press, 2008.

Fodor's Belize 2014. New York: Fodor's Press, 2014.

Hennessey, Hum. *Insight Guide Belize.* Germany: Langenscheidt Publishing Group, 2008.

Twigg, Alan. *Understanding Belize: A Historical Guide.* Madiera Park, British Columbia, CA: Harbour Publishing, 2006.

Woodward, Ralph Lee. *Central America: A Nation Divided.* New York: Oxford University Press US, 1999.

Works Cited

"Background Note: Belize." *U.S. Department of State Online.*

"Belize." *CIA World Factbook Online.* https://www.cia.gov/library/publications/the-world-factbook/geos/bh.html

"Belize: Overview." *Lonely Planet Country Guides.* http://www.lonelyplanet.com/worldguide/belize/

"Belize." *CIA World Factbook.* Washington, DC: CIA, 2014. https://www.cia.gov/library/publications/the-world-factbook/

"Belize." *Nations of the World.* Amenia, NY: Grey House Publishing, 2015.

Booth, John A., Wade, Christine J. and Thomas W. Walker. "Understanding Central America: Global Forces, Rebellion and Change." Jackson, TN: Westview Press, 2006.

Brignoli, Hector-Perez. "A Brief History of Central America." Berkeley, CA: University of California Press, 1989.

Chandler, Gary and Robert Reid. "Central America on a Shoestring." Oakland, CA: Lonely Planet Press, 2004.

Coates, Anthony G. and Olga F. Linares. "Central America: A Natural and Cultural History." New Haven, CT: Yale University Press, 1999.

Counihan, Carole and Penny Van Esterik. "Food and Culture: A Reader." New York: Routledge Publishing, 2007.

Eltringham, Peter. "The Rough Guide to Belize, 3rd ed." New York: Rough Guides, 2007.

Eltringham, Peter. "The Rough Guide to Central America 3rd ed." New York: Rough Guides, 2004.

"Fodor's Belize 2008." New York: Fodor's Press, 2008.

"Fodor's Central America, 3rd ed." New York: Fodor's Press, 2008.

"Government of Belize." Official Site. http://www.governmentofbelize.gov.bz/

Hennessey, Hum. "Insight Guide Belize." Germany: Langenscheidt Publishing Group, 2003.

"Population Statistics of Belize." *Statistical Institute of Belize Online.* http://www.statisticsbelize.org.bz/dms20uc/dm_tree.asp?pid=6

Twigg, Alan. "Understanding Belize: A Historical Guide." Madiera Park, British Columbia, CA: Harbour Publishing, 2006.

Woodward, Ralph Lee. "Central America: A Nation Divided." New York: Oxford University Press US, 1999.

Church interior in Costa Rica/Stock photo © OGphoto

COSTA RICA

Introduction

Costa Rica, which is Spanish for "rich coast," lies between the Pacific and Atlantic Oceans, with Central American neighbors Nicaragua to the north and Panama to the south. The country is known for its cash crops of coffee and bananas. It is one of the most popular tourist destinations in Central America.

San José is the capital of Costa Rica and the largest urban area in the country. The city was founded in the 18th century, when Costa Rica was a Spanish colony. After a brief civil war, San José became the capital of the country's independent government. The capital represents the center of Costa Rica's economy, particularly the tourism and ecotourism industries.

GENERAL INFORMATION

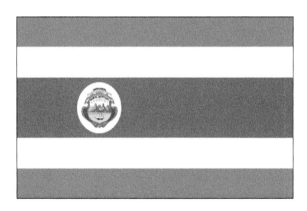

Official Language: Spanish
Population: 4,755,234 (2014 estimate)
Currency: Costa Rican colón
Coins: Coins are available in denominations of 5, 10, 50, 100, and 500 colones.
Land Area: 51,060 square kilometers (19,714 square miles)
Water Area: 40 square kilometers (15 square miles)
National Motto: "Vivan siempre el trabajo y la paz" ("Long live work and peace")
National Anthem: "Noble patria, tu hermosa bandera" (Noble homeland, your beautiful flag)
Capital: San José
Time Zone: GMT -6

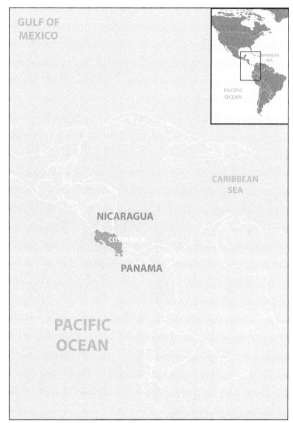

Flag Description: The flag of Costa Rica features five horizontal stripes of blue (top), white, red, white, and blue (bottom), with the country's coat of arms emblazoned to the left of center within the thicker central red stripe. The blue of the flag stands for the sky, opportunity, and perseverance; the white symbolizes peace and happiness; and the red signifies the blood shed for the country.

Population

About 91 percent of Costa Ricans are white or mestizo (mixed European or Amerindian descent). Three percent of the population is black, 2.4 percent is Amerindian, and one percent is of Chinese descent. Most Afro-Costa Ricans are the descendents of Jamaican immigrant workers who came to Costa Rica in the 19th century. The country is the adopted home to many immigrant groups from both Europe and the rest of Latin America. In the late 20th century, many immigrants from Nicaragua came to Costa Rica seeking work; as a result, between 10 and 15 percent

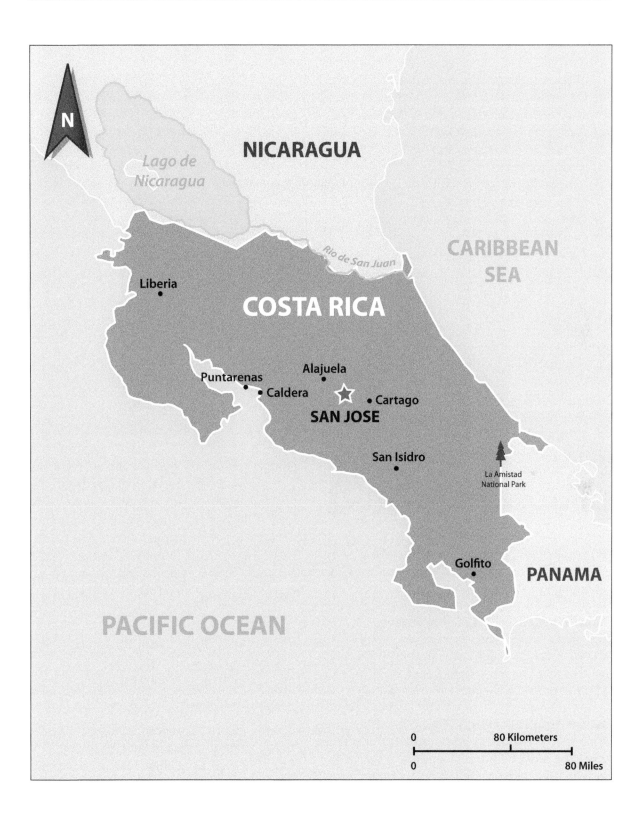

Principal Cities by Population (2011 Census):

- San José (288,054)
- Limon (61,075)
- Alajuela (42,975)
- San Francisco (20,209)
- Cinco Esquinas (64,842)
- Desamparados (33,866)
- Liberia (53,382)
- Puntarenas (115,019)
- Paraiso (57,743)
- San Vincente (30,998)

of the population is considered Nicaraguan. The legal immigrant population, most of whom are Nicaraguan, numbers over 400,000 people.

During most seasons of the year, the population increases by more than 10 percent due to an influx of temporary visitors from North America and Europe. Native Costa Ricans are locally known as "Ticos."

The San José metro area, including Alajuela, an important coffee processing center, accounts for more than half of the nation's population at just under two million residents. Other large urban centers include the Pacific port of Puntarenas, and the Caribbean port city Limon. About 65 percent of the population is considered urban. Costa Rica has one of the lowest emigration rates of all Central American countries.

Languages
Spanish is both the official and most common language, although English is widely used for business, particularly in the tourism industry. A Creole dialect is common among the minority of Jamaican immigrants who settled in Limon, along the Caribbean coast, in the 1800s.

Native People & Ethnic Groups
Costa Rica was once almost entirely forested. The dense hilly terrain did not support large native empires as in nearby Peru or Mexico. Spanish settlement displaced what few tribes were farming the central regions. Small groups remain in mountainous regions, such as the

Chorotega in the Northern Guanacaste province, and the Bribri, Cabecar, and Boruca in the Southern Talamanca region.

A 1977 law created 22 small Indian reserves in the country, recognizing eight different tribes. Today, Native Americans on the reserves make up less than 1 percent of Costa Rica's total population.

The majority of Costa Ricans are mestizos, or persons of mixed racial heritage, descended from a combination of Spanish and native tribal individuals. In addition, between 10 and 15 percent of the population is descended from Nicaraguan natives.

Religions
Roman Catholics made up more than 76 percent of the religious affiliation in 2000. Evangelical Protestant groups were a 14 percent minority.

Climate
Average temperatures vary widely from coastal subtropical regions to temperate regions at higher elevations. Most areas receive abundant annual rainfall, and seasons are generally divided into wet (May through November) and dry (December through April, often referred to as the summer season).

Average temperature in tropical Pacific costal regions is 32° Celsius (90° Fahrenheit), 28° Celsius (82° Fahrenheit) along the Caribbean coast, a mild 22° Celsius (72° Fahrenheit) in the central plateau, and about 17° Celsius (62° Fahrenheit) at higher elevations.

Annual rainfall along the Caribbean coast amounts to 2,500 millimeters (100 inches) or more, and about 2,000 millimeters (77 inches) in the central plateau. The higher elevations receive the most rainfall, up to 3,500 millimeters (140 inches). Extreme rainfall years in the coastal and mountainous regions can bring totals as much as 50 percent above normal.

ENVIRONMENT & GEOGRAPHY

Topography
Costa Rica is the second-smallest Central American country after El Salvador. In the south,

the country is only 120 kilometers (75 miles) wide, stretching to about 265 kilometers (165 miles) wide to the north. The coastline, mostly along the Pacific Ocean, is roughly 1,290 kilometers (802 miles) long.

Plains along both coasts lead to central highlands that average 900 to 1,800 meters (about 3,000 to 6,000 feet) in elevation. San José is at 1,150 meters (3,773 feet). A segment of the Andean-Sierra Madre mountain range bisects the country from north to south. The highest mountain peak is Cerro Chirripó Grande at 3,819 meters (12,530 feet). It lies 56 kilometers (34 miles) southeast of San José.

The highest volcanic peak is Irazú at 3,432 meters (11,260 feet), just east of San José. There are 122 volcanoes in Costa Rica, seven of which are considered active as of 2002. The Arenal volcano, near San Jose, which destroyed a village in 1968, erupted in 2000, killing one person and leading to the evacuation of about 600, and again in 2010. This active peak sits next to Lake Arenal, the country's largest natural lake. As with most areas of volcanic activity, the country is also susceptible to earthquakes; the April 22, 1991, quake measured 7.4 on the Richter scale.

Numerous short rivers have become favorites for white water rafting and kayaking. Rio Reventazón (145 kilometers/90 miles) and Rio Pacuare (108 kilometers/67 miles) empty into the Caribbean Sea. Rivers draining to the Pacific include the Rio Corobicí, Rio Sevegre, and Rio Naranjo.

San José is located at the geographic center of the country, in what is known as the central valley or "meseta central." The central valley is covered by volcanic soil that is excellent for agriculture. For that reason, the majority of the population has settled in the region.

Plants & Animals

Original stands of oak and other deciduous trees near the Pacific coast were almost completely wiped out by Spanish settlers, and replaced by more tenacious grasslands (savannahs). The Caribbean lowlands contain mangrove swamps.

The more impenetrable and inhospitable rainforests contain an overwhelming abundance of species, including about 800 varieties of ferns and more than 1,000 species of orchids. Common trees include balsa, cedar, ebony, and mahogany.

Among wildlife, birds and monkeys are most associated with Costa Rica. The country's 600 species of birds include the colorful quetzal, the macaw, and the toucan, along with eagles that prowl the upper reaches of the forest. Bats are also plentiful.

The four major species of monkeys in Costa Rica are the capuchin, howler, spider, and squirrel. Capuchins have been kept as pets in the United States and Europe and are recognizable as the stereotypical "organ-grinder monkey." Squirrels are the smallest, spiders are the most endangered, and howlers are the largest, typically weighing about 10 pounds. Other generally vegetarian mammals include sloths and tapirs. The principal hunter of the jungle was once the jaguar, but it is now an endangered species, as are sea turtles that nest on both coasts.

In 2000, the country's National Biodiversity Institute created a park area called INBioparque, north of San José at Santo Domingo de Heredia, to increase awareness of the endangered resources of the rainforest. The institute also has an agreement with the Merck pharmaceutical company to collect plant samples that may be used to create new drugs.

CUSTOMS & COURTESIES

Greetings

Most greetings in Costa Rica, whether friendly or formal, begin with a handshake. Costa Ricans tend to maintain direct eye contact while shaking hands. Among friends and family members, kisses on the cheek are common forms of greeting. In addition, male friends may hug one another.

Though Spanish is the official language of Costa Rica, the Ticos have developed their own variations on common Spanish expressions.

Costa Ricans often say "Buenas," which translates as "Good," as a basic greeting for all times of the day. In other Spanish speaking countries the speaker would add the time of day as in "Dias" ("Day") or "Tardes" ("Afternoon"). Young and informal speakers may also use the expression "Hola" ("Hi") as a greeting. The saying "Pura vida," meaning "Happy or pure life," has become the slogan of Costa Rica's tourism industry, but is also a popular expression among Ticos who use it as a greeting or a statement of general well-being. The expression "Twanys," which is slang for "Things are great," is a common answer to the question "¿Cómo estás?," or "How are you?" Among friends, the expression "Upe" may be used to say "Hello."

Gestures & Etiquette

Costa Ricans typically use a number of hand gestures to supplement verbal communication, and many of these gestures are different from those used in Western countries. For example, Costa Ricans tend to use their entire hand, rather than just the index finger, to point or indicate and object or person. Rubbing the thumb and forefinger together is a gesture that loosely means "hurry." This can also be expressed by clapping the back of one hand against the palm of the other hand while pulling both hands downward. Tapping or touching the elbow can mean "cheap," and is often used as an insult when someone is being miserly.

Direct eye contact is important to Costa Ricans, particularly as a sign of trust and honesty in communication. Costa Ricans are generally comfortable with close proximity and may stand closer, on average, than is customary in some Asian or North American cultures. Physical contact is common among friends of any sex during conversation.

It is typical to dress formally for business meetings and to make sure to use titles when addressing others. These include the titles Señor or Señora (Mister or Mrs.), and the honorific titles Don (for a man) and Doña (for a woman), typically in conjunction with the individual's surname.

Eating/Meals

Costa Ricans commonly eat three meals a day, roughly corresponding to the Western traditions of breakfast, lunch, and dinner or supper. Simple courses are served for the morning meal, including fruits, tortillas, rice, and eggs. Coffee, which is a major agricultural crop in Costa Rica, is served in the morning, and may also accompany the afternoon meal. The midday meal is generally small and may consist of leftovers from the previous night, or rice and beans, and fruits. The richest and most extensively prepared dishes are usually served during the evening meal. These include dishes of roasted meats and vegetables and other such main courses.

Costa Ricans conventionally use forks, knives, and spoons, but there are a variety of foods that can be eaten by hand. These commonly include foods wrapped in flour tortillas. Alcoholic beverages, including cocktails and beer, are often served with the midday and evening meals. As in most cultures, it is customary to wait until the table has been served before eating. It is also considered impolite to make loud chewing noises or to talk with food in one's mouth.

Visiting

When invited to a Tico home, it is advisable to bring a small gift for the host. Candy, alcohol, dessert items, and flowers are appropriate gifts for visiting. Flowers are also an appropriate gift. However, lilies should be avoided as they are commonly used at funerals or to express condolence. Visitors may also want to bring small gifts, such as toys and candy, for the host's children.

Costa Ricans often offer beverages to guests, including alcoholic beverages such as beer or liquor, and it is not considered offensive to politely refuse beverages. Occasionally, Costa Ricans may extend invitations out of a sense of polite custom rather than a genuine desire for company. It is therefore common to refuse a first invitation for a meal or social occasion in order to determine the sincerity of the offer.

LIFESTYLE

Family

The central unit of Costa Rican life is the nuclear family, commonly consisting of a mother, father and, typically, two children. In small towns, such as Filadelfia in the province of Guanacaste, Ticos often live in close proximity to extended family members, and may also have close bonds with members of the extended community. Children rarely leave home until they marry and may thereafter choose to settle in the same area as their parents, helping to maintain extended family structures. Compared to other Central and South American countries, Costa Rica has a high rate of marriage, and women generally marry before the age of 25.

The Costa Rican government initiated a nation wide campaign for family planning in the late 1960s that had a significant impact on the population. The average number of children per fertile woman decreased from seven to three between 1960 and 1990. Because of the nation's largely Catholic heritage, some Costa Ricans resist the use of contraceptives. However, poverty, homelessness, and overpopulation have convinced more Costa Ricans to begin using birth control. Families of three to five children are average, with larger family sizes more common in rural areas. The birth rate continued to drop in the 21st century. With the release of data from the 2011 Census, major concerns were expressed regarding fertility rate, which in 2014 had dropped further to 1.9.

Housing

Because of the growing number of expatriates and foreign developers in Costa Rica, the character of Costa Rican housing has changed since the late 20th century. In rural areas and small towns, many Costa Ricans live in simple one- to two-bedroom concrete and plaster houses, generally ranging from 100 to 150 square meters (1,076 to 1,614 square feet). Most Costa Rican houses do not have central heating or air conditioning, and are left open to the elements with ceiling and floor fans to circulate air. Hot and humid conditions are prevalent during much of the year, posing a problem for wood and fabric, which can develop mold unless kept dry by circulating air.

In urban areas such as San José and Límon, there are numerous poor districts, often referred to as shantytowns, where families live in corrugated tin housing with thatched roofs and few amenities. Because of the obvious housing shortage, the Costa Rican government has initiated programs to improve housing conditions for the urban poor. In affluent urban neighborhoods, security fences made of brick and/or concrete are common. In addition, many wealthy residents hire security to protect their property.

Food

Costa Ricans have access to a wealth of fresh food, including hundreds of tropical fruits and vegetables, fresh seafood from the Pacific and Caribbean, and a variety of farm-raised meats. The productive agricultural climate played a major role in the development of local cuisine. Tropical fruits—including pineapple, mango, papaya, melons, and plantains—and rice and beans and tortillas accompany most meals in Costa Rica. Coffee is served with both the morning and afternoon meal, and Costa Ricans generally drink locally grown and roasted coffees.

A typical dish in Costa Rica is gallo pinto, or spotted rooster, which contains black beans and rice, with various spices and other ingredients. Gallo pinto is typically served for breakfast, lunch, and dinner, with varying additions including eggs, ham, and chicken. While many restaurants serve a gourmet version of gallo pinto, it is a common peasant dish because it is simple to prepare, flavorful, and uses few ingredients.

Arroz con pollo (chicken and rice) is another popular dish in Costa Rica, and is served at nearly every restaurant featuring native cuisine. Arroz con pollo and a number of other dishes are often flavored with Lizano salsa, a sauce made from vegetables, sugar, salt, and a variety of hot peppers. The sauce was developed by the Costa Rican Lizano Company in the 1920s and has since become a common ingredient in a variety of Tico dishes. Most restaurants have Lizano sauce on the table in place of Tabasco or pepper sauce.

Mondongo is a type of soup made from beef intestine, vegetables, and spices. Mondongo is also a common dish throughout Central America and the Caribbean, and is prepared differently depending on the locality. A typical Costa Rican version usually contains vegetables that are common in Costa Rican agriculture, like chayote (a type of gourd), carrots, and cilantro. It may also have chorizo (spicy sausage) or other meats added for flavor.

Life's Milestones

Most Costa Ricans are Catholic and follow the major Catholic/Christian rites of passage, including baptism, communion, weddings, and funerals. Celebrations in Costa Rica typically involve feasting with family and friends. Birth, especially of a couple's first child, is a major cause for celebration and is generally followed by a large family celebration.

Some families celebrate a young woman's transition from childhood to adolescence (age 15 in Costa Rica) with a traditional quinceañera. This celebration, prevalent in Latin-speaking countries, typically involves a party wherein the young girl and friends engage in a traditional waltz. Birthday celebrations are generally small, involving only the immediate family.

Children often choose to remain in the home until marriage, with a wedding therefore traditionally symbolizing the transition to independence for many Costa Ricans. Women generally keep their family name after marriage. In addition, children are given the surnames of both parents, with the mother's name listed first, followed by the father's surname. Most anniversaries are not celebrated or observed until a couple has reached their 25th year of marriage.

CULTURAL HISTORY

Art

The culture and artistic traditions of Costa Rica's indigenous inhabitants largely disappeared after the arrival of European colonists in the 16th century. While some of the nation's Spanish colonists produced art in a variety of forms, a unique fine arts tradition didn't emerge until the 19th century. Traditional crafts, such as weaving and woodwork, are among the oldest continuous artistic traditions in Costa Rica.

The creation of decorated carretas (ox-carts) dates back to the late 19th century. Ox-carts were once used to transport coffee and other crops from the central valley—which boasts the best soil for agriculture—to the coasts for export and distribution. As the utility of ox-carts declined in the 20th century, craftsmen and women began painting and displaying the carts instead. As decorations became more elaborate, villages and towns began holding contests to judge technique. The tradition became so common that an ox-cart museum was established in Salitral de Desamparados, located outside the capital of San José. In fact, the construction and decoration of ox-carts has been recognized by the United Nations Educational, Scientific and Cultural Organization (UNESCO) as an intangible cultural heritage of Costa Rica.

In the 1920s, a new fine arts movement arose, drawing on European traditions but using traditional Costa Rican culture and lifestyle as its subject. Landscape painter Teodorico Quirós (1897–1977) is remembered as one of the leaders and pioneers of this movement. Collectively known as the "Group of New Sensibility," Quirós and his cotemporaries were among the first Costa Rican artists to produce paintings and sculptures that were uniquely Costa Rican. For example, Quirós painted scenes of Costa Rican life and the rural countryside. He later became dean of Costa Rica School of Fine Arts. Franciso Zúñiga (1912–1998) was the leading sculptor of the new school. His work, both paintings and sculpture, still features prominently in studies of Costa Rican artistic traditions. Another prominent painter of the era was Manuel de la Cruz Gonzalez (1909–1986), who is sometimes called the "Costa Rican Picasso" and was known for his impressionist style.

By the 1950s, Costa Rican artists were expanding the boundaries of the art movement with influences from new European styles, a progression, which continued into the 21st century. Among the most famous contemporary artists is Isidro Con Wong, the son of Chinese immigrants who migrated to Punterenas in the 1930s. Con Wong became one of the few Costa Rican artists to gain international attention with his blend of Asian and Central American elements and his use of magic realism (a genre of art in which magical aspects appear in normal settings). Another modern artist, Roberto Lizano (1951–), gained international fame in the 1990s for his unusual mixed media creations. Driven by Lizano and other contemporaries, Costa Rican art has developed past the point of imitation, and now holds a unique place in the Central American and global art scene.

Architecture

Costa Rica's architecture has suffered from the country's natural disasters, such as volcanoes and earthquakes, and many of its historic buildings have been destroyed. Spanish colonial architecture predominated during the 17th and 18th centuries, and is still evident in cities such as Liberia or Heredia. Heredia's Cara de Cultura, a single-story house once home to President Alfredo Gonzalez Flores (1877–1962), is a fine example of Spanish colonial architecture and hosts many cultural events.

The town of Barva, founded in 1561, also boasts a collection of 17th- and 18th-century homes with red tile roofs, as well as a Baroque-style church. The San Jose neighborhood of Amon contains many examples of colonial homes, as well as the 19th-century mansions of wealthy coffee plantation owners. Another 19th-century neoclassical treasure is the Teatro Nacional, which was built in 1897.

Drama

Costa Rica has shown a longstanding support for theater, exemplified by the huge National Theater completed in San José in 1897. Since 1970, it has been the home of the well-regarded National Symphony Orchestra. Today, the National Theater and other smaller theaters, such as the Melico Salazar Theater and the FANAL Theater, host local performing groups such as the National Opera Society, National Choir, National Youth Symphony, and dance troupes Compania Nacional de Danza, and Taller Nacional de Danza.

Music

Costa Rica has a rich musical culture. The Orquesta Sinfónica Nacional celebrated its seventieth year in 2010. The state-funded organization has an educational program that helps develop the talent of classical musicians within the country. The orchestra has also toured internationally.

Other musical traditions within the country include folk music, which has several forms. Many attribute the source of the folk music traditions to the Guanacaste province. The country's folk dance, the Punto Guanacasteo, originates here and is characterized by music from marimbas, chirimias, and the quijongo. In the Limon province, Afro-Costa Rican music predominates, with calypso and reggae beats.

Literature

There are few examples of Costa Rican literature before the 20th century. After Costa Rica became a Spanish colony, the indigenous population began a rapid decline from which it never recovered. By the time Costa Rica won its independence in the 19th century, a majority of residents were of Spanish descent. Spanish Costa Ricans, or "Ticos" as they are sometimes called, shaped the nation's only native literary movement.

One of the first Tico authors recognized outside of Costa Rica was Ricardo Fernández Guardia (1867–1950). Fernández Guardia published influential fiction, such as the celebrated story *Hojarasca* (1894). He became one of the most prominent historiographers in Costa Rica. Joaquín García Monge, who is famous for his short stories including *El Moto* (1900), is another of the pioneers of the modern Tico literary movement. As director of Costa Rica's Biblioteca Nacional (National Library), Monge was able to exert a strong influence over what Costa Ricans were reading, both for recreation and education.

In the 19th century, many Costa Rican writers imitated styles and settings common in European literature. This changed in the early 20th century when a "rural" literary movement began to surface. During this movement, writers began to focus on stories and characters more in keeping with daily life in Costa Rica. From the 1930s to the 1980s, Costa Rican literature evolved to include deeper, more substantive, themes. Costa Rican writers began to explore politics, family, and psychological roles through the characters of popular literature. Among the most prominent writers of the period was Carlos Salazar Herrera (1906–1980), whose short stories and novels were celebrated for their insightful exploration of life in Costa Rica.

While the "classical" literature of Costa Rica is largely rural in origin, Costa Rican literature began to reflect the effects of globalization and urbanization in the late 20th and early 21st centuries. Contemporary authors began to explore traditional themes while also drawing upon modern phenomenon—such as the growth of the ecotourism industry in the 1990s and the import of large numbers of expatriates in the 1980s—as influential milestones in the development of Costa Rica and its culture.

CULTURE

Arts & Entertainment

The Costa Rican government takes the development of the arts seriously, and places the responsibility for funding and overseeing artistic and cultural development with the Ministerio de Cultura, Juventud y Deportes de Costa Rica (Ministry of Culture, Youth and Sports). The ministry provides funding and support for public art projects and also helps to find work for young and emerging artists. The artistic community has flourished most in San José and the nearby city of Escazú, which have developed a number of prominent galleries and institutions to promote

the arts. These include the Center for Creative Arts, in Escazú, and the School of Fine Arts, located in San José.

Contemporary Costa Rican music and dance is a mix of Caribbean, African, and Latin American influences. A variety of Latin music styles, including salsa, merengue, soca, and cumbia, are common in Costa Rican clubs and dancehalls. Musical traditions also differ according to location, with slightly different traditions on the Pacific and Caribbean coasts. Reggae, and other Caribbean music, for example, is popular across the country, but more common on the Caribbean coast.

The Caribbean coast is also the most popular location for Afro-Cuban music, like the popular sinkit, a drum-heavy type of folk music. More common types of instrumentation have largely replaced traditional instruments, such as the ocarina, a flute-like ceramic wind instrument. Nonetheless, traditional folk music can still be found in some areas. In addition, the Ministry of Culture provides limited funding for artists who help to preserve native musical traditions. The province of Guanacaste is also known for its extant folk music and dancing community. There, musicians will sometimes use traditional instruments such as the quijongo, a single string instrument made from a gourd, in their performances.

While Costa Rican artisans have been producing impressive wood and fabric crafts for centuries, the growth of the tourism industry in the 1980s and 1990s encouraged an explosion in craft for profit enterprises. Visitors to Costa Rica can purchase crafts ranging from hand-carved wooden statues and dyed fabrics to painted feathers from some of the country's tropical birds. Much of the art produced for the tourist trade is of low quality, but some native craft traditions, such as feather painting and appliqué for fabric, have endured because of the demand for tourist merchandise.

Festivals and festejos populares (city fairs) occur almost weekly across various cities and towns, typically in honor of a patron saint. Most focus on music, food, and parades with horses and sometimes oxcarts. Many feature bullfights, although the bulls are not harmed in these show fights.

Football (soccer) is the sport of choice among Costa Ricans. The national team is La Selección. Matches bring about 20,000 fans wearing red team colors to Saprissa Stadium in San José.

Cultural Sites & Landmarks

Costa Rica has long been dependent on agricultural production for its economic stability. In the 21st century, tourism and services have emerged as a more important feature of the new economy. Because of ecotourism and national efforts to promote conservation, Costa Rica has preserved large portions of its forests as national landmarks. UNESCO has designated several natural areas in Costa Rica as World Heritage Sites.

The Area de Conservación Guanacaste, which is important for its biodiversity, encompasses more than 120,000 hectares (296,526 acres) of land and 70,000 hectares (172,973 acres) of marine habitat. It includes portions of rain forest, dry forest, secondary forest, and mangrove forest. The Talamanca Range-La Amistad Reserves/La Amistad National Park, which is maintained in cooperation between UNESCO, Costa Rica, and Panama, is another important preserve and World Heritage Site. It contains tropical forest and the home ranges of several of Costa Rica's remaining indigenous populations. Another national park of Costa Rica, Cocos Island National Park, was also designated as a World Heritage Site in 1997.

The capital of San José contains the vast majority of Costa Rica's important architectural and cultural landmarks. The Museo de Arte y Diseño Contemporáneo is the largest art gallery in Costa Rica, and occupies a 19th-century building that once belonged to the national liquor industry. Exhibits focus on emerging and modern artists, but there are also several exhibits focused on the history of Tico art. The Teatro Nacional de Costa, located in downtown San José, is the regular venue of Costa Rica's symphony orchestra. The venue also hosts frequent concerts from visiting musical and theatrical groups. The theater has been in continuous operation since 1897, and also attracts tourists because of the building's architectural

and historic significance. In addition, the oxcart museum located outside the capital also includes displays of traditional agricultural life in Costa Rica.

Downtown San José has a large public park, known as Parque Central, which is popular as a recreational area. The area surrounding the park has developed into a thriving commercial district driven by large numbers of tourists who visit San Jose each year. Near the park is the Plaza de la Cultura, or Culture Square, which contains a number of historic buildings and abuts a growing commercial area.

Libraries & Museums

San José boasts numerous museums and cultural centers. The Gold Museum located in downtown San José features hundreds of gold artifacts by pre-Columbian artisans. The Museo de Jade Fidel Tristán (Fidel Tristán Jade Museum), also in San José, features the largest collection of pre-Columbian jade artifacts in the world. The museum also features ceramics, tools, and other artifacts from the same period. Visitors to the museum are also offered a trip to the 11th floor where they can enjoy a panoramic view of the capital. Other museums include the Costa Rican Art Museum, which displays a large collection of local artists, and the National Museum in San José, also known for its collection of pre-Columbian artifacts.

Costa Rica maintains two national libraries, the National Library "Miguel Obregón Lizano" of Costa Rica (Biblioteca Nacional "Miguel Obregón Lizano" de Costa Rica), established in the late 19th century, and the National Library of Health and Social Security (Biblioteca Nacional de Salud y Seguridad Social), both in San Jose.

Holidays

Easter is generally the most significant holiday in Costa Rica, reflecting the Catholic majority. During the week preceding Easter Sunday, the nation practically shuts down, with many residents enjoying religious parades and taking advantage of the time off to visit popular beaches. Christmas is a similar celebration.

Other holidays include St. Joseph's Day (March 19), in honor of the patron saint of San José, and Virgen de los Angeles Day (August 2), in honor of the patron saint of Costa Rica. Costa Rica celebrates Independence Day on September 15.

Youth Culture

Costa Rican youth enjoy many different recreational and social activities. Sports are a major draw for Costa Rican children, with fútbol (soccer) being the most popular sport in the country. Even small villages with populations in the hundreds often have a soccer field where people of all ages gather to play and socialize. In fact, sports fields are often placed at the center of the village, signifying their central position in the culture.

The official age of legal employment is 15, though many children are asked to participate in family work at a much younger age. This is particularly prominent in rural and agricultural families, where children generally begin helping with agricultural and domestic work as soon as they are physically able. The driving age is 18, though many children learn to drive before this age. In addition, motorbikes, mopeds, and all-terrain vehicles (ATVs) are popular with youth in both urban and rural areas.

Costa Rica has a significantly developed beach culture, with sports such as surfing, parasailing and kayaking commonly enjoyed by both locals and tourists. Costa Rican youth often learn to swim at an early age. Fashion is also influenced by the climate and the prevalence of beach activities. Certain beach fashions such as shorts, sandals, and tank tops, which are synonymous with Western surf culture, are casual staples for young people. In urban areas, children may be more aware of fashion trends in Europe and the US, particularly when it comes to the clothing styles of Goth and punk subcultures.

SOCIETY

Transportation

Costa Rica has few options for public transportation, the most common of which are public buses and private taxi services. Buses travel from the capital of San José to many locations across Costa Rica, and along both coasts. There are two basic types of buses: "directo," which travel along express routes and make fewer stops, and "colectivo," which provide local service. Some buses have overhead luggage and storage.

Taxi and car rental services are the best option for accessing rural and remote areas. Taxis offer flexible rates and visitors are advised to negotiate price ahead of time, rather than waiting until the end of the trip. Rental car agencies are common in cities and most companies offer a variety of small, four-wheel drive vehicles. These are especially helpful as many Costa Rican roads are poorly maintained. Traffic moves on the right side of the road.

There are boats available in some areas that offer travel through rivers or along the coast. However, these are often recreational or luxury options, rather than a supplement to public transportation.

Transportation Infrastructure

Costa Rica's transportation infrastructure has been characterized as poorly maintained with insufficient investment. Between 2000 and 2006, less than 1 percent of Costa Rica's GDP (gross domestic product) was allocated to transportation. Nonetheless, in the early 21st century, some long-awaited projects are nearing completion and the country has received an infusion of foreign aid and loans to improve infrastructure. Thus, in 2014 infrastructure expenditures were 5.4 percent of GDP. After over 40 years in development—it was begun in 1962—the Costanera (coastal) Highway, connecting southern Costa Rica, was finished in 2010. Investment in the infrastructure has focused largely on improving the country's road system.

Costa Rica has two international airports, one in San José and one in Liberia. There are also flights available between the nation's two main airports and from any of a number of smaller airports around the country for domestic trips.

Media & Communications

Costa Rica enjoys a variety of local and independent media sources, including nine daily newspapers and many local tabloids and magazines. The most popular newspapers are *El Heraldo* and *Diario La Repúblico*, which are both Spanish-language publications. *The Tico Times*, Costa Rica's only English-language newspaper, is one of the most popular and widely read publications, particularly driven by the growing numbers of expatriates in the country. North American newspapers and magazines are also widely available in most urban areas.

A number of public and private television stations are widely available and cable television is broadcast in most parts of the country. Canal 13 is one of the nation's only public television stations, offering programming ranging from public access programs to news and educational programming. There are also a number of private television stations, including Teletica and Repretel, which offer Spanish-language programming. Cable and satellite television are available in most urban areas, as is Internet access. Though there are few sites offering high-speed Internet outside of San José, Internet cafés have become popular in many towns and cities. In addition, there are numerous radio stations in Costa Rica, with popular stations such as Radio Uno and Radio Dos, both offering commercial programming such as music and talk programs.

Costa Rica does not censor media content, though libel laws serve to control broadcast content through the threat of extensive penalties. As of 2014, there were nearly four million Internet users in Costa Rica, representing about 85 percent of the population.

SOCIAL DEVELOPMENT

Standard of Living

Costa Rica ranked 68th out of 187 countries on the 2013 United Nations Human Development Index, which compiles quality of life and standard of living indicators.

In 2014, Costa Rica's average life expectancy at birth was just under 79 years—76 for males and 81 for females.

Water Consumption

In 2012, Costa Rica measured 97 percent improved access to clean water—with 99 percent access in urban areas and 91 percent access in rural areas. In terms of access to improved sanitation, the country reported 94 percent access, with urban areas measuring 95 percent and rural areas measuring 92 percent.

A lack of sewage treatment facilities in some areas has led to the closing of beaches. The government is working to implement a national sewage treatment system.

Education

Costa Rica has one of the most literate populations in Central America. Public education began in the late 1800s. By 1920, approximately half of the population was literate. In 2011, the average adult literacy rate was 96 percent.

Nearly 100 percent of eligible students attend primary schools. Attendance in grades seven through nine is just over 70 percent. Most of the shortfall occurs in rural areas that lack facilities.

High school students in Costa Rica must pass a minimum skills exam, called the Bachillerato Test, to graduate and gain a chance at admission in one of four state universities. These include the University of Costa Rica (UCR) in San Pedro, the National University in Hereda, the Technical Institute of Costa Rica (ITCR) in Cartago, and the State Correspondence University.

These state-sponsored schools are generally considered the nation's best, but there are numerous smaller private colleges, most in or around San José, including the University Latina, University Autónoma de Centro America, and University Interamericana.

Women's Rights

Women are guaranteed equal rights under Costa Rican law. Generally, monitoring agencies have found that the penal code is sufficiently egalitarian, or characterized by equality, with regards to protecting women. However, because of persistent social norms, which give men superiority and authority over their spouses, women are often unwilling to address issues of abuse or exploitation by reporting violations to authorities.

Rape is illegal under Costa Rican law and carries penalties ranging from two- to 10-year prison sentences, depending on the severity and circumstances of the crime. More than 200 rape cases were reported in 2007, though monitoring agencies estimated that many instances were unreported largely due to prevailing cultural attitudes. Spousal abuse has been a continuing problem in Costa Rica. In 2007, the government enacted a new law recommending stronger penalties for spousal abuse and a sentence of up to 35 years for spousal homicide. The new law also established training procedures to teach police how to appropriately handle domestic violence and abuse cases.

Prostitution is legal in Costa Rica for all persons over the age of eighteen. As such, the sex tourism industry has grown in the 21st century. The penal code contains laws aimed specifically at protecting the rights of workers in the sex industry. Participation of underage girls in the sex industry has become a major problem, and police have been unable to prevent the exploitation of underage women as prostitutes.

Health Care

A national health care plan, initiated in the 1970s, uses two state systems to provide care. The Costa Rican Social Security System (Caja Costarricense de Seguro Social or CCSS) provides low-cost access to 250 clinics and emergency care at 29 hospitals. The National Insurance Institute (Instituto Nacional de Seguros or INS) offers more options at greater cost. There are also private hospitals, such as Clinica Biblica and Clinica Catolica.

GOVERNMENT

Structure

Costa Rica is a democratic republic. It gained independence from Spain in 1821. The popularly elected president serves for four years and works with a cabinet and two vice presidents. Costa Rica's unicameral legislature consists of 57 members elected to four-year terms. There is

government monopoly control over power generation, petroleum, and much of the health care, banking, insurance, and telecommunications industries. The powers of the presidency are limited in that the president has no veto power on the budget.

Political Parties

Several parties dominate Costa Rican politics. In the 2014 presidential election, the left-leaning Partido Acción Ciudadana (Citizen's Action Party) took the presidency in the run-off with 77 percent of the vote, also winning thirteen seats in the legislature with 24 percent of the vote. The socialist Partido Liberación Nacional (National Liberation Party or PLN) took almost 23 percent of the run-off presidential vote. In the parliamentary election of 2014, the PLN took 25 percent of the vote, winning eighteen seats. The Broad Front gathered 13 percent of the parliamentary vote, earning nine seats. The Partido de Unidad Socialcristiana (Social Christian Unity Party) won eight seats, the Partido Movimiento Libertario (Libertarian Movement Party) won four seats, and the Partido Renovación Costariccense (Costa Rican Renovation Party won two. Three other parties each won one seat in the legislature.

Local Government

Provinces are led by governor appointed by the president. The provinces are San José, Alajuela, Cartago, Puntarenas, Guanacaste, Heredia, and Limón. At the local level, popularly elected mayors govern along with city councils.

Judicial System

The Supreme Court's 22 magistrates are appointed to eight-year terms by the legislature. The high court is divided into four chambers addressing constitutional, criminal, civil, and merchant law issues. There are also appellate, appeals, and provincial courts.

Taxation

The government of Costa Rica levies corporate and personal income tax, as well as property,

property transfer, sales, and other taxes. Taxes are considered moderate, and the highest personal income tax rate is 25 percent.

Armed Forces

Costa Rica does not have a standing army. A small military contingency is maintained for matters of international peacekeeping and national law enforcement. The armed forces were abolished in 1948.

Foreign Policy

The relative stability of the Costa Rican economy, in terms of agricultural productivity and technology manufacturing, has allowed Costa Rica to avoid the political instability that has plagued many of its Latin American neighbors. Domestically, Costa Rica is a member of the Organization of American States (OAS), an international body representing the 35 independent nations of the Americas, and the Dominican Republic–Central America Free Trade Agreement (CAFTA-DR), a free trade agreement between the US, Dominican Republic, and numerous Central American nations. Internationally, Costa Rica is represented in the UN, where it strongly advocates environmental and human rights issues. In fact, Costa Rica is home to the international organization's peace university, the UN Affiliated University for Peace

Costa Rica has adopted a neutral stance with regard to international peacekeeping issues. In fact, the Costa Rican government officially proclaimed neutrality as its government policy in 1993. A prime example is provided by President Óscar Arias Sánchez who, during his first term from 1986 to 1990, helped to negotiate peace agreements at the end of the Nicaraguan Civil War. For his efforts, he was awarded the 1987 Nobel Peace Prize. Though a popular president and a strong international leader, Arias was forbidden to run for a second term by a long-standing constitutional amendment. (After it was abolished in 2004, Arias was elected to a second term in 2006).

Costa Rica has strong financial ties to the United States and Europe through its export industry. Almost 50,000 American expatriates live in Costa Rica and the U.S. accounts for just under 40 percent of Costa Rica's export revenues. Though Costa Rica is known for its agricultural exports, the country has also become internationally recognized for its environmental policies and efforts to protect natural resources. Costa Rica also has friendly relations with its Central American neighbors and has cooperated with Nicaragua and Panama to jointly protect natural resources and to prevent drug trafficking.

Dependencies

Cocos Island, which lies 480 kilometers (300 miles) off the Pacific coast of Costa Rica, is its only dependency. It is uninhabited and has been designated a World Heritage Site by UNESCO.

Human Rights Profile

International human rights law insists that states respect civil and political rights, and also promote an individual's economic, social and cultural rights. The United Nations (UN) Universal Declaration of Human Rights (UDHR) is recognized as the standard for international human rights. Its authors sought the counsel of the world's great thinkers, philosophers, and religious leaders, and were careful to create a document that reflects the core values shared by every world culture. (To read this document or view the articles relating to cultural human rights, visit: www.udhr.org/UDHR/default.htm.)

Costa Rica has a strong human rights record, and independent monitoring agencies have found that it meets and exceeds international guidelines with respect to protecting the rights of their citizens and visitors to their country. However, monitoring agencies such as Amnesty International have found several areas of concern.

While Costa Rica's penal code is in keeping with the principles of the UDHR, monitoring agencies have reported several significant problems with the legal system, including lengthy detentions while accused await trial, which is a violation of Article 9. One of the primary problems is that the police force received insufficient funding to allow for extensive investigation and to ensure adequate police coverage in all areas.

While Costa Rica has no official laws censoring the press, the penal code contains severe fines for libel. Press organizations have argued that these laws constitute a form of censorship and a violation of Article 19 of the UDHR. The government has recently announced intentions to revise the penal code to reduce penalties in libel cases.

The Costa Rican government recognizes child abuse and exploitation, which are prohibited under Article S1 and Article S25 of the UDHR, as a significant problem. For example, in 2014, there were more than 2,300 cases of child abuse reported. In urban areas such as San José and Límon, monitoring agencies have reported that children were particularly at risk for commercial and sexual exploitation. In 2007, Costa Rica adopted an amendment prohibiting child pornography, and extended the statute of limitations for child abuse prosecution. This effort symbolizes the country's dedication to protecting the rights of children.

Costa Rica has a small population of residents representing the nation's indigenous tribes, estimated at about two percent of the population as a whole. The effort to protect territory for indigenous tribes has been a controversial issue as the demand for land increases. Living conditions for indigenous persons has also been a continuing concern. Monitoring agencies estimate that more than 30 percent of indigenous persons live in inadequate housing and have little or no access to medical care.

ECONOMY

Overview of the Economy

Costa Rica's economy is based on the tourism and ecotourism industries, with the service section accounting for 72.5 percent of the economic production and employment in the nation. Agriculture accounts for 6.2 percent of the economy; major crops include bananas, coffee, beef, sugarcane, rice, and houseplants. Industrial production is 21.3 percent of the 2013 GDP.

Costa Rica is stable both politically and economically, making the country attractive to tourists and investors alike. The country is expected to benefit from the Central American Free Trade Agreement (CAFTA) with the United States.

In 2013, the country's gross domestic product (GDP) was estimated at nearly $61.4 billion USD, with a per capita GDP of $12,900 USD.

Industry

Industry overtook agriculture in the 1900s as the leading driver of Costa Rica's economy, due in large part to new incentives to spur foreign investment. Intel Corporation's 2,000-person facility inspired additional high technology investment from Acer and Microsoft. Proctor and Gamble employs about 1,000 in an administrative center that handles services from Canada through Argentina. Abbott Laboratories and Baxter Healthcare are two large health care products employers. Other industrial output includes food processing, textiles and apparel, and construction materials.

San José also supports a growing industrial sector. The major industries include electronics, food processing, banking, insurance, and tourism.

Labor

The labor force in Costa Rica was estimated at 2.2 million in 2013. The services sector made up the majority of the workforce at 64 percent, followed by industry and agriculture, at 22 and 14 percent, respectively (2006). The unemployment rate was estimated at 7.9 percent in 2013.

Energy/Power/Natural Resources

Whitewater enthusiasts have come into conflict with the government due to plans for additional dams to feed hydroelectric power plants. There were a dozen such plants as of 2004, providing most of the country's energy needs. Additional facilities have been used to export electricity to nearby nations.

Mineral and petroleum deposits remain largely untapped due to the difficulty of the surrounding terrain and government limits on exploration. Abundant rainfall and fertile soil in the central plateau region are Costa Rica's most exploited natural resource. The extensive rainforest is a resource for both products and tourism, while the coastline supports a small fishing industry.

Fishing

Costa Rica's Pacific coast is more important to the overall fishing industry than the Caribbean coast, as fishery production is higher in Pacific waters and there is a larger presence of high seas vessels. Commercial catches include tuna, sardines, and shrimp. Sport fishing is popular, and the country is a global destination for catching marlin and giant sailfish, among other species. Illegal fishing and overfishing remain significant concerns, and the Costa Rican government has come under criticism for lax regulation of the commercial fishing industry.

Forestry

Long ago, 99 percent of Costa Rica was covered by forest. This dropped to 85 percent in 1940, and to 35 percent in the early 21st century. Since that time, efforts to expand the forests (often related to tourism) have been successful, moving the percent forested closer to 51 percent, according to a UN study. Much of the land was cleared for cattle grazing, an industry that has lost its economic importance. The government is now cultivating the nation's ecotourism industry, and reforestation and conservation is part of that plan.

Costa Rica's conservation plan has been characterized as ambitious among other Latin nations, as it protects more than 10 percent of the country. The government's goal is to increase protection to 18 percent of the country's area, in addition to 13 percent of private land. The government is working with private landowners to implement sustainable practices. The government has also enrolled the country in a "rainforest conservation for emissions" program, where wealthier countries reimburse less affluent countries for preserving the rainforest.

Mining/Metals

Costa Rica's mining, like much of Central America's focuses on gold, silver, and some coal deposits. Open-pit gold mining has become an issue of concern among that nation's environmentalists who are concerned about the impact of cyanide and mercury used in that mining process. In 2010, President Chinchilla banned open-pit mining. The president's spokesperson claimed that the extraction of gold was not worth the costs to the environment and the ecotourism industry.

Agriculture

The central plateau region's mild climate and soil fertilized by volcanic ash are ideal for coffee production. Banana production, led by multinational firms Dole and Chiquita, is concentrated on the tropical plains regions along the Caribbean Sea.

Other important crops are sugarcane, cacao, and various tropical fruits and nuts.

Most of the country's large debt is tied to the 1978 collapse in worldwide coffee prices. Oil prices also soared at that time. The Costa Rican government began promoting foreign investment in order to diversify the economy, and more hydroelectric power plants were built to reduce dependence on imported oil. Both efforts have been successful.

Animal Husbandry

Common livestock include dairy and beef cattle, as well as poultry. Cattle ranching is widespread but controversial, as ranch lands increasingly encroach on forest reserves.

Tourism

Costa Rica's ecotourism industry is among the largest in the world, and the country is recognized as a global leader in sustainable tourism. The country supports a number of hotels, resorts, and scientific institutions. Because the country's economy is based on tourism, national parks and undisturbed wildlife habitats are among the country's most valuable resources. Services, including tourism, employ more than 70 percent of Costa

Rica's workforce. Tourism combined accounted for $2.6 billion in revenue for the country in 2014.

The tourist trade grew rapidly in the 1990s as ecotourists flocked to Costa Rica's national parks and forests. In total, there are 32 national parks, 13 forest reserves, and 51 wildlife refuges that make up 27 percent of total land area. Some of the most popular parks include Manuel Antonio National Park on the Pacific coast, and Poás National Park north of San José, where tourists can drive almost all the way to the rim of the Poás volcano.

Micah L. Issitt & John Pearson

DO YOU KNOW?

- Costa Ricans often refer to themselves as Ticos (men) or Ticas (women).
- It is estimated that Costa Rica's rainforests account for about five percent of all worldwide plant and animal species.

Bibliography

Booth, Johan A. *Costa Rica: Quest for Democracy*. Boulder, CO: Westview Press, 1999.

Cruz, Consuelo. *Political Culture and Institutional Development in Costa Rica and Nicaragua: World-making in the Tropics*. New York, NY: Cambridge University Press, 2005.

Daling, Tjabel. *Costa Rica in Focus: A Guide to the People, Politics and Culture*. Northampton, MA: Interlinke Publishing Group, 1998.

Eliot Greenspan. *Frommer's Easy Guide to Costa Rica 2014*. New York, NY: Frommer Media, 2014.

Helmuth, Chalene. *Culture and Customs of Costa Rica*. Westfield, CT: Greenwood Press, 2000.

Lonely Planet, and Wendy Yanagihara. Costa Rica. Oakland, CA: Lonely Planet Press, 2014.

MacKinnon, Dorothy. *Insight Guides: Costa Rica*. New York, NY: Langenscheidt Publishing Group, 2013.

Mavis Hiltunen Biesanz, Richard Biesanz, Karen Zubris Biesanz. *The Ticos: Culture and Social Change in Costa Rica*. Boulder, CO: Lynne Rienner Publishers, 1999.

McNeil, Jean, et al. *The Rough Guide to Costa Rica*. New York: Rough Guides, 2014.

Palmer, Steven Paul, Iván Molina and Iván Molina Jiménez. *The Costa Rica Reader: History, Culture, Politics*. Durham, NC: Duke University Press, 2004.

Works Cited

"Background Note: Costa Rica." United States Department of State. http://www.state.gov/r/pa/ei/bgn/2019.htm.

"BBC News—Country Profile: Costa Rica." BBC News Online. http://news.bbc.co.uk/2/hi/americas/country_profiles/1166587.stm.

"Costa Rica." CIA World Factbook Online. August 07, 2008. https://www.cia.gov/library/publications/the-world-factbook/geos/cs.html.

"Costa Rica." Human Rights Watch Online. http://hrw.org/doc/?t=americas&c=costar.

"Costa Rica." The Columbia Gazetteer of the World Online. New York: Columbia University Press, 2005. http://www.columbiagazetteer.org/public/Costa%20Rica.html.

"Costa Rica: Overview." Lonely Planet Press Online. http://www.lonelyplanet.com/worldguide/costa-rica/.

"Costa Rica—Information Related to Intangible Cultural Heritage." UNESCO Online. http://www.unesco.org/culture/ich/index.php?topic=mp&cp=CR.

"Costa Rica." *Nations of the World*. Amenia, NY: Grey House Publishing, 2015. http://centralamerica.com/cr/moon/moart.htm

"Instituto Nacional de Estadistica y Censos." Costa Rican Office of Statistics Online. http://www.inec.go.cr/.

Republica de Costa Rica. Official site of the Costa Rican government. http://www.casapres.go.cr/.

Sanchez Mora, Alexander. "El Modernismo Construction La Nacin: La Polemica Literaria de 1894 en Costa Rica." *Revista de Filologia y Linguistics de la Universidad de Costa Rica*. January 01, 2003.

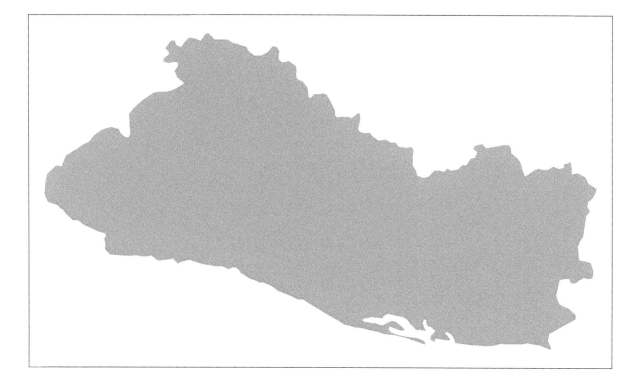

EL SALVADOR

Introduction

The smallest country in Central America, the Republic of El Salvador borders Guatemala, Honduras, and the North Pacific Ocean. Between 1524 and 1821, it was a Spanish colony. The mingling of Spanish settlers and Amerindian natives gave the country its modern-day character, both in ethnic and cultural terms.

Vast disparities of wealth and land ownership led to a devastating civil war (1979–1992) in which a right-wing military junta, funded by the United States, fought Marxist guerillas for economic and political control of the country. The years since the ceasefire have seen modest reforms, yet many of the root causes of the conflict remain.

Art occupies a central position in the culture of El Salvador. The country's civil war interrupted cultural production, but then became a major thematic subject of El Salvador's artists, especially in the realm of literature. Traditional arts and crafts, including ceramics, basketry, textiles, and masks, also continue to be practiced, and are often associated with a particular village.

GENERAL INFORMATION

Official Language: Spanish
Population: 6,340,000 (2013 estimate)
Currency: United States dollar
Coins: The U.S. dollar is divided into 100 cents. Coins are available in denominations of 1, 5, 10, and 25 cents, with a 50 cent and 1 dollar coin both rarely used.

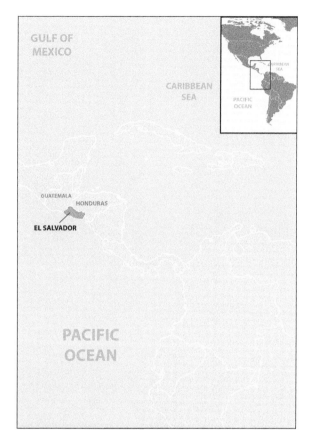

Land Area: 20,721 square kilometers (8,000 square miles)
Water Area: 320 square kilometers (124 square miles)
National Motto: "Dios, Union, Libertad" (Spanish, "God, Union, Liberty")
National Anthem: "Saludemos la Patria orgullosos" ("Proudly Salute the Fatherland")
Capital: San Salvador
Time Zone: GMT +6
Flag Description: The flag of El Salvador features two horizontal bands of blue separated by an equal horizontal band of white. El Salvador's national coat of arms is located in the center of the white band.

Population

El Salvador's population growth has slowed, with a decline in the number of youths and a slowly aging population. Life expectancy is 71 years for men and 78 years for women (2014 estimate). Over one million Salvadorans, or

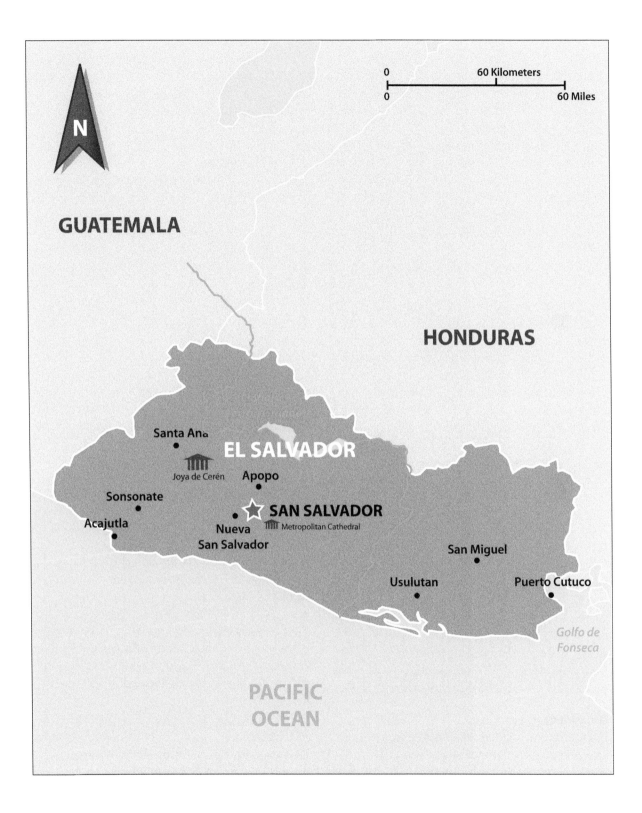

Principal Cities by Population (2014 estimates, unless noted):

- San Salvador (525,990)
- Soyapango (329,708)
- Santa Ana (176,661)
- San Miguel (161,880)
- Mejicanos (160,317)
- Santa Tecla (124,694)
- Apopa (112,158)
- Delgado (71,594)
- Sonsonate (59,468)
- San Marcos (54,615)

approximately 20 percent of the population, live abroad, mainly because of economic and social hardship within their native country. During the civil war, an estimated 75,000 Salvadorans were killed.

The average population density is approximately 299 persons per square kilometer (774 per square mile). Historically, the population was mostly rural, but today about 65 percent of the total population lives in urban centers (2011 estimate). One-quarter of the population lives in San Salvador and its environs, the most densely populated area of the country. (In 2011, the estimated population of the San Salvador metropolitan area was unofficially 2.44 million.) San Salvador is often cited as Central America's third largest city. Santa Ana, San Miguel, Mejicanos, and Soyapango are other important urban centers, the latter two being suburbs of San Salvador.

Approximately 86 percent of the population is mestizo, of mixed Spanish and Amerindian descent. The lower and middle classes are generally mestizo, whereas the upper class is of European descent. These Salvadorans account for only one percent of the population.

Languages

Spanish is the official language of El Salvador. Among the more educated, English is the most common second language. Traditional Amerindian languages include Pipil, Lenca, Kekchi, and Cacaopera, though these have very few known speakers.

Native People & Ethnic Groups

The indigenous population of El Salvador represents between five and 10 percent of the total population. Their ancestors, the Nahua people, arrived in the region around 3000 BCE, and were in control when the Spanish began their conquest.

Today, they are among the poorest inhabitants of the country and have accepted many cultural traits of the dominant mestizos, especially since a failed 1932 rebellion reduced their population considerably.

Mestizos represent the large majority of El Salvador's population. Minority ethnic groups in the country include French, German, Irish, and Italian.

Religions

Most Salvadorans are Christian. About 57 percent of the population identifies with the Roman Catholic Church, and much of the remainder is Protestant. Evangelical Protestant denominations have grown increasingly popular since the 1992 peace accord that ended El Salvador's civil war. Church rituals still permeate people's daily lives, though El Salvador is less conservative than its Central American neighbors.

During the 20th century, the Catholic Church began taking an increasing interest in the poverty of the lower classes and sought practical ways to relieve their plight. This movement, initially called Socialist Christianity, came to be known as Liberation Theology, and was commonly found throughout Central and South America.

During the 1970s and 1980s, the government persecuted the Catholic Church for its ostensible support of Communist ideals and subversive activities. Church figures, such as Archbishop Oscar Romero, were murdered during this period.

Each August, San Salvador is the epicenter of El Salvador's national patron saint festival, the highlight of which is a symbolic reenactment by the faithful of the transfiguration of Jesus Christ from mortal man to divine savior. An image of Jesus is processed atop a float through the thronged streets of San Salvador's historic district and then, in a part of the ritual known as la bajada ("the descent"), is lowered out of sight. The image then reemerges clad in glowing white garments symbolizing the transfiguration.

Climate

El Salvador has a tropical climate, with little variation between seasons. Precipitation is high between May and October (averaging 2,030 millimeters/80 inches); between November and April, the weather is generally warm and dry.

Temperature and moisture vary by elevation. Along the coastal lowlands, the hottest region, temperatures are between 25° and 29° Celsius (77° and 84° Fahrenheit), and humidity is low. The central plateau is cooler, with an annual average temperature of 23° Celsius (73° Fahrenheit). Annual average temperatures for the mountains are between 12° and 23° Celsius (54° and 73° Fahrenheit). Deforestation has caused hotter summers and shortened the rainy season.

El Salvador is prone to a range of natural disasters, from mudslides and hurricanes to violent earthquakes and volcanoes. In 2010, three tropical storms, Agatha, Alex, and Matthew, battered the country, causing massive flooding and the loss of nearly the entire bean crop in the nation. An earthquake measuring 7.3 on the Richter scale struck in 2014 causing many wall collapses and other damage to buildings. These natural disasters set the country's development even further back.

ENVIRONMENT & GEOGRAPHY

Topography

The terrain of El Salvador can be divided into three regions: the mountains (60 percent of the total area), the central plateau (25 percent), and the coastal lowlands. The Sierra Madre range, running east to west along the northern border between 1,600 and 2,200 meters (5,249 and 7,218 feet), has been deforested and eroded and is no longer suitable for cultivation.

The highest peak in El Salvador, the Santa Ana volcano, rises to an elevation of 2,385

meters (7,825 feet) in the northwest. Parallel to the Sierra Madre range, with the central plateau in between, is a range of more than 20 volcanoes, including San Miguel and Izalco, which have passed out of their most active stage.

The narrow central plateau has the highest population density, and is characterized by rolling hills and soil made rich from deposits of volcanic ash. The average elevation of this region is 600 meters (1,969 feet). The rolling coastal lowlands extend from the Gulf of Fonseca in the east for approximately two-thirds of the Pacific coastline; at that point, the range of volcanoes begins forming the coastline.

There are many rivers and lakes throughout El Salvador. Rio Lempa is the most important river and the only navigable one. It waters El Salvador's central plateau before flowing into the Pacific Ocean. Rio Lempa has been used to form several artificial lakes, Embalse Cerrón Granden being the largest. Torola, Goascorán, and Jiboa are other rivers which also flow into the Pacific. Many of the country's natural lakes are in volcanic craters, found in the highlands. Lago de Ilopango is the largest, at 70 square kilometers (27 square miles).

San Salvador is located in central El Salvador. The city stands at an altitude of 680 meters (2,240 feet) above sea level, on both sides of the Acelhuate River. It sits in a geologically active zone, in the shadow of several large hills and volcanoes, including Volcán de San Salvador, which last erupted in 1917. The land the city itself is situated upon, however, is largely flat.

Plants & Animals

Deforestation brought about by logging and agricultural production has decreased El Salvador's forests by about 85 percent since the 1960s, with only five percent of the total area remaining, thereby reducing animal habitats as well. Among the plants and trees still present are oak, balsam, rubber, pine, cypress, wild fruit trees, mahogany, several hundred types of orchid, and herbs.

Animals which have disappeared from the country include the jaguar and the crested eagle;

endangered animals include two types of bat, the giant anteater, and Baird's tapir. Monkeys, pumas, wild boar, ocelots, reptiles, and several hundred bird species still thrive in the country's mountains and forests, especially where protected by the government.

CUSTOMS & COURTESIES

Greetings
Greetings in El Salvador are typically modest, with handshakes being the most common. In addition, two people who have already met might simply nod their heads in greeting. When addressing a woman, a man will customarily wait for the woman to extend her hand in greeting before offering his own. More intimate greetings such as light hugs and kisses on the cheek are common among family and friends.

Spanish is the most common language in El Salvador and is spoken by more than 95 percent of Salvadorans. The most common greetings are "Buenos días" ("Good day" or "Good morning"), "Buenas tardes" ("Good afternoon" or "Good evening") and "Buenas noches" ("Good evening" or "Goodnight"). Like many Central American countries, Salvadorans pronounce words ending in "s" with an articulated "h" sound. The word "Buenos" ("Good") is therefore pronounced "Bwe-noh."

A small population in western El Salvador speak the Pipil language, an Amerindian tribal dialect. Among members of the Pipil, the language is referred to as "Nawat." In Nawat, a common greeting is "Yehyek tunal" (meaning "Hello"), and may be followed by "Ken tinemi?" ("How are you?").

Gestures & Etiquette
In comparison to Western cultures, Salvadorans are more comfortable with close proximity during conversation. Individuals generally stand less than an arm's length apart while talking, and direct eye contact is seen as a sign of sincerity and is therefore expected in daily conversation. Gestures such as pointing, particularly at a person, are considered rude, and many Salvadorans will use facial gestures in place of pointing with their hands. Pursing the lips toward an object or person is considered a more polite form of greeting than using the hand. To beckon a person, Salvadorans typically hold the hand up with the palm facing down. It is considered rude and/or aggressive to beckon to someone with the hand facing up.

Dress is casual in all but the most formal situations. In business situations, Salvadorans generally wear dark colors and dress conservatively. Timeliness is important, and it is typically considered rude and disrespectful to be late in formal or business situations, especially for a first meeting.

Eating/Meals
Most Salvadorans eat three meals a day. The morning meal is generally the smallest and lightest meal of the day. Typical morning dishes include beans, eggs, fruit, and tortillas. The midday meal, called "almuerzo," is usually the largest of the day. Roasted meats and vegetables are commonly served, and may be accompanied by salads, soups, and other small courses. Salvadorans often set aside more than an hour for their midday meal, including a period of rest and relaxation, before returning to work.

The evening meal consists of dishes similar to the afternoon meal, but generally in smaller proportions. Both the midday and evening meals are prime times for socializing among Salvadorans. Beer, sugar cane liquor, and other types of alcoholic beverages are commonly served with both afternoon and evening meals. Tropical beverages are very common in El Salvador, and include fresh fruit juices like tamarind and pineapple.

In rural communities, it is more common for Salvadorans to eat family-style, or communally, meals where guests serve themselves from common plates. It is unusual for food to be served in courses, and it is more common to serve single plates with a number of dishes mixed. As in many cultures, it is considered polite to sample all food and beverages offered by the host.

Visiting
In general, El Salvador is a poor country and most homes lack all but basic amenities. Despite

this fact, Salvadorans take pride in their hospitality. It is considered appropriate to compliment one's host on their appearance and the condition of their home. Small gifts are appreciated, but not expected, when visiting. Gifts such as flowers, candy, small pastries, or home accessories are the most common. In addition, Salvadorans tend to have a relaxed attitude toward punctuality in more informal and social settings.

LIFESTYLE

Family

Most Salvadorans live in extended families, with aunts, uncles, and grandparents sharing the same home or living in close proximity. Large families are the rule, with an average of three to four children per couple. In traditional Salvadoran culture, men are expected to work outside the home, while women are expected to manage domestic duties and child rearing. Even when not living in close proximity, Salvadoran society requires that extended family members be willing to aid in the support of children and mothers, either through direct assistance or by donating resources. Additionally, despite a greater proportion of women working outside the home in the early 21st century, most men continue to take little responsibility for domestic work and/or childrearing.

Most Salvadorans fall into one of two socioeconomic classes: wealthy landowners and poor laborers. The division between the wealthy and the poor has been a dominant feature of Salvadoran society since the Spanish colonial period. Poor Salvadorans suffer from a lack of employment and advancement opportunities, contributing to the need for travel. A disproportionate number of Salvadorans working for the government and in management positions are members of the social and economic elite, indicating the lack of mobility between socioeconomic castes.

Housing

More than 50 percent of Salvadoran houses lack flooring and adequate roofing. Houses are generally made of concrete and stone or a combination of concrete and wood. Wealthy families often tile their homes with slate or ceramics, while poorer families use more affordable materials, such as corrugated tin or simple, thatched roofing. The government has initiated programs intended to help poor Salvadoran families to improve housing conditions and pay for structural improvements. In addition, the tropical climate makes it unnecessary to install heating systems, and only wealthy members of society generally own air conditioning systems.

According to Habitat for Humanity, El Salvador is in the midst of a housing crisis in which more than 51 percent of the population lacks adequate housing. Habitat for Humanity estimates that more than 600,000 housing units are needed to address the current situation. In 2001, the housing crisis was further worsened by severe earthquakes, causing damaging to 20 percent of Salvadoran homes, of which more than 60 percent were in rural areas. Government aid was distributed first to families in rural areas. However, many rural families were forced to wait for years before they were able to repair their homes.

Food

The cuisine of El Salvador is similar to cuisines of neighboring Latin American cultures, with distinct native, African, and Spanish culinary influences. In particular, Salvadorans make extensive use of locally grown ingredients in their cuisine. Rice, beans, and maize (corn) are the staples of the Salvadoran diet and form the basis of most meals. Fresh tropical fruits are another important component to native cuisine, providing flavor and nutrition from an easily accessible source. Additionally, seafood and pork are commonly consumed, and popular and traditional dishes include turnovers and meat pies, tamales (seasoned meat and corn wrapped in husks or leaves), beef stews, and fried plantains.

One popular dish, casamiento, combines fried beans and rice with a variety of herbs and spices. Casamiento is an all purpose side and is often served as a main course, especially in rural families. Casamiento can be prepared with either black or red beans, and a variety of spices can be used, with chopped chilies and garlic being the most popular. Sometimes casamiento is served mixed with chicken and fried plantains. Another popular Salvadoran dish is the pupusa, which is a type of flatbread made of corn or rice flour and filled with cheese or meat. The pupusa is a traditional dish for the Pipil Indians, and was eventually absorbed into Salvadorian cuisine. Pupusas are often filled with chicharron, which is chopped and fried pork, similar to bacon. Other variations include pupusas stuffed with rice and beans, and sometimes filled with local gourds or vegetables.

A typical beverage in Salvadoran cuisine is atol de elete, which is a type of shake made from ground corn mixed with sugar, water, and sometimes cinnamon. Served either as a beverage or as a dessert pudding, atol de elete was traditionally served in the husk of a gourd, though most restaurants now serve it in glassware. Another beverage, known as chicha, is made from fermented corn flavored with a variety of floral or fruit extracts. The alcohol content of chicha depends on the aging process. New batches of chicha are generally sweeter while more mature varieties have a stronger alcohol flavor. Historians believe the Inca in Central America invented chicha.

Life's Milestones

Since El Salvador is predominantly a Roman Catholic nation, most Salvadorans follow Catholic traditions and rites of passage. As such, birth, baptism, communion, and marriage are the major milestones, marking the transition from childhood to adulthood. The birth of a family's first child is a cause for major celebration. Guests may bring small gifts or donate a small amount of money for the new parents.

As in many Latin American countries, Salvadorans celebrate a young girl's 15th birthday (often referred to as a quinceañera) with a special celebration. In Salvadoran culture it is known as the "La Fiesta de Roses," or "Festival of Roses," and includes a church ceremony followed by a party. Customarily, the girl of honor

wears a pink dress, which symbolizes innocence and youth. It is also common for the young woman to wear a red dress following the church ceremony, symbolizing womanhood.

Though marriage traditionally marks the transition to adulthood in the Catholic faith, a large number of Salvadorans forgo official services and engage, instead, in common law unions. Salvadoran law recognizes cohabiting couples as having certain rights, but also makes it easy for such couples to end their union without significant ceremony or penalties. If a couple decides on a church wedding, Catholic and local traditions make it difficult to dissolve the union, contributing to the growing number of common law unions in the nation.

CULTURAL HISTORY

Art

Traditional arts and crafts, often associated with a particular village, are practiced in the form of ceramics, basketry, textiles, and masks. Some of these traditions revolve around an individual founding artist, such as Fernando Llort (1949-), whose energetic style is now characteristic of the village of La Palma. He is often referred to as El Salvador's national artist.

The European influence in the arts was strong during the 19th century, with portraiture and religions paintings predominant in the genre

Villages are often identified through their arts and crafts.

of visual arts. The early 19th century also saw the opening of the country's first art schools. As the visual arts evolved, prominent themes include nationalism and indigenous identity. The Museo de Arte and the Museum of Anthropology house many examples of traditional Salvadoran art and artifacts. The Museo de Arte also features works from Spain and Mexico.

Architecture

El Salvador's architectural heritage has its roots in the country's pre-Columbian cultures. An ancient Mayan settlement remains near Santa Ana, once populated by the later Pipil (Nawat) culture. Known as the Joya de Cerén Archaeological Site, it was buried by a volcano in 600 CE and is a UNESCO World Heritage Site.

The country's architectural heritage is also characterized by the country's colonial period, perhaps best exemplified by the colonial architecture of the capital. Because of the city's geologically turbulent history, however, only a fraction of San Salvador's colonial-era heritage has survived. The city's oldest square, now called the Plaza Libertad (Liberty Plaza), was once anchored by elaborate Spanish-designed buildings dating to the capital's 16th-century origins. All of the original structures have succumbed to earthquakes or fire. Much of the country's modern architecture is built with earthquake resistance in mind.

Drama

El Salvador did not have a national film industry until the late 20th century, when two production companies, Radio Venceremos and the Revolutionary Film Institute of El Salvador, both of which concentrated on documentary films, were established. One of the first domestic films produced in the country was *El Salvador: The Pueblo Vencera* (*The People Will Win*), produced in 1981 by the Revolutionary Film Institute. It is considered a landmark achievement that contributed to the political and social tension that led to the Salvadoran Civil War (1979–1992).

The first decade of Salvadoran cinema saw the development of an industry concerned mainly with producing informative films about the Civil War. Though Radio Venceremos and the Revolutionary Film Institute once differed in political affiliation, the two studios joined to form the El Salvador Film and Television Unit in the early 1990s. Controlling television, film, and radio, the Film and Television Unit remains the major force in Salvadoran media, having evolved from a primarily political unit into a diverse company providing programming for both recreation and information.

Music

Like most Central American countries, El Salvador features a blend of European and native cultural influences. The dominant tribe in El Salvador at the time of Spanish colonization during the 16th century was the Pipil (Nawat), descendants of the Aztec tribe that once inhabited the region. After the Pipil were conquered, their traditions and customs were absorbed into the national culture. Spanish colonists later brought African slaves to El Salvador, and elements of African music were integrated into the country's cultural landscape.

During El Salvador's colonial period, Spanish authorities discouraged native music, fearing that native art and music could become the foundations of a nationalist movement. With the 1833 defeat of Anastasio Aquino (1792–1833), one of the last revolutionary Pipil leaders, native music all but disappeared. However, in the 1960s, a number of musicians began to return to traditional Pipil music and art in an effort to cultivate a native artistic tradition. The government also began to support the research and exploration of native arts to counterbalance European and American music, which was seen as having the potential to eclipse native traditions.

One of the most common types of music that is typically Salvadoran is Xuc. Xuc features the sacabuche, a woodwind instrument, and emerged in the 1940s. Traditionally, Salvadoran musicians use a variety of percussion instruments usually associated with African music, including small drums and wooden scrapers. Flutes and wooden drums also feature prominently. Western and

European instruments have also been incorporated into Salvadoran music, including the violin, guitar, and other stringed instruments. In the late 20th century, the music industry flourished as salsa, calypso, and reggae music became popular. In the early 21st century, hip-hop and reggaeton (a blend of dancehall and reggae music) emerged, becoming increasingly popular among urban youth.

Literature

Literature in El Salvador dates back to the arrival of the first printing press in the mid-17th century. The first printed works were religious texts attributed to Spanish monks living in the country. However, Salvadoran literature first emerged in the modern era, and one of the first Salvadoran writers to have an impact outside the country was Jose Maria Peralta Lagos (1873–1944). Writing under the pen name T.P. Mechin, Peralta Lagos published two famous works: *Burla Burlando* (*Mocking the Mocked*) in 1923 and *Brochazos* (*Brushstrokes*) in 1925. Writer and literary critic Italo Lopez Vallecillos (1932–1986) is another figure often associated with the early age of Salvadoran literature. Vallecillos was director of a publishing company known as EDUCA, which was important in the establishment of a more progressive, forward-leaning literary movement in El Salvador.

In the period immediately preceding the Civil War, there were a number of writers who gained fame by writing essays, poetry, and books with military, revolutionary, and political themes. One writer who became famous for political literature was Roque Dalton (1935–1975), a poet, essayist, and devout Marxist who remains one of El Salvador's most famous literary figures. Dalton wrote the famous *Las Historias Prohibidas del Pulgarcito* (*The Forbidden Stories of Tom Thumb*), published in 1975. In it, he tells the story of El Salvador's Spanish conquest through a mixture of literary styles, including poetry and journalistic accounts.

During the Salvadoran Civil War, a number of promising young poets and writers were killed because of their political beliefs or affiliation.

Among those killed were members of a literary society known as La Cebolla Purpura (The Purple Onion). The authors associated with this society were largely considered dangerous because of the revolutionary ideals they supported with their work. The end of Civil War in 1992 brought about a minor literary revolution, with the conflict itself becoming a prominent theme.

CULTURE

Arts & Entertainment

The Consejo Nacional para la Cultura y el Arte (Concultura) is the government agency responsible for promoting and facilitating artistic and cultural development in El Salvador. The council was established in 1991, and supervises five directorates, each with authority over certain aspects of the country's cultural development. The branch of Concultura with the greatest influence over the national arts scene is the Dirección Nacional de Artes, which operates the CENAR Art Academy, the nation's largest institute of arts education. CENAR teaches painting, sculpture, and performance arts.

Art and music both continue to serve an important role in daily life. In rural villages, music and dancing is part of all Salvadoran celebrations, and a major focus for community organization. While fine arts such as painting and sculpture are more common in urban areas, traditional crafts, including needlework and woodcarving, are popular across the country. Some Salvadorans make small crafts to sell in the cities, with this exchange constituting a major source of income for many people.

One of the major challenges facing the Salvadoran government is to preserve the artistic legacy of the Pipil tribe. Though Pipil art and culture is in danger of extinction due to a general lack of interest and the small size of the remaining Pipil population, Pipil artists are among the most popular and influential in the Salvadoran artistic community.

Fútbol (soccer) is the most popular sport. It is widely played in El Salvador, and local teams have numerous followers who fill stadiums for live matches. Basketball, boxing, tennis, and auto racing are also popular.

Cultural Sites & Landmarks

The city of San Salvador, which is El Salvador's capital and largest city, contains several sites designated by the Salvadoran government as national landmarks. The Palacio Municipal (Municipal Palace) was built in 1918 on the ruins of the original municipal palace, which was built in the Spanish colonial period. It served as the nation's first administrative capital building. Another famous landmark is the Catedral Metropolitana de San Salvador (Metropolitan Cathedral of San Salvador), built on the same site as the 19th-century Old San Salvador Cathedral, which burned to the ground in the 1950s. The Metropolitan Cathedral has become a symbol of the nation's Catholic heritage and was twice visited by Pope John Paul II (1920–2005).

In addition, the city is home to the exquisitely frescoed National Theater of El Salvador, as well as several monuments. The somber Monument to Memory and Truth memorializes the estimated 25,000 people who died or "disappeared" during El Salvador's long civil war. The memorial is one of the capital's most notable landmarks. Built of black granite, the 91-meter (300-foot) monument is inscribed with the names of the victims.

Several Salvadoran towns and villages have significant cultural importance due to their artistic traditions. For example, La Palma has become famous for hosting a school of art established by internationally renowned Salvadoran painter Fernando Llort (1949-). Llort is regarded as the national artist of El Salvador, and is known for his simple and colorful style, and his rural imagery. The town of Ilobasco is famous for ceramics, while the country town of San Sebastián is known for its textiles. Both ceramics and textiles are important artistic traditions in El Salvador.

In the highlands of El Salvador there is a mountain path known as the Ruta de las Flores (Route of Flowers), which has become increasingly popular as a cultural attraction. The Route of Flowers passes through several small towns, and is named for the numerous species of tall grass flowers that appear there after the rains. In addition, the colonial town of Suchitoto is also an important cultural destination, and one of the few places remaining in El Salvador to feature cobblestone roads.

Additionally, El Salvador is home to one World Heritage Site, Joya de Cerén. Located in the jurisdiction of San Juan, is an important archaeological site containing the preserved remains of a pre-Columbian farming community that was buried during the eruption of the Luguna Caldera volcano in 600 CE. The site also contains a number of excellent botanical specimens, allowing paleobotanists to investigate the use of plants in pre-Columbian culture. It was designated as a World Heritage Site in 1993 by the United Nations Educational, Scientific and Cultural Organization (UNESCO).

Libraries & Museums

San Salvador is home to several well known museums, including the David J. Guzmán National Anthropology Museum, which contains wide-ranging exhibits on the ancient Mayan civilization. It also houses the most significant archeological and ethnographical artifacts gathered from indigenous cultures throughout El Salvador. Additionally, the Museum of Popular Art and the Museum of Modern Art provide visitors with access to regional folk and contemporary artworks. The Museum of Words and Images displays manuscripts, objects, photographs, film, video, and works of art to document the Salvadoran search for truth and reconciliation in the aftermath of its troubled recent history.

The National Library of El Salvador serves as the country's legal depository and is located in the capital. Founded in 1870, it is the nation's largest library institution, with over 150,000 volumes. As of 2007, the country reported 225 public libraries and 26 university libraries. Foreign assistance has helped to grow the country's library system into rural and impoverished areas.

Holidays

The most colorful and widely celebrated holidays in El Salvador are Catholic. Villages, towns and cities annually recognize their patron saints with festivals involving processions, masses, music, games, and family gatherings. The most important saint day honors the country's patron, El Salvador del Mundo (The Savior of the World). It is held during the first week of August.

The other major religious holidays are the pre-Easter Holy Week, the day of the Virgin of Guadalupe (December 12), and Christmas. For Christmas, large nativity scenes are assembled, trees are decorated, and families gather to hold large feasts and exchange gifts. Dia de la Cruz (Day of the Cross), taking place on May 3, is amalgamation of pagan and Christian beliefs. Crosses are erected and adorned with flowers and fruit in order to encourage good crops.

Independence from Spain is celebrated on September 15.

Youth Culture

Salvadorans tend to marry young—at an average age of 19—resulting in a period of adolescence that is relatively short when compared to the U.S. In fact, more than 40 percent of women in El Salvador give birth to their first child by the age of 20. School is compulsory up to the age of 15.

Salvadoran youth typically enjoy a wide variety of music, from traditional Salvadoran and Latin American styles to imported music from Europe and North America. Some sociologists have noted that the emergence of hip-hop culture in El Salvador has served as an anchor for ethnic identification and association. Hip-hop music remains one of the most popular music styles for young Salvadoran boys. Additionally, while urban youth are typically exposed to a wealth of cultural influences, including imported music, literature, and film, youth in rural areas have fewer recreational options. Poverty, which affects four out of ten families in El Salvador, also limits the recreational options for young people.

One disturbing trend among youth in urban areas, particularly in San Salvador, is the increasing popularity of street gangs. Often, boys join these gangs for income, camaraderie, and protection from violence. Youth in many poor Salvadoran neighborhoods may also feel significant pressure to join their peers in gang-related activities. As a result, gang violence has become a major problem in El Salvador, and the government has been forced to include anti-gang laws into the penal code and to develop officer-training programs for police.

SOCIETY

Transportation

Public buses are the most common form of public transportation in El Salvador. Most are repurposed school or tour buses imported from the United States. Car rental services are available in all major cities and gas is available even in small, rural towns. Car travel can be expensive because of high gas prices, but allows easy access to smaller villages and more remote locations. There are a variety of private car and taxi services available in the cities and for travel between towns. It is also common to see hitchhikers along the major roads. Traffic moves on the right-hand side of the road.

Transportation Infrastructure

There are approximately 65 airports in El Salvador. However, only Aeropuerto Internacional de El Salvador, located 44 kilometers (27 miles) outside of San Salvador, handles international traffic. Comalapa is the largest airport in Central America and is also considered one of the safest airports in the world, due to the sophisticated radar system used. Other airports offer domestic transport, which are generally affordable and can be arranged on short notice.

While it is easy to travel between the major cities, travel to remote locations and small villages can be difficult because many roads have not been well maintained. In addition, over 80 percent of the nation's roads are unpaved.

Media & Communications

There are numerous daily, weekly, and monthly publications available in El Salvador. The major print news outlets include the daily newspapers *La Prensa Grafica* and *El Diario de Hoy*, and the evening paper *El Mundo*. Newspapers regularly run articles critical of the government and government policy without fear of reprisal. There are also a variety of magazines available in El Salvador, in both Spanish and English. International and English-language publications are also widely available in urban centers.

El Salvador has several major television stations, most of which are privately owned. The nation's most popular television stations, Teledos, Canal Cuatro, Canal Seis, and Agape TV, are all privately owned and offer a mix of entertainment and news. Cable and satellite television are generally only available in urban areas. El Salvador also has a diverse selection of radio stations, with programming ranging from Latin rock to talk radio. In addition, some of El Salvador's small towns and villages have their own radio stations, while others may share a single broadcast family with several surrounding towns. The largest radio station in the nation, Radio El Salvador, is state-run, and features a mix of public service programming and news.

Freedom of speech is guaranteed by the constitution of the republic and the government respects these rights, leading to a diverse selection of independent media outlets. In most urban areas, visitors have the option of television, radio, and Internet access. In rural areas, only radio and basic television are usually available. In 2012, an estimated 24.5 percent of the population (roughly 1,491,000 people) were considered Internet users.

SOCIAL DEVELOPMENT

Standard of Living

El Salvador ranked 115th out of 185 countries on the 2014 United Nations Human Development Index, which compiles quality of life and standard of living indicators.

Water Consumption

According to 2010 statistics from the World Health Organization (WHO), approximately 88 percent of the population of El Salvador has access to an improved source of drinking water, while 87 percent has access to improved sanitation. Both figures are below the regional average. The continuity of supply for water is low, and many households engage in meter sharing.

Education

Education for school age children between the first and ninth grades is free and compulsory in El Salvador. After the ninth grade, students can study for three more years towards an academic diploma, or choose vocational training.

The system has improved since the civil war years and has become more egalitarian. Large problems still loom, however. Attendance among the most disadvantaged sector of society is low; more resources are allocated for urban schools, and many students do not continue after grade nine. Total adult literacy in El Salvador was estimated at 85 percent in 2011.

Public institutes of higher education include the University of El Salvador, the Central American University, and the University of Don Bosco, all located within the San Salvador metropolitan area. There are also institutes for technical and teacher training and private institutes.

Women's Rights

Violence against women remains a serious problem in El Salvador. In traditional Salvadoran society, women are expected to be submissive to their spouses and to men in general. This male-dominated nature of traditional Salvadoran society makes it difficult to eliminate violence against women—particularly domestic violence—because women often fail to report abuse, fearing reprisal or criticism. Generally, a conviction for domestic violence carries a penalty of between one and three years in prison, depending on the circumstances and severity of the crime. However, interviews with Salvadoran men and women suggest that domestic abuse is not generally considered a serious crime, contributing to the belief that domestic abuse may be more common than indicated by official statistics.

Rape is illegal under Salvadoran law and carries a penalty of between six and 10 years imprisonment. There is a special statute extending the maximum sentence to twenty years for the rape of children, elderly or disabled persons. Spousal rape is not specifically addressed in Salvadoran law, but can be prosecuted under laws that apply to rape in general. Investigations by human rights organizations indicate that women are less likely to report spousal rape than rape by unrelated individuals. In addition, reports from victims suggest that police are not effective in investigating reports of rape, and are not supportive of victims who report rape. According to the U.S. Department of State, 461 rapes per year were reported during 2010-2012.

El Salvador has a law prohibiting sexual harassment with penalties ranging from three to five years in prison. The penal code also states that, in cases where the harassment involves a superior in a workplace, teacher or other authority figure, additional fines may be imposed. Investigations indicate that most incidents of sexual harassment are not reported due to cultural norms and fear of reprisal. Prostitution is legal in El Salvador, though the law prohibits facilitation and promotion. Though the penal code serves to protect sex workers from exploitation, it also prohibits prostitutes from seeking protection through a facilitator.

Salvadoran women represent more than 40 percent of the workforce, and on average earn less than men do, and are less frequently offered opportunities for advancement. In most industries, males hold a majority of the highest-paying and management-oriented jobs, while women dominate low-wage and domestic labor positions.

Health Care

El Salvador's health care system has improved since the end of the civil war, but still does not provide adequate care for a significant portion of the population. Medical services are dispensed in two ways: through an insurance program supported by workers and their employers, and by government subsidy programs.

There is a great disparity between the care received by the rich and poor, and an even greater disparity between urban and rural populations. Poor sanitary conditions and contaminated drinking water contribute to prevalent cases of dysentery and diarrhea as well as to cholera. Cases of dengue fever and leishmaniasis (parasitic disease) also occur. Furthermore, the infant mortality rate is high, and malnutrition is common among children.

GOVERNMENT

Structure

One positive effect of the civil war was greater participation in government along socioeconomic and ideological lines. The leftist movement, which once opposed the government with guerilla attacks, is now a legitimate political party in opposition to the right wing. This represents at least a partial break from the legacy of Spanish colonial rule, which established a small number of wealthy families and military elite to dominate every aspect of the country.

According to the 1983 constitution, El Salvador is a republic. The president, who is elected by popular vote to a single five-year term, is the chief of state and the head of government. He or she is responsible for selecting the cabinet, the Council of Ministers, pending legislative approval. A vice president is elected along with the president.

The unicameral legislature consists of 84 deputies. They are elected to three-year terms by popular vote. In addition to approving presidential selections, they are responsible for choosing Supreme Court justices.

Political Parties

Since the end of the civil war, it has been common for political parties to fracture and make new coalitions. Among the most prominent parties currently operating in El Salvador are the Farabundo Marti National Liberation

Front (FMLN), the National Republican Alliance (ARENA), the Christian Democratic Party (PDC), and the National Conciliation Party (PNC). Other parties include the Social Democratic Party, the Renewal Movement, and the United Democratic Centre.

Local Government

El Salvador has 14 departments. Departments are headed by a federally-appointed governor who serves a four-year term. Each of El Salvador's departments is subdivided into municipalities. Municipalities are administered by a council and mayor. Though some local power is vested in popularly-elected town councils, the national government maintains strong control of them.

Judicial System

The Supreme Court is the highest court in El Salvador. Among other duties, it reviews legislation and interprets the constitution. Each of the country's 14 administrative regions has its own civil and criminal courts. Minor civil conflicts are adjudicated by Justices of the Peace, who hear cases in personal courts. Larger criminal matters are reviewed by first instance courts comprised of three judges. The country's criminal justice system has its roots in 19th-century Spanish law.

Taxation

Individual taxes collected in El Salvador include an income tax, a capital gains tax, and property tax. The maximum tax on corporate profits in El Salvador is 30 percent. Tax revenue was an estimated 19 percent of the country's GDP in 2013. Corruption remains a problem at all levels of government in El Salvador.

Armed Forces

The Armed Forces of El Salvador consist of an army, navy, and air force. The voluntary age for military service is 16, while the age for selective conscription, lasting one year, is 18 (though compulsory service is considered voluntary in practice). In 2009, in response to increasing crime, armed forces personnel joined police on patrols through 19 municipalities with the highest rates of criminal activity. The Salvadoran armed forces were also the longest-serving Latin American armed forces to serve in the Iraq War.

Foreign Policy

Many of El Salvador's foreign policy commitments are designed to strengthen economic and military cooperation between El Salvador and its Central American neighbors. For example, El Salvador is a key member of the Central American Common Market (CACM) and the Central American Security Commission (CASC), which is active in a variety of initiatives designed to strengthen weapons control and arms traffic control. In 1994, El Salvador joined its Central American neighbors in forming the Alliance for Sustainable Development, also called Conjunta Centroamerica-USA (CONCAUSA). The goals of CONCAUSA include developing plans for sustainable development and agriculture, energy use and distribution, and to create and maintain productive avenues of change between all the Central American countries and the U.S. moreover, creating jointly administered territories with the goal of protecting key habitat and keystone species is another goal.

El Salvador is also active on the international stage, and is an active member of the United Nations (UN) and several specialized groups within the organization. El Salvador also plays a role in the World Trade Organization (WTO), and is in the process of negotiating more comprehensive trade agreements to strengthen its economy. While El Salvador has an ongoing territorial dispute with Honduras, involving the disposition of ocean territory within the Gulf of Fonesca, regular relations and communication have persisted between the two nations. Recently, both agreed to honor the border division determined by the International Court of Justice (ICJ). In addition, El Salvador is one of the few countries to maintain diplomatic relations with Taiwan (Republic of China) instead of the People's Republic of China.

Human Rights Profile

International human rights law insists that states respect civil and political rights, and also promote an individual's economic, social and cultural rights. The United Nations (UN) Universal Declaration of Human Rights (UDHR) is recognized as the standard for international human rights. Its authors sought the counsel of the world's great thinkers, philosophers, and religious leaders, and were careful to create a document that reflects the core values shared by every world culture. (To read this document or view the articles relating to cultural human rights, visit: http://www.udhr.org/UDHR/default.htm.)

While the penal code of El Salvador is in keeping with the principles of the UDHR, human rights organizations have recognized several areas of concern. Numerous reports indicate, for example, that members of the National Civilian Police (PNC) regularly commit crimes that violate provisions of the UDHR. According to the U.S. Department of State, in 2013 the PNC was charged with 324 human rights abuses, including murder, assault, and unlawful detention.

El Salvador's penal code guarantees free and fair public trials for those accused of crimes, in keeping with Article 11 of the UDHR. However, in many cases monitoring agencies have found that the judicial system is inefficient and that individuals are held in detention for long periods awaiting trial. Several monitoring agencies have also raised concerns about corruption in the judicial system.

The constitution of El Salvador guarantees freedom of speech, expression, and assembly to all citizens, in keeping with Articles 19 and 20 of the UDHR. However, representatives of Amnesty International (AI) criticized the Salvadoran government in 2007 for using anti-terrorism laws to violate the rights of political protestors. Though incidents such as the 2007 protest arrests are cause for concern, in general the Salvadoran government actively protects the rights of speech and expression. For example, the media has been free to explore political issues without significant censorship.

Several human rights organizations have criticized the government for doing little to find children lost or killed during the Salvadoran Civil War. It is estimated that there are hundreds of children who disappeared during the height of the civil conflict who have yet to be found or returned to their families. There is also some concern that child abuse remains common in some rural areas. This is largely attributed to cultural norms that allow fathers considerable freedom to use corporal punishment and discourage reporting familial abuse to authorities.

Lastly, the U.S. Department of State estimates that between 40,000 and 70,000 Salvadorans were killed during the Salvadoran Civil War and the violence that preceded it. The Mexico City Peace Accords brought an official end to the conflict in 1992, but violence continued to erupt sporadically for several years. Human rights monitoring agencies have expressed concern that the government has done little to address crimes committed during the civil war.

ECONOMY

Overview of the Economy

During much of the 20th century, El Salvador's economy and resources were controlled by a tight-knit group of families who led decadent lives while keeping the lower classes in poverty. The ensuing civil war devastated the economy, causing an estimated $2 billion worth of damage. Since the end of hostilities, the economic situation has improved due to expanding markets, the redistribution of land, and the diversification of products for export.

As of 2013, El Salvador's estimated gross domestic product (GDP) per capita was $7,500 USD. Approximately 36.5 percent of the population lives below the poverty line, but the middle class has broadened. Foreign aid and contributions from Salvadorans living abroad have helped reduce the country's enormous trade deficit.

Industry

Industry accounts for approximately 30 percent of GDP. Some sectors were damaged during the civil war, as guerillas attacked factories and infrastructure in order to weaken the government. The most commonly manufactured goods are food products and beverages, but El Salvador also produces tobacco products, petroleum products, leather, textiles, chemicals, and furniture. The industrial sector provides manufactured goods for domestic, regional, and, increasingly, foreign markets.

The capital's manufacturing sector turns out clothing, textiles, shoes, leather goods, construction materials, soap, tobacco products, furniture, chemicals, processed foods, and beer. However, remittances sent from Salvadorans living abroad, primarily in the United States, continue to outstrip the income generated by manufacturing exports.

Labor

El Salvador's labor force was estimated at nearly 2.74 million in 2013. The majority worked in the services sector, while 21 percent and 20 percent, respectively, were employed in the agricultural and industrial sectors. Unemployment stands at 6.3 percent (2013 estimate). Underemployment is also a problem.

Energy/Power/Natural Resources

El Salvador has deposits of gold, silver, limestone, copper, iron ore, lead, zinc, mercury, and gypsum, but mining operations remain small-scale. Logging has significantly reduced the once-extensive forests. Some of the remaining trees, such as cedar, oak, and mahogany, are cut for timber; others are protected in national parks.

Hydropower and geothermal plants were both devastated during the civil war but have reopened in recent years. Arable land remains the country's most vital resource.

The rapid deforestation has created serious environmental problems, including soil erosion and poor water quality. Water and soil have also been degraded by toxic waste dumping and pesticides, and the air in urban centers is polluted by traffic. Many people do not have access to clean water or proper sanitation, and trash disposal is poorly handled. Vestiges of the civil war, in the form of landmines and unexploded ordnance, dot the countryside.

Fishing

The Pacific Ocean supports a developing fishing industry, and El Salvador exports shrimp, tuna, mackerel, and swordfish caught off its shores. An estimated 30,000 tons of fish were produced in 2003. Sport fishing, particularly marlin fishing, is also becoming increasingly popular in the country.

Forestry

El Salvador is known as one of the most deforested countries in the Western Hemisphere. Efforts to promote legal and sustainable forestry continue. The country remains a leading producer of balsam.

Mining/Metals

Although the Canadian-based mining company, Pacific Rim, discovered valuable strains of gold and silver in Ecuador in the 1990s, conflicts over mining licensing prevented them from being exploited. Critics of the mining company contend that it is using money to influence the political process involved in accessing El Salvador's mineral resources. Allegations of violence and intimidation on the part of the mining companies have surfaced.

Agriculture

Agriculture accounts for 10 percent of El Salvador's GDP and employs 21 percent of the country's labor force. Traditionally, agriculture has been the mainstay of the Salvadoran economy and it is still important today. Approximately 32 percent of the land is arable. Coffee remains the most important crop but is vulnerable to international price fluctuations. Sugarcane, cotton, corn, beans, rice, cereals, fruits, and vegetables are also cultivated.

Animal Husbandry

Cattle and hogs are the most commonly raised livestock. Other livestock include goats, mules, and horses. Many animals are raised for the purposes of subsistence farming and for El Salvador's informal economy. Industrial animal production continues to face challenges related to infrastructure.

Tourism

El Salvador has had difficulty overcoming its image as a war-torn country prone to natural disasters, and the number of foreign visitors is limited as a result. Unlike in Caribbean countries, where tourism generates significant revenue, it only accounts for a sliver of El Salvador's GDP. Efforts are underway to promote the country's natural beauty and culture and to further develop its infrastructure.

For nature enthusiasts, El Salvador offers a varied landscape that encompasses mountains, volcanoes, a cloud forest, and Pacific coastline. Surfing, hiking, kayaking are popular sporting activities for visitors. Protected areas include the Montecristo Cloud Forest and the Cerro Verde National Park. Indigenous culture is on display at the Mayan ruins of Tazumal, while historic churches showcase the country's colonial heritage.

Micah Issitt, Michael Aliprandini,
Beverly Ballaro

DO YOU KNOW?

- "El Salvador" means "the Savior" in Spanish, a reference to Jesus Christ.
- Pedro de Alvarado was the Spanish conquistador who claimed El Salvador for the crown in the 16th century.

Bibliography

Boland, Roy. *Culture and Customs of El Salvador.* Westfield, CN: Greenwood Publishing Group, 2001.

Booth, John A., Wade, Christine J., and Thomas W. Walker. *Understanding Central America: Global Forces, Rebellion and Change.* Jackson, TN: Westview Press, 2006.

Brignoli, Hector-Perez. *A Brief History of Central America.* Berkeley, CA: University of California Press, 1989.

Fariña, Laura Pedraza, Spring Miller, and James L. Cavallaro. *No Place to Hide: Gang, State, and Clandestine Violence in El Salvador.* Cambridge, MA: Human Rights Program, Harvard Law School, 2010.

Jacques, Jaime. *El Salvador (Moon Handbooks).* Berkeley, CA: Avalon Travel, 2014.

Lonely Planet. *Nicaragua and El Salvador.* Oakland, CA: Lonely Planet, 2006.

Moodie, Ellen. *El Salvador in the Aftermath of Peace: Crime, Uncertainty, and the Transition to Democracy.* Philadelphia: University of Pennsylvania Press, 2010.

Negroponte, Diana Villiers. *Seeking Peace in El Salvador: The Struggle to Reconstruct a Nation at the End of the Cold War.* New York: Palgrave Macmillan, 2012.

Pederson, David. *American Value: Migrants, Money, and Meaning in El Salvador.* Chicago: University of Chicago Press, 2013.

Works Cited

Proyecciones de Poblacion, 2005-2010. *Central Office of Statistics El Salvador.* http://www.minec.gob.sv/

"Background Note: El Salvador." *U.S. Department of State Online.* http://www.state.gov/r/pa/ei/bgn/2033.htm

"El Salvador." *CIA World Factbook Online.* https://www.cia.gov/library/publications/the-world-factbook/geos/es.html

Boland, Roy. "Culture and Customs of El Salvador." Westfield, CN: Greenwood Publishing Group, 2001.

World Bank. "El Salvador: Rural Development Study." Fundación Salvadoreña para el Desarrollo Económico y Social. Washington D.C.: World Bank Publications, 1998.

Woodward, Ralph Lee. "Central America: A Nation Divided." New York: Oxford University Press U.S., 1999.

Counihan, Carole and Penny Van Esterik. "Food and Culture: A Reader." New York: Routledge Publishing, 2007.

Chandler, Gary and Robert Reid. "Central America on a Shoestring." Oakland, CA: Lonely Planet Press, 2004.

Coates, Anthony G. and Olga F. Linares. "Central America: A Natural and Cultural History." New Haven, CT: Yale University Press, 1999.

Bethell, Leslie. "Central America Since Independence." Cambridge, UK: Cambridge University Press, 1991.

Booth, John A., Wade, Christine J., and Thomas W. Walker. "Understanding Central America: Global Forces, Rebellion and Change." Jackson, TN: Westview Press, 2006.

Eltringham, Peter. "The Rough Guide to Central America 3rd ed." New York: Rough Guides, 2004.

"Fodor's Central America, 3rd ed." New York: Fodor's Press, 2008.

Penland, Paige and Gary Chandler. "Lonely Planet Nicaragua and El Salvador." Oakland, CA: Lonely Planet Press.

Montgomery, Tommie Sue. "Revolution in El Salvador: From Civil Strife to Civil Peace 2nd ed." New York: Westview Press, 1994.

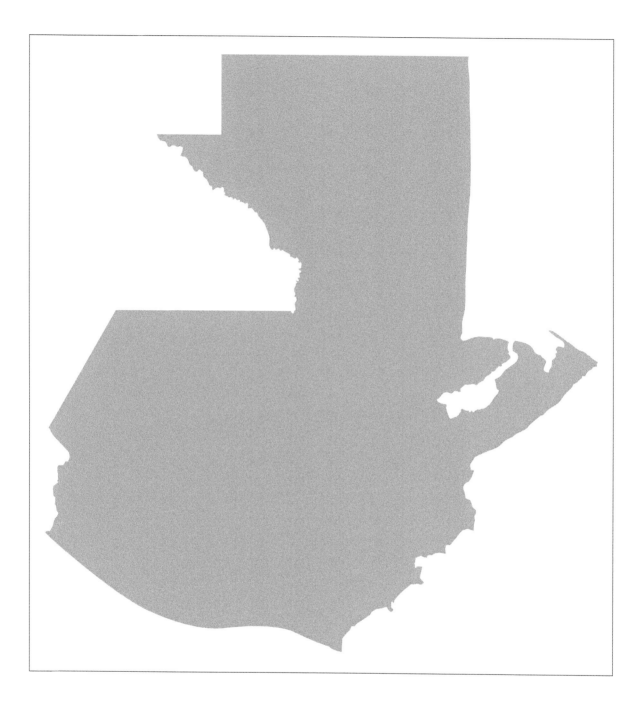

GUATEMALA

Introduction

The Central American Republic of Guatemala, located in the southern part of the continent of North America, is bordered by Mexico to the north, Belize to the northeast, and Honduras and El Salvador to the southeast. A constitutional democratic republic, Guatemala is comprised of twenty-two administrative divisions. It is the largest and most populous country in Central America.

The Maya peoples occupied Guatemala until the 11th century. Remnants of the Mayan culture remain in the form of ruins throughout Guatemala. In 1524, Guatemala was conquered by Spanish conquistador Pedro de Alvarado and became a Spanish colony. Guatemala won its independence in 1821 after three centuries as a Spanish colony. The Mayan culture remains strong in Guatemala, and celebrations based on the "Popol Vuh," a Maya creation story, are still observed.

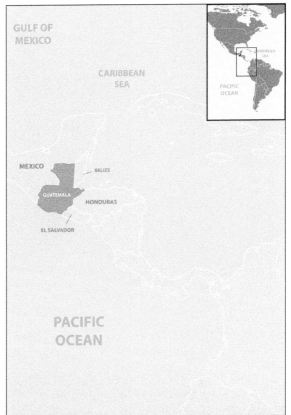

GENERAL INFORMATION

Official Language: Spanish
Population: 14,647,083 (2014 estimate)
Currency: Guatemalan quetzal
Coins: The Guatemalan quetzal is divided into 100 cents. Coins are available in denominations of 1, 5, 10, 25, and 50 centavos, and 1 quetzal.
Land Area: 107,159 square kilometers (41,374 square miles)
Water Area: 1,730 square kilometers (667 square miles)
National Motto: "País de la Eterna Primavera" ("Country of the Eternal Spring")

National Anthem: "Guatemala Feliz" ("Guatemala, Be Praised")
Capital: Guatemala City
Time Zone: GMT -6
Flag Description: The flag of Guatemala features three equal, vertical bands—two sky blue and one white. In the center of the white color band, which is located between the two blue color bands, is the Guatemalan coat of arms.

Population

Approximately 55 percent of Guatemala's population is considered Mestizo, which is mixed Amerindian-Spanish or assimilated Amerindian (called Ladino in Spanish). Approximately 43 percent of the population is Amerindian, with whites and others making up the final two percent of the population.

The population was greatly affected during the second half of the 20th century as the country experienced a 36-year guerrilla war. While the government signed a peace agreement in 1996 to put a formal end to the conflict, an estimated

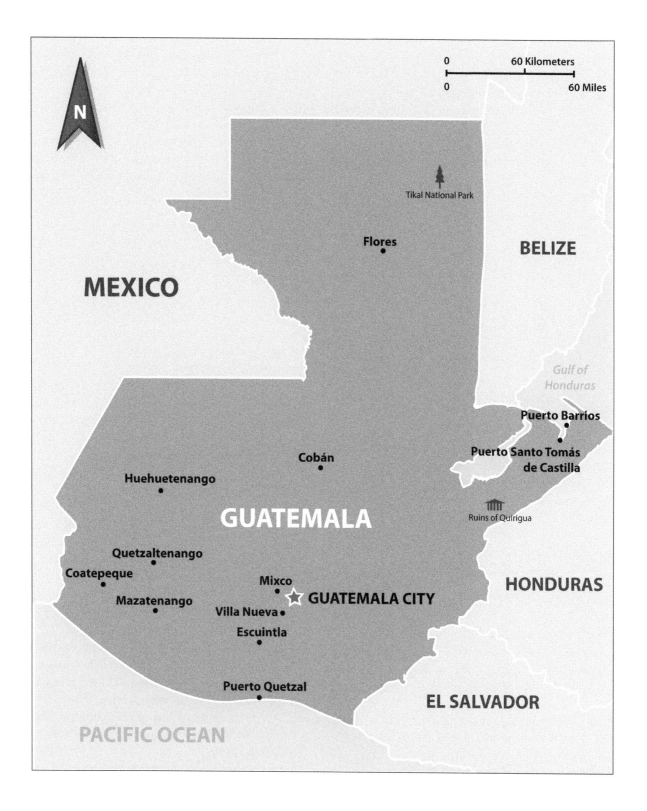

Principal Localities by Population (2013):

- Guatemala City (994,938)
- Mixco (473,080)
- Villa Nueva (406,830)
- Petapa (141,455)
- San Juan Sacatepéquez (136,886)
- Quetzaltenango (132,230)
- Villa Canales (122,194)
- Escuintla (103,165)
- Chinautla (97,172)
- Chimaltenango (82,370)

100,000 people died due to the war, which also created an estimated one million refugees. Many Guatemalans left the country for Mexico or the United States.

The population of the greater metropolitan area of Guatemala City is approximately 4 million and has grown rapidly thanks to a continuing influx of people moving to the capital from the nation's rural areas. Until the mid-1990s, most migrants moved to Guatemala City as refugees from a brutal civil war that had raged in the countryside for more than three decades. The end of the war in 1996—and the upsurge of foreign investment and economic growth it made possible—accelerated this migration trend among rural citizens. Many rural people continue to perceive Guatemala City as an escape from the chronic poverty and harsh living conditions associated with a traditional agrarian lifestyle.

Languages

Spanish is the official language of Guatemala, with the majority of the population speaking it as a primary language. An estimated 40 percent of the population speaks Amerindian languages, 23 of which are officially recognized. Some of the Amerindian languages are Quiche, Cakchiquel, Kekchi, Mam, Xinca, and Garifuna. In Guatemala City, English is widely spoken in business and educational settings.

Native People & Ethnic Groups

The Mayan people occupied Guatemala until the 11th century. Mayan ruins remain throughout Guatemala. The most well known of these is Tikal, which was uncovered by archeologists in the 1950s. The site includes over 300 separate constructions including monuments, statues, and hieroglyphics. After excavating Tikal, archeologists were able to recognize residential buildings, tombs, altars, and administrative buildings.

Today, Mestizos (Amerindian and Spanish) make up Guatemala's largest ethnic group. Minority ethnic groups in Guatemala include various Amerindian populations. Descendents of the indigenous Mayans, these groups include the Kaqchikel, Mam, and K'ichie. There are also small numbers of Italians, Germans, and Scandinavians in Guatemala.

Religions

Guatemala's constitution provides religious freedom for all citizens. Roman Catholicism is the predominant religion, but in recent years, Protestant groups have become more popular. Catholicism arrived with the Spanish during the 16th century, but Protestant missionaries have been working in Guatemala only since the 1960s. Mayan religious leaders maintain that a large portion of the population also participates in indigenous spiritual rituals or the incorporation of traditional indigenous rites into the practice of Christian worship.

Climate

Guatemala's climate varies greatly with changes in altitude and the seasons. The rainy season lasts from May to October, with the dry season lasting from November to April.

Above sea level, where the majority of the Guatemalan population lives, the nights are usually cool while the days are warm. The average temperature is usually around 20° Celsius (68° Fahrenheit). In the coastal regions of Guatemala, the weather is much warmer and more tropical, usually around 28° Celsius (83° Fahrenheit).

Rainfall also varies greatly between the costal and highland regions. Coastal areas usually receive about 1.5 to 2.5 meters (60 to 100 inches) of rain per year, while the highland areas typically see about one meter (52 inches) of rain.

ENVIRONMENT & GEOGRAPHY

Topography

Most of Guatemala's terrain is dominated by mountains with narrow costal plains, limestone plateaus, and volcanoes and jungles. There are no natural harbors on the west coast of the country.

Guatemala has over 30 volcanoes, which contribute to the likelihood of earthquakes in the region. Many of the volcanoes are massive and stand over 12,000 feet high. The highest point in the country is Volcan Tajumulco, at 6,777 meters (22,234 feet). Approximately 10 percent of Guatemala's total land area is preserved by the Maya Biosphere Reserve, which is composed almost entirely of tropical forest.

Guatemala has 644 kilometers (400 miles) of coastline, with black-sand beaches along the Pacific coast. There are also many rivers and lakes throughout the country. The Motagua, the Usumacinta, and the Chixoy are the longest rivers in Guatemala.

Located at an elevation of 1,493 meters (4,897 feet), Guatemala City sprawls over a large valley in the midst of Guatemala's rugged central highlands. Scattered throughout these highlands are some 33 volcanoes, including the Agua volcano, the forested 3,760-meter-tall (12,336-foot) cone of which is visible from all points in the capital. Although most of the 33 volcanoes are extinct, some remain active, including the Pacaya volcano, located 30 kilometers (19 miles) south of the capital's center. A 1998 eruption of the Pacaya volcano showered tons of volcanic sand and ash on Guatemala City, forcing the closure of the capital's airport. Pacaya erupted once again in 2014, forcing the evacuation of the 3,000 residents of El Rodeo and Patrocinio.

Plants & Animals

Guatemala is home to more than 8,000 plant species, including 600 species of orchids. The country is also home to 250 species of mammals and 221 bird species.

The national bird is the quetzal. The bird is considered sacred to the Mayan population of Guatemala, and has a prominent role in many Mayan legends. The quetzal has been seen as a symbol of freedom in Guatemala for centuries. An endangered species, the quetzal faces many threats including cattle ranching, deforestation, and a lack of water in its natural habitat.

There are 19 ecosystems throughout Guatemala, including cloud forests and rainforests. The country also has 30 protected national parks and biological reserves, which are intended to encourage sustainable tourism while preserving plant and animal resources.

Guatemala uses the money generated by tourism to fund protection efforts for the ecosystems. Some of the problems facing the plants and animals of Guatemala include soil erosion, water pollution, and the deforestation of the Petén rainforest (often called the "cradle of Mayan civilization").

CUSTOMS & COURTESIES

Greetings

Handshakes are the most common type of greeting in Guatemala between men and strangers meeting for the first time. Guatemalan handshakes are generally not firm, and are relatively brief. Men may kiss women on the cheek in greeting, and friends often embrace or exchange cheek kisses. Additionally, it is considered polite to rise from one's seat when greeting someone.

Spanish is the official language of Guatemala and most Guatemalans speak it as their primary language. When greeting, Guatemalans typically use the word "Buenos" ("Good") combined with a word to indicate the time of day, such as "Buenos días" ("Good morning"), "Buenas tardes" ("Good afternoon") and "Buenas noches" ("Good evening"). They might also ask "¿Como esta usted?" ("How are you doing?").

In addition to Spanish, there are more than a dozen distinct Mayan dialects used in Guatemalan society. Visitors may also encounter individuals who speak the Garifuna language in parts of Guatemala. The Garifuna are a people of mixed African and Caribbean heritage that reside along the Caribbean coasts of several neighboring Central American countries. Common greetings among the Garifuna include "Mábuiga" ("Hello"), "Buíti binafi" ("Good morning"), "Buíti amidi" ("Good afternoon"), and "Buíti ranbá weyu" ("Good evening").

Gestures & Etiquette

In conversation between members of the same sex, Guatemalans may stand close to one another. This is especially true of the Garifuna, who often stand in close proximity when conversing. Men addressing women may stand further apart on average in an effort to show respect. In general, Mayan people are more reserved and conservative than other subsets of Guatemalan society.

Guatemalans have a relaxed sense of time and punctuality in most situations. Parties, dates, and other social engagements are often scheduled within a range, rather than at a specific time. In business meetings, however, Guatemalans see tardiness as a sign of disrespect. Foreigners are often held to higher standards in regards to punctuality.

Hand gestures are important in Guatemalan communication, helping to emphasize meaning and indicate emotion. For example, Guatemalans typically do not cross their arms during conversation, as this is viewed as a sign of discomfort. When beckoning, the palm is held down while the fingers are moved back and forth. Similarly, when waving "goodbye," Guatemalans hold the hand up with the palm facing away from the person, and wave the hand with the fingers held together. As in other Central American countries, Guatemalans consider it rude to point with the fingers and often use lip pointing, which involves pursing one's lips toward an object of interest.

Eating/Meals

Guatemalans generally eat three meals a day. In rural and poor communities, families may limit themselves to two meals a day due to economic concerns. Most meals are served family style, with everyone serving themselves from communal dishes. Most major holidays are accompanied by family and/or community feasts, including the major Roman Catholic holidays.

The typical Guatemalan breakfast consists of light fare, including fruit, eggs, rice, beans, and bread. The midday meal is traditionally the largest of the day, and the prime time for socializing. In contemporary Guatemalan culture, the evening meal is gradually replacing the afternoon meal as the select time for business and social engagements. While lunch lasts for at least an hour, individuals now regularly set aside more than two hours for the evening meal. The evening meal, which is typically eaten between five and 10 o'clock, is generally light and can consist of leftovers from the midday meal. Additionally, some Guatemalan families may commonly stop work for a snack and drink in the early evening. Alcohol, including mixed drinks and beer, is commonly served at both social and business meals.

In formal situations, meals may more closely resemble dining in Europe or North America, where guests are served by their host and the meal is served in courses. However, Guatemalans typically serve their food on a single plate containing a variety of items. When eating dinner in a social situation, it is considered polite to comment on the host's food, and to try every dish offered.

Visiting

When visiting a Guatemalan home, it is customary to bring a small gift for the host, with common gifts including flowers, candies, and liquor. If invited to dinner it is acceptable to bring a dessert course. In Ladino culture, white is the color of both marriage and funerals, while the Mayans associate yellow with death. White and yellow flowers should therefore be avoided, as they are commonly used for funerals.

While some Guatemalans may offer to give guests a tour of their home, it is considered impolite to ask for a tour or to investigate areas of the house without accompaniment. In general, Guatemalans are regarded as friendly and gregarious in social situations, and typically treat their guests with respect and enthusiastic hospitality.

LIFESTYLE

Family

Guatemalans live in extended family groups that have historically formed the basis of neighborhoods and communities. This is important for newly married couples that often rely on the aid of extended family members for financial support and child rearing. Additionally, most families cannot afford to hire day care or babysitting services, and instead utilize parents and grandparents. It has become more common in the 21st century for both parents to work outside the home in Guatemalan families. After marriage, Guatemalan couples typically use a hyphenated combination of both individual's surnames, with the male's name appearing first. Guatemalan society also maintains an indigenous Maya population that, while generally integrated with the rest of the population, maintains unique cultural traditions.

As in many Central American countries, Guatemala has a tradition of masculinity or idealized manhood known as "machismo," in which men are expected to take a leading role in society. Though this feature of traditional Central American society is slowly changing, men in Guatemala still tend to take a dominant position when conversing, and women rarely travel unaccompanied. Though this tradition has negative connotations, it is still perceived as admirable in certain Latin American cultures simply because it deals with the virtues of manhood, as opposed to male dominance.

In 2006, the Guatemalan government passed a law to promote contraception and family planning. At the time of the law's passage, Guatemala had one of the highest birth rates in Central America, and also disproportionately high levels of infant mortality and malnutrition. According to 2008-2009 estimates, 20 percent of Guatemalans have two children by the age of 18, and 50 percent have had their first child by age 20.

Housing

Guatemala is a relatively poor country and most Guatemalans live in simple housing. In rural areas, one-room brick or concrete houses are common, and in urban areas, one-bedroom apartments or shared housing units are also prevalent. Even among the wealthy Ladino elite, homes tend to be simple by comparison to American or European-style houses, and typically consist of two or three bedrooms connected to a large, central living room. Wealthy families may also have gardens and yards that are protected by concrete privacy walls.

In some rural villages, Guatemalan families still live in traditional mud or clay houses known as bajareque (or bahareque) houses. The dwellings use wooden poles to support the foundation and the tin or thatched roof. Other poor families live in simple, single-room homes constructed from concrete blocks. In poor communities, most houses have earthen floors and few amenities, and families often share a single sleeping area. Some extended family groups choose to live in compounds, where several single-family homes are built close to one another. Often, residents of the compound may share sanitation facilities and other amenities.

Food

Guatemalan food blends elements of Spanish and indigenous cuisine, most notably the culinary traditions of the indigenous Mayans and the Garifuna. Guatemalan food is similar to the cuisines of neighboring Latin American countries. Corn is considered the staple of most Central American dishes, and is used in a variety of ways in Guatemalan cuisine, including making bread and tortillas. In fact, the most typical meal in Guatemala consists of tortillas, beans, and rice. Black beans (frijoles) are commonly served with nearly every meal and, when combined with rice, form a complex protein that is equivalent to diets with greater meat content.

"Desayuno chapin" (Guatemalan breakfast) usually consists of red and/or black beans served with tortillas and accompanied by a seasonal variety of fruit. Coffee is commonly served with the morning meal as well. Guatemalans are proud of their locally grown coffee, which is shipped internationally and has become prized by coffee connoisseurs around the globe.

A popular lunch dish, particularly in Antigua, is pepian, a thick stew made of meat and vegetables. The dish may contain chicken, beef, beef intestine or pork, slow cooked in a broth with salt, pepper, and spices. Pepian is usually served with rice, beans, and vegetables. More elaborate recipes also call for spicy peppers and/or tomatillo cooked into the stew. Chiles rellenos, which are mild green chili peppers stuffed with meat and/or vegetables, and usually covered in a red or green sauce with cheese, are also popular. There are dozens of varieties served in different parts of Guatemala, which may include stuffing options such as lamb, chicken, spicy sausage, yucca, carrot, plantain, and radish.

There are varieties of non-alcoholic beverages served in Guatemala, including licuados, which are shakes made with milk or water mixed with sugar and fruit juice. There are common tropical flavors available, such as pineapple and banana, and more exotic flavors such as guanabana and star fruit. Horchata is a common variety of licuado that combines sugar, rice milk, and cinnamon.

Life's Milestones

It is estimated that over half of the population of Guatemala—between 50 and 60 percent—is Roman Catholic and follow Catholic rites of passage, including baptism, communion, confirmation, and marriage. While Ladinos tend to be conservative in their adherence to Catholicism, many in the Mayan population follow only a few Catholic traditions, most notably baptism. In recent years, an increasing number of Guatemalans have responded to the work of Protestant missionaries; Protestants now make up 40 percent of the population. This demographic shift is expected to have a significant impact on local culture in the 21st century.

In Guatemala, as in many Latin American communities, families celebrate a young girl's 15th birthday with a special celebration, known as "la quinceañera." This celebration marks her transition from childhood to adolescence. The quinceañera is traditionally observed through a religious ceremony followed by a reception.

Often, the young woman will wear a special red dress in honor of the event. Couples in Guatemala tend to marry in their early 20s and most marriages are conducted according to Catholic tradition. It is customary for guests to a wedding to bestow small cash gifts to the bride and groom.

CULTURAL HISTORY

Art

The history of art in Guatemala can be divided into three distinct periods: pre-Columbian, colonial, and modern. The pre-Columbian artistic tradition includes the architecture and sculpture of the Maya, an ancient civilization that occupied parts of Mexico and Central American for more than 1,500 years. The Maya thrived in what is now present-day southern Guatemala. They were renowned for their highly developed fine arts, such as architecture, painting, and sculpture, and traditional crafts such as weaving, ceramics, and woodcarving. Remnants of Maya architecture, stone sculpture, and other types of art can still be found across the country.

In particular, archeologists have noted that Mayan art found in the Guatemalan highlands (in southern Guatemala) bears distinct characteristics that set it apart from Maya art in other areas, such as Mexico. The highlands also contain some of the oldest pyramid-like structures ever discovered. In 2002, archaeologists who were working at the San Bartolo site in northern Guatemala discovered the earliest known Maya painting—a mural depicting an ancient creation myth. Believed to be more than 2,000 years old, the mural is evidence that painting was highly sophisticated in early Mayan culture.

The Spanish conquest of Guatemala began in 1524, and the Spanish soon occupied large portions of the country. The development of Guatemalan colonial art thus mirrored the evolution of Spanish art. Artists in Guatemala began by imitating the old European masters, but slowly began to absorb elements of indigenous culture.

Modern Guatemalan art began to fully emerge in the 19th century. As Guatemalan artists returned after studying abroad, they retained foreign artistic traditions while simultaneously drawing inspiration from their daily lives in Guatemala. Carlos Merida (1891–1984) was one of the few Guatemalan artists to gain fame outside of Central America. Merida was a musician, painter, and sculptor who studied at the Instituto de Artes y Artesanias before traveling through Europe. He eventually settled in Mexico, where he became a prominent member of the Mexican mural painting movement. Merida was also one of the first Guatemalan artists to experiment with surrealism.

Architecture

Guatemala is well known for its stunning architecture, a remnant of the Spanish colonial era. The colonial architecture of Guatemala during this period reflected the baroque architecture of Spain. While most of this colonial architecture has disappeared, Antigua (the colonial capital of Guatemala) remains one of the best-preserved colonial cities in the world. The city, just outside of Guatemala City, is known for its more than 30 convents, churches, cathedrals, and monasteries. Many historic homes have also been preserved. It was designated as a World Heritage Site in 1979 by the United Nations Educational, Scientific and Cultural Organization (UNESCO).

Guatemala City also bears Spanish influence, and is laid out according to a grid pattern. (Streets that run north and south are dubbed avenidas; those that run east or west are known as *calles*.) The capital is subdivided into 21 numbered zones. Zone 1 contains the city's oldest churches and public buildings, many of them constructed in an elegant neoclassical style during the period of Spanish domination. Although long neglect has led to the decay or the collapse of many of the original structures, preservation efforts have been undertaken to protect what remains of the zone's colonial-era heritage.

Drama

Until the late 20th century, there was no significant native film industry in Guatemala. The first film produced in the country to gain international attention was the documentary *Vamos Patria a Caminar* (*Onward my Country*). Released in 1983, it was produced by a small, independent film company called Cinematografía de Guatemala.

Guatemala suffered under a series of military-led dictatorships from the late 19th century until the 1940s, and again during a civil war that began in 1960 and spanned over three decades. As a result, Guatemala's artistic community was largely stifled by stringent censorship and government control throughout this long period of time. With the restoration of relative government stability in the 1990s, a domestic film industry began to emerge.

The 1993 feature film *El Silencio del Neto* (*The Silence of Neto*), produced and directed by filmmaker Luis Argueta (1946-), tells the story of a young boy raised in the politically and socially tumultuous period of mid-20th-century Antigua. The film was a major milestone for the local industry and inspired a generation of young filmmakers to use the medium as an exploration of the nation's social and political history. Additionally, during the latter part of the 20th century, a number of documentary and historical fiction films investigating the Mayan genocide of the 1970s and 1980s also emerged. This politically charged subject would have been impossible to address during the nation's more repressive political periods, but has been the subject of some of the most internationally acclaimed films produced by Guatemalan filmmakers.

Music & Dance

The music of Guatemala has its origins in the musical traditions of the Mayan civilization and the folk music of the country's various indigenous populations, including the Garifuna. Following the Spanish conquest, music—along with other performance arts—served as a tool of the missionaries to educate the indigenous population. The national instrument is the marimba, a wooden xylophone-styled instrument. It is considered the principal instrument of Guatemalan folk music, and traditional marimbas were often built to accompany three or four musicians.

In 2005, UNESCO recognized the Rabinal Achí dance, a Mayan performance art involving masked dances and theater, as one of its Masterpieces of the Oral and Intangible Heritage of Humanity. The drama typically presents a narrative, depicting a creation myth or a subject of regional importance, which is performed in four acts. This dance tradition is performed during festivals or on Saint Paul's day, observed on January 25. It remains one of the more unique and preserved traditions of pre-Hispanic culture in Latin America.

Literature

Early literature in Guatemala included the manuscripts of the pre-Columbian Mayan civilization, which were mostly recordings of their history and myths. However, though Guatemala had a large population of indigenous residents, there were few examples of native literature until the aftermath of the Spanish conquest of the 16th century. A mestizo culture, a mix of European and indigenous heritage referred to as Ladinos, developed in Guatemala. It was within the Ladino culture that a native literary movement would develop.

Modern literature in Guatemala first received international acclaim with the works of Miguel Angel Asturias (1899–1974), who was Guatemala's first author to win the Nobel Prize in Literature. One of Asturias's best-known novels, 1949's *Hombres de maíz* (*Men of Maize*), combines Mayan myth with significant events in Guatemalan history to produce a unique depiction of Guatemalan life. Another modern Guatemalan novelist whose works have had an international impact is Rigoberta Menchú (1959-), who won a Nobel Peace Prize in 1992, and has become recognized as one of the most influential writers and women's rights activists to emerge from Guatemala. Menchú's life was the subject of the biography *I, Rigoberta Menchú* (1983), which has remained one of the most famous works by any Guatemalan artist, and helped to illuminate the plight of the Mayan people (her native ethnic group) to an international audience.

CULTURE

Arts & Entertainment

Modern Guatemala supports a variety of artistic traditions. A tumultuous political history has given Guatemalan artists a broad palate of potential political inspiration, while other artists use the beauty of Guatemala's natural environment as the subject of their work. For example, modern performance artist Regina Jose Galindo (1974-) became famous for her provocative performances, including dipping her feet in blood in front of the state capital to protest the Guatemalan dictatorship. Additionally, despite having a relatively small artistic community, Guatemalans are very proud of the accomplishments of native artists. The National Museum of Art in Guatemala has a large collection of modern art, in addition to the largest national collections of colonial and Amerindian art and artifacts.

In recent years, the Guatemalan government has begun to offer funding and endowments for artists, writers, and musicians who explore traditional and native culture with their work. Funding is most abundant for artists whose work is significant to the goal of protecting Mayan and Garifuna art and culture, as both cultures are thought to be in danger of extinction.

While there are few government- or state-sponsored programs for music in Guatemala, native music is also a source of national pride. Any festival or celebration in Guatemala is typically accompanied by live music and dancing. Guatemalan musical traditions are passed from teacher to student through informal education. There has been concern that, with the increasing urbanization of the Guatemalan population, native forms of music, and other artistic traditions, may face extinction.

The favorite sport in Guatemala is fútbol (soccer). Baseball, basketball, and bicycling are also popular. Bullfighting is also extremely popular, and bullfights are held in Guatemala City in October and December each year.

Cultural Sites & Landmarks

Antigua is one of the major cultural centers of Guatemala, due to the city's numerous well-preserved colonial structures and its status as an UNESCO World Heritage Site. Antigua was the national capital until a series of earthquakes—known as the Santa Marta quakes—ravaged the city, causing the government to abandon the site for a more stable location. The Merced Church provides an example of the decorative achievements of Guatemala's remaining colonial architecture. Elegantly crafted from stone and stucco, the church was finished prior to the earthquakes. Additionally, the Palace of the Captains General, which was built in the mid-16th century, was once the seat of the Spanish colonial government and is also the site of the national mint. Most of the structure was destroyed in the earthquakes of 1773, but has since been restored through a government rehabilitation program.

Tikal National Park is one of the largest biological reserves in the country, measuring 370 square kilometers (143 square miles). The park is famous because it contains the ruins of Tikal, a Mayan kingdom located in the midst of the jungle. The site is built around a stone pyramid, but also contains thousands of minor stone remnants of monuments, walls, and other Maya buildings. The reserve area has been reclaimed by nature in the centuries since the Maya abandoned the city, and is also now treasured for its biodiversity, including thousands of birds, mammals, reptiles, and insects.

Another important site for the preservation of Mayan culture are the ruins at Quirigua, which has been continually inhabited since the second century CE, and was the Mayan capital during one of the most notable periods of Maya prosperity. The ruins located at the site include a series of eighth-century sculptures and Maya calendars, which have been of enormous benefit to archaeologists studying the culture and history. Both the Quirigua site and the ancient Mayan ruins of Tikal, part of Guatemala's Tikal National Park, are designated as UNESCO World Heritage Sites.

Additionally, Guatemala's renowned biological and ecological diversity is on display at Lago de Atitlan (Atitlan Lake) in the Guatemalan Highlands. With a surface area of more than 130 square kilometers (50 square miles), Atitlan was formed in the basin left by a volcanic eruption that occurred thousands of years before humans inhabited the area. The area around the lake has been inhabited for centuries, and has become an agricultural zone due to its rich volcanic soil and plentiful irrigation. The region is also notable for the Maya archaeological sites found in the surrounding villages.

Guatemala City is celebrated for its churches. The Church of Our Lady of Mercy, which is noted for its colonial-era paintings and its gilded altarpieces, survived the earthquake that destroyed the old capital of Antigua and was transferred to the new capital. The capital's best-known church, however, is the neoclassical-styled Metropolitan Cathedral. Construction began on the Cathedral in 1782 but was not completed for another 85 years. Its interior is rich in religious paintings dating to the 17th and 18th centuries, some of which were originally brought to the New World by the Spanish conquistadors.

Libraries & Museums

Guatemala City is home to several noteworthy museums, including the National Museum of Archeology and Ethnology, which is dedicated to the study of the native peoples of the Americas. The city is also home to the Ixchel Indigenous Costume Museum, which offers exhibits of traditional costumes and textiles from throughout the country. The Popol Vuh Archeology Museum, which highlights artifacts from the three major periods of ancient Maya civilization, and the National History Museum, which documents Guatemalan history since 1821 when the nation officially achieved independence, can also be found in Guatemala City. The Natural History Museum, which features exhibitions of Guatemalan flora, fauna, mineralogy, and paleontology, as well as the Miguel Angel Asturias Cultural Center, which houses a museum of antique weapons and the National Museum of Modern Art, which features a large collection of contemporary Guatemalan painting and sculptures, are among the city's attractions.

The National Library of Guatemala dates back to the late 19th century, and serves as the legal depository for the country. Located in Guatemala City, the library is known for its modern style of architecture, which offers a stark contrast to the capital's colonial heritage.

Holidays

Guatemala celebrates a variety of secular and religious holidays. Each city and village has a patron saint, and once a year, members of the village will celebrate this saint on the designated feast day. These celebrations often include dancing, music, elaborate meals, and a processional.

Nationally recognized Guatemalan holidays include: Año Nuevo or New Year's Day (January 1); Semana Santa or Holy Thursday, Holy Friday, and Holy Saturday (variable); Día del Trabajo or Labor Day (May 1); Día del Ejército or Army Day (June 30); Día de la Asuncion or Assumption Day (August 15); Día de la Independencia or Independence Day (September 15); Conmemoración de la Revolución de 1944, or Revolution Day (October 20); Día de Todos los Santos or All Saint's Day (November 1); and Navidad or Christmas Day (December 25).

Youth Culture

The youth experience in Guatemala can differ markedly depending on ethnicity and social status. For example, among traditional Mayans, youth typically begin helping with family work at a young age and often marry before the age of 20. As a result, they have children in the same community as their parents unless forced to leave in order to find employment. Among the urban population and the Ladinos, young Guatemalans have a variety of choices in terms of recreation, employment, and relationships.

Due to high poverty rates, only 13 percent of Guatemalan children finish secondary school and few go on to obtain higher education. Guatemalan society is highly stratified, and these class structures manifest at the social level for Guatemalan youth. Among the conservative and economic elite, young people wear Western-style clothing, similar to children and teenagers in the United States. Among the Mayans, young boys and girls rarely speak to one another openly in public, and social brokering by family members precedes dating. In contrast, urban Guatemalans may engage in relationships and dating customs similar to those of American youth. Generally, most young Guatemalans typically socialize only with others of the same socioeconomic group.

Imported music, particularly from the U.S., has been popular in Guatemala since the 1980s. Guatemalan teens enjoy hip-hop, rock, and alternative music, and some local bands have begun to resemble some of the more popular U.S. music groups and artists. Many Guatemalan teenagers assemble at live music concerts or at dance clubs in the cities. In contrast, most Mayan children are exposed only to traditional music. However, even within Mayan communities, youth events often involve music.

Overall, the prevalent youth culture in Guatemala is difficult to define because of cultural and ethnic diversity, and because social stratification has effectively created distinct cultural subgroups. The ineffectiveness of the educational system, coupled with low rates of social movement within society, function to maintain this hierarchy.

SOCIETY

Transportation

When traveling throughout the country, the primary modes of transportation are private bus services and car rental services. Another common form of transportation in both urban and rural areas is the "chicken bus," so dubbed because locals often use the buses to transport livestock. Though they are easy to find, chicken buses can be dangerous both because they are often involved in traffic collisions, and because theft on the buses is common. Alternatively, travelers can book private passage in a taxi or minibus, or can choose to rent a car. Some minibus drivers specialize in transporting tourists to certain locations, including the Mayan ruins and the national parts. Vehicle traffic in Guatemala travels on the right-hand side of the road.

Transportation Infrastructure

Guatemala has 14,095 kilometers (8,758 miles) of roads, of which 4,863 kilometers (3,022 miles) are paved. This includes approximately 75 kilometers (47 miles) of expressway. A portion of the Pan-American Highway, also known as CA-1 or the "Interamericana," runs through Guatemala from the Mexican border through Guatemala City, and to El Salvador at the border of San Cristobal. The Pacific Coast Highway, also known as CA-2, also runs through a portion of Guatemala, while CA-9 runs through Guatemala City.

La Aurora International Airport, which is located in Guatemala City, is the nation's primary international airport. La Aurora was the first international airport established in Central America, and accommodates air travel from across Central America, the Caribbean, Mexico, and the U.S. There are 11 additional paved airports in Guatemala.

Media & Communications

Most of the communications infrastructure in Guatemala is government owned, including the telephone network. While the press has considerable freedom, most of the major print and broadcast networks are closely aligned with a particular political party or viewpoint. For example, the two largest newsprint sources in the nation, *Prensa Libre* and *El Grafico*, support the liberal and conservative political views, respectively.

There are four major broadcast television stations in Guatemala, including Canal 3 and Teleonce, both of which provide mixed entertainment and news content. There is a wide variety of cable networks available. All the major television stations, print sources, and radio stations are headquartered in Guatemala City, while some of the smaller cities support regional radio and publications. The nation's only government-owned radio station, La Voz de Guatemala, provides talk programs, music programming, and official government speeches and press releases.

Internet access has expanded slowly in Guatemala since 1990, as have cable and satellite television companies. In 2012, Internet usage was measured in 16 percent of the population. In cities such as Antigua and Guatemala City, visitors have a range of communications options available, including hotels and other retail locations, where individuals can access the Internet for a small fee.

Freedom of the press is enshrined in the Guatemalan constitution and is generally respected by the government. Guatemalan journalists and broadcasters often publish and broadcast information critical of the government, however. There is also significant corruption within the media and some reports indicate that media agents will accept bribes to support political or business interests. In addition, there have been reports that members of the media are sometimes threatened for publishing sensitive information.

SOCIAL DEVELOPMENT

Standard of Living

Guatemala ranked 125th out of 185 countries on the 2013 United Nations Human Development Index, which compiles quality of life and standard of living indicators.

Water Consumption

According to 2012 statistics from the CIA World Factbook, approximately 94 percent of the population had access to improved sources of drinking water, while 80 percent of the population had access to improved sanitation (below the regional average of 87 percent). Inconsistent service and water quality and coverage continue to be persistent issues, and a large percentage of households share metering. With 18 rivers originating in the central highlands area, the country, nonetheless, has access to ample water sources, though deforestation has contributed to the loss of available surface water.

Education

Education in Guatemala is universal and compulsory for children between the ages of seven and 14. However, there is a shortage of public schools, and many schools are privately operated. During the 1990s, there were 9,300 primary schools in Guatemala, with about 1.3 million students attending annually.

Guatemala has one of the lowest literacy rates in Central America. An estimated 76 percent of the population over the age of 15 is literate—81 percent of males and 71 percent of females. It can be difficult to obtain schooling in Guatemala because many people live in remote locations, and because laws requiring schooling are not enforced.

There are five main universities in Guatemala, all located in the capital city. The oldest and best known is the University of San Carlos, which was founded in 1676 in Guatemala City. Tuition is free for residents.

Women's Rights

Guatemala faces serious issues with regard to protecting women's rights. Although the constitution guarantees equality of the sexes and equal protection under the law, in practice, crimes against women are less often investigated and domestic violence remains common. Many critics allege that violence against women in Guatemala is associated with prevailing misogynist attitudes. In addition, sexual offenses were also considered a problem. In 2009, Guatemala had a rape rate of 2.9 percent. The penal code recommends sentences of between six and 50 years for rape. Until 2004, Guatemalan law allowed convicted rapists to avoid sentencing by marrying their victims.

Failure to report abuse is a major problem in the effort to prevent spousal abuse, domestic violence, and sexual crimes. Though domestic violence is prohibited, the penal code does not recommend specific sentences for domestic crimes. Amnesty International has reported that police and judges are unwilling to issue appropriate penalties for domestic crimes. In addition, there were no programs in place to train officers in how to respond appropriately to domestic disturbances. However, efforts to address domestic violence resulted in the establishment of the Program for the Prevention and Eradication of Intrafamily Violence. In addition, in November 2007, the government established eight new shelters for victims of domestic abuse, which provide sleeping quarters, food, childcare, and legal and psychological services.

There are no laws in place to prohibit or address sexual harassment, and instances are reportedly widespread. Gender inequality in hiring and harassment in the workplace have been cited as contributing factors to the relative scarcity of female managers. In the workforce as a whole, women earn less, on average, than male counterparts. In addition, women are more likely to be employed in low-wage positions.

Health Care

It is estimated that only 59 percent of the Guatemalan citizens have access to health care. This is due in part to the primitive conditions in the remote areas of the country, which are often economically depressed. The average life expectancy among Guatemalans is 70 years for men and 74 years for women (2014 estimate).

GOVERNMENT

Structure

Guatemala is a constitutional democratic republic. The government has a turbulent history of civil war and political unrest. It has been difficult for Guatemala to achieve democracy because of many military takeovers, civilian governments, and dictatorships. The Guatemalan Republic has been more stable since the constitution took effect in January 1986.

The Guatemalan government is headed by the chief of state, or president, who is elected (along with the vice president) to a four-year term by popular vote. The president then selects a Council of Ministers. Guatemala's legislative branch consists of the unicameral Congress of the Republic. Its 158 members are elected to four-year terms. The Congress elects the 13 justices of Guatemala's Supreme Court.

Political Parties

Guatemala has a multi-party system and most parties are small. Political parties include the Democratic Union (Unión Democrática), the Grand National Alliance (Gran Alianza Nacional), the National Advancement Party (Partido de Avanzada Nacional), and the Patriotic Party (Partido Partriota). The dynamic nature of Guatemalan politics is reflected in the fact that no single political party in Guatemala has held the presidency more than once.

Local Government

Guatemala is divided into 22 departments (administrative subdivisions). Each department is led by a governor who is appointed by the president. Departments are further subdivided into 332 municipalities, which are headed by mayors. Political power in Guatemala is highly centralized.

Judicial System

The Guatemalan judicial system was reformed following the end of the country's civil war in 1996. However, it is generally considered weak. Incidence of attacks on witnesses and destruction of evidence are common. Members of Guatemala's Supreme Court are appointed to six-year terms by the Republic Congress. Guatemala's criminal justice system is based on European law. Efforts have been made to prosecute former members of the military junta that once ruled the country.

Taxation

Guatemalans pay a progressive income tax rate that does not exceed 31 percent. Corporations can pay an income tax of five percent on their gross income or an income tax on 31 percent of their income. Other taxes include social security contributions, real estate taxes, and capital gains and withholding taxes.

Armed Forces

The armed forces of Guatemala are a defense-oriented military body that primarily focuses on external threats to the country. The military consists mainly of a land force, with small air force and naval contingents. In the early 21st century, the Guatemalan armed forces reduced its personnel significantly, cutting down from approximately 28,000 to roughly 15,500 soldiers. Conscription is limited to one or two years of service.

Foreign Policy

Guatemala is an active member of the international community and a member of several regional and international groups. In an effort to preserve biodiversity, considered one of the nation's chief resources, the Guatemalan government has made environmental protection a primary goal in the 21st century. Toward this end, Guatemala is a member of CONCAUSA (Conjunto Centroamerica USA). The organization was created in 1994 and concentrates on forming international agreements to conserve natural resources, promote the development of green energy, and create international consensus on environmental protection initiatives.

Guatemala, Honduras, Costa Rica, Nicaragua, and El Salvador have had a free trade agreement with Mexico, called the Mexico-Northern Triangle, since 2000. The agreement is designed to promote more equitable trade in the region. The ultimate economic benefit of the Mexico-Northern Triangle is still a matter of debate, but Guatemalan officials are optimistic that the agreement will bolster trade and economic diplomacy. Guatemala is also a founding member of the Central American Parliament (PARLACEN).

The most significant ongoing foreign relations issue for Guatemala is a dispute over the status of Belize. The dispute stems from Belizean independence, at which time Guatemala claimed ownership over the entire Belizean territory, while Mexico also claimed ownership over a portion of the territory. Though most Latin American countries initially supported Guatemala in the dispute, several nations gradually transferred their allegiance to Belize, beginning with Cuba in 1975. This support expanded to include many of Guatemala's neighbors, including the Sandinista government of Nicaragua. In 1980, the UN decided to officially support Belizean independence.

In response to international pressure, Guatemala has slowly amended its policies regarding Belize. In 1989, Guatemala sponsored Belize for membership in the Organization of American States (OAS). In 1991, the country officially agreed to recognize Belizean independence, though the border dispute had not been resolved. In 2009, both countries agreed to resume border negotiations under the arbitration from the International Court of Justice (ICJ). The nations were to hold simultaneous votes in April 2012 on whether to submit to binding resolution by the ICJ, but the vote has been suspended indefinitely.

While the U.S. and Guatemala have maintained strong diplomatic and economic ties, the U.S. government and monitoring agencies have criticized Guatemala for ineffectively protecting the rights and safety of citizens. Despite criticism, the U.S. and Guatemala have cooperated to create programs to address money laundering, drug trafficking, and other cross-border issues. Between 1997 and 2007, the U.S. committed more than $500 million (USD) to the ongoing peace process in Guatemala.

Human Rights Profile

International human rights law insists that states respect civil and political rights, and also promote an individual's economic, social, and cultural rights. The United Nations (UN) Universal Declaration of Human Rights (UDHR) is recognized as the standard for international human rights. Its authors sought the counsel of the world's great thinkers, philosophers, and religious leaders, and were careful to create a document that reflects the core values shared by every world culture. (To read this document or view the articles relating to cultural human rights, visit: http://www.udhr.org/UDHR/default.htm.)

The 36-year Guatemalan Civil War ended in 1996. Despite domestic and international efforts to promote the establishment of a functional democratic system, human rights abuses, high rates of violent crime, and high poverty levels have made it difficult for Guatemala to develop an effective and lasting government. In September and November of 2007, Guatemala held presidential elections, according to a two-round system. Reportedly, 26 political activists were killed in conjunction with the elections. The killings are a violation of Article 3 of the UDHR, which guarantees the right to life and freedom from persecution without regard to political affiliation.

Failure of the legal system to address violent crime is a major problem in Guatemala. For example, more than 5,000 people were killed in 2007, and only one percent of killings resulted in conviction. The murder rate fell each year, however, during 2010-2012. There were accusations the police played a role in some crimes, including the murder of three members of the El Salvadoran parliament in February 2007. Additionally, the national director of police resigned in September 2007, in response to allegations that police officers and members of the police director's bodyguards executed five young Guatemalans. Amnesty International (AI) reports that there were 195 attacks against human rights workers in 2007, many of which were campaigning for environmental issues.

Though the constitution guarantees humane treatment of prisoners, human rights organizations report that Guatemalan prisons lack critical resources and medical facilities, and that corruption within the prison system is widespread. In addition, overcrowding is significant, with approximately 14,990 prisoners detained in a system designed to accommodate an estimated 6,492 inmates. According to the U.S. Department of State, an internal evaluation of the prison system, conducted in May 2007, indicated that the penitentiary system was in danger of full collapse. Conditions in Guatemala's prisons are in violation of Article 5 of the UDHR.

AI also reported, in 2008, that instances of arbitrary detention and arrest, violations of Article 9 of the UDHR, commonly occurred in Guatemala. Some reports indicate that police routinely arrest suspects without judicial warrants, and that prisoners are often held for extended periods without trial. Additionally, though the constitution of Guatemala guarantees freedom of the press and expression, there were reported cases where individuals interfered with the activities of journalists, a violation of Article 19 of the UDHR. As of 2008, the government had not been implicated in threatening journalists. Generally, Guatemala maintains a positive record with regard to allowing free assembly, speech, and expression.

ECONOMY

Overview of the Economy

Guatemala's economy is generally weak in comparison to other Central and South American countries. In 2013, Guatemala's gross domestic product (GDP), the total of all goods and services produced by the country, was estimated at $81 billion USD. The per capita GDP was approximately $5,300 USD.

Approximately 54 percent of the population lives below the poverty line, and there is a large gap in the standard of living of socioeconomic classes in Guatemala. Although the Guatemalan government has made efforts to improve wealth distribution in recent years, the gap remains.

Guatemala's economy also reflects its society's deep, largely race-based, socioeconomic divide. However, the inequities in economic opportunity are not as pronounced in the capital as they are in the country's rural agricultural sector, which employs more than half of the Guatemalan national workforce.

Industry

The migration of largely uneducated people to Guatemala City has created a vast pool of cheap, unskilled labor that powers the country's manufacturing sector, most of which is concentrated in, and around, the capital. This rapidly growing workforce is predominantly female and young. Major components of this sector include sugar, food, and beverage processing as well as the manufacture of furniture, kitchenwares, textiles, automobile tires, pharmaceutical products, and other consumer goods.

The availability of cheap labor has attracted substantial foreign investment to Guatemalan factories. However, international critics have suggested that investors are forcing an exploited work force to tolerate low wages and oppressive working conditions.

Labor

In 2011, Guatemala's unemployment was estimated at 4.1 percent. However, this number does not reflect the fact that over half of Guatemalans live below the poverty line. Unemployment among Guatemala's youth is widespread. According to the United Nations World Food Programme (UNWFP), the country has the fourth highest rate of chronic malnutrition in the world.

Energy/Power/Natural Resources

Valuable resources in Guatemala include petroleum, rare woods, nickel, chicle, hydropower, and fish. The country is rich in iron ore, sulfur, and gold, little of which has been exploited by mining.

Environmental concerns in Guatemala include soil erosion and severe deforestation. Volcanoes and earthquakes pose a different type of environmental danger. Guatemala is highly susceptible to hurricanes and other severe weather because of its proximity to the Caribbean Sea.

Fishing

Guatemala's industrial fishing industry is based on the country's Atlantic coast. Although the country has a long coastal border along the Pacific Ocean, most of the fishing on Guatemala's Pacific coast consists of small-scale, subsistence fishing. Exported fishery products include tuna, shrimp, and lobster. Over 85 percent of the country's fishery products are provided by domestic fishing operations.

Overfishing and disregard for regulations have resulted in decreasing species populations in waters bordering Central America. However, efforts to introduce better technological resources to Guatemala's industrial fishing fleets continue.

Forestry

As of 2010, approximately 34 percent of Guatemala's land was forested and over half of the country's territory is considered fertile enough for forestry-related economic activity. However, illegal logging remains pervasive. It has been estimated that as much as half of the country's annual timber harvest is logged illegally. The government's National Protected Area Council continues to work with international agencies like the Rainforest Alliance to improve forestry regulations and law enforcement. Wood exported out of Guatemala includes cedar, mahogany, and rosewood. The United States is second to El Salvador as an export destination of Guatemalan timber.

Mining/Metals

Mining accounts for approximately two percent of Guatemala's GDP. An estimated 3,650 Guatemalans were employed by the country's mining sector in 2007. Exported mineral products include silver, clay, and iron ore. The work of several mining companies on Mayan territory has been met with protests and constitutional petitions. It has been alleged that mining in these areas constitutes a violation of the International Labour Organization's Rights of Indigenous and Tribal Peoples. According to allegations, mining companies rarely discuss their operations with indigenous people before undertaking projects on Maya lands.

Agriculture

The agricultural sector accounts for about 13.5 percent of Guatemala's GDP (2013 est.).

The most important agricultural products are coffee, sugar, and bananas. Other valuable crops include corn, rice, wheat, potatoes, tobacco, beans, and livestock such as cattle and chickens.

About 30 percent of the labor force works in agriculture, and approximately 20 percent of the land in Guatemala is used for agriculture. Approximately 65 percent of the arable land in Guatemala is taken up by only 2 percent of the country's farms, leaving very little land for smaller, less-profitable farms.

Animal Husbandry

Guatemala's primary livestock include cattle, sheep, pigs, and poultry, as well as rabbit. However, the country is not a major exporter of animal products and the majority of livestock produced in the country is used for domestic consumption. The demand for more grazing land is one of the factors behind continuing deforestation in Guatemala.

Tourism

Boasting many active volcanoes and some of the world's most impressive ruins, Guatemala is a popular tourist destination. Due to the country's turbulent past, some tourists have been hesitant to visit. Nevertheless, about one million tourists visit the Republic of Guatemala each year.

Tourist attractions in Guatemala City include its many art and textile museums, as well as the Maya art exhibits at the archaeological museum. There are also Mayan markets, which sell handmade items such as textiles, carved figures, and pottery, throughout the city. The ruins of Tikal and Huehuetenango are also popular tourist sites. In August 2010, The Guatemalan Tourism Institute was formed. The goal of the institute is to improve cruise ship traffic to Guatemala.

Micah Issitt, Ellen Wolterbeek,
Beverly Ballaro

DO YOU KNOW?

- The national instrument in Guatemala is the marimba, a type of wooden xylophone. A typical marimba is so large that six people can play it at once.
- The quetzal, the national bird of Guatemala, also lends its name to the country's unit of currency.

Bibliography

Grandin, Greg, Deborah T. Levenson, and Elizabeth Oglesby, eds. *The Guatemala Reader: History, Culture, Politics*. Durham, NC: Duke University Press, 2011.

Greenspan, Eliot. *Frommer's Guatemala*. New York: Wiley Publishing, 2007.

Jonas, Susanna. *The Battle for Guatemala*. New York: Westview Press, 1991.

Kubler, George. *The Art and Architecture of Ancient America: The Mexican, Maya and Andean Peoples*. New Haven, CT: Yale University Press, 1992.

Morrison, Terri & Wayne A. Conaway. *Kiss, Bow, Or Shake Hands: Latin America: How to Do Business in 18 Latin American Countries*. Cincinnati, OH: Adams Media Press, 2006.

Noble, John & Susan Forsyth. *Guatemala*. Oakland, CA: Lonely Planet, 2004.

Poverty in Guatemala. Washington, D.C.: The World Bank, 2011.

Rockwell, Rick J. & Noreene Janus. *Media Power in Central America*. Champaign, IL: University of Illinois Press, 2003.

Rough Guides. *Guatemala*. London: Rough Guides, 2012.

Shea, Maureen E. *Culture and Customs of Guatemala*. Westview, CT: Greenwood Publishing Group, 2001.

Tompkins, Cynthia and Kristen Sternberg. *Teen Life in Latin America and the Caribbean*. Westfield, CT: Greenwood Publishing Group, 2004.

Works Cited

"Background Note: Guatemala." *U.S. Department of State Online*. August 2008. http://www.state.gov/r/pa/ei/bgn/2045.htm

"Country Profile: Guatemala." *BBC News Online*. April, 2008. http://news.bbc.co.uk/2/hi/americas/country_profiles/1215758.stm

"Guatemala Human Rights." *Amnesty International Online*. http://www.amnestyusa.org/all-countries/guatemala/page.do?id=1011162

"Guatemala." *The World Factbook Online*. 22 June, 2014. https://www.cia.gov/library/publications/the-world-factbook/geos/gt.html

"Guatemala." *UNESCO Online*. http://whc.unesco.org/en/statesparties/gt

"Guatemala." *Washington Office on Latin America Online*. http://www.wola.org/?&option=com_content&task=blogsection&id=6&Itemid=&topic=Guatemala

"Guatemala." *World Health Organization Online*. (Accessed http://www.who.int/countries/gtm/en/

"Guatemala: Overview." *Lonely Planet Press Online*. http://www.lonelyplanet.com/worldguide/guatemala/

Blankson, Isaac A. & Patrick D. Murphy. *Negotiating Democracy: Media Transformation in Emerging Democracies*. Albany, NY: SUNY Press, 2007.

Grandin, Greg. *The Blood of Guatemala: A History of Race and Nation*. Durham, NC: Duke University Press, 2000.

Greenspan, Eliot. *Frommer's Guatemala*. New York: Wiley Publishing, 2007.

Inda, Jonathan Xavier, et al. *The Anthropology of Globalization: A Reader*. Boston: Blackwell Publishing, 2008.

Jonas, Susanna. *The Battle for Guatemala*. New York: Westview Press, 1991.

Kubler, George. *The Art and Architecture of Ancient America: The Mexican, Maya and Andean Peoples*. New Haven, CT: Yale University Press, 1992.

Morrison, Terri & Wayne A. Conaway. *Kiss, Bow, Or Shake Hands: Latin America: How to Do Business in 18 Latin American Countries*. Cincinnati, OH: Adams Media Press, 2006.

Noble, John & Susan Forsyth. *Guatemala*. Oakland, CA: Lonely Planet, 2004.

Rockwell, Rick J. & Noreene Janus. *Media Power in Central America*. Champaign, IL: University of Illinois Press, 2003.

Shea, Maureen E. *Culture and Customs of Guatemala*. Westview, CT: Greenwood Publishing Group, 2001.

Stewart, Iain, Mark Whatmore & Peter Eltringham. *Guatemala*. New York: Rough Guides, 2002.

Tompkins, Cynthia and Kristen Sternberg. *Teen Life in Latin America and the Caribbean*. Westfield, CT: Greenwood Publishing Group, 2004.

A local youth cycles large fresh fish in Utila, Honduras/Stock photo © Holger Mette

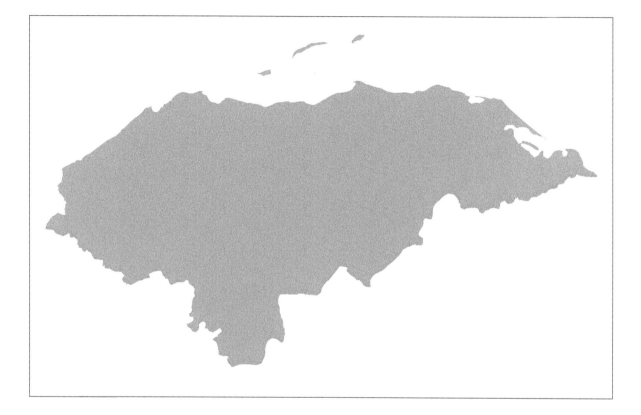

HONDURAS

Introduction

The Republic of Honduras is the second largest country in Central America. It borders Guatemala, El Salvador, and Nicaragua, as well as the Caribbean Sea to the north and the Pacific Ocean to the south. The country gained its independence from Spain in 1821, though it did not become a republic until 1982.

GENERAL INFORMATION

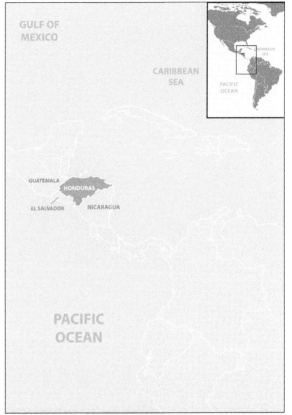

Official Language: Spanish
Population: 8,598,561 (2014 estimate)
Currency: Honduran lempira
Coins: The Honduran lempira is divided into 100 centavos. It is available in coin denominations of 5, 10, 20, and 50 centavos.
Land Area: 111,890 square kilometers (43,200 square miles)
Water Area: 200 square kilometers (77 square miles)
National Motto: "Libre, Soberana e Independiente" ("Free, Sovereign and Independent")
National Anthem: "Himno Nacional de Honduras" (Spanish, "National Hymn of Honduras")
Capital: Tegucigalpa
Time Zone: GMT -6
Flag Description: The flag of Honduras features a bicolor design, with two equal horizontal stripes of blue flanking a white interior horizontal stripe. Centered in the white stripe is a cluster of five stars (in blue) that represent the original five Central American provinces (El Salvador, Costa Rica, Nicaragua, Honduras, and Guatemala).

The blue bands represent the Caribbean Sea and Pacific Ocean, while the white represents the land between, as well as peace and prosperity.

Population

Honduran citizens are a diverse group of people. Roughly, 90 percent of Hondurans are mestizo, a mix of indigenous and European descent. Other notable ethnic groups include indigenous Indians (seven percent), and those of Arab, African, European, and Asian descent (three percent).

Most of the population resides in the mountainous, wooded interior of the country. The population density is 72 people per square kilometer (186 people per square mile). Despite Honduras' rich natural resources, the majority of the population is extremely poor. This is especially apparent in the rural areas, where more than half of the population lives.

Honduras has a young population. Almost 35 percent of the population is under 15, and more

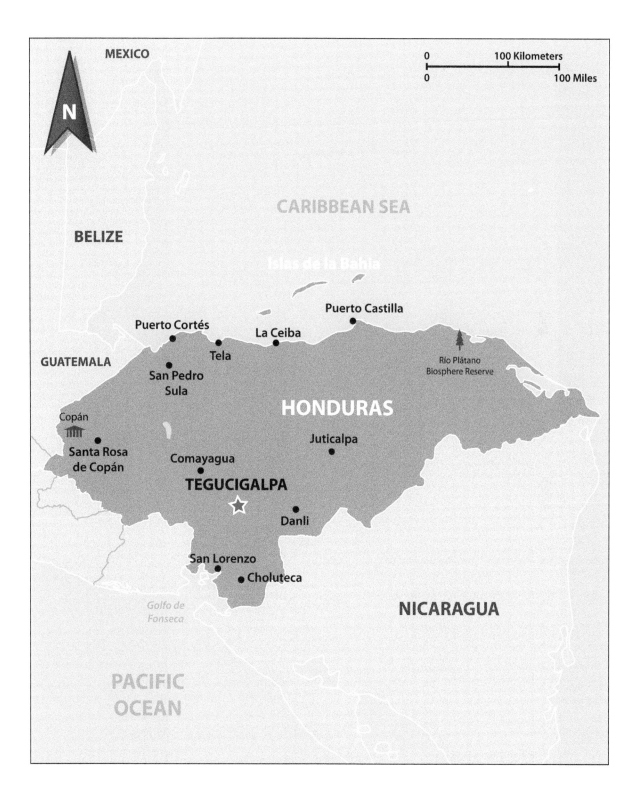

Principal Cites by Population (2014):

- Tegucigalpa (850,848)
- San Pedro Sula (489,466)
- Choloma (139,100)
- La Ceiba (130,218)
- El Progreso (100,810)
- Choluteca (75,872)
- Comayagua (58,784)
- Puerto Cortez (48,013)

than 20 percent is between the ages of 15 and 24. The average life expectancy is 69 years for males and 73 years for females (2014). The population growth rate was estimated at 1.74 percent in 2014.

Approximately 52 percent of the population lives in urban areas (2014). The major cities of Honduras include Tegucigalpa, the capital, as well as Comayagua, San Pedro Sula, Choloma, and La Ceiba. Unofficially, the population of Tegucigalpa is around 1.2 million, with hundreds of thousands more residing in the metropolitan area.

Languages

Although Spanish is the official language, English is also widely spoken in the cities. In addition, native Indian dialects are also present. Miskito is spoken by the Miskito Indians in the northeastern part of Honduras. Garifuna, a mix of African and Arawak Indian languages, is spoken by the Garifuna people, who are the descendents of African slaves and Arawak Indians.

Native People & Ethnic Groups

Before the Spanish invaded Central America and conquered Honduras, Mayan Indians lived throughout the country. The Mayans formed a great civilization, which spread across Honduras and Guatemala. From this ancient people come three distinct indigenous groups: the Miskito Indians, the Garifuna, and the Ch'orti' Maya Indians.

The largest group, the Miskito Indians, number more than 70,000 and make up seven percent of the modern population. They speak their own dialect, Miskito, as well as Spanish. The Garifuna are a mix of the native people with black slaves from Africa. They number around 80,000, and live along the eastern coast and in the Bay Islands. The Ch'orti' Maya Indians live along the Guatemalan border and are considered the modern day "Mayan Indians." They are known for their craftwork, especially pottery and dolls.

In addition to these groups, the Lencas are the largest indigenous group not related to the Mayans. They live in the southwestern area of Honduras, and are known for their exquisite pottery work.

Religions

Honduras supports freedom of religion. Christianity was established in the early 16th century by Spanish invaders, and it remains the dominant religion. Over 97 percent of the population is at least nominally Catholic. In keeping with the Roman Catholic influence, Honduras has a patron saint: the Virgin of Suyapa. Protestant denominations are also present.

Climate

Honduras has two separate climate zones; temperate in the mountainous interior and subtropical in the lowlands. However, the weather is generally hot and humid throughout the country, with average temperatures ranging from 20° to 32° Celsius (68° to 90° Fahrenheit). Humidity generally stays steady at 70 percent year-round.

Cooler temperatures are found in the mountains, where the capital of Tegucigalpa is located. The coolest time of year is from December to January. The rainy season lasts from September to February, and the dry season is between December and May.

Hurricane season begins in August and lasts through October. In 1998, Hurricane Mitch hit the country, killing thousands of people and leaving hundreds of thousands homeless, and causing billions of dollars in damage. Honduras is also prone to earthquakes, though these are less frequent than hurricanes.

ENVIRONMENT & GEOGRAPHY

Topography

There are four land regions in Honduras; the mountainous interior (60 percent of the country's area), the northern coast, the northeastern plain, and the southern coast.

The country's highest point is in the Cerros de Celaque mountain range, at 2,849 meters (9,347 feet) above sea level. Most of the soil in the northern coast region is not rich enough to support significant agriculture, though bananas are grown there. The area surrounding the Choluteca River in the southern coast region is fertile enough to support many farms and ranches. The Mosquito Coast, home to the Miskito Indians, is found in the tropical rainforests of the northeastern plain.

Tegucigalpa, the capital, is located in a small valley surrounded by the pine-covered mountains of south-central Honduras. The valley sits at an altitude of about 975 meters (3,200 feet) above sea level.

Honduras' territory includes the Bay Islands, off the northeastern coast, and the Swan Islands, off the north coast, both in the Caribbean Sea. Until 1960, Honduras and Nicaragua were involved in a boundary dispute. The International Court of Justice (ICJ) in the Netherlands eventually ruled in favor of Honduras. Another border dispute with El Salvador has largely been resolved over islands in the Gulf of Fonseca, but El Salvador still claims Conejo Island, which was not mentioned in the 1992 ICJ decision.

Plants & Animals

Honduras' landscape is naturally suited to support a variety of plants and animals. Its rainforest and coral reef are home to at least 173 species of mammals. Just over 5 percent of the country's land is totally protected.

Not surprisingly, many animals living in Honduras' rainforests are endangered or vulnerable. Endangered animals include the Ruatan Island agouti. Vulnerable animals include the American manatee, the Central American tapir, the Central American woolly opossum, the giant anteater, the Honduran fruit-eating bat, the Honduran small-eared shrew, and Van Gelder's bat, a species of vesper bat. Extensive slash-and-burn methods of clearing forest for farming have been a key cause of the growing danger to these animals and their habitats.

Honduras' plant life consists of forests of oak and pine in the mountains, Mangrove and palms in the coastal regions, as well as savanna grasses. Roughly, 65 percent of the land is forested.

Honduras includes part of the Mesoamerican reef. This reef stretches from the eastern coast of Mexico down through Honduras, and it is the largest coral reef in the Western Hemisphere. Many natural conservation groups, such as the International Coral Reef Action Network (ICRAN) and the World Wildlife Fund (WWF), are working together to preserve and improve the health of the reef.

CUSTOMS & COURTESIES

Greetings

Honduran men usually greet by shaking hands. Women may pat each other's arms in greeting, and it is common for female friends to exchange kisses on the cheeks. Greetings are important in Honduran culture and Hondurans often introduce themselves to every person in a room, rather than only greeting known individuals.

More than 90 percent of Hondurans speak Spanish as their primary language. As in many Central American nations, Hondurans tend to use the form "vos" in informal conversation, a convention that divides Central American Spanish speakers from those in Mexico and Spain. When greeting, Hondurans generally use the word "Buenos," ("Good") combined with a word to indicate the time of day, such as "Buenos días" ("Good morning"), "Buenas tardes" ("Good afternoon"), and "Buenas noches" ("Good evening"). To inquire about one's well being, Hondurans may say "¿Como esta usted?" ("How are you doing?").

There is a large population of Garifuna living in Honduras, some of who speak the native

Garifuna language, in addition to Spanish and/or English. Common greetings among the Garifuna include "Mábuiga" ("Hello"), "Buíti binafi" ("Good morning"), "Buíti amidi" ("Good afternoon"), and "Buíti ranbá weyu" ("Good evening").

A third language encountered in Honduras is Honduran Miskito, which is a blend of Spanish and the language of the Miskito ethnic group that occupies parts of the Atlantic coast of Nicaragua and Honduras. Travelers to Honduras may occasionally encounter Miskito Creole in the major cities, though it is relatively uncommon away from the Atlantic coast.

Gestures & Etiquette

Hondurans, like most Central Americans, use a number of distinct gestures in communication. When pointing, for instance, it is considered rude to use the fingers. Instead, most Central Americans use "lip pointing," which involves gesturing toward a person or object by pursing the lips in the general direction of the object of interest.

There are a number of other social comments made by using the index finger. For example, placing the index finger below the eye is a way of telling someone to be cautious, while placing the index finger on the elbow is a way of commenting that someone is being "stingy." When saying "No" or indicating a negative, Hondurans will shake the index finger rather than shaking the head. In addition, when beckoning to a person, Hondurans typically hold out the hand with the palm facing down and wave the fingers back and forth. (It is considered rude to beckon to someone with the palm facing up.) Similarly, when waving to a person, whether in greeting or farewell, it is customary to wave with the back of the hand facing the person.

In general, Hondurans engage in energetic and open communication. Individuals may stand close to one another, and males more frequently make physical contact when conversing. It is common, for instance, for male friends to pat one another on the arms and back during casual greetings.

As in most of Central America, Hondurans take a relaxed attitude toward time, except in business situations. In social meetings, it is acceptable to be late. Generally, Central Americans value relaxed, casual interaction and are less "task" and "purpose" driven. They tend to place high value on socializing and relaxing, which are believed to be healthy.

Eating/Meals

Most Hondurans eat three meals a day, with the largest meal generally served at midday. Most meals are eaten family style, with a single plate filled with a sampling of each item offered. Hondurans may say "Buen provecho" ("Good meal") before eating with friends and or family. Additionally, dining customs are markedly different in urban and rural areas. Most peasants will generally eat only enough to sustain them throughout the day while, in urban areas, eating for pleasure is more common and meals are generally more elaborate.

The morning meal typically consists of light fare, including fruits, beans, eggs, and bread. Plantations around Honduras produce world-renowned coffee, which is also served with the morning meal. Most dishes described as main courses are served at the midday meal. The staple Central American food is a mixture of rice and beans, which are served as an accompaniment to most meals. Roasted meats and vegetables, along with the staple rice and beans, are common with the midday meal, as well as the evening meal.

Many Hondurans hold meetings during the midday meal because the meal is the longest of the day. In addition, it is generally followed by a rest period before returning to work, allowing ample time to conduct business in a relaxed manner. Though Hondurans generally accept a certain level of tardiness, it is not advisable to be late to business meetings and is considered an insult to arrive more than 20 minutes late to a meal.

Visiting

Hondurans are generally friendly and inviting, and pride themselves on their hospitality. When visiting a Honduran home, it is considered polite to bring a small gift for the host. Wine, dessert items, flowers, or candies are common and acceptable choices as gifts for a host. When bringing flowers, lilies should be avoided as they are commonly used in funeral traditions and mourning rituals. As in most of Central America, it is considered rude to ask to tour a host's house or to investigate a home without permission.

LIFESTYLE

Family

Family life in Honduras is similar to that of most other Central American countries, in that Catholic traditions are typically blended with indigenous customs, and the social structure is commonly based on an extended family system. In traditional Honduran society, individuals usually married within similar socioeconomic castes and most marriages were arranged through an agreement between parents. Though modern marriages are more often based on individual choice, there are still social prohibitions in the early 21st century that make it unlikely for members of different socioeconomic backgrounds to marry.

More than 90 percent of Hondurans marry before age 30, and eventually have children. In Honduras, men and women combine surnames when married, using a hyphen to divide their names (traditionally, the man's name appears first). Divorce, infidelity, and unwedded reproduction, though prohibited by traditional Catholic values, have become common in Honduras, and are generally accepted in society.

In contemporary Honduras, it has become less common for men to assume full financial responsibility for their families. Instead, it is now more common for both parents to work outside the home. While most young couples prefer to establish themselves close to their extended families, the necessity to relocate for work threatens the traditional structure of Honduran communities. Additionally, Honduras is home to one of the largest homosexual populations in Central America. However, the country prohibits homosexual marriage, though the law allows same-sex couples to share a single residence.

Hospitals in Honduras rarely offer family planning services and contraception. The first government program to establish family planning services began in 1999, as a cooperative project between the Ministry of Health and the Population Council, a non-governmental organization (NGO). The Honduran Health Alliance (HHA) also operates several clinics across the country, providing counseling and family planning services at no cost.

Housing

Honduras is a country of deeply divided socioeconomic groups. At the highest levels of society, Hondurans live in villas (historically, upper class country dwellings), with multiple bedrooms and yards typically lined by fences. At the lower level of society, individuals live in concrete, single-room houses with earthen floors, and few amenities. As in much of Central America, Honduran families sometimes live close to one another in multi-family compounds, and with several houses sharing some basic facilities. In urban areas, houses are generally constructed from concrete and/or brick, while in rural areas, houses of mud and stone are common. Wooden houses are common in some parts of the country, but humidity and inclement weather make it difficult to maintain them.

Honduras is among the poorest and least developed countries in Central America, and almost 60 percent (2010) of the population lives below internationally designated poverty levels. An examination in 1999, conducted by Habitat for Humanity, revealed that more than 60 percent of the nation's residences did not meet international standards of adequacy. Additionally, in 1998, Hurricane Mitch destroyed more than 30,000 homes across the country. Although the government attempted to initiate a program to rebuild, after more than a decade many families were still without housing.

Food

The cuisine of Honduras is largely a blend of Mexican, Spanish, and indigenous customs and influences. Corn is the staple food of most Central American countries, which is considered a legacy of the region's Mayan heritage. Cornmeal is used to make tortillas, which form a central component of the Honduran diet. Beans and rice are the other major component of the local cuisine and, when combined with tortillas, form a complex protein that is equivalent to that of meat.

The plato tipico (typical meal) for breakfast might consist of eggs, black beans, and rice, accompanied by tortillas, fresh fruit, juice or coffee. Fried meats, such as sausage and ham, are also commonly served in the morning. Mondongo, a spicy soup made with tripe (beef or pork intestine), is a Caribbean-inspired dish that has become popular in Honduras and several neighboring countries. The soup usually contains a variety of local vegetables, which may include squash, cabbage, yucca, and sweet potato. Flavoring varies according to region and taste, and several varieties of pepper are used to give the soup a spicy flavor.

Another common dish is bistec, which is grilled or pan-fried steak, generally served with vegetables, rice, and beans. Bistec may be served with or without cheese and with various vegetable sides. Common varieties of bistec include bistec salteado, where the steak is marinated in pepper and spices before being grilled.

Among the Garifuna population, seafood forms a large part of the daily diet. The Garifuna often eat ceviche de pescado (fish ceviche), a dish made from raw fish soaked in citrus and served with garlic, spices, and a variety of vegetables and fruits. The Garifuna also make liberal use of conch, a type of crustacean, in their cooking. Conch fritters are balls of dough with pieces of conch cut and mixed into the batter before frying. Another common conch dish is conch soup, generally made with a coconut milk base mixed with spices.

Among non-alcoholic beverages served in Honduras, licuados (smoothies) are the most popular, and are generally made with fruit juice mixed with either water or milk. A variety of tropical flavors, including mango, star fruit, and tamarind, are available.

Life's Milestones

Most Hondurans are Catholic, and most families follow traditional Catholic rites of passage, including baptism, communion, confirmation, and marriage. In addition, many Hondurans observe the quinceañera, a celebration occurring on a young girl's 15th birthday that is meant to symbolize the transition to maturity. The celebration usually commences as a religious ceremony, and then culminates with a reception, similar to a bat mitzvah (the celebration of a girl's maturity—at age 12—in Jewish culture). Additionally, most of Honduras's Garifuna population also adhere to the Christian faith, and therefore follow similar traditions to the rest of the population.

Many Honduran children live with their parents until marriage, and continue to live close to their parents and their extended family after having their own children. In traditional Honduran society, marriage serves to distinguish the beginning of adulthood. However, in modern Honduran society, more couples choose to cohabitate without marriage. Typically, most marriages are conducted according to Catholic traditions and are accompanied by a family party and communal feast. Among the Garifuna, traditional roles have remained more pronounced. For example, Garifuna couples are more likely to marry before living together and to have children only after marrying.

CULTURAL HISTORY

Art

Before the arrival of the Europeans, Honduras was inhabited by a succession of indigenous cultures, or pre-Columbian civilizations. The most notable of these were the Maya, who inhabited western Honduras and flourished during the Classic period (150–900 CE) of Mesoamerica (a region stretching from Mexico to Honduras and Nicaragua). They established a major city at Copán in western Honduras, which reached its height during the fifth and ninth centuries. A variety of Mayan artifacts and architectural remnants have been discovered in Honduras, and the Honduran government has taken steps to protect Mayan archaeological sites as part of the nation's cultural heritage. Traditional crafts from the pre-Columbian period include ceramics, woodcarvings (particularly Mayan instruments), textile arts, and basketry.

Honduras also has a sizable population of Garifuna, a people of mixed Caribbean and African origin who reside along the northern coast and the Bay Islands (off Honduras' Caribbean coast). The Garifuna have a unique artistic heritage, and are particularly known for their music and dance, which combines African and indigenous traditions. One renowned form of music is called punta, a dance music based on vocals and traditional percussive instruments. Often, the music featured other traditional instruments such as a conch shell (stringed instruments were introduced by the Spanish), and the dances that accompanied it were based on the movement of the hips. Punta has evolved over the years, adding contemporary instruments such as the guitar and the saxophone, and a variation—called punta rock—is now a popular genre of world music.

Since most of the Garifuna in Honduras live in coastal communities, much of their unique art—such as paintings and the lyrics to their music—draws inspiration from their surroundings. In 2001, in recognition of the living cultural heritage of the Garifuna (who also live in Belize and Nicaragua), the United Nations Educational, Scientific and Cultural Organization (UNESCO) named their language, dance, and music an intangible cultural heritage (ICH).

Painting in Honduras largely emerged in the 17th and 18th centuries, during the country's colonial period, and was typically religious in nature. Following this period, the work of Honduran painter Pablo Zelaya Sierra (1896–1933), often considered the father of Honduran painting, marked the beginning of a unique native movement. He was one of the first Honduran artists to depict rural life in Honduras rather than imitating European artists. In 1949, the government of Honduras created the Art Pablo Zelaya Prize to be awarded to artists whose work serves to promote native culture.

By the early 20th century, most successful Honduran painters were using either a realistic or an impressionistic style, while still relying on Honduran life, wildlife, and scenery as their primary inspiration. Jose Antonio Velasquez (1906–1983) is one of the most famous artist, known for his landscapes and depictions of rural villages (his style is often referred to as primitivist painting). Velasquez's work gained international fame through its acceptance by the international botanical community. In fact, a collection of his paintings is maintained at the Zamorano Pan-American School of Agriculture in Honduras.

In addition to fine art, Honduras has gained a reputation for its native craft traditions. The most typical Honduran handicrafts are wooden sculptures, embroidery, and leather crafts. Though generally a commercial industry, some Honduran crafts have their origins in Garifuna and Mayan traditions.

Architecture

The architecture of Honduras has its roots in the ancient culture of the Maya (particularly their temple architecture), but was largely influenced by the Spanish, who combined Baroque and Gothic elements in their colonial architecture. This influence is particularly evident in the country's various Spanish churches and cathedrals, and the use of the typical Spanish plazas (open city squares) and red-tiled roofs, common in Honduras's old colonial towns and villages.

The architectural heritage of Honduras is perhaps best represented by the contrasting architecture of its capital and largest city, Tegucigalpa. For much of its history, the area now encompassing what is the capital of Honduras existed as two separate cities, Tegucigalpa and Comayagüela. Although the two cities, originally divided by the Choluteca River, merged together in 1938, they have retained their distinct characters. Today, Tegucigalpa is a blend of modern and colonial architecture and the nation's administrative, cultural, and economic capital.

The Tegucigalpa bank features most of the capital's colonial-era architecture and sites of historic interest. The Old Town, with its narrow, twisting streets, is built into the slope of a steep hill. It contains the capital's main thoroughfare, the Boulevard Morazán, along which most of the city's upscale commercial and business settings are concentrated. The Comayagüela bank, by contrast, is more industrialized and crowded, but less affluent. It features many shops and open-air markets that form the backbone of the capital's informal economy. Many of the half-million or so residents of Comayagüela live in impoverished settlements that sprawl from the city's edges into the foothills of the surrounding mountains.

At the center of urban Tegucigalpa are religious buildings dating from the Spanish colonial period. The San Francisco Church, for instance, was constructed in 1590 and is considered the oldest building in the nation. The La Merced Church, built in 1650, is one of several churches created by the Merced Order in Central America (a Roman Catholic religious order), and attracts visitors because of its architectural beauty.

The architectural heritage of Honduras also encompasses the country's many Maya ruins sites. The Copán ruins, in western Honduras, inscribed as a World Heritage Site by the United Nations Educational, Scientific and Cultural Organization, or UNESCO, are known for its monumental architecture, as well as the site's various step-pyramid-style architecture and palaces.

Drama

Western-style theater, different from ceremonial indigenous traditions, was introduced to Honduras by Spanish colonials, beginning with the work of Father José Trinidad Reyes (1797–1855). He began a tradition of staging pastoral dramas, called pastorelas, for the general public. These dramas often contained political, satirical, or musical elements, as well as a moral message. Luís Andrés Zúñiga (1878–1964) presented *Los Conspriadores*, a drama celebrating the Central American hero General Morazán in 1915. But theater languished in Honduras, in spite of the efforts of several playwrights such as Alonso A. Brito (1884–1925) and José María Tobías Rosa (1874–1933).

In 1961, a Spanish playwright, Andrés Morris (1925-1987), arrived in Honduras and produced works that were noticed more for their melodrama than their message. Morris tended to include social criticism in his work, which was a new aspect of theater in the country. Even though the country established a national theater in 1965, theater has not gained a stronghold. Efforts to establish the Comunidad Hondureña de Teatris or Honduran Theater Community lasted only six years, from 1982 to 1988, failing because of a lack of government support. One offshoot, the Festival de Teatro por la Paz (Theater Festival for Peace), endured and is held every two years in Santa Barbara.

Additionally, Father Jack Warner, a Jesuit priest, began the Teatro La Fragua in 1979. This theater company has three primary goals: to stage secular dramas, to teach the Gospel, and to develop Honduran productions that reflect the country's culture and experience. Warner's troupe travels to both cities and rural areas to fulfill their mission.

Music & Dance

Hondurans enjoy modern dance as well as folk dancing. The two main forms of native dance are the sique and the mascaro. Honduran music is a unique blend of indigenous, African, and European musical traditions.

The banguity or punta, music and dance of the Gaifuna people, is danced at wakes as a kind of "last dance" for the deceased. Other accounts claim that the punta is danced to celebrate the reincarnations that will come in the wake of the deceased's soul. Others claim that the punta is inappropriate at wakes because the punta was originally danced upon the death of an enemy.

Literature

Despite having a relatively small publishing industry, a number of native Honduran writers have made an international impact throughout the country's history. In fact, Honduras was one of the first Central American countries to attract attention for its literature. Lucila Gamero de Medina (1873–1964) was one of the first Honduran writers to gain international prominence, and wrote the first Honduran novel that was published. Most of her novels tell the stories of Honduran families living during the turn of the century.

Ramon Amaya Amador (1916–1966) became one of Honduras's most popular writers in the 20th century, and is now considered the country's most renowned author. As a former journalist and a worker on a banana plantation, Amador had a unique insight into the nation's cultural heritage. Amador's novel *Prision Verdes* (*Green Prison*), which talks about life on a plantation of the 1940s, has become one of the most famous books ever published in Honduras. Overall, much of Honduran literature has been overlooked internationally, as it generally deals with the political history and conflicts of the region.

CULTURE

Arts & Entertainment

Arts education is available in Honduras at both the secondary and higher education levels. There are few specialized schools offering arts education at the secondary level, and most are paid programs, including the School of Fine Arts in Tegucigalpa. The nation's largest art gallery, Nacional Gallerie de Arte, features an impressive collection of art ranging from prehistoric artifacts to modern painting and sculpture.

In the 21st century, Honduras supports a small but diverse artistic community, and a small number of Honduran painters and sculptors have gained national attention for their work. However, artists in Honduras are usually forced to find private funding, as sources for public and government funding are scarce. The Honduran government has recently begun to initiate a few programs to promote the exploration of Garifuna music and art in an effort to preserve that element of local culture.

Additionally, the craft industry is a major source of employment for individuals living in cities with significant tourist traffic. Native weaving, painting, wood sculpture, and other forms of craft art are sold by street vendors and in small retail shops. Though considered "commercial" rather than "fine" art, Honduran crafts are part of a tradition that stretches back to Mayan and other indigenous tribal cultures.

Many Hondurans enjoy sports, especially football (soccer), which is its national sport. Baseball and basketball are also popular.

Cultural Sites & Landmarks

Honduras is particularly renowned for its pre-Columbian history and its ecology. In fact, these two distinctions have earned the country recognition from UNESCO, which has designated two World Heritage Sites in Honduras: the Copán ruins, inscribed in 1980, and the Río Plátano Biosphere Reserve, inscribed in 1982.

The Copán Ruinas (Copán Ruins) are a famous Mayan archaeological site, located in northern Honduras. Archaeologists believe that the pre-Columbian city reached its peak between the fifth and ninth centuries CE, when it was the site of a flourishing culture. Among the architectural remnants at the site are several former religious monuments and a large square structure that archaeologists believe was once a sporting arena. Copán remains one of the three largest Mayan sites in existence.

The Río Plátano Biosphere Reserve contains hundreds of fish, bird, reptile, and mammal species that live only within the tropical rainforest habitat. The reserve is part of a watershed system that contains mountains, rainforest, and riverine habitat stretching an estimated 524,999 hectares (1,297,303 acres). In addition to its biodiversity, Río Plátano is home to more than 2,000 indigenous inhabitants, representing the native Central American tribes that first inhabited the region. The reserve also contains several important archaeological sites, including Mayan ruins and the site where explorer Christopher Columbus (1451–1506) first arrived on the mainland of the Americas.

Another historic site in Honduras is the capital of Tegucigalpa. The city was the center of several indigenous settlements before Spanish settlers occupied the region. Archaeologists believe that the name for the settlement was taken from an indigenous term meaning "silver hill." The region surrounding the city contains a number of productive silver mines. Just outside the capital lies the Gothic-style Basilica of Our Lady of Suyapa, the patron saint of Honduras. Stories of miraculous occurrences attributed to the saint draw thousands of the faithful to the shrine from all over Honduras and beyond.

Tegucigalpa's historic center is home to a number of churches built during the 17th and 18th centuries. Among the most notable is the baroque-style cathedral of St. Michael Archangel, which features an elaborate façade of columns and pillars, and is dedicated to Tegucigalpa's patron saint. The Iglesia de Nuestra Señora de los Dolores, whose stained-glass shows the influences of both African and indigenous American cultures, and the San Francisco church, which dates to around 1590 (making it the oldest structure in the city), are also of historical importance.

Tegucigalpa also has two famous monuments. The capital's central park contains a statue of the Central American political leader Francisco Morazán (1799–1842), a native son of Tegucigalpa and a Honduran national hero. The national park located on Tegucigalpa's northern side contains a massive hilltop statue known as Christ of the Picacho. Although the statue has been in place only since 1997, it has become one of the city's most distinctive landmarks. El Picacho Park also contains a traditional Asian garden, the gift of the Taiwanese government, and the Honduras National Zoo.

Additionally, the island of Utila, located 29 kilometers (18 miles) from the coast of Honduras, has become a major tourist attraction because of the island's natural beauty and biodiversity. Known to scuba diving enthusiasts around the world, Utila sits on the Mesoamerican Reef System, which is the second largest in the world after the Great Barrier Reef.

Libraries & Museums

Many of the country's premier cultural institutions are located in the capital, Tegucigalpa. The Museum of the Republic documents modern Honduran history, beginning with the country's 1821 achievement of independence from Spain. It includes a display of bullet-proof vintage limousines used by a succession of Honduran dictators. The Military History Museum displays personal possessions of past Honduran leaders, as well as both antique and modern weaponry, while the Sala Bancatlan features artifacts that document Honduran history. The National Art Gallery displays the work of Honduran painters from the colonial era to the present day. The Museum of Natural History includes exhibits of native birds, mammals, and reptiles, and highlights the extraordinary biodiversity of Honduras. The rich and ancient histories of the various Honduran indigenous cultures are on display at the Villa Roy National Museum, which features collections of traditional costumes and crafts and archeological objects.

The National Library of Honduras is located in Tegucigalpa, and dates back to the late 19th century.

Holidays

The Christian holidays of Christmas and Easter are widely celebrated in Honduras. Easter is a week–long celebration, known as Semana Santa or "Holy Week." In the capital of Tegucigalpa, religious processions crowd the city streets.

Feasts and parades to honor the saints are frequent. The largest of these, Suyapa Day, has occurred annually for centuries. Suyapa Day is celebrated for several days beginning on February 1. During this time, pilgrims travel to the Suyapa Basilica, which holds a statuette of the Virgen de Suyapa (Virgin of Suyapa). This statuette is believed by many to have the power to perform miracles.

Honduras' national Independence Day is observed on September 15, and celebrates the separation of Honduras from Great Britain.

Youth Culture

Sports are one of the primary recreational activities for Honduran youth, with fútbol (soccer) being the most popular. The Ministry of Sport and Culture is responsible for promoting interest in participation in sports, and also works to establish community sport centers.

Preferences in music and fashion among Honduran youth draw heavily from American pop culture. The fad of ear piercing among Honduran males, for instance, has been linked to influence from similar fashion trends among American teenagers. Similarly, hip-hop and rock music have been imported into Honduras and have become widely popular with young people. Dancing is a popular activity for Honduran youth, with a number of clubs in urban areas catering to teenage audiences.

Poverty contributes to the popularity of gangs (maras) and the prevalence of criminal activity among Honduran youth. It was estimated that between 2002 and 2006, there was a 90 percent increase in violent deaths among youth 23 or younger. To address youth gangs and violence, the Honduran government has enacted the Anti-Maras Laws, which recommend severe fines and jail time in an effort to deter children from gang activity. However, prominent human rights organizations oppose the laws and recommend that the government enact programs for rehabilitation. Little funding has been available, however, and a 2013 report by the U.S. Department of Justice notes that the Anti-Maras Laws have been ineffective in controlling the gang problems.

SOCIETY

Transportation

Buses are the most common form of public transportation in Honduras and the hub of the bus system is in the capital of Tegucigalpa. Many of the public buses in Honduras are repurposed school or cross-country buses imported from the United States. As such, many are in need of repair. Additionally, due to the frequency of crimes that occur on buses, visitors are typically advised to limit themselves to traveling along the main bus routes or to use private taxi or car rental services. Traffic moves on the right-hand side of the road in Honduras.

Transportation Infrastructure

The terrain of Honduras, which includes rapid changes in elevation and rugged mountain cliffs, has made it difficult to develop extensive passenger rail systems. There are currently 699 kilometers (434 miles) of rail in Honduras running between Puerto Cortez and San Pedro Sula. The bulk of the nation's rail system was constructed in the early 20th century, but agricultural companies such as the Cuyamel Fruit Company began constructing a rail system as early as 1910. The rail system is still primarily dedicated to transporting agricultural crops and connecting the capital with agricultural settlements in the north.

There are 13,600 kilometers (8,451 miles) of roads in Honduras, of which only 2,775 kilometers (1,724 miles) are paved. The main component of the highway system is the North-South Highway (Inter-Ocean Highway), which connects Puerto Cortez on the Caribbean side through Tegucigalpa and the capital region to San Lorenzo, on the Pacific Coast. The Inter-American Highway, which is part of the larger Pan-American Highway that links most of Central America, runs through Honduras for approximately 100 miles, and connects to El Salvador and Nicaragua.

Honduras has twelve airports with paved runways. Ramón Villeda Morales International Airport, in the city of San Pedro Sula, is the nation's largest airport and the hub for most international air traffic. The capital of Tegucigalpa is also open for modern air travel, but has not become the nation's principal port. Travelers can also obtain short flights within the nation for relatively low prices.

Media & Communications

All the major media outlets of Honduras are owned by one of five major families, effectively forming a media oligarchy. Each of the five major families is associated with one or more political groups, making media objectivity unlikely. For example, *La Prensa*, which is the most popular newspaper in the nation, and *El Heraldo* are both owned by the Canahuati family, and have allegedly promoted biased political reporting in trade for lucrative government contracts.

In general, the Honduran media system has been heavily constrained by political corruption, threats of violence, and laws that allow severe penalties for defamation. There are few governmental measures in place to protect the rights of journalists or media organizations. Media monitoring agencies report that journalists in Honduras often exercise self-censorship because of the defamation laws, which are heavily slanted against journalists. Under these existing laws, journalists may be required to reveal their sources and may also face significant fines if convicted of defaming public figures in the course of reporting the news.

Although the five major families also own and control most of the television and radio stations in the nation, increasing popularity and availability of cable and satellite television has begun to increase media options for affluent Hondurans. Internet coverage in Honduras is restricted to major cities but is not censored by the government and is generally considered to be free from political bias. However, because Internet usage is not widespread, it was limited to only an estimated 17.8 percent of the population in 2013.

SOCIAL DEVELOPMENT

Standard of Living
Honduras ranked 129th out of 185 countries on the 2013 United Nations Human Development Index, which compiles quality of life and standard of living indicators.

Water Consumption
According to 2012 statistics from the World Health Organization (WHO), approximately 90 percent of the population has access to improved sources of drinking water, while an estimated 80 percent has access to improved sanitation. Coverage gaps for both clean water and sanitation are prominent in rural areas. A National Policy on Water Supply and Sanitation was scheduled for implementation in July 2011, but a 2013 World Bank report called for a more robust policy and additional investment in water and sanitation infrastructure.

Education
Although the law in Honduras states that children between the ages of seven and 12 must attend school, this law is not enforced, especially in the rural areas. Problems contributing to low school attendance include a lack of school buildings, mandatory public school fees for uniforms and textbooks, and parents putting their children to work. Overall, attendance during those six mandatory years is 90 percent; however, that number drops to 35 percent when children reach high school age. The average literacy rate is 85 percent, according to a 2011 estimate.

There are many bilingual private schools that teach classes in both English and Spanish. However, these schools are found only in the major cities, and are financially out of reach for most people. Many middle class families struggle to send their children to these schools, as English fluency is a great advantage in finding a well-paying job.

Honduras has several universities. The largest, the National Autonomous University of Honduras, is located in Tegucigalpa. It was founded in 1847. The university also has a campus in San Pedro Sula. Another notable university, the Pan American Agricultural School, is located just outside Tegucigalpa. Chiquita Brands International, a company based in the United States, funds the agricultural school.

Women's Rights
Women's rights are enshrined in the Honduran constitution and the nation's penal code. However, violence against women, spousal abuse, rape, and other crimes remain common. According to a 2013 report by the U.S. State

Department, violent deaths of women increased by 246 percent between 2005 and 2012. In addition, the traditional "machismo" attitude, which holds that women are socially inferior to men, continues to dominate thinking in some parts of the country, and women are still expected, in some circumstances, to be subservient to men.

Rape is a public crime according to Honduran law, punishable by three–to–nine years imprisonment, and the state is free to prosecute without the involvement of a witness. Spousal rape carries the same penalties, but is administered through a different legal system that requires case-by-case evaluation. There is evidence to suggest spousal rape is underreported because of the social and cultural stigma attached.

Spousal abuse and domestic violence are classified as crimes with penalties ranging from two–to–four years imprisonment. In practice, authorities appear unwilling to prosecute spousal abuse and convictions are rare. The burden of proof in domestic violence cases is placed on the accuser, and police are often reluctant to prosecute unless there is obvious evidence of physical abuse.

Amnesty International estimates that domestic violence is one of the leading causes of female mortality in Honduras.

In 2007, the Honduran government invited several non-governmental organizations (NGOs) to assist in a program to train police officers in effective management of domestic violence reports. This system is supplemented by a few privately run facilities and several makeshift centers set up by NGOs. (There are only two public facilities, nationwide, that serve to shelter abused women.) Additionally, Honduran law prohibits sexual harassment and recommends between one and three years imprisonment depending on the circumstances. While Honduras is one of the few Latin American countries to aggressively penalize sexual harassment, monitoring agencies estimate that harassment is underreported because of cultural and social norms.

Women have fewer employment options and make less, on average, than men in similar positions make. Since the 1980s, rising poverty levels have forced many women to enter the workforce. Women commonly work as domestic servants or in the educational industry and there are relatively few women working in management positions. Women's rights organizations have called attention to reports that some women were required to take pregnancy tests before being considered for employment.

Health Care

Health care is not available to every citizen. Those who live in rural areas often do not have access to doctors or hospitals. Instead, they rely on herbal remedies from local healers.

Hondurans who live in the major cities have more options for health care, but it is expensive. Only the wealthy consistently receive quality health care. As a result, many Hondurans suffer from untreated diseases, and only one-quarter of the population survives past 30 years of age.

Due to widespread poverty, malnutrition is a serious problem throughout Honduras. Combined with a lack of both clean water and a modern sewer system, many Hondurans live their entire lives in ill health. Common illnesses include malaria and dengue fever, typhoid fever, tuberculosis, influenza, and pneumonia. HIV/AIDS is becoming more pervasive as well. As of 2005, 60 percent of all reported cases of AIDS in Central American were occurring in Honduras, which has only 17 percent of the total population of Central America.

GOVERNMENT

Structure

Honduras is a democratic constitutional republic, headed by a president. The president is elected every four years by popular vote and can serve only one term. The legislative branch of government consists of the National Congress, comprised of 128 members who each serve four-year terms. Honduras highest court is the Supreme Court of Justice. All Hondurans, 18 years and older, are required by law to vote.

Honduran history is full of military revolts against the government. Because of this,

Honduran presidents often served only short terms before being overthrown. It was not until 1981 that elections were held to elect a civilian president and governing body. However, the military still retains influence, and military leaders have veto power over the president's choice of cabinet members.

Political Parties

Two parties dominate Honduran politics, even though five parties were registered and participated in the 2013 elections. The winning party in the presidential election was the National Party (PNH), a center-right conservative party; the PNH garnered 37 percent of the vote in the presidential race and their candidate, Juan Orlando Hernández, won. In the congressional election, the PNH took 48 seats. Liberty and Refoundation, a leftist party, won 29 percent of the presidential vote and took 37 seats, The Liberal Party of Honduras (PNH), a center-right liberal party, and its presidential candidate took 20 percent of the vote and secured 27 seats in the congress. Four other registered parties are active in Honduras: the Anti-Corruption Party, the Democratic Unification Party, the Christian Democratic Party of Honduras, and the Innovation and Unity Party.

Local Government

The country is divided into 18 departments and nearly 300 municipalities. Governors, appointed by the president, oversee the departments, and are seen as an extension of the national government. Mayors oversee municipalities, along with a council, both of which serve four-year terms.

Judicial System

The Supreme Court of Honduras is the highest court in the country. Lower courts include appeals courts, as well as labor, tax, and criminal courts.

Taxation

The government of Honduras levies a flat personal income tax, as well as taxes on corporate income, rental income, capital gains, sales, and property. A social contribution tax is also collected. Both the top income and corporate tax rates are 25 percent.

Armed Forces

The armed forces of Honduras consist of an army, navy, and air force. There is no conscription, and 18 is the minimum age for voluntary service. In 2009, the armed forces participated in a coup that ousted President Manuel Zelaya.

Foreign Policy

Honduras is an active member of the international community, and most notably a member of the United Nations (UN) and the World Trade Organization (WTO). The United States is Honduras's primary trading partner and provided $9.8 billion (USD) in annual trade revenues in 2013. Honduras was one of the countries included in the US-Central American Free Trade Agreement (CAFTA), which was implemented in 2004. Additionally, the U.S. has a military base in Honduras, and both countries have cooperated successfully on joint counterterrorism and anti-drug trafficking operations. In return for cooperating with U.S. military operations, the U.S. government provides funding assistance for Honduras to help defray the costs of training and equipment for Honduran security forces.

Regionally, Honduras is an advocate for economic integration and cooperation among Central American states. Honduras holds membership in the Organization of American States (OAS), the Central American Parliament (PARLACEN) and the Central American Integration System (SICA). In terms of regional and national security, Honduras participates in the Conference of Central American Armed Forces (CFAC), and the Central American Security Commission (CASC).

The most significant international issue in Honduras is a dispute with El Salvador over the administration of maritime and inland territory surrounding the Gulf of Fonseca. The dispute resulted in a five-day military conflict in 1969 between Honduras and El Salvador, known as the 100-Hours War or the "Football War" (also known as the "Soccer War"). A peace treaty with El Salvador was brokered in 1980. The International Court of Justice (ICJ) awarded most of the disputed territory to Honduras in 1992, and a new border territory was created in 1998. Both sides agree that the issue has not been satisfactorily resolved. In 2007, the ICJ also addressed a long-standing border dispute between Nicaragua and Honduras, which had become a pressing issue in 1999 when Nicaragua placed a tariff on goods imported from Honduras.

Human Rights Profile

International human rights law insists that states respect civil and political rights, and also promote an individual's economic, social, and cultural rights. The United Nations (UN) Universal Declaration of Human Rights (UDHR) is recognized as the standard for international human rights. Its authors sought the counsel of the world's great thinkers, philosophers, and religious leaders, and were careful to create a document that reflects the core values shared by every world culture. To read this document or view the articles relating to cultural human rights, click here: http://www.udhr.org/UDHR/default.htm.

Honduras has numerous issues to address in regard to protecting human rights. Although the constitution guarantees freedoms in keeping with the UDHR, monitoring agencies such as the US-based Human Rights Watch and Amnesty International (AI) reported frequent violations of human rights and liberties. Little effort is made by the authorities to address continuing human rights issues.

The Honduran constitution guarantees freedom of speech and expression, in keeping with Article 19 of the UDHR. In practice, journalists have been threatened for expressing issues contrary to the government or of powerful economic groups. On the other hand, there appears to be little opposition to the activities of international media representatives. There have also been reports of widespread corruption among representatives of the media, who are criticized for accepting bribes to report news according to the political designs of parent companies and/or government representatives.

Monitoring agencies report that there are currently no measures in place to restrict or control Internet content, and the government does not actively monitor e-mail or other cyberspace activities. Though the Honduran government generally respects the rights of expression and assembly, there are laws in place that proscribe fines and imprisonment for speech that can be said to "incite" violence or rioting. Some rights organizations have criticized Honduras for maintaining laws that can be used to persecute persons engaging in assembly that may threaten governmental authority.

Amnesty International (AI) has reported that the government does not adequately investigate cases of violence or persecution directed against homosexuals. In 2000, for example, AI criticized the Honduran government for failing to investigate over 200 murders involving homosexual workers. Failure to ensure equality under the law is a violation of Articles 2, 3, and 7 of the UDHR.

There have been reports that human trafficking is a significant problem in Honduras, largely fueled by the global sex industry. Casa Alianza, an international nonprofit based in the United Kingdom and specializing in protecting street children in Latin America, estimates that as many as 20 or 30 children were transported across the border on a daily basis for the purpose of sexual exploitation in 2007.

Though the government prohibits physical and emotional abuse, there were reports that authorities occasionally used torture and physical abuse in criminal investigations. There have also been credible reports that individuals were regularly held in detention without due process. The prison system in Honduras is also a significant area of concern, and investigations have revealed severe overcrowding, inadequate nutrition, and inefficient medical and sanitary facilities. Thus, prison conditions in Honduras constitute a violation of Article 5 of the UDHR.

Arbitrary arrest and persecution are also pressing problems in Honduras. According to a report released by the Committee for the Defense of Human Rights in Honduras, more than 34,000 persons were arrested, detained or abused by government representatives under the government's Operation National Program. These abuses constitute violations of Article 9 of the UDHR.

ECONOMY

Overview of the Economy

Honduras is one of the poorest countries in the Western Hemisphere and the second poorest in Latin America. In 2013, the per capita gross domestic product (GDP) was estimated at $4,800 USD. While the official unemployment rate for the country is reported to be 4.5 percent (2013), the US Central Intelligence Agency reports that about 36 percent of the population is unemployed or underemployed. Unequal distribution of income is also a serious challenge.

The World Bank and the International Monetary Fund (IMF) have determined Honduras eligible for debt relief under the Heavily Indebted Poor Countries (HIPC) program.

The Honduran export economy is based mainly on agriculture—with the primary exports being coffee, bananas, clothing, and textiles. These agriculture-based products make the export market more vulnerable to natural disasters, and Hurricane Mitch in 1998 had a devastating and long-lasting impact on the nation's economy.

Remittances also account for 20 percent of the nation's GDP—to which the global economic crisis that began in 2008 has also had an impact.

Industry

Honduras trades mainly with the United States, El Salvador, Guatemala, and Mexico. Chief items for trade are sugar, coffee, textiles, clothing, and wood products.

Honduras has the world's second-largest maquiladora industry. Maquiladoras are factories that assemble imported parts to produce goods solely for export. Most maquiladoras are foreign-owned, and take advantage of inexpensive local labor. Still, these factories generate tens of thousands of much-needed jobs in Honduras.

Tegucigalpa serves as the main center of industry in Honduras. The capital's economy nonetheless reflects the struggles of a country that is one of the most impoverished in Central America. Over the past decade, city officials have promoted the growth of a light manufacturing sector that produces sugar and tobacco products as well as clothing and textiles. Tegucigalpa's job market has been unable to accommodate the waves of young, rural emigrants who continue to flock to the capital.

Labor

The labor force of Honduras was estimated at 3.507 million in 2013, with an unemployment rate reported as high as nearly 36 percent in 2008. Underemployment also continues to be a concern. Approximately 39 percent of the work force is concentrated in agriculture, while nearly 40 percent is employed in the services sector. Industry accounts for nearly 21 percent of the labor force.

Energy/Power/Natural Resources

Honduras is rich in natural resources, including timber, coal, fish and hydropower. Honduras is known internationally for its mahogany.

The country has extensive mineral deposits, including gold, silver, copper, lead, and zinc, but lacks the resources to exploit them. There are also large offshore reserves of natural gas and oil, but again, these remain unexploited.

Fishing

The Honduran fish export market generates $170 million (USD) per year. The fishing industry in 2010 lacks organization, oversight, and planning, and overfishing is a real concern. Shrimping is also a major contributor to the industry, accounting for an anticipated $200 million in 2010, with most exports going to the United States and Europe.

Forestry

Illegal harvesting is devastating Honduras's forests, with a 37 percent decrease in forest cover between 1990 and 2005. The large-scale deforestation rate more than quadrupled between 2007 and 2011. Poverty is claimed to be a persistent driver, as local farmers clear forests for fields, fuel, and grazing. Mining and illegal logging are also said to be contributing factors, as is the narcotics trade. Reports also claim that 85 percent of the nation's timber harvest is gathered illegally. International pressure to resolve issues of corruption and target resources towards planning and enforcement have been forthcoming, with limited success.

Mining/Metals

Precious metal mining in Honduras was at a standstill in 2009 due to decreased demand, investment, and consumption. In 2006 and 2007, mining accounted for 1.2 percent of GDP. This dropped to 0.8 percent in 2008 and 2009, with a dollar figure of $99.4 million USD reported in 2009.

Lead, silver, zinc, and gold are the major commodities in the mining sector.

Agriculture

Coffee and bananas are Honduras' two largest exports; together they account for approximately one-third of the country's total exports. The value of the country's coffee production can fluctuate wildly with changing international market prices. Most banana plantations in Honduras are owned by foreign interests. The effects of Hurricane Mitch devastated the local banana industry in 1998.

Other important agricultural products produced for export include citrus, beef, timber, and shrimp. Honduran farmers grow a variety of other crops, including corn, beans, cotton, rice, sugar cane, and tobacco. Corn is the most extensively grown crop in the country.

Animal Husbandry

With the help of the IAEA (International Atomic Energy Agency), the government of Honduras is working towards improving its livestock productivity. The agency is working with the government improve the health of livestock by assessing the nutritional value of grazing pastures and available food sources for livestock, improving reproductive techniques, combating disease, and introducing new laboratory techniques that might increase production.

Tourism

Tourism was a growing industry in Honduras, but due to the political unrest that followed the 2009 coup that deposed President Manuel Zelaya, many infrastructure efforts were put on hold and the industry suffered a downturn. In 2008, the industry reported a 70 percent decline; plans for an international airport in Copán were suspended. Signs of a recovery were evident, though, as Carnival Cruise Lines continued the construction of a dock in Roatán and a resort in the north continued.

The Bay Islands attract tourists from around the word. The islands are ideally suited for scuba diving and snorkeling in the extensive coral reefs. In the interior, tourists visit the country's Mayan ruins, especially the ruins of Copán, in the western part of Honduras. At the height of Mayan civilization, between third and 10th centuries, Copán was the empire's second-largest city.

La Tigra National Park, the country's first national park, lies just outside Tegucigalpa and is frequented by Hondurans and tourists alike. La Tigra is host to many rainforest animals; including tapirs, ocelots, pumas, and monkeys. Also near Tegucigalpa is the Cerro el Picacho national park, which features a large botanical garden and the 90-foot-tall statue El Picacho Cristo ("Christ Resurrected"), which lights up at night.

Micah Issitt, Rebekah Painter,
Beverly Ballaro

DO YOU KNOW?

- Honduras is the second-largest country in Central America. The largest is Nicaragua.
- It is estimated that humans have been living in Honduras for more than 8,000 years.
- The national bird of Honduras is the scarlet macaw.

Bibliography

Booth, John A. & Patricia Bayer Richard. *Latin American Political Culture: Public Opinion and Democracy.* Thousand Oaks, CA: CQ Press, 2015.

Chandler, Gary & Liza Prado. *Honduras & the Bay Islands.* Oakland, CA: Lonely Planet, 2007.

Cuddy, Thomas W. *Political Identity and Archaeology in Northeast Honduras.* Boulder, CO: University Press of Colorado, 2007.

Morrison, Terri. *Kiss, Bow or Shake Hands: Latin America: How to Do Business in 18 Latin American Countries.* Cincinnati, OH: Adams Media, 2006.

Humphrey, Chris. *Honduras.* Berkeley, CA: Avalon Travel Publishing, 2006.

Jensen Arnett, Jeffrey. *International Encyclopedia of Adolescence: A Historical and Cultural Survey of Young People around the World.* Boca Raton, FL: CRC Press, 2007.

Norsworthy, Kent & Tom Barry. *Inside Honduras.* 2nd ed. Washington, DC: Interhermispheric Resource Center, 1994.

Schulz, Donald E. *The United States, Honduras, and the Crisis in Central America.* New York: Westview Press, 1994.

Soluri, John. *Banana Cultures: Agriculture, Consumption, and Environmental Change in Honduras and the United States.* Austin, TX: University of Texas Press, 2005.

Tompkins, Cynthia & Kristen Sternberg. *Teen Life in Latin America and the Caribbean.* Westview, CT: Greenwood Publishing Group, 2004.

Works Cited

"Background Note: Honduras." *U.S. Department of States Online.* Bureau of Western Hemisphere Affairs. June 2008. http://www.state.gov/r/pa/ei/bgn/1922.htm

"Honduras and the IMF." *International Monetary Fund Online.* October 12, 2008. http://www.imf.org/external/country/hnd/index.htm

"Honduras." *UNESCO Online.* http://whc.unesco.org/en/statesparties/hn

"Honduras." *World Factbook Online.* 22 June, 2014. https://www.cia.gov/library/publications/the-world-factbook/geos/ho.html

"Honduras: Overview." *Lonely Planet Online.* Destinations. http://www.lonelyplanet.com/worldguide/honduras/

Chandler, Gary & Liza Prado. "Honduras & the Bay Islands." Oakland, CA: Lonely Planet, 2007.

Escure, Genevieve & Armin Schwegler. "Creoles, Contact, and Language Change: Linguistics and Social Implications." Philadelphia, PA: John Benjamins Publishing Company, 2004.

Hamovitch, Eric. "Honduras." Montreal, Quebec: Ulysses Publishing, 2000.

Humphrey, Chris. "Honduras." Berkeley, CA: Avalon Travel Publishing, 2006.

Humphrey, Chris. "Moon Handbooks Honduras." Berkeley, CA: Avalon Travel Publishing, 2003.

Jensen Arnett, Jeffrey. "International Encyclopedia of Adolescence: A Historical and Cultural Survey of Young People around the World." Boca Raton, FL: CRC Press, 2007.

Law Library of Congress. "Honduras Gang Violence: Report for the Department of Justice." Washington, D.C.: Library of Congress, 2013.

"Monitoring Country Progress in Drinking Water and Sanitation." Geneva, Switzerland: The World Bank, 2013.

Norsworthy, Kent & Tom Barry. "Inside Honduras 2nd Ed." Washington, D.C.: Interhermispheric Resource Center, 1994.

Schulz, Donald E. "The United States, Honduras, and the Crisis in Central America." New York: Westview Press, 1994.

Soluri, John. "Banana Cultures: Agriculture, Consumption, and Environmental Change in Honduras and the United States." Austin, TX: University of Texas Press, 2005.

Tompkins, Cynthia & Kristen Sternberg. "Teen Life in Latin America and the Caribbean." Westview, CT: Greenwood Publishing Group, 2004.

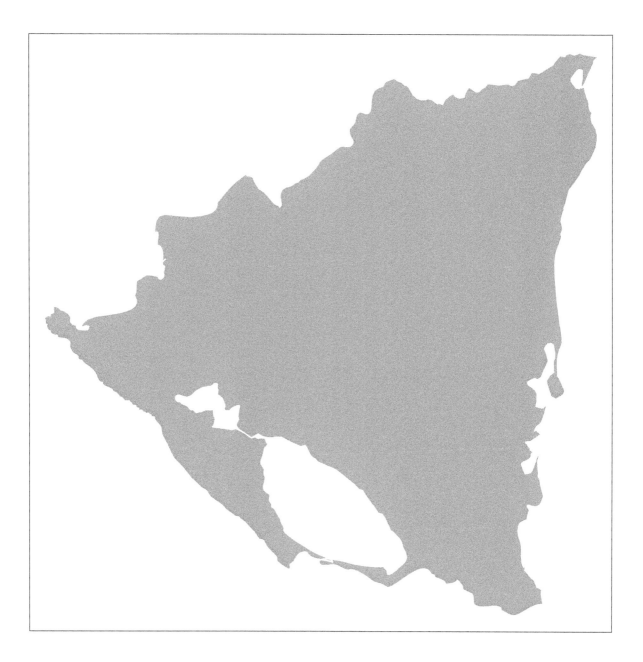

NICARAGUA

Introduction

The Republic of Nicaragua is the largest country in Central America, and one of the poorest in the Western Hemisphere. Bordered by Honduras and Costa Rica, it has coastline along both the Pacific Ocean and the Caribbean Sea. Nicaragua was once part of the Spanish empire, giving the country its dominant ethnic and cultural influence.

In the latter half of the 20th century, Nicaragua experienced a series of crippling natural disasters, as well as civil conflict. In 1979, the ruling dictatorship was overthrown and replaced by the Sandinista government, a socialist party that enacted a great number of programs aimed at improving quality of life concerns for the Nicaraguan people. They came out of power in 1990, and the country was faced with crippling debt and then a devastating hurricane in 1998. Political upheavals and natural disasters have taken their toll on Nicaragua, and today the country struggles with widespread poverty.

Tourists are drawn to Nicaragua for its culture and history, as well as its scenic beauty and animal life. Historic Granada and Leon both offer examples of colonial architecture, including several important cathedrals. The Volcán Masaya National Park, numerous nature reserves, the extensive coastlines, and islands locales are among the country's natural attractions.

GENERAL INFORMATION

Official Language: Spanish
Population: 5,848,641 (2014 estimate)
Currency: Gold Cordoba

Coins: One hundred centavos equal one cordoba. Coins are issued in denominations of 5, 10, 25, and 50 centavos as well as 1, 5, and 10 cordobas.
Land Area: 119,990 square kilometers (46,328 square miles)
Water Area: 10,380 square kilometers (4,007 square miles)
National Motto: "En Dios Confiamos" ("In God We Trust")
National Anthem: "Salve a ti, Nicaragua" ("Hail to You, Nicaragua")
Capital: Managua
Time Zone: GMT -6
Flag Description: Nicaragua's flag features the blue, white, blue pattern common to all Central American flags, recalling their former union. In particular, the Nicaraguan flag features three horizontal stripes in a blue, white, blue pattern with the center white stripe emblazoned with Nicaragua's coat of arms. White represents purity while blue represents the oceans on each side of the country.

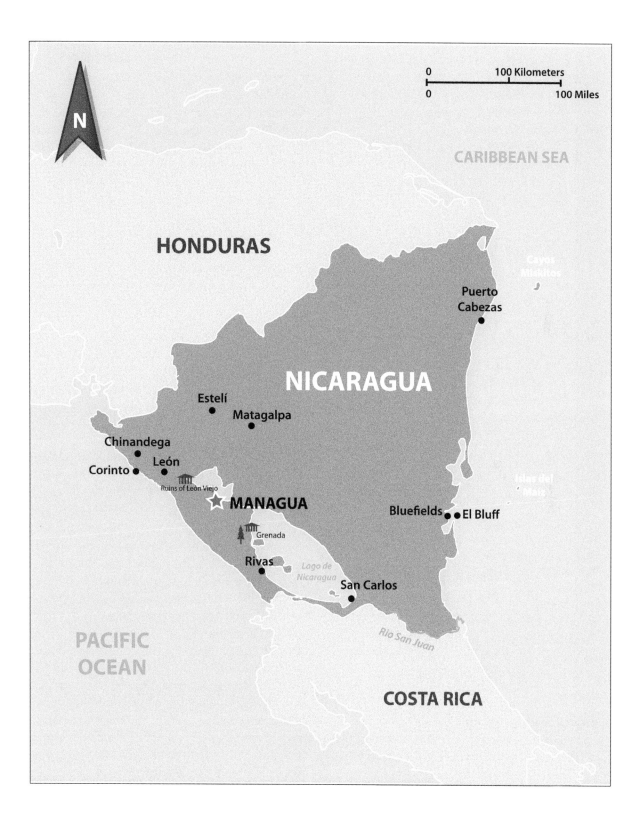

Principal Cities by Population (2012):

- Managua (928,621)
- León (147,199)
- Estelí (102,851)
- Tipitapa (98,453)
- Matagalpa (96,090)
- Masaya (92,745)
- Chinandenga (92,222)
- Granada (93,042)

Population

Nicaragua's population is young and growing. Life expectancy at birth is 70.57 years for males and 74.98 years for females (2014 estimate). The median age for the Nicaraguan population is 24.2 years; the country's birth rate is 18.41 per 1,000 residents and the population growth rate is 1.02 percent in 2014. According to the United Nations, Nicaragua has one of the highest birth rates in the Western Hemisphere.

Nicaragua's average population density is 42 persons per square kilometer (114 per square mile), but the population is concentrated along the Pacific coast. During the second half of the 20th century, Nicaragua's urban population began growing rapidly; 58.14 percent of the total population now lives in urban centers. Managua is the largest city with a metropolitan population numbering over 2.1 million people. León and Granada are important urban centers, but both are considerably smaller than the capital.

Languages

Nearly all Nicaraguans speak Spanish, but it is a second language for those who live in the Caribbean lowlands. English dominates among the African population, and Miskito is the most widely spoken indigenous language.

Native People & Ethnic Groups

Before the 16th century, Nicaragua was populated by various Amerindian tribes. The diseases brought by the Spanish seriously reduced their population, and survivors were forced into labor. Today, the Miskito, of mixed Amerindian and African blood, are the country's largest native group.

Other indigenous groups include the Sumu and the Rama. Their long neglect by the mestizo majority was somewhat reversed in 1980s, when the Sandinista government attempted to foster better relations by giving the Caribbean minorities more autonomy.

Mestizos, of mixed Spanish and Amerindian ancestry, comprise 69 percent of the population. The minority ethnic groups are European (17 percent), mixed African, (nine percent) and Amerindian (five percent). Mestizos and Europeans are concentrated along the Pacific coast and in the central highlands, whereas the other minorities are concentrated in the Caribbean lowlands. Those of African descent arrived in Nicaragua as escaped West Indian slaves.

Religions

Approximately 58 percent of Nicaraguans adhere to Roman Catholicism, the religion that predominates among the Mestizos and Europeans. Twenty-one percent of the population identifies as an evangelical or Protestant, many of whom live along the Caribbean coast, reflecting Britain's historical influence on the area. More than 15 percent of the population claims no religious affiliation.

Climate

Elevation rather than season affects the tropical climate of Nicaragua's three zones. The Pacific lowlands are hot and drier than the Caribbean coast. The average temperature is 27° Celsius (81° Fahrenheit), and the average rainfall ranges between 1,000 and 1,800 millimeters (40 and 70 inches). The central highlands receive a similar amount of precipitation but are cooler, with average temperatures between 16° and 27° Celsius (60° and 80° Fahrenheit). The rainy season lasts from May to October.

The Caribbean coast is the wettest region in all of Central America and very humid. It is also the region most prone to tropical storms and hurricanes. The rainy season brings more than 2,500 millimeters (100 inches) of precipitation, with higher totals along the southernmost stretch of the coast.

Nicaragua is prone to natural disasters. Volcanoes, earthquakes, hurricanes, tropical storms, and the ensuing landslides and floods have caused widespread damage. The earthquake of 1972 destroyed the center of Managua, and Hurricane Joan (1988) and Hurricane Mitch (1998) caused billions of dollars in damage, killed thousands of people, and left thousands homeless.

ENVIRONMENT & GEOGRAPHY

Topography

Nicaragua can be divided into the Pacific lowlands in the west, the Caribbean lowlands in the east, and the central highlands between them. In the south, the highlands taper down into the basin of the San Juan River, and the elevation approaches sea level.

Several volcanoes beginning near the Gulf of Fonseca and extending to Lake Managua break the narrow, flat lowlands along the Pacific. Running southeast from the Gulf is a depression in which Central America's two largest lakes formed: Lake Nicaragua and Lake Managua.

The long, narrow Caribbean lowlands account for over 50 percent of Nicaragua's total area. They are characterized by coastal plains, bays, lagoons, salt marshes, and ridges descending from the central highlands. Numerous islands dot the coastline.

Mountain peaks and deep valleys characterize the central highlands. The Cordillera Isabella range crosses the highlands and contains the country's highest peaks, several of which rise to 2,100 meters (6,890 feet).

None of Nicaragua's major rivers empty into the Pacific. The Rio Grande, the Escondido, the Coco, and the San Juan rivers flow into the Caribbean. The Rio Grande and its tributaries form the country's largest river system, but the Escondido is the most traveled.

Lake Nicaragua, the country's largest lake, gives rise to the San Juan River. It covers 8,000 square kilometers (3,100 square miles) and contains many islands and several volcanoes. The Tipitapa River, flowing from Lake Managua, connects the two bodies of water. Lake Managua covers 1,050 square kilometers (405 square miles).

Plants & Animals

Nicaragua is home to a rich array of tropical plants and animals, especially along the Caribbean coast and where protected by governmental decree. There are an estimated 6,500 plant species, many of them flowering, including several types of orchids. Fruit trees, pine, oak, mahogany, cedar and rosewood are a few of the trees found in Nicaragua; although the hardwoods are quickly disappearing.

Among Nicaragua's 200 mammal species are the armadillo, the three-toed sloth, the white-tailed deer, the ocelot, the jaguar, and the puma, as well as several monkey and bat species. Reptiles include venomous snakes, boa constrictors, iguanas, geckos, and sea turtles, which are hunted for their meat and eggs. Bird species, which number over 600, include parrots, hummingbirds, wrens, and hawks. The blue whale, the American manatee, the Central American tapir, and the giant anteater are listed as endangered or vulnerable.

The more exotic animal species are under the general threat of being captured for sale as pets. It is common for Nicaraguans to have wild animals as pets, and the country has been a major hub for selling them throughout the world. New legislation is aimed at protecting the animals from being trapped, kept as pets, and smuggled abroad.

CUSTOMS & COURTESIES

Greetings

Handshakes are the standard greeting in Nicaragua and tend to last longer than in some cultures. Friends may also exchange hugs, and it is common for men familiar with women to kiss both cheeks as a form of greeting. More than 90 percent of Nicaraguans speak a dialect of Spanish, known locally as "Nicañol." This dialect is similar to the Spanish spoken in other parts of Central America. For example, among the characteristic features of Central American Spanish is the use of the formal form "usted" and the informal "voseo" instead of "tu."

Nicaraguans use standard Spanish greetings but with slightly different pronunciations. In many expressions, ending in the "es" or "s" sound, the sound is dropped. When using the Spanish greeting "Buena," or "Good" to say "Hello," for example, Nicaraguan speakers typically drop the "s" sound, whereas Mexican speakers will usually say "Buenos." Nicaraguans also use the informal expression "Hola," meaning "Hi." In addition, "Adios," which is used to say "Goodbye," is also typically pronounced "ah-DEE-oh," as the speakers drop the "s" sound. Similarly, the expression for "Thank you," which is "Gracias," is commonly pronounced "GRA-cee-ah."

The Garinagu people, a population of West African and Caribbean descent who live in parts of Nicaragua and several nearby countries, have their own dialect. Known as Garifuna, it is a blend of Spanish and several African dialects. In Garifuna, the expression "Mábuiga" means "Hello." Alternatively, many greetings reference the time of day, as in "Buíti binafi" ("Good morning"), "Buíti amidi" ("Good afternoon") and "Buíti ránba weyu" ("Good evening").

Gestures & Etiquette

There is a variety of gestures commonly used in Nicaragua and other Central American countries. One of the most common is the expression for a failure to understand, which typically involves the scrunching of the bridge of the nose. Another gesture involves rubbing the two index fingers together, resulting in an expression that refers to money, while wagging the index finger vigorously with the arm extended is a sign that clearly means "no." Additionally, clenching the fingers and thumb of one hand with the arm outstretched means "crowded" or "full."

Since diarrhea has become a health problem due to polluted water, Nicaraguans have even incorporated a special gesture for its occurrence. This involves pressing the arm with the clenched fist upward against the body, and moving the arm up and down against the side of the body. Furthermore, many Nicaraguan hand gestures have been incorporated into the Nicaraguan sign language, a unique form of signing that originated in the 1970s. Nicaraguan Sign Language, or Idioma de Señas de Nicaragua, has been extensively studied by neurobiologists and linguists and has provided insights into the origin and development of language.

Generosity and polite behavior are highly valued in Nicaragua, as in most Central American cultures. In general, however, Nicaraguans are comfortable with informal behavior in certain contexts. In formal or business situations, the use of honorific titles, such as "don" for a man and "doña" for a woman are common. It is also considered rude not to directly acknowledge the presence of a familiar person, even if seeing them in passing.

It is considered inappropriate to be overly formal even in business meetings. Dressing tastefully is advisable, but many business meetings are handled in a relaxed manner, accompanied by friendly conversation, refreshments, and liquor. Western and Asian executives sometimes express frustration at the relaxed nature of Nicaraguan business, where meetings extend beyond their scheduled time and it is common for negotiations to be rescheduled. Additionally, it is not uncommon for a host to arrive late to a prescheduled business meeting.

Eating/Meals

Nicaraguans generally eat three meals per day, roughly corresponding to breakfast, lunch and dinner. Breakfast is generally light and always includes coffee, which is a major plantation crop in Nicaragua and a point of pride for locals. A variety of rice and bean dishes, certain types of fruit and eggs are also morning staples. Most meals are served with tortillas, which are as common as rolls and bread in other cultures.

The afternoon meal is generally the largest of the day. During this meal, many Nicaraguans take an hour or more to eat with friends and family. The afternoon meal is followed by a short siesta before returning to work. The evening meal is lighter than the afternoon meal and often accompanied by some form of alcoholic refreshment. In many Nicaraguan homes, leftovers from the afternoon meal are commonly served for the evening meal.

Visiting

It is considered polite to bring small gifts, including flowers, liquor, and candies, when visiting a Nicaraguan home. Lilies should be avoided as a gift as they are typically used to express condolence, and are thus used for funerals.

Generally, Nicaraguans are comfortable with informal speech, and are often loud and boisterous in social situations. Little time passes before Nicaraguans begin using informal terminology and reducing the average distance of social contact with new friends. Nicaraguan hosts usually offer beverages to their guests, and it is generally considered impolite to refuse. It is not uncommon for Nicaraguans to enjoy casual drinking any time during or after midday. In addition, coffee is a popular drink at all times of the day.

LIFESTYLE

Family

The nuclear family (loosely defined as a mother, father, and children) is the basic unit of kinship and society in Nicaragua. However, extended family is an important part of the social networks that exist in Nicaragua. Social status is important and is often linked to kinship and heritage. As such, it is common for members of certain prominent families to serve in politics or as community leaders for several generations.

The "compadrazgo" system is a tradition in many Latin American countries in which parents choose "godparents" from among their closest friends. This tradition, like marriage, creates bonds of extended kinship between families and creates stronger community links. Families linked through the compadrazgo system form an extended support network and often assist one another in times of crisis. Strategically choosing godparents for one's children is also seen as a way to increase the social status of the family.

Housing

Housing in Nicaragua varies considerably from urban to rural areas. In large cities, such as Managua, it is common for residents to live in apartments. Generally, these apartments contain one or two bedrooms. Single family-houses are more common in suburban and rural areas. Cities also have housing projects and multi-family buildings. Adequate housing has become a significant issue in Nicaragua in the 21st century, and organizations such as Habitat for Humanity have estimated that more than 300,000 new or completely reconstructed housing units are needed to meet the demands of the population.

Generally, most families live in relatively basic housing, and it is estimated that approximately 80 percent of Nicaraguans participate in the construction of their own homes. The Instituto Nacional de Estadística y Censos estimated in 2001 that more than 40 percent of Nicaraguan homes have dirt floors, and that only 30 percent have concrete walls. Roofing made of zinc is common (found in more than 60 percent of houses) because it is inexpensive. However, it is also generally of low quality. Because of high poverty rates and insufficient investment in housing improvement, less than 80 percent of houses have electricity and less than 30 percent have adequate indoor plumbing. Conditions in cities are better than those in rural areas, though thousands of urban residents also live below the poverty line and in substandard living conditions.

Food

The cuisine of Nicaragua is largely a blend of Pre-Colombian, immigrant (largely Caribbean) and Spanish traditions, and is often very similar to other Latin American cuisines. As such, corn is an important staple, and the use of rice, beans, and seafood is often prominent. For example, the popular dish, gallo pinto, which translates as "spotted rooster," provides an example of typical Nicaraguan cuisine. The dish is composed of rice and beans mixed and served with tortillas. The dish is very popular for breakfast, but may be served at any time of day. In addition, there are variations of the dish that might include roasted meats, vegetables, eggs, or fruit.

Picadillo is another common dish in Nicaragua. It is typically made from chopped beef or pork and often served with tortillas and fresh fruit. There are many varieties of picadillo, ranging in consistency from stew to soup. In Nicaragua, cooking the meat with sautéed onion, garlic, and spices and then adding other vegetables is a common way to prepare picadillo. The stew may be served with avocado or tomatoes.

While tamales are common throughout Central American and Mexico, the Nicaraguan tamale, called nacatamale, is generally larger and often served as a main course. The tamale filling is made from pork or chicken, and wrapped in dough made of corn meal and steamed in plantain leaves. Potatoes, peppers and onions are often mixed into the dough. The nacatamale has become one of Nicaragua's most famous dishes.

A common beverage in Nicaragua is pinolillo, which is a drink made from corn that is soaked and toasted, and milk, along with cacao. There are several varieties of pinolillo, including sweetened and unsweetened. Some Nicaraguan dishes call for pinolillo as a base for cooking. Pinolillo is one of the few dishes in Nicaragua that is not a part of the shared cuisine of neighboring Central American countries.

Life's Milestones

Many Nicaraguans are Catholic, and the major rites of passage are based on Catholic traditions. Birth and baptism are occasions for major family celebrations and are also the point at which most parents choose godparents for their children. Some families celebrate a young girl's 15th birthday, commonly called the quinceañera or quince años celebration, in Latin American cultures. This celebration typically consists of a party and a traditional waltz, which commemorate the young woman's transition to adulthood.

Both males and females tend to remain in the home, or living nearby, until marriage, which is considered the point of transition to adulthood in Nicaraguan culture. After marriage, most young couples remain close to their families, often living in the same village or city. Nicaraguans do not celebrate the anniversary of their marriage as in some cultures. However, major milestones such as the 25th and 50th wedding anniversaries are commonly celebrated with family feasts.

While some families celebrate birthdays annually, some follow the alternative Catholic tradition of celebrating "saint days." The celebration of saint days involves assigning one or more given names to each calendar day and celebrating all persons of that particular name on that appointed day. Each day in the tradition is also designated by the recognition of a Catholic saint. It is common in Central American cultures for families to celebrate either the birthday or the saint day, but it is considered uncommon to celebrate both.

CULTURAL HISTORY

Art

Nicaragua's artistic heritage can be traced to the Pre-Columbian era, a designation historians use to refer to the thousands of years of history in Central and South America before the arrival of European explorers. Nicaraguan ceramics are among the only lasting remnants of Nicaragua's Pre-Columbian artistic heritage. During this era, pottery was typically used as a commodity and was valued as highly as precious stones, metals, spices, and fabrics. After thousands of years, Nicaraguan artisans still produce some of the most highly valued pottery of any Central or South American culture.

After the Spanish conquest of Nicaragua in the 16th century, pottery making was largely discouraged, as were many links to the traditional culture of the native Nicaraguan tribes. It wasn't until the 20th century that artisans began exploring the techniques that once made Nicaraguan pottery such a valuable commodity. Today, artisans from towns such as San Juan de Oriente, near the capital of Managua, are known for their artisan pottery and decorated plates.

Architecture

Nicaragua's cities reflect the country's colonial history. In spite of the natural disasters that have plagued this Central American country, cities like León and Granada have retained a significant number of Spanish colonial structures, including churches, homes, and mansions. Nicaraguan colonial structures are characterized by asymmetrical construction, spiral columns, archways over doors, carved stone, or wood, intricate grill-work, and adobe, stucco or plaster finishes.

Because of the destruction wrought by both the earthquake of 1972 and Hurricane Mitch in 1998, Nicaragua's capital, Managua, lost its downtown, and much of the rebuilding of that city happened outside of the city center. The result is a sprawling metropolitan area. Scientists estimate that Managua will be hit with an earthquake every 50 years, and new structures are designed and built with that in mind.

Drama

The dramatic production known as El Güegüense, which is regarded as one of the oldest dramatic traditions in Central America, began as a "protest drama" in the 18th century. The satirical play combines elements of both Spanish and indigenous culture, and thereby serves as a record—in song, dance, and costume—of the cultural transformations that began in the 16th century. The drama, traditionally performed at the Feast of San Sebastian (an annual celebration in the nation's Catholic tradition), tells of meetings between colonial Spaniards and the country's native residents, represented by El Güegüense, the leader of one of the tribes. El Güegüense appears to cooperate with the Spanish, but cleverly finds ways to undermine their authority and rules. The character has become so well known in Nicaragua that natives use the expression "Güegüense face," to describe an attitude of insincere compliance.

Music & Dance

The blending of indigenous, immigrant, and European (Spanish) culture also features prominently in the development of Nicaraguan music and dance. While many regions have their own traditions, many characteristics are typically considered "Nicaraguan." These include certain styles of guitar strumming, the use of the marimba (percussion instrument), and chicheros, which are musical groups or street musicians prominently performing on brass instruments.

One particular style of dance and music often associated with Nicaragua is Palo de Mayo, found on the country's Caribbean coast. Considered both a style of dance and a music genre all its own, this theatrical form of dance music is featured extensively during the Palo de Mayo festival, held in May, and blends both Afro-Caribbean and European traditions. In addition, Nicaraguan polka, which has its roots in the polka traditions of Poland, is popular in northern regions. Historically, costumes have figured prominently in both folk and modern Nicaraguan dance and music.

Literature

Before the arrival of the Spanish, the native tribes of Nicaragua and neighboring Panama and Costa Rica used storytelling to preserve their history and culture. Though most of Nicaragua's native stories disappeared, a few were translated into Spanish. More importantly, the blending of Spanish and native culture eventually generated a unique literary tradition in the 1800s, when writers drew upon European literary forms but used Nicaraguan life as the setting for their literary works.

Nicaraguan literature is often renowned for its poetry. During the nation's turbulent political periods, poets chose to express their pain, anger, and frustration through epic lyrical compositions, with these poems often gaining international attention. The poet Rubén Darío (1867–1916), who is sometimes referred to as the "father of modernist literature," is one of the most famous Nicaraguans in history. He is particularly known for his political activity and revolutionary poetry and essays. Dario's image is featured in hundreds of paintings, sculptures, and has even been immortalized on the country's currency (the 100 Córdoba bill). Drawing from French poetic style, Dario's work became emblematic of the struggles of the Nicaraguan people, and encouraged an international audience to take interest in the culture of Nicaragua.

Granada, the eighth largest city in Nicaragua, and Managua, the nation's capital, are considered the two epicenters of art and literature in the country. Galleries, cafés, and bookstores in both cities showcase local talent and are a proving ground for young painters, poets, writers, sculptors and dramatists. Gioconda Belli (1948–) remains one of the nation's most famous poets and a well–known figure in international literary circles. Belli was the first Nicaraguan writer to address gender equality and gender roles in her writing. She has been recognized as one of the most important poets of the 20th century. Other famous Nicaraguan poets include Pablo Antonio Cuadra (1912–2002), and Julio Valle Castillo (1952–).

CULTURE

Arts & Entertainment
Cultivating the development of the artistic community in contemporary Nicaragua has not been a major priority for the Nicaraguan government. Generally, there are few assistance and/or training programs available for Nicaraguans interested in pursing arts education. Additionally, art education in primary and secondary school is basic, and the general education system does not recognize and cultivate artistic talent.

Managua contains the nation's most significant independent arts scene, largely through its gallery district where independent galleries display a variety of local artist's work. Galleries in Managua also display imported art and are one of the few places that aspiring Nicaraguan artists can go to seek exposure to the international arts scene.

Popular art forms in Nicaragua include primitivist painting, associated with the Solentiname Islands in Lake Nicaragua, and folk music. The Caribbean population commonly plays reggae.

Basketball, soccer, and volleyball are popular in Nicaragua, but baseball is the national sport. The sport is widely played, and the country's professional teams receive ardent support.

Cultural Sites & Landmarks
Nicaragua is famous for its ecological beauty and biological diversity. After years of military upheaval, the country has recently begun to build a significant ecotourism market and has started utilizing its resources to expand the services industry. In addition, the United Nations Educational, Scientific, and Cultural Organization (UNESCO) has designated the Ruins of León Viejo, the remnants of a historical Spanish settlement, as a World Heritage Site.

One of Nicaragua's famous ecological sites is the Miskitos Keys, a natural reserve containing 40 kilometers (24 miles) of coastal territory encompassing coral reef, marine meadows and dense tropical forest. The site features a large number of threatened and endangered species, including several varieties of marine reptile. Another renowned ecological area is the Volcan Masaya National Park, which contains a volcanic mountain with attached craters (Nicaragua is considered Latin America's most volcanic nation). The national park supports a unique assemblage of plants and animals that have evolved to survive and flourish in the volcanic rock and surrounding forest environments. Hundreds of species of reptile, plant, and small animals live in the volcanic scrub and forest surrounding the park, which is among the best preserved natural areas in Nicaragua. Both sites, along with the Bosawas Natural Reserve— famous for its cloudy forests—were submitted to UNESCO for consideration as World Heritage Sites.

The entire city of Granada is also tentatively awaiting inscription from UNESCO as a World Heritage Site. The city is considered an important site for the preservation of Nicaraguan culture. For example, the streets of Granada are filled with examples of colonial Spanish architecture blended with modern buildings and residential housing. The city, established in 1954, still houses many preserved military structures when it served as a military base for the Spanish colonial government. Granada also sits on the edge of Lake Nicaragua, and the areas surrounding the city, including lakes, streams, and several types of forest and lagoons, are protected for their biological diversity.

The Cathedral of León has been called the most important historic building in Nicaragua. Built in the 1800s, the building avoided major catastrophe and the central structure remained unchanged, establishing the cathedral as one of the best existing examples of Spanish cathedral design. The cathedral is one of several important cultural buildings remaining in León, which is the second largest city in the nation after Managua. In June 2011, the cathedral was added to UNESCO's list of World Heritage Sites. Other important Nicaraguan landmarks include the Fortress of the Immaculate Conception, a 17th-century Spanish fortification located in El Castillo now preserved as a monument, and the island of Ometepe, formed by twin volcanoes. The island is well known for its archaeological sites and wildlife.

Libraries & Museums

The National Museum of Nicaragua features prehistoric bones and pre-Columbian statues and ceramics, traditional arts, as well as exhibits highlighting the country's more modern accomplishments in the arts. The Acahualinca Footprints Museum centers on the discovery of 6,000-year-old footprints discovered in the late 19th century. Other archeological findings on display include mammoth footprints and other ancient artifacts.

Cathedral of León

The General National Archive houses the country's historical documents. Much of the collection was destroyed in a fire caused by the 1972 earthquake; the collection stands at over 10 million documents.

Holidays

The country's major holidays pertain to Catholic traditions. Each town and city has a patron saint whose day is marked by feasts, processions, and street parties. Holidays celebrated on a national scale are the pre-Easter Holy Week, Easter, All Soul's Day, the Immaculate Conception of the Virgin Mary (December 7 and 8) and Christmas, particularly Christmas Eve. Religious ceremonies, family gatherings, and festivals mark these events.

Nicaragua's independence from Spain (1821) is celebrated on September 15.

Youth Culture

Nicaraguan youth have a variety of opportunities for recreation and socializing. Similar to other young people around the world, Nicaraguan youth often become members of different social groups based on their popular culture preferences.

For example, a common teen group in Nicaragua is the "fresas," literally translated as "strawberries." The group is identifiable by a preference for expensive clothing and dress and the status indicated by their consumer choices. The fresas correspond roughly to socialites or "preppies" in North American culture. The "hippies," who avoid expensive consumer preferences for homemade clothing, fashion, and bohemian style, are opposite of the fresas in many regards. Similar to "hippie" culture of the US in the 1960s and early 1970s, most of the Nicaraguan youth who identify with this group are of middle-class origins.

Another aspect of Nicaraguan youth culture is known locally as "revelers," a term typically applied to youth united by their fondness for the club scene. The revelers support the dance music culture in the urban areas of Nicaragua, including electronic music, Latin disco and other forms of club music. The high cost of nightlife and fashion common to this group often means that revelers come from the higher social strata of society.

SOCIETY

Transportation

There are two major forms of public transportation in Nicaragua: public buses and private taxi services. The bus system in Nicaragua is extensive and serves remote towns and villages. Major hubs in cities such as Managua and Granada offer both express and local alternatives. Fares are typically affordable, and the bus system is widely used by both tourists and locals alike to travel throughout the country. It is also typical to see repurposed school buses serving the local bus routes in Nicaragua, especially in smaller cities and towns.

Rental cars are common and affordable in Nicaragua, and there are a variety of taxi services available in urban areas. Customers generally negotiate the price of a taxi ride in advance to avoid drivers who attempt to cheat their customers through faulty meters or exorbitant pricing.

Drivers in Nicaragua travel on the right side of the road.

Transportation Infrastructure

In comparison to some of its Central American neighbors, Nicaragua has well-maintained roads, making travel by automobile possible throughout most of the country, without the need for four-wheel drive. The Pan-American Highway, a continuous highway system that crosses and connects North, Central, and South America, passes through Managua and connects to Granada and other cities farther south.

In addition, Nicaragua has one international airport, the August C. Sandino International Airport, located near Managua, as well as smaller airports in other locations where passengers can book travel within the country.

Media & Communications

The relationship between the government and the media in Nicaragua has long been tense, especially during periods of military rule. International monitoring agencies still report that the Nicaraguan government occasionally attempts to interfere with the function of the media or to control the content of news broadcast and print sources.

The most diverse media source in Nicaragua is the radio. The country has more than 200 chartered radio stations, with Radio Corporación and Radio Mundial two of the most popular. Both radio stations are available in most cities and surrounding areas. The major political parties in Nicaragua are often supported by a small number of radio stations that, despite claims of impartiality, tend to display a political bias in their broadcast choices.

Nicaragua has three major Spanish-language newspapers, *La Prensa*, *Baricada*, and *El Nuevo Diario*. These three papers represent the most popular of more than 100 print publications. English-language publications, such as the *Washington Post* and the *New York Times*, are also available in Nicaraguan cities. During Sandinista control of Nicaragua, *La Prensa*, which was started in the 1920s, was seen as controlled entirely by the government. However, in the 1980s and 1990s, the newspaper began publishing articles that set itself apart from the government. *El Nuevo Diario* has been criticized for being controlled by the radical leftist political elements and is not considered by some monitoring agencies to be an independent source of news.

Nicaragua has several public television stations, including Nicavision Canal 12 and Televicentro Canal 2, both providing Spanish-language public programming. In urban areas, cable and satellite television are available, but not common. Internet service came to many Nicaraguan cities in the 1990s, and has become more common in the 21st century, extending from the cities to smaller towns and outlying areas. Managua, Granada, León and several other major cities have recently begun expanding and integrating high-speed Internet coverage.

SOCIAL DEVELOPMENT

Standard of Living

The country ranked 132 on the 2013 United Nations Human Development Index, which compiles quality of life and standard of living indicators.

Water Consumption

As of 2008, the WHO/UNICEF reported that approximately 98 percent of the urban population had access to improved drinking water, and 68 percent of the rural population had the same. As for the population's access to improved sanitation, statistics from the 2012 *World Fact Book* show that just over half the population, or 52.1 percent, had access to improved sanitation. A little over 63 percent (63.2) of the urban population had access to improved sanitation, as compared to 37 percent of the rural population.

Education

As of 2013, Nicaragua has one of the lowest levels of education in Central America, ranking 129th in the United Nations Human Development report. The literacy rate as of 2005 stood at 78 percent. Following the 1979 revolution, education became a top priority for the Sandinista government. A national literacy campaign was launched and money was poured into the educational system as a means to bridge the gaps between urban and rural areas and between rich and poor.

As the country descended into civil war, fewer resources were available for education, and counter-revolutionaries frequently attacked schools. The system still struggles to cope with the growing number of school-age children.

Primary education, comprising six grades, is free and obligatory. Many students, however, do not attend school or do not complete the primary grades. Except for the greater number of schools in rural areas, the gains made under the Sandinistas have evaporated.

Reforms at the university and college level also occurred during the Sandinista period. Emphasis was placed on agriculture, education, and medicine, and lower income students were able to attend. Nicaragua has several technical and private universities in addition to the National University, located in Leon, and the Central American University, located in Managua.

Women's Rights

As in many Latin American countries, Nicaragua has a history of male domination in domestic relationships. The lasting consequence of this cultural tradition is that women are less likely to report and pursue legal remedy in cases of spousal abuse, rape and other related crimes. While recent statistics indicate that women are becoming more comfortable with the idea of taking domestic issues to the police, the majority of domestic crimes still go unreported. In fact, the penal code did not effectively punish cases of domestic violence until the mid-1990s.

Rape carries a social stigma in many Latin American countries, which may be related to the idea of chastity in Catholic society. While the penal code prohibits rape, the penalties are relatively light and currently set between four months and nine years of imprisonment, except in cases where the victim is below the age of 10. Nicaragua has one of the highest rates of reported sexual abuse in Central America, and many believe that most instances are still unreported.

Prostitution is legal in Nicaragua and common in most cities. There are laws prohibiting underage girls, (below 18 years of age) from working as prostitutes, and surveys have found that the laws are generally well-enforced. A significant concern for Nicaraguan prostitutes is the scarcity of facilities and medical management, as many sex workers are unable to obtain access to effective health care.

There are few women's organizations in Nicaragua, but those that do exist have repeatedly criticized the government for doing little to create an environment of equality for female workers. Women often earn less than male counterparts in similar positions and are less frequently considered for advancement. However, Nicaraguan women have entered the workforce in large numbers in recent years, and comprise more than half of the public service sector.

Government support for family planning is weak, and has been since the 1970s. Abortion is illegal in the country. Family planning in Nicaragua has become a major concern for some non-governmental organizations (NGOs) and international human rights monitoring agencies. A 2006 study revealed that more than half of Nicaraguan women between the ages of twenty and twenty-four have at least one child.

Health Care

The Sandinista government also made health care a priority, and was successful in improving the quality and availability of care. Programs for health education, vaccinations, and community participation were enacted and new hospitals and clinics were built. These achievements were set back by the civil war, which limited government funding for health care in favor of defense and caused many injuries among the populace. The counter-revolutionary guerillas, moreover, often made hospitals and clinics their targets.

For approximately 90 percent of the population, the under-funded, under-equipped, and under-staffed national health care system is inadequate. Common illnesses, many of which are preventable, include diarrhea, dysentery, enteritis, tuberculosis, and malaria. The infant mortality rate is at 20.36 per 1000 live births (2014 est.), and children often suffer from malnutrition. Poor sanitation, lack of clean drinking water, and inadequate housing also contribute to the array of health problems. Most doctors and hospitals are found in urban centers, exacerbating these problems in rural areas.

GOVERNMENT

Structure

Nicaragua is a republic. Its 1987 constitution has been amended several times, most recently in 2014. There is universal suffrage for citizens sixteen years of age and older.

The president is chief of state, head of government, and commander-in-chief of the armed forces. The president and vice-president are elected by popular vote to a five-year term; at the end of his or her term, the president must wait at least one term before running for re-election. Presidential duties include the nomination of judges and the appointment of cabinet ministers.

The unicameral legislature, called the National Assembly, is comprised of 92 members, 90 of which are elected to five-year terms, as well as one seat for the former president and another for the runner-up in the most recent election. In addition to putting law into effect, the National Assembly is responsible for approving the presidential nominations and appointments.

Political Parties

Numerous political parties now operate in Nicaragua. In the 2011 election, the Sandinista National Liberation Front (FSLN) or Sandinista party, won a majority of votes, with 60.85 percent for their presidential candidate and 62 seats in the National Assembly. The Sandinistas are a socialist party who held power from 1979 to 1990. The Independent Liberal Party (PLI) earned 31.59 percent of the vote and took 26 seats in the National Assembly. The Constitutionalist Liberal Party (PLC) garnered 6.4 percent of the vote for their presidential candidate and landed two seats in the National Assembly. The Nicaraguan Liberal Alliance (ALN-PC) lost significant power, taking only .76 percent of the national vote and zero seats in the National Assembly. The Alliance for the Republic (APRE) took .36 of the national vote.

Local Government

Nicaragua is divided into 15 departments and two autonomous regions, Atlantic North and Atlantic South. The departments are divided into smaller administrative units, which are presided over by popularly elected mayors and councilors; the two autonomous regions have regional councils.

Judicial System

The Nicaraguan judicial system is comprised of civil and military courts. The Supreme Court is comprised of 16 judges who are responsible for interpreting the constitution and mediating disputes between the executive and legislative branches. They also appoint judges to the lower courts. Judges serve five-year terms.

Taxation

The Nicaraguan government levies income, rental income, capital gains, property, and asset taxes. Additionally, sales, social security, fuel, and value-added taxes (VAT) are also collected. Corporate tax on income comes in at about 30 percent.

Armed Forces

The Nicaraguan Armed Forces are comprised of an army, navy, and air force.

Foreign Policy

For the most part, Nicaragua has adopted a neutral stance in regard to foreign affairs. However, because Nicaragua is highly dependent on European and North American aid, the country has been influenced by the foreign policy of donor nations. For example, Nicaragua supported the U.S. in its "war on terror" initiatives beginning in 2001, even though several other Central American countries objected to this aspect of U.S. foreign policy.

Nicaragua is a member of the United Nations and several related organizations, such as the International Monetary Fund (IMF). Nicaragua is also heavily involved in the Central American Security Commission (CASC). The CASC is an alliance between Nicaragua, Costa Rica, El Salvador, Guatemala and Honduras to develop and initiate policies aimed at controlling the sale and distribution of arms, and to provide and protect national borders.

Nicaragua has several ongoing border disputes, including an unresolved issue with neighboring Costa Rica over ownership of territory along the San Juan River. Additionally, Nicaragua is engaged in similar territorial disputes with Honduras and Colombia over the ownership of ocean territory in the Caribbean Sea. All three issues have been submitted to the International Court of Justice (ICJ) for arbitration. More recently, Nicaragua broke diplomatic relations with Colombia following the Colombian military's incursion into Ecuador in March 2008. Relations were later re-established following a summit meeting one week later.

Human Rights Profile

International human rights law insists that states respect civil and political rights, and also promote an individual's economic, social and cultural rights. The United Nations Universal Declaration on Human Rights (UDHR) is recognized as the standard for international human rights. Its authors sought the counsel of the world's great thinkers, philosophers, and religious leaders, and were careful to create a document that reflects the core values shared by every world culture. To read this document or view the articles relating to cultural human rights, go to http://www.udhr.org/UDHR/default.htm.

Generally, the Nicaraguan government has consistently demonstrated its commitment to abide by the UDHR. Additionally, the penal code and governmental policies of the Nicaraguan government are in keeping with the principles of human rights. However, the policies and actions of the Nicaraguan government are not without criticism.

For example, international monitoring agencies have repeatedly noted cases in which Nicaraguan authorities subjected persons to unlawful torture and physical violence, which is a violation of Article 5 of the UDHR. In 2012, the Nicaragua National Police (NNP) Office of Internal Affairs registered 2,549 complaints of police abuse. Other problems with the penal and security systems include overcrowding of prisons and extended periods of incarceration while accused are awaiting trial.

In addition, while the penal system supports the right to a fair and public trial for all citizens—in keeping with Article 10 of the UDHR—monitoring agencies have repeatedly accused Nicaraguan judicial officials of corruption. There have also been reports that justices often appear to judge cases based on political affiliation.

While the government generally supports freedom of expression and the media, as stated in Articles 18 and 19 of the UDHR, reports of political and police interference with the media

have been commonplace. Many cases appear to originate from a failure to control police officers, who are accused of mistreating or preventing members of the press from effectively reporting on certain issues.

Furthermore, Nicaragua prohibits forced labor and bondage, as stated in Article 4, but monitoring agencies have occasionally lodged accusations of forced child labor. Though not common, instances in which parents forced children to panhandle or sold children to panhandling groups have been reported by human rights groups. While the government has been committed to ensuring child welfare, rampant poverty and a lack of funding for family and childrearing support have made it difficult to effectively guard children's rights.

ECONOMY

Overview of the Economy

Until the Sandinistas came to power in 1979, Nicaragua's economy was dominated by a small upper class that owned most of the land, received funding from the United States, and used the country's resources to increase its own personal wealth while keeping the lower classes in poverty. The Sandinistas attempted to redress these inequalities, with mixed success.

By the end of the civil war, the economy was in shambles and the infrastructure was damaged. The economic situation deteriorated further when the country was struck by Hurricane Mitch in 1998. However, following this natural disaster, many of Nicaragua's foreign debts were canceled.

Today, Nicaragua's economy is overwhelmingly based on agricultural production. One of the major sectors of Managua's economy involves the processing of crops such as coffee, cotton, tobacco, and sugarcane that are grown elsewhere in the country for export distribution. Textiles and clothing are also major exports. In all, approximately 60 percent of the country's production is carried out in Managua.

The country's per capita gross domestic product (GDP) is an estimated $4,500 USD (2013 est.).

Industry

Industry accounts for 25.5 percent of the GDP and employs 18 percent of the labor force. Nicaragua produces refined sugar, processed food, beverages, textiles, and chemicals. Products such as clothing and jewelry are assembled in local plants.

Labor

Approximately 42.5 percent of the Nicaragua's population lives below the poverty line, and unemployment stands around 7.2 percent (in 2013). Underemployment is a massive problem as well.

Managua's labor force has been estimated at around three million as of 2013. Many workers hold informal jobs that are unaccounted for in the city's official economic statistics. The labor force is characterized by several trends, including a low skill base, high underemployment and unemployment, and a reputation for competitiveness and high production.

Several international corporations, attracted by the large labor force and relatively low costs of operations, maintain factories in Managua. Accusations that some of these corporations operate sweatshops, in which employees are overworked and underpaid, have had little effect on often poor working conditions and few if any labor rights. Many of these corporations operate within the state-owned Las Mercedes Industrial Free-Trade Zone, where numerous products are assembled. The value of annual exports from this free-trade zone continue to grow, with $600 million (USD) worth of products generated in 2004.

Energy/Power/Natural Resources

Land is Nicaragua's most important natural resource. The region's many volcanoes have deposited ash into the soil, creating excellent conditions for agriculture. The country also has large tracts of forest, though these are quickly disappearing as the trees are taken for lumber and the land is cultivated for crops. Forest covers more than 40 percent of the land.

Approximately half of Nicaragua's energy needs are met by hydroelectric and geothermal plants that tap the country's rivers and volcanoes.

Fishing

The Caribbean Sea has traditionally provided fertile fishing grounds, contributing to both domestic and foreign consumption. Fish and spiny lobster are valuable catches. Pollution of some of the country's lakes, however, threatens fish habitats.

Forestry

Deforestation is a pressing environmental problem in Nicaragua. In addition to the loss of trees and animal habitats, it has led to the erosion of topsoil.

Mining/Metals

Nicaragua has significant mineral deposits, but only gold, silver, and salt are mined. Those that have not been exploited include copper, lead, phosphate, iron, tungsten, molybdenum, and antimony.

Agriculture

Agriculture accounts for 17 percent of the GDP and employs 29 percent of the population. Approximately 16 percent of the land is under cultivation.

Coffee has long been the country's major cash crop but is susceptible to international price fluctuations. It grows in the upper elevations of the central highlands. Other crops include sugar cane, a wide range of tropical fruits, corn, beans, rice, and peanuts.

Animal Husbandry

Cattle are the most common livestock, and are raised in the lower central highlands.

Tourism

Since the end of the war, the tourist industry in Nicaragua has grown steadily, except for an extended slump following the destruction wrought by Hurricane Mitch in 1998. Between 2007 and 2011 tourism in Nicaragua generated $612 million (USD). The country's infrastructure is basic but developing, and tourism is the second largest industry.

Tourists are drawn to Nicaragua for its cultural and political history, as well as its scenic beauty and animal life. Historic Granada and León both offer colonial architecture, including several important cathedrals. The Volcán Masaya National Park, numerous nature reserves, the extensive coastlines, and the islands in Lake Nicaragua and off the Caribbean coast are among the country's natural attractions.

Micah Issitt, Michael Aliprandi

<u>DO YOU KNOW?</u>

- Christopher Columbus sighted the Caribbean coastline of Nicaragua in 1502.
- The only freshwater sharks in the world are found in Lake Nicaragua.
- Evidence of human life around Lake Managua, within the modern city of Managua, goes back at least 6,000 years in the form of volcanically preserved footprints. These can be viewed at the Las Huellas de Acahualinca Museum.

Bibliography

Baracco, Luciano. *Nicaragua: The Imagining of a Nation from Nineteenth-century Liberals to Twentieth-century Sandinistas.* New York, NY: Algora Publishing, 2005.

Kinzer, Stephen and Merilee S. Grindle. *Blood of Brothers: Life and War in Nicaragua.* Cambridge, MA: David Rockefeller Center for Latin American Studies, 2007.

Penland, Paige, Gary Chandler and Liza Prado. *Nicaragua & El Salvador.* Oakland, CA: Lonely Planet Press, 2006.

Plunkett, Hazel. *Nicaragua in Focus: A Guide to the People, Politics and Culture.* Northampton, MA: Interlink Publishing Group, 2001.

Rogers, Tim. *Christopher Howard's Living and Investing in the New Nicaragua.* Berkeley, CA: Costa Rica Books, 2005.

Sabia, Debra. *Contradiction and Conflict: The Popular Church in Nicaragua.* Tuscaloosa, AL: University of Alabama Press, 2012.

Staten, Clifford L. *The History of Nicaragua.* Santa Barbara, CA: Greenwood Press, 2010.

Walker, Thomas W. *Nicaragua: Living in the Shadow of the Eagle,* 2d ed. Boulder, CO: Westview Press, 2011.

White, Stephen. *Culture and Customs of Nicaragua.* Westfield, CN: Greenwood Press, 2008.

Wood, Randy and Joshua Berman. *Moon Handbooks Nicaragua.* Berkeley, CA: Avalon Travel Publishing, 2005.

Works Cited

Baracco, Luciano. "Nicaragua: The Imagining of a Nation from Nineteenth-century Liberals to Twentieth-century Sandinistas." New York, NY: Algora Publishing, 2005.

Berman, Joshua and Randall Wood. "Moon Living Abroad in Nicaragua." Berkeley, CA: Avalon Publishing, 2006.

Kinzer, Stephen and Merilee S. Grindle. "Blood of Brothers: Life and War in Nicaragua." Cambridge, MA: David Rockefeller Center for Latin American Studies, 2007.

Penland, Paige, Gary Chandler, and Liza Prado. "Nicaragua & El Salvador." Oakland, CA: Lonely Planet Press, 2006.

Plunkett, Hazel. "Nicaragua in Focus: A Guide to the People, Politics and Culture." Northhampton, MA: Interlink Publishing Group, 2001.

Rogers, Tim. "Christopher Howard's Living and Investing in the New Nicaragua." Berkeley, CA: Costa Rica Books, 2005.

White, Stephen. "Culture and Customs of Nicaragua." Westfield, CN: Greenwood Press, 2008.

Wood, Carol. "Nicaragua." Montreal, CA: Ulysses Travel Guides, 1999.

Wood, Randy and Joshua Berman. "Moon Handbooks Nicaragua." Berkeley, CA: Avalon Travel Publishing, 2005.

"Instituto Nacional de Informacion de Desarrollo." *INEC Online.* http://www.inec.gob.ni/

"Nicaragua." *CIA World Factbook Online.* https://www.cia.gov/library/publications/the-world-factbook/geos/nu.html

"Nicaragua." *Nations of the World.* Amenia, NY: Grey House Publishing, 2014.

"Nicaragua: Overview" *Lonely Planet Travel Guides.* http://www.lonelyplanet.com/worldguide/nicaragua/

Vargas, Juan Carlos. "Nicaraguans in Costa Rica and the United States: Data from Ethnic Surveys," California Center for Population Research.

"Nicaragua." *UNESCO Online.* http://whc.unesco.org/en/statesparties/ni

"Languages of Nicaragua." *Ethnologue Online.* http://www.ethnologue.com/show_country.asp?name=NI

"Country Profile: Nicaragua." *BBC News Online.* http://news.bbc.co.uk/2/hi/americas/country_profiles/1225218.stm

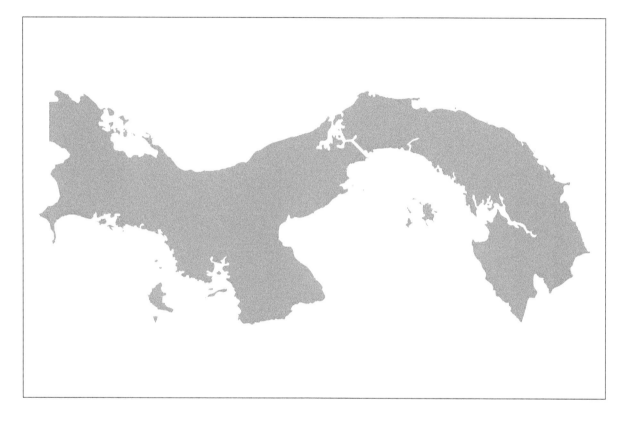

PANAMA

Introduction

Panama is a small country in Central America and is, in fact, an isthmus, or a connective piece of land between Central America and South America. Consequently, it has consistently functioned as an important location for trade during the past 500 years, a role solidified by the construction of the Panama Canal by the United States in 1914. Panama was the initial point of departure for the Spanish conquest of the Inca. In fact, until the 19th century, Panama remained a central departure point for gold and silver being shipped to Spain. It remains an important international shipping hub.

Given Panama's role as a crossroads between the continents of North and South America, its culture is a mixture of North American, Spanish, Native American and African influences. One of Panama's most significant artistic contributions is its music. Panamanian music is a mixture of styles and rhythms, including elements of salsa, Cuban "son" music, cumbia, reggae, soca, and calypso.

GENERAL INFORMATION

Official Language: Spanish
Population: 3,608,431 (2014 est.)
Currency: Balboa; United States dollar
Coins: The balboa is divided into 100 centésimos. Coins have been issued in denominations of one centesimo, and 1/10, 1/4, and 1/2 balboa.
Land Area: 74,340 square kilometers (28,702 square miles)
Water Area: 1,080 square kilometers (416 square miles)

National Motto: "Pro Mundi Beneficio" (Latin, "For the Benefit of the World")
National Anthem: "Himno Istmeño" ("Isthmus Anthem")
Capital: Panama City
Time Zone: GMT -5
Flag Description: The Panamanian flag is divided into four quarters. The top hoist-side quadrant is white with a centered blue star, while the upper-right quadrant is solid red. The bottom hoist-side quadrant is solid blue and the lower right-hand quadrant is white with a centered red star. The stars and four quarters represent the rival political parties (blue for Conservatives and red for Liberals) and white symbolizes peace.

Population

The majority of the population, about 70 percent, is mestizo, a mixture of Spanish and Amerindian ancestry. At the beginning of the 20th century, immigrants from the West Indies arrived in Panama to help construct the canal, and they make up about 14 percent of the population. 10 percent

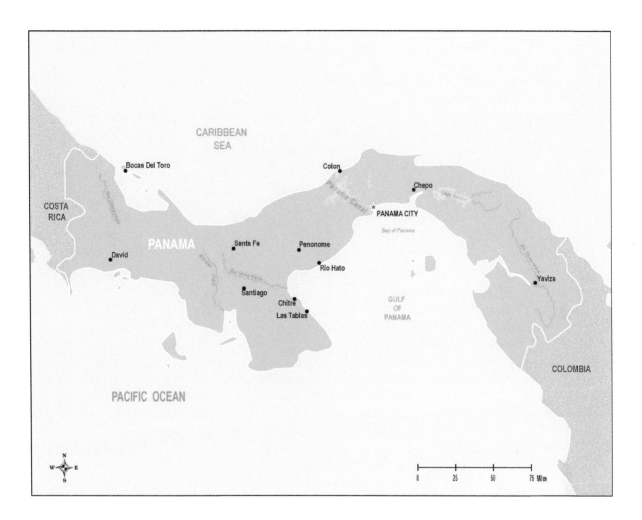

Principal Cities by Population (2012):

- Ciudad de Panamá (441,014)
- San Miguelito (355,313)
- Las Cumbres (suburb of Panama City) (112,992)
- Tocumen (107,625)
- Columbus (82,282)
- David (91,592)
- Arraiján (77,120)
- La Chorrera (61,469)
- Pacora (55,866)
- Colón (51,801)

is white, and about six percent are Amerindian. The people of Panama are called Panamanians.

More than half of the country's population lives in the corridor of industry between Colon and Panama City, in the center of the country. West Indians generally live in Panama City.

U.S. citizens working in Panama live near the Panama Canal Zone, a 16-kilometers (10-mile) wide stretch of land on either side of the canal. Until 1999, the zone was owned and run by the United States, as part of the provision for building and then securing the canal. The zone was officially abolished in 1979, and over the next twenty years, Panama and the US shared responsibility for the canal. Panama took complete control in 1999.

Approximately 40 percent of the population lives in rural isolation and practices subsistence agriculture, often relocating to farm fresher plots of land.

Languages

The country's official language is Spanish, though many Panamanians are bilingual, and English is spoken in the more urban areas near the canal. There are also seven indigenous languages, many of which are spoken on the comarcas, which are similar to Native American reservations in the United States.

Native People & Ethnic Groups

Taken together, native Amerindian groups account for roughly six percent of the total population.

Three major indigenous tribes include the Kuna, the Guaymi (Ngobe-Bugle), and the Choco (Embera and Wounaan) Indians. The most numerous of Panama's indigenous groups are the Guaymi Indians, who live primarily in the western provinces of Chiriqui, Bocas del Toro, and Veraguas. The next most populous indigenous group is the Kuna, who live mainly in the San Blas Islands and along the nearby coast.

Religions

Nearly 85 percent of the population is Roman Catholic. The number of Pentecostal churches has grown in recent decades. There is also a significant Jewish minority. Some Panamanians also practice Santería, a mixture of Catholic and West Indian religions.

Climate

Panama's weather varies greatly between the Caribbean and Pacific coasts. On the Caribbean coast, the annual rainfall ranges from 1.5 to 3.5 meters (60 to 140 inches), while the Pacific coast it ranges from 1 to 2.2 meters (45 to 90 inches). On the Caribbean side, the rainfall lasts nearly all year; on the Pacific coast there is a more definitive dry season, from January to April.

Because of the rainfall variations, the Caribbean side of the country features tropical rainforests, while the Pacific side contains the tropical savannas. The average temperature is constant throughout Panama, usually ranging between 24° and 29° Celsius (75° and 84° Fahrenheit).

ENVIRONMENT & GEOGRAPHY

Topography

Panama borders Costa Rica to the west, Colombia to the east, the Caribbean Sea to the north, and the Pacific Ocean to the south. The country can be roughly divided into four quadrants; a spine of mountain ranges that run the course of the isthmus splits the north and the south, and the Panama Canal divides the country into the east and west. The southwest quadrant has the largest number of settlements, and not surprisingly, the area around the canal has the most commercial activity and the largest population density.

The Tabasara Mountains lie in the western part of the country, and the Cordillera de San Blas is in the east. The highest peak in the country is Baro, an inactive volcano that reaches an elevation of 11,401 feet (3,475 meters) above sea level. Most of the mountains in Panama are comprised of volcanic rock.

There is an area of depressed land in the center of the country; this eventually became the canal site. The lowland areas lie on top of a layer of slate and shale. There are also approximately 1,600 islands off the country's Pacific coast.

In addition to the canal, which is controlled by a system of locks and dams, Panama has many short, shallow rivers, as well as two main lakes, the Gatún and the Alajuela.

Plants & Animals

Panama's wildlife population includes typically South American animals, such as sloths and anteaters, as well as tapirs, jaguars, and other traditionally North American species.

Common trees found in Panama's forests include cedar, mahogany, and cativo. Cacao trees grow in the hotter zones of Panama's mountain ranges, while coffee plants grow in the more temperate middle zones.

CUSTOMS & COURTESIES

Greetings

Panamanians are a formal people and typically greet one another in a reserved manner. Handshakes are common, and proper etiquette requires the use of "Señor" ("Mr."), "Señora" ("Mrs.") or "Señorita" ("Miss") in formal situations or when speaking for the first time. Once familiar, Panamanians will demonstrate respect and status differentiation through the use of honorific titles such as "Don" (for men) or "Doña" (for women) before an individual's first name.

Common polite verbal greeting shared by Panamanians include "Hola" ("Hello"), "Buenos dias" ("Good morning"), "Buenos tardes" ("Good afternoon") and "Buenos noches" ("Good evening"). Religious blessings, such as "Vaya con dios" ("Go with God") or "Adios" ("To God"), are common and said as kindnesses. In private, Panamanians may greet one another by embracing or offering a kiss on both cheeks.

Indigenous Panamanians, such as the Kuna, commonly greet one another with ceremonial dialogue called arkan kae. The dialogue includes formalized discussion of the chief's health, the state of the village, and updates about the lives of friends and family. This form of dialogue is particularly common when friends and family have not seen one another for a long time.

Gestures & Etiquette

In general, Panamanians use gestures familiar to most North Americans. For instance, Panamanians hail cabs with a wave of the hand, and raising the middle finger is considered taboo. One unique gesture among Panamanians involves pointing the lips as a way to direct attention to an object, person, or event. This lip-pointing gesture—with lips together and protruding an equal amount in a certain direction—is commonly used by the general public but is strongly associated with the Kuna Indians. The Kuna use hand gestures to add intensity to their conversations and have traditionally used their lips, rather than their index fingers, to point. The Kuna's lip-pointing is considered to be one of the clearest examples of the practice or gesture in the world and has been the subject of study by anthropologists.

Panamanians typically stand one to two feet apart when engaged in conversation. Eye contact is maintained while talking, but physical contact and touching is kept at a minimum. In particular, men and women rarely touch when talking to one another. Panamanians tend to dress formally and conservatively despite the hot and humid weather. Lightweight suits or camisillas (lightweight tunic shirts) are common dress for men. Panamanian women commonly wear modest skirts and dresses.

Eating/Meals

The majority of Panamanians generally eat three meals a day, though Panamanian farmers and other rural families will eat only two meals to accommodate the long agricultural work-day. Panamanian breakfast is typically hearty and simple, and is eaten at an early hour in rural areas. Breakfast foods and drinks typically include coffee with heated milk, tortillas with eggs, or deep fried breads. Panamanians farmers tend to eat a larger breakfast than Panamanians who live in urban regions.

Lunch is the main meal of the day. Whenever possible, families come together for this mid-day event to eat a multi-course meal. Common lunch foods include soup, fish, beans and rice, fried bread, and fruit. Lunch is traditionally followed by a short siesta (nap). Dinner typically consists of light fare, such as chicken or fish soup, salad and bread, and is generally eaten after dark. Panamanian farmers will eat a larger meal to compensate for having skipped a mid-day meal. Generally, Panamanians eat rice with most every meal, with fruit the most common snack.

Panamanians use their hands and utensils to eat depending on the setting and the food. Blessings and graces before meals are common. Within the Panamanian home, meals are generally served family style. The head of the family will traditionally say "Buen provecho" ("Good appetite") to signal that family and guests should begin to eat and partake in the host's hospitality.

Visiting

Panamanians visit one another for personal, religious and national holidays, often traveling long distances. If family members live close to one another, they will visit each other on a daily basis. Adult children bring their children to visit elderly family with great regularity. Generally, social visitors to a Panamanian home will be greeted with an offer of coffee or small sweet. Panamanians will also serve dinner guests first and offer them the largest portions.

Proper etiquette is important and generally observed when visiting someone's home in Panama. Visitors who are strangers to a house-hold should greet the head of the household with a bow of the head or handshake, accept offers of food and drink, and bring a small gift of wine or flowers. Visitors may also be given a small gift when leaving. It is also important to ask about the well-being of a host's family. Presents are not generally exchanged during business visits.

LIFESTYLE

Family

The typical Panamanian family is nuclear, and consists of two married adults and their offspring. Exceptions to this family unit include the Guaymi (indigenous people of western Panama) men, who tend to have multiple wives, and Panamanians in the lower socioeconomic classes, for whom a formal marriage ceremony is not a real priority. These couples sometimes have a formal ceremony later in life at the prompting of their children or their priest, but children of informal or consensual relationships are not treated any differently from those children whose parents were married in a church or civil ceremony. Kuna family structures and households are built around the elders in a family. In recent years, migration for work has created a new trend in which households are matriarchal.

Panamanians are very loyal to their families. The bond between parents, particularly mothers, and their children is sacred. Panamanians tend to socialize within their extended family network and visit family members frequently. For example, celebrations tend to be family occasions including parents, godparents, grandparents, cousins, aunts, and uncles. In addition, the family network serves as a source for business connections and work opportunities. Panamanian law also guarantees equal inheritance for all heirs regardless of gender or circumstance.

Housing

In Panama, urban housing is a mix of single homes and apartment buildings. Construction materials include brick, concrete, and stone. Rural housing is most often constructed of straw and thatch. The majority of rural Panamanians live in bohios, which are open-sided huts with thatched roofs and separate sections devoted to sleeping and cooking. Since the mid-to-late 20th century, overcrowding has been a common problem. In particular, Panama has a lack of affordable urban housing to accommodate an increasing migrant labor force and urban migration. In 2008, Panama secured a $30 million (USD) loan from the Inter-American Development Bank (IDB) for urban renewal and low-income housing in Panama City.

Food

A distinct fusion of Afro-Caribbean, Spanish and traditional influences, Panamanian cuisine is often exotic, and includes plentiful fresh seafood, tropical fruits, herbs, and comforting flavors. Staple ingredients include fish, shrimp, chicken, plantain, eggs, cheese, beans, citrus, and corn. Corn appears in many dishes as flour, oil, porridge, or whole kernel. Panamanians fry much of their food in corn oil.

Traditional breakfast dishes include hojaldras and tortillas. Hojaldras are deep-fried doughnuts sprinkled with sugar. Panamanian tortillas, which resemble pancakes, are thick deep-fried circles of flat bread most often eaten with eggs, cheese, or beans. Larger meals include sancocho, corvina and tamales. Sancocho is a Panamanian chicken stew made with one whole chicken, onion, cilantro, dried oregano, green pepper, potatoes, and corn on the cob. Corvina is a Panamanian sea bass often used in ceviche (a preparation of raw fish marinated in citrus). Panamanian tamales are ground corn meal and meat wrapped in a banana leaf. While tamales are steamed in other Latin American and Caribbean countries, Panamanian tamales are typically boiled.

Common side dishes include arroz con guandu, carimanola and plátano maduro. Arroz con guandu is a Panamanian rice and beans dish most often served with fish. (Guandu are a tiny green bean usually cooked in coconut water.) Carimañolas, are bread rolls made with yucca flour and stuffed with meat, vegetables, eggs, and spices. Plátano maduro are fried plantain slices

sweetened slightly with sugar. Popular desserts include cocadas and suspiros. Cocadas are cookies made of shredded coconut and sugar, while suspiros are cookies made of eggs, yucca flour, ground corn, cinnamon, and sugar.

Life's Milestones

In Panama, life's milestones correspond to Roman Catholic traditions and sacraments, which are activities that promote spiritual progress and growth. Important milestones include birth and death, baptism, communion, and marriage, all of which are typically observed or celebrated with religious rites.

In the Roman Catholic tradition, birth is celebrated with an infant's baptism, which is a sacrament performed to admit someone into the Catholic Church. The baptismal ritual involves a formal pronouncement by a priest, the verbal support of godparents, the sign of the cross made on the forehead of the baptized person, and the pouring of holy water on the head of the baptized person. Baptism requires the appointment of godparents. Panamanians choose godparents, called padrinos, in an effort to strengthen the infant's future social relationships and opportunities.

Confirmation and first communion are initiation rituals in the Catholic Church that mark the growing importance of faith and church in a young person's life. In Panama, weddings are usually held in a church and include a religious mass, as well as a celebratory party with abundant food and music. Funerals typically consist of a religious mass, a wake and a burial.

CULTURAL HISTORY

Art

Panama's best-known art forms are the product of the country's indigenous artisans. In particular, indigenous tribes such as the Kuna, Wounaan, and Embera create molas, tagua nut carvings, and woven baskets. Molas are a type of multi-color and multi-layer appliqué textile panel created by the Kuna. They are traditionally worn on the front or back of blouses of women from Panama's Kuna tribe and are an expression of artistic and ethnic identity. Prior to contact with and colonization by the Spanish, the Kuna painted geometric designs on their bodies. After colonization, the Spanish, particularly missionaries, provided the Kuna with fabric and encouraged the Kuna to paint and embroider their designs on fabric rather than decorate their bodies.

During the early 20th century, the Panamanian government tried to "Westernize" and modernize the Kuna people by controlling Kuna dress, customs, and language. The Kuna successfully resisted through violent revolt, as well as steadfast commitment to traditional dress and language. Molas are characterized by their reverse appliqué technique and most often depict abstract geometric designs reminiscent of traditional body painting, elements of the natural world, or Kuna legends. Today, the textiles, which are usually made and sold in pairs, are bought by art collectors, tourists, and museums from around the world.

Indigenous tribes in Panama carve the tagua nut into representations of birds and animals from Panama's Darien Rainforest. (The nut is also called vegetable ivory due to its resemblance to the animal ivory of elephants, whales and walruses.) Tagua nuts, which are harvested by artisans without harm to the tagua tree, are approximately the size of a chicken egg. Panamanians have historically used the tagua nut as material from which to carve buttons, jewelry, and dice. Contemporary tagua nut carvings are collected internationally and appreciated as an eco-friendly art form. Basketry is particularly celebrated among the Wounaan and Embera tribes. These artisans use nahuala and chunga plant fibers from the Darien Rainforest to weave their silk-like baskets.

Beginning with colonization, indigenous art was suppressed, and art and architecture followed European and Spanish styles and influences. Art during this early colonial period was also religious in nature. Though a native culture began to emerge in the 17th and 18th centuries, art still imitated European trends and movements. Art also witnessed a distinct African influence from the influx of slaves into the country. Indigenous art would reemerge in the 20th century as Panamanian artists strived to construct and identify with their nationality following independence.

Architecture

Historically, traditional rural homes in Panama reflect the needs of their particular culture. Guaymi Indians (in the west) live in circular structures made of wood and mud with palm leaf roofs and have summer dwellings close to the river. The Guaymi do not live in dense clusters, but are spread out. Kuna dwellings are rectangular in shape, sided with cane, and topped with palm leaves. Houses have a sleeping room and another room for a kitchen and storage. The Kuna live in close proximity to one another. Another indigenous group, the Choco Indians, are closely tied to the water and fishing. Because of their proximity to the water, their structures are often elevated and topped with palm fronds. Simple, open, and square, these dwellings are widely dispersed.

Spanish colonial architecture is evident in Panama City's Panama La Vieja (Old Panama), the remains of the first Spanish settlement on the Pacific. Panama City, in its history, was plagued by both pirate attacks and disease. In 1671, Henry Morgan, a privateer, attacked Panama City and burned it to the ground. The riches he sought, though, evaded him, as they had been taken from the city earlier, and were out of reach in a Spanish ship in the Gulf of Panama. After Morgan's attack, the city was relocated to the west on a rocky peninsula and a blend of styles prevailed, including French, Spanish, early American, and Art Deco. The United Nations Educational, Scientific, and Cultural Organization (UNESCO), named the old city a World Heritage Site because of its historic significance as a planned European-style city, the first on the Pacific.

Drama

Prior to independence from Colombia in 1903, there was no organized theater community in the country. Drama was dependent on international traveling troupes performing for the elite. It wasn't until 1908 that Panama had its own National Theater, which played host for a continual stream of traveling companies. Two other theaters opened in 1914 (Teatro Variedades) and in 1920 (Teatro El Dorado). These provided access to the same plays as the National Theater, but at a later date and a lower cost, opening up the theater to a larger socioeconomic audience than had been seen earlier. Throughout the 20th and 21st centuries, Panamanian theater has suffered from the country's various economic and political swings.

Music

Panamanian musicians have created distinctly Panamanian folk, jazz and calypso styles, and sounds. Panamanian folk music, which is often called tipico or pindin, is used to transfer local histories and stories from one generation to another. Popular folk songs or styles include the mejoranas, torrents, cumbias, puntos, vallenato and pasillos. Panama's folkloric music has a unique vocal sound that emerged after the arrival of the 16th-century Africans and Spaniards brought to Panama as slaves and forced laborers. Common instruments used to play Panamanian folk music include the mejoranera (a five–stringed guitar), the rabel (a three–stringed violin), the conga drum, and accordion. The accordion, in particular, is a very prominent sound in Panamanian folk music.

Throughout the 20th century, Panama, which saw an increase in foreign traffic and influence due to the construction of the Panama Canal, immigration and foreign military bases, developed its international music and art scene. As a result, the country developed two distinct musical traditions in the mid-20th century: jazz in the 1940s and calypso in the 1950s. Today, the annual Panama Jazz Festival, an internationally recognized festival which began in 2004, celebrates the sound of Panamanian jazz. Calypso, with its Afro-Caribbean beats and sentimentality, remains widely popular. Other forms of popular music in Panama include salsa, reggae, and merengue.

Dance

Panamanian dance has European, African, and indigenous influences. One of the most popular traditional Panamanian folk dances is called the tamborito, a classical Spanish dance with native rhythms and steps. The lead dancer and singer in the tamborito is called the cantalante. Back-up dancers, called the estribillo, support the lead dancer and singer by clapping, singing and drumming. The conga dance, with upright drums, provocative lyrics and sensual dance moves, is particularly popular in Panamanian communities of African descent, particularly on the northern coast. Dance styles such as mento and calypso are popular with Panamanians of Jamaican descent.

Panamanians folk dancers are typically attired in traditional dress, particularly the pollera and the montuno. The pollera is a typical dress for Panamanian women. It is a brightly colored dress embroidered with intricate designs and images. The montuno is a traditional Panamanian hat worn by men. Traditional dress for men also includes short pants and embroidered shirts.

Literature

Panama is a country with a high level of literacy and a strong national literary tradition that began in the colonial era, when writers were predominantly Spanish colonists. The majority of Panamanians speak and read Spanish as their primary language, and Panamanian literature is rarely translated into English or other foreign languages. As a result, Panamanian literature rarely reaches international markets. Notable Panamanian writers include María Olimpia de Obaldía (1891–1985), Guillermo Sanchez Borbon (1924-) and Ricardo Miró (1883–1940).

Obaldía was a poet and teacher whose best-known work was *Orquideas* (*Orchids*, 1926). Obaldía wrote poems on subjects such as maternal love and fidelity. It is contended that some of her best poems were written from the perspective of indigenous women. Obaldía was a member of the Panamanian Spanish Academy of Language, an organization which monitors the use of the Spanish language in Panama and recognizes particularly successful work of Panamanian literature. During her lifetime, she was awarded significant Panamanian awards for literature.

Guillermo Sanchez Borbon (who wrote under the pen name Tristan Solarte) was a poet, novelist, and journalist whose writing combined Panamanian legends with the detective genre. Borbon's best-known work was *El Ahogado* (*The Drowned Man*), first published in 1937. Ricardo Miró is often considered Panama's national poet and most significant literary figure. His work was influential in the country's independence movement and is often patriotic in nature. The annual Ricardo Miró National Literary Contest of the Republic of Panama was established posthumously in his honor.

CULTURE

Arts & Entertainment

Given Panama's role as a crossroads between the continents of North and South America, its culture is a mixture of North American, Spanish, Native American and African influences. One of Panama's most significant artistic contributions is its music. Panamanian music is a mixture of styles and rhythms, including elements of salsa, Cuban "son" music, cumbia, reggae, soca, and calypso. Panamanian musician and actor Rubén Blades has found success both at home and abroad. He ran for president of Panama in 1994.

The Panamanian government, as represented by the National Institute for Culture, supports Panamanian artists through grants, education and exhibits. Panamanian art is on exhibit at Panama's many art museums, including the Museo del Hombre Panameño, the Instituto Panameño de Arte, and the Museum of Colonial Religious Art. Ultimately, Panama's traditional clothing and textile arts express Panama's commitment to its folklore and culture and promote Panamanian art and culture worldwide.

Traditional Panamanian festivals transmit Panamanian dances, stories, and traditions from one generation to the next. Carnival, which begins the five days before Ash Wednesday, is cel-

ebrated in the interior of Panama. Congo, which is held in January, is celebrated in Panama's coastal cities by Panamanians of African descent. The May Pole ceremony is celebrated in Bocas del Toro by Panamanians of European descent. These dramatic festivals involve dances, shrines, pilgrimages, bonfires, rodeos, and parades.

Cultural Sites & Landmarks

Panama is home to a wealth of important cultural sites and landmarks that are spread throughout the country. UNESCO recognizes five particular sites in Panama as requiring international recognition and preservation efforts. They include the Archaeological Site of Panamá Viejo and the Historic District of Panamá, Fortifications on the Caribbean Side of Panama and Portobelo-San Lorenzo, Coiba National Park and its Special Zone of Marine Protection, Darien National Park, and La Amistad National Park. In 2015, the Archaeological Site and Historic Centre of Panama City was also submitted for consideration to the World Heritage List.

The Archaeological Site of Panamá Viejo, founded in 1519 by the Spanish, is the oldest European settlement on the Americas' Pacific Coast. It was replaced in the 17th century by a new settlement, officially recognized as the Historic District of Panamá. The "new town" is significant for its early urban planning and mixture of early American, French and Spanish architectural styles. The Fortifications on the Caribbean Side of Panama, particularly the Portobelo-San Lorenzo, provide visitors the opportunity to see and tour preserved 17th-and 18th-century Spanish military architecture. The Spanish built these fortifications as part of their effort to protect their interest in transatlantic trade.

Coiba National Park, along with its Special Zone of Marine Protection, is located on Panama's southwest coast. The Coiba National Park includes 39 islands, which are home to threatened animal species, such as the crested eagle. Scientists are particularly interested in the area's prolific evolution of new species. Darien National Park forms a land bridge between the continents of North and South America, and the park contains a wide range of protected habitats, including mangroves, swamps and tropical forests. Darien National Park is also home to two Indian tribes. The Amistad National Park is a protected area managed by Panama and Costa Rica. The Amistad National Park was created to protect the migration routes animals and four Indian tribes between Panama and Costa Rica. The park has the largest area of virgin rainforest in all of Central America.

Libraries & Museums

Most museums in Panama suffer from underfunding. The Museo Antropológico Reina Torres de Araúz serves as the country's best anthropology museum and boasts over 15,000 pre-Colombian artifacts, the museum is located near the National Metropolitan Park. The Museo del Canal Interoceánico de Panamá features artifacts related to the isthmus and the various efforts to build the Panama canal.

The National Library of Panama was established in 1942 and serves as a repository for publications of national importance.

Holidays

Since the overwhelming majority of Panamanians are Catholic, Christian holidays are an important part of the calendar. Another key holiday is Carnival, a festival celebrated before the Christian season of Lent.

Panama observes two Independence Days: November 3 commemorates independence from Colombia, and November 28 celebrates independence from Spain. November 10 marks the anniversary of the uprising against the Spanish in the Villa de Los Santos.

Youth Culture

Panama, a relatively prosperous and literate country, places a strong emphasis on educating its youth. In general, teenagers are expected to attend school and study regularly. Panamanian youth, from the ages of six to 15, attend free public school, while more affluent families may send their children to private school locally or abroad. The University of Panama, founded in 1935, is a state-sponsored university open to all Panamanian youth.

Panamanian youth typically follow North American and European cultural trends in fashion and music. Popular pastimes for youth include the cinema, attending concerts, and frequenting dance clubs and Internet cafés, while regional festivals are a social attraction in rural areas. Reggaeton, a hip-hop style of music originating in Puerto Rico that fuses rap and dance music, is particularly popular among youth. Many even contend that the reggaeton sound originated with the experimental sounds of El General, a Panamanian singer. Popular sports include baseball, football (soccer) and boxing, with many youth following North American professional sports leagues. Panamanian boys are given more freedom of movement and less direct supervision than Panamanian girls are of the same age.

SOCIETY

Transportation

In Panama, local transportation is mostly undertaken by car, taxi, van, or bus. Taxi prices are negotiated on a per-ride basis and should be determined prior to setting off for the destination. Bus travel is the most affordable transportation option for most Panamanians.

Drivers travel on the right-hand side of the road in Panama.

Transportation Infrastructure

High traffic Panamanian highways include the National Highway (connecting the Costa Rican border to the Colombian border) and the Trans-Isthmian Highway (connecting Colón and Panama City). The growth of Panama's road system is hindered by Panamas rugged terrain. International air travel is centered at the Tocumen International Airport and the Omar Torrijos International Airport.

Panama's most famous claim to transportation is the Panama Canal, which can be crossed by the Bridge of the Americas, which connects eastern and western Panama. It is a 77.2-kilometer

(48-mile) canal constructed in the early 20th century to allow ships to cross between the Pacific and Atlantic Oceans rather than travel around South America. The canal consists of a system of locks, which raise and lower ships depending on sea levels. (Lake Gatun, an artificial lake, is the reservoir of water used to raise and lower ships in the Panama Canal.)

Media & Communications

Panama has a well-developed media and communications system. As of 2007, the country maintained an extensive network of land telephone lines and an estimated 6.9 million subscribers to mobile phones, with 93 percent using a prepaid system. Panama's "teledensity" (the number of telephones per 100 persons) was over 90 percent. In addition, the Internet is growing in the number of users and providers. There are no government restrictions on the Internet, which was accessed by 45 percent of the population in 2012. Panama is also the location of a cable system, which connects the United States, Caribbean, Central America, and South America.

Independent media in Panama is generally free to express a wide variety of opinions and viewpoints. While Panamanian law protects freedom of speech and freedom of the press, the Panamanian government does work to control and influence the flow of information. In particular, the Panamanian government financially supports (through advertising revenue) the media outlets most sympathetic to the government's positions and people. The Inter-American Press Association (IAPA) and Reporters Without Borders (RWB) monitor and report on the Panamanian government's efforts to censor and influence the press. On the 2013 press freedom index compiled by RWB, Panama ranked 111th out of 179 nations.

SOCIAL DEVELOPMENT

Standard of Living

Panama ranks 65th out of 187 nations on the 2014 UN Development Index, a global indicator of development and quality of life.

Water Consumption

According to the CIA *World Factbook*, 94.3 percent of Panamanians have access to clean water (2012 est.) In 2012, 79.7 percent of Panamanians in urban settings had access to improved sanitation, while 52.5 percent of the rural population had the same.

Efforts to protect the Panama Canal Watershed are being supported by USAID/Panama. Critical ecosystems are threatened by agricultural and industrial pollution, as well as population growth—the result of a growing economy.

Education

Primary education in Panama is free and compulsory for children between the ages of six and 15. However, only one-third of the population over the age of 25 has completed primary school. The average literacy rate is approximately 94 percent.

There are two main universities in the country: the University of Panama, a public university, and the University of Santa Maria la Antigua, which is private. Both are located in Panama City. Technical colleges are also available, such as the Universidad Latino Americana de Ciencia y Tecnología.

Women's Rights

In Panama, women and men have the same rights under family and property law and the judicial penal system. In practice, however, Panamanian women have different levels of power, influence, and rights depending on their education, social status, geographic location and ethnicity. Regardless, their role and treatment in Panamanian society is changing as the economy grows through international trade and partnerships, providing Panama's educated women with increased opportunities.

New trade partnerships between Panama and foreign nations are also challenging existing Panamanian social customs and role expectations. International worker's rights organizations and women's rights organizations—particularly the International Gender and Trade Network

(IGTN), International Labor Rights Fund (ILRF), and the American Friends Service Committee (AFSC)—believe that Panama's new trade pacts, which call for a fast-track process of trade negotiations, harm Panamanian women. For example, new international trade pacts may increase the unemployment and worker exploitation issues facing Panamanian women. It may also decrease Panamanian women's access to essential public goods and services as a result of privatization and deregulation. These new partnerships possibly threaten the overall public health of Panamanian women by limiting the production and availability of generic medicines.

Women in Panama continue to experience human rights problems particularly involving domestic violence, sexual harassment, and human trafficking for sexual and commercial exploitation. Many Panamanian women are trafficked to Colombia to work as domestic servants or prostitutes. International human rights organizations cite the Panamanian government for failing to fight the problem of human trafficking through prosecution or victim assistance.

Domestic violence, which is criminalized under Panama's Family Code, is a large problem for Panamanian women and society. Violence against women is commonly accepted in Panamanian society, and convictions for domestic violence or rape are rare. Organizations, such as the Foundation for the Promotion of Woman are working to educate and assist victims of violence.

While Panamanian law prohibits sexual harassment in the work place or educational settings, sexual harassment is a normalized part of Panamanian society. Convictions for sexual harassment are extremely rare in Panama. In addition, women performing the same job as men are routinely paid 30 to 40 percent less than their male counterparts. Additionally, women work more often than men in service jobs, and men dominate the management and executive fields. The Panamanian government, as represented by the Ministry of Social Development and the National Directorate of Women, is working to educate Panamanian businesses about laws covering equal pay for equal work.

Health Care

Panama's health care system consists of hospitals, clinics and rural health centers, funded primarily by the state. The quality of public health in Panama has not kept pace with the growth of industry in recent decades. One of the major challenges continues to be ensuring proper sanitation and drinking water for Panama's rural population.

The average life expectancy is 78.3 (2014 est.) years—75.51 years for men and 81.22 years for women. The average infant mortality rate is 10.7 deaths per 1,000 live births (2014 estimate).

In the 1970s, the government began to establish rural health clinics. The quality of care in rural areas remains uneven, and the life expectancy and infant mortality rates reflect the disparity between urban and rural populations.

GOVERNMENT

Structure

Panama is a constitutional democracy with a popularly elected representative government. The current constitution was adopted in 1972. Universal suffrage for citizens 18 years and older has been in place since 1907.

The president and vice president are limited to a single five-year term. The unicameral legislative assembly is comprised of 71 members, who retain their positions for five years and can be reelected. The president selects the executive cabinet, and appoints judges to the Supreme Court.

Political Parties

Two parties dominate Panamanian politics, the Democratic Revolutionary Party (PRD) and the Democratic Change party (PCD). The PRD is a center-left party that led the One Country for All Alliance (UPPT) in the 2009 election. The UPPT coalition included the PRD, the Liberal Party, and the People's Party. They garnered 37.6 percent of the electorate in the 2009 presidential election and 40.6 percent of the legislative vote, giving them twenty-seven seats in the legislature. The

PCD led the conservative Alliance for Change (APC) coalition, which included the PCD, the Panamenista Party, the Patriotic Union party, and the National Liberal Republican Movement. In the 2009 election, the APC enjoyed 60 percent of the vote in the presidential election and 56 percent in the legislative election, resulting in the election of their candidate, Roberto Martinelli, as president and gaining 42 seats in the National Assembly.

In the 2014 election, conservative presidential candidate Juan Carlos Varela took 39 percent of the vote in a three-way race. However, Varela's coalition garnered just 12 of the 71 seats in Panama's new national assembly, while Martinelli's Democratic Change party kept its advantage with 29 seats. The Democratic Revolution Party took 21 seats.

Local Government

Panama is divided into nine provinces and five comarcas or indigenous zones. Governors appointed by the president oversee the provinces. The comarcas on the other hand, are semi-autonomous areas governed by tribal leaders and home to Panama's native population. The comarcas are: Emberá, Ngöbe-Buglé, Kuna de Madugandi, Kuna de Wargandi, and Kuna Yala. The zones are similar to the Native American reservations of the United States. In recent years, the indigenous zones have been threatened by industrial growth in Panama, with industry encroaching on protected tribal territory.

Judicial System

The Supreme Court is the highest court in Panama's civil law system. The nine judges on the court are appointed for 10–year terms. Courts of review and trial courts serve the civil and criminal system.

Taxation

Panama levies both income and corporate taxes, with the highest income rate at 27 percent. The corporate tax rate is 25 percent of net income. The government also levies value-added taxes (VAT), real estate, and transfer taxes.

Armed Forces

Panama does not have a standing army, and instead relies on the Panamanian Public Forces for domestic security. Panama has the ability to summon a temporary military force if necessary. The public force is comprised of police and security forces, as well as smaller air and maritime divisions.

Foreign Policy

Panama's foreign relations have historically been influenced by its geographical location (it rests between Colombia and Costa Rica on the isthmus joining North and South America) and the Panama Canal. In 1999, the U.S. turned over control and operations of the Panama Canal to Panama, while also closing all military bases on Panamanian soil. Since gaining control of the Panama Canal, the Panamanian government has worked to strengthen Panama's economic and political position through tax reforms, social security reforms, trade agreements, and tourism initiatives. In 2007, Panama began a $5.3 billion (USD) expansion project on the canal, which would double the size of the canal, allowing larger ships to pass through. The project was initially slated for completion in 2014, however, as of January 2014 the expansion was just nearly three-quarters complete and over budget. The expanded canal is now expected to open for business by the summer of 2015.

Panama's foreign policy has also focused on strengthening the nation's international presences and alliances. Panama is a founding member of the UN, and holds membership in the UN Security Council (UNSC), the World Bank, the IDB, the International Monetary Fund (IMF), Central American Integration System (SICA), and the Alliance for Sustainable Development (Conjunta Centroamerica-USA or CONCAUSA). Panama has also been an active participant in international agreements on climate change, desertification, endangered species, hazardous wastes, law of the sea, marine dumping, ozone layer protection, ship pollution, tropical timber, wetlands and whaling.

Panama's national economy is dependent on international trade, and the government has focused on growing trade by developing the Colón Free Trade Zone (CFZ), the largest free trade zone in the Americas. The city of Colón, a seaport near the Panama Canal, is a free trade zone developed in 1948. Imports and Exports registered in the Colon Free Trade Zone surpass five billion (USD) annually, directed towards a market of more than 525 million consumers. This free trade zone is a large contributor to the Panamanian economy, and has been successful in large part because of relaxed business requirements and the use of the U.S. dollar as its legal tender and relaxed business requirements. Panama's largest trade partners include the U.S., Netherlands, China, Sweden, the United Kingdom (UK), Costa Rica, Spain, Japan, and South Korea.

International disputes between Panama and neighboring countries focus on the drug trade. In particular, Panama and Colombia have disputed over Colombia's narcotics operations within Panama's borders. Since the turn of the 21st century, Panama has enacted a number of reforms focused on curbing drug trafficking, money laundering and similar illegal activities.

Human Rights Profile

International human rights law insists that states respect civil and political rights, and also promote an individual's economic, social and cultural rights. The United Nations Universal Declaration on Human Rights (UDHR) is recognized as the standard for international human rights. Its authors sought the counsel of the world's great thinkers, philosophers, and religious leaders, and were careful to create a document that reflects the core values shared by every world culture. To read this document or view the articles relating to cultural human rights, click here: http://www.udhr.org/UDHR/default.htm.

While the Panamanian government, in general, respects the human rights of citizens, areas of human rights concern and abuse do exist. For instance, international human rights organizations continue to monitor Panama's prison conditions, corruption, government control of the media, discrimination against women and ethnic minorities, human trafficking, violence against women, and child labor.

While the articles of the UDHR are generally supported by the Panamanian constitution, they are not always supported by the actions of the government or society. For example, there are numerous contradictions inherent in Panama's legal system. Panamanian law simultaneously prohibits discrimination on the basis of race, gender, disability, language or social status, and forbids immigrants from owning their own businesses as sole proprietorships. The Panamanian legal system offers immigrants who own businesses fewer legal protections than citizens who own businesses. Businesses found guilty of discriminating against people based on skin color or social status face fines of up to $1,000 (USD). However, the Panamanian government investigates and prosecutes very few cases of discrimination.

Article 16 of the UDHR, which states that men and women of any race, nationality or religion have the right to marry and establish a family, is supported by Panamanian law. In practice, racial and ethnic minorities—particularly Chinese, Middle Eastern and Indian immigrants—as well as indigenous people from the Embera-Wounaan, Ngobe-Bugle, Kuna, Bri-Bri and Naso communities tend to marry within their own groups due to language and cultural barriers. Laws prohibiting homosexual behavior and relationships exist, but are not generally enforced.

Article 18 of the UDHR, which supports the right to freedom of thought, conscience, and religion, so long as the practice of religion does not violate public morality, decency, or the public order, is also reflected in Panamanian law. Freedom of religion is protected so long as "Christian morality" and the public order are not challenged. There is no division between church and state, and Catholic theology is taught in public schools.

Article 19 of the UDHR, which guarantees the right to freedom of opinion and expression, is generally supported by Panamanian law, but challenged by the actions of the government. International media watchdog organizations have reported that the Panamanian government engages in efforts to control the free flow of information. The government financially supports (through advertising dollars) the media outlets that offer the best publicity for the government. The government does not censor Internet content or control academic or cultural expression.

Articles 27-29 of the UDHR, which invoke the need for national and international social, moral, economic and cultural support for the rights and freedoms set forth in this declaration, are supported by Panamanian government and law. The Panamanian government has created the human rights ombudsman's office to investigate human rights issues. It cooperates with independent groups in their investigations of human rights cases.

ECONOMY

Overview of the Economy
Though Panama has been a trading center for centuries, it has only become industrialized since World War II. The majority (roughly 78 percent, 2013 est.) of Panama's gross domestic product (GDP) is generated by the service sector, especially banking. Industry accounts for about 18 percent, while agriculture accounts for 3.7 percent (2013 estimate). Prior to the 1990s, U.S. activity in Panama accounted for five percent of GDP.

In 2013, the per capita GDP was estimated at $16,500 (USD).

Industry
Most industrial activity is concentrated in Panama City and the Colón Free Zone. The free zone resembles the "maquiladora" districts of other Central American countries. It is essentially central location for the production, warehousing, and export of chemicals, clothes, and machinery. Panama processes a few goods, namely fish, sugar, bananas, and cocoa products.

Trade focuses on importing machinery and fossil fuels, mostly from the United States. Panama exports bananas, shrimp, clothing, coffee, and sugar. Panama's largest trading partners include the United States, Germany, Japan, and other Central American countries.

Panamanian industry received a boost in 1970 when the Panamanian government granted tax exempt status to international transactions as part of an effort to increase offshore banking. By the 1980s, a great deal of foreign capital was being invested in the country, and Panama became Latin America's biggest financial center, housing branches of banks from all over the World. The national Bank of Panama was formed in 1970, but was reformed in 1998 to discourage money laundering in relation to the drug trade.

Panama also has a significant illegal drug trade based largely on its imports of cocaine and heroin coming from nearby Colombia.

Labor
The labor force in Panama numbers about 1.54 million people. Of that 2013 labor force estimate, 4.5 percent were unemployed. Of those employed, 64.4 percent find work in the service sector, 18 percent in industry, and 17 percent in agriculture.

Energy/Power/Natural Resources
Much of Panama's electricity is generated by hydroelectric dams. The country is also home to coral reefs, mahogany forests and mangrove swamplands. About one-sixth of the land is devoted to national parks and reserves. These include the eastern Darien province, as well as the La Amistad National Park, created in 1988. This park lies next to Costa Rica's Tala Maro Range.

Fishing
Fishing is a major industry in Panama and is its second largest export. The fishing industry focuses on shrimp, anchovy and herring, as well as artisanal fishing.

Forestry
Approximately 40 percent of Panama's area remains forested, though the wooded acreage has been cut in half since World War II.

Mining/Metals

Panama's mineral resources include salt, clay, and limestone, as well as gold and manganese. There are also deposits of copper that have not yet been mined.

Agriculture

Panama's soil is rich in clay, and in many areas crops cannot be grown without fertilization. Roughly seven percent of the land is arable. The most fertile soils in Panama are those found in the river valleys. Many subsistence farmers cultivate a tract of land until it is depleted and then abandon it in search of new land until the fertility returns. Less than one-third of Panamanian farmers actually own the land they work. The most common crops include sugar cane, bananas/plantains, corn, oranges, and rice.

Animal Husbandry

The country also exports beef and hides, and large cattle farms are concentrated in the south-western savannas. Some tropical rainforests have been cleared for cattle ranching.

Tourism

Panama's tourist trade is not as developed as in neighboring Costa Rica, but the country has its share of attractions. The expansion of Tocumen International Airport was completed in January 2012. The new, $100 million (USD) North Concourse has 12 additional gates to allow a 50 percent increase in passenger traffic. Cruise ship visits are being encouraged and account for a growing proportion of arrivals. Visitors to Panama can explore the tropical rainforests and wildlife while also enjoying the shallow Pacific coast waters. The country's small size makes it easy for tourists to visit the beaches as well as the central mountains with little difficulty. However, Panama's border with Colombia makes the eastern part of the country relatively unsafe for foreign travelers.

Simone Flynn, Barrett Hathcock

DO YOU KNOW?

- The United States initially considered Nicaragua for the location of an Atlantic-Pacific canal.

- Panamanian law requires that all workers receive an additional month's salary each year. It is called the "décimo tercer mes," or "thirteenth month."

- Panama has become a destination for birdwatchers. The country boasts over 972 species of birds, more than the US and Canada combined.

- Panama is one of the few countries where you can see the sun rise over the Atlantic Ocean and the sunset on the Pacific Ocean.

Bibliography

Carse, Ashley. *Beyond the Big Ditch: Politics, Ecology, and Infrastructure at the Panama Canal.* Cambridge, MA: MIT Press, 2014.

Casado, Matt A. "Overview of Panama's Tourism In The Aftermath Of The Turnover Of The Canal Zone." *Journal of Travel Research* 40.1 (Aug. 2001): 88.

Conniff, Michael L. *Panama and the United States: The End of an Alliance.* Athens, GA: University of Georgia Press, 2012.

Friar, William. *Panama.* Berkeley, CA: Avalon Travel, 2013.

Holston, Mark. "More Than a Canal: Panama Strives For Identity." *Hispanic* 13.1/2 (Jan. 2000): 104.

Perez, Orlando J. *Political Culture in Panama.* New York: Palgrave Macmillan, 2012.

Rough Guides. *Rough Guide to Panama.* London: Rough Guides, 2014.

Szok, Peter A. *Wolf Tracks: Popular Art and re-Africanization in Twentieth-Century Panama.* Jackson, MS: University Press of Mississippi, 2012.

Watson, Sonja Stephenson. *The Politics of Race in Panama.* Gainesville, FL: University Press of Florida, 2014.

Works Cited

"A Country Study: Panama." Library of Congress (2005). http://lcweb2.loc.gov/frd/cs/patoc.html.

"Background Note: Panama." U.S. Department of State (2008). http://www.state.gov/r/pa/ei/bgn/2030.htm.

"Culture of Panama." Countries and Their Cultures. http://www.everyculture.com/No-Sa/Panama.html.

"Food in Panama." Spanish Abroad (n.d.). http://www.spanishabroad.com/panama/panamacity/pc_food.htm.

Gullberg, Marianne. "Pointing. Where language, culture, and cognition meet." Gesture. 4.2 (2004): 235-248.

"Letter to Congress." International Gender and Trade Network (2007). http://www.citizen.org/documents/USGTNTPA2007final_1.pdf.

"Lip-pointing: A Discussion of Form and Function." Gesture. 1.2 (2001): 185-211.

"Panama." CIA World Fact Book. https://www.cia.gov/library/publications/the-world-factbook/print/pm.html.

"Panama." Nations of the World. Amenia, NY: Grey House Publishing, 2015.

"Panama." UNESCO World Heritage List. http://whc.unesco.org/en/statesparties/pa.

"Panama." Encyclopedia of the Nations (2007). http://www.nationsencyclopedia.com/Americas/Panama.html.

"Panama: Country Reports on Human Rights Practices." US Bureau of Democracy, Human Rights, and Labor (2006). http://www.state.gov/g/drl/rls/hrrpt/2006/78900.htm.

Sherzer, Jouel. "Ceremonial Dialogic Greetings among the Kuna Indians of Panama." Journal of Pragmatics. 31.4 (April 1999):453-470.

St. Louis, Regis and Scott Doggett. Panama. Footscray, Victoria: Lonely Planet, 2004.

Tompkins, Cynthia. Teen Life in Latin America and the Caribbean. Westport, CT: Greenwood Publishing Group, 2004.

"Universal Declaration of Human Rights." United Nations (1948). <http://www.udhr.org/UDHR/default.htm>.

"2005 Population Estimates for Cities in Panama." Mongabay (2005). http://www.mongabay.com/igapo/2005_world_city_populations/Panama.html.

SOUTH AMERICA

Angel statue in Buenos Aires, Argentina cemetery Recoleta/Stock photo © Grafissimo

ARGENTINA

Introduction

Argentina, known formally as República Argentina (Argentine Republic), is the second largest country in South America. Deeply influenced by the Spanish and Italian cultures, it is located in the southern half of the continent, and borders the Atlantic Ocean on its eastern side. Its neighbors are Uruguay, Brazil and Paraguay to the east, Bolivia to the north, and Chile, which runs along its entire western border.

Buenos Aires is the capital of the Argentine Republic, and is the nation's financial and cultural center. It is also one of South America's largest cities. Its graceful European-inspired architecture dominates much of the city, inspiring its cultural reputation as "the Paris of the Pampas."

GENERAL INFORMATION

Official Language: Spanish
Population: 43,024,374 (2014 estimate)
Currency: Argentine Peso
Coins: Argentine currency has five coin denominations; 5, 10, 25 and 50 centavo coins and a 1 peso coin. In 2001, 1 centavo coins were withdrawn from circulation. Commemorative 2 peso coins were minted in 1994 and 2007. A commemorative 5 peso coin was minted in 1994.
Land Area: 2,766,890 square kilometers (1,068,302 square miles)
Water Area: 2,796 square kilometers (1,079 square miles)

National Motto: "En Union y Libertad" (Spanish, "In Union and Liberty")
National Anthem: "Himno Nacional Argentino"
Capital: Buenos Aires
Time Zone: GMT -3
Flag Description: The flag of Argentina features 3 horizontal bands: two light blue bands framing a center band of white. The blue represents the sky, while the white represents the snow of the Andes Mountains. An image of the sun is located in the center of the flag, in the middle of the white horizontal band. This image, depicted as the Inca sun god, represents the country's movement for independence, which began on May 25, 1810.

Population

More than a third of Argentina's population lives in or around the capital, Buenos Aires. About 97 percent of the population of Argentina is descended from European immigrants, mostly from Italy and Spain, but there are large populations who are descended from settlers of German,

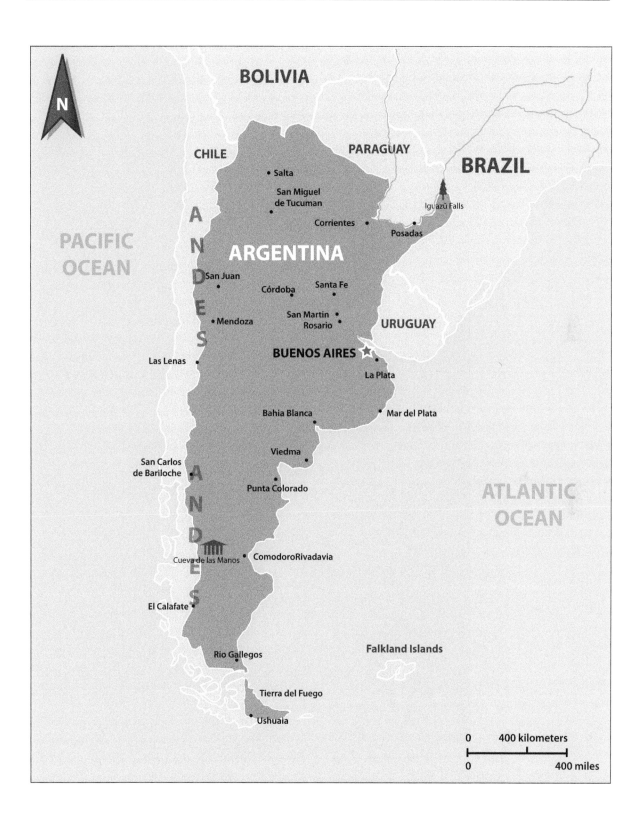

Principal Cities by Population (2014 estimate):

- Buenos Aires (3,050,700) [urban area total: 13,528,000]
- Córdoba (1,556,000)
- Rosario (1,283,000)
- Mendoza (957,000)
- San Miguel de Tucumán (868,000)
- La Plata (759,000)

Welsh, and Middle Eastern descent. Argentina has a small indigenous population of around 600,000. Most of these people are classified as mestizo, an ethnic mix of Indian and European ancestry.

Natives of Buenos Aires colloquially refer to themselves as porteños. The nickname is tied to the immigrant heritage of many of the city's inhabitants. More than 3.5 million immigrants disembarked in "El Puerto" (as Buenos Aires is known throughout South America) between the middle of the 19th century and the First World War.

Nearly half of these immigrants came from Italy and a third from Spain. Today, many porteños have Italian or German surnames and are fluent in various European languages in addition to Spanish.

Argentina ranks as the third most populous country in South America. Almost half of the country's total population lives in the province of Buenos Aires.

Languages

The official language of Argentina is Spanish, but some European and indigenous languages are spoken as well. The most common are English, Italian, German, and French.

Native People & Ethnic Groups

The largest groups of indigenous peoples in Argentina are the Collas, Chiriguanos, Tobas, Selk'namgon and Mapuches. Most live in the northern part of Argentina near the Paraguayan and Bolivia borders, but there are settlements found throughout the country. Quechua, Chiringua, Guarani, and other languages are spoken by indigenous Argentines.

Only in recent years have the conditions for native Argentines been anything above dismal. Since the earliest contact with European settlers, indigenous Argentines have been forced from their native lands. Populations have been decimated by genocidal attacks or otherwise marginalized by the majority white population, a similar circumstance which met the native peoples of North America during the same period between the sixteenth and nineteenth centuries. These conditions have continued, in rare instances, up to the present era.

Argentina maintains a National Plan of Indigenist Policy, which allows some protections for these peoples, but there are still many unaddressed grievances involving the political, environmental, and social conditions of indigenous peoples throughout the country. Argentina's indigenous population is estimated to be approximately 600,000, or about 1.4 percent of the country's total population. The largest indigenous group in Argentina is the Mapuche people.

Religions

Like most of the population of Latin America, the majority of Argentines are Roman Catholics. The Roman Catholic Church in Argentina was elated with the 2013 election of Cardinal Jorge Mario Bergoglio as the 266th pope, taking the name Pope Francis. Among majority non-Catholic religions in Argentina are Judaism and Protestant faiths (including many Jehovah's Witnesses), which when combined, make up four percent of the population.

Climate

Because of Argentina's topographic length from the midpoint of the South American continent to its tip near the South Pole (roughly equivalent in climate to the stretches of North America near the North Pole), its climate varies from subtropical in the north to subantarctic in the south.

The average annual temperatures in various regions range from 11° to 24° Celsius (51° to 75° Fahrenheit) in Buenos Aires, a sea-level city, to 8° to 24° Celsius (46° to 75° Fahrenheit) in Mendoza, which is higher in elevation than the capital. The average annual precipitation is 97 centimeters (38 inches).

ENVIRONMENT & GEOGRAPHY

Topography

There are three distinct topographical regions in Argentina: the Andes region along the western border; the Pampas, or treeless grasslands of central Argentina; and Patagonia, which stretches from central to southern Argentina, south of which lies the extreme tip of Argentina (and South America), Tierra del Fuego.

The Andes mountain range is shared with six other nations in South America, including neighboring Chile. The Argentine Andes contains the highest peak in the entire system, Aconcagua (also the highest in the Western Hemisphere), which rises to 7,130 meters (23,393 feet).

Central Argentina contains the Pampas region, which is home of several of Argentina's agricultural industries, including cattle farming and soybeans. The Patagonian region is a resource-rich, semi-arid plateau that has been a place of lasting fascination for world travelers and adventurers since Europeans first came across it in the early 16th century.

Argentine rivers include the Rio de la Plata, the Paraguay and the Uruguay, and the Rio Parana, which flows southward from Brazil and empties into the Atlantic Ocean.

Plants & Animals

Each of the regions of Argentina has distinct flora and fauna. The Pampas region is grassy, and has the largest variety of indigenous plant life in the country. The treeless regions (the plains and Patagonia, principally) of Argentina have several types of herbs and shrubs. Tropical plants such as palm, rosewood and lignum are found in the northeastern region, while cacti are common in the northwest. Carob and quebracho (white and red varieties) trees are also common in forested areas. Oak, araucaria, and cypress trees are also common.

Common animals found in the north include such large cats as jaguars, ocelots, and puma. In addition, the region includes monkeys, peccaries (known as javelinas in the southwestern United States) and tapirs. The mountainous regions are home to llamas, guanacos, alpaca and vicuñas. Common animals found in the plains region include hawks, armadillos, foxes, martens, and foxes.

Endangered species of Argentina include the short-tailed chinchilla, the Chacoan peccary, the South Andean deer, and the blue whale.

CUSTOMS & COURTESIES

Greetings

Argentine greetings are often elaborate. Women may exchange a kiss on the cheek, and men will typically kiss their close female friends. Men often exchange kisses with each other as well. The full embrace, called the abrazo, involves a hug, a handshake, and several pats on the back, and ends often with another handshake. It is in formal or business situations that only a handshake is used, typically accompanied by a nod to both men and women.

Appropriate salutations and formal titles almost always preface requests or formal conversations. For example, the Spanish pronoun "usted" is used to respectfully address someone in formal situations. Additionally, this pronoun may be used to address the elderly. In conversation, the informal variant is "vos," and the transition from "usted" to "vos" is almost immediate, but usually not before asking permission. Married and unmarried women are addressed as "señora" and "señorita," respectively.

Usually, Argentine names consist of the first name followed by the surname. However, sometimes there are two surnames—the mother's and the father's. In keeping with Spanish tradition, there may not be a surname at all. Many Argentines have two first names, but may use only one. Additionally, women usually attach their married name to their maiden with a "de." Argentines are also very fond of nicknames, which are often a sign of affection. Names are often shortened and diminutives are common.

Conversation in Argentina is generally polite. Out of courtesy, a person will often inquire about another's family and well being. Boasting or talking about money, specifically one's own finances, is typically considered crass, and all requests are prefixed by "permiso" ("excuse me"). Argentines also typically speak softly, and loud conversation is considered crude in private settings. Lastly, Argentines are also known for piropos, which is an often comical and poetic style of street flirtation, and thus not meant to be offensive. Considered a time-honored tradition in other Latin American cultures as well, these flirtations are usually spoken under the breath, or when someone is within close earshot.

Gestures & Etiquette

Argentines are characteristically considered a tactile people, and when talking, they often stand in very close proximity to one another. Additionally, during conversation, Argentines will usually pat the arm or shoulder of the other person, or touch their lapel. First impressions are also very important, so Argentines may commonly dress in a tasteful manner when in public.

Argentines often rely on body language to communicate, thus gestures and facial expressions are important. Pointing is considered rude, and the whole hand with the palm open is used to indicate something. Other common gestures include the cupping of one's hand, and touching the thumb and the fingers to make a point and then moving the hand back and forth, which is a sarcastic way of asking "what is this?" or "what do you want?" A sweeping gesture which begins under the chin and goes all the way over the head means "I don't know or care." The holding of one's thumb and middle finger together as if holding a pinch of salt and then tapping them with the index finger means "hurry up" or "a lot."

Good posture is also appreciated, and it is considered polite to stand upright and refrain from putting one's hands either in pockets or on hips. During conversation, Argentines typically maintain eye contact, and avoiding this is believed to be a sign of untrustworthiness. Smoking is also common, and eating in a public place or on public transportation is considered poor manners.

Eating/Meals

Meal preparation has traditionally been the responsibility of the housewife, but this is slowly changing, especially in urban areas. There are typically three main meals per day, but breakfast is usually very light, consisting of café con leche y medialunas (coffee with steamed milk and croissants), or toast with butter and jam. Lunch and dinner both feature heartier fare. While lunch traditionally consisted of three courses, this has changed in recent years, though dinner remains elaborate.

The popular time for lunch is around one o'clock in the afternoon, and although dinner may be taken at eight o'clock in the evening, it is usually an hour later. (On weekends, however, this may be as late as ten o'clock, and may continue to midnight.) Between meals, snacks, which are typically available at confectionaries and kiosks, are located throughout cities. Perhaps as a result of British influence, teatime is still observed, although less popularly than in the past.

The social and political life of Argentines often revolves around eating, and dining out is a popular activity. Though conversations over food or coffee are common, meals are strictly social events. As such, business is hardly discussed, even during formal business dinners. Argentines traditionally follow certain etiquette when eating in public. For example, hands are kept on the table, rather than in the lap, and the pouring out of wine is a ritual. Pouring with the left hand, for instance, is considered an insult. Family events such as picnics and barbeques are commonplace, and families typically convene on Sundays for an asado, or all-day barbeque.

Visiting

The tradition of hospitality is an honored one in Argentina. Offers to dine in Argentine homes are infrequent if the guest is not close to the family, and the host will usually offer to take the guest out for dinner. In such a case, the host traditionally pays for the meal.

When a guest is invited to an Argentine home, he or she is expected to arrive about thirty minutes late. In fact, arriving on time may be considered rude. However, a guest will be expected to be on time for lunch or an event which starts at a specific time. When entering a home, the guest is not usually expected to take their shoes off. At dinner parties, it is customary for the host to introduce his guests individually to all present.

The bringing of gifts for the hosts is also customary. These may be flowers—bird of paradise flowers are particularly popular gifts—or imported chocolates or whiskey. In general, the gift is expected to be of superior quality and craftsmanship, and in good taste. For example, the bringing of knives is considered to be a bad omen, as they are believed to signify the severance of a friendship.

LIFESTYLE

Family

Argentina traditionally has a very family-oriented culture, and devotion to familial ties is often considered a national trait. For Argentines, family is an all-inclusive term, and even distant relatives are considered family. In smaller, more rural towns, there is a special relationship between family and community, where the former is the cornerstone of the latter. Families tend to be large (usually consisting of extended family members), and marriage is regarded as the expansion of the family, rather than a creation of a separate one. Thus, children traditionally live with their parents after marriage, and may continue to do so well into middle age, or even permanently. Additionally, due to the large number of family members in one household, the idea of personal space or privacy is less important in rural families.

In Buenos Aires and other urban areas, living patterns, partly due to limited physical space, are different. The families tend to be nuclear (consisting of two parents and two children), and having more than two children is becoming less common. Additionally, both parents typically work, and the divorce rate is also increasing (which, as a result, has increased the number of single-parent households). Generally, urban parents have a comparatively limited participation in the daily lives of their children than in more rural families.

However, the communal and familial ties remain strong even in the urban centers, and children often live with their parents into adulthood. This is especially true for the less affluent families. It is also common for children to continue living with their parents while attending university. Sunday remains an important day in Argentine culture, and extended family typically meet almost every week for a barbeque. The generation gap in Argentine society is also considered minimal, and it is common for young and old alike to comfortably share ideas and converse freely.

Housing

In rural areas, a majority of the population resides on estancias, which are farming estates, or ranches in small agricultural towns and settlements. Houses may be built of adobe bricks. Some middle-class areas have traditional Spanish colonial-style streets, which are set out in grids around central squares. In modern cities such as Buenos Aires, the housing patterns vary according to social class. The upper classes live in wealthy European-style neighborhoods. In the suburbs of Buenos Aires, such as San Isidro and San Telmo, the houses are set amid large private grounds that are typically of modern design. Middle-class urban housing is more modest. The houses are of the more conservative design, and also reminiscent of European styles. (These styles were commonly brought over by Spanish, Italian, and French immigrants in the 12th century.)

Lining the outskirts of Buenos Aires are the villas, or shantytowns (informal settlements). Living conditions are typically poor in these neighborhoods, and basic necessities such as electricity and sanitation are often lacking. In fact, few villas have access to clean water. While some of the buildings are made of wood, the majority incorporate recycled materials.

Food

The cuisine of Argentina is heavily influenced by European food, most notably from Italy and Spain. The two cornerstones of Argentine cuisine are beef and pasta, and beef is typically consumed at least once a day, if not twice.

Argentines consider good beef their birthright, owing in part to the country's historical dependence on cattle and livestock ranching. Beef is eaten as *asado* (grilled barbecue), fried or boiled. In fact, almost every part of the cow is eaten in the parrillada, or mixed grill, including the chin chulines (small intestines), tripa gorda (large intestines), molleja (thymus gland or sweetbreads), and the ubre (udder), riñones (kidneys), costillas (ribs) and morcilla (blood sausage). Steaks are sometimes accompanied by chimi churri, a spicy marinade of olive oil, parsley, and garlic, or the salsa criolla, made of diced tomatoes, onions and parsley. While beef has become so popular that the word "meat" is used to refer only to beef, chicken, pork, and lamb are also consumed.

Empanadas, pie-like pastries are considered staple food of Argentine cuisine, and may be filled with beef, ham and cheese, hard-boiled eggs, vegetables or other fillings, and served warm. Due to Argentina's Italian influence, pasta has become a common food, with lasagne being quite popular. Another common dish is the noquis, an Italian dish of potato dumplings traditionally served with a marinara or white sauce. Locro is a popular and cheap stew, and traditionally made of butter beans, haricot beans, sweet corn, butternut squash, and chorizo (sausage).

Argentines thrive on pastries and sweets. Dulce de leche, literally "sweet milk," is made by boiling milk, vanilla, and sugar to obtain a caramel-like consistency. Facturas are small pastries topped with dulce de leche, jam, chocolate, or ricotta cheese, and are eaten as snacks at any time of the day. They include caras sucias, literally "dirty faces," which are encrusted with brown sugar, and media lunas (half moons), which are sweet, doughy croissants. Additionally other popular desserts include masitas, which are small, fancy confections; churros, Spanish-style fingers of deep-fried dough traditionally filled with dulce de leche; alfajores, cookies with a sweet filling that are topped with chocolate; and mil hojas, which are layers of fine pastry held together with dulce de leche and covered in margarine.

Lastly, Argentina has historically been a wine-producing country, and while both red and white wines are popular, the traditional drink is maté, which is tea made from a green Paraguayan herb. In Argentina, the ritual drinking of maté dissolves all socio-economic distinctions. Traditionally, a host fills a hollow gourd two-thirds of the way with maté, adds a little cold water to moisten it, and then lets it sit a while. Hot water is then poured into it, and the maté is then sucked through the bombilla (a metal straw). The gourd is then filled again and passed to the next person in the clockwise direction. Maté is sometimes sweetened with sugar.

Life's Milestones

An estimated 90 percent of Argentines are Roman Catholic. As such, many rites and milestones, such as birth, marriage, and death, adhere to Catholic traditions. However, other traditions originate from the regional Hispanic culture, including the quinceañera, a celebration of a girl's 15th birthday that marks her transition into adulthood. The girl is dressed in a new dress, usually pink, and is seated in front of a gathering of family and friends. The celebration includes with food and music, and involves a ceremony at the church.

Argentine weddings are often elaborate, and follow the European model. They usually consist of three separate ceremonies, including a church ceremony and a civil ceremony. The bride usually wears a traditional white dress, and it is not common to have a best man or bridesmaids as part of the ceremony (the parents of the couple may traditionally fulfill these roles). It is considered traditional for the bride's grandmother to give the bride a ring for her wedding, which she would have received from her own grandmother at her wedding. The rings are handed down from generation to generation, and are believed to bring love and happiness to the couple. It is considered a bad omen to lose the ring, as this signifies the end of the marriage.

Lastly, when a child reaches a school graduation age, parents may plan an elaborate celebration. This is considered to be an important milestone, and the child celebrates it with family and classmates. In addition, there are week-long school trips to mark the end of primary and secondary education.

CULTURAL HISTORY

Art & Architecture

The arts have been slow to develop in Argentina, and have only acquired a distinct Argentine identity in the latter half of the 20th century. In fact, until the colonial period of the 17th century, there was no precedent for the arts in Argentina. The cultures of the pre-Columbian era contributed textiles, metalwork, and ceramics. The latter often featured geometrical and fantastical imagery and designs. In addition, there is also evidence of ancient rock art—including engravings and pictographs—in various caves and locations in modern-day Argentina.

After the arrival of the Spaniards in the 15th century, the development of the fine arts was largely influenced by religion and European styles. In the 18th century, the Jesuits (a Roman Catholic religious order) encouraged music, painting and the plastic arts to some extent. However, the focus remained on producing religious ornaments, carvings, weaving, and other handicrafts. Additionally, many Argentine artists trained in Europe, and imported many aesthetic movements such as impressionism, academic naturalism, and cubism. None left a lasting mark on the local arts scene, and artists focused mainly on landscape and portraiture paintings. Two of the more prominent Argentine painters of this early period were Carlos Morel (1813–1894) and Prilidiano Pueyrredón (1823–1870); both helped establish a distinct artistic heritage in Argentina.

The fine arts received national recognition with the establishment of the Fine Arts Museum in Buenos Aires in 1896 (and later, the National Academy of Fine Arts). These institutions largely focused on architecture rather than painting, and Argentine fine art in general continued to lack originality. Certain art collectives also began to emerge, such as the Nexus group in 1907, though the artists affiliated with the collective considered themselves to be impressionists. However, by the second half of the 20th century, local art, still heavily influenced by Europe, began to acquire certain concrete characteristics that would develop into a distinct Argentine identity.

This began in the 1940s with the Madí Movement (also spelled as the MADI Movement), launched in Buenos Aires, and considered to be Argentina's first international arts movement. These works, which spread across numerous media and countries alike, focused largely on geometric objects, and often used vivid colors. In 1959, artists Eduardo Mac Entyre (1929–2014) and Miguel Angel Vidal (1928–2009) helped create another of Argentina's original art movements. They described the movement as generative art (or arte generativo) because each painting seemed to be creating another, and gave the illusion of volume through geometric designs. On the whole, art began to acquire a distinctly Argentine flavor. Many historians believe that it was the Second World War and the strong presence of Informalism (abstract expressionism) and other styles of abstraction that gave it the impetus it needed.

Modern Argentine art came to be characterized by a unique depiction of space and light, and feelings of solitude, emptiness, and loneliness. This modern Argentine art helped the nation survive the socio-political turmoil it faced under military dictatorship, and has contributed to the national recovery from this reign of terror by searching for the meaning of being Argentine.

Art has now become popular with the Argentines, and the galleries of Buenos Aires stand witness to the quality and breadth of the local artistic production. Artists have become confident of their own artistic identity and no longer rely on mimicking European trends. In fact, two of the largest auction houses in the world now regularly sell Argentine paintings, and the works of artists such as Antonio Berni (1905–1981) and Emilio Pettoruti (1892–1971) have fetched record prices. However, there is still minimal government sponsorship of the arts and a marked absence of fine arts schools.

As the indigenous population was essentially nomadic, there is no significant pre-Columbian architecture in Argentina. There is, however, some notable architecture from the Spanish colonial period, especially in cities such as Salta, Tacumán, Córdoba, Carmen de Patagones, and Quebrada de Humahuaca. Catholics and Jesuits contributed to local architecture by constructing colonial and neo-Gothic cathedrals and basilicas (churches), notably in the Andean northwest and the cities of Córdoba, Luján, and La Plata.

Modern architecture was slow to develop in Argentina because of an absence of government sponsorship. In the late 19th century, the architecture of Argentina, and especially Buenos Aires, followed European trends closely, as local architects were trained in Europe, and because of the strong European influence on the country. Strong reflections of this heritage can be found in the architecture of Buenos Aires, which has much more in common with Rome or Paris than it does with any other South American capital.

Innovation and experimentation were not encouraged, resulting in an eclectic mix of European styles. However, Argentine architecture began to distance itself from its nationalist, colonial rhetoric and moved toward a more modernist approach.

Alberto Sartoris (1901–1998), sent to Argentina on a cultural mission by Italy, became one of the most important figures of modern Argentine architecture. A visit by the famous French architect Le Corbusier (1887–1965) in 1929 was also immensely influential. From the 1930s onward, Argentine architects began to experiment with space and structure, producing buildings such as the Hall of Spectacle and Sounds (1942), the Bank of London (1960–66), and the National Library (1962). Modern Argentine architecture is now a unique blend of European influence and local culture. It is characterized by strong geometrical design, and the structures are influenced by modern technological advancements, producing tall, metal skyscrapers and glass-covered minimalist buildings.

Dance

Traditional and folk dance in Argentina, much like traditional Argentine folk music, varies by region, and includes the gato, the chacarera, the samba, and the escondida. These are sometimes accompanied by a guitar and drum, and mimic the rhythm of a galloping horse. The malambo is a popular folk dance, which focuses on the figure of the gaucho. The dance involves elaborate footwork, which is accompanied by spurs and handkerchiefs. The samba also involves the use of a handkerchief, but is danced by couples and follows a slower pace. Historically, the male partner used to cover his hand with a perfumed handkerchief so as to not touch his delicate female partner with his bare hands.

Argentines lay claim to the tango, a sensual, intricate ballroom dance characterized by a close connection between partners at the upper body, and elegant stepping motions and deft head movements. It originated in Buenos Aires in the 1880s, from the bars and bordellos frequented by European immigrants. To attract more customers, bordello owners hired musicians, whose soulful lyrics inspired dancing.

Tango Day is celebrated annually in Argentina on December 11th.

In its early years, the tango was unpopular with the Argentine elites, who found it vulgar. Over time, it evolved into the elaborate art form, and only after it gained wide popularity in Europe did it become popular in Argentina.

Today, Buenos Aires celebrates an annual Tango Day on December 11.

Theater & Film

Argentine theatre began to develop in the early 20th century. By 1951, there were over 28 legitimate theaters, which produced over a hundred shows. During the dictatorship of Juan Perón (1895–1974), satirical political theater, a popular genre, virtually disappeared, but it revived in the years that followed. Theater then became overtly critical of the government, its leaders and its policies.

Argentina was one of the first Spanish-speaking countries to develop a film industry, showing the first film in 1896. It was producing Spanish-language films as early as the 1920s, and gradually developed a monopoly over Spanish cinema, which it shared with Mexico. As Argentine films progressed, they varied in genre, ranging from westerns and gaucho dramas, to musicals and dramas. In particular, they began to differ from Mexican films in that they lacked the bittersweet quality of Mexican cinema. Argentinian films have won two Oscars, the last in 2009, when *El Secreto De Sus Ojos* (The Secret in their Eyes), won the best foreign language film award.

Handicrafts

There is a long and rich tradition of Argentine handicrafts, varying from region to region. Initially developed to serve a practical use, these mainly indigenous handicrafts included furniture making, textile weaving, leatherwork, and silverwork, among others. Many of these traditions are still alive today.

Indigenous groups, such as the Quichua-Santigueno people of the highlands and the Guarani people, are famous for their woodwork. Commonly produced items include furniture and small decorative items such as trays, vessels, and

shrines for local saints. The woodworking designs are strongly influenced by the local animal and bird life, and often incorporate animal skins. Many different woods are used to make the furniture, from the vinal and huinaj woods, to white quebracho, corob, ancoche, punua and garabato, cardón, palo santo, and other fine woods.

Textile weaving is another common craft. Many traditional weavers continue to produce mats, bed linens, wall hangings depicting local scenes, bags, socks, scarves, hats, sashes, and ponchos, among other items. Although technique and design vary according to region, some common designs are bold geometric, floral, abstract or linear. The influence of indigenous, Moorish, and British cultures is visible. Vibrant colors are often used, with reds being particularly popular. The weavers typically create their own dyes from local plants and trees; llama wool and other distinct and native animal fibers are often used.

The idealized figure of the gaucho, the Argentine rural cowboy, has historically influenced local culture and crafts, especially leather and silverwork. Craftsmen create boots, belts, horse reins, harnesses, horse-head dresses and saddles, which display a high level of skill and finesse. Ornate belt buckles, stirrups, saddle decorations and the gaucho's *facón*, an all-purpose knife with an ornate handle, are traditionally made of silver. Today, examples of local silverwork also include earrings, scarf rings, and maté vessels and straws. (Maté is a caffeinated beverage made from the Yerba maté plant, and is considered the national beverage of Argentina.)

Literature

Argentina boasts a long literary tradition. Initially, Argentine writing mimicked European traditions, as in the works of Domingo Sarmiento (1811–1888). In the 19th century, Argentine writers were preoccupied with socio-political subjects. This changed as they began exploring local topics and searched their own history for inspiration. The gaucho figure made a re-appearance in Argentine literature, which glorified the gaucho way of life, as in the epic poem "Martin

Fierro" by poet José Hernández (1834–1886). A nationalist strain also appeared in 20th century Argentine literature. Nowhere was this more prominent than in the work of Ricardo Rojas (1882–1957), an influential essayist, historian and literary critic.

Modern Argentine literature, however, is largely a reflection of Western culture. The most famous modern writer is Jorge Luis Borges (1899–1986), who perfected the novel and short story, and also wrote poetry and philosophy. Other popular contemporary writers include Eduardo Mallea (1903–1982) and Julio Cortazar (1914–1984), and poets Ricardo Molinari (1898–1986) and Alberto Girri (1919–1991). Philosopher Alejandro Korn (1860–1936) introduced German rationalist philosophy in Argentina.

Lastly, Argentine literary culture has developed hand-in-hand with the tradition of talleres literarios, or, literary workshops. These are held by established writers and provide the opportunity for burgeoning writers to introduce and polish their work. Most famous writers have both attended and held these.

CULTURE

Arts & Entertainment

Argentina has a thriving contemporary arts scene, centered in Buenos Aires. Carnival, held in the week before Lent, is celebrated in many Argentine towns, and combines the country's many artistic, dance and musical traditions. Although not as extravagant as the Brazilian Carnival, the Argentine version is called Fiesta de la Murgas, and is celebrated every weekend of February in Buenos Aires. As part of the festival, costumed street bands hold competitions, and the crowds dance to loud music and drums. A more extravagant version of the Carnival is held in the city of Gualeguaychú during January and February, which features floats and a new theme every year. Additionally, in the city of Salta, there is a large parade with caricatures of politicians, and water fights.

The 21st century has seen a flourishing of the fine arts in Argentina, and there are now numerous art galleries and cultural museums all over the country. The National Museum of Fine Arts has received a face-lift in recent years, and important centers such as the Centro Cultural Recoleta and the Centro Cultural Jorge Luis Borges have been established in Buenos Aires. In addition, the recently created Museo de Arte Latinoamericano de Buenos Aires (MALBA) plays an important role in collecting and studying modern Argentine art. Alternative art centers such as the Ricardo Rojas Center and the Klemm Foundation continue to make significant contributions to local art by sponsoring new artists.

Argentine cinema has taken a new direction with the dawn of the 21st century. In the late 1990s, the Instituto Nacional de Cine y Artes Audiovisuales (National Institute for Film and Audiovisual Arts) began an effort to fund young filmmakers. This marked the beginning in Argentine cinema of a tendency toward a new, gritty, urban, and anti-Hollywood rhetoric, popularly termed as "el nuevo argentine" (new Argentine cinema). A number of film schools were established in Buenos Aires, and the city annually hosts a number of international film festivals. These include the Buenos Aires Film Festival, held in April, the Mar del Plata Film Festival, held in March, and the Salta Film Festival, held in December.

The Teatro Colón in Buenos Aires continues to be the center of Argentine theatre. The city also hosts an annual Festival Internacional de Buenos Aires every September, a two-week celebration of international theater programs. The Teatro is also the center of classical music. One of the foremost opera and concert venues in the world, it has hosted musical legends such as Caruso (1873–1921), Chaliapin (1873–1938) and Arthur Rubinstein (1887–1982). It has produced composers such as Juan José Castro (1895–1968) and Juan Carlos Paz (1901–1972), and conductors such as Arturo Toscanini (1867–1957). Along with other musical organizations such as the Wagnerian Organization and the Argentine Philharmonic Association, it has cultivated a taste for European classical music.

Electronica (dance and club music) has become popular in recent decades, as has

American jazz. In recent years, Argentina has seen a revival of the tango, particularly among younger generations. Tango is a dance that originated in Buenos Aires, as well as Uruguay. It continues to be danced in the numerous milongas, or tango dance halls, in the city, and on the streets of Florida and San Telmo. Every year in October, Argentina hosts the World Tango Festival. Concentrated mainly in the neighborhoods of San Telmo, the festival is a weeklong celebration in which some of the best tango dancers from around the world take part.

Music is an important part of Argentine culture, and all types of music, from the indigenous to the classical, are enjoyed. Traditional music is known as folklorico, and is largely inspired by the classic music of the Andean highlands. Folklorico has many genres, such as the chamamé (which is accordion-based), chacarera (folk dance music popular in rural areas), and carnavalito (dance music, popular in the northwest, and which is believed to have its origins in pre-Hispanic culture). Other types of folk music include the milongas, the estilos, and the cifras, which are traditional gaucho songs. Performances of folk songs and dances, called peñas, remain quite popular.

Other popular forms of music include tango music and cuarteto. In Argentina, tango music traditionally includes a small orchestra featuring a bandoneón (an accordion-like instrument), two violins, piano and the double bass. It also sometimes incorporates the guitar and a reed instrument such as the flute. Cuarteto is another form of dance music developed in Córdoba in the 1940s, and is characterized by a catchy rhythm and a musical pattern known as the tunga-tunga. Because of the offbeat nature of the tunga-tunga and the lyrics of the cuarteto, it is not very popular among the upper classes, and is played frequently only in working-class bars, dance halls, and stadiums.

A recently popularized musical form is the cumbia villera, which is an amalgamation of the cumbia, a Colombian dance, and "gangsta" posturing characterized by punk and reggae overtones. It developed out of the villas, or shantytowns, of Buenos Aires, and is characterized by forceful lyrics dealing with topics such as poverty, marginalization, and the Argentine economic crisis.

Cultural Sites & Landmarks

Argentina is home to a wealth of cultural sites and landmarks, many of which date back to Argentina's pre-Spanish and colonial periods. Many of these sites have been designated as World Heritage Sites by the United Nations Educational, Scientific and Cultural Organization (UNESCO) for their cultural and natural importance. They include natural sites such as Quebrada de Humahuaca, a mountain valley that served as an important cultural route dating back to prehistoric times.

In Rio Pinturas, the Cueva de las Manos is a collection of cave art dating from 13,000 to 9,000 years ago. The name, which means "the cave of hands," is derived from the human hands stenciled on the walls. There are also a number of drawings of animals as well as hunting scenes. The artists are believed to be the hunter-gatherer peoples of Patagonia (a geographical region in southern South America). In Córdoba, there are several buildings dating from the Jesuit era of the 16th and 17th centuries. In addition to five estancias, or farming estates, the block contains religious and secular buildings. These include the university, the church and residence of the Society of Jesus. The architecture reveals a fusion of European values with indigenous culture. In addition, the collective-ruined Jesuit missions of the Guarini people were named a World Heritage Site in 1983.

Buenos Aires is considered the cultural capital of Argentina, and is home to many architectural wonders and museums. One of these is the Teatro Colón, an opera house built in 1908. The building is constructed in the Italian Renaissance style, with some French and Greek influences. The opera house holds about 3,500 people, and the acoustics are considered nearly perfect. The Colón has an adjoining museum, which displays mementos from the theater's long history. The Buenos Aires Obelisk, standing at 67 meters (220 feet), is perhaps the city's most iconic structure. It was constructed to mark the 400th anniversary of the city's founding, as well as the place where the Argentine flag was raised for the first time. According to tradition, local soccer teams come here to celebrate their victories, flying flags and honking horns.

The Plaza de Mayo is the city's main cathedral and the location of its numerous protests. Standing at its center is the Pirámide de Mayo, a small obelisk that marks the first anniversary of the nation's independence from Spain. On its north side stands the Banco de la Nación, the work of the famous architect Alejandro Bustillo (1889–1982). The Casa Rosada, or the "pink house," houses the office of the president, and the building owes its name to the color of its salmon pink walls.

Another famous square is the Plaza San Martín, where the residents of Buenos Aires, in 1807, put up a fierce resistance against British invaders. The square features a monument to the hero of that resistance, General José de San Martín. In addition, plaques honor participants in a more contemporary Argentine conflict: the 1982 war with Britain over the Islas Malvinas, also known as the Falkland Islands.

Other cultural landmarks include the Manzana de las Luces, or the Block of Enlightenment, which contains the oldest colonial church in the city, the 17th century Jesuit Iglesia San Ignatio. During the colonial era, this was the center of learning, and in 1912, a number of secret tunnels were discovered. Other important churches include the baroque Catedral Metropolitana, home to the tomb of the Argentine hero General José de San Martin (1778–1850), and the 18th century Basilica de Santo Domingo.

The Bosques de Palermo, a large wooded park located near many of Buenos Aires' foreign embassies, contains three artificial lakes and numerous gardens. It serves as a venue for many outdoor activities and events during the summer.

Lastly, Argentina is home to a number of national parks and natural sites, including the Iguazú, the Ischigualasto Provincial Park, and Talampaya Natural Park. The Los Glaciares National Park boasts high, towering mountains and glacial lakes, including Lake Argentina, which is 160 kilometers (99 miles) long. Argentina is also home to the Valdes Peninsula, an important nature reserve along the Atlantic coast which includes a diverse number of animal species.

Libraries & Museums

Important museums in Buenos Aires include the Museo Histórico Nacional, whose holdings offer perspectives on Argentine history from the 16th century to the present day, and the Fragata Sarmiento, a ship once used to train Argentine Navy students. The Museo del Arte Latinoamericano de Buenos Aires (MALBA), which opened in 2001, houses the world's finest collection of contemporary Latin American art.

Holidays

Argentine holidays include the Anniversary of General San Martin (August 17), which celebrates one of Argentina's founding fathers; Independence Day (July 9), which commemorates its 1810 independence from Spain; Revolución de Mayo (May 25), which celebrates one of Argentina's earliest attempts at independence; Malvinas Day (April 2), which honors veterans of war; Flag Day (June 20); and Christmas Day (December 25).

Youth Culture

Young Argentines are enamored with consumer culture, often paying keen attention to fashion trends and personal appearance. These youth are popularly known as "marquistas" because they buy only those products which are advertised by fashion magazines and on television. Body painting, piercing, and tattoos are also popular trends among young people. Additionally, while upper-class youth tend to follow international trends in fashion, the youth of middle-and-lower classes are less fashion-conscious, and generally follow simplistic and national trends in fashion and music.

Fútbol (soccer) is particularly popular with young people, and is unofficially Argentina's national sport. The national team has made the World Cup finals five time, the last in 2014 when it lost by one goal. Pato, a polo-like game played on horseback, is the national sport of Argentina, but it is seldom played. Rugby, polo, tennis, and field hockey are also popular sports. Dancing, or clubbing, is another popular activity among youth (clubs are typically open into the early morning, often until six o'clock). Generally, all types of music are popular, and Buenos Aires is often referred to as the electronica or techno capital of Latin America. The city hosts numerous raves and music conferences. Unlike North American or European culture, there is little emphasis on consuming alcohol.

The trend of literary salons, a literary workshop in a café setting, is returning to Buenos Aires. These gatherings provide youth an outlet to introduce their writing or music to their peers in a literary atmosphere. These are often equipped with Internet access. Other popular pastimes include playing video games and attending films and concerts. In addition, an increasing number of young Argentines are devoting their free time to working for non-governmental organizations (NGOs). However, many of Argentina's youth are also leaving to rediscover their European roots. In 2000, it was estimated that over 140,000 young professionals left the country.

SOCIETY

Transportation

Argentina has one of the most extensive transportation systems in South America. The country lays claim to inventing the bus system, and Buenos Aires has an extensive bus network.

The vehicle of note is the collectivo, a unique type of microbus that has its origin in Argentina. Roughly half the size of a typical city bus, the collectivo has a cartoon-like appearance and is commonly painted in vivid color combinations.

Additionally, since city traffic is often chaotic, certain streets are designated for pedestrian use only. Traffic-reducing measures such as speed bumps and closed streets have also been introduced.

Argentines drive on the right-hand side of the road. The U.S. Department of State warns travelers

to Argentina to be mindful of the risks of death and injury due to traffic accidents. Traffic laws are often ignored and speeding is common. It has been estimated that the country has the highest traffic mortality rate in South America.

Transportation Infrastructure

The road and railway system are both extensive, especially in the interior of the country, and larger cities such as Buenos Aires also feature subway lines. In fact, Buenos Aires has the oldest subway system in Latin America, opening its first line in 1913. Freight is usually transported by road, although some is also transported by rail or shipped between the country's coastal ports and along the Rio de la Plata and its tributaries. Water transportation includes high-speed catamaran and ferry service.

Buenos Aires is an important air terminal in South America, and three airports lie just outside the city limits. The Jorge Newbery Airport is the city airport, and serves domestic and regional airlines. According the U.S. Department of State, some domestic airline services can at times be unreliable.

Media & Communications

Argentine newspapers publish essays, short stories, literary criticism and poetry, with circulation rates remaining high in the early 21st century. The most notable dailies are *Clarin, La Nación,* and *La Prensa,* as well as the English-language daily *Buenos Aires Herald* and the Socialist daily *La Vanguardia.* Buenos Aires has also become an important publication center for Spanish books and periodicals.

The Argentine press has never been entirely free of government influence. During the years of the Perón dictatorship and military governance, freedom of expression was severely curbed. This censorship was imposed on all art forms, but the media suffered most as its journalists were threatened and attacked. However, an unprecedented free press accompanied the return of democracy in 1983. Popular media have since played an increasingly prominent role in politics, reporting on government incompetence and corruption, and televising government processes. However, media consolidation and government influence is still prevalent in radio and television, and some laws remain intact from Argentina's dictatorship. This has resulted in the emergence of independent and alternative media in the past several decades. For example, community television has used the Internet in recent years to broadcast a more working-class view.

There has been a steady increase in cellular telephone and Internet usage in recent years. In 2012, there were over 58 million cellular phone users, up from about 13 million in 2004. There was a similar increase in Internet users, increasing from about 6 million in 2004 to more than 13 million in 2009, with a corresponding development in necessary infrastructure.

SOCIAL DEVELOPMENT

Standard of Living
In 2014, the estimated Human Development Index rank of Argentina was forty-ninth out of 187 countries.

Water Consumption
It is estimated that 97% of Argentines have continuous access to healthy drinking water. However, the World Health Organization has also estimated that some 20 percent of the population lives without a connection to a water supply in their homes. Water dissemination and infrastructure is overseen by the National Agency for Water and Sanitation Works (ENOHASA), which operates under the authority of the Ministry of Public Works.

Education
Education in Argentina is compulsory for children between the ages of five and 14. Public schooling is free, but private education is available to those with the means to pay for it. Students wishing to continue beyond primary school may seek a secondary school education and then stand for a bachillerato (baccalaureate)

examination. Argentina has more than eighty public and private colleges and universities, including the Universidad de Buenos Aires, the country's largest.

Argentina's literacy rate for both men and women is almost 98 percent.

Women's Rights
Women in Argentina have historically enjoyed more equality than their counterparts in Latin America. Perhaps due to its European influence—Argentina is considered the most European of the South American nations—Argentina has a comparatively more modern view of gender equality. However, there remain areas of concern. In marital relations, for example, there have historically been double standards. The woman was expected to remain faithful to her partner while the man had a certain degree of latitude, and it was not uncommon for a man to have a casa chica, or mistress. Traditionally, it was also generally considered desirable for a young man to have considerable sexual experience before marriage, while a girl was expected to be a virgin.

Due to the influence of the Catholic Church, divorce was not legalized until 1987. Couples went to Uruguay or Chile to obtain divorce, and the status of remarriage (and that of any children born outside the first marriage) was doubtful. This caused more suffering for women (the legal guardianship of children was a male privilege until very recently). In modern society, however, these attitudes are gradually disappearing. Arranged marriages are no longer common, and marriage is left almost entirely to the couple.

Even though women did not get the right to vote until 1951, they had been given the right to own property earlier than in many other countries. Women also began to play a small but increasingly important role in politics in the mid-20th century. For example, the Socialist Party gave the women leadership roles, and the Union of Socialist Women (the Unión de Mujeres Socialistas) organized and rallied women long before they could legally vote. In particular,

Eva Perón (1919–1952), the second wife of President Perón—and popularly referred to as "Evita"—was a role model for women, and gave them the incentive to enter politics. She headed the ministries of health and labor, fought for women's suffrage, and founded a feminist political party in the 1940s. Today, women hold one-third of the Argentine congressional seats, and in 2007, Argentines elected Cristina Fernández de Kirchner, the country's second female president.

Women have historically been an important part of the workforce, and their role has been steadily increasing. Today, they account for 40 percent of the total labor force. However, they have never been equivalent to their male counterparts, especially in terms of wages. Until 1926, they were legally equivalent, under the Civil Code to minors or the handicapped, and were granted civil rights only because of socialist and feminist pressures. Historically, women have also been subject to abuse and exploitation by employers, and have been laid off more frequently than their male counterparts.

Health Care

The health care system in Argentina is divided into three subsystems: public, private, and social security (obras sociales). Life expectancy for Argentines is 77 years. Argentina has a relatively low infant mortality rate, and a median age of 29. It is estimated that less than one percent of the population is infected with HIV.

GOVERNMENT

Structure

Argentina achieved independence from Spain in 1816, and today it is a republic, with twenty-three provinces and one federal district (Buenos Aires).

The current constitution was written in 1853 and revised in 1994; there have been several periods in Argentine history when the government has either rescinded or otherwise altered the original constitution, but this practice ended after 1983.

There are three branches of government: executive, legislative and judicial. The president is elected to a four-year term, and may seek re-election once, but must sit out at least one term before seeking a third term of office. The president appoints his own cabinet officers and serves as the commander-in-chief of the military.

The controversial former president, Juan Perón (president, 1946–55 and 1973–74) was one of the most powerful political figures of 20th century Latin American politics. His nationalist policies were very popular among the Argentine working class, and his influence is still felt many years after his death.

Each province elects three senators to the National Congress for six-year terms. The Argentine legislative body is separated into the upper house and the Chamber of Deputies (elected for four-year terms). The president and the senate act in concert to appoint the nine justices who serve as members of the Supreme Court.

Since the start of the 21st century, there have been a series of economic and political crises leading to popular protests and a string of presidential resignations. The most recent crisis erupted in 2015, when a federal prosecutor filed a complaint accusing President Christina Kirchner and others of covering up the involvement of Iranian agents in a 1994 bombing of a Buenos Aires Jewish community center. In exchange for the cover up, it was alleged, Iran would supply oil to Argentina on a preferential basis. After filing the complaint, however, the prosecutor was found dead. Kirchner placed blame for his murder on her own country's Secretariat of Intelligence and dissolved the agency. Others were not so sure, and the matter continues to be investigated.

Political Parties

In recent years, the two major political parties in Argentina are the Partido Justicialista (Justicialist Party) and the Unión Civica Radical (Radical Civic Union).

The Partido Justicialista is a Peronist party, meaning its political philosophy is based on that of former Argentine President Juan Perón.

Peronism favors a strong centralized government and aims to combine nationalist policies with social democracy. Partido Justicialista split into two factions in 2005, one of which was led by Cristina Fernández de Kirchner, who was elected president of Argentina in 2007, and again in 2011.

The Radical Civic Union (UCR) is Argentina's more progressive party and is rooted in concepts of social democracy and social liberalism. In 2006, it was proposed that the party form an alliance with the political party led by Kirchner, but this idea was voted down. Although it placed third in the 2007 presidential elections, the party has since begun to fragment into disparate entities.

Many Argentine political parties will unite during elections under provincial electoral alliances. These alliances include the Propuesta Republican, Frente Progresista Cívico y Social, and Alianza Unión Córdoba.

Local Government

Each province of Argentina operates its own provincial government, the structure of which reflects the federal government structure. Each province has an executive, legislative, and judicial branch. At the municipal level, government systems vary between specific towns and cities.

Judicial System

The constitution of Argentina was established in 1853 and forms the basis of the country's judicial system, along with the Civil Code of Argentina, established in 1871. National issues of law in Argentina are addressed by the Supreme Court. Each province in the country also operates a provincial court. Critics of the Argentine Judicial System state that efforts to prosecute allegations of illegal behavior on the part of the police or military are regularly stymied by the government. Critics of the judicial system also comment on the delays inherent in its day-to-day operation.

Taxation

The government of Argentina collects taxes on personal income, which is a deferred tax, or one that is applied at the conclusion of the earnings year. Corporate taxes exist at a flat rate of 35 percent. In addition, the federal government implements a Wealth Tax of 0.5 percent. Excise taxes exist for many items, including tobacco, alcohol, soft drinks, and gasoline. In addition to federal taxes, provincial governments and municipalities collect taxes from individuals and businesses.

Armed Forces

The Armed Forces of the Argentine Republic, or the Fuerzas Armadas de la República Argentina is overseen by the President and the Minister of Defense. Argentina has an army, navy and air force, in addition to the Argentine National Gendarmerie. The gendarmerie and the Naval Prefecture operate a local level and are overseen by the Interior Ministry.

Foreign Policy

Since the late-20th century, Argentina's foreign policy has been impacted by a series of crises, from military dictatorship and defeat, to chronic debt and hyperinflation. The fluctuation between various policy extremes since 1983 has damaged the country's economic development. Argentina's foreign policy has been governed by a preoccupation with acquiring an international profile that many felt was unrealistic compared to the country's relative power. It is only in recent years that Argentine policy makers have recognized the need to focus instead on boosting economic development.

Regionally, Argentina's relations with Brazil and Chile have been marked by distrust and competition. In particular, Argentina has historically had territorial disputes with Chile, but has been an advocate of regional stability in recent years. Since 1991, it has been a part of the Mercosur trade group, a regional trade agreement (RTA) that includes the majority of South American nations, but its level of commitment has varied. However, Argentina has recognized the necessity of developing its economy and has used Mercosur as a vehicle for introducing itself into the world economy.

Internationally, Argentina has tried to advance its profile since the latter half of the 20th century, particularly by leaving the Non-Aligned Movement (NAM) in the 1990s. This was seen as an attempt to establish closer relations with more industrialized nations. A founding member state of the United Nations (UN), Argentina has been a strong supporter of UN peacekeeping, and has deployed troops to Haiti in 2004, and to East Timor and Kosovo. The country was reluctant to support the U.S.-led coalition into Iraq in 2003. However, Argentina was the only Latin American nation to participate in the Gulf War of 1991–92. Argentina is also considered a significant ally of the North Atlantic Treaty Organization (NATO). It has also been as strong advocate of non-nuclear proliferation, and has limited its use of nuclear technology.

Argentina's relations with the U.S. have also shaped its foreign policy. Argentina has supported the U.S. in the international fight against terrorism and drug trafficking. However, since 2003, Argentina has instead focused on regional ties and stability.

Dependencies

The province of Tierra del Fuego, separated physically from the rest of Argentina by the Strait of Magellan, includes the disputed territories South Georgia and South Sandwich Islands (SGSSI), and the Islas Malvinas, also known as the Falkland Islands. Argentina has maintained a territorial claim over the British-administered islands, a claim which stood as the origin of the Falklands War in 1982. Argentina's claim of sovereignty over these territories is ongoing.

Human Rights Profile

International human rights law insists that states respect civil and political rights, and also promote an individual's economic, social and cultural rights. The United Nations Universal Declaration of Human Rights (UDHR) is recognized as the standard for international human rights. Its authors sought the counsel of the world's great thinkers, philosophers, and religious leaders, and were careful to create a document that reflects the core values shared by every world culture. (To read this document or view the articles relating to cultural human rights, visit: www.udhr.org/UDHR/default.htm.)

In the 20th century, Argentina had an appalling human rights record. The dictatorial and military regimes carried out a reign of terror that resulted in a human rights crisis. Almost all Argentine governments have violated Article 2 of the UDHR, which guarantees the right to political opinion. For example, in 1974, during the government of President Isabel Martínez de Perón (the third wife of Juan Perón), the minister of social welfare, José Lopéz Rega (1916–1989), used a right-wing terrorist group, the Triple A, to eliminate the political left. Moreover, the military junta that ruled from 1976–1983 violated human rights in a manner that was unprecedented.

Under the guise of political repression, the military junta that ruled from 1976 to 1983 systematically violated human rights in a state-sponsored campaign known as the "Dirty War." It divided the country into five sectors, and put each under the command of different corps. Thus, it practiced its brutal regime of suppression as a military operation, leading to numerous abuses such as torture, arbitrary arrest and detention, and forced disappearances. In fact, there were over 300 clandestine detention centers in operation, and it has been estimated that over 30,000 people "disappeared" during this period. Blue-collar and white-collar sectors were targeted, with a special focus on students, professionals, journalists, lawyers, and those associated with disciplines such as psychiatry and political science.

The Jewish population was another target group, and it is estimated that the regime eliminated 10 percent of the Argentine Jewish population. Additionally, the regime altered the constitution, dissolved parliament, suspended political and trade unions and paralyzed legal institutions. Thus, the right to protest, as guaranteed by Article 20, was dissolved and victims did not receive a fair public trial, in violation of Article 10. The Argentine constitution recognized the protection of the rights of its citizens, and its sophisticated legal system recognized legal provisions such as habeas corpus. However, this was not upheld in practice, and these atrocities gave birth to a human rights movement in the 1970s, supported by the international community. This has led to a significant improvement in the human rights record of the country. Military leaders have been put to trial for their role in the reign of terror. However, some human rights concerns, such as poor prison conditions, remain.

ECONOMY

Overview of the Economy
Argentina has seen disappointing economic times since the 1980s and 1990s, including high levels of unemployment and inflation, decline in the value of its currency, and problems within its banking sector. Important economic reforms in the early 21st century, however, have made the economy more robust. For example, the privatization of formerly state-run utility enterprises made Buenos Aires increasingly attractive to foreign investors. In 2006, the country succeeded in paying off its International Monetary Fund (IMF) debt, which provided another boost to its economy. However, it still struggles with a billion-dollar debt to private investors.

It is predicted that Argentina's economy will make a recovery. The strengths of the Argentine economy include a sound foundation for growth and a diverse selection of native resources, including rich agricultural regions and a high literacy rate.

The per capita gross domestic product (GDP) was estimated at $18,600 USD in 2013, comparable to Hungary and Russia.

Industry
The major industries of Argentina include agricultural products (including cattle and wool), motor vehicle production, petroleum and natural gas, and timber. The major employment sectors are services and industry.

Important Argentine exports include edible oils, petroleum products and natural gas, cereals and feed, and automobiles. Its major trade partners are Brazil, the United States, China, Chile, and Germany.

Labor
With a labor force of around 15 million people, the unemployment rate, as of 2012, stands at 7.5 percent. The rate is expected to continue to decrease in the coming years.

Energy/Power/Natural Resources
Petroleum and natural gas deposits, timber, lead, zinc, tin, copper, iron ore, manganese, and uranium are Argentina's chief natural resources. Each year, Argentina extracts enough petroleum to meet the fuel needs of the entire country.

Fishing
Fish account for approximately one percent of Argentine exports. Argentine hake is caught in the largest numbers, but pollock is also caught in Argentina.

Forestry
Issues of environmental concern in Argentina include deforestation and desertification.

Mining/Metals
Argentina exported over $2 billion USD in minerals in 2007. The country's major mineral export is coal. Among the metals that are mined in Argentina are gold, silver, zinc, and copper. Mining is a growth industry in Argentina, with much of the industry operating in the country's northwest region.

Agriculture
Traditionally, agriculture has been a mainstay of the Argentine economy, owing in part to the richness and diversity of what can be grown or raised in the vast Pampas region. Most of the country's agriculture takes place in Pampas, which boast some of the richest soil in the world. Among the most important crops are sunflower seeds, wheat and cereal grains, lemons, grapes, and tobacco. Argentina ranks among the largest producers of grain in the world. The country is also a big

producer of soybeans. Roughly one-third of the country's farmland is devoted to this crop.

More than half of the country's total area is under cultivation. Buenos Aires features immense processing facilities where the country's wheat, wool, and leather products are prepared for export.

Animal Husbandry

Argentina ranks among the largest producers of livestock in the world. Livestock represent one of the most important industries in the Argentine economy, and includes beef cattle, sheep (especially for wool), pigs and horses.

Tourism

Argentina is rich in tourist attractions. Among the most notable destinations are Patagonia, the Andes, and the city of Buenos Aires, which is considered one of the most cosmopolitan cities in South America.

Other popular destinations are Iguazu Falls in the far northeast near the borders with Brazil and Paraguay, the beaches of Mar del Plata, and the city of Cordoba, which contains many unique examples of Argentine architecture. In 2012, 5.5 million tourist visits were recorded for Argentina, slightly off the previous year's record high.

Izza Tahir, Craig Belanger, Beverly Ballaro

DO YOU KNOW?

- The tango, which originated in Argentina and Uruguay, is also a very popular dance in Russia, Italy, Japan, and in Finland, where the Finnish tango was born.

- One of the most charismatic figures to come from Argentina was the second wife of President Juan Perón, Eva Duarte, better known as "Evita," a charismatic woman who helped his political career greatly by appealing to labor and women. Evita died young and was later immortalized in the musical *Evita*, by Tim Rice and Andrew Lloyd Webber.

- Avenida 9 de Julio in Buenos Aires is one of the widest streets in the world.

- The Casa Rosada ("Pink House") was painted pink at the end of the 19th century. According to one explanation, blending red and white (the colors associated, respectively, with the two rival political factions of the day) to produce pink symbolized a political truce. A more utilitarian theory holds that the building was painted with a wash of bull's blood, cheap and abundant in a city equipped with vast cattle processing facilities, and which the sun baked into a deep rosy color.

- An elaborate network of tunnels dating back hundreds of years was discovered under the oldest sections of Buenos Aires in 1912. The Manzana de las Luces tunnel system is rumored to have provided, in recent times, a hideout for truant students (the local slang for skipping school is ratearse, or "to hide underground like a rat"). Some historians have speculated that, in earlier centuries, the tunnels may have played a role in smuggling operations.

Bibliography

Auyero, Javier. *Routine Politics and Violence in Argentina: The Grey Zone of State Power*. New York: Cambridge University Press, 2007.

Fearns, Les and Daisy Fearns. *Argentina*. London: Evans Brothers Ltd., 2005.

Finkielman, Jorge. *The Film Industry in Argentina*. Jefferson (NC): McFarland & Company, Inc., Publishers, 2004.

Foster, David William, Melissa Fitch Lockhart and Darrell B. Lockhart. *Culture and Customs of Argentina*. Westport (CT): Greenwood Press, 1998.

Hamwee, Robert. *Argentina – Culture Smart!: The Essential Guide to Customs & Culture*. London: Kuperard, 2015.

Magrini, Cesar and Silvia Pellegrini. *Argentina in Art*. Buenos Aires: Ediciones Institucionales, 2002.

Nouzeilles, Gabriella, and Graciella Montaldo. *The Argentina Reader: History, Culture, Politics*. Durham, NC: Duke University Press, 2002.

Pastore, Daniela. *Argentina: Architecture*. Rome: Gangemi Editore, 2004.

Paz, Ricardo H. *Arts and Crafts of Argentina: Hidden Treasures from the Andean Highlands.* New York: Rizzoli International Publications, 2001.

Plotkin, Mariano Ben. *A Cultural History of Peron's Argentina*. Trans. Keith Zahniser. Wilmington (Delaware): Scholarly Resources Inc., 2003.

Roniger, Luis and Mario Sznajder. *The Legacy of Human Rights Violations in the Southern Cone: Argentina, Chile and Uruguay*. New York: Oxford University Press, Inc., 1999.

Romero, Luis Alberto. James Brennan, trans. *A History of Argentina in the Twentieth Century: Updated and Revised Edition*. University Park: Penn State University Press, 2013.

Ruggiero, Kristin Hoffman. *And Here the World Ends*. Stanford (CA): Stanford University Press, 1988.

Thomkin, Cynthia and Kristen Sternberg. *Teen Life in Latin America and the Caribbean*. Westport (CT): Greenwood Publishing Group, Inc., 2004.

Wright, Thomas C. *State Terrorism in Latin America*. Lanham (Maryland): Rowman & Littlefield Publishers Inc., 2007.

Works Cited

"Argentina." *CIA World Factbook*. Washington, DC: CIA, 2014. https://www.cia.gov/library/publications/the-world-factbook/

"Argentina." *Nations of the World*. Amenia, NY: Grey House Publishing, 2015.

"Argentina". World Heritage. <http://whc.unesco.org/en/statesparties/ar>

"Argentina-Amnesty International Report, 2008". Amnesty International. <http://www.amnesty.org/en/region/argentina/report-2008>

"Area and Population (Argentina)". Europa World Online. <http://www.europaworldonline.com/pub/entry/ar.ss.2>

"Buenos Aires." Encyclopædia Britannica. 2008. Encyclopædia Britannica Online. <http://www.britannica.com/EBchecked/topic/83533/Buenos-Aires>.

"Carnivals in Argentina". *Welcome Argentina*. < http://www.welcomeargentina.com/carnavales/index_i.html>

"Communications Media (Argentina)". Europa World Online. <http://www.europaworldonline.com/pub/entry/ar.ss.75>

"Festivals in Argentina". *Holidays Hub*. < http://www.holidayshub.com/argentina/festivals.html>

"Fine Art and Sculpture". *Argentina Autentica*. < http://www.argentinaautentica.com/fineart.php>

Frommer's. "When to go to Argentina". *The New York Times*. November 12, 2008. < http://travel.nytimes.com/travel/guides/central-and-south-america/argentina/when-to-go.html>

Henderson, Helene, Ed. Holidays, Festivals, and Celebrations of the World Dictionary. Detroit: Omnigraphics, Inc., 2005.

Mandel, Andrea and Jaime Campos. Passport Argentina. Novato (CA): World Trade Press, 2000.

Morrisson, Terri and Wayne A. Conaway. Kiss, Bow or Shake Hands: Latin America. Avon (MA): Adams Media, 2007.

New America Media. "Community Television in Argentina Defies Media Consolidation." <http://news.newamericamedia.org/news/view_article.html?article_id=90118a55ad7765adf04f74099a55d33a>.

Lonely Planet, Sandra Bao et al. Argentina. Oakland (CA): Lonely Planet Publications, Inc., 2014.

"Transport (Argentina)". Europa World Online. <http://www.europaworldonline.com/pub/entry/ar.ss.63>

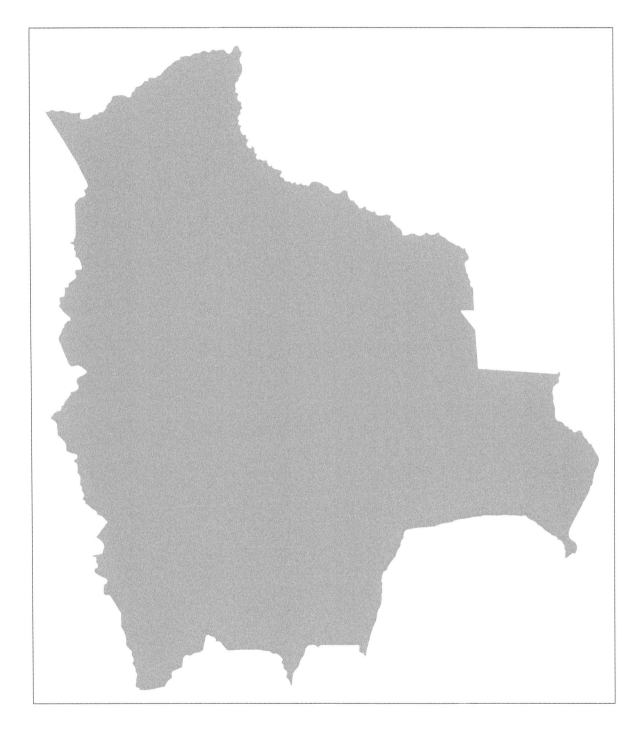

BOLIVIA

Introduction

Bolivia, or as it is officially known, the Plurinational State of Bolivia, is a landlocked country in the middle of South America bordered by Brazil, Paraguay, Argentina, Chile, and Peru. After a turbulent history of coups, serfdom, and poverty, the country now maintains a stable democracy with universal suffrage, increased educational opportunities, and a rising standard of living.

Bolivia's plurinational state was founded on the principle that each "nation" or culture within the region must be recognized and respected, and the country's culture reflects the wide diversity of its people. Bolivia is known for its traditional arts, and is particularly famous for its beautiful weavings. Each region has its own distinct designs and colors, some of them dating back to the Tiahuanaco culture, believed to have flourished from about 600 to 1000 CE, when it became part of the Incan Empire. Traditional Bolivian music is played on the zampona (pan flute), quena (flute), or charango (similar to a ukulele).

GENERAL INFORMATION

Official Language: Spanish, Quechua, Aymara (as well as thirty-four other languages)
Population: 10,631,486 (2014 estimate)
Currency: Bolivian boliviano
Coins: The Bolivian boliviano is subdivided into 100 centavos. Coins are minted in denominations of 10, 20, and 50 centavos, and 1, 2, and 5 bolivianos.

Land Area: 1,083,301 square kilometers (418,264 square miles)
Water Area: 15,280 square kilometers (5,899 square miles)
National Motto: "Morir antes que esclavos vivir" (Spanish, "We'd rather die than live as slaves")
National Anthem: "Himno Nacional" ("National Hymn")
Capital: La Paz (administrative), Sucre (legal and judicial)
Time Zone: GMT -4
Flag Description: The Bolivian flag is characterized by three equal horizontal stripes of red (top), yellow (middle), and green (bottom), with the coat of arms emblazoned in the center of the yellow stripe. The red in the flag represents the blood lost in the country's fight for independence, the yellow stands for the country's mineral wealth, and the green reflects the country's vegetation and fertility. In 2009, Bolivia's president, Evo Morales, declared that the "Wiphala," a square, multi-colored flag traditionally

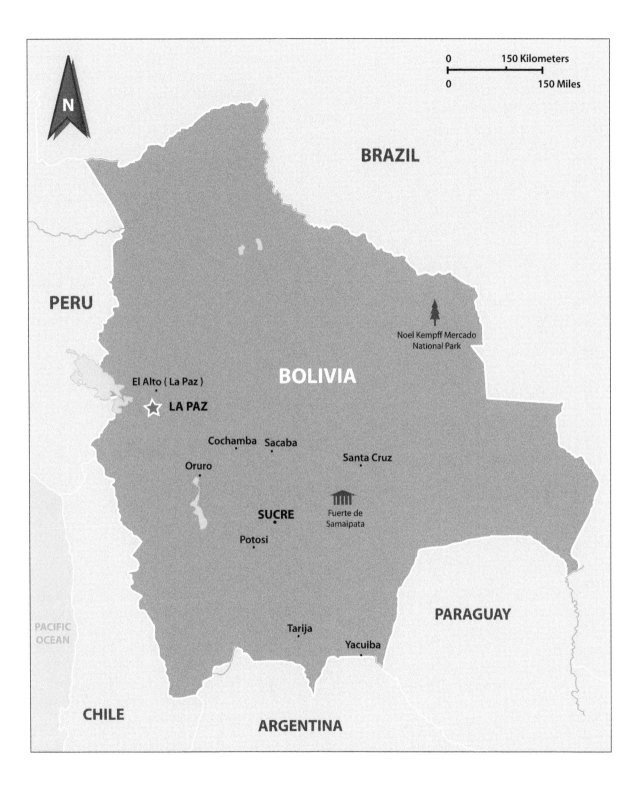

Principal Cities by Population (2012):

- Santa Cruz (1,441,406)
- El Alto (842,378)
- La Paz (757,184)
- Cochabamba (630,587)
- Sucre (237,480)
- Oruro (264,683)
- Tarija (179,528)
- Sacaba (149,570)
- Potosí (174,973)
- Yacuiba (61,844)

representing the indigenous peoples of the central Andes (particularly the Andean, Quechua, and Aymara peoples), be flown alongside the national tricolor. The declaration has been controversial, as the country boasts more than 30 native cultures.

Population
Quechua Indians account for 30 percent of Bolivia's population. The Aymara represent another 25 percent. A further 30 percent of the people are mestizo, of mixed Indian and European ancestry. Finally, 15 percent are of European descent. The minority (those with European names and features) constitute the middle and upper classes.

As of 2011, about 67 percent of the population lived in urban areas, with the heaviest populations in the administrative centers of the country's nine departments. Urbanization of the population is on the rise.

Languages
At least 39 languages are spoken in Bolivia; all of these languages are recognized in the country's new constitution, passed in 2009. Although these languages are all officially recognized, Spanish is, in fact, the language of education, government, and commerce, and the primary language of about 61 percent of the people. Quechua is spoken by 21 percent of Bolivians, Aymara by 15 percent, and the other three percent speak various other languages.

Native People & Ethnic Groups
The two main ethnic groups are the Quechua and the Aymara. The Quechua are descendants of colonizers sent by the Incas hundreds of years before the arrival of Columbus. They live throughout Bolivia, though they originated in the Altiplano region, or the high plateau.

The Aymara, believed to be descendants of the even older Tiahuanaco culture, live primarily in the departments (administrative divisions) of La Paz and Oruro. Both groups are intermingled with other, smaller ethnic groups.

Highland ethnic groups include the Urus, Qaraqaras, and Uamparas, who were part of Inca Empire. They retain their own customs and language, but have adopted some Quechua characteristics.

The Guaranis, who number approximately 75,000, are the largest lowland ethnic group. They live in southeast Bolivia. Other lowland indigenous people include the Chiquitano, Moxenos, Sirionos, Chimanes, Paiconecos, Ayoreos, and Mosetenes. These have united in regional coalitions because each group consists of only a few thousand people.

There are also about 30,000 black descendants of the numerous African slaves imported to work in the mines. This group has had a great influence on traditional dance in Bolivia. The typical heavy percussion in the dance music imitates the clink of chains worn by slave miners.

Religions
While there are some Protestant Bolivians (about five percent of the population—mostly Evangelical Methodists), 95 percent of the population identifies as Roman Catholic. Most Quechua and Aymara are Catholic, but they retain many religious customs from Incan days. The church provides education and owns a large stake in the communications media.

Climate
Although the climate varies widely across Bolivia's topographical zones, it shows little seasonal change. The Andes and Altiplano are dry and cool, with temperatures of 15° to

20° Celsius (59° to 68° Fahrenheit) during the day, dropping to 5° Celsius (41° Fahrenheit) at night. Polar conditions sometimes occur in the Andes. Frost appears on the shores of Lake Titicaca most months.

Annual rainfall in the mountains varies from 152 centimeters (60 inches) on the exposed heights to 64 centimeters (25 inches) in protected valleys. In the Yungas, the annual rainfall is from 70 centimeters (27.5 inches) to 80 centimeters (31.5 inches), and the humidity is high.

The northern lowlands receive plenty of rain from northeast trade winds, and daytime highs average 30° Celsius (86° Fahrenheit) all year round. The central lowlands are wet October through April, dry May through September, and hot always, with an average temperature of 25° Celsius (77° Fahrenheit). The surazos (cold southern winds) sometimes lower the temperatures by several degrees.

The Chaco has hot and dry conditions, with rain and humidity only from January through March.

ENVIRONMENT & GEOGRAPHY

Topography

Bolivia is bounded by Brazil on the north and east, Paraguay on the southeast, Argentina on the south, and Chile and Peru on the west.

Bolivia has several climatic and topographical regions. In the west is the cold and dry Altiplano (mountain plateau), an area 800 by 130 kilometers (about 500 by 80 miles), between the snow-covered coastal Andes and eastern Andes (Cordillera Occidental and Cordillera Oriental).

The Yungas region consists of hills and valleys to the east of the Andes, with plenty of water and semitropical rain forests. The llanos, or plains, are semitropical lowlands of the Amazon Basin, rich with grassland and rain forests, and always hot. The Chiquitos highlands in the southeast separate the Llanos from the Chaco, the dry, semitropical plains that Bolivia shares with Paraguay.

The country's highest point is Nevado Sajama, at 6,542 meters (21,463 feet). Its lowest point is Rio Paraguay, at an elevation of only 90 meters (295 feet).

The Guapore River rises in Brazil, where it is called the Itenez, and flows northwest, forming part of the border between Bolivia and Brazil. The river then empties into the Mamore River, which rises in the Andes and flows through Bolivia into Brazil. The Guapore is known for its clear water.

The Pilcomayo is the main river in the southeast. Rising in Argentina, it flows through the Chaco, forming part of the Argentina-Bolivia-Paraguay border, and eventually empties into the Paraguay River.

The famous Lake Titicaca lies in the northwest corner of the Altiplano, half in Bolivia and half in Peru. It is the world's highest navigable lake, at 3,821 meters (11,463 feet). The lake has an area of 8,300 square kilometers (3,205 square miles). Fishermen on the lake are known for their traditional boats made of totora reeds.

Plants & Animals

Bolivia is one of the dozen most bio-diverse countries in the world. More than 20,000 species of seed-bearing plants can be found there, along with more than 1,200 species of fern, 1,500 species of liverwort, and at least 800 species of fungi. In addition, there are 356 species of mammals, 1,400 species of birds, 600 species of fish, 266 species of reptiles, and 203 species of amphibians. Bolivia ranks fourth in the world in the number of butterfly species.

Chili peppers, locoto peppers, sweet peppers, potatoes, peanuts, beans, manioc, and a variety of palms originated in Bolivia. About 3,000 medicinal plants are used by locals, including albahaca (basil), used to treat cardiovascular problems; una de gato (cat's claw) used among other things to stimulate the immune system against HIV; and Taikiji kawayu (horsetail), with many uses, including treatment of wounds and uterine hemorrhage.

On the Altiplano live llama, alpaca, and vicuña. The cloud forests of the Andes are home to ocelots, collared peccaries, brown capuchin monkeys, nine-banded armadillos, brocket deer, and tapirs. Many of these animals are protected by the Tariquia Flora and Fauna National Reserve. The reserve also provides a safe home for many bird species, including Andean condors, whistling herons, Chilean flamingos, red shovelers, white-rumped hawks, osprey, great egrets, scaly-headed parrots, Andean pygmy owls, giant hummingbirds, spot-billed ground tyrants, toucans, and Bolivian military macaws.

In the northeast live river otters, capybaras, pink river dolphins, black and spectacled caiman, tapirs, gray and red brocket deer, silvery marmosets, pumas, jaguars, maned wolves, giant anteaters, spider and black howler monkeys, harpy eagles, storks, Amazonian umbrella birds, helmeted manakins, hoatzins, and more than 20 species of parrot.

The Amazon basin provides habitat for monkeys, pumas, jaguars, armadillos, and various reptiles, birds, and insects.

Endangered species include the Aceramarca Gracile Mouse Opossum (which is endemic to Bolivia), the short-tailed chinchilla, giant armadillo, giant otter, and pygmy short-tailed opossum. Animals listed as "vulnerable" include the spectacled bear, giant anteater, and Andean cat.

On the Altiplano grows ichu, a coarse grass. The rainforests are home to rubber trees, vanilla, sarsaparilla, saffron, and more than 2,000 species of hardwood trees. In the Noel Kempff Mercado National Park are orchids, bromelias, palms, mahogany, cedar trees, and rubber trees. Cactus grows in the dry altitudes.

CUSTOMS & COURTESIES

Greetings
Bolivians commonly greet one another in Spanish, Quechua, or Aymara. (Quechua and Aymara are native languages spoken most often in the Andean region of Bolivia.) Spanish is predominantly spoken in urban regions, while Quechua and Aymara, sometimes intermingled with Spanish words, are spoken in rural regions.

Spanish is almost always used in business contexts.

Spanish speaking Bolivians typically greet one another with "Hola" ("Hello"), "Buenos días" ("Good morning"), "Buenas tardes" ("Good afternoon"), "Buenas noches" ("Good evening") or "¿Cómo estás?" ("How are you?"). Quechua speaking Bolivians greet one another with "Askini punijuttata ("Welcome") or "Sumaj punchay" ("How are you?"); Aymara speaking Bolivians may greet one another with "Imaynalla" ("How are you?"). Spanish language farewells include the common expressions "Hasta luego" ("Until later"), "Chau" or "Adios." Quechua and Aymaran language farewells include "Q'ayaqama" ("See you tomorrow").

Proper etiquette requires the use of "Señor" (Mr.), "Señora" (Mrs.) or "Señorita" (Miss) in formal situations or when speaking for the first time. Once familiar, Bolivians will demonstrate respect and status differentiation through the use of the honorific titles of "Don" (for men) or "Doña" (for women) before a person's first name. In rural regions, friends often refer to one another as "campesinos" (peasant or farm worker friends).

Bolivians in urban areas will greet each other with a handshake, abrazo (embrace), or kiss on the cheek. Bolivians in rural regions shake or pat hands rather than kiss or embrace, and tend to use large hand or arm gestures very sparingly. Physical space between people is typically not protected or valued, and Bolivians tend to stand physically close to one another when talking. In addition, stepping away or turning one's back to another during a conversation is considered rude, and sustained eye contact and upright posture is the norm.

Gestures & Etiquette
Physical touch and gesturing, in general, is common and accepted in Bolivia. In particular, Bolivians pat backs, touch arms, and lean into people when engaged in conversation. Bolivians tend to speak quietly and use gestures to convey intensity of meaning. One common gesture, used to signal "no," is conveyed by rocking an open

hand back and forth, commonly known to mean "so-so" in the United States. Bolivians also find staring and pointing to be rude, and typically point by nodding their head toward the object of attention, rather than pointing with a finger or hand.

In general, Bolivians of Spanish heritage tend to be more informal and physically expressive than Bolivians of indigenous heritage. Bolivians communicate their status, language, and ethnic heritage through their particular form of dress. For instance, in the Bolivian countryside, proper dress etiquette for the Quechua and Aymara people involves traditional clothing. Traditional indigenous dress for men is striped ponchos, colorful shawls, and a chulla (a woolen cap with earflaps). Traditional indigenous dress for women is a skirt with many layers and apron, embroidered top and bombin (round, felted hat). Quechua and Aymara women also use squares of woven fabric to carry babies and other bundles on their backs.

Eating/Meals

Bolivians typically eat four meals a day including breakfast, tea, lunch, and dinner. Utensils rather than hands are used for eating nearly every food, including pizza and fruit such as bananas. During meals, social custom dictates that people keep their hands above their laps and refrain from asking for more food. In rural areas, Bolivians consider eating in front of strangers to be rude. This belief causes individuals at restaurants to eat facing the wall or with head tilted down. Within the home, meals are generally served in individual portions rather than family style. The head of the family will traditionally say "Provecho" ("Enjoy your meal") to signal that family and guests should begin to eat.

Breakfast is usually eaten at approximately eight o'clock and includes bread, butter, jam, and café con leche (coffee with milk). Celebratory or formal breakfasts may include cheese, quesillo (caramelized flan), or eggs. Tea may be eaten mid-morning (typically eleven o'clock) or mid-afternoon (typically four o'clock) depending on an individual's or family's daily schedule. Tea is a light meal of tea, coffee, and sweet or savory bread. Salteñas (pastry filled with beef, chicken, peas and carrots, potatoes, onions, olives, raisins or eggs) are a popular teatime snack.

Lunch is the main meal of the day. Families come together at the family home to eat a multi-course meal which generally lasts one to two hours. Common lunch courses include soup, main dish, fruit, and coffee or tea. Drinks include water, pisco (grape brandy), fresh-squeezed orange juice, or sweetened-powdered drinks.

Dinner is generally eaten late in the evening (typically between seven and nine o'clock). Informal dinners will be light—similar to the tea-time meal—while formal dinners will be similar to the typical Bolivian lunch, involve many courses, and may last late into the evening. Custom dictates that dinner guests will arrive 15 to 30 minutes late. Dinner guests will usually be served food first.

Visiting

Familial relationships are actively expressed and strengthened through informal, formal, and ceremonial visits between people and households. Adults spend significant amounts of time making visits to family and friends and receiving frequent guests in their own households. Bolivians bring gifts of flowers, wine, whiskey, and chocolate when visiting friends and family. Business associates may exchange small gifts of pens or items with company logos. Adult visitors to Bolivian households will generally be offered coffee, singani (Bolivia's national liquor), coco leaves or cigarettes.

In addition to frequent reciprocal household visits to strengthen family ties, Bolivians visit family and friends during birthdays, weddings, baptisms, funerals, holidays, and festivals. For instance, Bolivians visit one another for birthdays since parties held to observe the event are common. For adults, evening birthday parties include dancing, food, and cake late into the night. For children, daytime birthday parties are common. For most birthdays, gifts are opened after the guests have left the party.

Important national holidays for visiting include Christmas, Easter, and Bolivia's Independence Day. Important festivals for visiting include the Festival of the Cross, Carnival, and the Festival of Abundance. Distant relatives and friends will travel for weddings, baptisms, funerals, holidays, and festivals. Family fiestas (parties) are held for significant life and family events such as baptisms, weddings, and funerals. Traditionally, women schedule and lead social visits.

LIFESTYLE

Family

Bolivian families of Hispanic and Indian origin tend to be large and extended rather than small and nuclear (consisting of a mother, father, and their children). Bolivians reinforce their familial ties through family traditions such as formal visits to relatives, weddings, baptisms, and funerals. Bolivians also establish kinship connections to one another through compadrazgo (the extended set of relationships that link a child, the child's parents and his or her godparents). Compadres (those people linked through family and kin bonds) remain loyal to one another throughout their lifetimes. Compadres may link people of different classes and ethnicities. Bolivians also recognize that an individual's actions affect the wider group of family and friends.

Bolivia's large indigenous population, particularly the Aymaras, Quechuas, and Guarani, depend on family to protect against economic downturns. The indigenous family unit is generally stable, and indigenous families typically share resources such as food and labor. Intermarriage within indigenous kin groups and villages is common.

Housing

The majority of Bolivians live in detached family homes. Bolivian housing reflects the availability of natural resources, and contemporary houses tend to be constructed of local materials such as mud, stone, and reeds. Mud is used to make brick, stucco, and roof tiles, stones are used to construct walls and fences, while reeds are used for thatched houses. In rural areas, houses tend to be one story, while in urban regions, houses are often two stories. The top story is often left unfinished as a tax strategy, as unfinished houses are taxed at a lower rate than completed houses. Families with resources to protect tend to build tall masonry walls around their houses. Additionally, it is common for security and privacy walls to be topped with broken glass or other deterrents.

Food

Traditional Bolivian cuisine includes meat (often chicken or pork) and starches such as rice, potatoes, hominy (ground or crushed corn without the germ) or chuño (dehydrated frozen potato). Bolivian food includes local ingredients and reflects regional tastes. For instance, guinea pigs (referred to as cuy, cuye, or curí in Spanish) are a popular dish in the Andean highlands, and guinea pig meat is interchangeable with chicken meat in most Bolivian recipes. Visitors to Bolivia often miss out on the most authentic tastes and flavors of Bolivia as Bolivians tend to eat at home or private clubs more often than restaurants. Examples of traditional Bolivian dishes include chuño, salteñas, and picante de pollo.

Chuño is the staple food of Bolivians residing in the highlands of Bolivia. Bolivians eat chuño plain or integrated with other foods. Chuño phuti is a common side dish throughout Bolivia. Ingredients include chuño, fresh cheese, eggs, salt, onion, and oil. Bolivians enjoy salteñas as an appetizer. Salteñas are most often filled with potatoes, peas, and carrots. The crust of the salteña may be flavored with sugar or red pepper.

Picante de pollo (spicy chicken) is a favorite Bolivian main dish. Bolivian households tend to have their own variation suited to the tastes of the family members. Common ingredients include chicken, ground cayenne pepper, white onion, tomato, locoto (red chili pepper), green peas, parsley, cumin, oregano, black pepper, salt, garlic, broth, and oil. Picante de pollo is often served with steamed rice, boiled potatoes, and a tomato and onion sauce. Overall, Bolivian food tends to be spicy. In addition to the spice in the cooked food, Bolivian food is often eaten with llajua (Bolivian hot sauce).

Bolivian desserts range from local fruits, such as guapuru and achachairu, to European influenced recipes such as such as cinnamon sorbet, coconut macaroons, and arroz con leche (rice pudding).

Life's Milestones

For Bolivians, baptism and marriage represent the most significant milestones of a person's life. Godparents are chosen prior to an infant's baptism as a way to link households and families. In the Roman Catholic tradition, baptism is a sacrament performed to admit an infant into the Catholic Church. The ritual involves a formal pronouncement by a priest, the verbal support of godparents, the sign of the cross made on the forehead of the baptized person and the pouring of holy water on the head of the baptized person.

Marriage signifies the transition of men and women into adulthood. Traditionally, Bolivian marriage involves many customs, including courtship, betrothal, and a number of different wedding ceremonies. Many Bolivians adhere to the formal Roman Catholic marriage and mass, while other customs include the feast of the marriage godparents, the inheritance feast, the planting ritual, and the roofing ritual of the couple's home. The marriage process, with its many steps, strengthens familial ties through ritualized giving and receiving of food, money, and blessings. Generally, godparents are actively involved in both baptism and marriage.

CULTURAL HISTORY

Art

Bolivian artistic traditions date back to the region's pre-Columbian cultures, and include sculpture, ceramics, woodcarving, metalwork, embroidery, and textiles. Bolivia's fine arts are particularly influenced by the aesthetics of the ancient Inca civilization. (The Inca conquered the early inhabitants of the Andes mountain range in the 15th century.) For instance, the Inca preference for geometric designs on pottery continues to be reflected in contemporary Bolivian ceramics.

Bolivian embroidery and textiles, more than any other art form, have strong historical significance for Bolivians. Bird and horse motifs are common in Bolivian textiles and fabric arts. Two important traditional textile pieces include winchas—which are embroidered headbands traditionally worn by women under rounded felt hats in the Charazani region of Bolivia, and ch'uspa, which is a coca bag carried by men throughout the Andean region. The ch'uspa is used to carry coca leaves, as well as the lime ash which is added to the coca leaves before chewing. Chewing coca leaves is a traditional Bolivian remedy for fatigue or sickness.

Increasingly, traditional Bolivian arts such as textiles are made for tourist sale and export. For example, arpilleras (appliqué textiles depicting scenes of daily life) are a modern version of a traditional textile form. Arpilleras are commonly found in tourist markets and indigenous craft cooperatives around the world. The tourist trade in Bolivian textiles serves as a source of revenue for Bolivian women living in poverty.

Many Bolivian painters have arisen since Melchor Perez de Hoguin (1660–1732), a baroque-style painter, founded the Potosi Indigenous School of Painting in the 17th century. Another famous Bolivian painter associated with the School of Potosi is Gaspar Miguel de Berrio (c. 1706–1762), whose work incorporates religious themes and makes use of gold leaf. Other renowned Bolivian painters include Alejandro Mario Yllanes (1913–1960), an Aymaran miner who was awarded—but did not claim—a Guggenheim Fellowship, and contemporary painter Roberto Mamani Mamani (1962–), an Aymaran artist whose work is significantly based in Aymaran indigenous tradition and symbols. María Nuñez del Prado (1908–1995) was a well-known sculptor.

Architecture

Just as Bolivia's folk and fine art traditions were influenced by the Pre-Columbian Inca civilization, so, too, was the country's architectural heritage. The Incas developed sophisticated systems of roads, aqueducts, bridges, and buildings in the Andean region of Bolivia, and portions of this pre-Hispanic architecture remain today. Much of Inca architecture is derived from the Tiahuanaco, known for their monumental, public, and ceremonial architecture.

Bolivia's colonial period is another defining aspect of the country's architectural heritage. Within the constitutional capital of Sucre, for example, the narrow, winding streets are known for their white-washed, colonial-style buildings from the 18th and 19th centuries. One of the city's most notable landmarks is the Metropolitan Cathedral. Construction began on the cathedral in 1559, but the building was not complete until 1712. This long period of construction contributed to the building's mixture of Renaissance and Baroque architectural styles. In 1991, the United Nations Educational, Scientific and Cultural Organization (UNESCO) recognized Sucre as a World Heritage Site for the city's impressive colonial architecture, which includes its numerous civil and religious structures. Another World Heritage Site, the city of Potosi, is an example of the blend of indigenous and colonial (Baroque) architecture.

Drama & Dance

Bolivia's traditional dances are performed in a variety of contexts. They depict dramatic cultural and historical events that range from encounters and relationships between slaves, indigenous people, and Spanish colonists, to dramas depicting the actions of Andean warriors, devils, and soldiers. Historically, the dances have provided an opportunity to ritually act out historical tensions between social and ethnic groups as well as events such as war, courtship, and work. Popular Bolivian folkdances depicting historical events and relationships include the caporales, morenada (popular in the highlands), diablada (known as the rebellion of devil dance), tobas (an

indigenous folkdance), tinkus (a ritualistic and sacrificial performance staged as a "battle"), and tarqueada (performed in rural areas and of indigenous origins). Many of these dances are performed during Carnival and at regional festivals throughout the year.

Caporales is Bolivia's most traditional folkdance performed during Carnival and other festivals. It is accompanied by music called saya, and is an athletic dance that dates back to Spanish colonial rule in Bolivia. Dancers performing the caporales must be physically strong and, as a result of the physical demands of the dance, tend to be young. The dance movements represent the activities of colonial-era mine workers and foremen. The costumes worn to dance the caporales enhance the story. Male dancers wear costumes with heavy boots and whips reminiscent of the uniforms worn by the caporal (colonial-era Spanish guards). Female dancers wear costumes of colorful dresses, fancy shoes, and a rounded hat typical of the clothes worn by the wives of the caporal during colonial times.

Additionally, the boots worn by male dancers are traditionally adorned with cascabeles (bells). Bolivians debate whether the bells worn on the boots of male dances represent the chains worn by slaves or the end of Spanish slavery. Some Afro-Bolivians have protested the continued celebration and performance of the caporales in Bolivia on the grounds that the dance ridicules, rather than celebrates, Afro-Bolivian heritage.

Music

Bolivians express their culture and history through music. Bolivian music incorporates indigenous, African, and Spanish instruments and musical styles. Bolivian music often serves as accompaniment to a particular dance style or genre. For example, the huayño is a traditional genre of music and dance that dates to pre-Hispanic times and includes Andean folk music and dance styles. The sounds of the huayño include high-pitched vocals and numerous instruments such as the flute, harp, panpipe, accordion, saxophone, charango, lute, violin, guitar, harmonica, and mandolin. The huayño is a hybrid musical genre that can be adapted to the sounds of traditional folk music, as well as to contemporary Andean rock music. The dance of the huayño is considered a flirtatious style of dance, and typically performed by couples.

Traditional Bolivian instruments include the zampoña (pan flute), quena (traditional Andean wooden flute), bombo (drum), and reco reco (percussion instrument made of a carved gourd). Small stringed instruments such as the charango, charangón, ronroco, and hualaycho are also used. Bolivia's traditional folk music is performed with native instruments and celebrated at peñas (folk music shows) and regional celebrations throughout the country. For instance, Bolivian stringed instruments and flutes accompany the costumed devil-dancers who perform annually in the Oruro Carnival. The Bolivian Ministry of Education's Folklore Department supports and promotes Bolivia's traditional folk music as a means of strengthening and preserving Bolivian culture.

Literature

Early Bolivian literature is rooted in the pre-Columbian and Hispanic traditions of the region, and includes scientific, religious, legal, and creative works. For example, prized early writing includes *Arte de los Metales* (*The Art of Metalworking*) by Spanish priest Alvaro Alonso Barba (c. 1569–1661), which dates to 1640, and a 16th century-instructional guide to silver mining at Potosí.

During the 20th century, Bolivian poetry and fiction flourished. One of Bolivia's most celebrated 20th-century poets is Javier del Granado (1913–1996). Granado's important works include *Rosas Pálidas* (*Pale Rises*, 1939), *Canciones de la Tierra* (*Songs of the Earth*, 1945), *Vuelo de Azores* (*Flight of Azors* 1979), and *Cantares* (*Songs*, 1989). Granado is considered Bolivia's poet laureate, and is remembered through national holidays and commemorative street names.

Contemporary Bolivian literature is beginning to be recognized internationally in large part due to large-scale translation efforts. In particular, anthologies of Bolivian literature, such

as *The Fat Man from La Paz: Contemporary Fiction from Bolivia* (2003), are being translated into foreign languages and, as a result, gaining international audiences. The anthology includes works by well known contemporary Bolivian fiction writers Edmundo Paz Soldan (1967-) and Gonzalo Lema (1959-).

CULTURE

Arts & Entertainment

The role of the contemporary arts in Bolivia reflects the country's 21st century culture, traditions, collective experience, and social consciousness. Bolivians also use the performance arts to celebrate and commemorate Bolivia's indigenous, pre-Hispanic cultural heritage.

Bolivia's indigenous population uses the arts to gain and strengthen their identity. The historical disenfranchisement of the peasant majority has created deeply-felt ethnic tensions between groups. Regional and ethnic identities tend to be stronger than national identity, while racial tensions have become common. The arts, particularly cinema and festivals, work to elaborate on, as well as diffuse, racial tensions. They also serve to keep pre-Hispanic traditions alive and create new images of indigenous Bolivia. For instance, in 1986, the Cinematography Education and Production Center (CEFREC) was founded to provide filmmaking resources and training for historically oppressed indigenous communities in Bolivia. According to CEFREC, films, such as *¿Ahora de Quien Es La Verdad?* (*Whose Truth Is It Now*?), which combines indigenous origin myths and interviews with social movement leaders, have been made by indigenous communities to help tell their own stories and manage their own images.

In addition to cinema, festivals celebrate and preserve indigenous cultural heritage as well as provide an opportunity to ritually act out historical tensions between social and ethnic groups. Important Bolivian festivals, including Noche de San Juan (Night of Saint John), Virgin of Urkupiña Festival, and the Carnaval de Oruro (Carnival of

Ouro), blend Hispanic and pre-Hispanic traditions and elements.

Noche de San Juan, celebrated on June 21, was introduced by Spanish colonists but transformed by indigenous participants through the incorporation of pre-Hispanic traditions and elements. Bolivians use Noche de San Juan to celebrate the arrival of winter and the longest day of the year. Traditionally, Europeans use the Night of Saint John to celebrate the summer solstice and the arrival of summer. Celebrations include bonfires on the city streets, music and dance, and fireworks.

The Virgin of Urkupiña festival is held mid-August in the province of Quillacollo. The festival combines Hispanic (Catholic) and pre-Hispanic (pagan) religious traditions. The catholic-pagan rituals reflect the blending of artistic and religious traditions that occurred during the colonial era in Bolivia. The festival celebrates a local legend about a young shepherd girl who heard a celestial voice instructing her to gather and carry a heavy load of rocks to her home. The young girl's load of rocks was miraculously turned into silver.

The Carnaval de Oruro (Carnival of Oruro), which begins on the Saturday before Ash Wednesday, combines Hispanic and pre-Hispanic cultural and religious traditions. Carnaval de Oruro celebrates pre-Hispanic religious traditions and figures (such as Pachamama (Mother Earth) and Tio Supay (God of the Mountains) that have been cloaked in Catholic imagery and symbolism. Tens of thousands of people, particularly dancers and musicians, participate in the Carnaval de Oruro. Traditional dances performed throughout the multi-day festival include the caporales, diablada, morenada, and tinku. In fact, UNESCO recognizes Carnaval de Oruro as an intangible cultural heritage (ICH). The festival, along with the Andean Cosmovision of the Kallawaya—which is the healing arts of the Kallawaya, a group of indigenous healers in the Andes—were both listed as Masterpieces of the Oral and Intangible Heritage of Humanity.

Football (soccer) is very popular in Bolivia. Local leagues and informal games abound, and the national team has participated in World Cup competition. Famous soccer players include Marco Etcheverry, Ramiro Castillo, and Demetrio Angola. Volleyball, basketball, chess, and card games are also popular. On Fridays (known as "Bachelor Fridays"), men gather to play cacho, a dice game, or sapo, in which they try to shoot small metal game pieces into a frog-shaped goal.

Cultural Sites & Landmarks

The United Nations Educational, Scientific and Cultural Organization (UNESCO) recognizes six sites in Bolivia as requiring international recognition and preservation efforts. These sites include the city of Potosí; Fuerte de Samaipata (Fort Samaipata); the city of Sucre; the Jesuit Missions of the Chiquitos; Tiwanaku; and the Noel Kempff Mercado National Park.

Potosí, founded in the 16th century, was once an internationally important industrial city that produced silver ore for worldwide use. Areas of interest include the old colonial town, the Church of San Lorenzo, barrios mitayos (colonial-era neighborhoods where mine workers lived), and the manmade system of aqueducts and artificial lakes that once channeled water to hydraulic mills.

Fuerte de Samaipata is generally considered a religious or ceremonial site believed to have been built by a pre-Inca culture. Today it is an important archaeological site consisting of the old town center, residential district, and immense rock sculptures. The stone sculptures are believed to reflect the original settlers' highly developed religious belief system. It is believed that the distinct rock carvings found at the site have no parallel anywhere else upon the continent.

The city of Sucre was Bolivia's first capital. Settled by the Spanish in the 16th century, Sucre provides visitors with the opportunity to tour colonial era churches, including San Lázaro, San Francisco, and Santo Domingo. These churches showcase Bolivia's early architectural history of blending local and European styles. The historic city was Bolivia's third World Heritage Site, inscribed in 1991.

The Jesuit Missions of the Chiquitos was settled between 1696 and 1760. Chiquitos (which means "little ones" in Spanish) were a group of 31 local tribes. Local legend says that explorer Ñuflo de Chávez (1518–1568) called the tribes Chiquitos in reference to the narrow doors on their huts. These early Jesuit Mission settlements were built to reflect the ideal city concept of 16th-century philosophers. The remaining ensembles of "reducciones" (settlements of Christianized Indians) include San Francisco Javier, Concepción, Santa Ana, San Miguel, San Rafael, and San José.

Tiwanaku is a pre-Hispanic city in the southern Andes that predates the Inca civilization. Officially inscribed as Tiwanaku, the Spiritual and Political Centre of the Tiwanaku Culture, the archaeological site flourished as a city between 500 and 900 CE. Visitors to Tiwanaku will view important examples of pre-Hispanic architecture. The remains of the Tiwanaku Empire, particularly its massive buildings, suggest that the Tiwanaku Empire dominated the region during their day.

Noel Kempff Mercado National Park is one of the largest areas of protected land in the Amazon Basin. Visitors to the park will learn of its geological history dating back over a billion years, to the Precambrian period. The park's varied habitats include evergreen rainforests, palm forests, cerrado, swamps, savannahs, gallery forests, and semi-deciduous dry forests. Many of the parks habitats, which have been isolated for millions of years, shelter endangered species and ecosystems.

Libraries & Museums

The University of San Francisco Xavier in Sucre is significant both as a university and as the location of three of Bolivia's pre-eminent museums. The Anthropology Museum was established in 1943 and includes exhibits related to the folklore, archaeology, ethnography, and pottery of Bolivia. The Museum of Viceregal Art was founded in 1939; its exhibits include artifacts and pictorial works from colonial times. The Modern Art Gallery is the country's premiere modern art museum.

The Museum de la Recoleta is located in Sucre in a convent established by the Franciscan Order between 1600 and 1613. Over the centuries, the convent has also served as a barracks and a prison. The museum displays anonymous paintings from the 16th to 20th centuries.

The National Archive of Bolivia is located in Sucre. It contains documents dating back to the 16th century, including those of the Audiencia de Charcas (Spanish colonial court). The National Library is also located at Sucre; the nation's legal depository, whose origins can be traced back to 1825, is also located at Sucre.

Holidays

Independence Day (August 6) celebrates Bolivia's 1825 independence from Spain. Other national holidays include La Paz Day (July 16), which celebrates the 1548 founding of the city; Mary's Day (July 21); National Day (April 9), which commemorates the reestablishment of the National Revolutionary Movement in 1952; and El Dia de los Muertos (Day of the Dead), observed on November 1.

Many Inca holidays are also observed, often combined with Roman Catholic holidays. Alasitas, the Aymara festival for Ekeko, the god of abundance, is celebrated in January. May 27 is Heroínas de la Coronilla (Heroines of Coronilla), which commemorates the defense of Cochabamba by women during the war of independence.

Youth Culture

Bolivian youth culture is strongly influenced by the country's Inca and Hispanic heritage, as well as the current political and economic instability. The majority of Bolivian youths, like the population at large, live in poverty, and this socioeconomic status influences their culture, particularly their choice of fashion and music. For example, clothes are often secondhand, and popular music is often found locally. Youth clothing styles vary based on location as well. For instance, teens in urban areas wear American or European styles of jeans and sweatshirts, and teens living in rural areas follow local custom more closely and wear traditional dress.

Teens generally begin dating, usually with chaperones, at the age of 15. In cities, teens often gather in small groups at local plazas and squares to walk hand-in-hand and flirt. Popular youth leisure activities include playing football (soccer, the national sport), watching television, visiting friends, and participating in festivals.

The Bolivian government provides free public education up to age 14, or grade eight. Bolivia law also requires five years of primary school education. However, literacy and attendance remains low in rural areas as compared to urban areas. Recently, Bolivia has made an increased effort to incorporate information and communication technologies (ICTs) as an educational tool in primary and secondary schools.

SOCIETY

Transportation

Bolivians most often travel by car, bus, or taxi, and taxi vans are also common; car ownership in Bolivia, however, remains low, and the roadways are predominantly unpaved and poorly maintained. The Pan-American Highway, which links Peru with Argentina, crosses through Bolivia as well. For longer trips, the country has both eastern and western rail lines, as well as long-distance bus transportation. The weather, particularly rain, can have a severe impact on transportation, dividing Western and Eastern Bolivia and isolating remote villages, often for weeks. Traffic moves on the right-hand side of the road.

Transportation Infrastructure

Despite the sophisticated transportation systems (such as extensive regional road networks) developed hundreds of years ago by the pre-Hispanic peoples in Bolivia, modern Bolivia lacks an effective transportation infrastructure. Travel tends to be expensive and time consuming for Bolivians and tourists alike, and the lack of modern transportation infrastructure has prevented economic development in Bolivia. For instance, numerous agricultural areas have limited access to market towns, and roads are often impassable during the rainy season.

In 1988, Bolivia had an estimated 41,000 kilometers (25,476 miles) of roads, three percent of which were paved. By 2014, Bolivia had 80,488 kilometers (50,012 miles) of roads and 15 percent were paved. In urban centers such as La Paz, streets are often narrow and made of cobblestone. Servicio Nacional de Caminos (The National Road Service) was established in 1964 to supervise road planning, construction, and maintenance. Bolivia is seeking foreign aid, such as that given by the Inter-American Development Bank, to modernize Bolivia's road, train, and air travel systems.

Media & Communications

Bolivians depend on the growing media and communications industry to connect isolated regions and people. In 2012, Bolivians had 880,600 land telephone lines, 9.5 million mobile cellular connections, and an estimated 1.1 million Internet users. Telephone and Internet service is much more common in urban areas than rural regions. Bolivia's mountainous terrain limits the signal range of the majority of radio stations. The majority of television programming in Bolivia is Spanish-language foreign content. Bolivia's low literacy rates make radio and television more popular than newspapers. As of 2012, Internet usage extended to just over 10 percent of the population.

The Bolivian government has a long history of controlling, censoring, and punishing journalists and privately-owned media networks. In the 1980s, Hernán Siles Zuazo (1914–1996) was elected president, and freedom of the press (and freedom of expression in general) emerged as a shared ideal in Bolivia for the first time. Media content, particularly printed and televised media, is often strongly tied to political parties but does not generally result in government censorship or fines for journalists. Popular daily newspapers include *La Razon, Los Tiempos, El Deber, El Diario, Correo del Sur*, and *El Mundo*.

SOCIAL DEVELOPMENT

Standard of Living

Bolivia ranked 113th out of 187 countries on the 2013 United Nations Human Development Index, which compiles quality of life and standard of living indicators.

Water Consumption

The World Health Organization, which compiles data related to human development issues, indicates that 86 percent of the Bolivian population has access to clean water. Access to improved sanitation is very low, at 46 percent. Rural populations face more challenges when it comes to access to clean water and sanitation, and environmental health issues contribute heavily to deaths of children under the age of five. It has also been estimated that 80 percent of the curable diseases in Bolivia are caused by polluted water. Although the country has abundant supplies of water, very little drinkable water is available to the people. Privatization of water delivery has resulted in price increases and "water wars" among providers.

Education

The literacy rate in Bolivia is 91 percent overall—95 percent among men and nearly 87 percent among women. This represents a rapid increase as a result of education reform.

However, educational problems remain. Education is compulsory from age six to 14, but the reality is that rural girls are often registered but do not actually attend school, because education past basic reading and writing is not considered necessary for girls.

Because the weather is stable year-round, the school year has two one-month breaks instead of one long vacation in the summer. Teacher salaries are low, and frequent teacher strikes interrupt the school term.

Bolivia has 10 universities. The largest is the University of San Andres in La Paz. San Francisco Xavier University, in Sucre, is one of oldest in the hemisphere.

Women's Rights

The role and treatment of women in Bolivian culture is largely influenced by social custom. While women have equal legal rights to men, women do not have the same social status as men. Additionally, Bolivian women are often unaware of their legal rights. For instance, Bolivian custom, rather than law, prohibits land inheritance for women. Women also earn less than men for the same jobs, and common sectors of employment for women include the services, trade, and agricultural sectors. In addition, women often work as maids or farm workers, and girls often leave school early to work at home or seek outside employment to support their families.

Sexual harassment, a civil crime, is a common problem in urban and rural areas. Mental, physical, and sexual violence against women, though legally prohibited, is seldom enforced, and the requirement that victims testify against the accused is thought to deter victims from reporting incidents of rape. Despite laws against domestic violence, it is perceived to be a private rather than legal matter. Adult prostitution, legal for all those over the age of eighteen, is associated with human trafficking in women and forced labor.

Numerous organizations work to support and educate women about their legal rights, as well as offer social and medical services. The Maternal and Infant Health Insurance Program provides health insurance to child-bearing women, infants, and young children. The Vice Ministry of Women in the Ministry of Sustainable Development operates to support the legal rights of women. Influential women's rights groups include the Federación Nacional De Mujeres Campesinas De Bartolina Sisa (Bolivia National Federation of Campesina Women of Bolivia Bartolina Sisa) and Centro de Información y Desarollo de la Mujer (Center for Information and the Development of Women, or CIDEM). These two groups focus on developing equality among rural indigenous women as well as those in the urban working class. Groups encourage women to vote in elections (a right that Bolivian women won in 1938) and actively advocate for themselves in Bolivian society.

Health Care

Annual expenditure for health care in Bolivia is about $230 per capita. Health care providers are scarce, with only 1.2 physicians per 1,000 people and even fewer nurses. The infant mortality rate is 39 per 1,000 births (2014 estimate). Life expectancy in 2014 was an estimated 66 for males and 71 for females.

In 2009, the estimated maternal mortality rate was 290 per 100,000 births, and many more women die from botched illegal abortions. More than 50 percent of pregnant women are anemic. In recent years, community pharmacies have opened in many small towns.

GOVERNMENT

Structure

When the Spanish arrived in the 16th century, the Indians maintained their community organization, but were required to provide labor for the Spanish in return for "protection" and conversion to Christianity. This led to enslavement in the mines for many Indians.

With the help of Simón Bolívar, Bolivia gained its independence from Spain in 1825. The country is named in honor of its liberator. In the century after independence, Bolivia had 40 different heads of government. Coups were frequent, and six of the chief executives were assassinated in office.

In the Chaco War (1932–35), Bolivia lost most of the Chaco (an area encompassing the Paraguay River that would have given Bolivia access to the Atlantic Ocean) to Paraguay. A result of the Chaco War was a resurgence of nationalism.

The 1952 Revolution brought about universal adult suffrage, education reform, the end of serfdom, and the nationalization of mines. Although the middle class ruled instead of the oligarchy, the same system of favoritism and monopoly of the economy persisted.

Until 1982, Bolivia held the world record for the number of coups. Since then, the country has enjoyed a stable government. The president and vice president are elected every five years.

The legislative branch consists of the bicameral Congreso Nacional (National Congress). The 36 senators in the Camara de Senadores (Senate Chamber) are elected every five years from party lists by proportional representation. The Camara de Diputados (Chamber of Deputies) has 130 representatives, 77 of whom are elected directly and 53 from party lists by proportional representation.

Political Parties

Two parties dominate Bolivia's political landscape: the Movement for Socialism—Political Instrument for the Sovereignty of the Peoples (MAS-IPSP) and the Plan Progress for Bolivia—National Convergence (PPB-CN). The socialist MAS party came into power in 2006. The other major party is the PPB-CN, a party of the right. In the 2014 elections, the MAS garnered 61 percent of the vote, securing 88 deputy seats and 25 senate seats. The PPB-CN got 24 percent of the vote, winning 32 deputy seats and nine senate seats. The Christian Democratic Party won 10 deputy seats and two senate seats. The leader of the MAS, Evo Morales, was re-elected president in 2014, having served as president since 2005.

Local Government

Bolivia is divided into nine departments, led by directly elected governors. These departments are further divided into provinces and again into municipalities and cantons.

Judicial System

Members of the Corte Suprema (Supreme Court) and the Plurinational Constitutional Tribunal are the country's highest courts. The 12 members of the Supreme Court and 14 members of the Plurinational Tribunal are elected for six year terms, by popular vote, from lists approved by the legislature. The Plurinational Electoral Organ has six members appointed by the legislature and one by the president. Lower courts include District Courts, Council of the Judiciary, and Agro-Environmental Court.

Taxation

The Bolivian government levies taxes on income, rental income, capital gains, property taxes, a value-added tax (VAT), and corporate taxes. Personal income taxes are relatively low, and the top corporate tax rate is 25 percent.

Armed Forces

Bolivia's armed forces consist of three service branches: army, navy, and air force, with a strong national police force, acting as a fourth branch. Recently, under the government of Evo Morales, the armed forces have experienced a build-up of arms, including the purchase of a range of weapons and aircraft from both China and Russia. Morales defended the military build-up as a response to the "poaching" of Bolivia's natural resources and minerals. The armed forces also adopted a new slogan in 2010, taken from revolutionary Cuba: "Fatherland or death, we shall overcome!"

Foreign Policy

Bolivia's ability to be an international leader is largely limited by the country's landlocked status and economic dependency on foreign nations. In 2005, Bolivia received $582.9 million (USD) in foreign aid. In particular, Bolivia has received extensive economic aid from the United States since the 1950s, and at times, Bolivia has received more U.S. economic aid than any other Latin American country. Thus, U.S. economic aid and political influence has shaped Bolivia's economic and political development. For instance, in the 1970s, the U.S. suspended economic and military aid to Bolivia as a means of protesting Bolivia's narcotics and human rights problems. In an effort to regain support, Bolivian government transitioned into a more democratic and transparent system. However, under the Morales government, relations have deteriorated. He expelled the U.S. ambassador and then, in 2013, the U.S. Agency for International Development, effectively stopping American foreign aid.

Bolivia's weak international position is also highlighted by its decreasing territorial size. Due to big territorial losses in three wars—the War of the Pacific (1879–1883), the lesser-known Acre War (1903) and the Chaco War (1932–1935)—Bolivia's land claim is half what it was in the 19th century. Nonetheless, Bolivia depends on the good will of its border countries to reach ports for import and export purposes, and has been active in the Organization of American States (OAS). It is also an associate member of Mercosur, a regional trade agreement (RTA) established among Argentina, Brazil, Paraguay, and Uruguay. However, regional relations have been strained.

In the case of Argentina, Bolivia weakened relations by seeking to buy more natural gas than the country has money to pay for. Also, Bolivia and Chile disagree about the type and extent of access to the Pacific Ocean that Chile should allow. Chile grants Bolivia unrestricted maritime access for commodities such as natural gas, but denies Bolivia sovereign maritime access and control. In addition, Chile has rejected Bolivia's request to reestablish Bolivia's claim to the Atacama corridor (an area of land granted to Chile in an 1884 settlement). In October 2010, Peruvian president Alan García forged an agreement with Bolivian president Evo Morales to allow Bolivia to build a small port south of Ilo, in Peru. This piece of coastal land is large enough for a dock and the mooring of some vessels, as well as serving as a free trade zone.

A member of the United Nations (UN) since 1945, a newly democratic Bolivia improved its relationships with foreign nations beginning in the 1980s. For instance, Bolivia reached a new trade agreement with Brazil, and has worked to strengthen relations with numerous countries, particularly European countries, with the eventual aim of building trade agreements. Bolivia has trade relationships with Brazil, Argentina, the U.S., Colombia, Japan, South Korea, Chile, and Peru. Bolivia exports natural gas, soybeans and soy products, crude petroleum, zinc ore, and tin and imports petroleum products, plastics, paper, aircraft and aircraft parts, prepared foods, automobiles, and insecticides.

The 2005 presidential election of Evo Morales tested and weakened U.S.-Bolivia relations. For instance, President Morales refused to work with the U.S. ambassadors and the U.S. Drug Enforcement Agency (DEA) on ending narcotics trafficking in Bolivia.

Human Rights Profile

International human rights law insists that states respect civil and political rights, and also promote an individual's economic, social and cultural rights. The United Nations Universal Declaration on Human Rights (UDHR) is recognized as the standard for international human rights. Its authors sought the counsel of the world's great thinkers, philosophers, and religious leaders, and were careful to create a document that reflects the core values shared by every world culture. (To read this document or view the articles relating to cultural human rights, visit: www.udhr.org/UDHR/default.htm.)

Bolivia's constitution generally supports and respects the human rights of its population, particularly with regard to Article 2 of the UDHR, which states that everyone is entitled to legal rights and freedoms without discrimination. Unfortunately, in daily life in Bolivia, significant discrimination exists against women, indigenous people, Bolivians of African descent, and children. Major social problems in Bolivia include violence against women and children, human trafficking, and child prostitution and labor. Furthermore, laws are often unenforced due to a lack of resources or interest. For instance, Bolivia's Code for Boys, Girls, and Adolescents, which establishes the rights of children and adolescents, regulates adoptions, and protects against exploitative child labor and violence against children, is often left unenforced as government officials lack sufficient resources and support to investigate problems and claims.

Article 16 of the UDHR, which states that men and women of any race, nationality, or religion have the right to marry and to found a family, is supported in the Bolivian constitution. While Bolivia's constitution does not prohibit marriage between men and women of any race, nationality or religion, the choosing of a marriage partner is more often influenced by social customs and norms. In practice, Bolivians tend to marry within their socioeconomic and ethnic group.

Article 18 of the UDHR supports the right to freedom of thought, conscience, and religion, so long as the practice of religion does not violate public morality, decency, or the public order. Bolivia's constitution specifies religious freedom and protection. In practice, the predominance of Roman Catholicism in Bolivia influences religious practice. Roman Catholicism is Bolivia's official religion—priests, who have some degree of political influence, receive stipends from the government. All non-Catholic religions are required to register with the Ministry of Foreign Affairs and Worship and receive government authorization for religious practice. The application process, which is complicated and prohibitively expensive for poorer religious organizations, forces some religious groups to practice their faith unofficially and underground.

The Bolivian constitution supports Article 19 of the UDHR, which guarantees the right to freedom of opinion and expression. The Bolivian government generally respects freedom of speech by giving academics and journalists permission to express themselves as they see fit. Additionally, the Internet is not controlled or censored by the Bolivian government. However, exceptions to freedom of expression include pornographic books, magazines, and artwork, as well as insulting, defaming, or slandering public officials for carrying out their duties. Jail sentences for insulting, defaming, or slandering public officials for carrying out their duties range from one month to two years.

Articles 27-29 of the UDHR, which, in part, invoke the need for national and international social, moral, economic, and cultural support for the rights and freedoms set forth in the Declaration, are not reflected in mainstream Bolivian culture and society. Bolivian social and cultural norms and customs allow for widespread discrimination and unequal treatment of different social groups, ethnicities, and genders.

ECONOMY

Overview of the Economy

Unemployment remains a concern, and a large percentage of Bolivians are informally employed. Most are traders, artisans, or self-employed service-providers. These jobs are unregulated and untaxed. Setting up a legitimate business is extremely difficult in Bolivia, and the process is slowed by red tape. In 2013, income from exports stood at $12.16 billion USD. The per capita gross domestic product (GDP) in 2013 was an estimated $5,500 USD.

Industry

The services industry remains underdeveloped, and the banking and finance sectors suffer from weak regulation. The majority of the manufacturing industry is small-scale. Significant industries in Sucre, the constitutional capital, include mining, smelting, petroleum, food and beverages, tobacco, handicrafts, clothing, and tourism. The city also functions as an agricultural center for the barren areas of the high Andean plateau known as the Altiplano, supplying the mining communities throughout the region with much needed resources.

Labor

The labor force in Bolivia numbers 4.5 million people. Thirty-two percent of the labor force finds employment in the agricultural sector; 27 percent works in industry; and 41 percent of the labor force works in the service industry. The unemployment rate in 2013 was 7.4 percent.

Energy/Power/Natural Resources

Tin, natural gas, petroleum, zinc, tungsten, antimony, silver, iron, lead, gold, timber, and hydropower are among Bolivia's known natural resources. Tin-mining used to be the main industry, but natural gas has recently replaced tin in importance. Forty-five percent of export income, in 2011, was from hydrocarbons (primarily natural gas).

Industrial development has resulted in dangerous destruction of habitat through burning and pollution. Illegal hunting and replacement of local plants and animals with exotic species have also upset the ecological balance, especially in the fragile ecosystems of the Altiplano and the dry Andean forests. Slash-and-burn agriculture and overgrazing, also contribute to desertification and loss of biodiversity.

To stem this tide of destruction, Bolivia has formed the Sistema Naciónal de Areas Protegidas (National System for Protected Areas), or SNAP. The protected areas cover 17 percent of the country's land area.

Fishing

Bolivia, a landlocked nation, has a small fishing industry concentrated in the country's freshwater lakes and rivers. Most fishing is done for domestic consumption.

Forestry

About half of Bolivia's forests consist of primary forests. The government is aware of the threat of deforestation and has made strides to certify the management of its forests, both public and private, for both environmental and social standards, managing to certify over two million hectares of forests. As of 2006, certified forestry products accounted for $16 million in exports, since that time it has been a decreasing part of export income.

Mining/Metals

Mining activity is an important part of Bolivia's industry. In the first quarter of 2014, mineral revenues rose to $2.04 billion, accounting for 17 percent of the country's export revenue. Substances mined include tin, lead, silver, copper, antimony, zinc, sulfur, bismuth, gold, tungsten, salt, petroleum, and natural gas. In 2010, it was reported that the Cerro de Potosi Mountain, which houses the earth's largest silver deposits, is close to collapse. More than 4,000 tons of rock is removed from the mountain each day, as it has been a source not only of silver, but of lead and zinc as well.

Agriculture

Only 2.6 percent of the land in Bolivia is arable. Potatoes are the traditional staple crop, followed by corn (50 percent for home consumption, 50 percent for sale to animal-feed producers), rice in the lowlands (sufficient for domestic use, inferior quality for export), barley in the highlands (mostly for beer, 10 percent for fodder), and quinoa (a hardy grain that has been grown in the Andes for thousands of years).

Soybeans, coffee, coca, cotton, corn, sugarcane, and timber are other common crops.

Animal Husbandry

Small to medium-sized farms form the bulk of Bolivia's livestock industry. Livestock raised in Bolivia include cattle and poultry, as well as sheep, goats, llamas, and alpacas.

Tourism

As reported in 2013, tourism brings an estimated $378 million USD each year, and employs 775,000 people. Approximately 800,000 people visit more than 1,300 tourist sites in the country annually.

Popular sites include Lake Titicaca; the Yungas valleys; the Moon Valley rock formations; Cochabamba, the garden city; Potosi, mineral center, historic memorial and World Cultural and Natural Historical Site; Noel Kempff Mercado National Park in the northeast; and Tarija, famous for its flowers, wines and climate. Mount Chacaltaya, at 5,200 meters (17,060 feet), boasts the highest ski resort in the world. Because of the thin air, oxygen tanks are available for fainting skiers.

Sucre contributes to the tourism industry of Bolivia with its rich colonial history and architectural attractions. Sucre is also known for the exquisite handmade tapestries sold throughout the city and at the popular nearby Tarabucco market.

Simone Flynn, Ellen Bailey Lynn-nore Chittom

DO YOU KNOW?

- The University of San Francisco Xavier is considered the oldest university in the Americas. It was established two years prior to the founding of Harvard.
- In August 2006, Microsoft launched versions of Windows and Office in the Inca language of Quechua at an unveiling ceremony in Sucre.
- Just outside Sucre is the Cal Orck'o limestone quarry, remarkable for its preserved dinosaur tracks. One of the most unique attractions in Bolivia, these fossilized footprints were preserved in the rock layers within just two weeks of their formation in the sediment.

Bibliography

Albro, Robert. "The Culture of Democracy and Bolivia's Indigenous Movements." *Critique of Anthropology* 26.4 (Dec. 2006): 387–410.

"Bolivia: Risk Summary." *Latin America Monitor: Andean Group Monitor* 22.12 (Dec. 2005): 8-8.

"Bolivia's Time of Rebellion." *Foreign Policy* (July 2004): 76–76.

Canessa, Andrew. "A Postcolonial Turn: Social And Political Change In The New Indigenous Order Of Bolivia." *Urban Anthropology & Studies of Cultural Systems & World Economic Development* 36.3 (Fall 2007): 145–159.

Devine, Elizabeth. *The Travelers' Guide to Latin American Customs and Manners*. New York: Macmillan, 2000.

Farthing, Linda C. and Benjamin H. Kohl. *Evo's Bolivia: Continuity and Change*. Austin: University of Texas Press, 2014.

Hayden, Tom. "Bolivia's Indian Revolt." *Nation* 278.24 (21 June 2004): 18–22.

Kain, Ronald Stuart. "Bolivia's Claustrophobia." *Foreign Affairs* 16.4 (July 1938): 704–713.

Klein, Herbert S. *A Concise History of Bolivia*. 2nd ed. Cambridge: Cambridge University Press, 2012.

Lazarte, Jorge. "Bolivia's Gordian Knot." *Hemisphere: A Magazine of the Americas* 18 (Fall 2007): 28–31

Paulson, Susan. "Model Families Of Modern Development Cede To Alternative Bonds In Bolivia's Social Movements." *Urban Anthropology & Studies of Cultural Systems & World Economic Development* 36.3 (Fall2007 2007): 239–280.

"Presentation by the Communist Party of Bolivia to the International Meeting of Communist and Workers' Parties." *Nature, Society & Thought* 19.2 (Apr. 2006): 153–59.

Reed, James and Shafik Meghji. *The Rough Guide to Bolivia.* London: DK Publishing Inc., 2012.

Works Cited

"Andean Textiles." Helen Louise Allen Textile Collection (2008). <http://www.sohe.wisc.edu/depts/hlatc/pixelsexhibit/andean.html>.

"Background Note: Bolivia." U.S. Department of State (2012). <http://www.state.gov/r/pa/ei/bgn/35751.htm>.

"Bolivia." CIA—The World Fact Book (2014). <https://www.cia.gov/library/publications/the-world-factbook/print/bl.html>.

"Bolivia." *Nations of the World.* Amenia, NY: Grey House Publishing, 2015.

"Bolivia." City Population (2008). <http://www.citypopulation.de/Bolivia.html>.

"Bolivia." UNESCO World Heritage (2008). <http://whc.unesco.org/en/statesparties/bo>.

"Bolivia." Political Risk Yearbook: Bolivia Country Forecast (Jan. 2008): 1-18. Business Source Premier. EBSCO. <http://search.ebscohost.com/login.aspx?direct=true&db=buh&AN=31210420&site=ehost-live>.

"Bolivia." UNESCO World Heritage List (2008). <http://whc.unesco.org/en/statesparties/bo>.

"Bolivia - A Country Study." Country Studies Series by Federal Research Division of the Library of Congress (n.d.). <http://www.country-data.com/frd/cs/botoc.html#bo0013>.

"Bolivia: Country Report on Human Rights Practices." U.S. Department of State (2004). http://www.state.gov/g/drl/rls/hrrpt/2004/41750.htm.

"A Bolivian Menu." International Recipes (n.d.) http://marga.org/food/int/bolivia/.

"A Country Study: Bolivia." The Library of Congress Country Studies (2005). http://lcweb2.loc.gov/frd/cs/botoc.html.

"Chuño Phuti." Recipes Gallery (2008). http://www.boliviaweb.com/recipes/english/chuno.htm.

Dining Etiquette In Bolivia." BoliviaBella (n.d.). http://www.boliviabella.com/dining-etiquette.html.

Eigo, Tim. "Bolivian Americans." Multicultrural America (2008). http://www.everyculture.com/multi/A-Br/Bolivian-Americans.html.

Ellard, Mona. "Bolivian Housing" (n.d.). http://web1.msue.msu.edu/intext/Bolivia/housing.htm.

Hudson, Rex and Dennis M. Hanratty, editors. Bolivia: A Country Study (1989). Washington: GPO for the Library of Congress. http://countrystudies.us/bolivia/38.htm.

"History of the Dances and Descriptions." Boliviamanta (2008). http://www.madison.com/communities/boliviamanta/.

Meisch, Lynn A. Traditional Textiles of the Andes: Life and Cloth in the Highlands. Fine Arts Museum of San Francisco (2007). London: Thames and Hudson.

Provan, Alexander. "Race and Images in Bolivia." Culturekiosque (2005). http://www.culturekiosque.com/nouveau/cinema/indigenous_filmmakers_bolivia.html.

Sanabria, Harry. "Culture of Bolivia." Countries and Their Cultures (n.d.). http://www.everyculture.com/A-Bo/Bolivia.html.

"Social Etiquette in Bolivia." BoliviaBella (n.d.). http://www.boliviabella.com/social-etiquette.html

"Universal Declaration of Human Rights." United Nations (1948). <http://www.udhr.org/UDHR/default.htm>.

Samba dancer performs during Queen of Carnival competition, Brazil/Stock photo © Global Pics

BRAZIL

Introduction

Brazil is one of the most important and economically powerful nations in the Western Hemisphere, and it is the fifth largest nation in the world. It was originally a Portuguese colony, and has been influenced by indigenous, European, and African cultures. Not surprisingly, its cultural contributions are equally rich and varied. Brazil has given the world Rio de Janeiro's Carnival, life-sustaining rainforest ecosystems, the rhythms of samba, and one of the Seven Modern Wonders of the World.

GENERAL INFORMATION

Official Language: Portuguese
Population: 202,656,788 (2014 estimate)
Currency: Real (New banknotes were issued in February 2010)
Coins: Coins are available in denominations of 1, 5, 10, 25, 50 and a 1 real coin. Commemorative versions of the 1 real coin have been released in 1998, 2002, and 2005.
Land Area: 8,511,965 square kilometers (3,286,488 square miles)
Water Area: 55,455 square kilometers (21,411 square miles)
National Motto: Ordem e Progresso (Portuguese, "Order and Progress")
National Anthem: "Hino Nacional Brasileiro"
Capital: Brasília
Time Zone: GMT -3
Flag Description: The Brazilian flag features a yellow rhombus (diamond-shaped quadrilateral) centered in a green field. Within the

rhombus is a blue circle which portrays the night sky of the Southern Hemisphere, including constellations. There are exactly 27 white, five-pointed stars.

Population

Most Brazilians (approximately 85 percent) are classified as urban and live in coastal regions in or near such massive urban centers as Rio de Janeiro, São Paulo, Salvador, Belo Horizonte, and Brasília. The southeastern and northeastern parts of the country have the heaviest concentration of people, while the Amazonian region of Brazil is not as densely populated.

According to the Brazilian Institute of Geography and Statistics, nearly 48 percent of the Brazilian population defined themselves as white in 2010. The majority of the population is of Portuguese, African, or indigenous descent. As of 2014, the estimated median age is around 30, and average life expectancy is approximately 73.

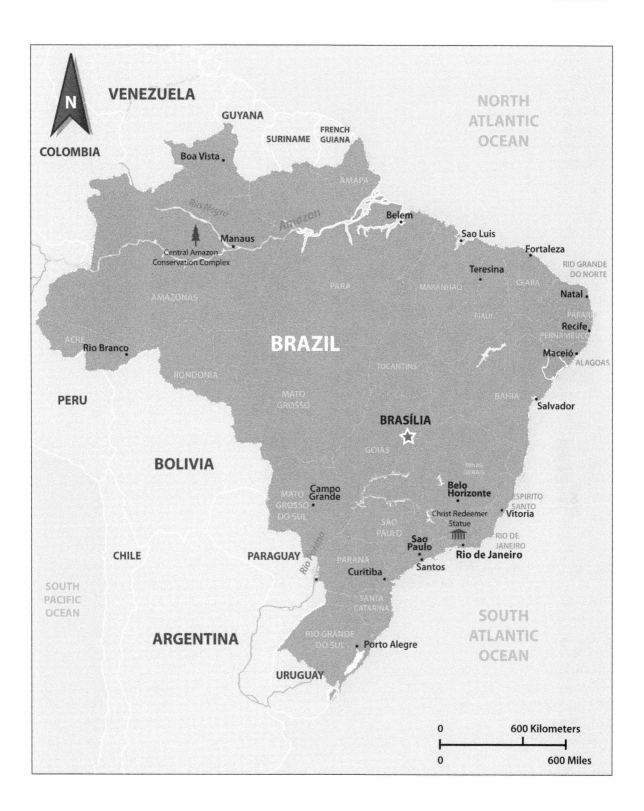

Principal Cities by Population (2014):

- São Paulo (11,788,959)
- Rio de Janeiro (6,453,682)
- Salvador (2,902,132)
- Brasília (2,754,765)
- Fortaleza (2,571,896)
- Belo Horizonte (2,491,109)
- Manaus (2,010,062)
- Curitiba (1,864,416)
- Recife (1,608,488)
- Porto Alegre (1,472,482)

Languages

The official language of Brazil is Portuguese, but other languages are common second languages for Brazilians, including English, Spanish, and French. In addition, there are over 100 Amerindian languages spoken throughout Brazil.

Native People & Ethnic Groups

The majority of Brazilians are an ethnic mixture of Portuguese (the primary European group to settle in Brazil), Africans (who arrived as slaves) and indigenous peoples, such as the Guarani and Tupi. In addition, there have been many other ethnic settlements in Brazil, including Asians, Middle Easterners, and Europeans.

Where once there were several million indigenous people in Brazil, now, in the early 21st century, they comprise a fairly small proportion of the total population, numbering approximately 300,000.

Among the more populous tribes are the Guarani, the Yanomami (who live along the Brazil-Venezuela border), and the Kayapo, who inhabit the eastern Amazonian region. Other tribes include the Ofaye, Banawa, and Awa. It has been estimated that as many as 50 or more Indian tribes still live in isolation in the Amazon region. Many of the indigenous languages of Brazilian Amerindians are endangered or have died out altogether.

Of major concern to many tribes, such as the Yanomami, are issues concerning both the rapid deforestation of the Amazon rainforest and indigenous land rights. Other issues include the ongoing battle for civil and economic rights. Governmental and private efforts are underway to improve economic and educational conditions among Brazil's indigenous people.

Religions

The primary religion in Brazil is Roman Catholicism, but because of the overall diversity of the population, many other religions are common, including Assemblies of God, Baptists, and Pentecostals. In addition to Christianity, other faiths such as Kardecism, blend Christianity and African spiritism.

Climate

Generally, the weather in Brazil has very little variation. Brazil is temperate in the southern portion, but is mostly tropical throughout the country. In the Amazon region, the climate is mostly wet, very humid, and has almost no dry periods. The average temperature in the north is 25° Celsius (77° Fahrenheit).

Rainfall in the north averages about 220 centimeters per year (90 inches), while in the grasslands region, it averages about 160 centimeters per year (60 inches). Heavy occasional rainfall and drought are common in the Sertão region.

Depending on topography, the climate can be varied: in Rio de Janeiro, which is coastal, temperatures in summer can be hot and humid; while in Brasília, which is inland, it may get as hot as in Rio de Janeiro, but not as humid.

ENVIRONMENT & GEOGRAPHY

Topography

Brazil is the largest country in South America, and borders every South American country except Ecuador and Chile. Along its northern border are French Guiana, Suriname, Guyana, Venezuela and Colombia; to the west are Peru, Bolivia, Paraguay, Argentina, and Uruguay. Its topography is equally varied.

Brazil is an equatorial country, but its long and mountainous northeastern coast stretches along the North Atlantic Ocean for 8,000 kilometers (4,971 miles), while its southeastern coast skims the South Atlantic. The northeast region contains a semi-arid desert known as the Caatinga. To the west, the Plantanal is the largest continental wetland in the world, and more than half of it lies in Brazil.

Several large rivers run through Brazil, including its most prominent, the Amazon River, which stretches from its source in the Peruvian Andes to its mouth at the Atlantic Ocean in the northern portion of the country. The Amazon is the longest river in the Western Hemisphere, and along with the Nile, one of the longest in the world; by volume, it is the largest river in the world. The Amazon River is narrow in some places, but several miles wide in others, and has more than a thousand tributaries. It also supports the immense Amazon rainforest and the thousands of native plant, animal and insect species found there.

South of the Amazon Basin are the Brazilian Highlands, an area of river valleys, hills, and mountains. The Cerrado is a tropical grasslands area in central Brazil. The highest point in Brazil is at Pico da Neblina, which is 3,014 meters (9,888 feet) high.

The capital Brasília is located in the highlands of Brazil's central western region. The area is largely composed of tropical grasslands and savannah called cerrado. Much of the grassland area surrounding Brasília is protected as national parkland. Brasília is isolated from the country's other major cities, located roughly 1,200 kilometers (740 miles) from the former capital, Rio de Janeiro.

Plants & Animals

Brazil has what may be considered the most diverse ecosystem on the planet.

In the south of Brazil, pampas, or grasslands, are common parts of the landscape, while caatinga, or low scrub, is prominent in the northeast area of Brazil. Cacti are also found in some areas of Brazil.

A wealth of tropical plants dominate the Atlantic and Amazon rainforest region; among the thousands of plants that live here are bromeliads, which provide their own tiny ecosystem for several kinds of insects; lianas, or climbing vines; orchids; and the Brazil nut tree. Many of the plants in the rainforest grow on other plants.

Of the hundreds of species of animals found in South America, most are indigenous to Brazil. Common animals of the rainforest include the macaw, iguanas, poison arrow frogs, toucans, and spider monkeys. More than 1,000 species of freshwater fish can be found in the Amazon.

Brazil is home to many other animals, including leopards, capybaras (the size of a large dog, they are the world's largest rodent species), tapirs and peccaries, and tens of thousands of insect species.

CUSTOMS & COURTESIES

Greetings

In Brazil, it is customary to shake hands with someone as a formal greeting. In more informal situations, people may kiss each other on the cheek. However, this custom varies by region and gender. For example, women might kiss and hug other women, men, and children, while men may only kiss children or close family members. Usually, men shake hands or give each other a slap on the back. In Rio de Janeiro, two light kisses, one on each cheek, is customary, while in São Paulo, only one kiss is typically given.

These gestures are frequently accompanied by the greeting "Tudo bom?" or "Tudo bem?" which means "How's it going?" Also, Brazilians may commonly greet each other using the time of day, such as with "Bom dia" ("Good Morning"), "Boa tarde" ("Good Afternoon") and "Boa noite" ("Good night"). If meeting someone for the first time, a person might say "É um prazer," or "Muito prazer em conhecê-lo." These expressions mean, "It's a pleasure to meet you."

When saying goodbye, Brazilians repeat the physical greetings, regardless of how much time passes in the company of others. In addition, they commonly say "Tchau" ("Goodbye") or "Até mais" ("See you later"). If parting at night, they may also say, "Boa noite" ("Good night"), which is used both as a greeting and farewell.

Gestures & Etiquette

Brazilians are very comfortable with physical contact, and it's common to see both men and women touching each other (patting knees or holding hands) in conversation. It is also common to attract another person's attention by lightly tapping them on the arm or shoulder, instead of by speaking.

Though Brazilians use some hand gestures, they also use ones that are understood in context, similar to sign language. For example, the thumbs up sign is frequently used to say "thanks" or "okay," in both formal and informal situations alike. There is a hand gesture for stealing, and another that means to do something quickly. In conversation, the person would use these specific gestures in lieu of words.

When referring to adults, it is polite to use "Senhor" ("Mr.") and "Senhora" ("Mrs"). When referring to someone of high social standing, Brazilians frequently use "Doutor" and "Doutora" ("Doctor"), even if that individual is not an actual practicing physician or Doctor of Philosophy (PhD). In addition, children often refer to familiar adults or adult family friends as "Tio" or "Tia," meaning "Uncle" and "Aunt," respectively.

Nicknames are used frequently in Brazil, often denoting a physical characteristic or referring to a particular memory about the person. For example, a heavier person might be called "Gordinho" ("Fatty"), while a short person might be called "Baixinha" ("Shorty"). Some nicknames are just shortened versions of full names, like Zé for José.

Other times, a person's city or state of origin is used as his nickname, like "Mineiro" for a man from the state of Minas Gerais, or "Carioca" for a person from the city of Rio de Janeiro. Many football (soccer) players use nicknames—like Careca, "the bald one," and Ronaldinho Gaúcho, little Ronaldo from the state of Rio Grande do Sul. However, most famous people, such as actors, models, and politicians, are often referred

to by their full names, an indicator of high social status.

Eating/Meals

Eating is a very important social activity in Brazilian life, and the company of others is almost as essential as the food. Brazilians believe it is good manners to sit at a table while eating, and for this reason almost never eat on the run or while walking around. Brazilians are very strict about hygiene, and will often bring their toothbrushes and floss to work to use after eating.

Lunch is the most important meal of the day, and is eaten at home with the family or at a restaurant with work colleagues. Since children go to school for half the day, they eat at home before or after classes. Frequently, co-workers will all choose a time to go out in groups for a leisurely lunch. Rice and beans is the most common meal for all social classes. Typically, the two dishes are mixed together and often topped with farofa, a flour-like substance made from manioc, a tuber vegetable.

Eating meals at home is reserved for family members and very close friends, while co-workers and acquaintances eat in restaurants or botecos, bars that serves food. A popular restaurant for lunchtime in Brazil is the "por quilo" (by kilo) restaurant. Here, patrons choose from a buffet of assorted dishes and pay by the weight of the food on their plate. Another Brazilian favorite is the churrascaria, or steakhouse, where many different types of meat are served rodizio-style, or all-you-can-eat.

Visiting

Brazilians are known for their hospitality, and will treat visitors like family. Family members will often stop by their relatives' homes unannounced, and visits by family and friends alike are quite informal. In the city, most apartments have intercoms, but in the countryside, where doorbells are scarce, it is customary to clap your hands outside the gate or front door in order to call to the person inside.

The host usually offers guests a coffee or a drink, and everyone sits in the sitting room or common area. Guests are rarely given a tour of the house and are expected to stay in the social rooms of the home. Also, the hosts ask the guest to participate in the family's activities that day, like going to a soccer game or watching a movie. When it comes to extended visits of more than a day, Brazilians insist that family members sleep at their home, regardless of space. In addition, it is not uncommon for Brazilians to offer their homes to mere acquaintances traveling to their city. In these cases, it is best for the guest to bring a small gift in exchange for the host's hospitality. However, when choosing a gift the colors purple and black should be avoided, since they are associated with mourning.

Timeliness is not a big issue in Brazil, and it is not uncommon for people to arrive late for a social gathering. In fact, the term "estou chegando" ("I'm almost there") is used to tell someone that you've almost arrived at your destination, but usually means you're still on the way or haven't left home yet.

LIFESTYLE

Family

Family is the core of social life in Brazil, and loyalty to one's family often comes before personal interests. In Brazil, "family" consists not only of the nuclear unit (typically a mother, father, and two children), but also uncles, aunts, cousins, grandparents, and sometimes even very close friends. Several generations ago, couples had many children, but the birth rate has declined in the late 20th century, in part due to the high cost of living. Since many older children are unable to afford their own homes, they often live with their parents until they are married.

Beginning in the 1960s, large waves of migrants from northeast Brazil, a largely impoverished region, began making their way to the wealthier south states, where they established squatter communities on forest land and in the outskirts of cities. This internal migration trend, which continued into the early 21st century, altered the family dynamics for the poorest

class of Brazilians, since it disrupted traditional extended family ties by scattering family members far from home.

Housing

In Brazil, housing in the countryside differs dramatically from housing in cities. In rural areas, people make an effort to show individualism, trying to make their house unique from others. These houses are usually small and simple and made from basic materials such cinderblock. Often, they are painted bright colors or decorated to give a distinctive look. In the city, however, most people live in apartments, where the home's interior is the only place to express individuality.

Security is an important factor in how people live, especially in cities where crime rates are higher, and urban housing reflects this reality. Most apartments have high fences, intercom systems, several locked doors leading to the inside of the building, and a doorman. Most middle-class and upscale apartments have 24–hour doormen. In lower-middle-class areas, people use barbed wire and broken glass embedded into walls around their homes to keep intruders out.

Another type of housing in Brazilian cities is found in favelas, or shantytowns. Despite the fact that these areas are quite poor, the houses are distinct. While some are precarious dwellings, made from nothing more than scraps of wood and sheets of tin, there are also small homes, built carefully from cinderblock and cement.

In Brasília, there are dense residential areas called superquadras. Each superquadra contains between eight and eleven blocks of residential units. Each superquadra was designed to be self-sufficient and contains its own schools, grocery stores, and other basic amenities.

Food

Contemporary Brazilian cuisine is a multicultural blend of international influences, most notably the Middle East, Africa, Japan, China and the U.S. Esfirra, which are meat pastries, are a popular Middle Eastern snack, while sushi is considered a food of the elite. Chinese cheese pastries are found in cafés countrywide, and typical fast food fare is widespread and popular. However, there are several typical traditional Brazilian dishes.

Feijoada, a stew of beans and meat eaten with rice, is the national dish of Brazil, As many as a dozen cuts of meat, such as bacon, sausage, tongue, and spare ribs, are simmered with black beans, spices, and vegetables. Today, Brazilians eat simple rice and beans several times a week, but feijoada is traditionally eaten on weekends, since it takes a lot of time to prepare. The dish was created in the 18th century by slaves in the southeast of Brazil, who were given the worst cuts of meat to live on. To make it tastier, the meat was simmered for many hours in a bean stew that became wildly popular with people of all social classes.

Acarajé is a traditional snack from the northeast of Brazil, the home of many people of African descent. In fact, acarajé is an African food that is still sold on the streets of Nigeria, a country in West Africa. Made with black bean paste, onions, dried shrimp, and chilli flakes, these fritter-like concoctions are fried in dende oil (palm oil), and served by women in traditional Bahian dress of long, flowing white dresses and white turbans.

Churrasco is a typical meal in southern Brazil, home of the gaúchos, or cowboys. Traditionally, different cuts of salted meat are slowly grilled on a spit over firewood. Once cooked, the meat is sliced into small pieces and eaten with rice or farofa (manioc flour). Churrascos (barbecues) are now a popular pastime not only in the south but all over the country, where families grill meat over the course of several hours and slice it into small pieces to share with family and friends. Other popular dishes are coxinhas (mock chicken legs), mugunza (a dessert made with hominy), and fish stew.

Life's Milestones

In Brazil, it is customary for young girls to have a coming-of-age party known as the festa de quince años, celebrated on their 15th birthday. This milestone is also known as quinceañera in other Latin countries. Traditionally, when a girl turns 15, her parents hold a celebration for family and friends. This celebration usually includes a large meal accompanied by alcoholic beverages and a cake. Depending on social class, this kind of party can range from a backyard barbecue to a catered event at an upscale hotel.

Weddings are another important cultural event in Brazil, which share many traditions with North America. These include the traditions of a white dress and cake, the bride and groom's first dance, and a honeymoon, called "lua de mel" in Portuguese. An interesting Brazilian wedding tradition is the cutting of the groom's tie. After slicing the tie, the pieces are often sold to the guests to raise money for the reception or the honeymoon.

CULTURAL HISTORY

The history of Brazilian culture is a fusion of Native American, African and European—particularly Portuguese—traditions and influence. Much of this unique culture has its roots in the country's colonial period (the 16th through the early 19th centuries). During this time, Brazil was heavily involved in the trans-Atlantic African slave trade. In addition, religion, namely Roman Catholicism, has also played a large role in shaping Brazilian culture.

Art

Though Brazil may be best known for its performing arts, it also has a rich history in the fine arts. Two of Brazil's most famous painters were Emiliano Di Cavalcanti (1897–1976) and Cândido Torquato Portinari (1903–1962). Though both were from the modernist movement, which was a cultural shift in Western society in the early 20th century, the painters used different approaches. Di Cavalcanti was known for his tropical landscapes and portraitures. Portinari created murals, and both artists concentrated on Brazilian history and themes. Another important painter from the modernist period was Tarsila do Amaral (1886–1973). A representative of early modernism and one of the few female Brazilian artists at the time, she focused on contemporary life in the cities and the countryside. In her work, she often distorted perspective and proportion to create human figures.

One of Brazil's most famous sculptors was Antônio Francisco Lisboa (1738–1814), also known as Aleijadinho (the Little Cripple). He lived during the colonial period and was a part of the Baroque movement, an artistic style that emphasized extravagance and curves. This style was principally used in churches and cathedrals in Brazil, and is featured prominently in their architecture. His most famous work was the Church of Bom Jesus de Matosinhos in Congonhas, where he carved 78 stone statues. Modernist Victor Brecheret (1894–1955) was another famous Brazilian sculptor. He was known for incorporating elements of indigenous folk art and mythology into his work. Many of his famous sculptures are located in his home town of São Paulo.

Music & Dance

Music and dance are integral parts of Brazilian culture. The dance form called capoeira developed between the late 16th century and the mid-19th century, during the peak of the African slave trade in Brazil. Scholars believe that capoeira was inspired by an Angolan dance called N'golo, which resembles a mixture of dance and martial arts. This dance was adapted by African slaves in Brazil, who used it as a form of resistance against slave owners. It is believed that the dance and choreography elements also helped to conceal slaves who were training for physical combat. Modern day capoeira performances commonly feature a circle of dancers, instrumentalists, and singers. Although it is distinctly Brazilian, the dance form is popular all over the world.

Samba is a deeply popular Brazilian dance that emerged with the development of samba music. The genre developed in the early 20th century among the black immigrant working class in the Brazilian city of Rio de Janeiro. Freed slaves flocked to the city from other parts of the country, bringing with them musical traditions from various African nations. Samba was born from these traditions and through the blending of numerous vocal styles and various types of percussion and guitar playing. Traditional samba instruments include the cavaco, a small four-stringed guitar; the caixa, a snare-style drum; and the repinique, a two-headed drum. It became popular worldwide in the 1940s, when it was exported to Europe and to the United States by artists such as Brazilian songwriter Ary Barroso (1903–1964) and singer Carmen Miranda (1909–1955). There are now numerous variants of both samba music and dance.

Today, samba is best known as a central part of the world-famous Brazilian Carnival celebration, the most famous of which is the Rio Carnival in Rio de Janeiro. Carnival is has origins in the customs of medieval Europe, but the Brazilian festival is largely a fusion of Portuguese, African, and indigenous traditions. The first festivals in Rio de Janeiro date back to the early 18th century.

The nationwide festival is also largely associated with Roman Catholicism because it is celebrated before the Catholic holiday of Lent, a 40-day fasting period leading up to Easter. Song, dance and costumes are the centerpiece of the Carnival tradition, though the festival varies by city and region. During the Rio Carnival, for example, 12 samba schools compete with other schools to determine which one is the best. Each school includes a large group of percussionists, singers and dancers, with a special theme, song and float, all accompanied by elaborate costumes.

Literature

Brazilian literature has its roots in the early colonial period, when missionaries and poets penned epic poems and lyrics about this new world and its indigenous peoples. Since that time, Brazilian literature has been largely influenced by European literary movements such as the Romantic Movement, a largely philosophical movement that flourished between the 18th and 20th centuries. It has also been shaped by social themes, such as the plight of its inhabitants and the country's move toward independence in 1822.

Some of Brazil's most famous writers include Joaquim Maria Machado de Assis (1839–1908), José Américo de Almeida (1887–1980), Jorge Amado (1912–2001), Garciliano Ramos (1892–1953), and Paulo Coelho (1947–). Machado de Assis, a prolific writer who never left Brazil, wrote modern novels, novellas, short stories, plays, essays, reviews, newspaper articles, and poetry. His most famous work is the novel *Memórias Póstumas de Brás Cubas* ("Epitaph of a Small Winner"), a story narrated by a dead man who recalls an unheroic life. Américo de Almeida was both a politician and a novelist. His works, of which 1928's *A Bagaceira* ("Trash") is the most famous, deal with the socioeconomic conditions of northeastern Brazil. The social content found in the works of subsequent Brazilian novelists is largely attributed to the influence of Américo de Almeida.

Jorge Amado also touched on politics until he settled on writing as a full-time career. Exiled twice for his political views, Amado returned to his homeland to write his greatest works, including *Dona Flor e Seus Dois Maridos* ("Dona Flor and Her Two Husbands") and *Gabriela, Cravo e Canela* ("Gabriela, Clove and Cinnamon"). Both novels take place in the northern state of Bahia, Amado's home, and include a large number of characters that all tie into the amorous misadventures of the female protagonists. Other famous Brazilian writers include Manuel Antônio de Almeida (1831–1861), largely credited with writing Brazil's first great novel, *Memórias de um sargento de milícias* ("Memoirs of a Militia Sergeant"). Prominent poets include Antônio Gonçalves Dias (1823–1864), largely perceived as Brazil's national poet (his lyrics are featured in the Brazilian National Anthem), and Mário de Andrade (1893–1945), associated with Brazil's modernist movement.

Film

Though Brazilian cinema had gradually been progressing since the turn of the 20th century, it first emerged in the 1950s with the advent of Cinema Novo, a film movement that largely focused on neorealism, or true life, and notably on themes of poverty. Some of the leading directors to emerge from this period include Nelson Pereira dos Santos (1928-) and Anselmo Duarte (1920–2009). Pereira dos Santos, who often filmed on low budgets using ordinary people as actors, is known as one of Latin America's most influential filmmakers. Duarte was one of the first internationally recognized Brazilian directors after his film *O Pagador de Promessas* ("The Prayer of Promises") won the highest prize at the Cannes Film Festival in 1962, the only Brazilian film to do so.

Brazilian films continued to receive widespread international acclaim outside of cinematic circles in the late 20th century. The first two movies on this scale were *Pixote* (1981) and *Kiss of the Spider Woman* (1983) by director Héctor Babenco (1946-). *Pixote* was about a homeless boy's struggles on the streets of São Paulo. In fact, the actor who portrayed the boy was a child from the streets who was killed by police just seven years after making the film. *Kiss of the Spider Woman* was filmed in São Paulo, but based on the novel by Argentinean writer Manuel Puig (1932–1990). The success of contemporary Brazilian cinema would continue into the early 21st century. However, national attendance began to decline in the 1980s and many theaters were closed.

CULTURE

Arts & Entertainment

While the fine arts and Brazilian literature and cinema continue to receive international acclaim in the early 21st century, the cornerstones of contemporary Brazilian popular culture are largely football (soccer), music, and the celebration of Brazilian Carnival.

Known as fútebol, or football, the national sport of Brazil is so deeply ingrained in popular culture that it extends to all parts of life, including religion, politics, and economics. Brazilians often refer to football as "o jogo bonito" ("the beautiful game"), which indicates its important place in Brazilian society. It also implies that Brazilian football differs from European or Latin American football in the playing style because it is considered both elegant and nimble, a performance art unto itself. Brazilian football also has some unique elements. Many city teams have an in-house Catholic priest, and sometimes, in addition, an Umbanda priest, of the Afro-Brazilian spiritist religion.

Besides samba, Brazil has produced several other genres of music in recent years, including bossa nova, forró, sertanejo, funk, axé, and MPB, which is popular Brazilian music similar to American pop music. Brazilian music is associated with synergy and evolution, based on a mixture of African and European influences that spawn new types of music. For example, bossa nova was a product of samba that developed in the 1960s, a slower, more relaxed tempo that became famous world-wide with Tom Jobim's song, "A Garota de Ipanema" ("The Girl from Ipanema"). Forró and sertanejo are typical of the rural and northeastern parts of Brazil. This music is similar to American country music, and also uses accordion and country-style guitar sounds. MPB emerged in the 1960s as a fusion of bossa nova, folk music, rock, and samba. Axé is a mix between samba, reggae, and African-style percussion that developed in the state of Bahia. This style of music is also at the core of another of Brazil's cultural foundations: Carnival.

While each Brazilian city or area has different Carnival traditions, the two most famous Brazilian Carnival celebrations take place in Salvador, in the state of Bahia, and the city of Rio de Janeiro. In Salvador, bands known as "trios elétricos" move through the jam-packed streets on trucks, playing axé and other music from the northeast. Famous singers and bands like Ivete Sangalo and Olodum lead revelers through the city for several nights before the Catholic season of Lent. Salvador's Carnival has stronger African influences, due to the high number of Afro-Brazilians in the region.

The Rio Carnival also involves music in the streets. Bands called blocos, similar to trio elétricos, parade in small sections of the city. The main event takes place in the Sambodrome, an avenue lined with bleachers in the downtown area. There, groups known as escolas de samba, or samba schools, participate in a competition that began in the 1930s. They compete by parading with several thousand members dressed in elaborate costumes on ornate floats playing samba songs written by the school's composers. At the end of the two-night event, judges use criteria based on the music, organization, costumes, and performance to declare a winner.

Contemporary Brazilian cinema continues to receive international recognition. The film *Central do Brasil* ("Central Station"), the story of a middle-aged woman from Rio de Janeiro who befriends an orphaned boy, was nominated for two Academy Awards in 1999. The 2002 film *Cidade de Deus* ("City of God"), a crime drama about growing up in a Rio de Janeiro favela, was nominated for four Oscars. The film *Carandiru* (2003) was lesser known but won international acclaim for telling the true story of a 1992 São Paulo prison riot. In 2010 and 2015, Brazilian films were nominated for Oscars in the best documentary feature category.

The film *Tropa de Elite* (2007), however, is considered one of the definitive Brazilian films of the new millennium. Based on a non-fiction novel about BOPE, a specialized police force, the film depicts the present-day war between drug traffickers and BOPE teams in Rio's slums. It inspired a great deal of controversy in Brazil, where the film's heartless and troubled protagonist was seen by some as a hero. In fact, the film's director was sued by police who wanted him to reveal his sources for the film.

Cultural Sites & Landmarks

The Christ Redeemer Statue in Rio de Janeiro is one of Brazil's most important cultural landmarks. It was voted one of the Seven Modern Wonders of the World in 2007. Located on Corcovado Mountain, the statue weighs 1,145 tons and stands 38 meters (124 feet) tall. The statue's construction was completed in 1931. The mountain top offers a 360-degree view of the city and has a chapel often used for weddings and baptisms.

Another Brazilian cultural landmark in Rio de Janeiro is Estádio do Maracanã (Maracanã Stadium). Built in 1950, this football mecca encompasses 304,000 square meters (3,272,228 square feet), and accommodates nearly 200,000 people, making it one of the largest stadiums in the world. The stadium hosted the World Cup in 1950, and is used today for national tournaments as well as concerts and special events. Pope John Paul II helped celebrate the 30th anniversary of the stadium's construction on January 26, 1981.

Apart from Rio de Janeiro (also known as "Rio"), another striking example of Brazilian architecture may be the country's capital city, Brasília. Brasília was originally planned as a city of 500,000. It was built between 1956 and 1960, in the shape of an airplane or a bird in flight. Brasília's features and layout are striking reminders of the influence of European art and architecture on South American culture.

Three Powers Square, located at Brasília's city center, is the seat of the Brazilian government. Three Powers Square is decorated with artwork from some of Brazil's most famous sculptors, and the buildings there were designed to enhance the city's skyline. In addition to Brasília, Brazilian cities offer many other fine examples of modern architecture, including the Museum of Modern Art in Sao Paulo and the Church of Pampuhla in Belo Horizonte.

Brazil is home to 19 World Heritage Sites, which are designated sites maintained by the United Nations Educational, Scientific and Cultural Organization (UNESCO). The historic town of Ouro Preto is designated as a World Heritage Site. Brasília, the capital of Brazil, and five other historic town centers in Brazil are also protected by UNESCO. They include the historic centers of São Luís, located on the island of São Luís, and Diamantina, in Minas Gerais.

Ouro Preto was founded in the 17th century and was the center of the Brazilian gold rush, becoming a prosperous and thriving metropolis. While the gold mines have since been emptied,

the Baroque churches and colonial architecture remain as a testament to Brazil's colonial history and past.

Nature is a powerful Brazilian landmark. Ouro Preto is also home to Iguaçu National Park, which is popular for its wildlife reserve and numerous waterfalls. The region is home to several endangered species, including the giant anteater and the glaucus mackaw bird. The park, which borders Argentina, features a 2,700-meter (8,858-foot) high waterfall, one of the highest in the world.

Since Brazilian territory constitutes roughly 60 percent of the Amazon rainforest, another important environmental area includes the Central Amazon Conservation Complex. This conservation area encompasses over six million hectares (nearly 15 million acres). As one of the largest protected areas in the Amazon, it is also one of the most biologically diverse regions in the world. UNESCO named it a World Heritage Site in 2000 to protect several endangered species, including the Amazonian manatee and the giant arapaima fish. The complex also includes the world's largest variety of electric fish. The conservation complex was extended from Jaú National Park, the largest forest reserve in South America, in 2003.

The Pantanal is another important wildlife area in Brazil. Located in the southwest, this UNESCO site protects nearly 188,000 hectares (464,000 acres), and includes one of the largest freshwater wetland areas on Earth. Since the Pantanal includes the headwaters of the two major rivers in the area, the Cuiabá and the Paraguay, fish stocks and water nutrients are systematically safeguarded.

Libraries & Museums
At 218 meters (715 feet), the Television Tower is Brasília's tallest building, and offers a panoramic view of the city from a viewing platform located 75 meters (264 feet) from the ground. The tower was designed by architect Lúcio Costa and constructed in 1967. The Television Tower also contains Brasília's famous Gem Museum, which boasts a collection of thousands of indigenous

gemstones. Brazil's National Museum, established in 1818, contains over 20 million items and artifacts. It is considered the largest museum of natural history and anthropology in Latin America. Other unique institutions include the Coffee Museum in the port city of Santos, Sao Paulo, the International Museum of Naïve Art of Brazil (MIAN), and the Afro-Brazil Museum (Museu Afro Brasil).

Brazil's national repository is the Biblioteca Nacional (National Library of Brazil). As of 2015, the institution housed over nine million items, including a UNESCO recognized collection of Brazilian photography.

Holidays

Brazilian holidays include Independence Day (September 7), Carnaval (February or March), Tiradentes (April 1), Proclamation of the Republic Day (November 15), and Christmas Day (December 25).

Youth Culture

Teenagers represent slightly more than ten percent of the total population in Brazil in 2007. Often, Western trends and fashions are popular, and popular youth culture activities include video games, sports, and shopping at the mall, all typical of most Western societies. Brazilian youth are also on par technologically with their Western counterparts, and instant messaging and Internet use is high.

Musically, Brazilian teens are largely fond of American pop, rock, and hip-hop, but most also listen to Brazilian music. Funk is a type of music that emerged from the favelas of Rio de Janeiro beginning in the 1970s that sounds like a mix of American hip-hop and electronic music. Funk parties, in which large dances are held on weekends, are very popular. Though held almost always in favelas, they draw a cross-section of young people from all walks of life.

Most high school students in Brazil attend school for only half the day, either in the morning or the afternoon. As a result, teenagers have more free time in the day for homework and leisure activities. Middle and upper class Brazilians usually use this time for activities like dance lessons, English courses and soccer leagues. Though many poor teens may not always have these same opportunities, many non-profit organizations in major cities have begun to provide similar activities for them.

Football (soccer) remains an important part of youth culture in Brazil. The sport was introduced to Brazil in the 1890s from the United Kingdom, and soon became popular throughout the country. Its appeal is universal, and people of all social classes play the sport in every area, from professional games with uniforms to a pick-up game in the slums. Competition between local and state teams is fierce, and fan support means not only wearing your team's jersey, but also hanging the team flag outside your house, joining the team's fan organization, and watching every game. For example, the Corinthians team fan group from São Paulo, once had 30,000 members.

SOCIETY

Transportation

In major cities, including São Paulo, Rio de Janeiro, Belo Horizonte, Brasília, Recife, and Porto Alegre, subway systems are in operation and extensive bus routes are available. Some cities also have metropolitan area above-ground train systems. Taxis are commonly available in all metropolitan areas. There is also a large network of interstate buses that allow for comfortable travel throughout the country.

Though automobiles are widely used, people of lesser means have to rely on other methods of transportation. Besides the metro and buses, people also use vans and kombis, which are white vans that carry multiple passengers in the same manner as a bus. However, these vans are usually run by an authorized company, while kombis are typically not. In favelas, people also use mototaxis, which are motorcycles that bring one or two people to their destination.

In the countryside and more rural areas, there are some buses, as well as flatbed trucks that run in a similar system to the kombis.

Brazilians drive on the right side of the road and all Brazilian states have seat belt requirement laws. Driving with flip flops is not permitted, and the use of cellular phones is limited to only "hands free" systems. According to the United States Department of State, intercity roads are considered very dangerous, and conditions in rural areas are also considered hazardous.

Transportation Infrastructure

Public transportation is highly developed in Brazilian cities, with more basic types of transport in the countryside. In addition, there are 50,000 kilometers (31,000 miles) of accessible inland waterways in Brazil, and many people in rural areas along the Amazon River and Basin use boats and ferries for transportation. Overall, Brazil's infrastructure is perceived as deficient and, at times, controversial—infrastructure improvements in the country's Amazon region have raised concerns about deforestation, for example. In preparation for the 2014 FIFA World Cup and the 2016 Olympics, Brazil planned major infrastructure improvements. This included projects such as a high-speed train connecting Sao Paulo and Rio de Janeiro. Ports also continue to be a primary focus of infrastructure improvement.

Major Brazilian airports include Guarulhos International Airport in Sao Paulo or Galeao International Airport in Rio de Janeiro, both of which handle most international flights. As of 2014, there were an estimated 4,000 airports or terminals.

Media & Communications

Television is the popular mode of media and communications in Brazil. Typically, TVs are everywhere, included in bars, restaurants, clubs and stores, sometimes even attached to the top of a mobile vendor stand. As such, most Brazilians receive their news from TV. Most viewers watch Globo, the largest TV network in Brazil and the fourth largest in the world. Other than the news, the most popular programs are telenovelas, which are soap operas that air Monday through Saturday during primetime. The viewership of

these programs includes both men and women alike. People also watch foreign movies dubbed in Portuguese, as well as sporting events, especially soccer.

Newspapers are another source of information, though most are regional, such as *Folha de São Paulo* and *O Jornal do Brasil*. Most newspapers are available online as well. Since the beginning of the 21st century, the Internet has become a fast-growing source of information and entertainment. In 2009, there were approximately 40 million personal computers and 75 million Internet users in Brazil. According to a 2010 study, Brazil has the highest participation rate on Twitter than any other country.

SOCIAL DEVELOPMENT

Standard of Living

In 2009, Brazil had a Human Development Index (HDI) value of just under 75, ranking it 79th out of 187 countries.

Water Consumption

According to a monitoring program by the World Health Organization and UNICEF, access to an improved water supply was at 97 percent in the early 21st century. Sanitation and water supply was low in predominantly rural areas. The National Water Agency (ANA) was created in 2000 to oversee water resources management.

Education

Education for Brazilians is compulsory between the ages of seven and 14. Public education is free. Approximately one-quarter of state and local tax revenue is given over to education throughout Brazil.

In recent decades, there has been much improvement compared with earlier periods when the education system was in need of major reform. As a result, the adult literacy rate rose from 81 percent in 1990 to 90 percent in 2010, primary school enrollment rates increased, and children tended to stay enrolled in school longer. In such population centers as Brasília, the literacy rate is much higher (93 percent) than in rural communities.

Important universities in Brazil include the Universidade de Sao Paulo, the Universidade de Federal de Minas Gerais, and the Universidade Federal de Rio de Janeiro.

According to 2010 estimates, Brazil's literacy rate was 90.4 percent.

Women's Rights

Though Brazilian women gained the right to vote in 1932, earlier than women in other Latin American countries, women's rights and professional options have been limited for decades. Brazilian society has always been one marked by machismo, a Latin American belief system in which women are expected to be submissive, and wives and daughters are expected to be obedient to husbands and fathers. Though upper class women sometimes managed to have careers in traditionally female occupations such as teaching and nursing, it wasn't until the 1970s that women began entering the workforce. Women of other social classes, particularly the poorest women, were relegated to unlivable wages and difficult living conditions. As such, domestic violence and single parenthood have become realities for many poor Brazilian women in the 21st century.

During the 1970s, women also began to protest against the military dictatorship, which ruled Brazil from 1964 to 1985. They began to demand better working conditions, especially for lower class women working long hours for very little pay. It was during this decade that women began to organize politically and to get involved in the feminist movement, which called for reproductive rights such as accessible contraception and legal abortion (abortion is still illegal under most circumstances). Women also faced the problem of political under-representation, since traditionally very few women entered politics.

Domestic violence is a significant problem, due to societal attitudes. Traditionally, violence against women wasn't considered a crime if the husband was "defending his honor," even in cases of murder. For example, a husband could kill his wife if he believed she had been unfaithful.

Though women have made this problem a political issue, it wasn't until 2006 that the legislature passed a law, known as the Maria da Penha law, specifically spelling out punishment for abusive husbands and outlining preventive measures for domestic violence. The law changed the Penal Code so that abusers would receive significant prison time and victims would receive certain legal rights. These rights included a six month leave of absence from work to recuperate and ensure the protection of children.

In the early 21st century, women have made strides in terms of economic representation and presence in the workforce. In 2011, for example, 42.7 percent of the workforce was female. More than 55 percent of women had jobs in 2010, an increase of 14 percent since 2001. Women's salaries increased faster than men's during the first decade of the 21st century. On average, women still make less than men. The average salary for a woman in 2010 was 56 percent lower than the average man's salary. Women in industrial jobs tend to earn considerably less than their male counterparts, while women in service jobs earn just slightly less than men.

Health Care

The Brazilian health care system serves as a model to many developing nations: Brazilians have a constitutional right to universal access to medical care. All Brazilians are guaranteed free coverage at either public or private medical facilities, and most private facilities are subsidized by the government. Between eight and nine percent of the government's budget is allocated to pay for these services. Most Brazilians take advantage of this unique health care system.

GOVERNMENT

Structure

The Federative Republic of Brazil is a federal republic. There are 26 states and one federal district, which is the capital city of Brasília in the state of Goias. The last major constitutional change was in 1988, when the Brazilian constitution was rewritten to include, among other important matters, provisions for the protection of wildlife and indigenous peoples.

The Brazilian government is comprised of executive, legislative, and judicial branches. The head of state, as well as the head of the government, is the president. The president appoints his/her own cabinet officers. Presidents and vice presidents are elected by popular vote to four-year terms. In 2014, Dilma Rousseff was elected to her second term as president.

The National Congress of Brazil is bicameral. The two legislative houses are the Federal Senate and the Chamber of Deputies. Members of these houses are elected by popular vote for eight-year and four-year terms, respectively. The judicial branch is comprised of three tribunals: the Supreme Federal Tribunal, the Higher Tribunal of Justice, and Regional Federal Tribunals.

Political Parties

Brazil has a multi-party system and is ruled by a coalition government. Among the many political parties operating in Brazil are the Brazilian Democratic Movement Party, the Workers' Party, and the Brazilian Labor Party. Party loyalty has been a concern, and in 2007, the Brazilian Supreme Court barred Congress members from party hopping. As of 2015, 28 parties are represented in the Brazilian Congress.

Local Government

Brazil has one federal district and 26 states, each ruled by a governor who must earn more than 50 percent of the vote. The states are further divided into municipalities, of which there are more than 5,500. Both state and local governments maintain a separation between the legislative and executive branches; municipalities have no judicial power.

Judicial System

The judicial system in Brazil, as framed by the Brazilian Constitution, is separated into federal and state branches, and is based on Roman codes. The main courts include the Federal Supreme Court, which oversees the constitution, and the

Superior Court of Justice, which upholds treaties and federal law. There are also five Regional Federal Courts. Courts and judges operate at the state level and are defined by that state's constitution, while municipalities have no judicial power.

Taxation

Brazil's taxation system allows for personal income to be taxed up to a maximum of 27.5 percent. In 2009, the corporate tax rate was 34 percent, which included a 15 percent basic tax. The federal, state, and municipal governments all have taxing powers. The federal tax administration agency is the Brazilian Revenue Service (RFB).

Armed Forces

The armed forces of Brazil are considered the largest in Central and South America. They include the Brazilian Army, the Brazilian Air Force, and the Brazilian Navy, and all operate under the Ministry of Defense. As the largest military presence in the rather peaceful region of South America, the armed forces have focuses more on civic duties and foreign relief operations, including the commitment of over 1,500 troops to the UN Mission for the Stabilization of Haiti following the devastating earthquake in January 2010. Brazil had assumed the command of the UN mission in Haiti in 2004.

Foreign Policy

Brazil is perceived as an emerging world power. With one of the largest populations in the world and the 10th largest economy, it wields considerable influence in both Latin America and abroad. One of Brazil's key foreign policies heading into the 21st century has been to strengthen its relationship to its neighboring South American countries. Brazil has also worked to maintain a strong presence in diplomatic relations between Latin America and the U.S. The U.S. considers Brazil a stabilizing force in the region due to is strong open economy and democratic government. Brazil's foreign relations, particularly its trade policy, are headed by the Ministry of

External Relations, which is often referred to as Itamaraty, since the ministry is headquartered in the Itamaraty Palace.

First and foremost, Brazil is considered a leader in Latin America, both politically and economically, and is known for having a history of diplomacy in the region. President Luiz "Lula" Inácio da Silva took office in 2002, and was the leader most involved in exercising modern Brazilian-style diplomacy in Latin America. He was a key participant in resolving political crises in Venezuela, Bolivia, and Ecuador, and worked closely with Colombian President Álvaro Uribe to combat drug trafficking. For example, President Lula hosted and participated in the mediation between Colombia and Ecuador in March 2008, when the two countries broke diplomatic relations over border incursions by Colombian troops. President Dilma Vana Rousseff, his successor, is from the same political party, the Worker's Party. She has continued good relations with the United States, except for the 2013 incident when she was confronted with allegations of U.S. spying on Brazilians.

Brazil has maintained friendly relations with the U.S., despite its opposition to the 2003 U.S.-led war in Iraq. Brazil has chosen an approach in which it has cooperated on certain issues instead of definitively allying itself with the U.S. For example, the two countries have worked together on matters of anti-terrorism and environmentalism, such as global warming. In 2007, Brazil and the U.S. reached an agreement to promote the international use and production of ethanol. In addition, the US is also an important trading partner; in 2012, 11 percent of all Brazilian exports were sent to the U.S., while almost 15 percent of Brazilian imports came from the U.S..

Outside of the U.S., Brazil has strengthened its economic relations with countries such as Russia and China. In fact, Brazil is the "B" in the acronym BRIC, a group of four developing countries—Brazil, Russia, India, and China—with the most economic potential. The four countries held a summit meeting in 2008 to strengthen their relations, although this joint effort faltered within a few years. The EU accounts for nearly 30 percent

of Brazil's international trade, and the country has become an important trading partner with the Netherlands and China, as well as the Pacific Rim.

Brazil continues to maintain a strong presence in important international organizations, including the International Monetary Fund (IMF) and the World Bank. Brazil is a founding member of the United Nations (UN) and the Union of South American Nations (USAN), a Latin American equivalent to the European Union (EU). Brazil is also a member of Mercosur, a regional trade agreement (RTA) among Argentina, Brazil, Paraguay and Uruguay. In addition, Brazil is responsible for a large amount of funding for Banco do Sul, or Bank of the South, a lending organization with the purpose of improving infrastructure and social initiatives in South American countries. Brazil also is involved in foreign aid and development work abroad, including providing monetary support for several African and Latin American countries, as well as leading UN peacekeeping troops in Haiti.

Brazil has also been a party to international legal disputes in the early 21st century. Recently, the country submitted a claim to extend its maritime territory, particularly the Brazilian Continental Shelf, to have the exclusive right to explore and use any resources found within. Brazil also maintains informal claims in Antarctica that overlap other territorial claims.

Dependencies

The Atlantic islands of Fernando de Noronha and Atol das Rocas Reserves are Brazilian. Located off the coast of Brazil, they were both inscribed as World Heritage Sites in 2001 for their wildlife importance and seascapes. Brazil also administers the volcanic Trindade and Martim Vaz archipelago and the St. Peter and St. Paul Rocks, a small cluster of rocky islets.

All of the islands are located in the South Atlantic Ocean, and only Fernando de Noronha is inhabited.

Human Rights Profile

International human rights law insists that states respect civil and political rights, and also promote an individual's economic, social, and cultural rights. The United Nations Universal Declaration on Human Rights (UDHR) is recognized as the standard for international human rights. Its authors sought the counsel of the world's great thinkers, philosophers, and religious leaders, and were careful to create a document that reflects the core values shared by every world culture. (To read this document or view the articles relating to cultural human rights, visit: www.udhr.org/UDHR/default.htm.)

Brazil struggles with human rights violations in several areas, namely public security, the judicial system, and land access. Many cities face serious problems with security and overcrowding, a violation of Article 3, the right to security of person, and Article 25, the right to an adequate standard of living. Underpaid and ill-prepared police have led to high levels of corruption in many urban police forces, as well as torture and excessive use of force with suspects and victims. High levels of crime in cities have caused armed conflict between police and drug traffickers, leading to many homicides and gun-related deaths in the poorest communities. For example, police killed at least 1,270 people in Rio de Janeiro alone in 2007. Nationally the number has been over 2,000 people killed annually by the police for the past decade. Shantytowns, or informal settlements or slums, on the outskirts of major cities have exacerbated these problems.

Paramilitary militias have also become a problem, in which retired or off-duty police officers have taken control of shantytowns by extorting residents. These groups have also been accused of high levels of violence in the poorest parts of cities. The judicial system has failed to fully address and condemn human rights violations. In violation of Articles 7 and 8, which both deal with equal protection under law, police killings are rarely fully investigated. In addition, investigations do not often led to the full prosecution of human rights violators. For example, an officer accused of orchestrating the murder of 111 prisoners in a São Paulo prison riot in 1992 was absolved in 2006. No other suspects were ever brought to trial.

In addition, Brazil's prison system has come under attack for violating certain articles, namely Article 25, due to overcrowding, and Article 5, which deals with inhuman treatment and punishment. In fact, overcrowding, abuse by guards and police, and poor sanitary conditions have become the norm for many prisons. Furthermore, women have suffered in the penitentiary system, including rape, torture, and being forced to share cells with men.

Another human rights issue in rural Brazil is the killing of land activists, violating Articles 5, 6, 7 and 13. The poorest part of Brazil, the northeast, has seen homeless and landless people fighting for their rights, struggling with attacks and evictions, while the government has done little to help. In 2006, 4,000 families in the state of Pará were forcibly evicted from their land, while 25 land activists were killed in the same state in the same year. In addition, people from the landless workers movement, the MST, have continually been the target for police in rural areas.

ECONOMY

Overview of the Economy

With a diversified economy that produces agricultural products, such as soy, wheat, and beef, and manufactured products, such as aircraft, automobiles, and ethanol, Brazil had a gross domestic product (GDP) of $2.41 trillion (USD) in 2013. An economic power among Latin American nations, Brazil is the third largest manufacturer of petroleum in South America (after Mexico and Venezuela), and the largest manufacturer of petrochemicals in the region.

Economic expansion has been a focal point for the Brazilian government in the early 21st century, but these efforts were hampered by the 2008-09 global financial crisis. Brazil has responded to the crisis nationally by granting tax cuts to manufacturers and reducing interest rates from the Central Bank. Brazil remains the major recipient of foreign direct investment in the region.

Industry

Brazil also has a growing manufacturing and industrial sector that accounts for nearly one-third of the country's GDP. The major industries include textiles, tourism, chemicals, lumber, tin, steel, motor vehicles, and industrial machinery. A number of international automobile manufacturers have established plants in Brazil and the country also specializes in manufacturing aircrafts for international customers.

Brazil's main exports are transport equipment, shoes, soybeans, iron ore, coffee, and automobiles. Brazil is also one of the world's leading gem producers. As of 2013, the industrial sector accounted for 26.4 percent of the GDP.

Labor

The unemployment rate of Brazil is 5.7 percent (as of 2013). Brazil's labor force is vast and accounts for the success of many of its industries during rough economic periods. The largest sectors for employment are services, agriculture, and industry.

Energy/Power/Natural Resources

Brazil has many natural resources; among the most important resources are bauxite, gold, iron ore, copper, timber, rubber, Brazil nuts, palm oil, limestone, sea salt, and tin.

Other areas of concern are the air and water pollution in such cities as Rio de Janeiro and São Paulo, illegal trade in wildlife, and wetlands degradation.

Fishing

Brazil is not a major exporter of fish or seafood. Freshwater fish account for about one-fourth of the country's total catch. In 2010, it was estimated that Brazil produced about 1.26 million tons of fish per year. In February of 2009, the Brazilian government announced its intentions of self-sufficiency in the production of seafood, and to make Brazil a more prominent exporter of fish. In February 2010, Brazil committed $17 million to enhance the protection of the country's fishing zones.

Forestry

Of major concern to environmental activists around the world is the continuing deforestation of the Amazon rainforest: this practice is quite destructive to animals and plant species, and may even have a detrimental effect on the planet's atmosphere.

Mining/Metals

Brazil is one of the largest global producers of iron ore, bauxite, nickel, and zinc, among other metals. Recently, Brazil has sought to diversify its mining industry and to seek foreign investment. The mining industry remains robust with a 2013 update to the mining laws, which removed the uncertainty which mining companies had faced.

Agriculture

Brazil's agricultural industries account for nearly one-third of its export revenues. Brazil's most important crops include coffee, soybeans, wheat, rice, corn, sugar cane, cocoa, oranges, and bananas.

Animal Husbandry

Beef is the major livestock industry in Brazil, followed by pigs, poultry, sheep, and goats. In fact, since 2005, Brazil is considered the leading exporter of meat, and held 20 percent of the world's beef production in 2012. Poultry and beef make up the majority of foreign sales for the Brazilian livestock and meat industry. Since 2007, there has also been considerable consolidation in the industry, including some 30 takeovers.

Tourism

Thanks to the vast holiday offerings in Brazil, including ecotourism in the Amazon Basin and festivals such as Carnaval in Rio de Janeiro, its tourism industry is quite large. In 2003, a ministry of tourism was created, and that same year over four million people visited Brazil. In 2012, tourism generated $6.9 billion USD and created 1.87 million jobs. With the World Cup in 2014, Brazil expected that number to increase by 50 percent. More than 5.6 million tourists are forecasted in 2012.

The most popular destinations in Brazil include the beach resorts in large coastal cities such as Rio de Janeiro and São Paulo, and in the state of Ceara; the Tocantins region, which bridges the Amazon Basin to other regions in Brazil, such as the Pantanal; the Amazon itself; the Festival Folcorico de Parintins; a wealth of sites that offer a glimpse into Brazilian history, such as the city of Ouro Preto, center of the Revolution of Minas Gerais; and the various other regions in Brazil which offer cultures and landscapes unique unto themselves.

Rachel Glickhouse, Craig Belanger,
Micah L. Issitt

DO YOU KNOW?

- Brazil was the center of the Portuguese kingdom in the early 19th century, when the Portuguese royal family under King John VI fled to Rio de Janeiro during the Napoleonic Wars.

- Nearly all of the navel oranges grown in the United States are descended from two trees brought to California from Brazil in 1875. One of them is still planted in Riverside, California.

- Brasília is the largest urban city to be named as a World Heritage Site by UNESCO and is also the only heritage city built in the 20th century. UNESCO not only honored Brasília for its urban structure but also for its attention to green space as a requisite for comfortable living.

- Football (soccer) is the most popular sport in Brazil. The Brazilian international team has won the World Cup five times. Brasília is home to two football teams, Sociedade Esportivo de Gama and Brasilienese Futbol Clube.

Bibliography

Eakin, Marshall C. *Brazil: The Once and Future Country.* New York: St. Martin's Press, 1997.

Bourner, Richard. *Lula of Brazil: The Story So Far.* Berkeley: University of California Press, 2008.

Crocitti, John J. and Robert M. Levine, *The Brazil Reader: History, Culture, Politics.* Durham: Duke University Press, 1999.

Fausto, Boris and Sergio Fausto. *A Concise History of Brazil.* 2nd ed. Cambridge: Cambridge University Press, 2014.

Hanchard, Michael. *Racial Politics in Contemporary Brazil.* Durham: Duke University Press, 1999.

Hemming, John. *Tree of Rivers: The Story of the Amazon.* New York: Thames & Hudson Inc, 2008.

Scheper-Hughes, Nancy. *Death Without Weeping: The Violence of Everyday life in Brazil.* Berkeley: University of California Press, 1992.

Skidmore, Thomas. *Brazil: Five Centuries of Change.* New York: Oxford University Press, 1999.

Rocha, Jan and Francis McDonagh. *Brazil: Inside Out: People, Politics and Culture.* Rugby, United Kingdom: Practical Action Publishing, 2014.

Rough Guides, Clemmy Manzo, Kiki Deere, Stephen Keeling, and Daniel Jacobs. *The Rough Guide to Brazil.* London: DK Publishing, Inc., 2014.

Underwood, David. *Oscar Niemeyer and the Architecture of Brazil.* New York: Rizolli, 1994.

Works Cited

Bellos, Alex. Futebol: The Brazilian Way of Life. London: Bloomsbury Publishing Inc, 2002.

"Biography." Official Site: Paulo Coelho. 2007. <http://www.paulocoelho.com.br/engl/bio.shtml>.

Bosio, Aline. "Participação de mulheres no mercado de trabalho apresenta ligeira queda." Reporter Diario. <http://www.reporterdiario.com.br/index.php?id=63175>.

Branco, Sandra. A Quick Guide to Customs and Etiquette. Portland: Kuperard, 2005.

Brasil. Rio de Paz. Rio de Paz. 22 May 2008. <http://www.riodepaz.org.br/artigos_pesquisas/relatorios/brasil/brasil1.pdf>.

"Brazil." Amnesty International. 2007. <http://www.amnesty.org/en/region/americas/south-america/brazil#report>.

"Brazil." CIA - The World Factbook. <https://www.cia.gov/library/publications/the-world-factbook/geos/br.html>.

"Brazil." *Nations of the World.* Amenia, NY: Grey House Publishing, 2015.

"Brazil, Russia, India, and China (BRIC)." Investopedia. 25 July 2008 <http://www.investopedia.com/terms/b/bric.asp>.

"Elite Squad: the movie that shook Brazil." The Telegraph 18 July 2008. Telegraph. 18 July 2008. <http://www.telegraph.co.uk/arts/main.jhtml?xml=/arts/2008/07/18/bfjose118.xml>.

Edwards, Todd L. Brazil: A Global Studies Handbook. Santa Barbara: ABC-CLIO Inc, 2008.

Ferrari, Bruno. "Brasil chega a 40 milhões de computadores." PLANTÃO INFO. 4 June 2007. <http://info.abril.com.br/aberto/infonews/062007/04062007-15.shl>.

"IGUAÇU NATIONAL PARK, BRAZIL." United Nations Monitoring Programme. 22 July 2002. 10 June 2008 <http://www.unep-wcmc.org/sites/wh/iguacu.html>.

"Instituto Brasileiro de Geografia e Estatistica: Cidades." IBGE. <http://www.ibge.gov.br/cidadesat/default.php>.

Jones, Caryn Gracey. Teens in Brazil. Minneapolis: Compass Point Books, 2007.

"LEI Nº 11.340." Presidência da República. 7 Aug. 2006. <http://www.planalto.gov.br/ccivil_03/_ato2004-2006/2006/lei/l11340.htm>.

"Maracana." Riotur. Riotur. <http://www.rio.rj.gov.br/riotur/pt/atracao/?CodAtr=1966>.

McGowan, Chris, and Ricardo Pessanha. The Brazilian Sound: Samba, Bossa Nova, and the Popular Music of Brazil. Philadelphia: Temple UP, 1998. <http://books.google.com/books?id=7MFD-EoTR7MC>.

Poelzl, Volker. Culture Shock Brazil: A Survival Guide to Customs and Etiquette. Tarrytown: Marshall Cavendish Corporation, 2006.

Ribando, Clare. CRS Report for Congress: Brazil-US Relations. Rep.No. Foreign Affairs, Trade & Trade Division, Wilson Center. Wilson Center. <http://www.wilsoncenter.org/news/docs/rl33456.pdf>.

Rohrig Assuncao, Matthias. Capoeira: the History of an Afro-Brazilian Martial Art. New York: Routledge, 2005. <http://books.google.com/books?id=SgbsnNRObuoC>.

Rohrig Assuncao, Matthias, and Mestre Cobra Mansa. "A Danca Da Zebra." Revista Da Historia Da Biblioteca Nacional Mar. 2008: 14-21.

"Seção: Banda larga e VOIP." Teleco. <http://www.teleco.com.br/internet.asp>.

Sheen, Barbara. Foods of Brazil. Farmington Hills: Kidhaven Press, 2007.

Stefano, Fabiane, Larissa Santana, and Marcelo Onaga "O retrato dos novos consumidores brasileiros." Exame 23 Apr. 2008: 20a-b30.

Taylor, Mark. "Brazil: Gestures." Gringoes. <http://www.gringoes.com/articles.asp?id_noticia=1008>.

Ventura, Alexandre. "Do Objetivo Religioso à Vocação Turística." O Dia. 10 June 2008 <http://odia.terra.com.br/especial/outros/cristo70/historia.htm>.

Vincent, Jon S. Culture and Customs of Brazil. Westport: Greenwood Press, 2003.

"UNESCO World Heritage Centre." 11 June 2008. UNESCO. <http://whc.unesco.org/en/list>.

http://www.brazilsf.org/brazil_culture_eng.htm

Wulff Castle in Viña del Mar, Chile/Stock Photo © roccomontoya

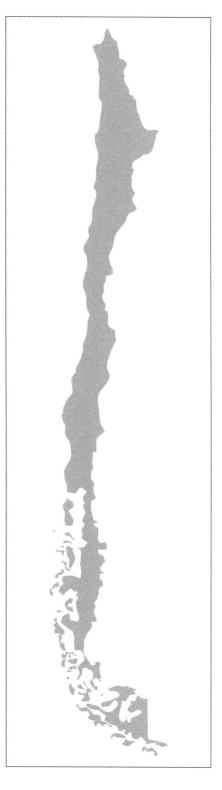

CHILE

Introduction

Chile is a long, narrow country located on the southwestern coast of South America. It is bordered by Argentina, Bolivia, and Peru. The country's climate varies from desert-like conditions in the north to cooler temperatures in the south. Chile is well known around the world for its exports of fruit, wine, and copper. Its government is a democratic republic that is led by a president whom is elected by the general public.

Chile underwent radical upheavals during the latter half of the 20th century; from having the first elected socialist government to enduring nearly two decades of political violence under the regime of General Augusto Pinochet. The neo-liberal economic policies that the Pinochet dictatorship put in place transformed the country, leading to widespread international investment, an expanded industrial base, and widespread consumerism.

While some economists praise the neo-liberal policies that continue to transform the country, others point out the numerous negative effects, including the high cost of living, the inability of the impoverished to make headway, and the prominent role of international corporations in the economy.

GENERAL INFORMATION

Official Language: Spanish
Population: 17,363,894 (2014 estimate)
Currency: Chilean peso

Coins: Coins are available in denominations of 1 and 5 pesos, which are rarely used, and 10, 50, 100, and 500 pesos.
Land Area: 743,812 square kilometers (287,187 square miles)
Water Area: 12,290 square kilometers (4,745 square miles)
National Motto: "Por la razon o la fuerza" (Spanish, "By reason or by force")
National Anthem: Himno Nacional de Chile (Chilean National Anthem)
Capital: Santiago
Time Zone: GMT -4
Flag Description: The flag of Chile features a horizontal band of red beneath a horizontal band of white. The left section of the white band includes a blue square and a five-pointed star. The red represents the blood that was shed during Chile's fight for independence. The white represents the snow covered Andes mountain range. The blue square is a representation of the Pacific Ocean and the sky. The national values of progress and honor are symbolized by the five-pointed star.

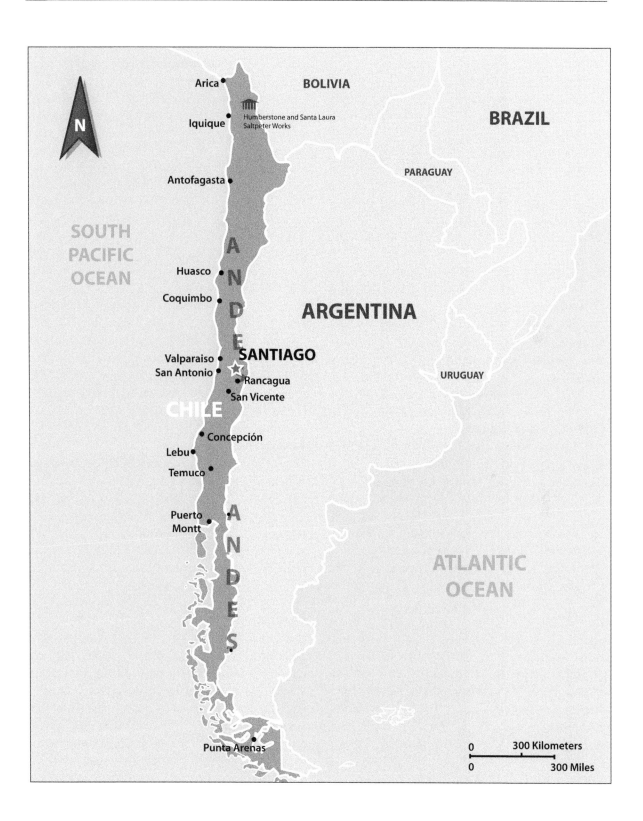

Principal Cities by Population (2014 Estimate):

- Santiago (4,837,295)
- Puente Alto (510,417)
- Antofagasta (309,832)
- Viña del Mar (294,551)
- Valparaíso (282,448)
- San Bernardo (249,858)
- Temuco (229,129)
- Concepción (215,413)
- Rancagua (212,695)

Population

The people of Chile are primarily white and white-Amerindian. There is a large mestizo (mixed) population due to Chile's long history of marriage between European settlers and the native population. Spaniards came to the country looking for gold in the 16th century and quickly saw the agricultural potential in central Chile. In the 19th century, many other Europeans settled in Chile including Germans, Italians, and Croatians.

Approximately 89 percent of Chileans live in the country's urban areas. In recent years this trend has been reinforced by population increases in the country's cities, which is likely to continue for economic and cultural reasons. The metropolitan area of Santiago, the capital, is home to 40 percent of the population. Other large cities include Viña del Mar, Valparaíso, and Concepcíon.

Languages

Spanish is the most common language in Chile, and is spoken by approximately 17 million people. Native populations often speak Spanish in addition to their traditional languages. Other languages spoken in Chile are Aymara, Huilliche, Mapudungun, Qawasqar, Quechua, Rapa Nui, and Yamana.

Native People & Ethnic Groups

Native groups in Chile controlled the land before the European colonists arrived. When the Spaniards first attempted to claim rule over

Chile in the 16th century, they were met with profound resistance, especially in the south among the Araucanian or Mapuche people. Their protest against Spanish rule persisted for 350 years. After the Indian wars of the 19th century, Mapuches moved into 2,000 reservations. Some of the reservations on which they were settled include Caitin, Meleco, Valdivia, Arauco, Bio Bio, and Llanquihue.

Today, about 1,369,500 Chileans are considered native peoples. They live mainly in the south, on Easter Island, and in the mountains in the north. The Mapuche are the most populous indigenous group in Chile, though they include several other native groups in their numbers. The Mapuche, whose name means "people of the land," live primarily in the southern Lake District. Temuco, a city in this region, is often considered the cultural capital of the Mapuche.

Other native groups in Chile are the Aymara in the north (population 35,000), the Papa Nui (3,000), the Atacamenos (4,000), and the Quechua, Colla, Alacalufe, and Yagan.

Religions

Christianity is the dominant religion in Chile. While an estimated 66 percent of Chileans are Catholic, approximately 17 percent are Protestant. Other religions in the country include Jehovah's Witness, Mormon, Jewish, Muslim, and Orthodox. Since the latter half of the 20th century, the number of Protestants has increased due to evangelical conversions.

Climate

Because of Chile's geographical extremes, the weather varies significantly throughout the country. Coastal Chile has very mild weather all year round, while Northern Chile is largely arid, but generally cool. Northern Chile receives very little rain; averages are often just above one centimeter (.5 inches). The average winter temperature in Northern Chile is a mild 17° Celsius (63° Fahrenheit), while summer temperatures average 28° Celsius (82° Fahrenheit).

Southern Chile has a significantly wetter climate; the area receives over 500 centimeters

(200 inches) of rain every year. Clouds hang low over head, and the average summer temperature is mild at 17° Celsius (63° Fahrenheit). Winters are a little colder in Southern Chile, with temperatures averaging 8.5° Celsius (47° Fahrenheit). A major characteristic of Southern Chile's climate is the number of hours the sun is visible during each season; in summer, which occurs in December, the sun shines for nearly 20 hours.

Central Chile has a Mediterranean climate, characterized by very warm, arid summers. Winters, though mild, bring the most precipitation, including snow, which occurs mostly in inland Chile. At the beginning of winter in central Chile, which begins in June, temperatures hover around 14° Celsius (58° Fahrenheit). Summers are generally warm; the temperature is usually around 29° Celsius (85° Fahrenheit). In the mountains, temperatures are generally cooler, though the snow cover for most of Chile's mountains is found at high altitudes.

ENVIRONMENT & GEOGRAPHY

Topography

The Pacific coast runs along the entire length of western Chile. On the east lie the Andes Mountains and the border with Argentina and Bolivia. The highest point in the country is Nevado Ojos del Salado at 6,880 meters (4,275 miles). The country borders Peru to the north.

The geographical extremes of the country (mountains, low valleys, and coastal regions) create varying climates. In the north is the Atacama Desert, one of the driest places in the world. In the central region, the rich, temperate valleys are highly favorable to farmers. The city on the southern tip, Punta Arenas, is the southernmost city in the world.

The Andes Mountains cover one-third of Chile. In the southern part of the country, there are many active volcanoes including Cerro Azul, Copahue, Llaima, Villarrica, and Cerro Hudson. The diverse landscape of Chile is also prey to earthquakes, tidal waves, volcanic eruptions, floods, avalanches, and landslides.

Chile contains several Pacific islands, including Easter Island, the Juan Fernandez Islands, and the Diego Ramirez Islands. Chile also claims a portion of Antarctica, which the United States does not currently recognize.

Flowing from the north, Chilean rivers include the Loa, Huasco, Coquimba, and Limari. In the central portion of the country, the major rivers include the Mapoche, Maule, and Maipo. The Bio-Bio is the major river in the south. The Lake District, a region in south-central Chile, is a popular vacation destination.

Plants & Animals

There are 36 national forest reserves in Chile. Some of the most common trees are the southern beech, the monkey puzzle tree, and maiten. Chile has a rainforest located in the Valdivian Coastal Range in which there are alerce trees, with a lifespan of up to 4,000 years. There are 2,400 plant species in central Chile, though there is much barren land in the north. The copihue is Chile's national flower.

In Chile, the diversity of wild animals is as wide ranging as the country's geography. Penguins abound in the southern tip of Chile, and mountain lions roam many of the mountainous regions. There are also four different types of camel, including llamas, alpacas, wild guacanos, and vicuñas, in the north.

Some of the rare mammals found in Chile include chilote foxes, colo colo or mountain cats, and the chinchilla, an animal that almost went extinct due to the market value of its pelt. Rare birds found in the south include magellanic woodpeckers and green-backed firecrown humming birds, as well as pink flamingos. Whales and seals are abundant in the waters off Chile.

CUSTOMS & COURTESIES

Greetings

Chile is a traditional country, and greetings, and social interactions usually follow a specific protocol. The customary greeting between a man and a woman, and also between two women, is a kiss on the cheek; Chileans, unlike Europeans, will only kiss once. Two men will generally shake hands, and close friends and relatives might give each other a hug or a pat on the shoulder. These greetings are usually accompanied by the appropriate reference for the time of day: "Buenas dias" ("Good morning") "Buenos tardes" ("Good afternoon") or "Buenos noches" ("Good night").

In addition, Chileans are quite formal when greeting someone for the first time. To show respect, Chileans will use the formal "usted" when speaking directly to a person. The informal command "tú," which is the informal for "you," is used in less formal situations and when among peers. Also, the terms "don" and "doña" are use when greeting someone as a sign of respect and to indicate seniority.

Gestures & Etiquette

Generally, Chileans are more restrained than their South American neighbors. They are very outgoing when among friends and peers, but usually maintain a sense of formality in most social situations. Although Chileans are often indirect in their communication styles, they can become very animated and assertive when emotional. Chileans also take pride in their socializing skills and generally are polite. It is common for Chileans to greet each individual at a gathering as a sign of courtesy, and to help make everyone comfortable.

Because family plays such a prominent role in Chilean life, it is common for conversations to start with questions about the general welfare of an individual's family. In informal settings, Chileans tend to stand close to the person with whom they are conversing. Direct eye contact is considered polite in all social circumstances. Talking in a loud, boisterous voice is frowned upon, and most Chileans place great value on self-control.

Chileans are very proud of their country and the progress they have made in recent decades. However, many Chileans share a sense of isolationism because of their country's remote location. In addition, the Pinochet era still weighs heavily on most Chileans. Conversations about Pinochet, human rights violations, and politics in general can occasionally become heated.

Gestures or behaviors to avoid include yawning without covering one's mouth, which is considered inappropriate. Also, holding one's hand with the palm up and fingers curled is considered a vulgar gesture, and should be avoided.

Eating/Meals

Desayuno, or breakfast, in Chile is traditionally a light meal consisting of toast, tostados, or bread topped with jam or butter. Although served in hotels and restaurants, eggs are rarely eaten in homes. Children drink milk or energy drinks such as Milo. Adults often have café con leche with their breakfasts. Café con leche is made by combining a half-cup of coffee with a half-cup of hot milk, and then sweetened with sugar.

Lunch, or almuerzo, is the main meal of the day in Chile, and is usually eaten between one and two o'clock. A typical Chilean lunch is comprised of two courses. The first is usually a salad or soup, often a stew called cazuela. The main course is usually a meat or fish dish served with vegetables. In smaller towns and rural areas, businesses often shut down during the lunch period, though this is not common in urban areas and cities.

People in Chile also may eat a light and late afternoon meal called "once." This small meal may also be eaten in the early evening. Similar to the tradition of English afternoon tea, once generally consists of tea with bread and jam, sandwiches, pastries, or some type of cake. Once is often the time when Chileans invite friends to their homes to socialize. For dinner, Chileans usually serve one large main course, either a fish or meat dish. Dinner, or la comida, is generally served no earlier than eight o'clock, and is often served later. Because most Chileans eat a very hearty lunch, dinners are usually smaller, or consist of lighter fare.

Visiting

Chileans are generally very hospitable and often invite guests to their homes. Chileans are known for their lack of punctuality for social occasions, however, so it is considered appropriate to arrive 15 to 30 minutes late to a host's home. Guests should bring a small token of appreciation, such as a bottle of wine, flowers or a small dessert. In general, living rooms are for socializing and entertaining guests (and often lack a television), and most dinner invitations revolve around conversation. Proper attire for social gatherings is more formal than in other countries, and hosts and guests are usually expected to dress quite nicely. In addition, hats are not worn indoors and guests should never walk barefoot in a host's house.

Chileans follow the European custom of serving dinners late. Main courses for meals are served no earlier than eight o'clock, and many dinner parties continue late into the night. It is Chilean custom for a guest to announce that he or she must leave. This usually happens 10 or 15 minutes before the guest actually leaves. Hosts take the announcement as a sign that the person is having a good time and is finding it difficult to leave.

LIFESTYLE

Family

The family structure in Chile has traditionally been the center of life for most Chileans. Although the country has changed dramatically since the 1980s, the family continues to play a crucial role in society. Children, including teenagers, generally spend a great deal of time with their parents, usually sharing evening meals. In addition, families usually gather with grandparents and other close relatives on weekends.

In general, Chileans are very affectionate within their families, and young children are especially doted upon. The youngest child is often of particular importance, and the term regalón is used to describe this special child within the family. The term is generally positive in connotation, and refers more to pampering than spoiling. Grown children in Chile commonly continue living with their families until they are married, or move to another city or region for employment.

With the markedly improved economy in Chile since the 1990s, many Chileans have seen their standard of living rise. However, there remains a widening gap between wealthy and poor families. Since Chilean families do not historically mix with families of different income levels—for example, the children of wealthy parents attend exclusive schools and usually socialize only with their peers—close family ties in Chile have increased class-consciousness among Chileans.

Housing

Homes in Chile vary depending on socioeconomic factors and their geographic locations. In the northern Andean regions of Chile, houses are commonly built using the traditional adobe mixture of straw and mud. In the southern regions of Patagonia, the typical home is a wood frame house sheathed with metal walls and a tin roof. Homes in the Lake Region often resemble Swiss cottages or German timber-framed homes, reflecting a European-influenced Alpine style. Outside urban areas, most homes in Chile do not have central heating, and gas, kerosene, or electric heaters are instead used for heat. In some rural communities, many homes are still heated with the fogón (open fire) or the cocina económica (wood-fired kitchen stove).

Most middle-class families living in Santiago and other large cities in Chile live in apartments. Because earthquakes have destroyed much of the colonial buildings over the last two centuries, many apartment buildings are very modern in style and construction. Apartment complexes in upscale neighborhoods often contain large rooms, balconies, gardens, and sometimes swimming pools. Some of these residences are guarded, and provide services such as porters and gardeners. Many families that live in older or historic sections of cities reside in traditional homes. These homes were built in the colonial style, often characterized by a central courtyard surrounded by living quarters.

Food

Traditional Chilean cuisine is a combination of indigenous and European culinary influences.

Most traditional Chilean dishes are very hearty and usually made from local ingredients. The humita is a Pre-Columbian dish that is made with the common, locally-grown Chilean corn. This dish is prepared by mashing the corn, mixing it with herbs, and then wrapping the mix in a cornhusk and steaming it. Curanto is one of the most uniquely Chilean dishes. Developed on the island of Chiloé, curanto is a feast of shellfish, meat, potatoes, and bread that is layered between leaves of pangue (giant rhubarb), traditionally cooked in a hole in the ground over charcoal and covered by stones. It is prepared by a family and served to friends and neighbors as a gesture of thanks for help with a large project.

Chile's location on the Pacific Ocean has made seafood a staple of the Chilean diet. Chileans eat seaweed, crab, clams, abalone, conger eel, oysters, and a wide variety of other seafood. Many of the sauces and soups that Chileans eat are also seafood-based. Erizos and picorocos are two unusual types of seafood that Chileans eat. Picorocos live in tube-shaped shells from which their beaks protrude. Chileans eat the picorocos by pulling them out of their shells by the beak and then swallowing them raw.

Chileans typically eat a considerable amount of meat, especially beef. Parrilladas, a large plate of barbecued meat cuts and sausages, are popular dishes at gatherings. A parrillada includes the intestines, stomachs, hearts, and other parts of the animal. Prieta (a blood sausage) is a common accompaniment to the parrillada. A traditional and popular beef dish is bistec a lo pobre (poor man's steak). This is a steak topped with fried eggs and served with french fries and onions (either sautéed or fried), and sometimes boiled rice.

Empanadas are perhaps the favorite snack in Chile. Empanadas are half-moon shaped pies made of bread dough or a puff pastry that can include various types of fillings. Empanadas are either fried or baked. The most common empanada in Chile is the empanada de pino, which is oven baked and filled with onions, meat, hard-boiled eggs, sultanas (grapes), and olives.

Life's Milestones

Because roughly 66 percent of Chileans are Roman Catholic, the majority of key milestones in Chilean culture are rooted in the Catholic tradition. Celebrating a new birth involves giving presents and large bouquets of flowers. While in the hospital, Chilean nurses often shave the heads of newborn babies in a belief that this will aid the future growth of the baby's hair. Baptisms are important family affairs that involve a church ritual followed by a large lunch or dinner. Rural Chileans celebrate a baptism with a much larger feast. Traditionally, guests are presented with a pink or blue sugar rose topped with a small figure of a baby.

As a child matures, the sacraments of first communion and confirmation become central milestones. In addition, Chileans celebrate birthdays as well as their patron saint's day. Another significant milestone is mandatory military service. All Chilean males must serve in the military when they reach the age of 18. However, military service for women is not compulsory, and only recently have women been allowed to serve.

All couples wishing to get married in Chile must be recognized by the civil registry. An official from the registry performs a quick ceremony and presents the couple with a Libreta de Familia (family book), in which the union is legally recorded and where information about births and deaths in the future can be added. Most couples also have a religious service to celebrate a wedding. The majority of Chilean weddings are Catholic ceremonies.

Unlike in many other countries, weddings in Chile traditionally do not include wedding parties. Instead, the bride and groom are accompanied by a padrinos de matrimonio (madrina—woman; or padrino—man), usually a parent or very close friend. Following the church service, couples celebrate with a reception. Upper-class families often have two lists of invited guests: those invited to the ceremony only and those invited to both the church service and the reception. In smaller or more rural locations, receptions often turn into large community events. Wedding guests consult listas de novio (wedding lists) to help buy gifts for the bride and groom. These lists are published in local newspapers on a regular basis. Chileans avoid giving money or gift certificates as wedding gifts, as this is seen as demonstrating a lack of thoughtfulness or care.

CULTURAL HISTORY

Art

Chilean culture is a blend of indigenous and European influences, beginning with the arrival of the Spanish in the 16th century. Often marginalized today, the indigenous peoples of the region, such as the Mapuches (Araucanians), Picundhes, Cuncos, and Atacameños, also played a pivotal role in shaping Chile's artistic heritage. For example, Mapuche artisans used silver coins that the Spaniards brought to Chile in the 17th century to create their unique jewelry. Melted down, the silver was worked into a variety of decorative jewelry, including head and chest pieces, as well as decorations for horse harnesses. Contemporary craftsmen continue this tradition by making replicas with ancient Mapuche designs.

In addition, textile craftsmanship is one of the most important elements of the Mapuche and other indigenous cultures. Weaving skills are typically passed on from generation to generation by mothers teaching their daughters. Mapuche craftswomen still use the witral, or upright loom, to create large weavings such as the pontro or frazada (blanket) and the lama or alfombra (rug). The traditional Mapuche method of weaving has been enhanced by the introduction of sheep wool, new designs, and other methods of weaving. Clothing and ceremonial garments, such as chamantos and colorful mantas, have become uniquely Chilean.

Fine arts such as painting and architecture were rooted in European traditions. Painting evolved from landscape art to concepts and themes that began to establish a Chilean identity, largely by embracing the Pre-Columbian and indigenous cultures. Beginning in the early 20th century, with a group of artists known as Generación del trece (Generation of 1913), Chilean artists started to depict Chilean life, focusing on local customs and social issues. During this time, the visual arts began to make a noticeable impact, and more modernist and aesthetic movements such as abstract art and cubism followed. Some of the best-known Chilean painters include abstract artist Roberto Matta (1911–2002) and Camilo Mori (1896–1973), both of whom received Chile's National Prize of Art (awarded annually since 1944.)

Architecture

Architecture in Chile represents a wide range of styles and historical periods. One of best known structures in Santiago is the Iglesia San Francisco. The church, originally built in 1586, dates back to the days of Spanish colonialism. The Museo Artequin in Santiago is renowned for its large glass windows and domes and its clay walls that are influenced by traditional Chilean building practices. The structure was designed for the 1889 Paris Exposition.

Chile's Ministry of Foreign Affairs is now located in the former National Congress building, a large example of neo-classical architecture that has been restored several times since its construction in the early 19th century. Many old buildings in Chile have been damaged or destroyed over time by recurrent earthquakes.

The Remota Hotel in Patagonia is a celebrated example of modern architectural design. The luxury facility, which was designed by native Chilean architect Germán del Sol, incorporates elements of the surrounding landscape and mixes modern design with elements of traditional Chilean folk culture.

Drama

The Chilean film industry, in the years before the dictatorship, was one of the most experimental in Latin America. However, like their musician counterparts during the Pinochet era, many filmmakers went into exile to escape the binds of creative oppression. Alejandro Jodorowsky

(1929-) was a leading director who made quirky films that often mixed genres. Miguel Littín (1942-) was nominated for an Academy Award in 1983 for his movie *Alsino and the Condor* (1981), and Europe-based directors Patricio Guzmán (1941-), known for his documentaries, and Raúl Ruiz (1941-2011), who directed over 40 films, both gained international respect for their works.

Contemporary Chilean filmmakers are exploring their country's turbulent history and trying to come to terms with it through their art. *Machuca* (2004), directed by Andrés Wood (1965-) tells the story of two young boys during the Pinochet coup, while the film *Sub Terra* (2003), directed by Marcelo Ferrari, examines the horrific working conditions and exploitation of miners in 1890s Chile and their struggle to unionize. In addition, Chile's emergence in the new global culture has been highlighted by the popularity of movies for younger audiences, with Sergio Castilla's 2001 film *Te Amo (Made in Chile*) one of the first titles to reach this market.

Music

Before the arrival of Europeans, the most common music of the Mapuche was the tayil. Performed only by women, the tayil recall a man's ancestral lineage and are a part of the rituals led by female shamans, who are perceived as intermediaries between the natural and supernatural worlds. Women perform the tayil using small lip movements, with each woman singing her own melody at her own speed and pitch level.

Traditional Mapuche musical instruments are the kultrún drum, and the trutruka, a long bamboo trumpet played by men for ceremonial events. The Spanish brought guitars and new styles of music that blended with the indigenous music to create a mixed, or mestizo, Chilean music. The tonada style is often called the quintessential Chilean song. These songs are performed solo or in duets and can be played for a variety of functions. In addition, traditional Andean music was the musical backdrop for what became known as the Nueva Canción style, which blossomed in Chile in the 1960s. Nueva Canción often utilized ancient rhythms and Pre-Columbian traditional instruments.

The cueca is the national dance of Chile, and is thought to have derived from Peruvian dances. The cueca is accompanied by guitar, accordion, and tambourine, and simulates the courtship of a woman who refuses the advances of a man. The dance uses the symbolism of a hen and rooster. Male dancers hold handkerchiefs to emphasize their movements.

The role of the arts, particularly music, in Chile steadily increased following the Pinochet regime. A great number of performing artists left Chile as the Pinochet administration punished anyone who was believed to be encouraging subversive activities or questionable education outside of the mainstream. The La Nueva Canción Chilena (New Chilean Song Movement) combined elements of traditional Chilean folk music with inspirational and often politically charged lyrics that reflected the problems of the times. Violeta Parra (1917–1967) was one of the genre's most famous performers, and "Gracias a la Vida" ("Thanks to Life") her most enduring song. Victor Jara (1932–1973) was another prominent Nueva Canción musician who protested government corruption through his music. Jara was imprisoned by the Pinochet regime and eventually murdered. Other performers, such as the bands Quilapayún and Inti-Illimani, and Los Prisioneros, went into exile and helped focus attention on the Pinochet government through their music.

Literature

Chilean writers have made valuable contributions not only to Latin American literature, but also to world literature as well. Poetry has long been one of the dominant genres in Chile. A 16th-century poem, "La Araucana," written by a Spanish soldier stationed in Chile, is considered the first Chilean poem. Chilean poetry reached its apex in the 20th century, when two Chileans captured Nobel Prizes in Literature. Gabriela Mistral (1889–1957) was a schoolteacher when she began writing poetry. Mistral wrote poems about everyday life and explored topics such as motherhood, children, death, and love. Her most famous collection of poems is *Desolación* (*Despair*), published in 1922. In 1945, Mistral became the first South American writer to win the Nobel Prize in Literature.

Pablo Neruda (1904–1973) is Chile's most famous literary figure. Born Neftalí Ricardo Reyes Basoalto, he began writing poetry at a young age, changed his name, and eventually found work in various diplomatic posts that took him around the world. Neruda's most famous works include *Twenty Love Poems and a Song of Despair* (1923) and *Heights of Machu Picchu* (1943). A communist, many of his poems are political in nature and explore issues such as poverty and the plight of factory workers. Neruda was awarded the Nobel Prize in Literature in 1971 and died two years later.

Many of Chile's prominent contemporary novelists were forced into exile following the 1973 Chilean coup (which established the military dictatorship of Augusto Pinochet). Jorge Edwards (1931-), like Neruda, was a diplomat as well as a writer. *Persona Non-Grata* (1974)*, his most famous book, describes his experiences in Cuba. Ariel Dorfman (1942-), a novelist critic, playwright, and human rights activist, was exiled by the Pinochet regime. His play *Death and the Maiden* (1991) was an international success. The play explores the confrontation between a prisoner and her torturer. Isabelle Allende (1942-) is one of South America's most popular contemporary novelists. Another political exile, Allende's novels often draw on Chile's history and her memories of her homeland. Among her works are *The House of Spirits* (1985)*, Of Love and Shadows* (1988), and *My Invented Country* (2003).

CULTURE

Arts & Entertainment

Today, Chile is alive with newfound creative energy in artistic expression. The contemporary music scene in Santiago has become a hotbed of diverse musical styles that transcend the traditional Chilean genres. In the aftermath of the dictatorship of Pinochet, the international music scene all but ignored Chilean music. In response, musical artists and industry leaders created a vibrant network of independent record labels. Pop, rock, punk, electronica, hip-hop, and traditional Chilean folk music are explored and experimented with by contemporary Chilean performers. La Ley, Los Bunkers, and Los Tres are the most famous bands to have emerged from the new Chilean music scene.

By and large, Santiago is the major center for arts and entertainment in Chile. Many symphonies and operas, as well as contemporary musicians and dance companies, find large audiences for their productions in the capital. Santiago is also the main site for local, national, and international artists to display their work in museums and galleries. Another cultural city often frequented by the wealthy is Valparaíso, a coastal resort.

The most popular professional sport in Chile is football (soccer). Chile has a national team called La Roja, as well as city-based teams, the most famous of which are all located in Santiago. The soccer season begins in March and ends in December. Games take place on Saturday, Sunday, and Wednesday. Other popular sports include horseback riding, horseracing, tennis, Palin (a Mapuche sport similar to field hockey) fishing, and rodeo.

Cultural Sites & Landmarks

Santiago, the capital, is often considered the cultural hub of Chile. The capital is famous for its bohemian nightlife, traditional neighborhoods, and historical downtown. In the city center is Santa Lucia Hill, also known as Huelen, where the city was founded in 1541. Another major downtown landmark is the Plaza de Armas, the central square; the Metropolitan Cathedral, dating to 1745, rises on its west side. Chile's recent political upheavals are also commemorated in Santiago in the form of several monuments and memorial sites. These include the statue of former President Salvador Allende in Constitution Square, a memorial to the 3,000 people who disappeared or were executed under the dictatorship, and the memorial complex at one prominent site of detention and torture called Villa Grimaldi.

The Atacama Desert, considered the driest desert in the world, occupies much of northern Chile. The center of this unique habitat is considered absolute desert, with some locations having possibly never received a drop of rain since measurements were first recorded. Climate conditions in the region make it an ideal location for astronomical observatories. Completed in 2011, the Atacama Large Millimeter Array (ALMA) consists of 66 radio antennae, and is generally considered the most ambitious radio telescope project yet developed. Prior to its construction, there were already two observatories in the desert, and the region is also home to a human settlement, the village of San Pedro de Atacama, which boasts an archaeological museum and a Spanish church dating back to 1577.

The archipelago of Chiloé, and its main island, Isla Grande de Chiloé, contains abundant wildlife and unique architecture. Originally inhabited by indigenous peoples, the Spaniards took control of the islands in 1567. Subsequent occupation by Jesuit missionaries in the 17th and 18th centuries helped to blend European and indigenous cultures. Of special note are 16 wooden churches that were listed as World Heritage Sites in 2000 by the United Nations Educational, Scientific and Cultural Organization (UNESCO). The churches are made entirely of native timber and are characterized by the blending of prominent woodcarvings and the baroque art of the religious mission style.

Located in Patagonia, in southern Chile, is Torres del Paine National Park. The park gets its name from the towering granite pillars that rise from the Patagonia Steppe. The park has been a part of UNESCO's biosphere reserve system since 1978 (classifying the park as a UNESCO World Biosphere Reserve). Torres del Paine contains a variety of landscapes, including mountains, forests, rivers, lakes, and glaciers. The park is also renowned for its flora and fauna, and features such wildlife as ostrich-like birds called rhea, Andean condors, and flamingos.

Easter Island is located 2,200 miles west of Chile in the Pacific Ocean. Chile gained control of the island in 1888, in the years following the War in the Pacific. Easter Island, or Rapa Nui as it is known by the original Polynesian inhabitants, is most famous for the hundreds of large stone carvings of human torsos that are found on the island. These carvings, called moai, are scattered around the island, some standing upright with their backs to the sea and others in various stages of completion. The moai range in size, with some as large as 18.2 meters (60 feet), and weigh as much as 80 tons. Carved with primitive basalt tools known as toki, completed moai were transported to stone platforms called ahu. Many archaeologists believe the moai were constructed as a way to worship the dead ancestors of the island's inhabitants.

Much of Easter Island is protected within the Rapa Nui National Park, which is also included on the UNESCO World Heritage List. In fact, in addition to Rapa Nui National Park and the wooden churches of Chiloé, Chile has three other World Heritage Sites. They include the historic section of the Seaport City of Valparaíso, due to its architectural legacy; the historic mining town of Sewell, a remote town connected by stairs and also considered a national monument; and the Humberstone and Santa Laura Saltpeter Works, which are two historic saltpeter refineries (saltpeter was commonly used in explosives and fertilizer).

Libraries & Museums
Among Santiago's most significant museums is the Museo Chileno De Arte Precolombino, which is housed in the former Royal Customs House that dates from 1807. The museum is known for its collection of Pre-Columbian artifacts that provide a look at indigenous life and culture before the arrival of the Spanish. Among the 1,500 objects on display are Chinchorro mummies, pottery, jewelry, and ceramic art. Other museums include the Museo Nacional de Bellas Artes (the National Museum of Fine Arts), and the Museo de la Solidaridad, which celebrates the socialist movement that brought

President Salvador Allende (1908-1973) to political power in 1970.

The Biblioteca Nacional de Chile (National Library of Chile) was built in 1925 in central Santiago. The library his home to a vast collection of books, government archives, and historical manuscripts. The Universidad de Chile and the Universidad Católica de Valparaíso are considered two of the country's main academic libraries.

Holidays

Chile celebrates many major public holidays. They include: New Year's Day (January 1); Good Friday; Easter Sunday; Labour Day (May 1); Navy Day (May 21); Corpus Christi (floating); St. Peter and St. Paul (June 29); Assumption Day (August 15); Independence Day (September 18); Army Day (September 19); Discovery of America (October 12); All Saint's Day (November 1); Immaculate Conception Day (December 8); and Christmas Day (December 25).

Youth Culture

In the early 21st century, Chilean children between the ages of six and 17 are leading the country into the Internet age. Chileans have become Latin America's greatest per-capita consumers of digital technology—including cell phones, cable television, and Internet broadband accounts—and access the Internet at higher rates than other South Americans. In addition, the use of Internet photo-sharing networks and websites by Chile's youth has exploded, and Chilean teenagers typically use these Internet meeting sites and tools such as instant messaging to organize and publicize large gatherings and parties.

As in many other cultures, Chilean youth also have their various subcultures. One such subculture that has garnered negative press in the new Internet age includes teenagers called "Pokemones." Generally, these youth are characterized as Internet-savvy, and the subculture is loosely based on androgynous fashions and Japanese anime culture. This subculture has also been linked to increasing sexual activity among youth, prompting the Chilean education ministry to implement a new sex education curriculum.

SOCIETY

Transportation

Air and road travel are the most widely used forms of transportation within Chile. The country's five major highways are paved and fairly well maintained. They include Chile Highway 5, which constitutes a large section of the Pan-American Highway and connects Chile to Peru. Chile's bus system operates throughout the country and includes international service to Bolivia and Argentina. Automobile traffic in Chile travels on the right-hand side of the road. In Santiago, vehicular restrictions are often announced in an effort to mitigate the city's air pollution problem.

Chile's railway system is operated by the state-owned company Empresa de los Feffocarriles del Estado (EFE). In the past, railways were a widely-used source of transportation among Chileans, but their use has declined in recent years as road and air travel have become dominant. Nonetheless, EFE operates train stations throughout the country and provides rail service to Peru and Bolivia.

Ferry services are available from the middle of the country to southern areas of Chile.

Transportation Infrastructure

Chile's mountainous terrain and its long length have challenged efforts to develop and maintain an efficient nationwide transportation system. Two railroad systems were built in the late 19th and early 20th centuries. The northern route connected La Calera and Iquique and the southern network connected La Calera with Puerto Montt. However, many of Chile's railway lines are now abandoned or in poor condition. Two well-traveled electric railway lines run from Santiago to Talca, Chillán, and Temuco. These lines are operated by Empresa de los Ferrocarriles del Estado (State Railway Enterprise).

The key seaport entry in Chile is Valparaíso. Santiago is served by the port at San Antonio, which handles copper exports and agricultural products. In addition, Chile's long coastline is dotted with many smaller ports that accommodate ferry traffic. Again, the mountainous terrain often makes ferry service to Chilean Patagonia and Tierra del Fuego the most accessible mode of transportation.

The main roadway in Chile is the Pan-American Highway, which stretches for roughly 3,379 kilometers (2,100 miles) and connects Arica with Puerto Montt. Secondary roads veer off from the Pan-American Highway to link with various cities. In addition, all-weather roads connect several cities in Chile with major urban centers in Bolivia and Argentina.

To ease congestion and reduce pollution, Santiago has invested in overhauling its public transportation systems. As well as building several thoroughfares that parallel the cities main streets, the new Transantiago bus system coordinates the entire system with the Metro (subway) system. Santiago's Metro system opened in 1975 and transports close to a million riders each day. In a state of constant expansion, the Metro operates five lines with 64 miles of track. Modern payment systems such as electronic fares and smart cards have also been implemented.

Media & Communications

The press in Chile is dominated by two large organizations, Consorcio Perodístico (Copesa) and Empresa El Mercurio. These two groups control many national and local publications. *El Mercurio* is the oldest daily newspaper in Chile and is perhaps the most influential. *La Tercera,* also based in Santiago, is the other prominent paper. *The Santiago Times* is a key English-language publication that reports on issues important to Chile. This paper is part of the Chilean Information Project (CHIP), a news and travel resource for the country.

Freedom of the press is provided in the Chilean constitution, and a 2001 press freedom act abolished many of the restrictions that the Pinochet-era government placed on the press.

With more than 20 million radios in use in Chile—picking up more than 1,000 stations—radio is the most popular medium in the country. The state-operated Radio Nacional de Chile is the most listened-to station in Chile. Radio Cooperativa is also a widely heard station throughout the country. Universidad de Santiago provides broadcasts of Voice of America News and the BBC News.

As of 2008, Chile had the highest rate of computer and Internet usage in Latin America. About 59 percent of Chileans have access the Internet. For the majority of Chileans who cannot afford a home computer, Internet cafés have opened throughout the country, even in some of the smaller towns.

SOCIAL DEVELOPMENT

Standard of Living

Chile ranked 41st out of 187 countries on the 2013 United Nations Human Development Index, which compiles quality of life and standard of living indicators.

Water Consumption

Fresh water is widely available in Chile. In 2014, the World Health Organization (WHO) estimated that 99 percent of the country has access to water. Although Chile's water infrastructure was government-operated for decades, today it is owned an operated by private companies. Drinking water standards are set by the Ministry of Health.

Education

Children begin school at the age of seven in Chile. After that point, school attendance is mandatory for the next eight years. Due to the Chilean seasons, the school calendar runs from March to December. Students have their summer break from January to March and a winter vacation for two weeks in July. To accommodate all of the students, many schools operate during two shifts. The first shift usually runs from 8:15 am to 1:15 pm, and the second shift from 1:30-6:30 pm.

Private schools enjoy a high enrollment rate, with over 60 percent of the primary and secondary students in 2011. This was because they were viewed as the highest quality of education in Chile, even though, all schools must follow a nationally standardized curriculum. Most students in private schools are assisted with their expenses, having been given government vouchers. However, in 2014, with the return to power of President Michelle Bachelet, the administration sought to limit private schools in order to help fund public schools at a higher level. When fully enacted, the change would transform the educational system created in the 1980s. Foreign language instruction often includes English, French, and sometimes German. High schools are either geared towards the arts and sciences or vocational training.

The Prueba de Aptitud Academica is a required test for those students who wish to continue on to university. There are over 60 colleges and universities in Chile, including Universidad de Chile, Universidad Central, Universidad de Ciencias de la Informatica, and Universidad de las Americas. The literacy rate among Chileans is an estimated 98 percent among both males and females.

Women's Rights

Since the end of the Pinochet era, women in Chile have made great advances and have become more influential and active in almost all aspects of society. In particular, several landmark events have changed the status of Chilean women. In 2005, Michelle Bachelet (1951-) was elected the first female president of Chile, and filled half of her cabinet positions with women. (She was defeated in 2009, but won the 2013 election.) An array of laws passed in the early years of the 20th century has also strengthened women's legal status. These include strict laws against sexual harassment and domestic violence, as well as a realignment of divorce rights.

Nonetheless, women continue to constitute a lower percentage of the workforce; in 2011, roughly 47 percent of Chilean women were actively employed outside the home, far below the average of other Latin American countries.

Although women in Chile receive about the same level of education as men, many women prefer to remain in the home and raise families. Others supplement the family income by working informal jobs, such as street vendors, fruit-pickers, or maids. The majority of Chilean women tend to work in nursing, teaching, and secretarial positions. Women have moved into high-profile careers in law, medicine, and journalism, but the number of women holding managerial roles in industry remains low. As of 2014, 16 percent of the Chile's legislature is made up of women, and few women hold elected or authoritative positions at local levels.

Although the Chilean government has promoted the cause of equal rights for women, traditional attitudes toward gender roles still serve to work against the full exercise of women's rights in the country. Machismo (excessive virility or masculinity) is not as strong in Chile as it is in other Latin American countries. However, the family and the traditionally held role of women remains the most important social unit in Chile, and most women view marriage and motherhood as the most important aspect of their lives. In 1990, the Chilean government created the Servicio Nacional de la Mujer (SERNAM—National Office for Women) to promote women's involvement in society. The head of SERNAM holds a cabinet position in the president's administration. Discrimination, education, employment opportunity, health, and family development are all issues SERNAM has addressed since its formation.

Women have the same rights of men under family and property law, yet women are still subject to discrimination under Chile's obscure marriage laws. Chile's "conjugal society" marriage arrangement gives husbands the right to administer joint property. A 1994 law enacted a community property system in which each spouse maintains control of the assets they brought into the marriage. However, unless couples declare themselves a community property couple, they are automatically registered as a conjugal society couple. In 2006, nearly 60 percent of all marriages were conjugal society partnerships.

Health Care

The Chilean Health Care System has several interwoven branches, but is primarily based on the Sistema Nacional de Servicios de Salud-SNSS (National System of Health Services). The SNSS is almost entirely funded and controlled by the government and serves every Chilean citizen. Care is either partially subsidized or free of charge depending on the patient's income and ability to pay. The system also oversees fundamental public health services and manages public inoculations as well as maternal-infant care.

Other important branches of healthcare augment the initiatives of the SNSS. The National Health Fund (Fondo Nacional de Salud-Fonasa) allows citizens to direct some of their income to the fund and choose their primary care doctors. However the fund is still run under the auspices of the SNSS.

The Security Assistance Institutions (Mutuales de Seguridad-MS), funded primarily by employers, is made up of hospitals and treatment centers that treat work-related accidents. The Institute of Public Health and Preventive Medicine (Instituto de Salud y Previsional Prevencion-Isapre) allows workers to direct their income toward private insurance. Most professionals in the healthcare field maintain a private practice and work within the SNSS.

GOVERNMENT

Structure

Chile is a federal republic with a constitution. Presidents are elected by a national vote held every four years. There is also a bicameral National Congress, made up of a Chamber of Deputies (4-year terms)) and a Senate (8-year terms), in which all ex-presidents serve for life. The Supreme Court has 21 members. Laws must be approved by both bodies of the National Congress, as well as the President.

Major political power struggles in the early 1970s resulted in a military takeover in 1973, after which a period of military rule lasted until 1990. At this point, democracy was reestablished. Before the coup, five parties dominated Chile: the Christian Democratic Party, the Socialist Party, the Communist Party, the National Party, and the old Radical Party.

Political Parties

The political organizations that participate in Chile's multi-party system are organized under two main coalitions: the conservative Coalition for Change and the Christian, left-leaning Concert of Parties for Democracy. National political parties register in the Santiago Metropolitan Region. There are eight national political parties in Chile. These include the Independent Democratic Union (Unión Demócrata Independiente), the Christian Democratic Party (Partido Demócrata Cristiano), National Renewal (Renovación Naciónal), Party for Democracy (Partido Por la Democracia), the Socialist Party (Partido Socialista de Chile), the Social Democrat Radical Party (Partido Radical Socialdemócrata), the Communist Party (Partido Comunista de Chile), and the Progressive Party (Partido Progresista).

Other political parties are registered in particular administrative regions of Chile, as opposed to the entire country. These regional parties include MAS-Region (MAS-Región), the Green Ecologist Party (Partido Ecologista Verde), the Humanist Party (Partido Humanista), and the Equality Party (Partido Igualidad).

Local Government

On the local level, Chile is comprised of 13 districts that are referred to by Roman numerals, with the exception of Santiago. These areas are governed by intendants and provincial governors. Chile also has 345 local municipalities which are headed by mayors, but local politicians are overshadowed by the power of the federal government. Municipalities are subdivided into administrative units known as communes. Chile's 346 communes are overseen by municipal councils. Municipal councilors and municipal mayors serve four-year terms.

Judicial System

Chile's legal system is based on Spanish law. The country's judicial system is comprised of a collection of police courts, military tribunals, criminal tribunals, and courts. The Supreme Court of Chile is the highest and most powerful judiciary in the country. Below the Supreme Court sits the Constitutional Court and a system of 16 courts of appeal.

Chile instituted a new code of criminal procedure in 2000. The aim behind the reformation of the country's criminal justice system was the replacement of the inquisitional, secretive prosecution code that was in place since the early 1900s and through the years of the Pinochet regime. The implementation of this new system occurred between 2000 and 2005.

Taxation

The government of Chile collects a variable income tax that ranges from zero to 40 percent annually. In addition, taxes are collected from individuals for private retirement funds, administrative fees, healthcare, and unemployment insurance. A value-added tax (VAT) of 19 percent is also collected. Chile's tax system is administered by the Servicio de Impuestos Internos (Chilean Tax Service), the Tesorería General de la República (the Treasury), and the Servicio Nacional de Aduanas (the Chilean Customs agency). Several bills to amend the tax system were initiated in 2014, increasing corporate taxes and giving some relief to middle-class citizens.

Armed Forces

Chile's armed forces consist of the Chilean Navy, the Chilean Army, and the Chilean Air Force. Military service is mandatory for male citizens 18 years of age, and can last up to two years. Beginning in the early 21st century, the Chilean military has made many large-scale arms purchases, including aircraft, tanks, and ships. Overall, the Chilean armed forces are considered to be one of the largest and most sophisticated military systems in the Latin American region.

Foreign Policy

Chile's two main foreign policy goals are to preserve peace and respect international law. In the wake of the Pinochet era, Chile's government strives to promote democracy, human rights, gender equality, respect for ethnic and

cultural diversity, and free trade throughout the world. The Chilean government supports many international resolutions and treaties, including the UN Conference on Disarmament (CD), the Organization for the Prohibition of Chemical Weapons (OPCW), the Nuclear Non-Proliferation Treaty (NNPT), the Kyoto Treaty, and the Anti-Personnel Mine Ban Convention (referred to as the Ottawa Convention). Chile is also a founding member of the UN, and maintains membership in organizations such as the Asia-Pacific Economic Cooperation (APEC). In terms of trade, the country is an associate member of Mercosur, a South American regional trade agreement (RTA), and has established free trade with the European Union, the United States, and Korea. In January 2010, Chile became the first South American country to join the Organization for Economic Cooperation and Development (OECD).

Chile's most pressing foreign policy issues, however, are regional. Although Chile has the most stable economy in South America, energy supply remains a serious concern, and many within the government consider it a national security priority. Hydroelectric dams are the country's main domestic source of electric power. These are massive infrastructure projects that take many years to construct and can result in great human and geological upheaval. Consequently, many Chileans are pushing the government to secure reliable sources of imported natural gas. The most direct route for a pipeline would be through neighboring Bolivia. However, Bolivia lost 250 miles of Pacific Ocean coastline in a late 19th-century war with Chile, and the two countries have disputed the territory since. Chile has allowed Bolivia to ship goods tariff-free through Chile's ports, but a complete agreement on the land remains unresolved. Until the issue is resolved, Chile is forced to purchase natural gas from Argentina. However, Argentina has restricted and at times reduced the amount of gas sold to Chile in order to meet its own demand.

Chile has not fought a war since the War of the Pacific (1878–1883) and faces no realistic military threat in the early 21st century. In fact,

Chile's stable and vibrant economy and strong military have made it a leader in South America. In addition, in 1958, the government established the Copper Law, which automatically gave 10 percent of all copper revenue from the state-owned National Copper Corporation of Chile (CODELCO)—the world's largest producer of copper—to the country's armed forces. As copper prices rose dramatically, Chile's armed forces were given a multi-billion dollar windfall. Since 2000, the armed forces have upgraded their weapons systems with F-16 fighter aircraft from the US, tanks from Germany, and warships from the Netherlands. For many Chileans, a great concern is checking the autonomy with which the armed forces operate. Traditionally, the armed forces have existed as almost a separate entity, operating under very little government control or legislative oversight. These concerns may grow as the government expands its copper production facilities, earmarking even greater streams of revenue for the cash-rich armed forces.

Dependencies

Easter Island and the Juan Fernandez Islands have constitutional status as "special territories" of Chile. The islands are located in the South Pacific Ocean off the northern coast of the country.

Human Rights Profile

International human rights law insists that states respect civil and political rights, and also promote an individual's economic, social and cultural rights. The United Nations (UN) Universal Declaration of Human Rights (UDHR) is recognized as the standard for international human rights. Its authors sought the counsel of the world's great thinkers, philosophers, and religious leaders, and were careful to create a document that reflects the core values shared by every world culture. (To read this document or view the articles relating to cultural human rights, visit: www.udhr.org/UDHR/default.htm.)

Overall, Chile has made great strides in overcoming the human rights abuses that marked the oppressive Pinochet era. Past abuses remain fresh in the minds of many Chileans, however. In 2004, the government released a long-awaited report on the Pinochet era that exposed the deaths or disappearances of more 3,000 citizens. The report also concluded that torture at the hands of the police and military was a common practice between 1973 and 1990. In addition, the government forced the military and the Chilean Supreme Court to issue apologies for their roles in the atrocities.

Chile's constitution is generally in line with Article 2 of the UDHR. It guarantees the equality of all its citizens before the law, regardless of race, religion or gender. Chile is a very homogenous society. Racism exists, but it is often subtle. A 2008 report from Amnesty International (AI) noted the need of the Chilean government to address the discrimination against the indigenous Mapuche people living in Temuco and Calama. Chilean law gives indigenous people a voice in determining decisions affecting their lands, cultures, and traditions. However, government policies and cultural discrimination have limited indigenous people's ability to participate. Private companies, as well as the Chilean government, recently have had clashes with the Mapuche over land ownership issues.

Article 5 of the UHRD states that no one shall be subject to torture and cruel, inhuman, or degrading treatment. Non-governmental agencies (NGOs) continue to receive reports of abuse and mistreatment of prisoners and citizens by the Carabineros de Chile (national police), Chile's investigative police (known as the PICH), and prison guards. These abuses open wounds for many Chileans as they try to come to terms with the human rights abuses during the Pinochet regime. Outside organizations, including AI, are pressing the Chilean government to prosecute those responsible for human rights crime and to fully compensate the tens of thousands who suffered.

Although freedom of religion, outlined in Article 18, is generally protected in Chile, some non-Catholic religions face discrimination. About 70 percent of Chileans are Roman Catholic, and the Church wields great influence in Chilean society. Until recently, only Catholic chaplains were provided for Chile's armed forces. Protestant and evangelical chaplains have been integrated into the services, but non-Christian religions are still not represented.

ECONOMY

Overview of the Economy

While declining over the past decade, trade dominates the economy of Chile, according to the World Bank, accounting for 33 percent of the gross domestic product (GDP), or the value of all of the goods and services produced. The estimated GDP of Chile was $335 billion USD in 2013, while the per capita GDP was $19,100 USD.

Santiago, the capital, one of the most economically successful cities in Latin America, is of inestimable importance to the economy of Chile, as it generates roughly 45 percent of the country's gross domestic product (GDP) and serves as its financial center.

Industry

Mining has declined in importance in recent years, but is still a major source of economic activity in Chile. Other important economic sectors are financial services, transportation, mining, and construction.

Most of Chile's industries are concentrated in or near the capital of Santiago and are focused on processing the country's wealth of natural resources, including copper, nitrates, and iron. Construction is also an important sector of the economy. This industry is supplied by factories that produce cement and other building materials. Other industries include food and beverage processing and textiles.

Exports contribute substantially to the overall economy. In 2013, Chile exported $78.94 billion USD in copper, fishmeal, fruits, wood products, paper products, fish, and wine. In recent years, wine has been an increasingly valuable export. Major export markets include the United States, the European Union, Japan, China, Korea,

Mexico, and Brazil. Most Chileans work in community services, commerce, or industry.

Labor

Chile's service industry is the country's largest employment sector. However, unemployment remains a significant problem. An estimated 10 percent of the total workforce is unionized, however at the end of 2014, the president introduced new laws supporting unionization. Although regulations regarding minimum pay and safe working conditions have been established by the Ministry of Labor, problems related to child labor and unsafe working conditions persist.

Energy/Power/Natural Resources

Chile has abundant natural resources including copper, timber, iron ore, nitrates, precious metals, and hydropower. In fact, Chile produces more copper than any other country in the world, and the metal plays an important role in the country's economy, accounting for 20 percent of the GDP in 2013. An estimated 40 percent of known copper deposits in the world are in Chile, however, the remaining copper is more expensive to mine than were the previously worked deposits.

There are 30 national parks in Chile. In fact, national parks account for 10 percent of the country's entire area. However, mining and deforestation threaten many of Chile's natural resources. Increasing air and water pollution add to the country's environmental concerns.

Fishing

Fishing is an integral part of Chile's economy and culture. The country's fishing industry produces a variety of species from its long coastline, including salmon, mackerel, sardines, herring, ling, langostinos, shrimp, and clams. Fishing represented an estimated 0.4 percent of Chile's GDP in 2011 and is the country's third-largest export industry.

In 2008, Chilean salmon began to be effected by a virus. Millions of salmon were killed and thousands of individuals employed in the fishing industry lost their jobs. Many biologists reported that the disease was a result of unsanitary fishing practices, although the Chilean government refuted this claim. In March 2010, the industry was further damaged by a tsunami that resulted in widespread damage to fishing vessels at ports in Concepcíon. However, in 2014, fishing's contribution to the economy rebounded sharply, rising 10.7 percent.

Forestry

Twenty percent of Chile is covered by forests, representing an estimated 15.9 million hectares. The logging industry serves as southern Chile's main economic activity. Primary forest products that are exported include cardboard, paper, cellulose, and lumber; earnings for exports were projected at $10.1 billion USD for 2013.

Mining/Metals

As recently as 2013, the mining industry accounted for nearly 60 percent of all Chilean exports. Chile remains the leading global producer for copper, lithium, sodium nitrate, and iodine. Chile is also a producer of gold, silver, and borate minerals. In 2013, mining represented just over 20 percent of Chile's total GDP. Mining, particularly of copper, is largely concentrated in northern Chile and in the Andes mountain range.

Chile's mining industry received worldwide attention in August 2010 after the collapse of a gold and copper mine near the city of Copiapo; trapped 33 men. The miners remained underground for 69 days before each was rescued by an international team of engineers, mining experts, and doctors. The incident became a global media event and the rescue of the miners was celebrated by Chilean communities worldwide. However, some commentators stated that the incident should result in more attention being paid to poor working conditions within the Chilean mining industry.

Agriculture

Though less influential than mining, agriculture is a major source of exports, and also contributes to the national food supply. There are currently 2,297,000 hectares (5,674,000 acres) of arable and permanent cropland in Chile. Of this land, 273,000 hectares (674,000 acres) are farmed organically.

Important crops include grapes, apples, pears, onions, wheat, corn, oats, peaches, garlic, asparagus, and beans. Apples, apricots, cherries, and plums are some of the leading exports to the United States.

Animal Husbandry

Livestock, including sheep, beef cattle, hogs, goats, horses, mules, llamas, and alpacas, are raised in rural areas. Much of the livestock industry is concentrated in Chile's central region. It is estimated that 90 percent of the premium beef sold in Chile is domestic, and Chile has experienced a rise in exports of premium beef, particularly Kobe beef. However, in the five years prior to 2013, beef production declined in Chile by 23 percent, while imports increased by 44 percent.

Tourism

Tourism is a major industry in Chile. Over three and a half million visitors came to the country in 2012, and with continued growth total tourist receipts, in 2013, were about $2.5 billion USD. Popular destinations include Vina del Mar and the Andean lakes in south-central Chile.

Chile is famous for its white-water rafting and kayaking, especially in the southern part of the country. Robinson Crusoe Island and Easter Island are two favorite Pacific vacation spots. Other outdoor activities enjoyed by visitors to Chile include wine tours and whale watching. The government of Chile has made significant financial investments in the tourism industry in recent years in the effort to increase its potential as a revenue source.

In 2013, an estimated 3.2 percent of employed Chileans had jobs in the country's tourism industry.

Michael Carpenter, Kim Nagy,
Michael Aliprandini

DO YOU KNOW?

- Chile is the longest (north-south) country in the world, stretching 4,200 kilometers (2,609 miles).
- Chilean seasons are directly opposite those of North America. That is, the Chilean summer begins in the end of December, and winter begins in late June.

Bibliography

Angell, Allan. *Democracy After Pinochet: Politics, Parties, And Elections, in Chile.* Washington, DC: Brookings Institute Press, 2007.

Caistor, Nick. *Chile in Focus: A Guide to the People, Politics and Culture.* Northampton, MA: Interlink Books, 2002.

Chatwin, Bruce. *In Patagonia.* London: Penguin Classics, 1977.

Constable, Pamela, and Arturo Valenzuela. *A Nation of Enemies: Chile Under Pinochet.* New York: W.W. Norton & Company, 1993.

Hutchison, Elizabeth Quay, Thomas Miller Klubock, Nara B. Milanich, and Peter Winn, eds. *The Chile Reader: History, Culture, Politics.* Durham, Duke University Press Books, 2013.

Joelson, Daniel. *Tasting Chile: A Celebration of Authentic Chilean Foods and Wines.* New York: Hippocrene Books, 2004.

Lagos, Ricards, Bill Clinton (Foreward by), Blake Hounshell, and Elizabeth Dickinson. *The Southern Tiger: Chile's Fight for a Peaceful and Democratic Future.* New York: St. Martin's Press, 2012.

Rector, John L. *The History of Chile.* New York: Palgrave Macmillan, 2005.

Shafil Meghji, Anna Kaminski, and Rough Guides Staff. *The Rough Guide to Chile.* London: DK Publishing, Inc., 2012.

Silver, Katherine. *Chile: A Traveler's Literary Companion.* Berkeley, CA: Whereabouts Press, 2003.

Ray, Leslie. *Language of the Land: The Mapuche in Argentina and Chile.* Copenhagen: IWGIA, 2008.

Works Cited

"Chile Seeks Energy Independence." ISA Consulting website. http://www.isaintel.com/site/index. php?option=com_content&task=view&id=35

"Chile." CIA World Factbook. Online. Accessed October 25, 2008. https://www.cia.gov/library/publications/the-world-factbook/geos/ci.html

"Chile." Encyclopedia Britannica. 2008. Encyclopedia Britannica Online. http://www.britannica.com/EBchecked/topic/111326/Chile.

"Chile." *Nations of the World.* Amenia, NY: Grey House Publishing, 2015.

"Chile." World Gazetteer website.

"Churches of Chiloé." UNESCO World Heritage website. http://whc.unesco.org/pg.cfm?cid=31&id_site=971

"Foreign Policy." Embassy of Chile in Australia website. Online. Accessed November 10, 2008. http://www.embachile-australia.com/en/brief/foreign.html

"Native American music." Encyclopedia Britannica. 2008. Encyclopedia Britannica Online. <http://www.britannica.com/EBchecked/topic/1350772/Native-American-music

"The List: The World's Forgotten Territorial Disputes," July 2006. Foreign Policy Magazine website. http://www.foreignpolicy.com/story/cms.php?story_id=3534

Chile: Major Human Rights Reform Must Mark Bachelet Remaining Time in Office. *Amnesty International USA.* Press Release November 7, 2008. http://www.amnestyusa.org/document.php?lang=e&id=ENGPRE200811078029

Barrionuevo, Alexei. "In Tangle of Young Lips, a Sex Rebellion in Chile." September 13, 2008. New York Times website. http://www.nytimes.com/2008/09/13/world/americas/13chile.html?_r=4&oref=slogin&pagewanted=print

"The Mystery of Easter Island." January 9, 2003. BBC News Channel. http://www.bbc.co.uk/science/horizon/2003/easterisland.shtml

Beech, Charlotte, Jolyon Attwooll, Jean-Bernard Carillet, Thomas Kohnstamm. Chile and Easter Island. London: Lonely Planet, 2006.

Bernasconi, Colette. "An Indie Label Under Every Rock." Revolver Magazine, November 2008. http://www.revolver-magazine.com/live-music-scene/34-live-music-scene/100-an-indie-label-under-every-rock.html

"Chilean Crafts Foundation" website. http://www.artesaniasdechile.cl/artes2/elaboracion6.htm

Estrada, Daniela. " Forestry Industry Sows Poverty, Study Says." Inter Press Service. August 26, 2010. IPS News website. http://ipsnews.net/news.asp?idnews=52622

"Frommer's Travel Guides" website. http://www.frommers.com/destinations/santiago/A29843.html http://www.world-gazetteer.com/wg.php?x=&men=gcis&lng=en&des=wg&srt=npan&col=abcdefghinoq&msz=1500&geo=-52

"Chile: Usage and Population Statistics". *Internet World States website.* Online. http://www.internetworldstats.com/sa/cl.htm

Mauleon, Rebeca. "Chile." National Geographic Online. http://worldmusic.nationalgeographic.com/worldmusic/view/page.basic/country/content.country/chile_56

Perrone, Caterina. "Chile—Culture Smart!" London: Kuperard, 2007.

Roraff, Susan, and Laura Camacho. Chile—Culture Shock!: A Survival Guide to Customs and Etiquette. Tarrytown, NY: Marshall Cavendish, 2007.

Sanchez, Alex. "Chile's Aggressive Military Arm Purchases Are Ruffling the Region, Alarming in Particular Bolivia, Peru and Argentina." August 7, 2007. Council on Hemispheric Affairs website. http://www.coha.org/2007/08/chile's-aggressive-military-arm-purchases-is-ruffling-the-region-alarming-in-particular-bolivia-peru-and-argentina/

"Chile: Country Reports on Human Rights Practices—2007, released by the Bureau of Democracy, Human Rights, and Labor." *U.S. Department of State.* March 11, 2008. http://www.state.gov/g/drl/rls/hrrpt/2007/100632.htm

"Statistics and Indicators on Women and Men." *United Nations Statistics Division website.* July, 2008. http://unstats.un.org/unsd/demographic/products/indwm/tab5d.htm

Vesilind, Priit J. "The Driest Place on Earth." National Geographic Magazine website. August 2003.

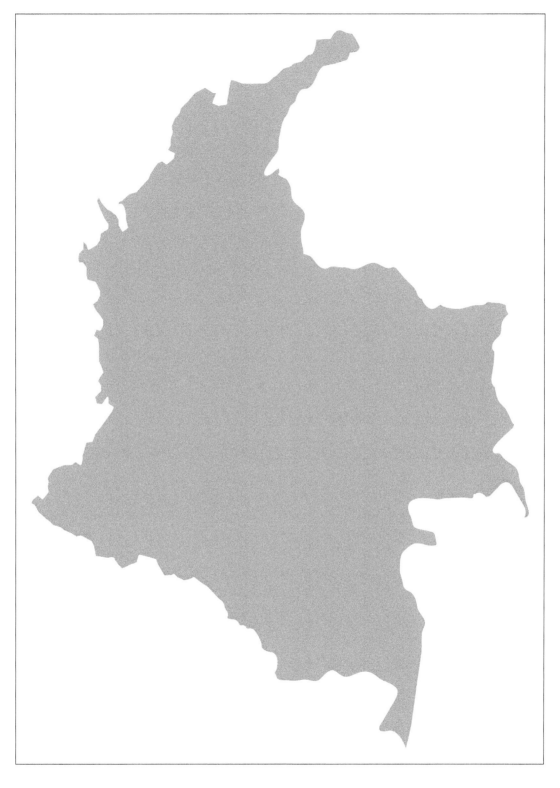

COLOMBIA

Introduction

Colombia is a republic in South America surrounded by Venezuela and Brazil to the east, Ecuador and Peru to the south, and the Pacific Ocean, Panama, and the Caribbean Sea to the west and north. Colombia's long history of social unrest is well documented. However, the country is one of the more stable democracies in South America, having experienced free elections for the last fifty years. Famous for its production of coffee, Colombia is also one of the world's largest coal exporters. It is also well known as a center in the international drug trade. A country driven by conflict between leftist guerilla groups and right-wing paramilitary groups, in recent years the paramilitary units have disbanded and the conflict has been at a standstill.

GENERAL INFORMATION

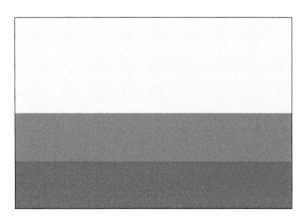

Official Language: Spanish
Population: 46,245,297 (2014 estimate)
Currency: Colombian peso
Coins: Coins are available in denominations of 50, 100, 200, 500, and 1000 pesos, with a rarely used 20 peso also in circulation.
Land Area: 1,109,104 square kilometers (428,227 square miles)
Water Area: 100,210 square kilometers (38,691 square kilometers)
National Motto: "Libertad y Orden" ("Liberty and Order")

National Anthem: "Oh Gloria Inmarcesible" ("Oh Glory Unfading")
Capital: Bogotá
Time Zone: GMT -5
Flag Description: The flag of Colombia is a tricolor of yellow (top), blue (center), and red (bottom). (The yellow stripe is twice the width of the other two stripes.) The yellow of the flag stands for the country's gold reserves; the blue represents the sea shore; and the red stands for the blood of Colombian patriots.

Population

Colombia's population is not concentrated in any one central city. Although Bogotá, Medellín, Cali, and Barranquilla are major cities, there are 37 other cities with a population of 100,000 or more. Most of these cities are located in the highlands, where about 78 percent of Colombians now live.

Seeking better living conditions and safety from the guerrillas, many people have migrated from rural to urban areas. Today, only two percent

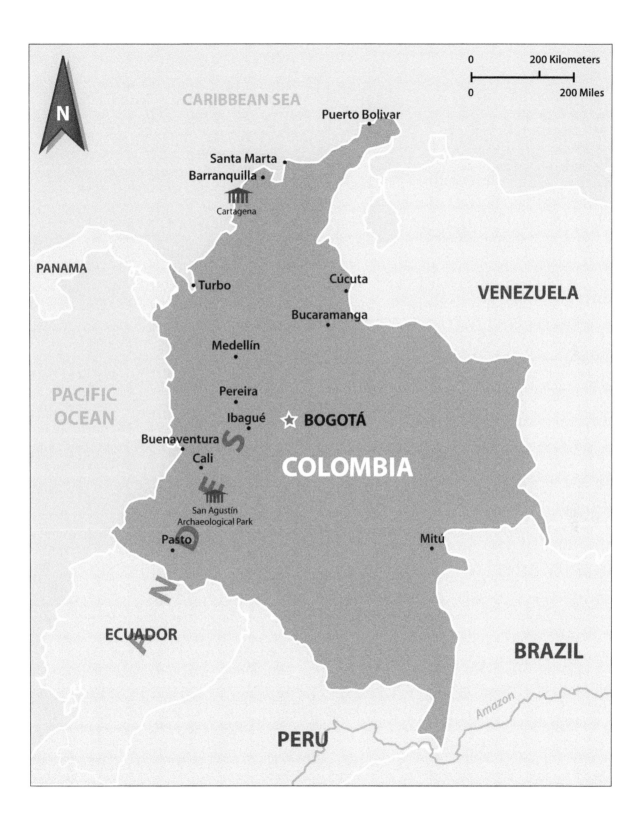

Principal Cities by Population (2011):

- Bogotá (8,743,000)
- Medellín (3,694,000)
- Cali (2,453,000)
- Barranquilla (1,900,000)
- Cartagena (988,000)
- Cúcuta (637,000)
- Soledad (661,851)
- Bucaramanga (1,120,000)
- Ibagué; (553,524)
- Soacha (511,262)

of the people live in the rural Llanos and Amazon regions that dominate two-thirds of the country.

Mestizos, of mixed European and Native American descent, make up most of Colombia's middle class and account for over half of the population (about 58 percent). Whites account for nearly 20 percent of the population, yet claim many of the government and high level business occupations. Blacks and mulattos (of black and European descent) make up less than 20 percent of the population, with Zambos (of black and Native American descent) and Native Americans accounting for less than five percent of the population.

Colombia has a fairly young population, with over 68 percent of its people between the ages of 15 and 64, and roughly 25 percent under the age of 14 (2014). Life expectancy is about 78 years for women and 72 years for men, with a population growth rate of 1.07 percent (2014).

Languages

Most of the country's inhabitants pride themselves on speaking the purest form of Spanish, however, local accents can be detected in some regions on the Caribbean coast.

Native People & Ethnic Groups

Native Americans account for about one percent of Colombia's modern population, as most of their ancestors died or vanished after the arrival of the conquering Spanish. Today, there are still about 50 different Native American groups living in Colombia, with the largest being the Guajiro.

Native Americans are virtually the only Colombians who do not speak Spanish. Native languages include Arawak, Chibchan, Carib, and Tupi-Guarani. Found mostly in the sparsely populated lowlands or remote mountainous regions, the native population still uses nearly 200 different dialects.

Religions

Approximately 90 percent of Colombians are Roman Catholic, while Protestants, Jews, and practitioners of native religions account for the remaining 10 percent. Recently, a trend toward conversion to the Jehovah's Witness, Mormon, Calvinist, and Lutheran faiths, especially among the poor, has contributed to nearly three million Colombians leaving the Catholic Church.

Climate

Colombia experiences various climatic conditions. While most of the country is in the Northern Hemisphere, the southern region stretches into the Southern Hemisphere, and each side of the equator brings its corresponding seasons. For the most part, however, the conditions are wet and tropical.

Most of the rainfall occurs during the summer. The eastern lowlands and Caribbean and Pacific lowlands are tropical, with hot temperatures and an average annual rainfall of over 100 centimeters (40 inches). The north and northwest regions experience drier winters, with the mountain regions experiencing a complex mix of conditions. Weather conditions can vary greatly over short distances, due to altitude, position, and level of exposure to winds and the sun. One slope might face winds that bring rain, while the sheltered side of the slope remains much drier.

Climatic differences are seen in the natural vegetation and type of crops produced in a given area. The influence of the Andes produces weather conditions ranging from extreme heat to permafrost in areas above 4,570 meters (15,000 feet).

Because of the city's elevation, and its proximity to the equator, Bogotá, the capital, has a mild, temperate climate, with a year-round average temperature of 14° Celsius (57° Fahrenheit). June and July are the city's wettest months. Precipitation is sporadic throughout the rest of the year. Bogotá's climate is subject to the drastic changes caused by the El Niño (The Boy) and La Niña (The Girl) storm systems.

ENVIRONMENT & GEOGRAPHY

Topography

Colombia has two distinct topographical areas. The Andes Mountains dominate the western part of the country, while the lowlands expand over two-thirds of the east. Most of the population lives in the shadow of the Andes, leaving the lowlands lightly populated. While Colombia is bordered by two bodies of water, most of its ports are located on the Caribbean Sea, where a large portion of the population lives.

The Andes consist of three ranges, or "cordilleras," all of which follow a south-to-north direction. The Cordillera Oriental is known for its high basins, one of which is home to Colombia's largest city, Bogotá. The elevation of this plateau is approximately 2,600 meters (8,500 feet), placing the capital in a cool climate zone.

The highest range is the Cordillera Central. Pico Cristobal Colon is the highest peak, at 5,776 meters (18,950 feet). This range is home to several active volcanoes as well, the highest being Tolima at 5,215 meters (17,110 feet). The volcano has not erupted since 1829. The northern tip of the range rises above the snow line. There are many small populated valleys at several different elevations, but unlike the Cordillera Oriental, this range is sparsely populated.

The Cordillera Occidental is the lowest and narrowest of the Andes ranges, with its highest peak reaching 10,000 meters (32,800 feet). As the range gently slopes into the Caribbean coastal plain, it is partially covered by deposits from the rivers that drain the Andes into the area. The deep and narrow Cauca River valley runs between this range and the Central range. The Cauca River and adjacent valleys are home

to two of Colombia's most populous areas, Medellín and Cali.

The expansive eastern lowlands that cover most of Colombia are dominated by the Orinoco River in the north and the Amazon River in the south. To the west, the lowlands still have elevated areas influenced by the fringes of the Andes and the Guiana highlands. The elevation enables most of the land to remain above the floodplains of the many rivers that cross it. Almost all of the inhabitants of the lowlands live on or near the edges of the rivers. To the east, traveling is difficult. The rivers connect the eastern lowlands to the foot of the Andes Mountains, often providing the only route to the lowland areas.

Bogotá is in the middle of Colombia, atop a plateau in the Andes, at an elevation of 2,650 meters (8,660 feet). The plateau is generally referred to as the sabana (savannah) de Bogotá, although it is not technically a savannah. The city lies at the base of the Guadalupe and Monserrate mountains and several smaller hills, which limit the city's ability to expand outward. The Bogotá River runs through the city from the north to the south, culminating in the Tequendama Falls. There are many tributaries to the Bogotá River, which has allowed the farmland in Bogotá and the surrounding areas to thrive.

Plants & Animals

Despite widespread logging activity, Colombia is still rich in plant and animal life. Colombia is home to the world's widest variety of birds, with 1,754 species living within its borders. These include ducks and other fowl, tropical birds such as toucans, parakeets, and parrots, and larger birds such as buzzards, condors, and eagles.

Brazil is the only other country that is home to a wider variety of plant species than Colombia. Common trees include coconut palms, rubber trees, bamboo, and tropical hardwoods.

The secret to the country's impressive biodiversity is its wide range of habitats. Few countries can match Colombia's diversity with its mountains, lowlands, seas, lakes, deserts, and swamps.

CUSTOMS & COURTESIES

Greetings

In Colombia, greetings are usually profuse and public, and accompanied by inquisitive phrases toward the other party. These include phrases such as "¿Que tal?" ("How are things?") or "¿Como le va?" ("How's it going with you?") or "¿Que mas?" ("What else?"). In formal or business settings, Colombians prefer the handshake; among acquaintances and friends, the embrace, or abrazo, is used by both men and women. Between sexes, it is common to kiss a woman on the cheek only upon first introduction. The phrase "Con mucho gusto" ("With much pleasure") is typically used when meeting a new acquaintance.

When saying goodbye, Colombians often use the Italian word "Ciao." In rural areas, or among practicing Catholics, it is not uncommon to receive a blessing such as "Dios le bendigo" ("God bless you"), or even "Vaya con Dios" ("Go with God") before separating.

Gestures & Etiquette

Colombians typically like to refer to themselves as a passionate people, and they exhibit this in numerous ways. In group situations, animated conversations are normal and Colombians tend to use both body language and expressive hand gestures on points of emphasis. In addition, music and dancing is a very popular part of Colombian custom, and it is common for men and women to dance salsa, meringue or vallenato as a way of socializing and friendship.

Colombians tend to have fluid concepts of time and distance. European or American standards of being punctual and keeping to a particular schedule are generally more relaxed in Colombia. Sunday, for instance, is a day of rest in Colombia, and most stores and shops remain closed for the entire day. Even words such as "ahora" and "ya" (both meaning "now") can oftentimes be variously interpreted as either "now," "in five minutes," or "later on in the week." Similarly, when giving directions, Colombians will use the term "cerquita" (meaning "close by") that does not necessarily correspond to commonly accepted standards of distance.

While Colombians are generally engaging and eager to talk about their country, they are reticent and particularly sensitive about their international reputation. In general, Colombians avoid conversation regarding the drug trade and civil disturbances. In addition, when addressing others, Colombians use a variety of nicknames and diminutives, or a shorter or affectionate term, with other people. For example, foreigners are generally called "gringo" or "mono" ("monkey"), with both words used as terms of endearment rather than to offend. Common diminutives include ones which are formed in Spanish by adding the suffix "ito" to a word. For example, "mono" becomes "monito."

Additionally, when speaking among themselves, Colombians call each other names which might be considered vulgar in other cultures. It is common to hear derogatory terms for a person's race or sexual orientation routinely employed in conversation, but on the whole these terms are not used as an insult. Instead, they are used in a humorous, friendly manner. However, this is mostly common among younger people. When addressing elders, Colombians are more consciously formal. They often use the formal Spanish terms "señor" or "señora" for the elderly, or even the more formal and dated "don" and "doña," which translate to "lord" and "lady."

Eating/Meals

Eating in Colombia is heavily influenced by the country's Spanish heritage. Breakfast, called desayuno, tends to be a light meal consisting of a broth or soup and bread or tortilla, followed by coffee or chocolate. Lunch, called almuerzo, is the largest meal of the day, with people generally returning to the family home to eat together. While declining as a custom in urban areas, Colombians still typically observe the practice of the post-meal "siesta," or nap, in rural areas. This break can last up to two hours in the afternoon, usually between 1 p.m. and 3 p.m.

Dinner, called cena, is a smaller affair than lunch, and is consumed later in the evening after people return home from work. Sunday is the day of the family meal when extended family members gather together to eat a large lunch. In urban areas, Colombians also frequent cafés in the afternoons to have a tinto (coffee) and meet with friends. In addition, cities usually host numerous street vendors, who sell everything from whole meals to sweet snacks and treats.

Visiting

Colombians generally offer a houseguest a coffee or beverage upon first arrival. While not compulsory, guests generally bring a small gift such as a postre (cake) or flowers for the host. Visits are considered occasions for socializing and conversing, and it is common for most informal or little visitas (visits) to last several hours. Among friends, it is expected to make polite inquiries into the health of family members. While the practice is largely fading, before entering a house sometimes guests are supposed to ask for permission to enter by inquiring "¿Con permisso?" ("With permission?") from the owner.

LIFESTYLE

Family

Like many other Latin American cultures, Colombians have historically emphasized strong family ties. Traditionally, the Colombian family incorporated a wide range of distant relatives, including cousins, uncles, aunts, and other distant relations. Thus, the family unit is more akin to a clan rather than the nuclear family that is common in Western cultures. Families could also be defined as patriarchal, meaning that much of the traditional authority was delegated to male members of the family. Traditionally, the males worked in business and industry to financially provide for the family while the female family members retained control over domestic affairs. As a result, Colombian homes often resembled small communities with several generations residing under the same roof. In addition,

children remained at home until marriage, and it was not uncommon for unmarried women to live their entire lives in the same family household.

Increased urbanization and a modernizing economy have changed elements of this family structure in Colombia. However, the basic concept remains, though this type of traditional living arrangement is frequently becoming a luxury of middle-class households that have the financial resources to permit large families in one house.

Furthermore, the continued civil strife within Colombia has brought much disruption and fragmentation to rural communities, forcing many families to flee to urban areas. The increased cost of living and stark economic realities of urban Colombia have forced many women to abandon traditional roles and work outside the home. Traditional concepts of marriage and child-rearing have also changed significantly, and the numbers of single-parent households has increased in recent years.

Housing

With the advent of Spanish colonization, Colombia developed architecture and housing that was heavily reliant on Castilian styles. Castile was a historical region of Spain, and the architecture of the ancient kingdom was heavily influenced by the French. This style featured such architectural devices as stained glass and buttresses. Castile buildings often consisted of a series of rooms built around an inner courtyard patio. Roofs were sloped and tiled and many houses were built using natural materials such as wood, stone, or adobe (a sun-dried clay brick). In rural areas of Colombia, many variants of this housing style remain today. However, the worsening economic conditions and extreme poverty affecting many rural populations have caused the number of shanties and shelters constructed out of wood to increase.

Twentieth-century urbanization has introduced new building trends into Colombian cities. Increased migration into cities led to a vertical housing boom, in which urban residential living trended upward. Under this development trend, vast areas of Colombian cities were re-made by the construction of numerous apartment towers and public housing complexes. In addition, roughly 70 percent of such urban housing is registered as privately owned and occupied. However, a thriving rental market also exists.

Many major cities, including Bogotá and Medellín, have witnessed the growth of large slum districts, or "shantytowns," on the city outskirts. The growth of these informal towns can be largely attributed to internal displacement, or forced migration. Currently, Colombia has one of the worst rates of internal displacement in the world. The majority of these slum districts are characterized by a lack of proper sanitation, running water, or even electricity. Housing in these areas is generally poorly constructed, and often made out of discarded lower-grade building materials.

Food

Colombian cuisine is traditionally heavily influenced by local tastes, and each region is famous for its distinct local dishes. As a result, there is nothing that could be considered a national Colombian cuisine. Instead, the various regions offer up a medley of different tastes and flavors.

In Bogotá, for example, the culinary specialty is ajiaco, which is a type of chicken soup. It is prepared by roasting together a whole chicken on the bone and several chunks of corn on the cob. Two to three different types of potatoes are cooked together with the chicken. An herb known as guasca is also added for flavor. After cooking for several hours in a broth, the soup is served with a side of heavy cream, rice, and avocado.

Medellín serves up a plate from its region known as the bandeja paisa. A typical bandeja paisa consists of grilled steak, chicharrón (fried pork rind), red beans, white rice, chorizo (sausage), a fried egg, and an arepa (tortilla). A slice of avocado and a grilled plantain are served as an accompaniment. This enormous meal was once nominated to be the national dish of Colombia, but protests from other regions left it as a specialty of the Antioquia region.

From the Tolima region come tamales, which are enjoyed around the country. Tamales consist of a plantain leaf stuffed with cornmeal, yellow peas, pork, eggs, and chicken. Several other different fillings can also used. Lechona is also another Tolima specialty. It consists of a whole roast pig stuffed with rice and vegetables.

Along the Colombian coastline, fish and lobster are an integral part of the cuisine, generally served fried and with lemon, rice, and fried plantains. Sancocho stew is a medley of fish, seafood, plantains, yucca, potatoes, and various other vegetables. Colombia also enjoys a long growing season, and the country harvests a dazzling array of tropical fruits which are served in a variety of juices and salads or just plain.

Life's Milestones

As is the custom in other Latin American cultures, Colombians celebrate the quinceañera, which is typically a young woman's 15th birthday. The quinceañera is a coming-of-age celebration and often begins with a celebratory mass at church followed by a large fiesta, or party, for the young woman and her friends. It is common for family members and guests to offer gifts. The young lady celebrating her quinceañera typically dresses up in either a white or a blue dress, and wears a crown or tiara on her head. A set of tacones (high heels) is traditionally given to her by her parents. They symbolize to the community that she is no longer a child, but a woman of the world. At the party, there is often a customary first dance with the father, and live music is provided by a band of either mariachi or vallenato musicians.

CULTURAL HISTORY

Art

Colombia is a country of diverse peoples and unique regional and local cultures. This is mainly due to Colombia's highly rugged and mountainous geography, which separates and isolates cities and towns. In every region and town, Colombians are extremely proud of their local culture and orient their national Colombian identity on a local scale.

The visual arts began in Colombia with the pre-Columbian indigenous tribes that lived along the coast and in the hinterlands (the inner land lying beyond the coast). Some of these tribes were known for their advanced metalworking, particularly with gold. Several of their intricate sculptures, ornaments, and jewelry have survived to the present day. Other tribes, such as those of the San Agustín culture (1–900 CE), used natural materials such as sandstone and limestone to sculpt several large monoliths and statues that depicted tribal deities and native flora and fauna.

Following colonization by the Spanish, Colombian arts were heavily influenced by the Roman Catholic Church, which commissioned and constructed large cathedrals and chapels in the Spanish settlements. Within these centers of worship were paintings and sculptures that were influenced by the baroque style of European art. The baroque style is characterized by grandeur and elaborate detail and realism, and often includes religious themes. It was popular in Europe beginning in the 17th century.

Colombian visual artists of the 20th century have drawn upon these trends. Foremost among these artists is the painter and sculptor Fernando Botero, who has gained a worldwide audience through his highly stylized paintings and sculptures. These works typically depict his subjects as morbidly obese. Botero has related in interviews that his artwork owes a debt to the 17th-century baroque art he saw displayed in the churches of his native city. Museums in Bogotá and Medellín house large collections of his work.

Other prominent visual artists have received international accolades for their work. The Bogotá photographer Juan Manuel Echavarría has become a renowned photographer for his photos and videos chronicling the endemic violence afflicting Colombia. The painter Miguel de la Espriella, better known by his pseudonym "Noble," has become popular for his brightly colored figurative scenes that depict the Colombian coast and countryside. Many Colombian artists today still work with the same materials their ancient ancestors used to make pottery and jewelry, and art galleries are numerous in the country, with over 100 galleries located in Bogotá alone.

Architecture

Bogotá is perhaps best representative of Colombia's architectural heritage. Much of the city's architecture is old and reminiscent of the Spanish colonial style, including the gold art that was common in the early days of the conquistadors (Spanish conquerors). However, Bogotá is also home to many modern high rises and skyscrapers, and the contrast of these two worlds is what makes the cityscape so unique. Bogotá's streets are laid out in a grid, with several plazas throughout. "Calles" run from east to west, while "carreras" run north to south, parallel with the hills.

Drama

Pre-Colombian theater consisted of ceremonial rituals of music and dance. With the arrival of the Europeans came a new form of theater. The first Colombian play was a one-act play by Fernandez de Valenzuela, the *Láurea crítica* (The Critical Laurel Wreath, 1629), a satire of baroque language.

In the 19th century, theater became more established, and Spanish productions were staged in the country, and the costumbrismo style developed. Costumbrismo was a realistic style depicting everyday life, sometimes in a satirical or moralistic manner. Successful playwrights of this genre were Luis Vargas Tejada (1802–1829), José María Samper (1828–1888), and José María Vergara y Vergara (1831–1872). Comparatively, Colombian theater did not advance as well as that in Argentina or Mexico, and troupes from those countries and Europe competed with fledgling national efforts.

In the 20th century, playwrights such as Antonio Alvarez Lleras, Emilio Campos, and Luis Enríque Osorio began creating a distinctly Colombian voice that reflected the country's political and social reality. After World War II, Colombian artists embraced the work of

European existentialists and surrealists who advocated for more experimental theater. Works began to reflect the social unrest within the country, such as the growing divide between rural and urban populations, as well as the differences between the wealthy and the poor. During La Violencia (1948–1958), a period of repression and conflict within Colombia between supporters of the Colombian Liberal Party and the Colombian Conservative Party, the theater community became engrossed in the country's internal conflicts. The Cuban Communist revolution also had a profound influence in Colombia, which saw the advent of Nuevo Teatro, a movement that sought inclusiveness of communities, marginalized peoples, and the disadvantaged. The government instituted a crackdown on some of these efforts, classifying them as subversive, and some playwrights lost teaching posts.

In the 1980s, theater in Colombia began to reflect what was happening globally in the dramatic arts—with the staging of productions from playwrights such as Edward Albee and Neil Simon. The Iberoamerican Theater Festival (FITB) was established in 1988, the brainchild of Fanny Mikey and Ramiro Osorio. Held biannually, it was meant to spotlight the work of Latin American artists; it has grown beyond Latin America to become an international showcase for performing arts.

Music

Historically, Colombia is home to many distinctive music styles that vary from region to region. Many of these styles have devoted adherents who celebrate their musical passions through dances, concerts, and festivals throughout the country.

Cumbia is a type of folk dance and music that is considered the country's national dance music. Originating in Colombia's Caribbean region among African slaves, cumbia is a dance and music style that fuses both African and Indian rhythms. Cumbia music typically relies on heavy percussion to provide an underlying beat while accordion, guitar, and flute give melody and rhythm to the song. This national style is thought to have evolved from a courtship dance between

African slaves and was historically regarded as music for the lower classes.

Vallenato is another popular folk music typically associated with Colombia. Like cumbia, it also stems from the country's Caribbean region. When translated into English, it means "from the valley." Traditional vallenato consists of three instruments: a caja vallenata, which is a small handheld percussion drum; a guacharaca, which is a small ribbed stick that is played by scraping a playing fork along the edge; and an accordion, which represents the most recent addition. The music is generally played in a variety of different formats, the most popular of which are son, paseo, merengue, and puya. Vallenato lyrics are often written in a narrative fashion, and tell everyday stories about coastal life and romance.

In addition, salsa music, which incorporates various Caribbean musical styles, enjoys enormous popularity in Colombia. While not invented in Colombia, it is nevertheless especially popular in the cities of Calí and Medellín, where numerous homegrown Colombian salsa artists and dancers have gone on to gain national and international fame. In the late 20th and early 21st centuries, several Colombian singers, including Shakira, have become world famous through their fusion of traditional Colombian music and modern popular music such as rock and roll.

Literature

Historically, much of Colombia's literature is religious, and Colombian literature did not gain great prominence until the 20th century. During the 1960s, Colombia and the rest of Latin America began to receive international recognition for its writers and literature. Foremost among Colombian writers is Gabriel García Márquez. In such works as *One Hundred Years of Solitude* and *Love in the Time of Cholera*, García Márquez perfected a form of writing known as magical realism. This style describes magical or fantastic events in a style that relates them in a factual, realistic narrative. For his many contributions to literature, García Márquez was awarded the Nobel Prize for Literature in 1982.

CULTURE

Arts & Entertainment

In the early 21st century, Colombia witnessed a tremendous upsurge in support for the public arts. In fact, numerous festivals, conferences, and celebrations have been staged throughout the country since the latter half of the 20th century.

The international recognition accorded to author Gabriel García Márquez has brought great acclaim to Colombia itself. Hoping to capitalize on this interest in Latin American literature, Bogotá holds an annual Feria del Libro (Book Fair), which attracts publishers, agents, and writers from all over the world. This event has become the third largest book fair in Latin America. In fact, there were over 415,000 visitors in attendance in 2012. In conjunction with the Hay Festival held in the United Kingdom (UK), Cartagena hosts the Hay Festival Cartagena every January. At this event, numerous journalists, politicians, intellectuals, and writers come together to discuss world affairs and the importance of the arts in relation to contemporary events. Since 1991, Medellín has held the international Festival de Poesia (Festival of Poetry). This festival invites poets from around the world to read their work.

There are also a number of festivals celebrating the dramatic arts. The biennial Festival Iberamericano de Teatro de Bogotá (IberAmerican Theater Festival of Bogotá) invites theater groups from around the world to perform in the city. Additionally, Colombia hosts two international film festivals. Having celebrated its 50th year in 2010, the Cartagena Film Festival has highlighted the works of numerous Latin American film directors including Lucía Puenzo, Antonio Eguino, and Jorge Durán. The Bogotá Film Festival is held every April and concentrates more exclusively on international films.

In addition, many of these festivals receive government funding. However, there has always been a lesser known, but thriving, underground arts scene in Colombia. This has existed primarily in opposition to established and official channels of the arts.

The first real underground arts scene came about with a literary movement called Nadaism (Nothing-ism), which was principally inspired by the poet Gonzalo Arango. This movement, developed during the 1950s, expressed opposition to all traditional forms of culture and society. This bohemian spirit still thrives in many of the underground arts communities in Colombia. For example, coinciding with the official IberAmerican Theater Festival, is the underground Festival Teatro Alternativo de Bogotá (Alternative Theater Festival), which places greater emphasis on native, homegrown Colombian talent. The festival invites greater audience participation. Numerous other underground festivals have also been established.

Cultural Sites & Landmarks

Throughout Colombia's history, many major cities such as Bogotá, Cali, and Medellín have not preserved much of their colonial heritage. However, smaller cities and towns have largely managed to preserve many of the country's historical and cultural landmarks.

Located along the Caribbean coast, the port and city walls of Cartagena were designated a United Nations Educational, Scientific and Cultural Organization (UNESCO) World Heritage Site in 1984. Founded by the Spanish in 1533, Cartagena was initially constructed as a fortress. Historically, it served as the major shipping point through which Colombian and Peruvian gold and silver were shipped to Spain. The heavily fortified walls of the city helped protect the bastion of El Castillo de San Felipe (the Castle of Saint Philip) and the city from numerous attacks. The stone walls also helped to shape and contain the growth of the city, and have been meticulously preserved throughout the centuries. Cartagena is also known for its Spanish colonial architecture.

Another nearby UNESCO site is the small northern city of Santa Cruz de Mompox. Founded in 1537, Mompox served as the religious and administrative base for the region. Located along the banks of the Magdalena River, Mompox was an important river port that linked the coast with the Colombian interior. Silting, in which a waterway is obstructed by deposited silt or sediment, caused the port to close down in the early 20th century. As a result, Mompox languished from a lack of commercial development. However, this led to the preservation of the city's Spanish colonial architecture.

The large Iglesia de San Francisco (Church of Saint Francis), with its lavish interior, is the oldest church in Mompox, and was constructed during the 16th century. Mompox is also home to the nearby Iglesia de Santa Barbara (Church of Saint Barbara). The church is known for its Moorish architecture (a branch of architecture that expanded from Islamic architecture), evident in the building's octagonal tower. Several other churches in the area help make Mompox a cultural heritage center for Colombia. The city also houses the Casa de Gobierno (Government House), formerly a priory for the Jesuits. It continues to serve as the administrative offices for the city.

In southern Colombia there are two additional UNESCO sites: San Agustín and Tierradentro, both of which preserve indigenous culture. San Agustín is an archaeological park containing several sandstone sculptures carved by pre-Columbian indigenous tribes. Archaeologists have dated some of these sculptures and statues back to 3300 BCE. Possibly founded by the same tribes of San Agustín, Tierradentro is a site of an indigenous funerary complex. The site also contains several rock sculptures as well as red, white, and black colored wall paintings that decorate the interior of the tombs.

The other major archaeological site in Colombia is the Ciudad Perdida (Lost City), located in the mountains of the Sierra Nevada near the city of Santa Marta. The site was only recently discovered in 1972. Believed to be founded between 500 and 700 CE, Ciudad Perdida was an enormous indigenous settlement that thrived for more than two centuries. Archaeological excavations have revealed large numbers of terraces and winding paved paths which suggest a densely populated indigenous

city that functioned as a trading city between tribes of the mountains and the coast.

Libraries & Museums
The capital of Colombia is home to many of the country's museums, including the Archeological Museum and the Museum of Modern Art, as well as institution such as the National Astronomical Observatory and the Botanical Institute. The Santa Clara Museum, which was once a church, has several large, restored frescoes. The Old Bogotá neighborhood is home to the Gold Museum, which has the world's largest collection of pre-Colombian gold artifacts.

Holidays
National holidays in Colombia include a few that North Americans would recognize such as New Year's Day, Labor Day, and Columbus Day. Other national holidays include Independence Day (July 20), the Battle of Boyaca (August 7), and the Independence of Cartegena (November 11).

Youth Culture
Youth culture in Colombia is similar to that found in other Latin American countries. However, the ways in which young people spend their leisure time are often dictated by gaps in disposable income among different parts of the population. In rural areas and in some urban centers, people begin working at a very young age to either help support the family or to earn extra money.

Among the middle and upper classes in Colombia, young people have more options. Larger cities feature numerous bars, clubs, and discos catering to young people; dancing is one of the most popular activities among Colombian teenagers. For those of the upper echelon of society, fincas and estancias (farms and ranches) exist outside the city and are common destinations on the weekend for groups of young people. Among young women, in particular, there has been a growing trend toward cosmetic surgery. In many Colombian cities, there is a growing market for cosmetic surgeries, for those who can afford it.

SOCIETY

Transportation

Most Colombian cities have a system of private bus and taxi lines to transport people through the city. Privately owned buses, known as collectivos, are used as a reliable system of transport for a majority of urban workers. The larger cities in Colombia have invested in public transportation systems that are run by municipalities. Bogotá, for example, has a public bus system, the Transmileno, which continues to expand service into new areas. Additionally, the city of Medellín constructed a light rail system, the Metro, which, with a 2012 expansion has two lines, 29 kilometers (18 miles) and 38 kilometers (24 miles) in length. Bogotá has also restricted car use in the city and increased bicycle and Bus Rapid Transit (BRT) traffic, as well as creating public pedestrian spaces. Many parking spaces have been demolished and wider sidewalks have been put in their place.

The Pan-American Highway is a major thoroughfare that runs through Bogotá, and connects it with other urban areas. A railroad system connects the city with Colombia's two coasts, on the Caribbean Sea and the Pacific Ocean. Bogotá is also where Avianca, the first South American commercial airline, is based. Traffic in the country moves on the right-hand side of the road.

Transportation Infrastructure

Up until the 20th century, transportation was difficult in Colombia due to the rugged nature and terrain of the high Andes Mountains. Commerce and transport were typically confined to the navigable rivers. However, increased investments in public infrastructure have gradually led to the creation of an extensive network of rail lines and highways. In recent years, there has been significant investment in road construction. According to 2011 report, there are 163,000 kilometers (101,283 miles) of roads in Colombia, of which 64 percent are paved.

Stemming from Bogotá, three major highway systems unite the Caribbean, eastern, and central regions. During the 1990s, however, most of these highway systems were susceptible to crime and insurgents, who used the highways for kidnapping and extortion purposes. However, an increased military presence has greatly enhanced security on the highways and now a variety of private bus companies offer service between cities.

However, the railroad network in Colombia has declined significantly in recent decades due to heightened security concerns and lack of private investment. While some commerce continues along the rails, most of it is confined to the Atlantic coast, where an extensive rail transport system hauls coal to nearby ports for overseas export. In addition, Colombia still utilizes its rivers and inland waterways as methods of transport. On both the Pacific and Atlantic coasts, commercial and passenger boats regularly travel the waterways. In the Amazonía region of southern Colombia, where limited road networks exist, river transport is crucial for the movement of goods and people through the region.

Media & Communications

While there are numerous newspapers, radio stations, and television channels in Colombia, control of these media outlets remains concentrated either in the hands of the government or among a few private companies. Under the 1991 constitution, freedom of speech is a public right officially protected by the law, and no outright official censorship exists. Nonetheless, Colombia remains a precarious place for journalists. More than 50 journalists were killed in the past 10 years and many more were victims of death threats and physical intimidation. In 2014, the non-profit Reporters Without Borders, an organization dedicated to journalist safety, ranked Colombia 126 out of 180 countries in terms of journalist safety and freedom of speech.

A government agency, the National Television Commission, regulates all television programming and issues operating licenses for private television stations. Caracol TV is the largest privately owned television station in Colombia and provides news coverage as well as general programming. Its major private competitor is RCN, which provides news coverage and entertainment programming. The Colombian government still operates two public television stations, Señal Colombia and Canal Uno, which provide public access television as well as government programming. In addition, the major cities operate small local television channels, such as the channel, CityTV, operating in Bogotá.

The largest circulating newspaper in Colombia is Bogotá's *El Tiempo,* which is owned by the Spanish conglomerate Grupo Planeta. The other Colombian daily is *El Espectador*, which has only recently returned to daily publication after a severe financial crisis in 2001. There are a variety of other daily city papers, the most famous of which is Medellín's *El Colombiano*, but many of these smaller papers suffer circulation problems.

Internet usage has been increasing in Colombia, with 2014 statistics measuring about 53 percent usage among the population. These numbers have been increasing and many government initiatives exist to provide greater Internet access to poor and rural areas.

SOCIAL DEVELOPMENT

Standard of Living
Colombia ranked 98th out of 187 countries on the 2013 United Nations Human Development Index, which measures quality of life and standard of living indicators.

Water Consumption
According to 2012 statistics from the World Health Organization (WHO), approximately 97 percent of the population has access to improved sources of drinking water, while an estimated 85 percent have access to improved sanitation; both percentages are below the regional average.

Education
Primary school in Colombia lasts for about seven years, and all children between the ages of six and 12 are expected to attend. Upon completion of primary school, students may continue on to secondary school and eventually attend one of Colombia's universities, technical schools, or other institutes of higher education. Over the past 50 years, the rate of illiteracy has dropped from 50 to seven percent.

In 2009, the government faced student protests and riots in Bogotá and Medellín in response to the government's under-funding of higher education and the low quality of education offered in its universities. In 2009, it was reported that the country only had 7.1 master's or PhD degree holders per 1 million residents. The country greatly expanded its spending education, going from 0.4 percent of GDP in 2009 to 4.4 percent in 2012.

Women's Rights
The 1991 constitution guarantees a woman's right to work and to fair and equal pay, as well as granting and guaranteeing property ownership, divorce, suffrage, and public office. In Colombia, women are increasingly joining the ranks of doctors, lawyers, business executives, and politicians. However, while these rights are guaranteed under the constitution, in practice they are not always respected.

Traditionally, Latin cultures have been patriarchal societies, meaning they were marked by the established supremacy of a father or male figure. Women were expected to remain in the home and manage the domestic affairs for the family. While the 1991 constitution has accorded women greater freedom in this respect, it remains difficult to alter several centuries of entrenched thinking. Women have entered the work forces in increasing numbers, either by choice or by necessity, but attitudes toward this new phenomenon vary. According to reports issued by World Economic Forum, in 2014, there was a 44 percent salary gap between men and women in most Colombian industries. In addition, while sexual harassment is legally prohibited in Colombia, women have no legal recourse if subjected to harassment.

Continuing civil conflict has affected all of Colombian society, but women have been particularly targeted in rural areas by security forces, insurgents, and paramilitaries. There have been numerous reported cases of rape and torture perpetrated against women in these areas. Additionally, domestic violence against women remains a constant and chronic problem in Colombian society. Studies indicate that nearly 41 percent of Colombian women are victims of domestic abuse at some point during their lives. Further statistics estimated that 20,000 women had been victims of sexual violence in 2010. Despite having legal recourse, a 2011 survey found that 73 percent of the women choose to remain silent about physical abuse, due to the lack of action by authorities.

The trafficking of women and prostitution remain problems in Colombia. Child prostitution in particular is a huge problem. A 2001 UN report stated that 35,000 young girls were working as prostitutes in Colombia. In addition, international crime syndicates and Colombians are widely suspected of cooperating in trafficking women abroad to serve as prostitutes in Europe, North America, and Asia. However, government prosecutors have been notoriously lax in indicting people for human trafficking.

In addition, abortion remains illegal in Colombia and punishable by up to three years of incarceration for both patient and practitioner. However, this trend might be changing. In May 2006, high courts in Colombia amended the law to permit abortion in cases where the mother's life is threatened, or in situations where the pregnancy was a result of rape or incest.

Health Care

Colombia has a social insurance system. As it is in the United States, the health care system is funded largely by employers, workers, and the government. Most industrial workers enjoy a host of benefits including maternity, dental, and accident insurance. A shortage of doctors and hospital beds remains a challenge, with most of the doctors concentrated in the larger cities. Malaria and yellow fever pose major health threats in some areas of the country.

GOVERNMENT

Structure

Colombia has a democratic system of government, sharing the basic structure of the system employed by the United States. The constitution, which was rewritten in 1991, calls for executive, legislative, and judicial branches. The executive contains the president, his cabinet, and a vice president as well. The president serves a four-year term.

The Senate and House of Representatives make up the legislative branch. The 102 members of the Senate and the 166 members of the House are elected at the same time as the president. Politically, Colombia is divided into 32 departments, with at least two representatives from each serving in the House or Senate. Minority groups are also represented with seats reserved for Native Americans, blacks, and guerrillas.

Political Parties

Colombia boasts a multi-party system, with several parties having influence in the government. In the parliamentary elections of 2014, the Partido de la U (Party of the U), a liberal conservative party, gained about 16 percent of the vote and secured 39 seats in the Chamber of Representatives and 21 in the Senate. The Partido Conservador Colombiano (Colombian Conservative Party) gained 13 percent of the vote and secured 27 and 18 seats in the representative and senate bodies, respectively. The Partido Liberal Coloabiano, a center-left party, took 14 percent of the vote in the representative race, taking 37 seats, and 12 percent in the Senate race, winning 17 seats. The Centro Democratico party took 20 seats in the Senate and 12 in the Chamber of Representatives.

Local Government

Local government in Colombia is comprised of 32 departments and one capital district. Each department is then divided into municipalities and then subdivided into corregimientos.

Departments are administered by a directly elected governor and council; municipalities are led by a mayor and council; corregimientos (smaller than a municipality) have their own administrator. Large cities have been designated districts, which also means they have local administration.

Judicial System

The judicial branch of government is ruled by four high courts: the Supreme Court, the Constitutional Court, the State Council and the Superior Council of the Judiciary, as well as superior and municipal courts.

The Senate and House of Representatives elect the Supreme Court Justices for life. The Supreme Court is divided into four chambers that address civil, criminal, labor, and constitutional matters.

Taxation

The Colombian government levies taxes on personal and corporate income, value-added, stamps, financial transactions, patrimony (wealth), as well as local taxes. Taxes are relatively moderate, with the highest corporate and personal income tax rates at 33 percent.

Armed Forces

The Military Forces of Colombia consist of an army, naval forces (including a marine infantry and coast guard), and an air force. Military conscription exists; as of 2004, the service obligation was 18 months, beginning age 18. For over four decades, the armed forces have engaged rebel and paramilitary groups in the country's rural areas, most notably Fuerzas Armadas Revolucinarias de Colombia (Revolutionary Armed Forces of Colombia, FARC) and the Ejército de Liberación Nacional, (National Liberation Army, or ELN).

Foreign Policy

Due to internal civil problems, Colombian foreign relations reflect the domestic conflicts that persist within the country. Historically, Colombia has held strong relations with the United States.

At the turn of the 20th century, the proximity of the Panama Canal and increased American investment in Colombia by corporations such as the United Fruit Company, led to a regular American diplomatic presence in Colombia. This involvement increased throughout the century and reached a high point with the advent of the "war on drugs" launched by the U.S. in the late 1980s. The massive drug eradication campaign was implemented to destroy the supply of illicit drugs, mostly cocaine, being smuggled from Colombia to the U.S.

In 1998, this campaign reached a new stage with the launch of "Plan Colombia," a multi-billion dollar foreign aid package to Colombia that involved direct American military aid. This included aerial fumigation, or the use of lethal gases, and military training to the Colombian government for the destruction of narcotics. Under the administration of President George W. Bush, U.S. foreign aid increased to Colombia. That aid is often used to directly combat political insurgents within Colombia. These strong ties with the U.S. have somewhat isolated Colombia from the rest of Latin America. However, the proposed 2015 U.S. budget allocates less than half as much foreign aid to Colombia as was appropriated in 2011.

Colombia still maintains economic and diplomatic connections with Europe, in particular with Spain. However, Colombia has sustained strained relations with the European Union (EU) because of Colombia's military solution to the civil conflict within its borders. Despite European concerns, Colombia has been awarded numerous foreign aid packages from the EU, and a brisk commercial trade exists between Colombia and the European continent.

More problematic have been Colombia's foreign relations with its fellow Latin American nations. One long-standing dispute has been Colombia's sovereignty over the islands of San Andres and Providencia, two Caribbean islands claimed by Nicaragua. International mediation has failed to provide a solution to the problem.

More recently, Colombia has experienced tension with the neighboring states of Venezuela and Ecuador. Both countries are under the control of leftist leaders, in particular President Hugo Chavez of Venezuela. Colombia has routinely accused both countries of sheltering Colombian insurgents and their supporters. In return, Chavez has routinely accused Colombia of being a "colony" of, or too dependent on, the United States. These tensions almost broke out into full-scale war during the Andean Crisis of 2008, when Colombia launched an aerial attack against a Colombian insurgent camp located in Ecuador. This violation of territorial sovereignty was roundly condemned by Ecuador and Venezuela, both of which mobilized troops along the Colombian frontier. A roundtable of diplomatic consultations averted war, but relations between all three countries remained strained.

Colombia is a full member of several Latin American diplomatic and trade organizations including the Organization of American States (OAS) and the Andean Community. On an international level, Colombia is a part of the UN, the International Monetary Fund (IMF) and the World Bank.

Human Rights Profile

International human rights law insists that states respect civil and political rights, and also promote an individual's economic, social, and cultural rights. The United Nations (UN) Universal Declaration of Human Rights (UDHR) is recognized as the standard for international human rights. Its authors sought the counsel of the world's great thinkers, philosophers, and religious leaders, and were careful to create a document that reflects the core values shared by every world culture. (To read this document or view the articles relating to cultural human rights, visit: www.udhr.org/UDHR/default.htm.)

Beset by civil conflict since the mid-20th century, Colombia has had a very mixed record on human rights. In 1991, in an attempt to bring greater transparency and political rights to the country, Colombia ratified a new constitution. On paper, the Colombian constitution is an ideal model for the protection of human rights, with over five chapters and 85 articles explicitly dedicated to the protection of human rights. For example, the rights of all minorities, especially indigenous groups, are protected in the constitution and several new branches of government were created to guarantee human rights for the Colombian people.

However, while human rights are protected on paper, the internal conflict in Colombia has led to multiple abuses of human rights. According to the 2013 annual report issued by Amnesty International, serious abuses of human rights are still a persistent problem, and are typically perpetrated by three particular groups: the paramilitaries, the guerrillas, and the security forces.

The two main guerrilla groups are the Fuerzas Armadas Revolucinarias de Colombia (Revolutionary Armed Forces of Colombia, FARC) and the Ejército de Liberación Nacional, (National Liberation Army, or ELN). Partly communist in orientation, both guerrilla groups have been in existence since the 1960s. Both groups derive significant revenue from drug smuggling, extortion, and kidnapping. It is estimated that more than 700 kidnapping victims continue to be held against their will by the FARC, and as recently as 2008, three Americans held hostage by FARC since 2003 were rescued from captivity. In addition, both the FARC and the ELN have targeted government officials and civilians for assassination and both groups have been tied to large-scale massacres of peasant families throughout the country. Since 2012, a strong, but not totally successful, effort has been made to end the conflict. This has reduced the violence, but, as of 2015, not produced an end to the conflict.

Paramilitary groups arose during the 1980s in reaction to the waves of guerrilla attacks and kidnappings in the country. Largely funded by private citizens and drug traffickers, the paramilitaries soon began to score notable victories against the guerrilla insurgents. The largest paramilitary group, the Autodefensas Unidas de Colombia (United Self-Defense Forces of

Colombia, AUC) became heavily involved in the drug trade and extortion. The AUC is also responsible for several notorious civilian massacres and extrajudicial killings in which hundreds of families, and in some cases, entire villages have been killed.

During 2004-06, the Colombian government pushed for paramilitary demobilization. This was severely criticized by international observers as political amnesty for paramilitary human rights violations. Documented cases of cooperation between Colombian government security forces and the paramilitaries were also uncovered. This was brought to light in 2006 with the so-called "parapolitico" scandal, in which signed documents and court testimony revealed high level meetings between Colombian politicians and paramilitary leaders. Over 31 Colombian politicians were implicated in the scandal, including many politicians with ties to the administration of President Alvaro Uribe (2002–2010).

Colombian security forces have also been implicated in numerous human rights abuses, including extrajudicial killings, torture, and rape. However, the Colombian government has shown extreme reluctance to investigate these allegations. International pressure and independent investigations by the Colombian judiciary have highlighted many of these abuses.

Migration
Colombia's net migration rate in 2010 was -0.68 migrants per 1,000 residents. Forced displacement, as well as economic, political, security, and social pressures, have contributed to both voluntary and involuntary internal migration. The entrenched armed conflict in the country has evolved to become a conflict involving territory as much as it is ideological.

ECONOMY

Overview of the Economy
Colombia, once known primarily as a coffee-producing country, has successfully diversified its economy. Today, petroleum ranks as its principal export. Other important exports include coffee, vegetables, chemicals, coal, textiles, fresh-cut flowers, bananas, sugar, gold, emeralds, and cattle.

In 2013, Colombia's gross domestic product (GDP) was estimated at $369.2 billion USD. The per capita GDP was estimated at $11,100 USD.

Colombia is a member of two trade organizations: the Andean Community, and the Group of Three, which includes Mexico and Venezuela. Its main trading partner is the United States.

Industry
Mainly smaller operations, Colombia's manufacturers generally produce goods for domestic consumption. Manufacturing activity accounts for about 38 percent of the country's yearly national output. Cotton spinning mills are the largest-scale manufacturers. Other manufactured items include foodstuffs, clothing, and footwear, ceramics, tobacco products, iron and steel, and transportation equipment.

Manufacturing is a key component of Bogotá's economy. The city produces textiles, machinery, tires, electrical equipment, chemicals, and pharmaceuticals, as well as food and drink. Bogotá also has a thriving publishing industry, as well as a major stock exchange.

Labor
Colombia's labor force was estimated at roughly 23.75 million in 2013, with an unemployment rate of 9.7 percent, down from 12 percent in 2009. Approximately 62 percent of the labor force is employed in the services sector while the agricultural and industry sectors averaged 17 and 21 percent of the collective work force, respectively (2013).

Energy/Power/Natural Resources
Colombia's reputation as an agricultural country often hides the fact that it is rich in minerals and energy sources. South America's largest producer of gold, Colombia also accounts for nearly half of the world's high-quality emeralds. The country ranks among the world's leaders in oil

reserves, and is Latin America's largest producer of coal.

Deforestation, as a result of intense logging efforts, has plagued Colombia's once lush landscape, while over-hunting has affected almost every animal species in the country. To combat this problem, national parks have become increasingly widespread in hopes of restoring the landscape.

In the major cities, Colombia has the same environmental challenges, especially air pollution caused by vehicle emissions, faced by any industrialized nation. This problem is particularly critical in Bogotá. Deforestation from logging efforts and soil and water quality damage from overuse of pesticides have taken a toll on the countryside as well.

Fishing

While Colombia's catch is comparatively small, its fisheries industry enjoys an international market. Tuna fishing is the leading industry, and much of the nation's catch is used for export. Along with tuna, other major catches include shrimp, white fish (snapper, grouper, etc.), anchovy, herring, crayfish, and conch. Shrimp and shark stocks are threatened by overfishing. Aquaculture products include shrimp, tilapia, rainbow trout, cachamas, bocachico, and carp.

Forestry

Of Colombia's total area of 282 million acres, 148 million are forested. The Colombian government has established the goal of expanding that area by reclaiming 2.7 million acres. The country's timber needs have largely been filled by imports.

Mining/Metals

Petroleum and coal are the main mineral products of Colombia. The country now produces enough petroleum to provide for all of its own energy needs, while still having significant amounts to export. As one of the world's largest exporters of coal, in 2013, Colombia produced about 85.5 metric tons. Most of the coal originates in a single mine on the Guajira peninsula.

Other minerals mined for export include gold, silver, emeralds, platinum, copper, nickel, and natural gas.

Agriculture

Coffee was once Colombia's principle money maker, but it has been surpassed by petroleum. Export earnings from coffee have fallen nearly 70 percent since the 1980s. Since 2000, output has dropped by 25 percent due to the economy and an increase in temperature in the region.

Coffee plantations cover about one million hectares (approximately 2.5 million acres) of Colombia's mountainous areas at altitudes of 900 to 1,800 meters (about 3,000 and 6,000 feet). There are nearly 150,000 small coffee plantations operating in the county today. Other cash crops include cacao beans, sugarcane, tobacco, cotton, bananas, and cut flowers.

Animal Husbandry

Livestock has exceeded coffee in terms of its share of exports. Cattle are providing meat as well as leather. Colombia has the fourth highest cattle population in Latin America and is among the top 13 cattle producers in the world. Its beef industry is poised for further growth in the early 21st century. Beef, poultry, and pigs dominate the livestock industry.

Tourism

Colombia offers a multitude of options for the traveler. Its mountains, beaches, rivers, and cities the country should be a popular vacation spot. However, Colombia has gained a reputation as an unsafe destination due to news of drug dealers, kidnappings, and guerilla violence.

Tourists who decide to visit Bogotá are treated to colonial churches and museums nestled among the modern architecture of the capital city. The Caribbean coast near Cartagena is home to historic Spanish forts, and islands boasting coral reefs that are ideal for snorkeling. The town itself is famous for its Spanish colonial architecture.

Medellín is the largest city in the northwest region, and is dominated by two distinct landscapes: the rainforests and the mountains. While Medellín is an industrialized city, Santa Fe de Antioquia, 50 miles to the northwest, retains the look and feel of the Spanish colonial period.

With a decline in negative publicity, 2013 began what Colombian officials hope is a continual dramatic increase in tourism, hosting three times the number of tourists than was the case a decade earlier. This included an increase in spending to 5.4 percent of GDP, as compared to 1.9 percent in 2008. Investment programs in 2008 and 2011 seem to be producing benefits, and the Colombian government hopes to increase employment in this area by 50 percent within the next four years.

Jeffrey Bowman, Christopher Stetter,
Alex K. Rich

DO YOU KNOW?

- Bogotá has one of the largest urban bicycle path networks in the world, at 303 kilometers (188 miles).

- The biennial Iberoamerican Theater Festival, the largest theater festival in the world, is hosted in Bogotá.

Bibliography

Gallon, Gustavo and Christopher Welna, *Peace, Democracy and Human Rights in Colombia*. Terre Haute: University of Notre Dame Press, 2007.

Graham, Patrick. *Go Before You Die: A Road Trip Through The "New" Colombia*.

Harper's Magazine 316.1893. February 2008.

Guillermoprieto, Alma. *Looking for History: Dispatches From Latin America*. New York: Vintage, 2002.

Hylton, Forrest. *Evil Hour in Colombia*. London: Verso Press, 2006.

Kohn, Robert and Landon Robert. *Colombia (Country Guide)*. London: Lonely Planet, 2006. [7th edition to be printed in September, 2015]

LaRosa, Michael J., German R. Mejia, and Pamela Murray (Foreward by). *Colombia: A Concise Contemporary History*. Washington: Rowman & Littlefield Publishers, Inc. 2013.

Lessard, Marc. *Colombia: Ulysses Travel Guide*. Toronto: 1999.

Livingstone, Grace. *Inside Colombia: Drugs, Democracy and War*. New York: Rutgers University Press, 2004.

Pollard, Peter. *Footprint Colombia Handbook: The Travel Guide*. London: Passport Books, 2001.

Rough Guides. *Colombia Rough Guide Snapshot South America*. London: Penguin Group, 2013.

Williamson, Edwin. *The Penguin History of Latin America (Penguin History)*. London: Penguin Books, 1993.

Works Cited

http://www.freemedia.at/cms/ipi/statements_detail.html?ctx id=CH0055&docid=CMS1146652393458&year=2002

http://worldmusic.nationalgeographic.com/worldmusic/view/page.basic/genre/content.genre/vallenato_798

http://www.nytimes.com/2006/05/24/opinion/24weds3.html

http://www.ewakulak.com/index.php?option=content&task =view&id=190&Itemid=25&lang=en

http://www.igac.gov.co:8080/igac_web/contenidos/division_politico_administrativa.jsp?idMenu=109

http://www.dane.gov.co/censo/

http://www.unhchr.ch/tbs/doc.nsf/(Symbol)/a315ebc5b6f67 01d80256562005306ad?Opendocument

http://news.bbc.co.uk/2/hi/americas/7188509.stm

http://news.bbc.co.uk/2/hi/americas/1738963.stm

http://www.state.gov/g/drl/rls/hrrpt/2001/wha/8326.htm

http://www.equalitynow.org/english/campaigns/un/unhrc_reports/unhrc_colombia_en.pdf

http://hrw.org/wr2k3/americas4.html

http://www.colombiajournal.org/colombia111.htm

http://news.bbc.co.uk/2/hi/americas/1138712.stm

http://news.bbc.co.uk/2/hi/americas/country_profiles/1212798.stm

http://news.bbc.co.uk/2/hi/americas/1212827.stm

https://www.cia.gov/library/publications/the-world-factbook/geos/co.html

http://www.unhchr.ch/tbs/doc.nsf/898586b1dc7b4043c1256 a450044f331/f663d6b606af4a41802568e7004ca9fa/$FI LE/G0040076.pdf

http://www.amnesty.org/en/library/asset/AMR23/018/2008/ en/cf385c32-3edb-11dd-9656-05931d46f27f/ amr230182008eng.pdf

http://www.amnesty.org/en/region/americas/south-america/colombia

http://www.colombiasupport.net/

http://www.pbi-colombia.org/1132.html?&L=1%3FL%3D1 %3FL%3D0%3FL%3D0

http://poorbuthappy.com/colombia/

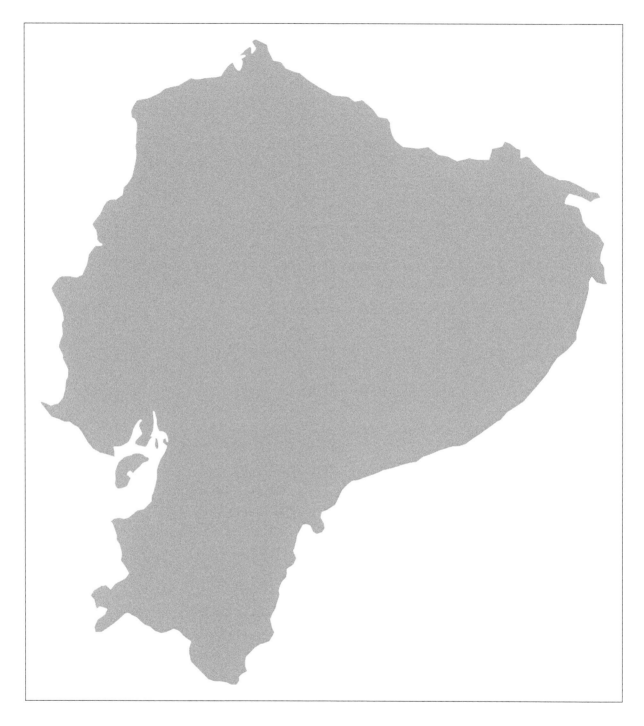

ECUADOR

Introduction

Ecuador, which in Spanish means "equator," is so named because the equator passes through the country. Once a colony of Spain, Ecuador struggled toward democracy for more than a century. Although the country has had more than 15 constitutions and has been governed by presidents, dictators, and juntas, its government has been relatively stable for over 50 years.

One of the smallest countries in South America, Ecuador boasts more biodiversity than most countries in the world. Within its small territory, Ecuador has islands, rainforests, deserts, snowcapped mountains, and valleys. The country's territory includes the Galápagos Islands, located several hundred miles off its coast. Ecuador is also home to several protected environmental areas.

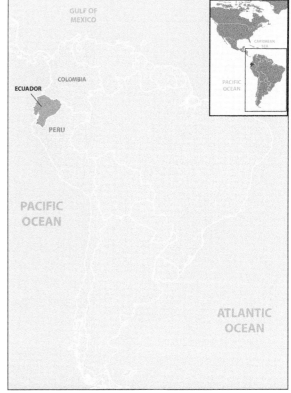

GENERAL INFORMATION

Official Language: Spanish
Population: 15,654,411 (2014 estimate)
Currency: United States dollar
Coins: The U.S. dollar is divided into 100 cents. Coins are available in denominations of 1, 5, 10, and 25 cents, with a 50 cent and 1 dollar coin both rarely used.
Land Area: 283,561 square kilometers (109,484 square miles)
Water Area: 6,720 square kilometers (2,594 square miles)
National Motto: "Dios, patria y libertad" (Spanish, "God, homeland and liberty")

National Anthem: "Salve, Oh Patria" ("Hail, Oh Fatherland")
Capital: Quito
Time Zone: GMT -5
Flag Description: The flag of Ecuador, known as "La Tricolor," has three horizontal bands of color: one gold (double width), one blue, and one red. In the center of the flag, the coat of arms of Ecuador is featured. The coat of arms depicts a condor with outstretched wings.

Population

Approximately 70 percent of the population of Ecuador lives in urban areas. Nearly half of the people live on the coastal plains, and almost as many live on the plateaus and in the valleys of the Andes. Only about 600,000 people live in the tropical rainforest to the east of the mountains. An estimated 25,000 or more Ecuadorians live in the Galápagos Islands, and the population of those islands is expected to double every 11 years.

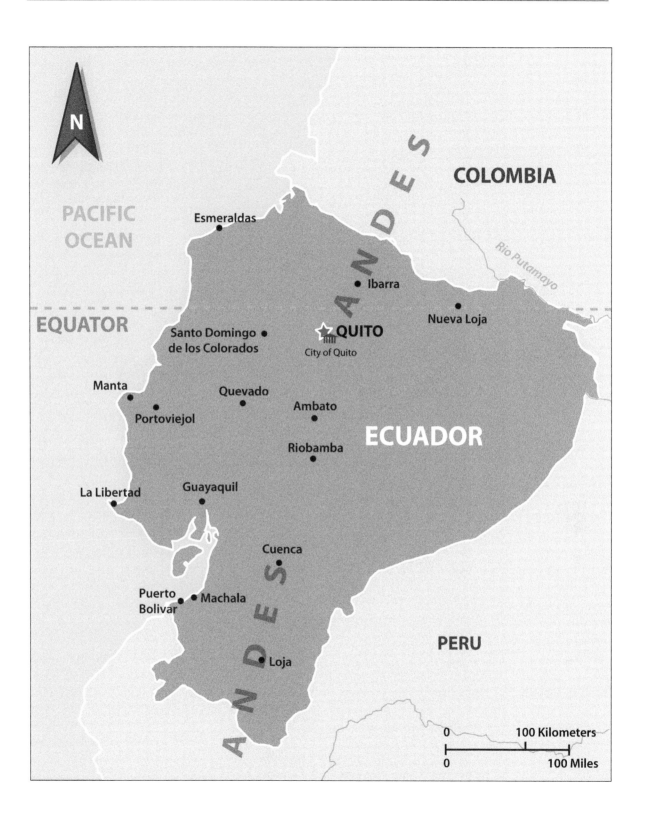

Principal Cities by Population (2010):

- Guayaquil (2,291,158)
- Quito (1,619,146)
- Cuenca (331,888)
- Santa Elena (305,632)
- Machala (241,606)
- Durán (235,769)
- Portoviejo (223,086)
- Manta (221,122)
- Loja (180,617)
- Ambato (178,538)

Gauyaquil is the largest city, with a population of 2.3 million (2010). Quito, the capital, has a population of approximately 1.6 million (2010). Other major cities include Cuenca, with a population of 332,000, and Santa Elena, with 305,000 residents. Roughly 25 percent of the population lives below the poverty line (2013).

Ecuador is home to over fourteen indigenous groups, which maintain their own customs and language. About 72 percent of the population is mestizo (a mixture of indigenous Amerindian and Spanish descent). Another 15 percent is Amerindian, seven percent of the population is black, and six percent is of European (mainly Spanish) descent.

Languages
Although Spanish is the official language, Quechua is commonly spoken in Ecuador. Additional Amerindian languages are also spoken in the country. Many residents of Quito speak English, especially in tourist and business settings.

Native People & Ethnic Groups
Pre-Columbian Ecuador was home to many tribes and cultures, including the Valdivia, Machalilla, Chorerra, Narrio, Tiaone, Jama-Coaque, La Tolita, Bahia, and Guangala. Many types of objects made by these peoples, including female figurines and ceramics, tools of stone and quartz, and obsidian spears, survive today.

In the late 15th century, the Inca from Peru conquered much of what is now Ecuador. The Inca united many of the tribes and taught them Quechua, the Incan language. The Spanish conquered the territory in 1534, and the native people were forced into slave labor on the large haciendas (plantations). Spaniards who settled in the coastal lowlands imported African slaves. Intermarriage between Spanish men and Amerindian women produced a large population of mestizos.

Ecuadorians of European descent are among the wealthiest and most powerful people in the country. Many are absentee landowners of large haciendas. Others are engaged in business or trading. Ecuador's Amerindians have very little power or money. They maintain their traditional languages, clothes, and customs. Many work unpaid on haciendas for the privilege of using small plots of land for themselves. Some Amerindian women earn money by weaving or pottery-making.

Mestizos, the largest ethnic group in Ecuador, often work as day laborers, harvesting bananas or cacao (cacao seeds are used to make chocolate and cocoa). Some plains mestizos clear small plots of land in the forest to feed their families. As the soil wears out, they migrate. Mestizos in the Andes often own their land. Others work for hire as laborers, servants, and shopkeepers.

Religions
More than 90 percent of the Ecuadorians are Roman Catholic, but indigenous groups often mix Christian beliefs with traditional beliefs. Quito, the capital, features a sizeable Mormon presence and a small Jewish community. There has been an upsurge of converts to various evangelical Protestant denominations in the early 21st century, particularly among the city's poorest residents.

Climate
The climate of Ecuador depends largely on elevation. The lowlands are hot and humid, with average temperatures of 23° to 26° Celsius (73° to 79° Fahrenheit). The Andes are cool,

with temperatures ranging between 13° and 18° Celsius (55° and 64° Fahrenheit). The higher elevations are colder and snowcapped. The Galápagos Islands experience the greatest climatic variation, with temperatures ranging from 22° to 32° Celsius (72° to 90° Fahrenheit). Ecuador receives 140 centimeters (55 inches) of rain annually, mostly in the lowland areas. The southern coast and the Galápagos receive only light rain.

ENVIRONMENT & GEOGRAPHY

Topography

Ecuador is about the size of the state of Colorado. It is bordered on the north by Colombia, on the east and south by Peru, and on the west by the Pacific Ocean. The Galápagos Islands, 960 kilometers (600 miles) offshore, are also part of Ecuador.

The country has four topographical regions: the coastal lowland, the Andes highland (or Sierra), the eastern lowland (or Oriente), and the Galápagos. The coastal lowland is a flat plain of mud and sand washed down from the mountains. The northern part is wet and swampy, while the southern part is desert. Between these two zones grow tropical rainforests. Much of the forested area has been cleared for crops.

The Andes highland consists of two parallel ridges of mountains traversing the country from north to south. High plateaus lie between the ridges, and some of the peaks are volcanic. The eastern lowland is an undeveloped area of thick tropical rainforest. Travel is mostly by boat on the region's many rivers.

The Galápagos Islands, the inspiration for Charles Darwin's theory of natural selection, are mostly volcanic peaks, rising as high as 12,500 meters (5,000 feet). The islands comprise an area of 7,800 square kilometers (3,000 square miles). They are known for their exotic animals and plants.

Ecuador's highest point is Mount Chimborazo, a volcano in the Andes, rising 6,267 meters (20,561 feet) above sea level.

The rivers of Ecuador are short but navigable. The Rio Esmeraldas flows through the northern coastal lowland for 80 kilometers (50 miles) to the Pacific. The Rio Guayas, formed of tributaries from the Andes, flows for 156 kilometers (100 miles) through the southern part of the coastal lowlands into the Pacific. The Guayas is part of one of the largest river systems on the west coast of South America.

The Río Pastazas, 644 kilometers (400 miles) long, rises in the Andes and flows south and east through the eastern lowland to the Río Maranon in Peru, one of the headwaters of the Amazon. The Río Napo, 885 kilometers (550 miles) long, flows through northeast Ecuador to northeast Peru.

Quito, the capital, is located 25 kilometers (15 miles) south of the equator, on the slopes of the Guagua Pichincha, an active volcano in the Andes mountains of northern Ecuador. The long, narrow river valley in which Quito lies is not only dotted with volcanoes, but is also prone to earthquakes. A powerful earthquake struck the capital in 1797 and killed 40,000 people.

Plants & Animals

Ecuador is home to nine percent of the world's animal species and 18 percent of its birds. Among Ecuador's birds, the most famous is the rare king vulture. Others include the harpy eagle, which is known to snatch monkeys out of treetops; the hoatzin, the only species in its family; and numerous varieties of macaws and toucans.

Common animals include two species of tapir (the largest native mammal), jaguars, ocelots, monkeys (including woolly, spider, and squirrel monkeys), armadillos, sloths, anteaters, and rodents (including the capybara, the world's largest rodent).

The rainforests host many varieties of tree frogs, including the poison-arrow frog. Anacondas, the heaviest snakes in the world (weighing up to 440 pounds), and caimans, a type of crocodile, also inhabit the rivers, as do river dolphins and manatees. Fish typically found in Ecuador's waters include piranhas, stingrays, and electric eels. Humpback whales and tropical fish are found in the waters off the coast.

The Galápagos Islands are home to giant tortoises, penguins, sea lions, iguanas, yellow and black marine turtles, frigate birds, blue-footed boobies, albatrosses, white-tipped sharks, sperm whales, bottlenose dolphins, and whale sharks. Many animals and plants of the Galápagos are found nowhere else in the world.

Ecuador also has 10 percent of the plant species in the world. The rainforests are home to 10,000 plant species, including 25,000 species of trees and 2,725 species of orchids. Grasses and frailejones (a kind of short tree) are found at high elevations of the Andes. The Galápagos Islands also host 600 native plant species and 250 introduced species.

CUSTOMS & COURTESIES

Greetings

Most Ecuadorians speak Spanish, which is the official language used in all official and educational capacities. However, the Spanish spoken in Ecuador varies according to region. Ecuadorian Spanish is closest to the Castilian Spanish spoken in Spain, with several minor phonetic differences. In coastal communities, Ecuadorian Spanish speakers often drop the second half of many common words and do not always pronounce the "s" at the end of words. The saying "Adios" ("Goodbye"), for example, is therefore pronounced 'Ah-dio' on the Ecuadorian coast.

The most common Spanish greetings are "Hola" ("Hello") and "¿Como estas?" ("How are you?"). Alternatively, Spanish speakers may use the word "Bueno" or "Buenos" ("Good") followed by the time of day, as in "Buenos Días" ("Good Morning"). Ecuadorians also commonly blend English words and phrases into their Spanish.

In addition to Spanish, a number of Ecuadorians speak Quechua, a Native American language indigenous to the Andean people. Quechua is actually represented by various dialects, one of which was adopted by the Inca Empire. Common expressions include "Rimaykullayki" or "Napaykullayki" ("Hello"), and the phrase "Windía" ("Good morning"). Additionally, "Ima hinalla" ("How are you?") is also commonly used.

When it comes to non-verbal greetings, both men and women commonly greet by shaking hands. Compared to North American and European behavior, Ecuadorian handshakes are generally light, with little or no pressure exerted. Close friends and family may exchange kisses upon the cheek, or may embrace upon greeting.

Gestures & Etiquette

When compared to North Americans, Ecuadorians tend to stand closer on average, and more frequently make physical contact while speaking. In contrast to other cultures, most Ecuadorians will always take the time to exchange pleasantries in any conversation, including when greeting street vendors and other service personnel. It is considered rude to ignore even vague acquaintances in passing.

As in many Latin American countries, it is considered impolite to show the palm of one's hand to other people. Therefore, Ecuadorians use the back of the hand to beckon someone forward and to wave in greeting or farewell. Ecuadorians also take a relaxed attitude toward punctuality, and tend to schedule meetings and social engagements within a range of time rather than at a certain hour.

Eating/Meals

Most Ecuadorians eat three meals a day, corresponding to breakfast, lunch, and dinner in North America. Meat and grains are staples of the Ecuadorian diet, and may be served at any time of day. Cuisine and customs differ among the Amerindians (descendents of the pre-Columbian cultures of the Americas), who may typically eat only two meals a day. Most meals are served "family style," a communal style in which guests serve themselves from shared dishes. Formal meals (as well as in restaurants) are often served in courses, ranging from appetizers (botanas) to entrees.

Breakfast (desayuno) is typically a light meal, with local coffee and/or fruit juice accompanied by rice and beans, eggs, and some form of pastry. The typical Ecuadorian breakfast in rural areas is generally a mix of grain and meat, of which chicken and lentils or chicken and beans are common varieties. The largest and most important meal of the day is typically lunch (almuerzo), often the only meal of the day that is served in courses. Social and business gatherings are commonly scheduled during the midday meal, followed by a short period of rest before returning to work (though this social custom is fading in recent years). Individuals may begin with appetizers, followed by soup and then a main course of rice, beans, and some form of meat.

By contrast, the evening meal (merienda), which is typically served between six and 10 o'clock, is often light, consisting of leftovers from the midday meal or light fare, including cheese, bread, and cold meat. Wine, beer, and spirits may be served with either the midday or evening meal.

Visiting

When visiting an Ecuadorian home, it is considered common courtesy to compliment the hosts on the appearance of their home. Ecuadorians show gratitude with effusive displays, and guests are advised to clearly indicate their pleasure at being invited to a social function. Additionally, when invited for dinner, it is considered polite to accept and sample any food or drink offered by the host, as outright rejection may be perceived as a comment on the quality of the food.

It is appreciated, but not expected, for visitors to bring gifts for their hosts, including liquor, candies, and pastries. Flowers are a good gift, but lilies should be avoided, as they are most commonly associated with death and funerary customs. When the hosts have children, it is also considered polite to bring small gifts, including toys or candy, for the host's children. The apparent amount of money spent on the gift is seen as a reflection of the guest's socioeconomic status, and visitors therefore take care when choosing gifts.

LIFESTYLE

Family

As in many Latin American nations, extended family groups are the basic unit of society in Ecuador. Young couples tend to live close to their families, unless forced to migrate to find work. This phenomenon poses a threat to the stability of Ecuadorian (and, to an extent, other Latin American) communities. In traditionally Ecuadorian culture, it was not uncommon for three generations of a single family to a share a house. Among the Amerindian cultures, most individuals live in rural environments and observe the same cultural norms as their ancestors. In urbanized environments, life choices vary and individuals more frequently choose to settle further from the security of extended family groups.

With the birth of a new child, the parents and grandparents choose godparents for the newborn child. This system, known as "compadrazgo" because parents and godparents refer to each other as "compadres," allows the family to extend the influence of their family by integrating friends and distant family members who may have superior financial or social influence. In this way, parents help to ensure the security of their children while widening their own influence within society.

In contrast to families in the United States, Ecuadorian families define their personal success partially in reference to their network of friends and family. To maintain these ties, Ecuadorians frequently hold and attend social gatherings involving family and community. Any holiday or a notable family accomplishment is seen as sufficient reason to hold a family or community event.

There are significant differences between Ecuadorian women and men in terms of their expected roles within the family and society. While Ecuadorian men are expected to be the social and economic leaders of the family, women are expected to play a supporting role, while maintaining control over all domestic issues. This system, often cited as "machismo," (which also refers to an exaggerated sense of masculinity) has been deteriorating in the 21st century, partially due to the need for both parents to join the workforce in order to meet economic needs.

Housing

Ecuador is an economically depressed nation that suffers from a housing crisis. It is believed that more than 18 percent of the population (estimated at more than 12 million) lives in substandard housing. A disparity between the wealthy and poor of Ecuador is evident in the differences between types of housing. The wealthy elite of Ecuador, many of whom are expatriates from Europe and America, sometimes live in lavish villas complete with security guards and manicured green spaces. Wealthy farmers sometimes occupy "hacienda" buildings left over from or modeled after the agricultural estates used by Spanish colonists. Spanish-style haciendas are easily recognizable by their white walls and red or brown tile roofing.

However, the vast majority of Ecuadorians live in modest one- or two-family houses, typically constructed of concrete, brick, or wood. More than 60 percent of houses have some sanitation facilities, though Habitat for Humanity estimates that a majority of Ecuadorian houses have insufficient sanitation. In urban areas, families also have the option of renting space in apartment buildings or living in shared housing communities, with a few houses connected to shared yards.

In the poorest communities, Ecuadorian families live in traditional houses made of wattle-and-daub with dirt floors. Wattle-and-daub is an ancient building technique in which wattle refers to interwoven wood, and daub refers to packed clay, soil, or other such substances. Corrugated tin or tile roofing and cement walls are gradually replacing the thatched roofing in many Ecuadorian houses. A large number of houses in rural areas are also built from flattened bamboo, among the most ecologically sound and easily renewable housing materials.

In September 2008, the Ecuadorian government ratified a new constitution containing a provision that guarantees every citizen the right to "adequate and dignified housing," and "water and sanitation." Ecuador was the first country in the region to constitutionally guarantee housing rights and, although the amendment will not itself remedy the housing crisis, it is expected to ensure that any new laws proposed will be in keeping with adequate housing standards.

Food

Ecuadorian cuisine is a blend of European and indigenous traditions, and varies according to the three main regions: the Pacific coast, the Andean and central highlands, and the Oriente region of the Amazon. For example, the coastal region features more seafood dishes, while the central communities tend more towards potatoes, pork, and grains, and the Amazon region features more tropical and exotic fare. In general, tropical fruits, beans, and rice are staple side dishes, and Ecuadorian entrees generally consist of some type of roasted or fried meat, commonly beef and chicken, found throughout the country.

On the Ecuador coast, ceviche is a common dish, and is typically made of seafood soaked in citrus and served with chopped vegetables. Ceviche is served with corn or rice and may also be accompanied by plantains. Another traditional seafood dish is called fanesca, made with fish and grain mixed with peanuts and spices. The dish is mostly served at celebratory feasts, but can also be found at many Ecuadorian restaurants. Among the most unique food served in Ecuador is cuy, a traditional dish that consists of roasted guinea pig. Cuy served with vegetables and lentils or with plantains, and is a common dish in the Andean highlands, where there are large populations of indigenous people. The Amazon region, however, features more adventurous fare, and includes exotic animals from the rainforest.

Quinoa is one of the most common grains served in Ecuador, and has a history dating back to the time of the Inca. Similar to millet, quinoa is a common breakfast food and is also often served as an accompaniment to chicken and other roasted meat dishes. Another common dish is Ecuador is the empanada, a fried dough shell filled with meat, vegetables, and/or cheese. While corn flour shells are most common, Ecuadorians sometimes make empanadas verdes, which use plantain flour and have a distinct flavor. Common fillings include yucca, onion, chicken, pork, and cheese. There are also sweet empanadas filled with fruit and seasoned with sugar or honey.

For refreshment, many Ecuadorians drink batidos or "smoothies," which are shakes made from fruit juice or other flavorings mixed with either water or milk. Among the most popular varieties of batidos are tamarind and mango. A more distinctive drink is chicha, which is made from fermented corn or yucca. Chicha is an indigenous drink that was traditionally made with human saliva as a key ingredient.

Life's Milestones

Ecuador is a predominantly Catholic country and most families celebrate the traditional Catholic rites of passage, including birth, baptism, communion, and marriage. Baptism is a cause for celebration in Ecuador, and is also the time when Ecuadorians choose godparents for their children. Most Ecuadorians celebrate baptisms with a communal meal and guests traditionally donate small cash gifts to the parents to aid in child rearing expenses. After the baptism, young couples may move into a separate house or may, as is traditional in some parts of the country, continue living with their parents.

Many Ecuadorian families observe a young girl's fifteenth birthday with an event commonly known as a quinceañera. This celebration traditionally marks the transition to adulthood, and celebrates the young girl's entry into society. Common in many Hispanic Catholic families, the quinceañera consists of a church ceremony, followed by a social gathering which typically features feasting and dancing.

Marriage is a major milestone in Ecuadoran culture. Ecuadorian Catholic weddings typically involve a church ceremony followed by a family celebration, where traditional foods may be served accompanied by dancing and drinking.

As in the U.S., guests are expected to purchase small gifts or to give money to the new couple to help them establish a new life together. Most Ecuadorian women will drop their own surname in favor of their husband's paternal surname, while some chose to keep their own surname combined with their husband's name.

CULTURAL HISTORY

Art

Ecuador has a rich artistic tradition dating back to the tribes that occupied the region before the arrival of European colonists. One of the most prominent of these pre-Columbian cultures is the ancient civilization of the Inca. Known for their architecture—which, when combined with Spanish influences, became a significant artistic heritage of Ecuador—the Inca also produced highly developed and aesthetic textiles, ceramics, metalworking, and stone sculptures. Other prehistoric and indigenous cultures, such as the Valdivia and Quitus cultures, respectively, were also known for their distinctive architecture and early ceramic crafts. For example, the Chorerra culture is noted primarily for its pottery, but also for its lifelike sculptures and whistling jars. The Machalilla culture produced long, thin, spouted jars, high-necked jars, and earthenware bowls.

Following European colonization of the New World, the Spanish occupied Ecuador in the 16th century, bringing Catholic religious traditions and European artistic techniques to the fine arts of architecture, painting, and sculpture. A unique feature of the early Ecuadorian art culture was the Quito School of Art, which blended Spanish religious imagery and baroque styles with indigenous tribal influences.

Catholic missionaries trained local artists to produce paintings, statues, crucifixes, murals, and other decorative objects to adorn Quito's numerous churches. By the mid-18th century, as many as 30 art guilds operated in the capital. They turned out hauntingly realistic pieces of art that blended European and indigenous influences, such as paintings of the Last Supper in which Christ and the apostles are portrayed seated at a table laden with humitas (a traditional dish of stuffed, steamed cornhusks), rather than the conventional bread and wine. The exquisitely detailed religious statues crafted by the Quiteño artists are famous for their realism, produced by the use of glass eyes, actual human hair and eyelashes, moveable limbs, and robes made of fine, locally woven fabrics.

Most of the paintings and sculptures produced by artists working in the Quito School were decorated with gold leaf, a gilding technique used by both the Spanish and the native tribes of Ecuador. Sculptor Manuel Chili (1723–1796) is one of the pioneers and best-known representatives of the Quito School, which dominated the arts scene until the 18th century.

Over the centuries, as intermarriage and other factors lead to deeper unions between the indigenous and colonial residents of Ecuador, artistic culture developed new characteristics. In the 20th century, artists began concentrating on depicting revolutionary figures and Ecuador's struggle for independence. Many of the works created during this period are considered national treasures, both because of their artistic excellence and because they serve as a record of the sociological transformations in Ecuador. Painter Eduardo Kingman (1913–1998) exemplifies the revolutionary period in Ecuadorian art, as well as the prominence of indigenous expressionism. Kingman used his paintings to explore the suffering of the indigenous people during colonization and the transition to independence. The nation's best known modern artist is painter Oswaldo Guayasamín (1919–1999), whose works depicted much about the lives of Ecuador's indigenous peoples. Modern aesthetics such as abstract expressionism, conceptualism, and minimalism would follow, and all have their own unique influence on Ecuadoran art.

Architecture

Quito, the capital of Ecuador, is perhaps best representative of the country's architectural heritage and is still shaped by its colonial heritage. The distinctive aesthetic of many of Quito's religious and public buildings—characterized by vibrant colors, ornate designs, and the lavish use of gold and other precious substances—reflects the capital's history of conquests by the Incan and Spanish empires. Spanish colonial-style architecture is particularly apparent in the city's red-tile rooftops, balconies, and central courtyards. The blending of European colonial culture and indigenous influences gave rise to a unique Quiteño style and turned Quito into one of the most significant centers of religiously-themed art in the Americas. (The wealth of European architecture and indigenous artistic influences, in fact, has led some to dub Quito "the Florence of the Americas"). Quito's carefully restored heritage remains a magnet for tourists and scholars interested in the intersection of Old and New World cultures. In the nation's largest city, Guayaquil, an 1896 fire destroyed most of the colonial buildings. Modern Guayaquil is a mixture of modern skyscrapers and impoverished residential areas.

Drama

Ecuador was a popular destination for Spanish and Mexican stage companies throughout the 1920s and 1930s. In the mid-1930s, a form of play known as "Estampa Quiteña," or "Quito sketch," became widely popular. These short comedic sketches, not unlike modern situation comedies, focused on the lives of Ecuador's middle class. Ernesto Albá was a popular actor of this period and genre. Ecuadorian playwrights, Francisco Tobar Garcia and José Martinez Queirolo, became widely known for both their creative and administrative work in the country's theater culture during the 1950s and 1960s. Garcia and Queirolo not only wrote theatrical works, but also organized and financed production companies, and were public advocates of the dramatic arts.

The Bolivar Theater (Teatro Bolivar), which was constructed in Quito in 1933, is a well known venue for theatrical performances in Ecuador. The theater features musical works, film, and dance performances throughout the year. Other theaters in Ecuador include the

National Theater, the Teatro Sucre, and the Malayerba Theater.

The Malayerba Theater Group has been active for over 30 years and is known widely for productions that explore regional social issues. The group's production *Tirenle Tiera* (Let's Forget It) took up the issue of domestic violence. Playwright Maria del Rosario Frances, who immigrated to Ecuador from Spain, has written a large number of works for the Malayerba Theater Group. In addition to performing in their theater, the group performs work in poor, rural communities, orphanages, and prisons.

Music

Ecuadorian music can be categorized by two umbrella terms: traditional music (born out of the indigenous communities and pre-Columbian cultures) and Spanish music (a product of music imported from Spanish immigrants beginning in the 16th century). In general, most Ecuadorian music has become a blend of European, indigenous and, to a certain extent, African traditions. More than 50 percent of the population is of mixed origin, and a full 25 percent are descendants of one of the nation's indigenous cultures.

Spanish music in Ecuador includes traditional Spanish folk music, usually played on a variety of stringed, wind, and percussion instruments. Folk music differs according to geographic area, with penas (music clubs) on the coasts playing a distinct brand of folk music from those in the inlands. Nightclubs around Ecuador also play modern Latin music styles such as samba, salsa, and rumba. Afro-Ecuadorian marimba music is also very popular.

The most famous and distinct type of music in Ecuador is the traditional folk music of the Andean peoples. Featuring a variety of flutes and other wind instruments combined with drums and a few stringed instruments, the music of the Andes has an unusual and highly unique sound that has inspired artists around the world. Traditionally, Andean music was played entirely on flute-like instruments such as the rondador, a type of bamboo pipe. However, modern Andean music includes a variety of imported instruments. For example, the charango—which uses five double strings and an armadillo shell as a sound-producing chamber—is an Andean instrument developed in imitation of the stringed instruments introduced by the Spanish. Because of ecological concerns, modern charangos are usually made of wood.

Literature

Ecuadorian literature had minimal impact before the 19th century, when writers of the revolutionary period began producing works of social and political criticism. Juan Montalvo (1832–1889) was an essayist and novelist who used his work to call attention to the dire political problems of mid-19th century Ecuador. His best-known books include *Siete Tratados* (1882), which is considered the first native work of serious political importance, and *Capitulos que se la olvidaron de Cervantes* (1895), which was an attempt to imitate the famous *Don Quixote* by Spanish novelist Miguel de Cervantes (1547–1616).

Ecuadorian literature is also characterized by an "indigenous" genre carried on by a new generation of young writers during the 20th century. One particular group of writers—part of a literary group known as the "Grupo de Guayaquil" (Group of Guayaquil), since they all hailed from Guayaquil—formed the so-called "realist school." Writers of this school focused on social realism and used Ecuadorian life as their central subject and theme. Among the best-known realist novels from the period is *Los que se van* (*Those Who Go Away*), a collaborative effort of stories by three authors: Demetrio Aguilera Malta (1909–1981), Joaquin Gallegos Lara (1911–1947), and Enrique Gil Gilbert (1912–1973). The novel describes the struggles of the indigenous people in western Ecuador.

Ecuador's most famous literary figure is perhaps Jorge Icaza Coronel (1906–1979), whose works deal with political themes, especially the relationship between modern and indigenous culture in Ecuador. His 1943 novel *Huasipungo* is considered one of the classics of Ecuadorian literature, and addresses the plight of a group of Indians persecuted and killed by colonial immigrants. Modern Ecuadorian literature continues to serve as a vehicle for social and political criticism within the country. Nelson Estupinan Bass (1912–2002) was an Afro-Ecuadorian writer whose works explore ethnic relations in Ecuador and the history of the nation's socio-economic castes. Bass is considered one of the nation's most prominent writers.

CULTURE

Arts & Entertainment

Ecuador's traditional folk arts and crafts, which include Inca wood and stone carvings, are considered part of the nation's cultural heritage. As Ecuador has attempted to build its tourist industry, traditional arts and crafts have gained importance. Crafts such as panama hats, which are made in the towns of Montecristi and Cuenca, are enormously popular with tourists. Panama hats have been made in Ecuador for more than 100 years, but were named after the Panama Canal, where the Ecuadorian hats were first sold to foreign visitors.

Art from the Quechua people in the Tigua region of the Andes has also become famous in Ecuador and around the world. The Quechua, who are descended from the Incas, use techniques developed by the Incas in conjunction with modern and imported artistic forms. Julio Toaquiza (1946–), a laborer and artist from the region, is credited with beginning the Quechua art movement in the 1970s. At the public market, he began selling landscape paintings that were painted on the traditional Quechua canvas—stretched sheep skin. Following Toaquiza's example, dozens of Quechua artists began producing works for sale, often depicting elements of Inca spirituality or the landscape and lifestyle of the highlands.

Tigua art has since gained an international reputation, helping to renew interest in studying the lives and culture of the Incan descendants in Ecuador. However, there remain few opportunities for government funding or arts education in Ecuador. The government provides minimal funding for those studying traditional art in an effort to preserve indigenous culture. Most artists, especially those studying Amerindian arts or crafts, learn through artisan internships or through informal lessons. Native music, including Andean folk music, is also passed from student to teacher through informal lessons.

Football (known as soccer in the United States) is Ecuador's national sport. Volleyball, which is played with a heavier ball than in America, and with three people on each team, is another popular sport. Pelota nacional is a traditional game in which two teams hit a small ball back and forth while a third team tries to intercept it. This game is generally played by older Ecuadorians.

Cultural Sites & Landmarks

The United Nations Educational, Scientific and Cultural Organization (UNESCO) designated Quito as a World Heritage Site in 1978. The city was founded in the 17th century by Spanish immigrants on the ruins of the Inca Empire of Quitus, which existed in the 13th century. However, there are no Inca remains in Quito and most of the buildings were established during the colonial period. While some buildings date back to the 16th century, much of the city was damaged or destroyed in a 1917 earthquake and has since been restored. Despite the earthquake, the city is considered to have the best-preserved historic center of any city in Latin America.

The Cathedral of San Francisco, established in 1535, is one of the most famous landmarks in Quito and is Ecuador's largest church. Built in a Spanish colonial style, the cathedral is decorated with dozens of religious-themed paintings from some of Ecuador's master painters of the colonial period. The cathedral also provides one of the best examples of the "Baroque School of Quito," which blends European (namely Italian, Spanish, Moorish, and Flemish) and indigenous architectural elements.

Independence Plaza, an outdoor park with monuments commemorating the shift to independence, is a popular destination for both residents and tourists living in Quito. Near the plaza is one of Quito's other famous religious monuments,

La Basilica. This large neo-Gothic style church is notable for its tower, the tallest in Ecuador. A major restoration of the Basilica began in 1992. In all, there are over forty churches and monasteries in Quito's historic downtown centre.

UNESCO has also recognized the historic center of Santa Ana de los Ríos de Cuenca as a World Heritage Site because of the small city's history of Renaissance-style urban planning. Established in 1557, the city has since become an important agricultural center. Many of Santa Ana's buildings were constructed in the 19th century, giving the city a classical, colonial style.

The island system of the Galápagos, located approximately 1,000 kilometers (621 miles) from the South American mainland, is considered one of the most important natural historic sites in the world. The Galápagos are famed as a "natural laboratory" for the study of evolution, which began after British naturalist Charles Darwin (1809–1882) visited the islands in 1835. Darwin used examples from Galápagos fauna and flora to illustrate his theory of evolution by natural selection. Along with the historic city of Quito, the Galápagos Islands also became one of the first World Heritage Sites in the world when they were inscribed in 1978. More than 30 years later, scientists continue to use the 19 islands of the Galápagos to study natural selection and evolution.

Other natural sites in Ecuador include Mount Chimborazo, the country's highest mountain, reaching more than 1,980 meters (6,500 feet) at its peak. The name of the mountain is taken from an indigenous term meaning "mountain of snow." Chimborazo is located in Ecuador's "Avenue of the Volcanoes," which has become an important site for volcanologists and explorers interested in mountaineering. The mountain is located within Sangay National Park, which was designated as a World Heritage Site in 1983 in recognition of the park's unique animal and plant life and geological features.

Libraries & Museums

Quito is home to many acclaimed museums, including those of the Museo Nacional del Banco Central del Ecuador (National Museum of Central Bank) and Casa de la Cultura Ecuatoriana (The House of Ecuadorian Culture) complexes. These cultural institutions house extensive collections of pre-colonial pottery, sculpture, and golden Inca treasures, as well as exhibits devoted to Ecuadoran history and colonial, republican, and contemporary art. They also feature collections of musical instruments, art, and clothing from indigenous cultures.

Other notable museums include the Convent Museum of San Francisco, which showcases religious sculpture, paintings, textiles, and furniture dating from the 16th century, and the Guayasamín Museum, devoted to the works of Oswaldo Guayasamín (1919–1999), an internationally acclaimed painter and sculptor of indigenous descent, as well as the Ecuadorian Museum of Natural Science, Museum and Library Aurelio Espinoza Pólit, and Colonial Art Museum.

The National Library of Ecuador, or Biblioteca Nacional del Ecuador Eugenio Espejo, is located in Quito. It dates back to the late 18th century and contains over 70,000 volumes of books. Other libraries of note in Quito include the Biblioteca Central Pontificia Universidad Católica del Ecuador, Biblioteca del Banco Central del Ecuador, and Biblioteca Ecuatoriana Aurelio Espinosa Polit.

Holidays

Official holidays observed in Ecuador include Labor Day (May 1), Independence Day (August 10), Guayaquil's Independence Day (October 9), Mourning for the Deceased Day (November 2), and Cuenca's Independence Day (November 3).

Ecuador celebrates its history with the observance of the Battle of Pichincha (May 24), and the Foundation of Quito (December 6).

Youth Culture

Children in Ecuador have diverse recreational options. Sports are popular with children of all ages and football (soccer) is the national sport. Amateur leagues across the country invite young girls and boys to play soccer at public parks or soccer fields at schools or public recreation centers. As there are few recreational venues specifically catered to teens, youth gather in front of stores or their schools at night to socialize. In general, Ecuadorian teenagers tend to gather according to socioeconomic groups, and recreational choices often depend on the social group. Additionally, most youth are expected to work outside the home or to help with family duties at a young age.

Ecuadorians are legally allowed to marry at age 12 for young girls, and age 14 for boys. It is estimated that approximately 30 percent of children are married by age 19. Surveys indicate that few Ecuadorians pay attention to sexual health or preventative measures, and the government has initiated public health programs to promote the use of condoms and to communicate with teenagers about reproductive responsibility.

In urban areas, the use of Internet cafés, shopping, and frequenting dance clubs remain popular youth activities. Both North American and South American movies are screened, with many translated into Spanish. Ecuadorian teens also enjoy a tremendous variety of music from traditional Latin music to American rock and hip-hop. Disc jockeys in Quito and other cities play a variety of music and most have broadcast programs aimed at teenage audiences. Electronic music has also become popular in the cities and is a regular feature of the local dance club scene.

SOCIETY

Transportation

Buses are the main mode of public transportation throughout Ecuador. Affordable Ecuadorian buses also tend to be crowded and commonly suffer frequent breakdowns. Some local buses allow villagers to transport small livestock on the buses, contributing to the nickname "chicken buses." In the capital of Quito, an electric trolleybus line is a unique transportation fixture. Built in 1994, the line runs on reserved lanes and features platform loading. In addition, private

transportation services such as taxis are common, and most cities have companies offering private car/minibus rental services. Boat travel also remains a common and necessary means of travel in Ecuador, particularly in the Amazon regions. Traffic in Ecuador moves on the right-hand side of the road.

Transportation Infrastructure

Ecuador has 43,670 kilometers (27,135 miles) of roads, of which 6,472 kilometers (4,021 miles) are paved. A portion of the Pan-American Highway runs through Ecuador, where it is known as Troncal de la Sierra, passing through Quito and connecting to the nation's other highways. Ecuador has several international airports out of its nearly 100 paved airports. Most international air traffic from the U.S. and Europe travels through Airport Mariscal Sucre, located in the northern portion of Quito near the financial district.

Media & Communications

There are dozens of newspapers and periodicals in Ecuador, many published only within certain areas. The most prominent newspaper in the country is *El Comercio* (*Commerce*), which is published in Quito and specializes in news and political coverage. The tabloid style paper *Hoy* (*Today*), which is also headquartered in Quito, provides daily and local news, in addition to sports and entertainment coverage.

Ecuador also has a diverse list of radio stations, featuring native and imported music and news. In Quito, Latin music programs are the most popular broadcasts, followed by imported music and news programs. In the Andes, there are a number of radio stations producing programs in the Quechua language. Among the most popular Andean radio programs is "La Voz de los Andes" ("Voice of the Andes"), which provides music, Andean news, and other information.

Ecuador has access to a few local television stations in addition to cable and satellite television options. There are four major networks in Ecuador: Ecuavision, Garmavision, Telecentro, and Teleamazonas, all of which offer entertainment programming as well as national and international news. In addition to the four major networks, there are several smaller, locally produced networks offering a variety of programs, many produced within Ecuador. Most television broadcasts in Ecuador are in Spanish, but there are also a variety of English programs available on some channels.

There is no censorship in Ecuador, with one notable exception: individuals are legally forbidden from discussing Ecuador's territorial disputes through publication, broadcast, or Internet sources. Internet access is widely available in Quito and other larger cities, and the government does not monitor Internet communication. However, Internet penetration remains low, with an estimated 12.6 percent of the population classified as Internet users in 2009. Projects are underway to expand Internet coverage to additional cities.

SOCIAL DEVELOPMENT

Standard of Living
Ecuador ranked 98th out of 185 countries on the 2014 United Nations Human Development Index, which measures quality of life and standard of living indicators.

Water Consumption
According to 2012 statistics from the World Health Organization (WHO), approximately 86 percent of the Ecuadorian population has access to improved drinking water sources, while 83 percent has access to improved sanitation. Nonetheless, contaminated drinking water and lack of proper sanitation remains a concern throughout some regions of the country. In 2014, The Law of Water Resources and Use of Water went into effect, ending four years of debate over water reform. Though the law prohibits the privatization of water, it has been criticized for allowing exceptions in the case of emergencies, which might place too much power in government hands.

Education
School attendance is compulsory for children ages five to fourteen, but pre-school is optional. Primary education begins at age five and lasts for seven years. Secondary education is provided in two three-year cycles.

All government-run schools in Ecuador are free. Amerindian languages are used for instruction in some rural schools. The literacy rate was 91.6 percent overall (93 percent among men and 90 percent among women) as of 2011. University education lasts up to six years. The University of Cuenca, the nation's oldest, was founded in 1867. The country's largest university is Universidad Central in Quito.

Women's Rights
Domestic violence remains a significant and ongoing problem in Ecuador. Domestic abuse carries penalties of up to seven days in prison in addition to fines. Police also have the power to impose restraining orders to protect women in the home and at their place of work.

In 2007, there were 30 special police offices handling women and family issues, including domestic violence. The National Commission on Women (CONAMU) was also empowered to hear complaints directly and forward information to the prosecutor's office for investigation. CONAMU has offices in every province and also offers outreach and psychological services for abused women. Women also have the option of counseling or legal support through government-appointed social workers or representatives of non-governmental organizations (NGOs) active in Ecuador. Some women's rights groups have objected to provisions within the penal code that require a woman to produce a witness if filing a complaint of abuse and/or spousal rape. NGOs and social work representatives report that abuse is unreported due to social norms prohibiting women from taking aggressive action against their husbands, and because many women believe that their grievances will not be adequately addressed by the police.

Sexual harassment is considered a crime, but according to rights organizations, it remains common. The National Women's Council is empowered to create policies that address women's rights issues, including current policies and penalties for issues like sexual harassment. The government's efforts to combat sexual harassment appear to be earnest. It provides public education programs regarding sexual harassment laws and penalties and free counseling for women who wish to report harassment in the workplace.

The constitution holds that women and men are equal before the law and prohibits discrimination on the basis of gender. However, NGOs and women's groups within the country, such as the Office of Gender and the National Women's Council, report that women receive less that 70 percent of the pay that men receive in the same positions. In addition, there are fewer opportunities for advancement and economic achievement for women in Ecuador. Disparities in achievement were the result of pervasive cultural attitudes, and a basic belief, on the part of many Ecuadorians, that men are more capable and competent than women in professional capacities.

Health Care

Overall life expectancy for Ecuadorians is 76 years; 73 years for men and 79 years for women (2014 estimate). The infant mortality rate is approximately 20 deaths per 1,000 live births.

Malnutrition and dysentery are common public health problems, and improperly prepared seafood has been blamed for cholera outbreaks. Cases of hepatitis B typically occur in rural areas.

Auxiliary health-care personnel staff rural posts in small communities. Medium-sized communities are served by health professionals in small health centers. Urban health centers serve the residents of the larger provincial capitals. Only the largest cities have hospitals.

Ecuador has 1.7 doctors per 1,000 people. The annual per capita health expenditure is $652 USD (2012).

GOVERNMENT

Structure

Ecuador is a republic with universal suffrage at age eighteen. Voting is compulsory for literate citizens between the ages of 18 and 65. For others, voting is optional.

The president is chief of state and head of government and is directly elected by popular vote. The president may not be elected to consecutive terms, but may run again later. The president appoints the 16-member cabinet. The unicameral Congreso Nacional (National Congress) has 100 members, who are elected by popular vote in each province. They serve four-year terms.

Justices of the Corte Suprema (Supreme Court) are usually elected by the full Supreme Court. However, in December 2004, the Congreso Naciónal replaced all the justices by a simple majority vote.

Political Parties

Ecuador's parliament is comprised of numerous political parties. The country's multi-party system requires that coalitions between parties be formed and prevents one party from gaining too much political influence. Parties include the PAIS Alliance, the Social Christian Party, the Democratic People's Movement, the January 21 Patriotic Society Party, the National Democratic Coalition, and the Ecuadorian Roldosist Party.

Local Government

Ecuador is divided into 24 provinces that are led by provincial councils. Provincial councils oversee the administration of public works and municipal budgets. Council members are elected to four-year terms by popular vote. Provinces are subdivided into cantons and parishes. Cantons are led by political chiefs. Parishes are led by political lieutenants. Each level of local government is overseen by Ecuador's executive branch of government.

Judicial System

Ecuador's Supreme Court, the country's highest court, has 30 justices. These judges preside over 10 chambers. Each chamber contains three judges. Ecuador also has a Fiscal Tribunal, which oversees legal matters related to tax collection and tax obligation. The country's Contentious Administrative Tribunal presides over legal conflicts related to public administration. Each of these three judicial branches are based in Quito.

Taxation

Citizens of Ecuador pay an income tax, though income tax is often not collected from the country's poorer workers and those that work in the country's informal economy. Married couples are required to file joint income tax forms. Other taxes include inheritance taxes, municipal property taxes, and real estate taxes. Corporations operating in Ecuador play a flat income tax of 22 percent. Oil companies in Ecuador pay a higher tax on profits.

Armed Forces

The Ecuadorian armed forces consist of an army, navy, and an air force. Selective conscription is the law, though currently suspended. The minimum age for military service is 20 and the length of obligation is one year. Active personnel numbered nearly 40,000 in 2008. Ecuador has sourced its weapons from regional neighbors such as Brazil and Chile and, to a lesser extent, Russia and China. In 2010, the United States supplied an estimated $1.2 million worth of military supplies to the Ecuadorian armed forces, though relations have been strained, resulting in the expulsion of all 20 U.S. Defense Department employees in April 2014. In September 2014, Ecuador signed a military cooperation agreement with China, which included $4.8 million in assistance to Ecuador's military.

Foreign Policy

Ecuador takes an interest in international politics and has been a member of the United Nations since 1945. Ecuador also plays a prominent role in regional affairs, and holds membership in the Organization of American States (OAS), the Latin American Energy Organization (OLADE), and the Andean Community of Nations (CAN), among other regional organizations. Ecuador has strong relations with the United States, both through financial investment and through mutual interest in combating drug trafficking. The U.S. also remains Ecuador's primary trading partner, purchasing more than $5 billion (USD) in Ecuadorian produce and other products annually. In addition, the U.S. government has consistently contributed to financial aid packages and development assistance for Ecuador, totaling more than $30 million (USD) in 2007 alone. There are nearly two million Ecuadorian citizens living in the U.S. and more than 20,000 former U.S. citizens living in Ecuador.

Ecuador endured a major financial crisis in 1991, partially due to a lack of predictable and reliable access to key resources, most notably petroleum. Though Ecuador has natural petroleum reserves, an inability to effectively refine fuel has forced Ecuador to import gasoline, further straining limited financial resources. Ecuador has asked to be readmitted into the Organization of Petroleum Exporting Countries (OPEC). The country was expelled from OPEC in 1992 when it they failed to pay annual revenues. The request to join OPEC has been criticized by some nations, including the U.S., because of Ecuador's relationship with Venezuela.

Ecuador's long-standing territorial dispute with Peru ended in 1998, in a peace agreement brokered by the U.S. and a group of military observers from neighboring nations. Ecuador also has longstanding issues with Colombia regarding both drug trafficking across the shared border and illegal migration of Colombians into Ecuador. In 2008, Ecuador was involved in a diplomatic crisis, known as the Andean diplomatic crisis, after Colombian troops executed a raid against leftist rebels across the Ecuadoran border. The 2008 government under President Rafael Correa, who assumed office in 2007, organized a new set of policies known as Plan Ecuador, which includes hiring additional border security and encouraging development along the border to protect the Ecuadorian citizens from the threat of Colombian drug cartels. Under the Correa government, Ecuador's relationship with the United States has become strained, resulting in the shut down of the U.S. Agency for International Development programs in the country.

Human Rights Profile

International human rights law insists that states respect civil and political rights, and also promote an individual's economic, social and cultural rights. The United Nations (UN) Universal Declaration of Human Rights (UDHR) is recognized as the standard for international human rights. Its authors sought the counsel of the world's great thinkers, philosophers, and religious leaders, and were careful to create a document that reflects the core values shared by every world culture. (To read this document or view the articles relating to cultural human rights, visit: http://www.udhr.org/UDHR/default.htm.)

The government of Ecuador generally respects the rights of its citizens, in keeping with the UDHR, though monitoring agencies have identified several areas of concern. One of the most pressing problems in Ecuador is the failure to address the human rights practices of the banana industry. Ecuador's plantations produce nearly 25 percent of banana imports for the U.S. and Europe, supplying major companies like Dole Foods, Del Monte, and Chiquita Brands. Surveys have found that the banana industry is rife with labor concerns, including underage laborers—in some cases as young as eight years old—and dangerous working conditions. In addition, investigations found that the banana industry prevents workers from forming unions, a violation of Article 20 of the UDHR.

Monitoring organizations such as Amnesty International (AI) have alleged instances of torture and cruel, degrading treatment on the part of Ecuadorian police and security forces. Monitoring agencies have also alleged that police and penal personnel have occasionally committed murder without adequate investigation, a violation of Article 3. According to the U.S. Department of State, instances of abuse and violence committed by law enforcement were sufficiently isolated and are not indicative of a widespread problem. However, the U.S. has recommended that the Ecuadorian government increase efforts to monitor police activities.

Though the penal code requires that police fill official reports within 24 hours of arresting a subject, reviews indicate that police occasionally arrest suspects without due process and that suspects may be held for long periods without trial. Some monitoring agencies have reported that Ecuadorian authorities occasionally imprison suspects for long periods on questionable charges. Long pretrial detentions and questionable trial procedures are also significant human rights concerns, and some monitoring agencies have alleged corruption within the judicial system.

The condition of the Ecuadorian prison is also an area of significant concern, as inadequate sanitation and overcrowding are common, all violations of Article 5 of the UDHR. Investigations have found that conditions are better in the central regions than in coastal areas, where prisons have significantly older facilities with fewer modern amenities. In 2013, the U.S. Department of State estimated that more than 24,722 prisoners were being detained in facilities designed to hold only 12,089 prisoners.

While trafficking in persons is illegal according to the Ecuadorian constitution, there were credible reports indicating that individuals were trafficked to Italy, Spain, Colombia, and Venezuela for the purposes of underage prostitution. The Ecuadorian government's failure to protect children is a violation of Article 25 of the UDHR.

ECONOMY

Overview of the Economy

Oil accounts for approximately half of Ecuador's export income. However, this dependence on one product makes the economy vulnerable to fluctuations in the world market. In 2000, Ecuador adopted the U.S. dollar as its official currency, in an effort to stabilize its economy and lower its foreign debt. Since that time, inflation has decreased, and the economy's rate of growth has increased. The per capita gross domestic product (GDP) is $10,600 USD (2013 estimate).

Industry

In addition to the production of fuel oil, gasoline, and other petroleum products, important industries in Ecuador include cement, pharmaceuticals, textiles, and processed foods. Ecuador is the leading exporter of bananas in the world, the world's second largest shrimp producer, and a leading producer of balsa wood.

Quito is one of Ecuador's major hubs for industrial production. The capital's manufacturing sector turns out pharmaceuticals, textiles, and leather goods, as well as gold, silver, and wooden decorative objects and handicrafts.

Export revenues amount to $25.48 billion USD (2013 estimate) and are growing. Major exports include petroleum and petroleum products, food, live animals, and cut flowers. Asian countries are Ecuador's largest trading partners.

Labor

According to 2013 statistics, the urban labor force of Ecuador is estimated to number 6.953 million. The unemployment rate declined from 8.5 percent in 2009 to 4.2 percent in 2013. The majority of the labor force works in the services sector—an estimated 70 percent in 2005.

Energy/Power/Natural Resources

Petroleum is Ecuador's main natural resource. Substantial oil deposits were discovered in the northeastern part of the country in the 1960s, and Ecuador was a founding member of the Organization of Petroleum Exporting Countries (OPEC). The country's other resources include fish, gold, hydropower, and timber.

Environmental concerns include water pollution, desertification, deforestation, and soil erosion. Perhaps worst of all, wastes from oil production have polluted fragile ecological areas in the Amazon Basin and on the Galápagos Islands.

Fishing

Fishing has been a part of Ecuadorian culture for centuries. Tuna, marlin, herring, and mackerel are caught in the country's coastal waters. In addition, shrimp is one of Ecuador's major export products. In recent decades, widespread shrimp fishing has had a negative impact on other fish stocks.

The country is also becoming a popular sport-fishing destination. There are numerous charter-fishing operations in Ecuador, most of which focus on marlin fishing.

Forestry

Ecuador provides over 90 percent of the world's balsa wood. The country's forest sector employs an estimated 5.7 percent of the overall labor force. The export of wood products contributed an estimated $250 million in 2012. Wood products, including balsa and timber products, accounted for an estimated one percent of Ecuador's GDP in 2012. Although 15 percent of the country's forests are protected, illegal logging of the country's Amazon forests continues and the country has the highest deforestation rate in South America.

Mining/Metals

Crude petroleum represented 50 percent of Ecuador's total exports in 2012. Non-fuel mineral exports represent less than one half of one percent of Ecuador's exports. The country's small metal mining industry produces copper, silver, gold, and limestone.

Agriculture

Approximately one-third of Ecuador's workforce is employed in the agricultural sector. The main crops are bananas, cacao, coffee, oil palm fruit, sugar cane, oranges, and rice. Crops for domestic use include beans, corn, potatoes, and wheat, most of which are grown in the Andes highland. Balsa wood, mahogany, and other tropical woods are also important.

Animal Husbandry

Cattle are raised for meat and dairy products. Livestock accounts for an estimated 40 percent of Ecuador's agricultural GDP. Products include beef and veal, milk, poultry, pork, and some eggs and hides. Approximately 560,000 metric tons of meat was produced in Ecuador in 2002. Due to increasing demand and improved animal breeding infrastructure, livestock is considered a growth industry in Ecuador.

Tourism

Tourism, particularly ecotourism, is growing in importance in Ecuador. Each year, more than 600,000 tourists visit the country, generating revenues of approximately $430 million USD.

Popular activities for tourists include mountain climbing (including volcanoes), mountain biking, bungee jumping, hiking, rafting, kayaking, diving, snorkeling, surfing, windsurfing, jet skiing, paragliding, fishing, and horseback riding. Indigenous markets in villages and international car races around Lake Yaguarcocha are also of interest. Other tourist sites include the colonial cities of Quito and Guayaquil.

Tourists like to stand in the northern and southern hemispheres at once at Mitad del Mundo ("Middle of the Earth"), a popular tourist site in the Andes. Ecotours take visitors to the tropical rainforests, the Galápagos Islands and the Andes Mountains.

Micah Issitt, Ellen Bailey, Beverly Ballaro

DO YOU KNOW?

- Guagua Pichincha, an active volcano that lies only 21 kilometers (13 miles) to the west of Quito, blanketed the city with more than 25 centimeters (10 inches) of volcanic ash during its 1660 eruption. The volcano last erupted in 1999, again depositing significant amounts of debris on the city. One of Quito's most famous churches, La Merced, was built in the 17th century to commemorate the resilience of Quito's people in the face of the volcanic danger faced by the capital's inhabitants.

- Many Ecuadorians enjoy fishing for large catfish called bagre, found at the bottom of rivers. These fish can weigh up to 100 kilograms (221 pounds). They are caught using rope and a hook big enough to catch a shark.

Bibliography

Ades, Harry and Melissa Graham. *The Rough Guide to Ecuador and the Galapagos*. New York: Rough Guides, 2013.

Becker, Marc. *Pachakutik: Indigenous Movements and Electoral Politics in Ecuador*. Lanham, MD: Rowman & Littlefield, 2011.

Crowder, Nicholas. *Culture Shock! Ecuador: A Survival Guide to Customs and Etiquette*. Tarrytown, NY: Marshall Cavendish, 2009.

de la Torre, Carlos and Steve Striffler, eds. *The Ecuador Reader: History, Culture, Politics*. Durham, NC: Duke University Press, 2008.

DeTemple, Jill. *Cement, Earthworms, and Cheese Factories: Religion and Community Development in Rural Ecuador*. Notre Dame, IN: University of Notre Dame Press, 2012.

Handelsman, Michael. *Culture and Customs of Ecuador*. Westport, CT: Greenwood Publishing Group, 2000.

Hurtado, Osvaldo. *Portrait of a Nation: Culture and Progress in Ecuador*. Lanham, MD: Madison Books, 2010.

"Lonely Planet." *Ecuador and the Galapagos Islands*. Oakland, CA: Lonely Planet Press, 2012.

Roos, Wilma and Omer van Renterghem. *Ecuador in Focus: A Guide to the People, Politics and Culture*. Northampton, MA: Interlink Publishing Group, 2000.

Works Cited

"Censos De Poblacion y Vivienda." Estadísticas Sociodemográfica. *INEC Online* http://www.inec.gov.ec/web/guest/ecu_est/est_soc/cen_pob_viv.

"Ecuador's New Constitution Leaves the Past Behind." *Habitat for Humanity Online*. September 28, 2008. http://www.habitat.org/lac_eng/newsroom/2008/09_28_08_Ecuador_eng.aspx

"Ecuador 2013 Human Rights Report." *U.S. Department of State Online*. http://www.state.gov/documents/organization/220651.pdf.

"Americas." *Human Rights Watch Online*. http://www.hrw.org/en/americas 'Ecuador.' *World Factbook Online*. Central Intelligence Agency. 22 June, 2014. https://www.cia.gov/library/publications/the-world-factbook/geos/ec.html.

"Ecuador Travel Information and Travel Guide." *Lonely Planet Online*. http://www.lonelyplanet.com/ecuador.

Trigger, Bruce G., et al. 'The Cambridge History of the Native People of the Americas: South America.' New York: Cambridge University Press, 2000.

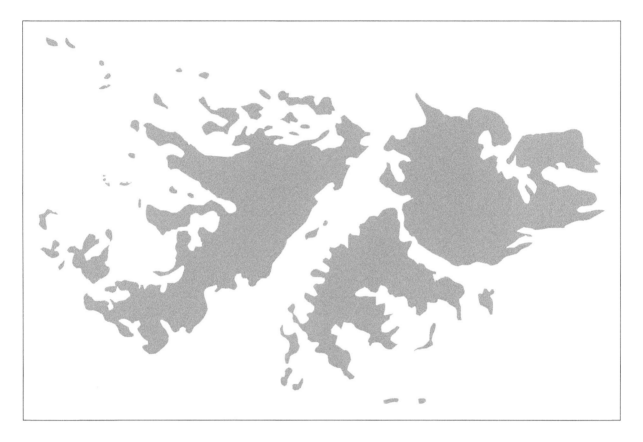

FALKLAND ISLANDS

Introduction

The Falkland Islands is an archipelago, or group of islands, in the South Atlantic Ocean, east of the southern tip of South America. Although the islands are situated geographically within Argentina's Patagonia region, the Falkland Islands is an overseas territory of Great Britain. The islands are inhabited by a mostly British population known as Falkland Islanders. The islands take their English name from the official who authorized Britain's 1690 expedition to the islands.

The sovereignty of the islands has been in dispute since the early 19th century. Argentina attempted to reclaim the Falklands from the British during the Falkland Islands War in 1982. Although Argentina no longer seeks to take the islands by force, Britain has refused to enter into talks regarding the islands' ownership.

GENERAL INFORMATION

Official Language: English
Population: 2,840 (2012 estimate)
Currency: Falkland Islands pound (FKP)
Coins: The Falkland Island pound is available in £1 and £2 coin denominations. The Falkland Island pound is subdivided into pence; coins are issued in denominations of 50, 20, 10, 5, 2 and 1 pence.
Land Area: 12,173 square kilometers (4,700 square miles)
National Motto: "Desire the Right"
National Anthem: "God Save the Queen"
Capital: Stanley

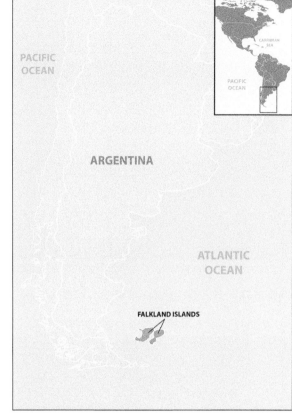

Time Zone: GMT -5
Flag Description: The flag of the Falkland Islands is blue and features an imprint of the United Kingdom's Union Jack in its canton. Printed in the flag's right hand field is the Falkland Islands' coat of arms, which features a sheep, a ship and the island's motto: "Desire the right."

Population

Falkland Islanders primarily inhabit East Falkland and West Falkland, the two largest islands. There are roughly 200 smaller islands, most of which are uninhabited. About 2,100 residents live in Stanley (also called Port Stanley), the small capital located on the eastern coast of East Falkland. Like many towns on the islands, Stanley is a seaport.

All areas outside of the town of Stanley are collectively referred to as "Camp." Whether living in Stanley or Camp, most families are self-sufficient and live on farms. Other major towns include Port Howard, Goose Green, and Weddell.

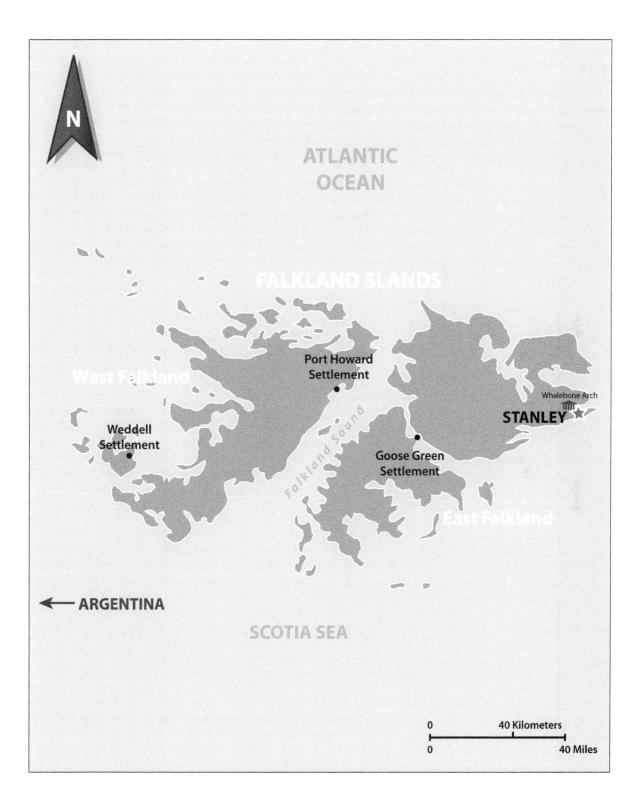

Principal City by Population (2006):

• Stanley (2,115)

The census estimate of the Falkland Islands' population does not include a group of roughly 2,000 British soldiers that have been garrisoned on East Falkland since 1982. These soldiers, located at the Mount Pleasant airport, are casually referred to as "squaddies."

Falkland Islanders are considered full British citizens.

Languages

English is the official language of the Falklands and Falkland Islanders, who are also referred to as Kelpers. They are primarily white and English speaking. The minority immigrant population, mostly from South America, speaks Spanish.

Native People & Ethnic Groups

The Falkland Islands were uninhabited by humans until they were settled by the French in 1763. While they have been occupied by various ethnic groups from Europe and South America throughout history—the British, Spanish, and Dutch all claim to have discovered the Falkland Islands first, some time during the late 16th or early 17th century—the small population of the Falkland Islands is now almost entirely made up of people of British ethnicity. A small group of South American immigrants constitute the only minority population. Most of this group hails from Chile. A small number of immigrants from the island of Saint Helena have also come to the Falkland Islands.

In the past, islanders have referred to themselves as "Kelpers," although this term is no longer used. The term was a reference to kelp, a type of seaweed prevalent in the region. The term "belonger" is used for individuals who have relocated to the islands from the UK.

Religions

Most Falkland Islanders practice Christianity. The Anglican and Roman Catholic churches are the most common denominations, and there are several churches located in Stanley.

Climate

The South Atlantic climate of the Falkland Islands is cold, windy and humid throughout the year. Average annual temperatures on the Falkland Islands are around 3° Celsius (37° Fahrenheit) during the winter and 8° Celsius (47° Fahrenheit) during the summer.

The Falkland Islands receive a large amount of precipitation. It rains lightly about 250 days of the year, generating an annual average of 60 centimeters (24 inches). It also snows on the islands throughout the entire year, with the exception of the summer months of January and February. Snow accumulation is very low, however.

ENVIRONMENT & GEOGRAPHY

Topography

The Falkland Islands are mountainous and covered with marshes and rocky terrain. An underwater plateau connects the islands to Argentina's mainland.

The two largest islands, East and West Falkland, have distinct topographical features. East Falkland consists of a southern lowland area of marshes and pastures, and a mountainous northern terrain known as Wickham Heights. Wickham Heights is the site of Mount Usborne, the highest point in the Falkland Islands at 705 meters (2,312 feet). The lowlands and the heights are separated by two large fjords running across East Falkland.

West Falkland features mountainous terrain, the Hornby Mountains, in its eastern area. This range includes the islands' second-highest peak, Mount Adam, which at 700 meters (2,296 feet) is barely shorter than Mount Usborne. The lowlands of West Falkland contain many of the islands' natural deposits of clay, sandstone, slate, and quartzite.

East and West Falkland are divided by a body of water known as the Falkland Sound. There are many natural inlets and harbors formed by the coastline, but there are no significant mainland lakes or rivers. One famous cove is Gypsy Cove, located only four miles outside Stanley and renown for its colony of Magellanic penguins.

Plants & Animals

The Falkland Islands are home to nearly 500,000 sheep. Other forms of livestock, such as cattle, goats and horses, are also raised in large numbers on the islands' farms.

There are many species of birds on the Falkland Islands, including geese, caracaras, cormorants, oystercatchers, snowy sheathbills, and several varieties of penguins. Common marine animals include elephant seals, sea lions, fur seals, orcas, and dolphins. In addition to a large population of squid, there are many species of fish in the waters surrounding the islands.

Plant life on the islands primarily consists of grass and wildflowers. There are almost no trees on the Falkland Islands, due to the extremely windy climate that prevents growth. Some trees have been imported to the island and planted in Stanley, and are surrounded by wind shields.

CUSTOMS & COURTESIES

Greetings

Historically conceived as a British outpost, the Falkland Islands follow British customs and language. However, the way English is spoken on the Falklands differs, and the island accent has been compared to that of Australia, but with its own distinct broad twang. In addition, while English is the official language of the Falklands, a sprinkling of Spanish lingers—a residual trace of Argentina's past presence on the islands. For example, Spanish words are sometimes spoken in conjunction with British terms, as in "Cheers che," meaning "Goodbye friend." Additionally, Falklanders are known to speak in a slow and deliberate manner.

Local vocabulary in the form of informal nicknames is common. For example, Falklanders refer to themselves as Kelpers, a term they coined,

which derives from the mass of kelp (seaweed) that ribbons the coastline.

British military forces have increased their presence on the Falklands after the 1982 conflict. Troops are somewhat isolated from the civilians, and short deployments give them little chance to forge close ties with islanders. Thus, soldiers began referring to the islanders in a slightly derogatory manner by calling them Bennies. This particular nickname derives from the simple-minded character of Benny Hawkins, featured on a popular British TV program *Crossroads*. Benny wore a wool cap similar to those sometimes worn by islanders. However, the locals coined their own term for the soldiers, referring to them as Whennies, as in the soldiers' talk of "When I was in Cyprus" or "When I was in Cairo," and so forth. Soldiers are most commonly referred to as squaddies, and no one seems to mind this designation.

Gestures & Etiquette

Falkland Islanders typically follow British customs in matters of gesture and etiquette, and as such are not given to expressive hand or arm gestures as they speak. In fact, etiquette in Stanley is very similar to any large English village. However, as a culture with a shorter history, much of it agricultural, islanders are not as formal or ritualistic as those in the UK. Generally, islanders seem to treat each other with kindness, as evidenced by the negligible crime rate in the Falklands. In fact, British immigrants, which are increasing in number, commonly cite safety for themselves and their children as a top reason for their relocation to the Falklands.

A certain island etiquette has also developed on the Falklands, much of it largely influenced by environment. For example, a typical sign of Falkland etiquette derives from the response to stranded drivers who find themselves "bogged" in the peat-rich land of "soft camp." Rocky areas are referred to as "hard camp." Thus, islanders commonly respond to any distress calls with tow ropes and boards, expecting nothing in return.

Island etiquette has also been known to extend itself in other ways. When young, sometimes underfed, Argentine soldiers occupied the islands during the 1982 conflict, islanders were known to smuggle food to these hungry teenagers.

Eating/Meals

Falkland Islanders typically eat three meals a day, but have also developed food traditions unique to the region. One such tradition is called "smoko," which is a between-meal break of coffee or tea and home-baked goods. The term was originally coined by sheep-shearers not just in the Falklands, but in Australia and New Zealand as well, and probably referred to a smoking break. More popular in the island's rural areas, smoko traditionally occurs at around 10:30 in the morning, but some Falklanders also indulge in an afternoon smoko at 4:00, corresponding to the time that Britons might typically have tea. "Out to lunch" signs are common in Stanley in the early afternoon, when many shopkeepers close down an hour or two for a mid-day meal.

Although the Falklands are not renowned for their cuisine, islanders are known for having a diet largely composed of comfort foods. Those who come to live on the islands may be subject to what has been dubbed the "Falkland Stone" (one stone, a pre-metric British unit of weight, equals 6.35 kilograms or 14 pounds). It is often said that within a year of living on the islands, one stands a good chance of gaining a stone.

Visiting

Falkland Islanders pride themselves on their hospitality, which is particularly noticeable in the sparsely populated countryside (only 400 of the Falklands' 2,800 residents live in Camp). Visitors in Camp may well find themselves invited in for a meal. Before the tourist trade boomed, visitors would often be invited to spend the night, free of charge. Then, a gift of rum—a favorite drink of islanders—was acceptable compensation. While free room and board have largely disappeared, the hospitality of Falklanders has not. However, Camp is where certain customs still apply.

Since there is very little public land on the Falklands, traveling off the roads—few of them paved— generally means one is on private land.

Getting permission ahead of time is advisable. When coming across a gate, it is island etiquette to leave it as found—either opened or closed. When entering a home, it is considered polite to remove shoes and boots. In addition, when nearing animal sanctuaries, wildlife is typically given the right of way. Furthermore, handling animals should be avoided, as this can result in a fine of up to £3,000 FKP ($6,000 USD).

LIFESTYLE

Family

The Shackleton Report, written in 1977 and updated after the war in 1982, was the first and perhaps lengthiest report on social aspects of life in the Falklands. Written by Lord Edward Shackleton, son of explorer Ernest Shackleton, the report was commissioned by the British government to report on the future of the Falklands. At that time, the low premium on education and the difficulties associated with living in isolated locations were cited as having a negative influence on family life.

Teachers would visit remote locations every few weeks, relying on grade school students to self-motivate and complete their assignments in the interim. Then, as it remains today, students in Camp would board in Stanley once they reached high school age. While boarding school is certainly not unknown in British culture, it does splinter the family. Furthermore, those wishing to attend college must do so abroad, generally in England. A high divorce rate—as high as 50 percent among new marriages—was also cited as disruptive to family life. Alcoholism was also reported as high. As for the next generation, Shackleton noted that teenagers reported a lack of interest in island life and a desire to leave.

However, a now-thriving economy has helped to change some of the negative aspects highlighted in the Shackleton Report. First, further investment from the UK allowed island farmers who had once been tenants working for absentee landlords to became landowners themselves. Second, the fishing industry became the primary income generator—more than tourism, stamps and the wool industry. The creation of an expanded 320-kilometer (200-nautical-mile) fishing zone allowed islanders to collect money from foreign fishing vessels. Third, this infusion of wealth led to an overhaul of the basic services on the islands, particularly the addition and renovation of schools and the paving of roads. In fact, with a per capita income of £25,000 ($50,000 USD), Falklanders are now considered one of the wealthier populations in the world, collectively.

Housing

Roughly 15 percent of Falklanders live on the 85 sheep farms located in Camp, with the remainder residing in Stanley. In either location, all homes are constructed to withstand the harsh and cold climate associated with the Falkland Islands. More importantly, since the Falklands rest at the juncture of the cold waters of the Antarctic and the warmer waters to the north, violent winds and waves can be common. In addition, without a nearby continent to slow down air movement—Argentina is closest at 563.3 kilometers (350 miles)—westerly winds often lash at the islands at an average rate of 17 knots (20 miles) per hour.

Generally, Falkland houses are renowned for being brightly painted with immaculately maintained gardens. Within homes, propane or kerosene is the most popular heat source, though the plentiful peat found on the islands was once burned as the main fuel source. Over 70 of the farms in camp are powered by wind turbines, and the government has plans to power nearly a quarter of Stanley's electricity using a wind farm.

Due in large part to annual fishing license revenues—as high as £25 million ($50 million USD) annually —Stanley has seen a big increase in housing. In fact, housing in the capital doubled in size between 1993 and 2003, with over 100 new homes being built to the east of town, often called East Stanley or Stanley to the East. In 1998, the government of the Falkland Islands started a program to encourage the construction of private homes. This government initiative led to a boom in the housing construction market with many new timber kit houses being imported, largely from Scotland. These houses range from single bedroom bungalows to large houses with four or five bedrooms. Often the style of cladding and colors vary immensely. In addition, according to the Falkland Islands Development Corporation, the cost of the average new home in 2008 was £100,000 ($200,000 USD).

Food

For the most part, Falkland cuisine is comprised of mostly standard British fare. Beyond the typical British dishes such as fish and chips (battered fish and fried potatoes, traditionally cod), meat pies, and bangers and mash (sausage, potatoes, and gravy), cuisine on the island is also largely based on lamb and mutton dishes, since sheep are plentiful. In fact, mutton, which is the meat of domestic sheep, is eaten so often that it is sometimes referred to as "365."

Although the Falklands are surrounded by waters teeming with fish, little of it is eaten by the locals. Rather, much of their fish is imported frozen. However, squid, trout and Atlantic Rock Cod (known locally as mullet) are popular fishes that often figure prominently in the local cuisine. Another popular dish, upland goose paté, is based upon the upland goose, a plentiful bird on the island. Other popular dishes and light fare common to the Falklands include sausage rolls, porridge, toast and marmalade, and bacon sandwiches.

Although the Falklands are predominantly considered British in terms of language, culture and food, immigrants from Chile and St. Helena, an island 4,000 kilometers (2,500 miles) to the northeast, have also influenced the local cuisine. For example, asado, which is meat slow-roasted on a spit over a fire, is becoming more commonplace. The meat is generally not marinated, with salt being the only seasoning used before and during cooking. The traditional Chilean sandwich chacarero—homemade bread, grilled steak or chicken, steamed green beans, Muenster cheese, tomatoes, avocado spread, salt, pepper and hot sauce—is popular as well. Empanadas, a popular snack in Chile and Argentina, consist of baked or otherwise cooked dough and are filled with vegetables, cheese, egg, or meat.

Life's Milestones

For the most part, Falklanders adhere to British customs and traditions when celebrating milestones or life events. Christianity is the dominant religion on the islands, particularly the denomination of Anglicanism. As such, religious rites of passage are commonly observed. Since getting to church can be a challenge for those in Camp, church services from Christ Church (Anglican), St. Mary's (Catholic), and the Tabernacle (Baptist) are alternately recorded and broadcast by local radio on Sunday evenings.

One unique aspect practiced on the islands is the use of the weekly newspaper, the *Penguin News*, as a personal message board. Often, the personals page in the newspaper is also where visitors to the islands post their good-byes, notices of thanks, and wistful, if largely unfulfilled, assertions that they shall return. Birthday and wedding announcements, some complete with photos, also regularly appear in the newspaper.

CULTURAL HISTORY

Art

Historically, the culture of the Falkland Islands was largely imported rather than developed, as there was no indigenous population. Since 1833, when the United Kingdom reasserted its claim to the islands, the cultural life of the Falklands has very much reflected these roots. From Scottish dancing to gardening to iconic red phone booths dotted about the capital, the culture of the Falkland Islands has been decidedly British. In addition, knit products such as sweaters constituted the major craft of islanders.

Prior to the Falklands War in 1982, in which Argentina unsuccessfully invaded the islands, one artistic endeavor that was already strongly established on the islands came in a small but highly sought after art form: the postage stamp.

The Falkland Islands first began issuing stamps in 1878. Due to a great surge in overseas interest that the local post office could no longer manage, the Philatelic Bureau was established 100 years later, in 1978. The war provided a huge boost of activity among collectors, to the point that stamp sales also became a major source of income for the islands.

Architecture

The architecture of the Falkland Islands is also decidedly British, when not distinctly influenced by the environment and available resources. Victorian-era (1837-1901) architecture is evident in the capital of Stanley, particularly in the Jubilee Villas, a row of four townhouses. Another architectural echo of Britain's Victorian era is the capital's police station. However, these architectural styles are mostly in contrast to the rest of the seaside capital.

Stanley's overall architectural look is that of a Scottish seaside town, with a distinctive Falklands flair. Due to an 1890s fire regulation outlawing wooden roofing, all the roofs and some of the facades, or exteriors, are made of corrugated metal. Known as "wriggly tin," many of the roofs are brightly painted. In fact, the Falkland Islands are known for their colorfully painted houses. Most Stanley buildings are either of this wood and tin variety or made from prefabricated "kits" shipped from Britain. Brick was considered too expensive to import and the local stone too difficult to quarry. A lack of native trees on the islands necessitated that any wood used be imported.

The rural areas outside of Stanley are known as Camp, from the Spanish word "campo," meaning countryside. Again, as building materials were difficult to come by, many of the 19th-century farmhouses are prefabricated wooden buildings shipped from overseas. Timbers from wrecked ships as well as corrugated metal were used to reinforce and protect the structures.

Drama

While adventure and wildlife were the prevalent themes of pre-1982 travelogues and nature films about the Falklands, the war sparked many internationally acclaimed dramas which continue to be made in the early 21st century. The 2005 Argentine film *Iluminados Por El Fuego* (*Blessed by Fire*), an account of the trauma suffered by young Argentine soldiers, won best film at the Tribeca Film Festival. The film centers on the harrowing conditions suffered during the brief but bloody war, and the grim aftermath for those young men who came home to a populace unhappy with their defeat. Also in 2005, the British film *An Ungentlemanly Act* mixes dark humor and real-life events to show the war as it erupted from the perspective of Falkland Governor Sir Rex Hunt.

Falklands: The Islanders' War, filmed on the island for the History Channel, is yet another addition to the growing library of award-winning war films based on the Falklands War. The 2008 documentary weaves together interviews and wartime footage to tell the story of the Argentine occupation from the islanders' point of view. Generally, literature concerning the Falklands falls into three main categories: personal narrative of life on the islands, the 1982 conflict (including poetry), and the natural world that predates both.

Music

The Falklands War provided inspiration for many British musical artists, including Roger Waters of the rock band Pink Floyd and Elvis Costello. The war has also been addressed in material recorded by punk rock bands such as The Clash, New Model Army, and The Exploited.

Literature

Prior to the Falklands War, much of what was written about the islands was non-fiction, and it related mostly to the Falklands' diverse and prolific animal life, most notably penguins, albatrosses and seals. After the war, however, a wealth of fiction, nonfiction, and poetry books concerning the war were written. Famous writers who have written about the war included Argentinian writer Jorge Luis Borges (1899–1986), French novelist Pierre Boulle (1912–1994) and British playwright Steven Berkoff (b. 1937–). The war

also became the subject of both film and television, including numerous British television programs and Argentinian films, including *Los chicos de la guerra* (1984), the first film made in Argentina about the war.

CULTURE

Arts & Entertainment

The Falkland Islands do not have an entertainment scene typical of most developed nations. There are no playhouses, movie theaters, or formal art galleries. Nevertheless, there is an artistic community of local poets and painters, and nature photography is one of the most popular art forms among Falkland Islanders. Another, more unusual mode of artistic expression is taxidermy, which is even featured as an exhibit at the Falklands Islands Museum. The exhibit contains albatross, petrel, which is a seabird, and several species of penguins.

Scottish music, a longtime favorite on the islands, remains a popular contemporary genre. Scottish dances are held frequently at Stanley's elementary school, and the town hall hosts old-fashioned dances, as well. However, the core of the islands' music scene is the Trough, a music venue constructed by local musicians and others. Completed in 1994, the venue is home to many local musical stars and visiting musicians.

Entertainment on the islands primarily consists of outdoor activities. Sports such as hiking, climbing, mountain biking, and sea-kayaking are popular. Other popular sports on the Falkland Islands are animal-related, and include horse racing, bull riding, and sheepdog trials. The Falklands also competes internationally in competitive sheep shearing. The oldest club on the islands is the Falkland Islands Rifle Association.

The Stanley Stadium, serving the Falkland Islands national football (soccer) team, holds about 1,000 people, roughly a third of the permanent residents. The Falkland Islands Community School in Stanley was built in 1992 at a cost of £10 million ($20 million USD). The facility serves as the community library, art gallery, and local recreational area, complete with a 25-meter (88-foot) heated swimming pool.

Cultural Sites & Landmarks

Stanley, the capital of the Falkland Islands, is considered the only city in the Falklands, and the main seaport. Located on East Falkland, it is the southernmost capital in the world. The capital is renowned for its small houses with brightly colored roofs. In addition, many of the modestly sized cottages from the 1800s remain standing in Stanley. One notable exception to the small-scaled buildings built in the capital is the Christ Church Cathedral, a centrally located massive brick and stone building. Opened in 1892, it replaced Stanley's Trinity Church, which was destroyed in an 1886 landslide caused by unstable peat, a mud-like, nutrient-rich fuel source that covers much of the islands. The church, which also has a corrugated metal roof, remains one of Stanley's most photographed landmarks. Other churches include the simple, plain St. Mary's Church, a classic example of Falkland Island architecture.

Rarely used brick was also essential to another project, Jubilee Villas. Built in the late 19th century in homage to Britain's Queen Victoria, this row of townhouses were seemingly plucked out of a London suburb and deposited into the southern hemisphere. The island's police station, originally built in 1873, serves as another cultural landmark in Stanley. It was severely damaged by friendly fire during the Argentine invasion. In 2008, it was renovated and modernized into a three-cell facility. The façade's historic aspects were maintained. Stanley's most recognizable icon, however, may be the Whalebone Arch. Fashioned from the jawbones of two blue whales, the sculpture was erected in 1933 to mark 100 years of British rule.

The Falkland Islands are also known for their numerous shipwrecks. There are over 200 hundred 19th-century ships, many of which were en route to California during the Gold Rush, sunken in the waters surrounding the Falklands. The rusted hulks serve as reminders of the treacherous waters around Cape Horn, the southernmost

tip of South America. Many attribute the large number of shipwrecks still visible to a lack of motivation among Falklanders to repair the ships since metal from the wrecks could be harvested and recycled into much-needed building materials. In fact, among sea captains, Stanley historically developed a reputation as a high-priced, slow-moving port to avoid. Today, scuba divers are allowed to peer at the ships. However, with winter water temperatures of around 4° Celsius (39° Fahrenheit) and summer temperatures of 14 degrees Celsius (57° Fahrenheit), a wetsuit is advised year-round.

Port Howard is the second largest settlement on West Falkland, and has a permanent population of about 20. The settlement offers a fascinating view of life on a sheep station, or farm. It is considered the Falklands' oldest farm. The former manager's house, a grand and picturesque building which now serves as a lodge, is a convenient base for nearby hiking, horseback riding, and fishing.

The Falklands have seen much violent conflict. The capital of Stanley has many commemorations and memorials to the soldiers and sailors who have died on the islands. West of town lies the 1918 Battle Memorial, a standing pillar that commemorates the end of World War I as well as the sailors who died in the sea battles that were waged by the Royal Navy in the waters off the Falklands. Closer to town, the Liberation Monument is a tribute to the 255 British servicemen who died in the 1982 conflict. Another tribute to the Falklands War is the 1982 Memorial Wood, which lies east of the town, where people have planted 255 trees to recognize the sacrifices of the fallen.

Libraries & Museums

Just west of Stanley is the Falklands Islands Museum, which details the history of life on the Falklands. The museum also contains comprehensive information about the scientists who traveled farther south to the Antarctic. In fact, famous explorer Sir Ernest Shackleton (1874–1922) stayed on the Falkland Islands in 1916 while coordinating a rescue of his men from

Elephant Island, an ice-covered island 940 kilometers (580 miles) south of the Falklands. Shackleton stayed at the governor's home, a rambling 1845 residence that is still in existence today. It is believed that Shackleton even remarked that he felt colder while staying on the Falklands than he had during his exploration of Antarctica.

Holidays

Most public holidays observed in the Falkland Islands are related to the Falkland Islands War. The most significant public holiday is Liberation Day, which is celebrated on June 14, the anniversary of the day in 1982 when British forces ousted Argentine troops.

On January 10, Falkland Islanders observe Margaret Thatcher Day, which commemorates the British prime minister who successfully protected the islands during the Falkland Islands War. The birthday of the Queen of England is observed on April 12 as a public holiday.

Youth Culture

It can be argued that education plays a significant role in the development of youth culture on the Falklands due to the small population. Public school is free and compulsory from age five until 16, and there are no private schools. The Stanley secondary school has about 160 students ages 11 to 16. Although the Education Ordinance of 1989 allows for corporal punishment of boys 11 and up—provided there is parental consent—no students have been hit since the law was enacted.

Graduates of the Falkland Islands Community School can either take advantage of a vocational training program or go on to college at the government's expense. About half the graduates choose to study abroad. Many of these students go either Peter Symonds College or Chichester College in England, as the Falkland Islands Government will pay their tuition to those two schools. Since the 1982 conflict, with its influx of money for social and educational programs as well as its reinvigoration of Falkland pride, young islanders seem intent on

staying on the islands or returning if they attend college abroad.

Where once there was little in the way of community-sponsored recreational activities, the Stanley Leisure Centre, completed in 1992, along with movies and bowling at the Mt. Pleasant military base, offer opportunities for fun that earlier generations didn't have. However, films typically debut at the base some three months after they've opened nationally in England. Like their predecessors, though, young people have a wide array of athletic and recreational activities to choose from, including the popular Moto-cross Club and the Stanley Rifle and Pistol Club. For youth 18 and older, the consumption of alcoholic beverages is legal and bars are a popular meeting place.

Underage smoking has become an issue on the Falklands. Interestingly, the age at which children are legally allowed to drink alcohol, as long as they are in a private place, is five. As such, underage drinking has increasingly become an issue on the island.

Youth aged 14 and over are legally permitted to have part-time employment. Babysitting and working in the shops are common seasonal jobs. Sixteen- and 17-year-olds can marry, but parental consent is required. The minimum age for enlistment in the Falkland Island Defense Force is 17, and no parental consent is needed.

SOCIETY

Transportation

Transportation is a nonissue in Stanley, as all the major sites are within walking distance. However, traveling around the rest of the Falklands is a challenge. Of the nearly 800 kilometers (500 miles) of road in the Falklands, only a small fraction is paved. East Falkland, the more populous of the two major islands, has several paved roads; West Falkland has none. For those driving on either island, four-wheel drive vehicles or motorcycles are considered necessary modes of transportation, since being stuck in the peat is an ever-present threat.

The fastest mode of transport, particularly for those wishing to visit some of the smaller islands, is the state-controlled Falkland Island Government Air Service (FIGAS). It is operated more like a phone-ahead taxi than a standard airline, and pilots not only take travelers to their remote destinations, they generally narrate and inform as they fly the nine-seat planes to any of the 35 landing strips across the islands.

International flights fly from and to Mount Pleasant Airport (MPA). Mount Pleasant Airport also functions as a UK military base. Service to the UK, chartered by the UK's Ministry of Defense, operates six times a month. There are also weekly flights between MPA and Santiago, Chile. Overall, the islands have six airports, two of which have paved landing strips. When traveling to the Falkland Islands, visitors must provide proof of sufficient funds and be in possession of a ticket to their destination of origin. All airport landing strips in the Falkland Islands are dirt or grass, except the airports in Stanley and at Mount Pleasant.

Automobiles travel on the left–hand side of the road in the Falkland Islands, in the same manner they travel in the United Kingdom.

Transportation Infrastructure

Since the late 20th century, when the selling of fishing licenses to foreign vessels increased revenue, the administration in Stanley has invested heavily in improving the infrastructure around the islands. Roads connecting the interior of the islands to the capital have vastly improved and the dock and port facilities have been thoroughly modernized and expanded. This increased harbor capacity has led to a surge in tourism. A cross-sound ferry service between the two main islands was established in 2008, linking Port Howard in West Falkland and New Haven in East Falkland.

Media & Communications

Aside from the three-digit emergency and directory assistance numbers, phone numbers in the Falklands are only five digits long. Cell phones were introduced in December 2005 and by 2012 there were 3,450 lines.

The Falkland Islands Radio Service (known until 2005 as Falkland Island Broadcasting Service, FIBS), provides radio broadcasts of news, weather, music and other programming. Falklanders can also listen to British Forces Broadcasting Service, targeted for military personnel. The Falklands' single newspaper, the weekly *Penguin News*, provides domestic and overseas news of note to islanders, along with charts on that week's fish haul, the international wool market report, classified ads, letters to the editor, and television and radio listings.

The Internet arrived on the islands in 1997. The government reports that by 2009 there were approximately 2,900 computers with Internet access. The online Falkland Island News Network, part of the South Atlantic Remote Territories Media Association (SARTMA), covers news concerning islanders. One special feature of the website is a weekly roundup of how the islands are being covered in the overseas press. The Uruguay-based Mercopress online news service focuses on financial and political news of several South American countries, as well as nearby territories. The British Broadcasting Corporation (BBC) provides some online news coverage, and islanders regularly listen to BBC broadcasts on radio as well. There is no local television station, and all programming is produced abroad.

SOCIAL DEVELOPMENT

Standard of Living

The Falkland Islands are not specifically ranked on the United Nations Human Development Index, which measures quality of life indicators. The islands, however, are an Overseas Territory of the United Kingdom, which was ranked 21st in the 2009 index.

Water Consumption

Tap water on the Falkland Islands is clean and is considered safe to drink. However, the Center for Disease Control (CDC) recommends that travelers to the islands drink only boiled or bottled water. Bottled water at local shops can be expensive, as it is imported.

Education

Children on the Falkland Islands are required to attend free, government-run schools from ages six to 15. Most students attend public school in Stanley. Some students that live in Camp receive their lessons via the internet, radio or telephone. Teachers make occasional trips to the Camp settlements to provide private tutoring for students. Most students continue their education at a secondary school that was built in Stanley shortly after the Falkland Islands War.

The government of the Falkland Islands offers grants to students so that they can attend university in the United Kingdom.

Women's Rights

The constitution of the Falkland Islands guarantees women full rights under the law. However, women's suffrage was not granted until 1949. Nonetheless, women serve in significant roles as representatives in the islands' government. In fact, of the five legislators representing Stanley as of 2008, two were women, and the Falkland Islands representative in the UK was also a woman. Women are also represented on the police and defense forces, the fire brigade, cultural institutions and in the sciences. Although the islands were not directly involved in World War II, 150 male and female islanders volunteered for overseas duty in the British Armed Forces. Furthermore, a 1996 census reported that nearly one-quarter of all households were run by women.

Health Care

Falkland Islanders benefit from their healthy environment and locally-grown foods. Residents are provided with government-funded health care. Pensions are provided by the government for retired citizens aged 64 and older. There are no serious health epidemics or diseases endemic to the islands. The islands' only hospital is located in Stanley.

One serious threat to the safety of Falkland Islanders is the presence of roughly 17,000 explosive landmines that remain from the Falkland Islands War. The landmines have been located and are marked with warning signs, which prevent most mine-related injuries.

GOVERNMENT

Structure

The ownership of the Falkland Islands was in dispute for centuries before the war in 1982. The islands have been claimed by a number of other nations, including France and Spain, and have been officially under British sovereignty since 1833. The constitution of the Falkland Islands was written in 1985.

Despite being a British territory, the Falkland Islands are self-governing. The islands are governed by English common law, and the observed chief of state is the monarch of Great Britain. However, there is a governmental structure specific to the Falkland Islands. The local government is headed by the governor, who holds the highest political power on the islands.

The Falkland Islands have a unicameral legislature. This consists of the 10-member Legislative Council, which is overseen by the governor. Voters elect eight of the 10 members of the Legislative Council. The remaining two members are the chief executive and the financial secretary, both of whom are appointed by the governor. The monarch of Great Britain appoints the governor.

The judicial branch of the government is made up of the Supreme Court, the Magistrates Court, and the Court of Summary Jurisdiction. The age of suffrage on the islands is eighteen.

Political Parties

The Falkland Islands are self-governing, but they remain a territory of the United Kingdom. There are no political parties that are unique to the Falklands.

Local Government

The UK's representative in the Falklands is the governor general; he, in turn, represents the

Falklands to the UK government in London. A chief executive acts as an administrator, ensuring day-to-day management of the islands' business, as well as proposes policy to the Legislative Assembly. The Legislative Assembly is comprised of eight members, having four-year terms. Three members of the Legislature are elected to the Executive Council, which consults with the governor.

Judicial System

The judicial system of the Falkland Islands mirrors that of England and Wales. The Supreme Court of the Falkland Island has unlimited jurisdiction and is headed by a Chief Justice. Civil court matters are often not decided by a jury, but are instead decided by a judge. In criminal cases, the defendant can opt for their case to be tried by either a jury and judge or just a judge. The islands do not have their own bar or law society, and many individuals who hold roles in the island's courts have significant career experience in the UK.

Taxation

Falkland Islanders pay a personal allowance tax. A medical tax, known as the Medical Service Levy, is also charged. The islands also have a Retirement Pension system, which requires a weekly contribution from all workers. Private sector employers on the Falklands pay routine Payments on Account of Tax (POAT). Corporations operating on the island pay a 21 percent tax rate, which changes to 26 percent after the first million FKP earned. Non-resident oil companies operating in Falklands territory play the full 26 percent tax.

Armed Forces

Because it is a territory of the UK, the Falkland Island's main defense organization is the British Armed Forces, also known as the Armed Forces of the Crown. Personnel and equipment in the region is overseen by the Commander of the British Forces South Atlantic Islands (CBFSAI). In addition, the islands also have a part-time volunteer army, known as the Falkland Islands Defense Force (FIDF).

Foreign Policy

The sovereignty of the Falkland Islands, one of Britain's overseas territories, continues to be the center of a diplomatic dispute between Argentina and Great Britain. The islands are internationally recognized as being a colony of Great Britain, which formally established a colonial presence in 1833. However, Argentina claims that an Argentinean colony was expelled from the islands prior to the establishment of British rule. Contemporary Falkland Islanders claim to be British, and have full British citizenship due to the British Nationality Act of 1983.

In 1982, the dispute between Argentina and Great Britain became violent. The Falkland Islands War began when Argentina invaded the islands on April 2, 1982. The war evoked strong patriotic sentiment on both sides. Argentina surrendered on June 14 after nearly two and a half months of conflict. However, Argentina has yet to relinquish its claim of sovereignty, stating that it had island settlements there in the early 1800s.

Nearly 1,000 people died in the Falkland Islands War. In addition, there was an unusually high suicide rate among soldiers who fought in the war in the years after it ended. As of 2002, a UK veterans' support group reported that at least 260 British servicemen had killed themselves—more than the 255 soldiers who were killed in action. And as of 2006, an estimated 400 Argentinean veterans had taken their own lives. That's more than half the number, 650, that died during the conflict itself. Many soldiers have suffered post-traumatic stress disorder, and the Argentines in particular were said to have been abused by their superior officers, then shunned back home for their defeat.

Although they remain eligible for Argentinean citizenship, the majority of Falkland Islanders reject Argentina's claim of sovereignty over the territory. Britain maintains control over the defense of the islands. Falklanders were also granted the right to self-determination, or self-governance. The United Nations (UN) has maintained that an open dialogue should continue between the two countries to resolve the dispute.

Aside from Argentina, Chile is the Falklands' closest South American neighbor. Although officially neutral during the war, Chile reportedly gave the UK surveillance information in return for discounted military aircraft. A link between Santiago and Stanley continues to this day in the form of weekly flights between the two capitals.

Two important issues affecting the foreign policy of the Falkland Islands are fishing rights and tourism, both of which are a large source of capital. Fishing vessels, notably from Spain, Taiwan and Korea, are ever-present in the waters that surround the islands. However, both the tourism and fishing industry have had negative effects on the environment in recent years. For example, in May 2008, a Korean trawler caught fire, dumping a reported 150 tons of oil into the pristine Berkeley Sound. In addition, the recent explorations for oil in the region have led Argentina to oppose any sanctioned drilling or extraction in the islands.

The British oil group Desire Petroleum began drilling for oil off the Falkland Islands in February 2010.

Human Rights Profile

International human rights law insists that states respect civil and political rights, and also promote an individual's economic, social, and cultural rights. The United Nations Universal Declaration of Human Rights (UDHR) is recognized as the standard for international human rights. Its authors sought the counsel of the world's great thinkers, philosophers, and religious leaders, and were careful to create a document that reflects the core values shared by every world culture. (To read this document or view the articles relating to cultural human rights, visit: http://www.udhr.org/UDHR/default.htm.)

In the aftermath of the Falklands War and the Shackleton Report, the Falkland Islands were able to forge a constitution based both on external advice and internal knowledge. Indeed, advice from the Shackleton Report was the catalyst for some of the greatest changes made on the Falklands. That constitution, created in 1985 and revised since, begins with language aimed at protecting the fundamental rights and freedoms of the individual, striving to ensure that all people on the islands—regardless of race, sex, place of origin, religion, political opinions, etc.—are accorded equal rights under the law. This goal is in accordance with Article 2 of the UDHR.

In 2003, the UN's own Committee on the Elimination of Racial Discrimination reported that the laws of the Falkland Islands, designed to outlaw racial discrimination, are indeed observed, respected, and actively enforced. The report further states that complaints of racial discrimination are rare. It commends the government on seeking to integrate immigrants by promoting their inclusion in the police force, the all-volunteer Falkland Islands Defense Force, and the judicial branch, as well as charitable and athletic associations. The report also praises island news outlets, principally FIRS and the *Penguin News*, for relaying information of use and interest to island minority groups.

Article 18 of the declaration, which addresses freedom of religion, is guaranteed in the constitution. Three percent of Falkland Islanders are members of the Baha'i faith, a religious group that has faced persecution elsewhere. Article 19, concerning the freedom to express one's opinion, is likewise a right of Falkland Islanders. Regardless of foreign birthplace—be it the UK or elsewhere—one must reside on the islands for seven years before applying for full and permanent rights to the islands. In keeping with prejudice-free schooling for all as stated in the declaration's Article 26, the UN report notes that all schools on the islands have zero tolerance for racism.

A favorable review from the UN notwithstanding, representatives of the Falklands continue to take issue with that organization's refusal to accord them the right of self-determination. Rather, the UN perceives the Falklands as a territory whose sovereignty remains in dispute. More recently, in June 2008, in what has become an annual protest to the UN's Special Committee on Decolonization, an island representative railed against the UN, particularly the perceived treatment of islanders as though they were akin to children involved in a divorce custody battle.

ECONOMY

Overview of the Economy
The Falkland Islands are a considerably wealthy territory with no unemployment. The Falkland Islands War had a positive, long-term effect on the economy. The estimated gross domestic product (GDP) in 2007 was $164.5 million and the per capita GDP was $55,000.

Industry
There is a limited manufacturing sector in the Falkland Islands' economy. Wool products account for most of the processed and exported goods. The service sector is far more significant than manufacturing in the industrial sector. Most service jobs are in government, which is the largest employer on the islands.

In recent years, the development of offshore oil resources has provided a boost to the islands' industrial sector. These oil deposits have also improved economic relations with Argentina, as the two governments have collaborated in developing the region's oil resources.

Major exports are entirely agricultural. Wool is the islands' most important exported commodity. Animal hides and meat are exported as well. Imports include fuel, food, drink, building materials, and clothes. The islands' major trading partners are the United Kingdom, Spain, Italy, and the Czech Republic.

Labor
There is relatively no unemployment in the Falkland Islands; workers are often recruited from the United Kingdom for jobs that cannot be filled by the small workforce of roughly 3,000 Falkland Islanders. The government remains the territory's largest employer.

Energy/Power/Natural Resources
The Falkland Islands does not have an abundance of natural resources. Fish, squid, wildlife, calcified seaweed, and sphagnum moss constitute the major natural resources.

Since 1998, exploration of the waters off Stanley for deepwater oil fields has increased.

Six test wells brought back some positive results and there is speculation that the Falklands basin contains rich potential for future oil development. Future testing is needed to determine the viability of any major offshore oil drilling.

Fishing
The coastline's many harbors allow for a healthy commercial fishing industry. Squid are fished more than anything else. An annual revenue equivalent of $40 million USD is generated by the sale of fishing licenses to commercial fishing vessels. However, one of the major environmental concerns on the islands is the problem of over-fishing by unlicensed boats.

Mining/Metals
There are small amounts of valuable minerals throughout East and West Falkland, including deposits of galena with a high silver content, and white sand which can be used for glassmaking. Fuel resources include peat and large offshore oil deposits.

Agriculture
Historically, agriculture has been the largest sector of the Falkland Islands' economy. Approximately 99 percent of the land on the islands is devoted to farming. In recent decades, however, fishing has overtaken farming in terms of revenue. Vegetable crops remain a vital agricultural commodity.

Animal Husbandry
Sheep and dairy products are vital agricultural commodities. Sheep were introduced to the islands in the late 19th century, and the 600,000 or so sheep in 2008 outnumber Falklanders 400 to 1. The Falkland Islands also has the world's only commercial herd of reindeer not affected by plutonium radiation from the 1986 Chernobyl nuclear reactor meltdown in Ukraine.

Tourism
Tourism is an important sector of the Falkland Islands' economy. The country benefits greatly from eco-tourism, as wildlife is the islands' biggest

tourist attraction. On average, 30,000 people visit the Falkland Islands each year. Stanley has only one hotel, few restaurants and bars, and no theaters.

One notable tourist attraction is Darwin Cemetery. The memorial burial grounds are located at Goose Green, where a significant battle in the Falkland Islands War was fought. The remains of a downed Argentine aircraft are located at this site as well.

Until 1999, tourism was inhibited by the fact the Falkland Islands were closed to air traffic from Argentina. From 1982 to 1999, the only Argentine citizens allowed into the Falkland Islands were those visiting the graves of relatives buried at Goose Green.

Hope Killcoyne, Richard Means,
Jeffrey Bowman

DO YOU KNOW?

- Charles Darwin was one of the first British visitors to the island in 1834 and personally named some of the landmarks around Port Stanley.

- During the Falklands War, the Argentine military changed all the place names of the locations on the island.

- The Argentine name for the islands, Islas Malvinas, is derived from the name given to the region by French explorers from Saint-Malo, France, and from translations of British names to Spanish.

Bibliography

Bernhardson, Wayne. *Patagonia, Including the Falkland Islands.* Emeryville, CA: Avalon Travel, 2005.

Cawkell, Mary. *The History of the Falkland Islands.* London: Anthony Nelson, 2001.

Hastings, Max, and Simon Jenkins. *The Battle for the Falklands.* New York: W. W. Norton & Company, 1983.

Hodgson, Bryan. "The Falkland Islands—Life After the War." *National Geographic.* March 1988: 390 - 411.

Ritchie, Harry. *The Last Pink Bits.* London: Hodder and Stoughton, 1997.

Shackleton, Lord Edward, R.J. Storey, and R. Johnson. "Prospect of the Falkland Islands." *The Geographic Journal.* 143.1 (March 1977): 1-13. 16 Jul 2008. <http://www.jstor.org/pss/1796671>.

Strange, Ian J. *The Falklands: South Atlantic Islands.* New York: Dodd, Mean & Company, 1985.

Wheeler, Tony. *The Falklands and South Georgia Island.* Oakland: Lonely Planet, 2004.

Winchester, Simon. *Outposts: Journeys to the Surviving Relics of the British Empire.* London: Hodder and Stoughton, 1985.

Works Cited

"Consolidated Version of the Falkland Islands Constitution." http://www.worldstatesmen.org/falkland. 1997. FIG. http://www.worldstatesmen.org/Falkland_order1985.pdf

"Falkland Islands Government" (Official Site). 07 Jul 2008. FIG. http://www.falklands.gov.fk/

"UN Convention on the Rights of the Child, Overseas Dependent Territories and Crown Dependencies of the UK." 29 May 2000. United Nations.

"Falklands Focus" 82, 83 Jan 2008 http://www.falklands.gov.fk/falklands-focus-issue-82-january-2008/; http://www.falklands.gov.fk/falklands-focus-issue-83-july-2008/

"Committee on the Elimination of Racial Discrimination," 13 Mar 2003. United Nations. http://www2.ohchr.org/english/bodies/cerd/

Johnston, Lisa. "Falklands' cruise season new record: 67.700 visitors," MercoPress. Independent News Agency. http://en.mercopress.com/2008/04/09/falklands-cruise-season-new-record-67-700-visitors

"Falklands Questions Answered," BBC News/UK 07 Jun 2007. British Broadcasting Corporation. http://news.bbc.co.uk/2/low/uk_news/6683677.stm

"Argentines protest at drilling plans." Penguin News [Stanley] May 2, 2008, V19.No51: 1 "Their Island Story, Argentina and the Falklands, Bitter Memories and a Popular Cause." The Economist Vol. 383, Issue 852307 Apr 2007.

Brock, J. "Falklands Forum Held in London." Falkland Islands News Network. 18 Apr 2007. http://www.falklandnews.com/text/public/story.cfm?get=4451&source=323

Rohter, Larry. "25 Years after War, Wealth has Transformed Falklands," New York Times 01 Apr 2007. http://www.nytimes.com/2007/04/01/world/americas/01iht-falklands.1.5099287.html?pagewanted=all&_r=0

Pascoe, Graham, Peter Pepper. "Getting it Right: The Real History of the Falklands/Malvinas. A Reply to the Argentine Seminar of 3 December 2007." May 2008 1-40. http://www.wildisland.gs/atlantis/gettingitright.pdf

Borders & Southern on the up." Penguin News [Stanley] May 23, 2008, V20.No02: 3.

"Chile 'helped UK over Falklands'," BBC News 25 06 2005. http://news.bbc.co.uk/2/hi/americas/4622565.stm

Cockwell, Jenny. "Comment by Managing Editor." Penguin News [Stanley]May 23, 2008, V20.No02: 2.

"Ocean 8 is lost." Penguin News [Stanley]May 23, 2008, V20.No02: 2.

Where was FIG action on oil spill asks Falkland Conservation?" Penguin News [Stanley] May 30, 2008, V20.No03: 1, 3.

"US scholar: Falklands 'right' to self-determination is a confusing and misleading obstacle to peace." Penguin News [Stanley] May 23, 2008, V20.No02: 9.

Dear Paula. "We Don't Sit Here Doing Nothing," BBC News, International Version 13 Jun 2007. British Broadcasting Corporation. http://news.bbc.co.uk/2/hi/uk_news/6743645.stm

Bingham. John. "Captivated by Windswept Beauty at the End of the Earth," StainesNews.co.uk 15 May 2007.

"Staines, Ashford & Egham News," Staines Informer and Leader. http://www.stainesnews.co.uk/staines-ashford-lifestyle/tm_headline=captivated-by-windswept-beauty-at-the-end-of-the-earth&method=full&objectid=19106808&siteid=106484-name_page.html

"Saved, but Still Fearful." Time Magazine 09 Aug 1982 23 http://www.time.com/time/magazine/article/0,9171,925649-5,00.html

"Firefighting in the Falkland Islands. (Brigade Profile).," Allbusiness.com 01 Feb 2003. http://business.highbeam.com/2380/article-1G1-225792397/firefighting-falkland-islands-falklands-islands-fire

"Falkland Islands." Worldwide Guide to Women in Leadership. 26 Jan 2008. www.guide2womenleaders.com. http://www.guide2womenleaders.com/Falkland_Islands.htm

"World War II: Falkland Islands Commemorates Involvement in World War II." Filahome 29 Jun 2005 http://www.filahome.nl/e/stamps/0506-world-war-2.htm

Ratliff. William. "Everyone wins from a compromise; The Falklands, 25 years later.(Opinion)," International Herald Tribune 02 Jul 2007. http://www.independent.org/newsroom/article.asp?id=1993

Valente. Marcela. "Argentina: Malvinas/Falkland Manoeuvres and Memories," IPS 30 Mar 2007. Inter Press Service News Agency. http://ipsnews.net/news.asp?idnews=37167

Billen, Andrew. "Mrs T and sympathy: Andrew Billen on the BBC play that took 15 years to reach our screens. (Television).." New Statesman 15 Apr 2002 http://business.highbeam.com/794/article-1G1-85007843/mrs-t-and-sympathy-andrew-billen-bbc-play-took-15-years

Steiner, Christopher. "The Falklands. Again?." Forbes v181 i9 05 May 2008 42. http://www.forbes.com/forbes/2008/0505/042a.html

Inglis, Alison, Jason Lewis. "Falklands.Info." 16 Jul 2008 http://www.falklands.info/index.html

Cocroft, Wayne. "Images of the Cold War: Combat Art." Conservation Bulletin 44 2003.

Beckman, Jeremy. "Southeastern Falkland Islands seen as highly Prospective." Offshore vol 66, issue 11 Nov 2006 58-60. http://www.offshore-mag.com/display_article/278105/9/ARCHI/none/none/1/Southeastern-Falkland-Islands-seen-as-highly-prospective-/

Hills, Ann. "Anchoring the Past in the Falklands." History Today 41, 7 Jul 1991 4-5. http://www.historytoday.com/ann-hills/anchoring-past-falklands

Robertson, Janet. "Special Committee of 24 on Decolonisation." United Nations General Assembly. United Nations, New York. 08 June 2008.

Stevens, Richard. "Special Committee of 24 on Decolonisation." United Nations General Assembly. United Nations, New York. 12 June 2008.

"An Ungentlemanly Act." Dir. Stuart Urban. Perf. Ian Richardson, Rosemary Leach, Bob Peck. DVD. BFS Video, 1991.

"Iluminados por el Fuego (Blessed by Fire)." Dir. Tristan Bauer. Perf. Gaston Pauls, Virginia Innocenti. DVD. Koch Lorber Films (USA), 2005.

"Our Malvinas Islands." Dir. Raymundo Gleyzer. DVD. Facets Video, 1965.

https://www.cia.gov/library/publications/the-world-factbook/geos/fk.html

http://wwwnc.cdc.gov/travel/destinations/falkland-islands.aspx

http://www.fightingpigband.com

http://www.guardian.co.uk/uk/2010/feb/22/falkland-islands-oil-drilling-begins

http://web202.ssvc.com/radio/ (British Forces Broadcasting Service)

http://www.firs.co.fk/ (Falkland Island Radio Service)

www.sartma.com (South Atlantic Remote Territories Media Association)

http://www.mysterra.org/webmag/falkland-islands/history.html (Travel web magazine)

Introduction

The Cooperative Republic of Guyana is the only English-speaking country in South America. It is one of three countries (along with Suriname and French Guiana) on South America's northeast coast known as the Guianas. The population of Guyana consists of several ethnic groups, including many Amerindians. Guyana is an Amerindian word meaning "land of the waters."

GENERAL INFORMATION

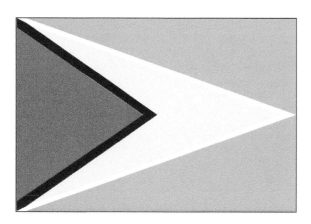

Official Language: English
Population: 799,600 (2013 estimate)
Currency: Guyanese dollar
Coins: Coins are issued in denominations of 1, 5, and 10 dollars.
Land Area: 196,849 square kilometers (76,000 square miles)
Water Area: 18,120 square kilometers (7,000 square miles)
National Motto: "One People, One Nation, One Destiny"
National Anthem: "Dear Land of Guyana"
Capital: Georgetown
Time Zone: GMT -4
Flag Description: Guyana's flag is called the Golden Arrowhead. It features a white-bordered golden triangle (the arrowhead) on a green background, and another equilateral triangle of red (with a black border) superimposed on top of that. The flag's green background represents the country's agriculture, while the white represents the rivers, as well as the country's potential. The gold of the arrow signifies the country's mineral wealth (gold), black symbolizes endurance, and red, the zeal of its people.

Population

Over 90 percent of the population of Guyana lives in the coastal plain, which comprises roughly five percent of the country's entire area. Within the region, Georgetown is the most populous city; about one-third of Guyana's population lives in or near Georgetown. Other major cities include Linden, which is known for its bauxite and gold mines, and New Amsterdam, an industrial port southeast of Georgetown.

Languages

English is the primary and official language in Guyana, and is spoken by more than 90 percent

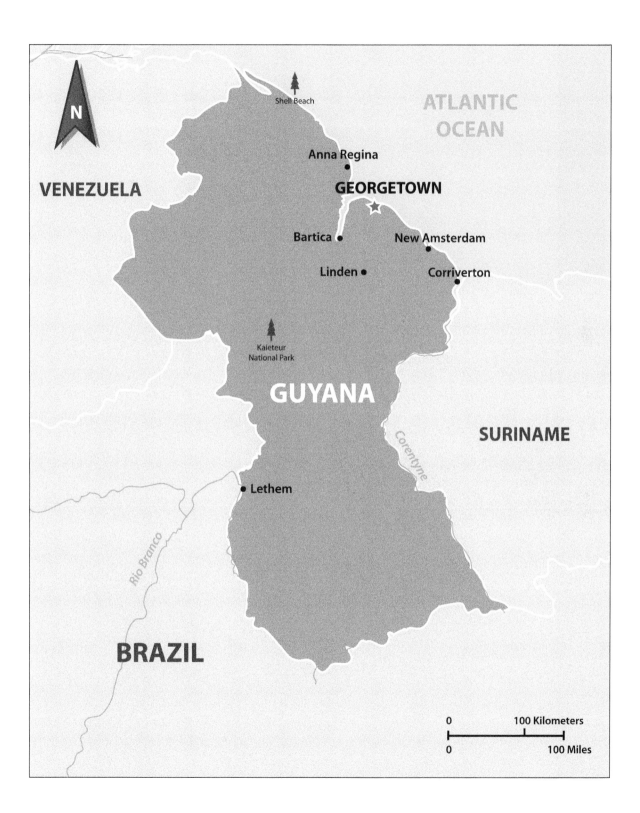

Principal Cities by Population (2014 unless otherwise noted):

- Georgetown (235,017), 2009
- Linden (Mackenzie) (44,690)
- New Amsterdam (35,039)
- Anna Regina (12,448)
- Bartica (11,157)
- Skeldon (5,859)
- Rosignol (5,782)
- Mahaica Village (4,867)
- Parika (4,081)
- Vreed-en-Hoop (3,073)

of the nation's residents. Guyanese Creolese is a creole form (often called Guyanese Creole), with elements taken from Hindi, various African dialects, and Amerindian terms. French, Hindi, and Urdu are also used in some portions of the capital.

Native People & Ethnic Groups

Guyana has been called the "Land of the Six Peoples" because of its diverse population. Today, there are five main ethnic groups in Guyana. Amerindians, or American Indians, are the native people, while the other four groups emigrated from Africa, East India, Portugal, and China. The Indo-Guyanese (people of East Indian descent) and the Afro-Guyanese (people of African descent) are the two largest groups in Guyana; East Indians comprise the largest ethnic group at over 43.5 percent of the population, while African descendants comprise 30 percent of the population. Almost 17 percent of Guyana's people are of mixed descent: either mulattoes (part African, part European) or douglahs (part African, part East Indian).

In Guyana, there are roughly 50,000 Amerindians living in nine tribes. These are the Arawak, the Akawáio, the Carib, the Patamona, the Makushi, the Arekuna, the Warao, the Waiwai, and the Wapishana. Originally, the Amerindians were semi-nomadic, and settled in family villages. Today, most Amerindians live in the highlands in the southwest.

The Guyanese Amerindians typically live in thatched-roof huts. This population finds itself between two worlds, trying to maintain its indigenous culture while simultaneously trying to gain an economic foothold in a changing world. Many families work on farms, where they cultivate the root vegetable cassava; the harvesting of palm hearts and the sale of captured native birds are also primary sources of income. The Amerindian community is working towards creating sustainable industries that can allow them to maintain their cultural integrity and support their families.

Many petroglyphs (ancient drawings carved onto rocks) tell the history of the Amerindians in Guyana.

Religions

Christianity, Islam, and Hinduism are the major religions within Guyana. Census surveys in 2002 indicated that over 55 percent of that population practiced some form of Christianity, while 28 percent of the remaining population was practicing Hinduism and just over seven percent identified as Muslim. Indigenous tribal religions are practiced in some communities, but are uncommon in the cities.

Climate

Guyana has a tropical climate, with high temperatures and high average rainfall. Temperatures are warm throughout the year, averaging 27° Celsius (80° Fahrenheit). The coastal plain receives an average of 229 centimeters (90 inches) of rain, while the inland forest and highlands regions receive about 178 centimeters (70 inches). The wet season spans from February to August, and the country sometimes suffers droughts in late August or September.

In the capital of Georgetown, the climate varies little from season to season. The daily temperature ranges from 23° to 30° Celsius (74° to 86° Fahrenheit) with high average humidity and frequent rainfall. The rainfall is a product of cool ocean currents meeting warmer air currents in the tropical doldrums.

ENVIRONMENT & GEOGRAPHY

Topography

Guyana has three topographical regions: the coastal plain, the inland forest, and the highlands. The coastal plain is the strip of land on the northeast shore where the majority of the population lives. The country's major cities, including the capital, Georgetown, are located in this region. However, most of the coastal plain is farmland, and contains sugarcane and rice crops.

More than 80 percent of Guyana is covered in dense tropical jungles, while the remaining landscape is divided between tropical savannah and coastal plains. The highlands in the southwest contain the savanna grasslands and several mountain ranges, including the Pakaraima Mountains and the Kanuku Mountains. Most of Guyana's Amerindian population lives in this 15,500 square kilometer (6,000 square mile) region.

The highest point in Guyana is atop Mount Roraima, which reaches its peak at 2,772 meters (9,094 feet). There are many rivers throughout Guyana, the longest of which is the Essequibo. This river flows down the center of the country for 1,014 kilometers (630 miles). Other major rivers are the Demerara, the Courantyne and the Berbice, which, like the Essequibo, flow north to south. Several waterfalls are found along Guyana's rivers. These include Kaiteur Falls, Great Falls, King Edward VII Falls, and Marina Falls.

Plants & Animals

There are three kinds of forests in Guyana: mangrove, hardwood, and tropical rainforests. The mangrove forests are found along the coast and consist of mangrove trees growing in swamps. Most of the mangrove forests are behind the coastal plain, along the rivers. In these watery habitats, the Victoria Regis (Victoria Amazonica) water lily thrives as the largest aquatic leafed plant in the world. The Victoria Regis water lily is also Guyana's national flower, and is featured on the national crest.

Hardwood forests are found further inland, near the savanna grassland. Hardwoods are large trees that grow in sandy soil and have expansive root systems. The wood from these trees is one of Guyana's most valuable exports.

The tropical rainforest is in the west and south of Guyana near the Brazilian and Venezuelan borders. Common rainforest trees include the greenheart and the mora. Some other plants native to Guyana's rainforest are the liana vine and the highly poisonous urari vine.

The rainforest is also home to many of Guyana's animal species. Native bird species include parrots and macaws. There are many species of insects in the tropical habitat, including the morpho butterfly and the parasol, or "leaf-cutter" ant, which is responsible for destroying vast amounts of vegetation.

Guyana's rivers and coastal waters are home to many freshwater and saltwater fish. Piranhas and the native lukanani are found in the rivers. Larger fish, such as the arapaima, are caught offshore as a part of Guyana's fishing industry.

CUSTOMS & COURTESIES

Greetings

While greetings in Guyana are often spoken in English, the pronunciation is different from the common English spoken in North America and Europe. For example, the greeting "Hello" is pronounced "Ello" in Guyanese Creole. Guyanese grammar is also unique, and can sometimes confuse non-native English speakers. The phrase "How are you doing?" for instance, is commonly phrased "How yuh do?"

In addition to Guyanese Creole, there are numerous other languages spoken in parts of Guyana, including Arawak and Carib dialects, several native African dialects, and Hindi. In larger urban areas, Portuguese has become increasingly common due to the cultural influence and influx of immigrants from nearby Brazil. In Portuguese, the greeting "Ola" ("Hello") is commonly used. The phrase "Tudo bem?" ("How are you?") is another popular greeting.

While cheek kissing is a common non-verbal greeting in many South American countries, handshakes are more common in Guyana, though they are typically perceived as not as firm as in other cultures. Among good friends, it is common for individuals to embrace when greeting.

Gestures & Etiquette

While Guyanese society is superficially similar to the culture of other Caribbean nations, Guyanese culture also has much in common with other South American countries. In general, the Guyanese people take a relaxed attitude toward scheduling and social engagements, though it is still considered rude to be late for business meetings. Social and business engagements are often seen as structured within a span of time, rather than at a specific hour.

Guyanese use a number of hand and facial gestures when speaking. Some gestures are similar to those in Latin American countries, such as waving with the back of one's hand and avoiding showing the palm of the hand. Other gestures are borrowed from African culture, such as the "cut eye" gesture. This gesture involves glancing at a person or object, and then closing the eyes and turning away. The gesture is meant to communicate hostility and is considered an insult.

Eating/Meals

Most Guyanese eat three meals a day. The morning meal is generally served between six and 10 o'clock, and may include coffee, some type of bread or grain, and roasted meat. The midday meal is typically larger and more substantial than the morning meal, and many Guyanese eat curries, or soup, in the afternoon. The evening meal, which is generally served between five and ten o'clock, may consist of the same dishes served in the afternoon. For many Guyanese, there is little difference, in terms of quantity or content, between the daily morning, midday, and evening meals. Generally, Guyanese tend to eat large, hearty portions, including meat, vegetables, and a variety of spicy sauces with Indian, Caribbean, and African influences.

Most Guyanese meals are served "family style," with all individuals serving themselves from communal dishes. In some ethnic populations, and in many restaurants, eating is more formal, with meals served in courses. Most celebrations, including holidays, are accompanied by communal feasting. In addition, Guyana makes its own coffee, beer and liquor, and most locals drink domestic beverages. Drinking is acceptable with any meal, but most people will generally drink only with the afternoon and evening meals. Business may be conducted at any time of day and meetings may be organized to accompany morning, midday, or the afternoon meals

Visiting

The Guyanese people tend to be informal in terms of rules of etiquette when meeting for social occasions. If invited to a Guyanese home, it is considered courteous to bring a small gift, such as liquor or pastries. If the host has children, it is also advisable to bring small toys or candy for the children, though this is not required. As in most cultures, it is considered impolite to request a tour of a host's home, and visitors are instead advised to wait for their host to offer a tour.

LIFESTYLE

Family

Both the Indo-Guyanese and Afro-Guyanese ethnic groups tend to live in extended family communities, where several generations live in close proximity. However, this common characteristic of Guyanese family life has begun to change as more Guyanese are forced to travel in search of work, making it more difficult to settle near members of their extended families.

Despite religious traditions, within both the Hindu and Catholic communities, that favor monogamous marriage, more than 30 percent of Guyanese children are born out of wedlock. It has become common for Afro-Guyanese to engage in a series of semi-monogamous relationships, and to parent one or more children before marriage. Among the Indo-Guyanese, marriage is more common, but more than a third of marriages end in divorce.

In households where men are absent, or where a couple has divorced, women often continue to live in close association with extended family, forming female kin groups in many towns and cities. Women rely on grandparents, aunts and close friends to aid in child rearing and to serve as a crucial economic buffer in times of need. The prevalence of family and friend networks contributes to the stability of Guyanese communities, though scarcity of work has also meant that many women are forced to travel in order to find jobs.

More than 60 percent of Guyanese mothers are young, and the average age when they give birth to their first child is 20.8 (2009 est.). Poverty forces most young parents to enter the workforce and reduces the number of Guyanese who attend college. In addition, more than 60 percent of Guyanese live in rural environments and are employed in agriculture or manual labor, contributing to high rates of poverty.

Housing

There is a critical housing shortage in Guyana, and in 2003 it was estimated by Habitat for Humanity that more than 20 percent of Guyanese were squatting illegally. Squatting is the act of inhabiting an abandoned and unoccupied space. As concrete and brick are difficult to obtain in Guyana, most houses are made of wood. Although wood construction is affordable in Guyana, many houses suffer from extensive weather damage. In addition, most Guyanese families live without adequate plumbing and sanitation, a contributing factor to infant and child illness.

Rural Guyanese villages are typically no larger than a square mile of houses and crops. Many of the villages are ethnically homogenous, owing to the settlement patterns put in place during the colonial period, when African and Indian communities were established in separate areas. In urban areas, concrete housing is more common, though most families live in small, single-room dwellings. Many families in rural areas also

have kitchen gardens, where tenants and home-owners grow some of the food eaten by the family. A smaller number of families have livestock living on their property for personal consumption or to sell at local markets. One of the major difficulties faced by rural Guyanese families is a lack of adequate drainage systems. Many villages suffer from flooding, which causes significant housing damage, loss of property and food crops, and can be a factor in transmitting disease.

In Georgetown and other cities, some Guyanese families choose to rent apartments rather than houses. Apartments in Guyanese cities often have superior amenities to private houses, but are generally smaller by comparison. Since 2000, the Guyanese government has been working to convert public land into additional housing projects for poor families. Economic assistance from the International Monetary Fund (IMF) and from the United States has been helpful in establishing housing improvement projects. There are also a number of non-governmental organizations (NGOs), like Habitat for Humanity, working in Guyana to address the housing shortage.

Food

Guyanese cuisine features a distinct blend of various ethnic and cultural influences, most notably African, East Indian, Asian and Caribbean, as well as Amerindian and European (particularly British and Portuguese). It is often largely based on Creole traditions and seafood (due to the country's location along the northern coast of South America). Rice is one of the staples of Guyanese cuisine, and is usually cooked with coconut milk and served with vegetables. The typical rice dish, with coconut and beans, is called rice cookup, and is commonly served as a side dish. Another staple is roti, a type of fried flatbread that is often used to sop up the various curries that accompany many Guyanese dishes.

One of the most famous Guyanese dishes is the pepperpot, which is any variety of slow-cooked meat, lamb, goat, beef, or chicken, served in a spicy stew made from onions, peppers, and cassareep, a fermented sauce made from ground cassava. Pepperpot is generally spicy and may be served with rice, vegetables, and roti. In addition to standard meats, Guyanese may also eat several local animals, including the paca and agouti, which are large rodents found across South America. Wild game is a common component in Amerindian food and is also served in a number of restaurants in Georgetown and other cities.

Fish and seafood is a major component of the Guyanese diet, especially for people living on the Atlantic coast or along one of the nation's major rivers. Salted fish, deep-fried or dried, is common as a snack or meal. Some Guyanese prefer their salted fish served with a curry sauce while others eat it plain with bread. Fried fish with curry and rice cookup is a popular dish, and typically served in restaurants across Guyana. The nation's curries blend Asian and Indian influences to create unique mixtures of spice and peppers.

For a snack or a dessert, many locals eat pholourie, which is a piece of fried bread served with sweet chutney. The bread is generally made from split pea or lentil flour and the sauce is usually either mango or tamarind.

Life's Milestones

Though Guyana has an ethnically diverse population, Christianity and Hinduism are the dominant religions. At the turn of the 21st century, over half of the population—more than 55 percent in 2002—were Christian, and thus followed traditional rites of passage, including baptism, communion and marriage. For example, the birth of a couple's first child is generally accompanied by a gathering of family and friends for a meal and a celebration. Extended family networks are important in Guyana, and parents often choose godparents for their children in a strategic manner intended to increase the family's social influence.

Guyanese weddings almost always involve music and dancing, in the African, Indian, and Creole populations. While some Guyanese hold their weddings at churches, other families, especially those located some distance from a church, may hold the wedding at the home of the bride's family. It is tradition for guests to present the bride and groom with monetary gifts, or contribute a dish to the wedding feast.

Among the Amerindian population, weddings are often more traditional. Folk songs passed down through generations are sung to commemorate the new couple's marriage and special dishes are served. Individuals may also engage in wedding dances, with all attendees invited to participate. Both the Carib and Arawak tribes have long traditions of incorporating music and dance into wedding celebrations, and these traditions have been extended to the Indo- and Afro-Guyanese populations as well.

In addition to the celebration of Christian and Hindu milestones and holidays, Guyanese also celebrate Mashramani, or "Republic Day," on February 23, with a major celebration that usually includes food, dancing, music and drinking with friends and family. Mashramani, or "Mash," which celebrates Guyanese independence, is a national holiday. Among the Hindu population, the Deepavalli, or the "Festival of Lights," is another festive occasion, and is usually observed in November.

CULTURAL HISTORY

Art

The arts in Guyana are rooted in the culture of the Amerindians, the pre-Columbian indigenous population of the Americas. Their contributions to art are seen in pottery, jewelry, textiles, sculpture, basketry and other traditional crafts. From this early influence arose the aesthetic traditions of the indigenous Carib and Arawak tribes. Two of more than a dozen tribes that inhabited the region, the Carib and Arawak produced a wide variety of art, including wood and stone sculpture, painting, and weaving. Modern Guyanese art then developed as the product of several separate strains of cultural influences. It was historically informed by imported art from Europe—particularly the Netherlands and England—and African and East Indian art brought during the slave trade.

European colonists began arriving in the late 16th century, bringing realistic painting, and sculpture to Guyana. African slaves began arriving in the early 17th century, along with new wood and stone sculpture techniques. Indentured servants began arriving in the 19th century, adding another layer to Guyana's creole culture. Creole is a term often used to describe a culture that has a mixed European and African heritage, particularly among former colonies where the slave trade was prominent. With the arrival of each group, new artistic techniques were introduced, and the changing culture provided inspiration for a new generation of artists.

After the long transition to independence, which occurred in the late 1960s, Guyanese artists began exploring the cultural and artistic traditions of the Amerindian tribes. (Prior to independence, Guyana was known as British Guinea). This led to the emergence of a native art movement in the mid-1970s. The Roots and Culture Gallery in the capital of Georgetown became an important center for native artists examining traditional Amerindian art. Works from the gallery were shipped worldwide for exhibit beginning in the 1980s. Among the artists who helped to create the native art movement was Philip Moore (1921–2012), best known for his 25-foot bronze sculpture called the 1763 Monument, which commemorates the famous 18th-century rebellion against the Dutch government.

The Guyanese Department of Culture fostered the burgeoning native art movement by purchasing the work of artists such as Moore, and installing representations of native art in the National Gallery, housed at the Castellani House in Georgetown. (The Castellani House is named for architect Cesar Castellani, who designed many of the prominent buildings in Guyana). Over the decades, the native art movement has become more complex and varied. Modern artists such as Winston Strick use native art as a model while exploring modern artistic ideas. Strick, credited with leading the modernist movement in Guyana, specializes in leather sculpture, and is one of the few Guyanese artists to have gained an international following.

Other prominent contemporary artists include Stanley Greaves (1935–), a painter and sculptor celebrated throughout the Caribbean and who was recognized by the Guyana Folk Festival Committee in 2002; Aubrey Williams (1926–1990), who once lived with the indigenous Warao; and Ronald Savory, one of the first Guyanese artists to use Amerindian motifs and themes in his work.

Architecture

Guyanese architecture is largely a mixture of colonial and traditional elements, though modern styles have defined urban areas in recent years. For example, much of the city of Georgetown's architecture is of wooden, colonial design, including both Dutch and English colonial styles, and each year a number of new, modern buildings are constructed. Some of the city's oldest buildings are constructed on brick stilts to prevent flooding.

Drama

Guyana's theater community was launched in 1957 with the establishment of the Guyana Theater Guild and the construction of the Theatre Guild Playhouse. Prior to this, drama depended on traveling North American and European troupes. The playhouse promoted the generation of distinctly Guyanese productions, played on stage and on the radio, by such writers as Frank Pilgrim.

In 1972, Guyana hosted the first Carifesta (Caribbean Festival of Arts), a Caribbean cultural event that showcases the works of Caribbean artists, writers, and musicians. In 1972, 25 countries participated, and the impetus of the event helped nurture the arts scene in Guyana. In 1976, another arts center was established, with a new theater featuring 1,000 seats. In the 1980s, writer Ron Robinson (1946–) founded the professional theater group, Theater Company. Guyana boasts contemporary playwrights such as Jan Carew (1920–2012), Michael Gilkes (1933–), and Ian Valz (1957–2010).

Music

Until the late 19th century, the Guyanese population was divided into ethnic pockets with little cultural blending between social groups. As the linguistic and cultural borders began to break down, new musical styles emerged, mixing elements of indigenous, European, African, and Indian musical traditions. While each ethnic group still maintains its own folk traditions, several musical styles have become predominant in Guyana. Calypso, which is a blend of African and Caribbean music, became one of the most popular styles in the country. Soca, which is a Caribbean musical style that has become popular in contemporary dance clubs, is similar to calypso, but uses heavy, pulsating rhythms to achieve a heavier sound. Modern calypso and soca artists may use electronic instrumentation to supplement the traditional drums and wind instruments used in each genre's traditional forms.

The Indo-Guyanese population, descendants of the East Indian workers who were brought to Guyana in the mid-19th century, developed their own unique forms of music. These include chutney, which is a blend of traditional Indian folk music with Caribbean and African-inspired rhythms. Chutney has become one of the most popular styles in 21st century Guyana, and modern artists have also begun experimenting with North American- and European-influenced styles to expand the genre. For example, some chutney artists incorporate hip-hop beats in their music to give it a modern sound. Some in Guyana have combined chutney with soca, blending Caribbean rhythms with Hindi lyrics and Indian instrumentation.

Literature

One of the first Guyanese writers to have an international impact was Edgar Mittelholzer (1909–1965), who published more than 25 books between 1940 and 1965. His most famous series of novels, *Kaywana,* tells the story of Guyana's colonization and transformation through the trials of a single family. Mittelholzer's novels provided a first glance of Guyanese life to international readers, and he was perceived as an inspiration to a generation of young writers who began working in the 1960s and 1970s.

Novelist Wilson Harris (1921–), who began publishing in 1960, became one of the most celebrated Caribbean writers in history. Beginning with his first novel, *Palace of the Peacock* (1960), Harris used his characters to delve into the deep cultural blending that gave rise to the mestizo culture prevalent along the South American coast. (The mestizo culture is a blend of European and Amerindian elements). Among other subjects, Harris used his books to speak about the divisions between Indo- and Afro-Guyanese in the villages and cities of Guyana. E. R. Braithwaite (1920–), a Guyanese expatriate who, with a doctorate in physics from Cambridge, was unable to secure a position due to his race and took a job teaching school in London's East End after serving in World War II. He wrote the autobiographical *To Sir With Love* about his experiences, which was made into a major motion picture in 1967.

Throughout the 1970s and 1980s, the most accomplished Guyanese writers used their works to explore ethnic and cultural relations. For example, celebrated Guyanese poet Cyril Dabydeen (1945–) introduced readers to a view of Guyanese life through the eyes of the Indo-Guyanese residents in his book of poems *Dark Swirl* (1986). A few other Guyanese poets have also achieved international fame, including Martin Carter (1927–1997), whose poetry collection *Poems of Resistance* (1954) has become an often-cited example of revolutionary political poetry. Carter, who was of mixed European, Indian, and African descent, generally concentrated on political poetry, but also published romantic and introspective poems in his collections. His work has become famous throughout South America.

In 1987, President Desmond Hoyte (1929–2002) created the Guyana Prize for Literature, an award given annually to artists whose work furthers the development of the native literary movement. Novelist Wilson Harris and poet

Martin Carter were both posthumously awarded the prize for their accomplishments. Other recipients have included Cyril Dabydeen, and Guyanese poet and playwrights Fred D'Aguiar (1960–) and Elly Niland (1954–), the latter winning as recently as 2007 for her second collection of poetry, *Cornerstones.*

CULTURE

Arts & Entertainment
While the Guyanese are proud of native artists, whose works have become nationally and internationally known, there remain few opportunities for arts education and funding in Guyana. However, limited government funding is available for artists whose work is seen as important for promoting or preserving indigenous culture, such as the work of artists depicting Amerindian spirituality through painting and sculpture. The National Gallery of Art, in Georgetown, is the only national gallery dedicated to promoting national art. Only the leading painters and sculptors in Guyana are able to install work in the National Gallery.

Despite few opportunities for formal education, artistic traditions remain strong within the various ethnic communities of Guyana. In the Indo-Guyanese community, for instance, chutney music, which blends Indian folk songs with Caribbean rhythm and instrumentation, is passed from teacher to student in an informal manner. Chutney is a proud part of Indo-Guyanese history because it has helped to preserve the native language of Indian immigrants, who arrived in Guyana speaking Hindi and Bhojpuri.

Guyana's music scene is a reflection of the overall cultural and ethnic diversity of the population. In addition to several unique varieties of Amerindian music, Guyana has a strong African and Afro-Caribbean music scene, and a vibrant East Indian pop and traditional music community. In Georgetown and other urban areas, imported music from the United States and Europe has become increasingly popular with young audiences.

Cricket is Guyana's most popular sport. Cricketer Clive Lloyd is Guyana's most revered athlete. Soccer, boxing, tennis, volleyball, and rugby are commonly played as well, and car, horse, and bicycle races are well attended.

Cultural Sites & Landmarks
Often known as the "land of the six peoples," Guyana has a rich cultural heritage that is a mixture of indigenous (largely Amerindian), African, East Indian, and European cultures. As such, many of the cultural sites and landmarks in Guyana are related to these distinct ethnic groups. However, despite its size, Guyana remains a relatively underdeveloped nation. The capital of Georgetown is the only city in Guyana with urban character, with less than 300,000 residents.

Georgetown is notable as a tourist attraction because of its natural beauty—the capital is situated on the coast of the Atlantic Ocean—and its well-preserved colonial architecture. Notable landmarks include Saint George's Anglican Cathedral, which is located in central Georgetown. The cathedral is considered the second largest wooden church in existence, and one of the largest wooden structures in the world. Designated as a national monument, the famed cathedral—built in the 19th century—is prized as one of the finest existing examples of colonial British architecture in the New World. Other popular landmarks in Georgetown include the Stabroek Market, a large market housed in an iron structure that serves as a commercial and social hub for city residents (and which is visible from a distance because of a large red clock tower at the center of the market), and the Demerara Harbour Bridge, a floating toll bridge.

Guyana is particularly renowned for its natural beauty. Recognizing the importance of the natural environment to the nation's legacy, the government of Guyana has set aside several large national parks and national preserves. Kaieteur National Park is one of the largest national parks in Guyana, and contains Kaieteur Falls, which at 226 meters (741 feet) is one of the tallest waterfalls in the world. The park is situated on the Guyana Shield, an ancient geological formation that forms the basis of a tropical plateau. The park also contains prime rainforest habitat, which is home to thousands of exotic and diversified flora and fauna.

Guyana is also known as the "land of many waters," in recognition of the important role Guyana's largest rivers—the Essequibo, the Demerara, the Berbice, and the Corentyne—played in the development of the national economy and culture. (Guyana, in fact, derives its name from an Amerindian word meaning "land of many waters.") The Demerara River, in eastern Guyana, flows for 346 kilometers (230 miles) to the Atlantic Ocean, and forms the backbone of the nation's historic shipping and transportation system. The Demerara linked Georgetown to the nation's sugar plantations during the colonial period, and still serves as a route for shipping sugar to the coast. The Essequibo River is the nation's longest river, running for more than 1,000 kilometers (621 miles) to the Atlantic through a large estuary with numerous islands. Both the Demerara and Essequibo rivers run through miles of native rainforest and flood plain habitat that is home to numerous species of animals and plants, many of which are endemic to Guyana.

Lastly, Guyana has nominated five sites as World Heritage Sites as designated by the United Nations Educational, Scientific, and Cultural Organization (UNESCO). Shell Beach, located on the Essequibo coast, has been recommended because of its importance as an example of Guyana's Atlantic coast ecosystems. Shell Beach also serves as the breeding ground for four species of marine turtle, including the endangered leatherback turtle (Dermochelys coriacea), which is the largest species of turtle in the world. The other submitted sites are the St. Georges Anglican Cathedral, Fort Zeelandia, Georgetown City Hall, and Georgetown's Plantation Structure and Historic Buildings.

Libraries & Museums

In 1868, the Royal Agricultural and Commercial Society established the National Museum of Guyana. It was originally founded to house samples of natural resources (minerals, soils, seeds, etc.), flora, and fauna from the country, as well as an ethnological catalog (artifacts of a social and cultural nature). A fire in 1945 destroyed all but the archives and ethnological collections. Many of the collections have been restored and the museum has an impressive natural history collection, as well as natural science sections.

The Guyana National Library acts as the country's national library and a repository for the country's printed material.

Holidays

Republic Day, which takes place on February 23, is Guyana's biggest national holiday. The celebrations on this day, which include parades and calypso music, commemorate the founding of the republic in 1970.

Independence Day is celebrated on May 26, which is the anniversary of Guyana's independence from British rule in 1966. The Afro-Guyanese community is honored August 1st on Freedom Day, which celebrates the end of slavery in 1838.

In addition to these secular celebrations, Guyana also observes a number of Christian, Hindu, and Muslim holidays. The biggest Hindu holiday is Divali, which is the Hindu Festival of Lights. The holiday honors the Hindu goddess Lakshmi. Muslims in Guyana celebrate the holiday of charity known as Id al-Adha, or the Festival of Sacrifice, and the ritual of daily fasting during the month of Ramadan.

Youth Culture

Like many Caribbean nations, the most popular sport in Guyana is cricket. This sets Guyana apart from many of its South American neighbors, where football (soccer) is the most popular sport. Guyanese boys and girls often begin playing cricket at the elementary school level, and many continue in secondary school. Guyana is a member of the West Indies Cricket Board (WICB), along with Jamaica, Antigua, the Leeward Islands, Windward Islands, Trinidad and Tobago, and Barbados. The local professional team is known as the "Windies."

Imported music and media from North America has become increasingly popular with Guyanese youth since the 1990s. Hip-hop music is popular with youth in urban areas, and some Guyanese have begun to combine hip-hop with native forms of music, such as chutney and rumba. Additionally, Indo-Guyanese youth may spend more time listening to chutney and Indian ethnic music, while Afro-Guyanese may spend more time listening to calypso and Afro-Cuban music. Guyanese teenagers are also fond of fashion from the U.S. and Europe, including hairstyles and fashion accessories.

As in most cultures, recreational choices vary according to socioeconomic status and ethnic identity. Teenagers in Guyana tend to gather into ethnically homogenous peer groups, which is a result of the social divisions in Guyanese communities. Though there is more ethnic blending in urban areas, many Guyanese primarily socialize with members of their own ethnic groups. Lastly, high crime and poverty rates place many Guyanese children at risk of becoming involved in a growing gang culture. Gangs are most prevalent in urban communities around Georgetown. Youth gang crime and violence have hindered the development of the tourism industry, and continue to pose a problem for an already overburdened police force.

SOCIETY

Transportation

The most common forms of public transportation in Guyana are privately owned minibuses and taxis, especially in urban areas. Georgetown, which is the hub of the transportation network, is organized into grids, with each minibus and taxi licensed to operate within a certain zone. Downtown Georgetown, along the Avenue of the Republic, is the most reliable place to find public transportation. The capital is also the hub of the national highway system.

In addition to road traffic, travelers in Guyana can use ferries and private boats to travel along either the Atlantic coast or one of the nation's rivers. Ferries are common and affordable along the Demerara, Berbice, and Essequibo Rivers, and also serve to connect Guyana to neighboring countries.

Drivers in Guyana travel on the left-hand side of the road.

Transportation Infrastructure

Guyana has 7,970 kilometers (4,952 miles) of roads, of which 590 kilometers (367 miles) are paved. With funding from the World Bank, the government of Guyana is in the midst of trying to develop its highway system, including the construction of a highway linking Guyana with Brazil. The highway extension project is part of a massive rehabilitation program intended to boost the Guyanese economy. Several bridge projects have also been completed, such as the Berbice River Bridge, the world's sixth longest floating bridge at its completion in 2008, and the Takutu Bridge connecting Guyana with Brazil. Also part of Guyana's ongoing economic development in the early 21st century is the establishment of deep-water harbors connected to both the Essequibo and Demerara Rivers. Once established, it is expected that commercial nautical traffic will increase significantly in those areas.

Cheddi Jagan International Airport is the nation's primary hub for international air travel, located less than one hour from Georgetown by automobile. In 2007, the nation had nine airports with paved roads, all of which offered affordable airfare for travelers seeking passage within the nation, with many offering short trips to Brazil, Suriname and other neighboring nations.

Media & Communications

Guyana has three daily newspapers, each filling a different niche. The *Stabroek News* is a private publication that is generally considered the most objective and reliable of the three daily newspapers. In fact, reporters for *Stabroek* have sometimes accused the Guyanese government of interfering with their ability to report news seen as unfavorable to the leading political group. The *Kaieteur News* is also a private publication, but is considered a tabloid-style daily, and thus focuses on news with wide popular appeal and sensationalized photography. The *Guyana Chronicle*, is the nation's state-run publication, and is widely considered to be under the control or influence of the nation's leading political party. In addition to the three leading publications, there are a number of international and niche publication available in Guyanese cities, especially in Georgetown, which is the hub of the national media industry.

There are 16 television networks available in Guyana, most of which rebroadcast U.S. television programming. Cable is available in Georgetown and some of the other cities, but is generally prohibitively expensive for local residents. Most stations broadcast local news, while a few also broadcast US and British Broadcasting Corporation (BBC) programs in the morning and evening.

Internet coverage is incomplete in Guyana and limited to the more developed cities such as Georgetown. As of 2012, an estimated 35 percent of the population had access to the Internet. There are no government laws restricting Internet access and some of the larger companies also maintain websites for their customers.

SOCIAL DEVELOPMENT

Standard of Living
The country ranked 121st out of 185 countries on the 2014 United Nations Human Development Index, which compiles quality of life indicators. The population has a high infant mortality rate, low life expectancy, and low population growth.

Water Consumption
According to UNICEF (2011), 95 percent of Guyana's population has access to clean water. The difference between rural and urban populations is improving, with rural populations measuring about 93 percent access and urban populations measuring about 98 percent access. Access to improved sanitation lags behind, measuring 84 percent for

the entire country, with 88 percent improved access in urban areas and 82 percent in rural areas.

Education
Guyana has one of the highest literacy rates in the Western Hemisphere. Roughly 98 percent of residents over the age of 15 can read and write English. Children are required to attend school from age six to age 14, at which point some students continue on to secondary education. While Guyana has achieved its universal primary education goal, it still struggles with funding for secondary education.

Schooling in Guyana is provided free of charge through the university level. The country's universities include the University of Guyana and the Institute of Distance and Continuing Education. Several colleges help citizens train in specific disciplines such as teaching, agriculture, and business.

However, in recent years, lack of funding has resulted in a general decline in the quality of education.

Women's Rights
Domestic abuse and violence against women is a serious problem in Guyana, where a lack of police and inadequate measures of protection and prevention continue to place women at risk. According to the constitution, women are guaranteed equal rights, equal protection, and freedom from persecution. In practice, however, authorities fail to adequately address violence against women.

Domestic violence is considered a criminal act, with penalties established under the Domestic Violence Act of 1996. According to the penal code, women are entitled to protection from police and social services to help deal with abuse and violence. Evaluations by non-governmental organizations (NGOs), conducted in 2013, indicate that conditions have improved since the establishment of the 1996 statutes, but that domestic violence remains common. Moreover, monitoring agencies have found that less than five percent of domestic violence cases result in convictions, and have cited failure to properly train law enforcement officials as a leading factor. When polled, a majority of Guyanese police believed that domestic violence is a private matter that should be resolved without police intervention. According to the U.S. Department of State, a shortage of officers contributes to the failure to address domestic issues.

Though the constitution prohibits workplace discrimination based on gender, the relative disparity in achievement between male and female counterparts in similar positions indicates that women are less likely to be considered for advancement. Recent surveys have also found that women earn less, on average, than their male counterparts in the same positions. There is no legal protection against sexual harassment in the workplace, which is a major issue of concern for women's rights organizations.

Health Care

One of Guyana's biggest dilemmas is the prevalence of many deadly tropical diseases. With only 30 hospitals and a ratio of one doctor for every 2,000 residents, fighting disease in Guyana remains difficult. Among the most common diseases are AIDS, typhoid, tuberculosis, yellow fever, malaria, hepatitis, gastroenteritis, elephantiasis, intestinal parasites, and dengue fever.

Guyana's health epidemic is made worse by poor public facilities, lack of general hygiene, and contaminated water. The Guyanese government has tried to improve sewer drainage and water treatment, but lacks the funding to implement a nationwide health care plan.

GOVERNMENT

Structure

Since obtaining its independence from Great Britain in 1966, Guyana has functioned as a democracy. Nevertheless, it is considered a republic within the British Commonwealth. The prime minister is the head of the government, but has less power than the president. The president, as chief of state, appoints the prime minister (who also acts as vice president) and the

65 members of the National Assembly, which is overseen by the prime minister.

The age of suffrage in Guyana is 18. Voters select a party, not a candidate, to support. Once elected, the party's president serves a five-year term, and may choose to extend his or her term by one year up to five times, leading to a ten-year presidency. One person may serve an unlimited number of presidential terms.

Guyana's unicameral National Assembly is made up of a total of 65 members, 40 who are elected in a national election based on proportional representation and 25 that are elected regionally by proportional representation.

Political Parties

Although there are five main political parties, two parties—the People's Progressive Party and the People's National Congress—have dominated the government since independence. The two parties represent the Indo-Guyanese and the Afro-Guyanese populations, respectively. The racial tensions between the two ethnic groups have led to political discord, mainly because each group asserts their right to full representation in the government.

In the 2011 elections, the People's Progressive Party garnered more than 48 percent of the vote and secured thirty-two seats in the legislature. The Partnership for National Unity, a coalition between the People's National Congress and several smaller parties, received 41 percent of the vote and 26 seats in the legislature. The Alliance for Change, a reform party, garnered ten percent of the vote and four seats in the assembly. The Guyana Action Party and the United Force also hold one seat in the legislature.

Local Government

There are ten political regions in Guyana. In these regions, local residents elect 12 to 35 members to their Regional Development Council (RDC). Municipal governments govern municipalities, Neighborhood Development Councils (NDCs) govern neighborhoods, and councils govern villages

Judicial System

The Guyanese justice system finds its foundations in English common law. The nation's highest court of appeal is the Caribbean Court of Justice, and the High Court is the secondary court. The magistrates' courts handle civil and criminal matters.

Taxation

The government of Guyana levies taxes on income, income on investments, capital gains, and property. Additionally, participation in the country's national insurance and social security services is compulsory and those contributions are due monthly. Taxes are also levied on corporate income.

Armed Forces

The Guyana Defense Force is comprised of an army, air force, and coast guard. Voluntary service may begin at age 18 and defense expenditures accounted for 1.09 percent of GDP (Gross Domestic Product) in 2012.

Foreign Policy

Guyana is an active member of the international community, with strong diplomatic ties to the Caribbean, as well as to South America, Europe and the U.S. In particular, Guyana enjoys strong trade relations with the U.S. and the European Union, and is a member of the UN Development Program (UNDP), the World Health Organization (WHO), and the Organization of American States (OAS). Guyana is also considered one of a few mainland countries to be a part of the Caribbean region, and the secretariat of the Caribbean Community and Common Market (CARICOM), which Guyana helped found, is located in Georgetown. Guyana has also been a member of the Non-Aligned Movement (NAM) since its inception, and hosted the 1972 conference of NAM nations.

Guyana remains the only English-speaking country in South America, and U.S.-Guyanese relations have been strong since the nation gained its independence. The U.S. is one of Guyana's strongest trading partners and has also been a source of financial support for the struggling country, donating to a number of causes including the development of infrastructure and programs to combat HIV/AIDS. Additionally, Guyana allows the U.S. military to conduct training exercises within its borders and, in exchange, military personnel help with infrastructural projects. As recently as 2007, Guyanese and U.S. military personnel were cooperating to improve drainage systems in the country.

In 2008, Guyana had two transnational border disputes, both stemming from unresolved issues that originated under British colonial control in the 19th century. Guyana's border dispute with Suriname is the older of the two. It began as a conflict between the Netherlands and England over the legitimacy of a 1799 treaty formed by the then-governors of Suriname and Berbice (a former Dutch colony), in what is now Guyana. The central facet of the conflict is the possession of territory immediately to the west of the Courantyne River. The discovery of offshore oil in the disputed territory initially fueled the conflict. In 2004, after the Guyanese and Surinamese military engaged in several armed conflicts over possession of the area, both nations agreed to take the conflict to the UN. In 2007, the UN courts determined that the area should be split into the Suriname-Guyana Basin, with both nations having some control and access to oil and other resources.

Another ongoing dispute with Venezuela dates back to the first attempt to map the British territory in the 1840s. At that time, it was argued by Venezuela that the territory west of the Essequibo River was Venezuelan territory (British authorities claimed it as part of Guyana). The border dispute was settled temporarily in the 1890s, with the help of American diplomats, but reignited in the 1960s and resulting in minor military conflict between the two nations. Violence subsided but the issue was never fully resolved, and neither nation has been able to develop the area.

Human Rights Profile

International human rights law insists that states respect civil and political rights, and also promote an individual's economic, social and cultural rights. The United Nations (UN) Universal

Declaration of Human Rights (UDHR) is recognized as the standard for international human rights. Its authors sought the counsel of the world's great thinkers, philosophers, and religious leaders, and were careful to create a document that reflects the core values shared by every world culture. (To read this document or view the articles relating to cultural human rights, visit: http://www.udhr.org/UDHR/default.htm.)

In general, Guyana has a positive record in terms of protecting and promoting human rights for its citizens. The constitution of the republic guarantees equal rights and equal treatment, in accordance with the UDHR. The majority of human rights abuses reported by monitoring agencies such as Amnesty International (AI) and Human Rights Watch appear to be isolated instances.

Members of the Guyanese military, known as the Guyana Defense Force (GDF), and members of the state police have been accused of violating Article 5, freedom from cruel and/or inhumane treatment, and Article 9, guaranteeing freedom from arbitrary arrest. Monitoring agencies have reported that police and GDF members sometimes use excessive force and may detain some suspects for long periods before trial or without due cause. Instances of police and military abuse are not common, and government officials have claimed that they are the result of certain unfit personnel rather than indications of a dysfunctional penal system.

Conditions in Guyanese prisons fail to meet internationally recommended standards of human rights and are in violation of Article 5. Internal reports indicate that overcrowding and insufficient facilities are the primary issues with the penal system. In addition, because the judicial system suffers from severe delays, individuals may be detained for pre–trial periods extending several years.

Though the constitution guarantees Guyanese citizens the right to privacy, reports from monitoring agencies indicate that police have sometimes violated the privacy of individuals acting without permission from judicial authorities. Instances were sufficiently rare to be considered isolated incidents but indicate, to some

monitoring agencies, that greater police oversight is required. There was no indication, in 2008, that the police regularly monitored phone and Internet communications.

Child abuse, child prostitution, and trafficking in children for the sex trade were also problems in Guyana, as reported by monitoring agencies and internal child welfare organizations. There have been reports that some children, especially from rural areas, have been forced into underage labor, a violation of the penal code. In addition to articles protecting the rights of citizens, the state of children in Guyana is a violation of Article 25 of the UDHR guaranteeing that mothers and children deserve special consideration and protection. To improve the condition for local children, the Guyanese government partnered with the United Nations Children's Fund (UNICEF) in 2005 to create the Child Protection Monitoring System. The program was intended to be fully functional by 2010 and will help prevent child abuse and exploitation in all forms.

Migration

Guyana's net migration over the period from 2010-2014 was -32,770. That means that Guyana is losing both skilled and unskilled workers, often due to a lack of economic development.

ECONOMY

Overview of the Economy

Guyana's economy and gross domestic product are based on the production and export of six principal products: sugar, gold, bauxite (aluminum), shrimp, timber, and rice. The area surrounding Georgetown houses some of the country's major industrial complexes, including mines, factories and agricultural production facilities.

Guyana has been in a state of economic crisis since the 1980s. Former president Forbes Burnham restructured the government into a cooperative republic. He intended to end privately-owned industry so that all industry would be owned and operated by the government, wanting to turn Guyana into a socialist economy. This eventually caused the economy to collapse, leaving Guyana in debt to many foreign nations and the International Monetary Fund (IMF).

Burnham's successor, Desmond Hoyte, attempted reconstruction, but Guyana still faces a number of economic problems, such as high unemployment (11 percent in 2007) and a low standard of living. The economy has rebounded from the global recession that began in 2008. The estimated per capita gross domestic product in 2013 was $8,500 USD, which represents a steady increase since 2009.

Guyana is a member of the Caribbean Community and Common Market (CARICOM), a trade association of 20 countries. In addition to CARICOM nations (including Jamaica, Barbados, and Trinidad and Tobago), Guyana's primary trading partners are the European Union, Canada, the United States, and Japan.

Industry

Mines in Aroima, Linden, and the Berbice River region provide bauxite and gold, two of Guyana's main exports. These and other materials are processed by the country's manufacturing sector, which also produces textiles, machinery, rum, and pharmaceuticals.

Guyana suffers from having a low population, which inhibits economic growth. The main problem is that there are too few people in the labor force (accompanied by a high net migration rate) for industries to effectively exploit natural resources, such as the abundant hardwoods in the forests.

Labor

Most of Guyana's workforce is employed in the service industry, and agriculture is the largest sector of Guyana's economy. According to the CIA World Factbook, the workforce was estimated at 313,100 in 2009. That same year, the unemployment rate was estimated at 11 percent. Unemployment remains a concern in Guyana, and some estimates place the unemployment rate as high as 25 percent. Regionally, Guyana also has one of the highest rates of outward migration of skilled laborers.

Energy/Power/Natural Resources

Bauxite is one of the most abundant minerals found in Guyana. Used in the production of aluminum, it has been an important export for the country. The rainforest has many greenheart trees, which are used in building wharves because of the wood's resistance to salt water.

Other minerals and metals can be found in the sand and soil around Guyana's riverbeds. Some freelance laborers known as "porkknockers" make their living by digging for gold and diamonds.

Fishing

Seafood is an important part of the Guyanese diet, which commonly includes shrimp, trout, and snapper. Guyana's fishing fleet focuses on inshore fishing, within 60 kilometers (37 miles) of the shore. Industrial fishing focuses on shrimp, particularly seabob. Shrimp exports are rising—they comprise more than 50 percent of the country's fishery exports—and in 2014, totaled approximately $57 million. Because of catch limitations, Guyanese fishermen anticipate a reduction in their trawler fleet.

Forestry

Guyana is one of the world's most forested nations; the inland forest covers 85 percent of Guyana's area, and contains roughly 1,000 different varieties of hardwood trees. Guyana has one of the lowest deforestation rates in the world—as of 2014, deforestation rates are estimated at less than 0.068 percent annually. Commercial species, however, make up a small amount of the overall volume, and logging is very selective.

Mining/Metals

Bauxite and gold are two major Guyanese exports. The state owns all mineral rights, and foreign investment has increased since the late 20th century. As much of the mining occurs in the interior of the country, indigenous peoples are disproportionately affected by mining efforts. Mercury pollution due to mining efforts is having an impact on Guyana's environment. Mining efforts are also posing a threat to unique wildlife habitats and Amerindians are pressuring the government to develop policies that protect indigenous populations and their communities, as well as unique natural habitats.

Agriculture

Sugarcane and rice crops account for 45 percent of Guyana's exports, making agriculture the largest sector of Guyana's economy. Almost all of the sugar and rice fields are located in the country's coastal plain region. Since the plain is four feet below sea level, irrigation is essential to the protection of farmland. Sea walls, dikes, and drainage systems keep the crops from being flooded by the ocean.

Animal Husbandry

Guyana's livestock industry is essentially undeveloped. Government efforts to expand pasture land, large-scale corn production (for feed), and increase of veterinarian services are being implemented in order to further develop the industry, particularly in the areas of cattle, small ruminants, pigs, and poultry.

Tourism

Tourism is not a substantial sector of Guyana's economy. Due to the lack of hotels, damaged roads, and poor funding, Guyana's tourism has been limited. The tourists who do visit the country are drawn to the natural beauty of its waterfalls, savannahs, and rainforest. However, though Guyana is rich in natural resources such as these, the eco-tourism industry has only recently begun to play a significant role in the economy. As the site of the country's only international airport, the capital of Georgetown receives the majority of Guyana's tourism, hotel, and recreational revenues.

Micah L. Issitt, Richard Means

DO YOU KNOW?

- The British Guyana Magenta stamp is one of the world's most rare and valuable postage stamps. The stamps were first issued in 1856 and were produced in limited numbers. As of 2007, only one example was known. The stamp was purchased by John E. DuPont in 1980 for $935,000.

- Andrew "Six Heads" Lewis became the first Guyanese boxer to win a world championship title in 2001.

- The area surrounding Guyana's Mount Roraimi is said to be the inspiration for Sir Arthur Conan Doyle's classic novel *The Lost World* (1912).

Bibliography

Abrams, Ovid. Metegee: *The History and Culture of Guyana*. East Orange, NJ: Ashanti Books, 1998.

Cambridge, Vibert C. *Musical Life in Guyana*. Jackson, MS: University Press of Mississippi, 2015.

Gafar, John. *Guyana: From State Control to Free Markets*. Hauppauge, NY: Nova Publishers, 2003.

Hinds, David. *Ethno-politics and Power Sharing in Guyana: History and Discourse*. Washington, D.C.: New Academia Publishing, 2011.

Hollett, Dave. *Passage from India to El Dorado: Guyana and the Great Migration*.

Madison, NJ: Dickinson Univ Press, 1999.

Manuel, Peter Lamarche. *East Indian Music in the West Indies: Tān-singing, Chutney, and the Making of Indo-Caribbean Culture*. Philadelphia, PA: Temple University Press, 2000.

Rabe, Stephen G. *U.S. Intervention in British Guiana: A Cold War History*. Durham, NC: University of North Carolina Press, 2008.

Ramdin, Ron. *Arising from Bondage: A History of the Indo-Caribbean People*. New York: NYU Press, 1999.

Smock, Kirk. *Guyana: The Bradt Travel Guide*. Bucks UK: Bradt Travel Guides, 2011.

Works Cited

Abrams, Ovid. "Metegee: The History and Culture of Guyana." East Orange, NJ: Ashanti Books, 1998.

Arnold, James A. et al. "A History of Literature in the Caribbean." Philadelphia, PA: John Benjamins Publishing Company, 2001.

Arnold, James A., Julio Rodríguez-Luis, Vera M. Kutzinski, Ineke Phaf-Rheinberger, J. Michael Dash. "A History of Literature in the Caribbean." Philadelphia, PA: John Benjamins Publishing Company, 2001.

"Background Note: Guyana." *United States Department of State Online.* Bureau of Western Hemisphere Affairs. http://www.state.gov/r/pa/ei/bgn/1984.htm

Chanan, Michael. "Cuban Cinema." Minneapolis, MN: University of Minnesota Press, 2003.

Gafar, John. "Guyana: From State Control to Free Markets." Hauppauge, NY: Nova Publishers, 2003.

Gafar, John. "Guyana: From State Control to Free Markets." Hauppage, NY: Nova Publishers, 2003.

Gates, Henry Louis. "Africana: The Encyclopedia of the African and African American Experience." New York: Basic Civitas Books, 1999.

"Guyana: Country Reports on Human Rights Practices 2007." *United States Department of State.* Bureau of Democracy, Human Rights and Labor. http://www.state.gov/g/drl/rls/hrrpt/2004/41763.htm

"Guyana." *The World Factbook Online.* https://www.cia.gov/library/publications/the-world-factbook/geos/gy.html

Hollett, Dave. "Passage from India to El Dorado: Guyana and the Great Migration." Madison, NJ: Dickinson Univ Press, 1999.

Kurlansky, Mark. "A Continent of Islands: Searching For The Caribbean Destiny." New York: Da Capo Press, 1993.

Kurlansky, Mark. "A Continent of Islands: Searching For The Caribbean Destiny." New York: Da Capo Press, 1993.

Manuel, Peter Lamarche. "East Indian Music in the West Indies: Tān-singing, Chutney, and the Making of Indo-Caribbean Culture." Philadelphia, PA: Temple University Press, 2000.

Manuel, Peter Lamarche. "East Indian Music in the West Indies: Tān-singing, Chutney, and the Making of Indo-Caribbean Culture." Philadelphia, PA: Temple University Press, 2000.

Palmerlee, Danny, et al. "South America on a Shoestring." Oakland, CA: Lonely Planet, 2004.

Rabe, Stephen G. "U.S. Intervention in British Guiana: A Cold War History." Durham, NC: University of North Carolina Press, 2008.

Ramdin, Ron. "Arising from Bondage: A History of the Indo-Caribbean People." New York: NYU Press, 1999.

Smock, Kirk. "Guyana: The Bradt Travel Guide." Bucks UK: Bradt Travel Guides, 2008.

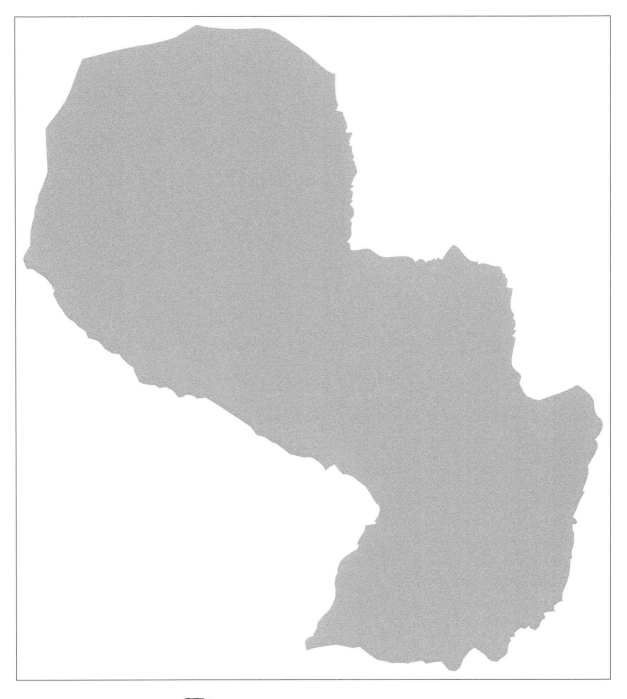

PARAGUAY

Introduction

The Republic of Paraguay is located in the south-central region of the South American continent. Its neighbors are Argentina, Bolivia, and Brazil. Paraguay's culture and history are deeply influenced both by European traditions, especially Spanish, and indigenous traditions of the Guarani. Both Spanish and Guarani are official languages in Paraguay, and the country's very name comes from the Guarani language, and may refer to the Paraguay River, which flows through the center of the country.

Paraguay is a relatively poor nation, one that emerged only recently from decades of political oppression and economic instability. Tourism is relatively low, except from neighboring Argentina.

GENERAL INFORMATION

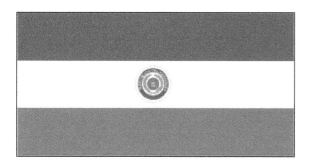

Official Language: Guarani, Spanish
Population: 6,703,860 (2014 estimate)
Currency: Guarani
Coins: Coins are available in denominations of 50, 100, 500 and 1,000 guaraníes.
Land Area: 397,302 square kilometers (153,399 square miles)
Water Area: 9,450 square kilometers (3,648 square miles)
National Motto: "Paz y justicia" (Spanish, "Peace and justice")
National Anthem: "Paraguayos, República o Muerte" (Spanish, "Paraguayans, Republic or Death")
Capital: Asunción

Time Zone: GMT -4
Flag Description: Paraguay's flag consists of a horizontal, triband design of red (top), white (middle), and blue (bottom) stripes. Centered in the white band is a national emblem—the national coat of arms on the obverse side and the seal of the treasury on the reverse side. Paraguay is only one of two nations—the other being Moldova—to have two different emblems on their national flag.

Population

Paraguay's population is largely descended from intermarriage between the Spanish and the local Guarani people. Approximately 95 percent of Paraguayans are "mestizo" or of mixed Spanish-Guarani background. This blending is partly the result of the European colonial and Jesuit missionary policies between the sixteenth and eighteenth centuries. Very few people are solely Guarani, due in part to intermarriage and also to of deaths from European diseases.

There are large Korean, German and Japanese immigrant communities, along with small Italian

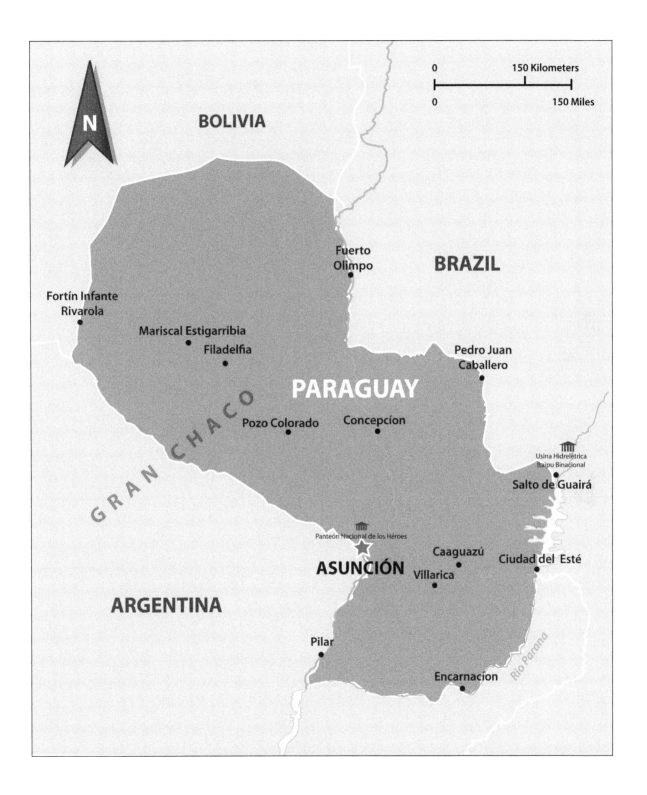

Principal Cities by Population (2012):

- Asunción (544,309)
- Ciudad del Este (396,091)
- Capiatá (366,998)
- Luque (361,662)
- San Lorenzo (320,878)
- Limpio (201,245)
- Ñemby (192,224)
- Lambaré (151,484)
- Fernando de la Mora (143,524)

and Polish communities, and some communities of people originating from Lebanon, Taiwan, and Hong Kong.

Most of Paraguay's population lives in the eastern part of the country, and an estimated 63percent of the population is urban. The Chaco Desert to the west is home to very few inhabitants apart from scattered Mennonite communities. Asunción, founded by the Spanish in 1537, is Paraguay's largest city. In fact, the Asunción metropolitan area is home to about 22 percent of Paraguay's total urban population. As of 2011, Asunción had an estimated population of 2.139 million. The city has served as the capital of Paraguay since colonial times, and it is Paraguay's major economic, cultural, and educational center.

Languages

Unlike many other Latin American countries, the native language is spoken by a large percentage of the population, with as many as 40 percent speaking only Guarani. Perhaps as much as 90 percent of the population can speak Guarani. Both Spanish and Guarani are official languages, though Spanish is the language of commerce and government. Spanish tends to predominate in urban areas, while Guarani is more widely spoken in rural areas.

Guaraní is one of the few indigenous American languages that does not face the threat of imminent extinction. Many Asunción residents consider their knowledge of Guaraní a point of cultural pride. The capital's residents sometimes

blend Guaraní and Spanish together within a conversation or even within a single sentence, in a mixed dialect called Jopara.

Native People & Ethnic Groups

Prior to Western contact, Paraguay's native population was a collection of tribes speaking the Guaraní language. Though known for their fierce fighting abilities, the Guaraní were able to coexist more or less peacefully with the Spanish, and intermarried with them extensively. The work of the Jesuit missions, as well as the role of sympathetic Spanish colonial officials, ensured that the Guarani language and cultural traditions would survive into modern times.

Despite the widespread use of their language, however, the Guaraní themselves suffer from high rates of unemployment and suicide, and are among the country's poorest people. Besides the Guaraní, the western Chaco region is home to various small indigenous groups. These include the Guaycurú, Lengua, Mataco, and Zamuco peoples.

Among the German immigrants are approximately 15,000 Mennonites, who settled in the western Chaco region in the early 20th century to practice their way of life in peace. One of the main Mennonite settlements is the town of Filadelfia, capital of the Boquerón department.

Religions

As a result of the Spanish colonial era, the population is around 90 percent Roman Catholic. As in other Latin American countries, Catholicism has assimilated some of the indigenous religious traditions. There are also small numbers of Protestants, many of them Mennonite settlers.

Climate

Paraguay's climate varies sharply depending on the region. The eastern part of the country is temperate, and in parts subtropical. Some eastern areas are subject to flooding from the fall through spring. Temperatures average around 35° Celsius (95° Fahrenheit) during the summer. Winter temperatures often drop to 5° Celsius (41° Fahrenheit). The western region, particularly the Chaco, is semi-arid, despite the presence of jungles and marshland.

ENVIRONMENT & GEOGRAPHY

Topography

A landlocked nation, Paraguay is located along the Paraguay River in the south-central part of South America. It is surrounded by Argentina, Bolivia, and Brazil. Paraguay has two main regions: the eastern uplands, home to most of the population, and the largely uninhabited western plain known as the Chaco or "Gran Chaco" (Great Chaco).

The two regions are divided by the Paraguay River, which flows roughly through the center of the country. The eastern region is covered by grasslands and woodlands, and is watered by the Paraguay and Paraná Rivers. The country's lowest point is 46 meters (151 feet) above sea level, at the confluence of the two rivers. The highest point is Cerro Pero, which rises 842 meters (2,762 feet) above sea level.

The Chaco, which extends into Argentina and Bolivia, is a vast region of dry plains, marshes, jungles, and thick forests. The name derives from the Quechua word for "hunting land." Part of the Chaco is a heavily wooded region known as the Chaco Boreal. The Chaco is also home to Defendores del Chaco National Park. The Mennonites who settled in the Chaco during the early 20th century had to work extremely hard to fight back the undergrowth in order to build their communities. Paraguay and Bolivia fought the "Chaco War" from 1932–1935 over control of the region, in part because of the discovery of oil there.

Plants & Animals

The Chaco region is home to many wild species, including large predators such as the jaguar, puma, and South American red wolf. Other large wildlife species include the tapir and giant armadillo. The yacaré or Paraguayan alligator makes its home in the country's waters.

Bird species include the wood stork, the parrot, and rare Chacoan peccary. Flamingos and hummingbirds are also frequently spotted.

On the grassland portions of the Chaco, cattle-ranching is a common activity. The Chaco Boreal is a heavily wooded section of the Chaco; common plant species include the guebracho tree, the lapacho tree, and the passion flower.

CUSTOMS & COURTESIES

Greetings

In Paraguay, it is common for strangers or casual acquaintances to greet by shaking hands. If a man and woman are well acquainted, then they might kiss each other on both cheeks. It is important to know that this often consists of a kissing sound when both parties touch cheeks. The same is true of two women who know each other well, while men who are already acquainted will typically shake hands warmly. Relatives will embrace and kiss on both cheeks as well. In a business setting, the shaking of hands is more appropriate unless two people are very familiar to each other, in which case a light embrace is appropriate. Failing to great people warmly when meeting them, or to leave graciously, is considered disrespectful in Paraguayan culture.

Gestures & Etiquette

Paraguayans typically express a very open body language and maintain a different concept of personal space than what is customary in North American culture. For example, touching another person for emphasis during a conversation is common in Paraguay, and placing a hand on another's arm to gain their attention, or standing within inches of another person while conversing, is considered normal.

A particular aspect of social etiquette in Paraguay involves the use of a certain pronoun in conversation. For example, a specific pronoun, "usted," is used when conversing with a stranger. This pronoun is also commonly used when conversing with superiors in business and educational settings, as well as with elders. "Usted" remains the appropriate pronoun to use unless the other person gives permission to use the more familiar pronoun, which is the "tú" form. Formal titles are common in Paraguay as well. Doctors, professors, lawyers, and other professionals are referred to by their titles and full names, while university graduates are often referred to as "licenciado" (men) or "licenciada" (women) to honor or clarify their status.

Composure and how one carries oneself is important in Paraguay. Generally, subtlety is prized over being overtly direct. A more cautious approach to conversation is valued and accepted, with the goal of avoiding conflict or tension. Good posture is also crucial, and it is considered poor taste to prop one's foot on furniture or other objects whether sitting or standing. This less direct approach also applies to business interactions.

Eating/Meals

Breakfast in Paraguay often consists of light fare. For example, a simple pastry or roll with butter taken with a cup of cocido, a hot drink made from sugar, milk and maté, is common. (Maté is a brewed stimulant drink similar to coffee.) Traditionally, lunch is a long affair for most Paraguayans; children and workers alike return home for the midday meal. In urban areas in Paraguay, particularly among the upper and middle classes, the main evening meal is often eaten late, or after dark. In more rural areas and among the lower-income classes in Paraguay, dinner is held somewhat earlier, and eating times in general can be more varied. Traditionally, children are fed before adults eat to accommodate an earlier bedtime. Mealtimes and customs, of course, vary by region and socioeconomic status, and have changed with the advent of globalization.

Visiting

When invited to a person's home, one symbol of acceptance is the offering of maté from a shared bowl. Traditionally, brewed maté is poured by the host into a gourd-like container called a guampa. A metal straw, called a bombilla, is inserted into the guampa, which is then shared. If a Paraguayan invites someone to share in the guampa, it is a sign of hospitality and a desire for the guest to stay and socialize. Additionally, offering a gift to the host or the host's children is customary in Paraguay. Flowers or candies (especially from Argentina) are valued, and children enjoy receiving toys (particularly those from the United States).

For meals, it is more common for families or individuals to invite friends over for dinner in urban areas. In more rural areas, meals are typically shared on holidays and special occasions. When Paraguayans serve meals to guests, they serve a full plate and will offer seconds persistently. Leaving some food on an unfinished plate is considered the most polite action at a meal; it tells the host that the guest has been fed to his/her satisfaction.

LIFESTYLE

Family

In Paraguay, the concept of family and kinship is important. Kinship is a loose term, and can be extended to direct blood relations as well as godparents, god-children, or people formally or informally adopted. Most Paraguayan families remain patriarchal. In the early 21st century, approximately 80 percent of all children are raised in two-parent families, with the majority of single-parent homes matriarchal. Single parenthood is far less common in rural areas.

In Guaraní society, kinship ties with maternal relatives are slightly more important than those with paternal relatives. In rural areas, a wedding is considered to be an expensive undertaking, with the obligation to host distant blood relatives and a celebration that may include hundreds of townsfolk and those related by blood. In many cases, consensual marriages are more common among the poor and lower classes. These informal marriages are similar to common-law marriages in Western cultures, and do not involve a religious or civil ceremony.

Housing

Housing in urban areas, particularly for the upper and middle classes, involves single-family homes, apartments and condominiums, typically outfitted with modern amenities. The well-being of the poor in many regions has improved in terms of housing quality and access to clean water, telephone service, and electricity. Dwellings in rural areas typically consist of structures built with thatched roofs and wood walls, often exposed, as well as mud, cement or plaster.

Improving rural housing materials is directly tied to public health in the rural countryside in Paraguay. In recent years, international disease specialists have worked on improving rural housing in Paraguay to reduce Chagas' disease, a chronic, blood-borne illness that infects seven million to eight million people worldwide, mostly in Latin America (2014 estimate). The insect that carries the parasite that causes the disease embeds itself in thatched roofs, wall cracks, and wood. Plastering wood surfaces and using non-thatched roofs, along with insecticide spraying, reduces Chagas' disease.

In 2008 alone, journalists documented numerous protests among the urban and rural poor for improved housing and land rights. In one particular protest that occurred in December 2008, two women allowed themselves to be crucified and carried through the streets of Asunción as a demonstration to force the federal government to release more than $1 million (USD) for low-income housing.

Food

The cuisine of Paraguay has both Guaraní and European influences. Traditional dishes include sopa Paraguaya, a corn mash with cheese, milk, onions and meat, palmitos (hearts of palm), and chipa, a cornbread made with cheese and eggs. Chipa guazu is made from a special sweet corn that is available twice a year in Paraguay (during the sweet corn harvests), and is similar to a corn soufflé or casserole. Dinner foods traditionally rely on meat, with Argentinean beef a very popular dish in the form of asado (an open fire cooking technique). Stews featuring beef are popular, and are often served with rice, bell peppers and onions.

While corn is a common ingredient in Paraguayan dishes, cassava is another staple. Cassava, also known as manioc or yucca, is a starchy food made from the root of the cassava plant. Finely-ground cassava is used to make tapioca flour, and cassava is used in much the same way as flour. Beans and peanuts are two other common crops in Paraguay, and local dishes often feature these foods.

While you can find modern fast food restaurants in major cities in Paraguay, the local version of a quick meal is the empanada, a meat- or cheese-filled pastry, and the milanesa, a breaded and fried piece of meat or fish. These items are often sold by street vendors in major cities in Paraguay and other parts of South America.

Life's Milestones

Paraguay, like many Latin American countries, is predominantly Catholic, with many traditions and social customs rooted in Roman Catholicism. During infancy, virtually all Catholic children are baptized, and the parents choose godparents for the baby. This system of godparenting, or co-parenthood, is called compadrazgo, and holds symbolic meaning among the upper and middle classes. Traditionally, the godparents pay for the baby's baptism, and are expected to give the child reasonably generous gifts each year. The godparents are also tasked with raising the children and caring for them financially should their parents die. Among the lower classes, this expectation is much stronger.

As in other Latin American countries, girls typically observe their 15th birthday with a celebration known as the quince años. A symbol of a girl's transition to womanhood, the quince años typically includes a religious ceremony followed by a festive party. Certain customs associated with the quince años include the wearing of flat shoes, which are then replaced by high heels (another symbol of womanhood) as part of the ceremony.

CULTURAL HISTORY

Art

The art of Paraguayans is heavily influenced by pre-Columbian indigenous tradition and culture. The Guaraní, who inhabited the land during the arrival of the Spanish in the early 16th century, were particularly influential. Some of the oldest samples of artistic styles in Paraguay involve crafts designed for daily use. Basketwork, for example, served two purposes: baskets are used in daily life to hold items and transport goods, while at the same time decorated as an art form. Native Guaranís used native plants such as the pindo palm to weave baskets for various needs. They used certain patterns and shapes to make these items distinct and expressive.

Feathers also played an important part in Paraguayan native art, and were largely used in elaborate Guaraní headdresses (called the "jeguaka"). Guaraní medicine men, called shaman, also wore detailed cloaks made of feathers. Other traditional indigenous crafts included ceramics, woodcarving, embroidery, and lacework. In fact, lacework has become a distinct art form in Paraguay, and the city of Itaguá in Paraguay is famed for its intricate lacework, called ñandutí.

With the advent of colonialism, religious themed art became prevalent. Early Jesuit missionaries established art schools in Paraguay, blending local artistic styles with European religious themes. Paraguay's relative isolation has allowed artistic styles from the 16th and 17th centuries to prevail. Religious art typically depicts saints and includes functional church pieces, such as pulpits and furniture, infused with a classic baroque style.

The fine arts did not fully develop in Paraguay until the 19th and 20th centuries, and were heavily influenced by European styles. Modern art forms such as painting and sculpture also began to adopt indigenous themes while breaking sharply from religious depictions. One of Paraguay's most famous painters is Pablo Alborno, who painted portraits and landscapes. Educated in Europe at the turn of the 19th century, Alborno studied in Venice and Rome, emulating Renaissance styles. His portraits and landscapes are impressionistic portrayals of his subjects. In the early 1900s, native Paraguayan artists and new European immigrants began to push for cultural development in the capital of Asunción, in particular the creation of a national museum, The National Museum of Fine Arts was founded in 1909. By the later 19th century, architects and artists helped to design and build structures in Asunción that mimicked Europe's finer baroque structures.

Architecture

Like many Latin American countries, Paraguay's architectural heritage is influenced by Spanish colonialism, with modern architecture somewhat slow to develop due to a lack of government support or sponsorship. A good example of colonial architecture can be found in the capital of Asunción, where elements of classic Spanish architecture include red-tiled roofs and the use of plazas, as well as patios, an important feature of medieval Spanish architecture.

Drama

Paraguayan theater and drama is often described as a blend of Guarani and Spanish culture, complimented by a variety of European styles of drama. Early on, dedication to theater in Paraguay was generally lackluster, and most if not all early Paraguayan playwrights were not known outside their native country. Early plays were mostly imported from Spain, and include operettas (light opera) and religious plays.

As Paraguayan theater evolved—Paraguay's national theater was founded in the second half of the 18th century, but lacked identity until the 20th century—one of the foremost dramatists was the Argentinean-born Jose Arturo Alsina (1897–1984). Alsina's work shows influences of European playwrights such as Henrik Ibsen and Julio Correa (1890–1953), who wrote in the Guaraní language and is considered the founder of Guaraní theater. Significant elements of Paraguayan drama include myths and folklore. For the most part, Paraguayan drama lacks the historical movements and schools that many other countries experienced or developed.

Music & Dance

Perhaps the most famous musical style from Paraguay is guarania, a sentimental musical form that involves slow rhythms and beats. It is often matched with a slow dance performed by couples. It was created in the early 20th century by Paraguayan composer José Asunción Flores (1904–1972). The main instruments used in guarania music are the Paraguayan harp and an acoustic guitar, though an electric guitar has also been incorporated into modern versions. Paraguayan polka is another popular music style. Similar to European polka, the Paraguayan version involves a dancing audience and has an upbeat and intense rhythm. However, unlike traditional polka, it does not involve any singing and often uses a three-part (ternary) musical structure (traditional polka uses binary, or two-part, rhythms).

The Paraguayan harp is the national instrument and is distinct from other harps. The harp itself dates back to the 16th century in South America. The strings spread upward from the instrument's center, and it produces very deep bass tones compared to other harps. Guitars and the Paraguayan harp are the most common instruments used in Paraguayan music and dance performance, but wind instruments such as wood flutes and whistles are also common. Percussion sounds, made by rattles and bells, are typically used for background beats.

Literature

Paraguayan literature is rooted in the oral traditions of the Guaraní and other indigenous groups. In terms of literature, the native language has persisted in written form since the early 1700s, when Jesuit missionaries documented the oral tradition. Throughout the 19th and 20th centuries, Spanish-language literature prevailed. During the military dictatorship of Alfredo Stroessner (1912–2006), Guaraní literature became an underground movement, emerging publicly after Stroessner was ousted in 1989. Late 20th-century writers such as Felix de Guarania (1924–2011) documented the experience of rural Paraguayans in novels, poems, and plays, much of it written in Guaraní and performed in the language.

Paraguay's history of strict rule, particularly throughout the 20th century, has been strongly influential in the development of its national arts and literature. For example, dissent against the government was considered a violation of the law, and the arts were used to express covert dissent or to openly critique the government, often with tremendous and dire consequences.

One of Paraguay's most famous writers from the 20th century was Augusto Roa Bastos (1917–2005), whose work critiqued Paraguay's history of military dictatorship and oppression. A former journalist in the 1930s and 1940s, Roa Bastos fled Paraguay for Argentina in 1947 after clashing with Stroessner. His most famous novel, *Yo, el Supremo* (*I, the Supreme*, 1974), examined the inner mind of Paraguay's first dictator, José Gaspar Rodríguez de Francia, who ruled from 1814 through 1840. Roa Bastos was part of the magic realism movement of Latin American literature in the 20th century, a literary genre in which the real life and the supernatural coexists. He won the Cervantes Prize (awarded among Spanish-speaking nations) for outstanding Spanish-language literature in 1989, the only Paraguayan writer to do so.

Another notable Paraguayan author is Gabriel Casaccia (1907–1980), often called the founder of the modern narrative in Paraguay. A contemporary of Roa Bastos, Casaccia's most famous novel, *La Babosa* (*The Slug*, 1952), was part of the modern realism movement. Poetry is another popular art form that was also used as a form of political protest. Much of Paraguay's literature is written in Guaraní, though generally translated into Spanish as well. In some cases, writing is published in Jopara, a mixture of Guaraní and Spanish that is commonly used in Paraguay. Twentieth-century Paraguayan poetry was often published in Jopara, with poets such as Félix Fernández (1897–1984) and Teodoro S. Mongelós (1914–1966) popularizing this style.

CULTURE

Arts & Entertainment

As with other aspects of Paraguayan culture, art forms and entertainment are largely a mix of the indigenous and immigrant cultures. Asunción, the capital city, is the main cultural center. The country is known for its exquisite handicrafts, particularly "spiderweb lace" (ñandutí). The word "ñandutí" is Guaraní for "spider web," and the lacework resembles a fine web. The lacework is typically characterized by a large circle at the center of the lace pattern and a series of smaller circles, or medallions, around the centerpiece. In ñandutí, the lacework is woven on a frame, producing its unique look. Each pattern is different, and various colored threads can be used to produce colored lace. The center of ñandutí production is the city of Itagua, and this particular art form is a source of pride for Paraguayans, in addition to being a source of income. Similarly, the city of Itá is also famed for its ceramicists.

Cultural Sites & Landmarks

The Jesuit Missions of La Santísima Trinidad de Paraná and Jesús de Tavarangue are two major cultural landmarks in Paraguay dating back to the 16th century. The Jesuits were Roman Catholic priests who took vows of poverty and chastity and dedicated themselves to missionary work. They were particularly active in the Rio de la Plata section of Paraguay (where Paraguay and Brazil meet), where they created missions and large plantations. The missions of La Santísima Trinidad de Paraná and Jesús de Tavarangue are no longer operated by church officials. However, they are considered historical landmarks that show the architecture and the impact of the Jesuits on the native populations. Collectively, the two missions represent Paraguay's only World Heritage Site, as designated by the United Nations Educational, Scientific and Cultural Organization (UNESCO).

Asunción, Paraguay's largest city and capital, is a cultural landmark unto itself. Founded in 1537, it is considered one of the oldest cities in South America and contains nearly 500 years of various architectural styles. Asunción is laid out in the grid pattern typical of cities of Spanish colonial origin. Many of the original colonial structures, however, were destroyed during modernization efforts dating back to the early 1800s. The Spanish influence is reflected in the city's tree-lined avenues and large public squares, as well as in common architectural flourishes such as balconies, patios, and red-tiled rooftops.

Historic landmarks in Asunción include the Panteón Nacional de los Héroes (National Pantheon of the Heroes), a pink-domed building which imitates French baroque architecture; the Gran Hotel de Paraguay, the capital's oldest and most famous hotel; and the Catedral Metropolitana (Metropolitan Cathedral), built in 1687. The city is also home to several museums, including the Casa de la Independencia Museum, one of the last examples of colonial architecture.

Paraguay is also home to several important national parks and nature reserves, including the Mbaracayú Forest Nature Reserve (MFNR). This site is part of a large rain forest called the Interior Atlantic Forest (IAF), and is the largest section of the IAF in Paraguay (it also covers southeastern Brazil and northeastern Argentina). The forest is a mixture of different environments, with wetlands, high rainforests, and deep river valleys all within its borders. Scientists from around the world study wildlife, plants, and biology in the forest, and the reserve is particularly famous for the variety and uniqueness of its bird population. Parque National Tinfunké was the site of many battles in the 1932-1935 Chaco War. Fought between Paraguay and Bolivia in Paraguay's northwest corner, the Chaco War involved control of the Gran Chaco, an area believed to be rich in oil. Paraguay designated Parque National Tinfunké a national park in 1956. Both the MFNR and the Parque National Tinfunké are tentatively listed for inclusion on UNESCO's World Heritage List.

One of Paraguay's more unique landmarks is situated on the border between Brazil and Paraguay. The Usina Hidrelétrica Itaipu Binacional is the second-largest hydroelectric dam in the world, built in 1984. It was the largest dam until the development of the Three Gorges Dam in China in the early 21st century. The plant provides more than 90 percent of Paraguay's energy and was named one of the Seven Wonders of the Modern World by the American Society of Civil Engineers (ASCE).

Libraries & Museums

The National Library of Paraguay (Biblioteca Nacional), located in the capital of Asunción, was established in 1887. Important museums in Paraguay include the Casa de la Independencia Museum, which commemorates the country's independence, and the National Museum of Bellas Artes, which shares a building with the National Archives. Museums dedicated to indigenous art include Andrés Barbero Ethnographic Museum, located in Asunción, the Guido Boggiani Museum, located in San Lorenzo, and the Museum of Indigenous Art. Other important cultural institutions include the Cultural Center of the Republic in Asunción, which displays a variety of artistic mediums throughout Paraguay's history.

Holidays

Paraguay's national holiday is Independence Day (Dia de Independencia), May 14, which commemorates the country's independence from Spain. June 12 commemorates the armistice ending the Chaco War of the 1930s. August 15 celebrates the founding of Asunción in 1537.

A largely Roman Catholic country, Paraguay also celebrates many Catholic Holy Days, including the Three Kings Day (Dia de Tres Reyes), or Epiphany, on January 6, and the Feast of the Immaculate Conception on December 8.

Youth Culture

As of 2014, 26 percent of Paraguay's population is under the age of 14 and youth culture in the capital is vibrant. Brasilia Street is one section of the city that is popular for affluent youth, and includes restaurants and nightclubs. Open-air restaurants are particularly popular among the younger urban professional class, while teenagers and young adults tend to flock to discos,

some of which stay open until early morning. Most major cities have busy urban centers with coffee houses and Internet cafés that are dominated in the evenings by the younger generation.

Like most youth cultures, Paraguayan youth are becoming more technologically savvy in the early 21st century. Cell phones are becoming increasingly common, and the culture associated with text-messaging is strong in the capital and surrounding urban areas. Graffiti is one form of communication in youth culture that has persisted over time. During Alfredo Stroessner's dictatorship, graffiti was used as a political tool for underground communication. In more recent years, urban graffiti has shifted from political discourse to artistic expression among the city's working-class youth.

SOCIETY

Transportation

Buses are the main mode of public transportation in Paraguay. There are three types of bus service: fixed bus stop service, in which buses stop at bus stops; "flag stop" service, in which buses stop when waved down; and "executive" service, a more direct, higher level of service (and more expensive). Long-range buses from city to city are generally clean and modern, and may include amenities such as food service and bathrooms. In urban areas, subways and taxis are frequently used, and bicycling is becoming more common. In the rural areas, horse-drawn wagons and buggies are not uncommon. Traffic moves on the right-hand side.

Transportation Infrastructure

Though Paraguay has an extensive highway network connecting the various regions, many highways feature only one lane, and outside of major cities, many roads remain unpaved. The primary highway, the Trans-Chaco Highway, was completed in the late 1980s and represents one of the longest stretches of paved road in the country.

Paraguay's railroad infrastructure has never been widespread, focused mainly on one extensive track between Asunción and Encarnación. Instead of railway dependence, Paraguay's economy focuses on waterways for travel. With an extensive network of rivers and canals, the country uses water passage for transportation of goods and people, with shipping companies from Brazil and Argentina managing the bulk of traffic. The port of Asunción is the major point for goods flowing in and out of Paraguay. While Paraguay has more than 800 small airports, only a small majority have paved runways for plane landings. The major international airport into Asunción is the Silvio Pettirossi International Airport. Most air travel into Paraguay arrives via Brazil or Argentina.

Media & Communications

Under President Alfredo Stroessner's reign, the media was tightly censored and many journalists left Paraguay for other countries, such as Argentina. In many cases, media outlets began practicing self-censorship as a protective measure against government interference. After Stroessner's ouster in 1989, some self-censorship remained, but by the early 1990s, Paraguay no longer experienced problems with a free press.

As of 2013, fixed telephone subscriptions per 100 inhabitants was 5.9, and mobile subscriptions per 100 inhabitants was 103.7. Telephone centers, at which patrons sit in a small booth and are assisted by operators for a small fee, are the primary method for telephone access for the vast majority of Paraguayans. These centers are common in urban areas, but may require some degree of travel in rural areas. Internet access has been slow to spread in Paraguay as well. Internet service providers face laws that prevent private providers from using state-owned and state-run telephone and fiber optic cables. At the same time, the Paraguayan government has collected taxes to upgrade communications technology, but has not invested in the material upgrades needed to expand Internet access outside of major urban centers.

In 2008, news reports from Paraguay claimed that COPACO, the only Internet provider in Paraguay, was censoring certain websites,

redirecting traffic from political sites to another, opposing site. News outlets reported the initial claims, and then later reported that the redirects had stopped. COPACO denied any censoring or redirection. According to the United Nations, about 27 percent of the population has access to the Internet.

SOCIAL DEVELOPMENT

Standard of Living

As of 2014, Paraguay ranked 111 out of 182 nations on the United Nations Human Development Index (HDI), a global standard of living indicator.

Water Consumption

According to UNICEF's 2011 annual report, Paraguay achieved the MDG for drinking water and access to improved drinking water supply networks from 44 percent in 1997 to 75 percent in 2010. However, goals for improved sanitation remain a problem. Gaps persist between urban and rural areas (87 percent against 58 percent). For improved sanitation, urban coverage is 91 percent while rural coverage is only 39 percent.

Education

Paraguay's public education system is relatively unequal, due to the poverty of the country. Nine years of education are compulsory, and most children (around 92 percent) attend the elementary grades. Many, however, do not attend secondary schools. Conditions are poorest in rural areas.

Despite these problems, overall literacy is around 94 percent. There is an ongoing debate about the role of Guarani-based education in Paraguay, and what the nation's overall language policy should be.

The country has several public and private universities. There are four campuses in the public National University (Universidad Nacional) system; the oldest is the National University of Asunción (Universidad Nacional de Asunción), established in 1890. The leading private university is the Catholic University (Universidad Católica), also in Asunción.

Women's Rights

As of 2008, women represented nearly half—an estimated 49.6 percent—of the population of Paraguay. Their struggle for equal rights began in the 20th century, and was galvanized by the right to vote in 1961. In 1992, over three decades later, Paraguay established a cabinet-level women's bureau, led by the minister (sometimes called secretary) for women's affairs. The first person appointed to this post also became the first female cabinet secretary in Paraguay's history. Additionally, 20 percent of electoral roles are now reserved for women (the positions tend to be the lowest-ranking spots, however), and 10 percent of all seats in parliament are filled by women. In 2008, the first female candidate for president, former education secretary Blanca Ovelar (1957-), ran as a viable presidential candidate.

In Paraguay, over one-third of women aged 15 and older participate in the work force in the early 21st century. However, work life is different for women in rural areas. According to the Food and Agriculture Organization of the UN (FAO), women own approximately 20 percent of all rural land. This is important to note, since women could not legally own land or hold the title until the passage of the 2002 Agrarian Act. Most rural women work as subsistence farmers, growing food for their families or for barter. Less than half of female rural workers earn money for their work and may not be counted in official labor force totals.

Urban women who earn hourly wages or a salaried income typically earn less than 60 cents on average for every dollar men earn. Women with college degrees typically earn only 70 cents for every dollar earned by their male counterparts. As of 2008, women hold only eight percent of all public government jobs and nearly 10 percent of professional and managerial jobs in Paraguay. Social security provides paid maternity leave for women who work in jobs covered by the policy. However, these women receive half their salary for twelve weeks. Women living in urban areas in Paraguay typically have greater access to birth control and reproductive health services.

A 2000 law made domestic violence a crime and provides penalties for physical violence. However, women's groups complain that the law is not enforced. These groups also point to the lack of telephone hotlines, shelters, and financial aid for domestic violence victims. In addition, Paraguayan women are vulnerable to human trafficking. The same 2000 law criminalizing domestic violence also made trafficking women and children illegal. According to the International Organization of Migration (IOM), 85 percent of trafficking in Paraguay is related to the sex trade.

Health Care

Paraguay's public health system is somewhat undeveloped. Most hospitals are located in the capital. During the mid-1990s, two-thirds of the population still did not have clean drinking water, partly because of inadequate sanitation.

Within Guaraní communities, traditional remedies and healers are still prominent. The Guaraní have suffered particularly high rates of suicide, which have been linked to despair over political and economic discrimination, including the illegal seizure of their lands.

GOVERNMENT

Structure

Under Paraguay's 1992 constitution, which limited presidential power, the president is popularly elected to a five-year term. Re-election is not allowed. The president is both the head of government and the head of state.

Paraguay has a two-house legislature, the members of which are elected by popular vote to five-year terms. Elections are held at the same time as the presidential elections. The upper house, known as the Senate (Camera de Senadores), has 45 members. The lower house, or Chamber of Deputies (Camera de Deputados), has 80 members.

Political Parties

Since the late 19th century, Paraguayan politics have been dominated by struggles between two political parties. The Colorado Party, or National Republican Association (Asociación Nacional Republicana), has held power since 1948. The main opposition party is the Liberals, known officially as the Authentic Radical Liberal Party (Partido Liberal Radical Autentico, or PLRA), which has become increasingly influential in the early 21st century. The last elections were held in 2013 when Horacio Cartes for the Colorado Party won 48.45 percent of the vote, garnering 44 seats out of 80. The PLRA won 27 seats, the UNCE won two seats, and all other political parties won less than five seats.

Local Government

Each of Paraguay's nineteen departments is headed by a governor or government delegate, appointed by the president. Asunción is governed as its own department. Departments are further divided into municipalities, which are limited in their governance.

Judicial System

The nine-member Supreme Court of Justice (Corte Suprema de Justicia) is the nation's highest court. The members are appointed by the president and the Senate, from a list of candidates proposed by the Council of Magistrates (Consejo de la Magistratura). The Supreme Court of Justice has the power of judicial review over legislation. Other courts include appellate courts and courts of first instance of administrative, civil, criminal, and commercial jurisdiction, as well as military courts.

Taxation

Paraguay's low tax rates include a capped corporate and income tax rate of 10 percent. Other levied taxes include a value-added tax (VAT) and a property tax.

Armed Forces

Paraguay's armed forces consist of an army, air force, and navy. Military service is compulsory for males up to one year, at the age of 18.

Foreign Policy

Much of Paraguay's foreign policy is structured around its position in South America. As one of two landlocked countries in South America (Bolivia being the other), Paraguay frequently negotiates with neighbors that have access to ocean ports to work on trade and economic issues. With two large neighbors—Argentina and Brazil—and with few natural resources by comparison, Paraguay has also had to work to protect its existence in the shadow of these larger countries. Additionally, two regional conflicts—the War of the Triple Alliance in the 19th century and the Chaco War in the 20th century—have left legacy issues in the 21st century in terms of border disputes, national pride, and economic stability.

Paraguay's strong history of government by military dictatorship has also affected foreign policy on a wider scale. Paraguay's long-standing dictator, Alfredo Stroessner, ruled Paraguay as an isolationist state from 1954 to 1989. An exception to this policy was engagement with South American neighbors for such multinational infrastructure projects such as the hydroelectric dam at Itaipu. During Stroessner's administration, Paraguay also refused to maintain any diplomatic relations with communist or Marxist states. Thus, Paraguay would not recognize fellow Latin American countries such as Cuba or Nicaragua (with the only exception being Yugoslavia, which was non-aligned).

Stroessner was removed from office in 1989 by a military coup, and foreign relations developed slowly. By the early 1990s, Paraguay's diplomatic relations with the U.S. focused on anti-drug efforts, with financial aid sent to Paraguay in an effort to reduce drug production and drug trafficking. The Tri-Border Area, where Paraguay, Brazil, and Argentina meet, has long been considered an area of concern for all three countries, particularly as a hotbed of drug and arms trafficking. In 2005, an agreement was signed allowing U.S. soldiers to train in Paraguay (the agreement also gave immunity to U.S. personnel operating on Paraguayan soil). The 2005 agreement allowed U.S. soldiers to evaluate the area, but Paraguay's neighbors, expressed concern that the U.S.-Paraguay foreign relations decision was a prelude to further U.S. involvement in the area. Since the 2001 U.S.-led "war on terror" relations between the U.S. and Paraguay have become strained, mostly by the U.S. decision to focus its anti-terrorist activities in the Tri-Border Area.

In the early 21st century, Paraguay has continued its policy of refusing to recognize communist states, and has maintained no ties with countries such as Cuba, North Korea, or China (Paraguay recognizes the Republic of China on Taiwan). However, Paraguay has stated it intends to strengthen relations with Middle Eastern countries, particularly Iran. Paraguay remains a member of various prominent international and regional organizations, including the UN and the Organization of American States (OAS), as well as regional trade agreements such as Mercosur (common market of the south).

Human Rights Profile

International human rights law insists that states respect civil and political rights, and also promote an individual's economic, social and cultural rights. The United Nations Universal Declaration on Human Rights (UDHR) is recognized as the standard for international human rights. Its authors sought the counsel of the world's great thinkers, philosophers, and religious leaders, and were careful to create a document that reflects the core values shared by every world culture. To read this document or view the articles relating to cultural human rights, click here: http://www. udhr.org/UDHR/default.htm.

Paraguayans experienced extensive human rights abuses under dictator Alfredo Stroessner. Stroessner suspended constitutional protections and used kidnapping, torture, murder, threats and totalitarian oppression to rule Paraguay, controlling the media and limiting information about disappeared dissidents. The dictator also welcomed war criminals, such as the infamous Nazi torturer Josef Mengele (1911–1979) and deposed Latin American dictators, Anastasio Somoza García (1896–1956) of Nicaragua and

Juan Perón (1895–1974) of Argentina, to settle in Paraguay. Paraguay did not extradite war criminals under Stroessner.

In 1992, the "Archives of Terror" were made public. The government documents detailing the kidnappings, torture and murders of alleged dissidents and protesters during Stroessner's administration confirmed reports from international human rights groups that Paraguay had violated basic international human rights laws. The archival documents also revealed information concerning Operation Condor, a coordinated multinational government effort on the part of Paraguay, Argentina, Chile, Bolivia, Brazil, and Uruguay to track dissidents in exile in other countries for the purpose of detaining and punishing them. In 2003, Paraguay created a Truth and Justice Commission (CVJ) to investigate Paraguay's human rights abuse record. The investigation into 400 cases is ongoing, and more than 3,000 people remain unaccounted for, or "disappeared."

Paraguay's recent human rights record era has improved dramatically. According to recent U.S. reports, the widespread and gross human rights abuses from the former dictatorship are no longer a pervasive issue in Paraguay. However, some human rights issues remain. These include various forms of torture and other repressive measures carried out by authorities, intimidation of journalists and public officials, and the trafficking of women and children. Human rights observers note that Paraguay's human rights record could be improved by enforcing existing laws that protect freedom of expression, workers' rights, children from labor exploitation, and citizens from law enforcement abuse. Human rights groups have also targeted Paraguay in recent years for its prison conditions.

ECONOMY

Overview of the Economy

Paraguay's economy has been somewhat sluggish in the early 21st century, following decades of political and economic instability, as well as the Latin American monetary crisis of the late 1990s. After a period of slight contraction, the economy resumed modest growth. The economy fell 3.8 percent in 2009, as lower world demand and commodity prices caused exports to contract. The government reacted by introducing fiscal and monetary stimulus packages. Growth resumed at 13 percent level in 2010, but slowed in 2011–2012 as the stimulus subsided and severe drought and outbreaks of foot-and-mouth disease led to a drop in beef and other agriculture exports. The economy took another leap in 2013, largely due to strong export growth.

Paraguay's gross domestic product (GDP) was an estimated $45.9 billion USD in 2013. Just over 20 percent of this was connected with agriculture, while around 17 percent was related to manufacturing.

Industry

Industry in Paraguay is limited to the processing of local products such as cotton and wood. Paraguay's main exports are agricultural products including soybeans, cotton, meat, and animal products. Hydroelectric power is also exported.

Paraguay imports many manufactured items, particularly consumer goods. These are often resold, at lower prices, to visitors from neighboring Latin American countries.

The Paraguayan economy depends heavily on those of neighboring Brazil, Argentina, and Uruguay, fellow members of the South American free-trade union. Brazil received roughly one-third of Paraguay's exports. The United States and the European Union are other important trading partners.

Alongside the formal economy is an immense informal or "underground" economy based heavily on smuggling and narcotics trafficking. The United States Department of State believes that Paraguay's black market may be as large as the formal economy.

Labor

Paraguay had an estimated labor force of 3.19 million in 2013. Over half of the labor force—55 percent—was employed in the services sector,

followed by agriculture (around 26 percent) and industry (about 18 percent). The unemployment rate was an estimated 6.6 in 2013.

Energy/Power/Natural Resources

Paraguay has rich natural resources, including hydropower, fertile soil, timber, and minerals. The Paraná River is a major source of hydroelectric power; the Itaipú Dam and the Yacyretá hydroelectric project were both completed in the 1990s.

The main minerals mined in the country are iron, manganese, and limestone. Despite the still-rich stands of timber, the country suffers from deforestation. Increased human settlement has also meant extensive water pollution and shrinking wetlands.

Fishing

Mostly, landlocked Paraguay's fishing industry serves to meet domestic needs and demand, and remains a minor industry focused on freshwater fish.

Forestry

Paraguay has the potential for a robust and sustainable forest industry due to the fact that its trees display a high rate of growth. Deforestation, however, remains a concern, and an estimated 0.5 percent of the country's forest cover was lost between 1990 and 2000.

Mining/Metals

Paraguay's mineral industry accounted for less than one percent of the country's GDP in the early 21st century. The industry mostly centered on cement production and minerals such as gypsum, limestone, marble and other ornamental stones, clays, and kaolin.

Agriculture

Paraguay's economy remains heavily agricultural, with around half of all workers employed in farming. Less than eight percent of the land is arable. The Chaco is generally non-arable, though with great effort Mennonite immigrants have established farms in that desert region.

The main crops in the formal economy include commodities such as cotton, sugarcane, and soybeans, as well as meat and dairy products. In the black-market economy, Paraguay is a major producer of cannabis, largely for the South American market.

Animal Husbandry

Cattle continue to be a main industry of Paraguay, with beef exports accounting for a large part of Paraguay's agricultural sector. Other important livestock raised include horses, pigs, and sheep.

Tourism

Paraguay has relatively limited tourism, with most visitors coming from the neighboring Latin American countries. A major draw is the availability of low-cost consumer goods. Travel and tourism contributes around four percent of GDP and accounts for around four percent of employment. The number of visitors grew to 465,000 in 2010 from 416,000 in 2007.

One of the most popular tourist destinations is Asunción, with its many historic buildings and lively cultural life. The Chaco region, with its exotic wildlife, is home to a national park, the Parque Nacional Defensores del Chaco (The Defenders of Chaco National Park).

Melanie Zoltan, Eric Badertscher,
Beverly Ballaro

DO YOU KNOW?

- Roland Joffe's 1986 Academy-Award winning film *The Mission* touches on the history of Jesuit missionary work with the Guaraní in the regions of what is today Paraguay and Brazil. During Asunción's annual June celebration of the Festival of Saint John, revelers indulge in a number of activities including walking barefoot over a bed of hot coals; dousing a wire-and-cloth ball in flammable liquid, setting it afire, and tossing it into a crowd of willing participants who try to kick the ball away to avoid getting burned; and observing a midnight burning of a fireworks-filled effigy of Judas Iscariot.

Bibliography

Bosrock, Mary Murray. *Put Your Best Foot Forward-South America (Put Your Best Foot Forward)*. Saint Paul: International Education Systems, 1997.

Ceasar, Mike. "Guarani from tongue to tome." *Americas* (English edition): July-August 2002.

Chaffee, Lyman. "The Popular Culture Political Persuasion in Paraguay: Communication and Public Art." *Studies in Latin American Popular Culture. (*1990): 127–148

Grow, Michael. *The Good Neighbor Policy and Authoritarianism in Paraguay: United States Economic Expansion and Great-Power Rivalry in Latin America during World War.* Lawrence, Kansas: University Press of Kansas, 1981.

Hanratty, Dennis. Paraguay: *A Country Study.* Washington, DC: Department of the Army, 1990.

Horst, Rene Harder. *The Stroessner Regime and Indigenous Resistance in Paraguay*. Gainesville, FL: University Press of Florida, 2007.

Lambert, Peter, and Andrew Nickson, eds. *The Paraguay Reader: History, Culture, Politics*. Durham, NC: Duke University Press, 2013.

Lewis, Paul H. *Paraguay Under Stroessner.* Chapel Hill, NC: University of North Carolina Press, 1980.

Lewis, Paul H. *Socialism, Liberalism, and Dictatorship in Paraguay (Politics in Latin America)*. Westport, CT: Praeger Publishers, 1982.

Miranda, Carlos R. *The Stroessner Era: Authoritarian Rule in Paraguay.* London, England: Westview Press, 1990.

Mora, Frank O. *Paraguay and the United States: Distant Allies.* Athens, GA: University of Georgia Press, 2007.

Rule by Fear: Paraguay After Thirty Years Under Stroessner. New York: Human Rights Watch, 1985.

Service, Elman R. and Helen S. Service. *Tobati: Paraguayan Town.* Chicago: The University Of Chicago Press, 1954.

Warren, Harris G. *Rebirth of the Paraguayan Republic: The First Colorado Era, 1878-1904 (Pitt Latin American Series).* Pittsburgh: University of Pittsburgh Press, 1985.

Works Cited

"Canada. Centre for Intercultural Learning, Foreign Affairs and International Trade." Paraguay—Intercultural Issues. <http://www.intercultures.ca/cil-cai/intercultural_issues_print-en.asp?lvl=0&ISO=PY>.

"Cultural Center of the Republic." Paraguay. <http://www.cabildoccr.gov.py/index.php>.

Dangl, Benjamin. "The U.S. Military Descends on Paraguay." *The Nation*. 12 July 2006. <http://www.thenation.com/doc/20060717/dangl>.

Díaz, Natalia Ruiz. "PARAGUAY: Agreement with Rural Activists Puts End to Protest." *IPS Inter Press Service*. <http://ipsnews.net/news.asp?idnews=44622>.

Encyclopedia: Paraguay. History.com. <http://www.history.com/encyclopedia.do?articleId=218604>.

Improved Housing and Spraying to Fight the Spread of Chagas' Disease. *International Development Research Centre*. 13 March 1998. <http://www.idrc.ca/en/ev-26951-201-1-DO_TOPIC.html>.

Logan, Sam and Matthew Flynn. "U.S. Military Moves in Paraguay Rattle Regional Relations." *Americas Policy Program Special Report*. 14 Dec. 2005. <http://americas.irc-online.org/am/2991>.

"Paraguay." *CIA World Factbook*. Washington, DC: CIA, 2014. https://www.cia.gov/library/publications/the-world-factbook/.

Paraguay. *Nations of the World*. Amenia, NY: Grey House Publishing, 2015.

"Paraguay. Statistics and Census." <http://www.dgeec.gov.py/>.

"Paraguay.com. Arts and Culture." <http://www.paraguay.com/arts_and_culture/indigenous_art.php>.

Sciscioli, Alejandro. "PARAGUAY: Internet Access? What About Just a Telephone?". IPS Inter Press Service. 18 Nov. 2005. <http://ipsnews.net/news.asp?idnews=31087>.

Thousands of People March in Paraguay for Agrarian Reform and Housing Rights. *Real World Radio*. 31 March 2008. <http://www.radiomundoreal.fm/rmr/?q=en/node/24955>.

"Trends in Latin American Networking. Internet in Paraguay." University of Texas at Austin Latin American Network Information Center. <http://lanic.utexas.edu/project/tilan/countries/par/>.

UNESCO World Heritage. Jesuit Missions of La Santísima Trinidad de Paraná and Jesús de Tavarangue. *United Nations*. <http://whc.unesco.org/en/list/648>.

UNESCO World Heritage. Mbaracayú Forest Nature Reserve. *United Nations*. <http://whc.unesco.org/en/tentativelists/1845/>.

UNICEF. At a Glance: Paraguay, Statistics. *United Nations*. <http://www.unicef.org/infobycountry/paraguay_statistics.html>.

United Nations. Food and Agriculture Organization. La Mujer en la Agricultura, Medio Ambiente y la Producción Rural. *InterPress Service*. <ftp://ftp.fao.org/docrep/fao/007/ad933s/ad933s00.pdf>.

U.S. Department of State. Paraguay. *United States*. <http://www.state.gov/r/pa/ei/bgn/1841.htm>.

"Women nailed to crosses in Paraguay to demand housing." *USA Today*. <http://www.usatoday.com/news/religion/2008-12-05-paraguay-crucifixions_N.htm>.

"Virtual Library of Miguel de Cervantes." *Paraguayan Literature*. <http://www.cervantesvirtual.com/portal/paraguay/>.

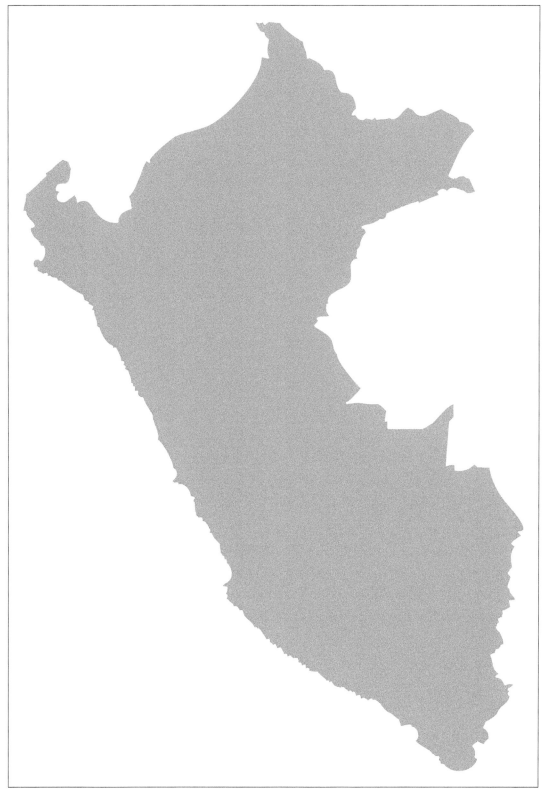

PERU

Introduction

The Republic of Peru is a west coast nation in South America. The Pacific sits along its west coast, Ecuador stands to the northwest, Colombia to the northeast, Brazil and Bolivia to the west, and Chile to the south. Peru is known for its biodiversity and boasts the second largest area of tropical forests in Latin America, with 10 percent of the world's total plant species and over 1,800 bird species. The government is making a concerted effort to protect the country's biodiversity while still availing itself of the economic benefit of its natural resources.

The culturally and scientifically advanced Inca Empire was situated in what is now Peru, but this once vast culture was mostly destroyed by Spanish conquistadors during the 16th century. The ruined city of Machu Picchu, called the "Lost City of the Incas," is one of the most famous cultural and historic attractions in South America. Peru achieved independence from Spain in 1821. Today, it is considered one of the most important economic powers in Latin America.

GENERAL INFORMATION

Official Language: Spanish, Quechua
Population: 30,147,935 (2014 estimate)
Currency: Nuevo sol
Coins: One hundred centimos equal one nuevo sol. Coins in Peru are issued in 1, 5, 10, 20, and 50 centimos and 1, 2, and 5 nuevo sols.

Land Area: 1,279,996 square kilometers (494,209 square miles)
Water Area: 5,220 square kilometers (2,015 square miles)
National Anthem: "Somos libres, sesmoslo siempre" (Spanish, "We are free, let us always be so")
Capital: Lima
Time Zone: GMT -5
Flag Description: Peru's national flag is a vertical triband, with red (symbolizing the blood shed in achieving independence) stripes on the left and right and a white (symbolizing peace) middle band with the coat of arms of Peru in the center.

Population

The majority populations of Peru are Amerindian (around 45 percent of the population) and mestizo (37 percent of the population), followed by smaller populations of whites (15 of the population) and blacks, as well as some Chinese and Japanese.

The largest cities in Peru are Lima, Arequipa, Trujillo, Chiclayo, and Piura. Most of the

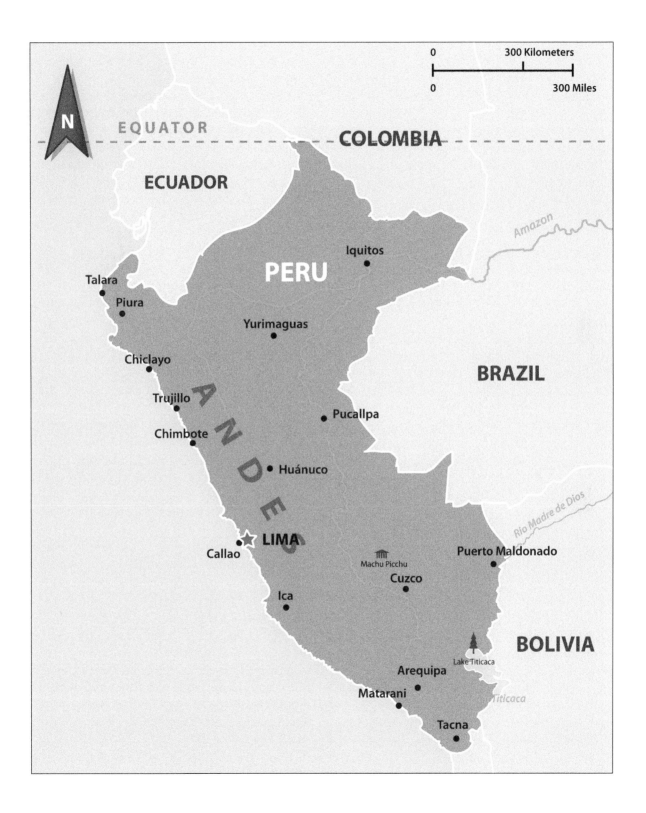

Principal Cities by Population (2012):

- Lima (9,130,000)
- Arequipa (959,763)
- Trujillo (789,175)
- Chiclayo (540,706)
- Piura (407,109)
- Iquitos (405,511)
- Cusco (371,448)
- Chimbote (335,141)
- Huancayo (330,373)
- Pucallpa (272,616)

non-Amerindian or mestizo population of Peru lives in urban areas, while the rural areas are primarily populated by indigenous and mestizo peoples. About 75 percent of the population lives in urban areas. The economic, social, and political disparity between the indigenous peoples of Peru and the wealthy white population is a source of continued conflict in Peruvian society.

The class system in Peru is complex: not only is there evidence of widespread class distinction between whites and non-whites, there are also many levels of it between mestizos and indigenous peoples, and among indigenous tribes.

Languages

Peru's official languages are Spanish and Quechua. Additionally, many other native languages are spoken by the large Amerindian and mestizo populations, including Aymara. Some languages have only a handful of native speakers, while others are more widely spoken.

Native People & Ethnic Groups

Historically, the indigenous people that had the most effect on Peru were the Inca, who held a vast empire that stretched between the equator and southern Chile in the 15th and 16th centuries. Inca civilization was one of the most advanced in the Western Hemisphere prior to the arrival of European explorers, who took only a few years to decimate the population and wipe out all possibility that the Inca Empire would ever rebuild itself.

Most of Peru's indigenous peoples are poor and lack political representation, as is true of many indigenous populations throughout South America. In fact, Peru ranks third internationally for the greatest population of "uncontacted" or "isolated" tribes. The Quechua and Aymara peoples of Peru also suffer from poor public health conditions and reliance on manual labor for their income. The indigenous peoples who live on the eastern side of the Andes Mountains and along the Amazon basin are ethnically distinct from the Amerindians who live in the Peruvian highlands.

In the late 20th century, two violent indigenous groups gained support in Peru: the Sendero Luminoso (Shining Path), led by the insurgent Abimael Guzman (captured in the early 1990s), and the Movimiento Revolucionario Tupac Amaru (Tupac Amaru Revolutionary Movement), named for the last Inca leader. Although neither party gained much political power in Peru, there has been widespread popular support (as well as large resistance at times) among indigenous peoples for their efforts. Both groups are considered terrorist organizations.

In the early 21st century, indigenous people in Peru are fighting for increased participation in decisions relative to oil and mining operations on ancestral lands. In 2010, then President Alan Garcia refused to sign a law that would grant indigenous people more power in these decisions, however since taking office in 2011, President Ollanta Humala has vowed to better the plight of indigenous peoples

Religions

As in most of Latin America, the majority religion in Peru is Roman Catholicism, practiced by more than 80 percent of the population. About 12 percent is comprised of Protestant denominations, as well as several non-Christian religions, including Judaism and Islam. Buddhism and Shintoism are commonly practiced among Peru's Asian population.

Climate

Peru has a diverse climate, containing many of the world's different climate types within its borders. Generally, the climate of Peru follows its regions: cold and dry in the high Andes region, arid from the western slopes of the Andes to its coast, and tropical in the Amazonian region. The mixture of the cold Humboldt Current, and the warmer El Niño, also affect its climate dramatically.

The rainy season lasts from October to March, bringing an annual rainfall of about 86 centimeters (34 inches), although some regions receive much more than that on average. In the eastern section of the Andes, rainfall can be as high as 406 centimeters (160 inches) per year.

The average temperature along the coastal plains is 20° Celsius (68° Fahrenheit). The sierra region has a temperature range of −7° to 21° Celsius (20° to 70° Fahrenheit). In Lima, the average annual temperature is 19° Celsius (66° Fahrenheit), while in Cusco, the average temperature is 12° Celsius (54° Fahrenheit).

ENVIRONMENT & GEOGRAPHY

Topography

Peru is home to two of the most significant geographic features in the Western Hemisphere: the Andes Mountains and the Amazon River. The Andes mountain range, or the sierra, bisects the western coastal and desert-like region, or costa, from the eastern region, which is part of the Amazon River basin known as La Selva.

The Amazon River originates in the Andes as a stream at Nevado Mismi, a fact which was finally confirmed in 2001 by researchers after years of speculation. From Nevado Mismi, the Amazon is formed by the Ucayali and the Maranon rivers, and then flows east roughly 6,400 kilometers (4,000 miles) to the Atlantic Ocean.

Along the coast is the Sechura Desert, where 52 rivers flow into the Pacific Ocean from the Amazon. Lago (or Lake) Titicaca, the highest navigable lake in the world, sits on the Bolivian-Peruvian border in the southeast. The highest point in Peru is at Nevado Huascaran, which is 6,768 meters (22,205 feet) high, in the Cordillera Blanca. Other ranges in the Peruvian Andes include the Cordillera Occidental, Cordillera Oriental, and Cordillera Central.

Lima is Peru's capital. It has an area of about 70 square kilometers (27 square miles). The city is located west of the Andes, on the southern bank of the Rímac River, 13 kilometers (8 miles) inland from the Pacific Ocean. It is surrounded by the Peruvian coastal desert, which has almost no native plant or animal life. Lima's landscape, like most of Peru's coast, was formed through glacial erosion, in a process that continues to this day, and is a constant threat to the city, in the form of earthquakes and cliff deterioration.

Plants & Animals

Peru is a place of extraordinary biodiversity. The mountain regions of Peru include forests of mahogany, cedar, rubber and cinchona trees, as well as sarsaparilla and vanilla plants. Mesquite, cactus, and eucalyptus plants are common in the desert region. Other trees include the strangler fig, cacao and Brazil nut trees, the ayahuasca vine, cassava, and many other tropical plants.

Llamas, vicuñas and alpacas (historically important to Peruvians as domesticated animals), are common in mountainous regions. Peru is also home to more bird species than any other country in the world, including condors, macaws, hummingbirds, hoatzin (a mysterious and possibly prehistoric bird) and many others. Jaguars, howler monkeys, tapirs, sloths, agouti and capybara are common Peruvian rainforest animals.

Endangered or threatened animal species include Anderson's mouse opossum, the short-tailed chinchilla, the yellow-tailed woolly monkey, the blue whale, the Incan little mastiff bat, the giant armadillo, the giant otter and the marine otter.

CUSTOMS & COURTESIES

Greetings

Peruvian culture, as with most Latin American cultures, is considered very warm. Commonly, a greeting or conversation may begin with "¿Como estás?" ("How are you?) or "Buenos dias" ("Good day"). Another common greeting in

Peru is the more informal "¿Que tál?" (loosely, "What's happening?").

When meeting friends or acquaintances, greetings typically consist of a handshake or a kiss on the cheek. When the friends are two men, a handshake is in order. Among women, a kiss on the right cheek is appropriate. Sometimes two men will exchange a kiss on the right cheek if they are related, though this is usually reserved for a father and son. In business settings, a handshake usually takes the place of a kiss for women. However, depending on the company, this rule is sometimes ignored in favor of the traditional Peruvian custom of warm greetings.

When arriving at a social function or party, the new arrival is supposed to greet every single guest in the appropriate fashion. The new arrival will circle the group shaking every man's hand (if the new arrival is a male as well) and kissing every woman's cheek. Even if two people have never met before, they are still expected to greet each other as described.

Gestures & Etiquette

In Peru, non-verbal gestures play a significant part of every-day communication. Most gestures would be familiar in Western cultures, while others would not. Peruvians may speak to one another closely, with little personal space. Additionally, eye contact is critical and can sometimes seem like staring to those unfamiliar with the practice. (Amerindians are shyer, and avoid eye contact.) Concerning etiquette, Peru's warm culture generally implies a higher sensitivity towards others than is found in other cultures. One example of this cultural difference is when giving somebody something. If someone is seated at a desk, it is considered customary and polite to place the item on the desk, not allowing the item to leave the hand until the item has safely arrived on the desk

Eating/Meals

Peruvians typically eat three meals. While dinner is the primary meal in most Western cultures, lunch is its equivalent in Peru. Lunch, like dinner, is traditionally a social occasion not to be rushed.

Typically, lunch may consist of a soup, an entrée and a beverage. For the average Peruvian, lunch is a feast, while dinner often amounts to a lighter meal or snack.

Traditional silverware—fork, knife, and spoon—is commonly used in Peru. Generally, Peruvians rarely eat with their hands. Sandwiches and salteñas (pastries often filled with meat and other ingredients), neither of which are commonly eaten, are among the only foods eaten with the hands.

While meals certainly differ from region to region, the typical Peruvian plate consists of rice, potato, meat and an accompanying sauce. Lime and ají, a spicy sauce made from peppers, eggs and oil, are commonly served on the side. The potato is actually native to Peru. It was introduced to Europe in 1536, after the Spanish colonized South America and brought the potato crop back with them.

Visiting

The social aspect of life is very important to Peruvians. Friends are often invited over or may show up unannounced. When invited for a meal, it is considered polite to bring a gift. Aside from the all-important lunch, Peruvians find many reasons to organize small get-togethers and social events, with birthday parties particularly popular. In addition, it is not uncommon for kitchen or living room furniture to be moved to accommodate a dance floor.

At parties and in social situations, it is customary for all the guests to drink together. For example, there might only be typically two glasses for all the guests to share in a rotation. Two guests on opposite sides of the rotation will fill their glasses and, upon finishing, pass the same glass to the guest on the right. If the guest is a woman, the male is expected to fill the glass and serve her.

LIFESTYLE

Family

Peru is a predominantly Catholic country and has a fairly patriarchal family culture. As such, gender roles follow traditional customs, with the father as the head of the household and the mother handling domestic duties. With an average of 5.1 persons per household, families in Peru are also considerably larger than in some other countries. Children typically live at home with their parents until they are married, though males sometimes live alone before marriage. Women, however, rarely move out of their family home until they have married. With the urbanization of the country in the 21st century, these traditions and customs are changing.

It is common for affluent families to employ a maid or servant, known as an empleada (employee). These domestic servants are typically responsible for cleaning and cooking, and often serve as nannies for the children. They are usually women from poorer or rural areas looking to establish new lives and opportunities in cities such as Lima, Arequipa or Trujillo.

Housing

Many of Peru's houses and buildings are made of adobe, a mixture of straw and clay in brick form. According to the International Development Research Centre, 65 percent of the rural population and 35 percent of the urban population reside in buildings made of adobe. However, adobe is not effective in withstanding earthquakes, and Peru is particularly prone to these. Certain cities experience tremors on a regular basis, in addition to experiencing major earthquakes every few years. In 2007, Pisco experienced a devastating earthquake, which killed more than 500 people and injured more than 1,000. For this reason, vertical architecture is rare in Peruvian cities—with only a few exceptions in Lima—and houses and apartment buildings are rarely more than three or four stories in height.

Besides single family homes and apartment buildings, squatter neighborhoods are common in big cities. These informal settlements are also called shantytowns, and are typically built by people who are destitute or homeless. These constructions are often made with whatever materials can be found, such as sheet metal, cardboard and wood planks, or other discarded materials.

These communities are common due to the high amount of impoverished Peruvians who travel to large cities looking for work. Shantytowns rarely have water or electricity.

Food

Peruvian cuisine developed from a fusion of different cultural and historic influences. Peru's unique geography is also central to its cuisine, as it allows for a diverse number of crops, most notably maize (corn), potatoes and tomatoes. All of these were introduced as staple foods to Europe from the Americas following Spanish conquest. As these cultures blended, the Spanish brought rice into the equation. The Spanish also brought with them the cultivation of olives, fruits and vegetables, including vine grapes, asparagus, oranges, and figs, to name a few.

A further blending of the culinary traditions of Chinese and Japanese immigrants resulted in the emergence of stir-fry (resulting in the term chaufa, or Peruvian Chinese food). In fact, Peru has a strong Asian influence, and has the most Chinese restaurants of any Latin American country. Peru's long coastline and the farmed Andean trout of the mountains account for the prevalence of fish and seafood in Peruvian cuisine. Peruvian food is known for its many spicy dishes; staple dishes often feature rocoto (hot peppers) or its sauce derivative known as ají, made from the ají pepper.

Unique and traditional Peruvian dishes include ceviche (raw fish marinated in lime juice, served with sweet potato, onions, seaweed, maize, peppers), cuy (roasted or fried guinea pig, often in peanut sauce), and salchipapa (a fast food plate of french fries topped with a chopped-up hot dog and covered in ketchup, mustard, mayonnaise and ají). Ceviche is a popular staple in Peru's coastal regions, while cuy is a more traditional dish commonly served in the regions around the Andes. Other well-known Peruvian dishes include ají de gallina (shredded chicken with a cream sauce), lomo saltado (fried and seasoned beef or steak strips, typically served with potatoes, tomatoes, onions and peppers), chupe (fish stew), and caucau (typically tripe with potatoes).

Popular Peruvian alcoholic beverages include aguardiente and pisco, a liquor made from grapes. The country's most famous cocktail, the pisco sour, has become quite popular outside of Peru in recent years. Chicha de jora is a fermented beverage made from corn that is often served with lunch. It has a sour taste and a slight amount of alcohol. Chicha morada is a sweeter, non-alcoholic brew derived from corn.

Peru also has various unique fruits native to the Amazon rainforest. Many Peruvian fruit juices are uncommon in other parts of the world, including maracuya, guava, lucuma, cherimoya, and camu camu. In fact, lucuma is the most popular flavor for ice cream in Peru—more so than chocolate, vanilla, or strawberry. Inka Kola is the most famous Peruvian soft drink brand. It is a bright yellow, bubble-gum flavored soda that is now owned by Coca-Cola.

Life's Milestones

Many celebrations in Peru are quite similar to those in the rest of South and North America. Approximately 90 percent of the population is Catholic, making a child's baptism very important. In Peru, a girl's 15th birthday is also a major life milestone. Known as the quinceañera or quince años, the 15th birthday represents the transformation of a girl into a woman, and is typically marked by an elaborate celebration. Traditionally, families throw a large party for relatives and friends. The occasion is similar to a sweet 16 party in American culture.

Baby showers are also significant celebrations in Peruvian culture. In the United States, baby showers are typically only attended by the female friends and relatives of the mother-to-be. In Peru, however, baby showers are lively parties attended by men and women. Drinks and food are served as both parents open gifts for their unborn baby.

CULTURAL HISTORY

Art

Peruvian art is as diverse and unique as the various cultures, geography, and political climates that have inspired and shaped it. Historically, art in Peru dates back to the pre-Columbian period, when ancient Andean civilizations flourished prior to the arrival of Europeans. These civilizations developed arts such as ceramics, weaving and metallurgy. Today, items such as pottery, jewelry, baskets, and leather are still made in the traditional fashion. This era was also known for its architecture and sculptures.

Traditional crafts flourished in the Peruvian countryside. Rugs and ponchos are the most renowned, and are still sold to tourists in almost every Peruvian city. The bright, multicolored rugs and ponchos are woven using traditional methods. Often, ponchos are still used to wrap babies up and carry them like a backpack. Brilliant pinks, blues, turquoises and oranges are featured prominently in stripes and cross-patterns.

Peruvian painting emerged with the onset of European influence and culture. The Cusco School, comprised of 17th- and 18th-century painters, is perhaps the best-known Peruvian visual arts tradition. Mestizo (people of mixed ancestry) and indigenous students studied European paintings and sculptures and produced works with religious and Gothic influences. Most of these paintings were done anonymously.

The indigenist movement of the early 20th century was a significant awakening of the Peruvian mentality to the plight of the rural poor. Artists featured images and stories of the indigenous peoples of Peru, particularly raising awareness of issues of injustice. The underlying ideas grew and spread to Brazil, Colombia, and Mexico, as there was a widespread oppression of indigenous peoples by modernizing governments in these countries. The movement helped spur a newfound recognition and inclusion of indigenous populations in society. While this approach was eventually subject to criticism in the 1960s, many necessary reforms were brought about by the painters, authors, and sculptors of the indigenist movement.

José Sabogal (1888–1956) is the country's most famous painter. Sabogal, a native of the Andes Mountains, shocked Peru with his bold portraits of indigenous people. He is largely credited with starting the country's indigenous movement. Other Peruvian artists associated with advancing the indigenous movement include Fernando de Szyszlo (b. 1925-), renowned for his work in plastic arts (art that is typically molded). José Carlos Ramos (b. 1948-) is probably the most famous among modern Peruvian artists. His paintings vary from abstract, typical Peruvian imagery that explores the country's native culture, to erotic paintings and woodblocks in the Japanese style.

Architecture

The ancient architecture of pre-Columbian civilizations, such as the Incas, is referred to as preconquest art and architecture. Much of this was burned down or compromised with the arrival of the Europeans, most notably by Spanish conquistador Francisco Pizarro, who conquered the Inca Empire (1439–1533). Nonetheless, these ruins remain a part of Peru's national architectural identity. Machu Picchu is perhaps the most famous of what remains, a sprawling jungle retreat built with large stones using no mortar. Saksaywaman, believed to be an Inca fortress in the city of Cusco, is another impressive example of Inca architecture.

The Spanish Baroque style—characterized by grandeur and the appeal to emotion rather than intellect—is commonly seen in cathedrals and plazas in many Peruvian cities. Many Peruvian churches bear the Spanish characteristic of intricate stonework and design on the façade (building exterior). Particularly noteworthy in Peruvian architecture is the city of Arequipa. Known as La Ciudad Blanca (The White City), the downtown area was built of a white, volcanic rock known as sillar. La Catedral and Santa Catalina are the two primary points of interest when touring the colonial buildings in downtown Arequipa. In fact, Arequipa's Plaza de Armas, which features La Catedral, has been designated a World Heritage Site by the United Nations Educational, Scientific and Cultural Organization (UNESCO).

In northeast Peru, most houses and buildings are built on stilts due to the risk of flooding in the Amazon basin. Modern Peruvian architecture has adopted modernist styles, including the vertical architecture of skyscrapers in Lima. However, this form is limited due to the prevalence of earthquakes. In addition, many modern buildings constructed in the 20th and early 21st centuries are characterized by eclecticism, or the combination of several architectural styles or theories.

Drama

Peru's early drama took place in religious settings, as morality plays and religious stories. Festivities during the Corpus Christi festival (60 days after Easter) often included plays staged in Lima's main plaza. As Peru's importance as a Spanish territory grew, Peruvians began to enjoy the work produced by those responsible for Spain's Golden Age, dramatists such as Pedro Calderón de la Barca (1600–1681) and Agustín Moreto y Cavana (1618–1669). The theater also supported work by local playwrights, even some in the Quechua language.

In the early 18th century, Marques de Castell dos Rius was appointed viceroy to Peru by Philip V. Upon his arrival in Peru, he established his own private theater within his palace. He commissioned members of his entourage to write plays for him, some of which still exist, such as *Love, the Ghost* (Amor el duende). Pedro de Peralta Barnuevo (1664–1743) rose to prominence under the viceroy's patronage by borrowing themes and stories from the work of others.

In the mid-18th century, an earthquake demolished a great portion of Lima, resulting in the reconstruction of El Coliseo, an early theater. This newly constructed theater, the New Coliseum, was completed in 1749. Another theater was built in 1793, where both Spanish and indigenous dramas were staged. Peru's successful fight for independence (1824) did nothing to hamper the dramatic scene in Lima. In fact, Peruvian theater flourished. Playwrights such as Felipe Pardo y Aliaza (1806–1868), Manuel Ascenzio Segura (1805–1871), and Pedro Paz Soldan (1839–1895) produced a great number of plays and created a strong and respected foundation for Peruvian theater.

The early 20th century was also a successful one for Peruvian drama, with playwrights such as Julio de la Paz (1888–1925) and Ladislao Meza (1892–1925) and Jose Chioino (1898–1960) ushering in a Modernist movement. In the mid-20th century, works by Sebastian Salazar Bondy (1924–1964) and Enrique Solari Swayne (1915–1995) explored darker topics of identity and disillusionment as well as proved a vehicle for social commentary. A National Theater was established and peripheral organizations supporting the dramatic arts began to emerge in the 1930s and 1940s, including the Association of Amateur Artists, the Theater of San Marcos University, the Actor's Union, and the National School of Scenic Art.

Music

Before Spanish colonization, Peruvian folk music typically involved many bamboo wind instruments. Later, the Spanish tradition of stringed instruments (guitar and violin) and the African emphasis on percussion combined to form the distinct sounds heard in Peru today.

Huayño is the popular folk music of the rural Andes Mountains. Typical instruments include the queñas (bamboo flute), zampoñas (panpipe) and charangos (stringed instrument). The typical dance resembled an American folk dance, with partners circling each other and linking arms. Chicha is a style of music believed to be derived from huayño and Colombian cumbia (folk music and dance). Chicha features surf guitars, synthesizers, and distinctive melodies. Música criolla and landó are two types of music developed by the Afro-Peruvian population incorporating the cajón, a wooden box sat on and used as a drum.

Generally, more typical forms of Latin music are popular on the radio and on dance floors in contemporary Peru. Colombian salsa and cumbia, as well as reggaeton from the Caribbean islands and Central America, are common.

Dance

A number of folk dances remain popular in Peru, including the Marinera, a courtship dance, which is practiced all over the country. The Tondero originated in the north and is a dance between couples, illustrating the pursuit of a chicken by a rooster. The Festejo Dance is a dance by black Peruvians that historically chronicles their struggles and triumphs. Other folk dances include the Alcatraz, Huaylash of Carnival, Carnival of Canas, Huayno Dance, and the Tarpuy Dance.

Literature

Peruvian literature is rooted in the oral traditions of pre-Columbian civilizations and the European influences of the country's colonial history. Early literature that developed in Peru often chronicled the region's history. One notable early Peruvian writer was Ricardo Palma (1833-1919), who wrote about colonial Peru and is credited with developing the tradiciónes (traditional) genre, short stories that combine fiction with history. Another prominent Peruvian writer was the poet José Santos Chocano (1875–1934).

Most famous among Peruvian artists is the writer and novelist, Mario Vargas Llosa (1936–), often considered one of the most significant Latin American authors of the 20th century. Vargas Llosa's more famous works include *La Ciudad Y Los Perros* (literally "The City and the Dogs," but published in English as "The Time of the Hero") and *La Fiesta Del Chivo* ("The Feast of the Goat"). The former is a novel inspired by Vargas Llosa's time at a military academy, and is critical of the military hierarchy and lack of personal growth. The latter describes the perspectives of different characters in different generations around the assassination of Dominican Republic dictator Rafael Leónidas Trujillo (1891–1961). In 2010, Llosa won the Nobel Prize in Literature.

Other famous Peruvian writers include Alfredo Bryce Echenique (b. 1939–), Julio Ramón Ribeyro (1929–1994), José Maria Arguedas (1911–1969), Ciro Alegría (1909–1967), and contemporary author Daniel Alarcón (b. 1977–). The most famous poet from Peru is Cesar Vallejo (1892–1938), who is considered one of the best Spanish-language poets of the 20th century.

CULTURE

Arts & Entertainment

The contemporary Peruvian art scene is very complex and diverse, thanks to the influence of various unique cultures over hundreds of years. These have included the Incas and pre-Columbian tribes of the region, the Spanish and other European cultures, the current indigenous peoples of the Andes and other rural areas, the Afro-Peruvian community in Lima, and the mainstream mestizo Hispanic culture. All of these have blended to create more of a collage of different styles rather than one "typical" Peruvian style.

Traditional musical instruments include flutes, panpipes, drums, guitars, fiddles, and horns. The national instrument is the charango, a type of mandolin. Important Peruvian cultural figures of the recent past include authors Mario Vargas Llosa (also an unsuccessful presidential candidate) and César Vallejo; artists José Carlos Ramos, José Sabogal, and Fernando de Szyszlo; and opera singer Luigi Alva.

As for contemporary television and cinema, the film industry remains somewhat underdeveloped in Peru. Peruvians generally watch movies from other countries, and television is mostly comprised of dubbed American shows or international Spanish language programs. While Peruvian cinema and television are completely undeveloped industries, Peru does have a thriving theater scene that has existed since Spanish colonization.

Sport entertainment is also popular. Peruvians are fond of football (soccer), volleyball, bullfighting, horse racing, and cockfighting.

Cultural Sites & Landmarks

Peruvian culture is derived from a mix of the Incas, the Spanish who colonized Peru, and the Hispanic character that has emerged since. As such, Peru has a rich cultural heritage. In addition to the historic center of Arequipa, Peru features nine other World Heritage Sites as designated by UNESCO. The country is also home to a diverse geography and numerous natural wonders, highlighted by the tropical Amazon rainforest, the extreme heights of the Andes Mountains, a Pacific Ocean coastline, and the Sechura Desert.

Machu Picchu, called the "Lost City of the Incas," is one of the most famous cultural and historic attractions in South America. The ruins lie in the Urubamba Valley, where the Andes converge with the Amazon rainforest. The city is a maze of intricate stonework and architecture set among the lush, green mountains of the region. The Incas kept Machu Picchu a secret from the Spaniards during the colonization of Peru, and the ancient city was eventually forgotten. In 1911, Hiram Bingham (1875–1956), an American explorer from Yale University, discovered the ruins, reportedly by accident. However, it was reported in June 2008 that a German businessman named Augusto Berns found Machu Picchu in 1867, looting and selling its artifacts in Europe. It is reported that an estimated 2,500 tourists visit Machu Picchu every day.

Cusco, a city of almost 350,000 in the Andes Mountains with an elevation over 3,322 meters (10,900 feet), was the ancient capital of the Inca Empire. It is often the starting point on the trek to Machu Picchu, and is also designated as a World Heritage Site. The cobblestone streets and Spanish architecture built on Incan stone foundations make Cusco into a year-round tourist destination. Another popular attraction outside the city is the statue of Cristo Blanco (White Christ), which overlooks the city.

Also located high in the Andes Mountains, along the border between Peru and Bolivia, is Lake Titicaca. At an average elevation of 3,657 meters (12,000 feet), it is the highest navigable lake in the world. Near the port city of Puno, the lake features man-made islets on which the people of the Uro tribe still maintain a traditional existence. It is said the native people made these islands to escape war with the Incas. Lake Titicaca is also home to the unchanged culture of the Taquile people. The Taquile are known for their rich textiles, and in 2005 their textile arts were proclaimed an Intangible Cultural Heritage by UNESCO.

Located in the desert south of Lima, along the Pacific coast, are the mysterious Nazca lines, 70 images that can be fully viewed only from above. It is believed the ancient Nazca culture (900 BC–600 CE) constructed these images—which include a spider, a condor, a lizard, a hummingbird and a human referred to as an astronaut—as a gift to the gods. The lines were made by removing dark gravel from the ground, exposing the lighter sand underneath. Since there is virtually no wind, the lines are still visible today, and are also designated as a World Heritage Site.

Libraries & Museums

The Pueblo Libre district is home to most of Lima's museums, including the Museo Nacional de Antropología, Arqueología e Historia, and the Museo de Oro del Perú, both of which have numerous artifacts from Lima's ancient civilizations on display.

Holidays

Holidays in Peru include religious and public holidays: Holy Week, a Christian Easter-week celebration in March and April; Feast of San Pedro y San Pablo, or Saints Peter and Paul (June 29); Peruvian Independence Day (July 28-29); the Feast of Santa Rosa de Lima, or Saint Rose of Lima (August 30); a commemoration of the Battle of Angamos, a naval battle in which Chile was victorious over Peru (October 8); and El Señor de los Milagros, or Lord of the Miracles (October 20).

Youth Culture

The youth culture of Peru is very typical of the rest of Latin America. Music and dancing is common at parties, and Peruvian youths enjoy a variety of music, including salsa, cumbia, chicha, reggaeton and American pop music. Because of the below average economic situation, most young people do not have the luxuries of computers and video games at home. However, every neighborhood of every city has Internet cafes with computers for rent. There are also houses which rent time on Xbox, Playstation and other popular video game consoles. Football

(soccer) remains the most popular sport by far. However, Peru's national teams are rarely competitive, and haven't qualified for a World Cup since 1982.

Private school enrollment is much more common in Peru. Because many Peruvian families do not earn much money, several private institutions cater to these families by offering lower tuition costs. All schools—public and private—require students to wear school uniforms. Education is mandatory for 11 years, and most Peruvian youths graduate high school at 16 years of age.

Gang activity is an unfortunate byproduct of Peru's economic conditions. Young people in big cities often join gangs to avoid dysfunctional family lives, to earn desperately needed money, or to gain respect in a society which many Peruvians believe doesn't afford much opportunity for the disadvantaged poor.

SOCIETY

Transportation

Transportation is a difficult area to improve in Peru because of its geographic extremes. The Andes and the Amazon rainforest are almost impenetrable by highways or railroads. As such, plane travel is necessary in many parts of Peru. The Pan American Highway, which runs from Ecuador to Chile, cuts through Peru. Most other freeways are poorly maintained, and accidents, often fatal, are not uncommon. Drivers in Peru travel on the right

None of the major cities in Peru have a light rail train system, so getting around can be difficult. However, taxi fares in all the cities besides Lima are typically inexpensive. Cities do have public transportation in the form of buses, called combis. The size of these buses ranges from that of a 15-passenger van to old Volkswagen (VW) buses. The insides are hollowed out with benches against the walls and rails along the ceilings for standing passengers. Passengers enter through a door behind the driver's seat, which is managed by a cobrador, or attendant. The cobrador is responsible for collecting money and announcing the destination to pedestrians on the street. However, combis can be extremely crowded and uncomfortable.

Transportation Infrastructure

Lima's public transit system is somewhat antiquated, including the oldest rail line in South America. The city streets are generally overcrowded with cars and buses, which tend to be small and poorly maintained. The need for better public transportation has led to a thriving amateur taxi industry. Plans for more sophisticated subway and/or elevated train systems have been proposed, but little progress has been made since the 1990s.

In 2009, the Peruvian government announced that it would invest about $3.3 billion (USD) in transport infrastructure. The nation's port authority, the Autoridad Portuaria Nacional (APN), announced that its 2009 investment would result in about $1 billion (USD) in port improvements; it is also moving towards privatization of port concessions. Construction on the Trans-Oceanic or Inter-Oceanic Highway is nearly complete as of early 2015. The road will connect Brazil and Peru and facilitate commercial traffic between the two nations. Concerns have been raised over the environmental impact of this project.

Media & Communications

The Peruvian constitution guarantees free speech for media and private individuals. However, the government has taken questionable steps in silencing critics throughout its history. The press was particularly censored in the 1970s under the rule of a military junta, and journalists faced severe penalties for criticizing the government. Reporters suffered more subtle forms of intimidation during the 1990s as well, under the Fujimori government. In the 21st century, the government generally respects the right to free speech.

El Peruano, founded in 1825 by Simón Bolívar (1783–1830), an important figure in Latin America's independence, is Peru's oldest newspaper and the official government paper. *El Comercio* and *La República* are also among Peru's most respected newspapers, with

El Comercio having the widest circulation among the three. Peru also has numerous tabloid style newspapers, characterized by their graphic and racy content. These tabloids can be seen on almost every city corner, displayed on the counters and walls of street vendors.

Because of the high levels of poverty, radio is the most important communications medium in Peru. Many people cannot afford televisions or Internet-connected computers. As such, every city features many radio stations for music and talk, and new frequencies are often not available to be licensed. A little more than 25 percent of the population has Internet access, although an expanded Internet network is gradually developing.

SOCIAL DEVELOPMENT

Standard of Living

Peru ranked 82 out of 187 on the 2014 United Nations Human Development Index, a global standard of living indicator.

Water Consumption

According to the World Health Organization and UNICEF in 2014, 85 percent of Peruvians had access to clean water and 71 percent had access to improved sanitation. These numbers fail to account for the disparity between urban and rural populations, as well as economic disparities. Ninety-one percent of the urban population had improved access to water compared to 65 percent of the rural population. In terms of sanitation, 81 percent of the urban population enjoyed improved sanitation to 38 percent of the rural population. Within cities, socioeconomic factors have an impact on access to water, with entire neighborhoods lacking access and suffering from higher prices for water. Peru faces challenges in terms of sanitation as well, with three quarters of wastewater going untreated.

Education

Peru's constitution allows for free and compulsory schooling from the primary school level through age 16. As of 2013, the literacy rate among Peruvians is an impressive 89.6 percent, nearly double the rate during the 1950s. Rural Peruvians are less likely to attend high school because of the lack of regional educational resources, but a high percentage of urban Peruvians attend secondary school.

Among the country's most important colleges and universities are the National University of San Marcos in Lima (also one of its oldest), the National University of Central Peru in Huancayo, the National University of San Agustin in Arequipa, and the National University of San Antonio Abad in Cusco.

Women's Rights

Women do have the right to vote in Peru. In fact, voting is mandatory for all adults between the ages of 18 and 70. However, Peru's record on women's rights is generally regarded as poor. On average, the female literacy rate in Peru is lower than the male rate. In addition, rape, domestic violence, and general abuse against women have long been a problem in Peru. In fact, a 2012 survey reported that 62 percent of Peruvian women had been battered, and 47 percent were abused sexually. Complicating matters is the fact that prosecuting abusers and rapists has proved ineffective.

Another study showed that single mother households were twice as likely to live in extreme poverty—defined as families of four surviving on $1 (USD) per day—than households headed by single men. Politically, women have some representation. However, there are many regions with no women representatives. As of 2013, according to a report by the World Economic Forum, Peru ranked 80 out of 131 countries in terms of gender equality.

Moreover, Human Rights Watch has criticized the government of Peru for not providing adequate access to therapeutic abortion. (Therapeutic abortion is an abortion performed in order to save the mother's life, or because giving birth would endanger the mother's health.) In addition, maternal mortality rates are among the highest in Latin America, and sexual harassment

in the workplace has only recently been made illegal, though critics have argued that the law is rarely applied. Prostitution is legal in Peru for women 18 years of age or older.

One important front in the struggle for women's rights concerns domestic workers. Domestic service is largely an undesirable job, usually entailing difficult job conditions. Most domestic servants work seven days per week, and many do not earn a salary. Instead, they work for room and board. Peruvian law guarantees one day of rest for these women, as well as a monetary benefit. However, these laws have proven difficult to enforce. Peruvian law also requires the host family to provide health care for the domestic servant. However, it is estimated that less than half of domestic servants actually have health care.

From 1996 through 2000, the Fujimori government led a campaign to sterilize poor, rural women of Peru. According to the British Broadcasting Corporation (BBC), government doctors performed approximately 215,227 sterilizing operations on women and 16,547 male vasectomies. Witnesses claimed that they were deceived about the nature of the operation, while others said they were offered financial incentives and food. Still others claimed to have been threatened with fines if they did not undergo the operation. The sterilization campaign was eventually dropped due to international pressure and criticism.

Health Care

A very high percentage of Peruvians are impoverished (as much as half the population, by some estimates), and many do not have adequate health care. Many have little or no access to primary health care services. As a result of some government health reforms, infant, and maternal death rates have decreased since the 1990s. Universal health care for Peruvians may be a goal of the government, but it is far from becoming a reality. The total health expenditure per capita is far below many other countries in the region (but above Nicaragua, Bolivia and Haiti). The average life expectancy among Peruvians was 73 years in 2014.

GOVERNMENT

Structure

Peru, a constitutional republic, is divided into 25 regiones (regions) and one constitutional province (Lima). The government is divided into executive, legislative and judicial branches.

The president, or constitutional president, of Peru is its chief of state and head of the government; there are also two vice presidents. The president is elected to one five-year term and may seek non-consecutive re-election. The Cabinet of Ministers and the prime minister are appointed by the president.

The legislative branch is comprised of the Congreso, a unicameral congress made up of representatives who serve five-year terms.

Political Parties

The country's most powerful political parties include the Union for Peru (Union por el Peru), a liberal/centrist party, and the Partido Aprista Peruana party (also known as the American Popular Revolutionary Alliance), a center-left party. In the 2011 congressional election, Peru Wins, dominated by the Peruvian Nationalist Party garnered 47 seats and Froce 2011, dominated by National Renewal took 37 seats. Electoral Alliance Possible Peru took 21 seats, the Alliance for Change took 12 seats, the National Solidarity Alliance took nine seats and the American Popular Revolutionary Alliance took four seats.

Local Government

The country is divided into 25 regions and the province of Lima. Regions are divided into provinces, and provinces are divided into districts, each having its own mayor and council. Lima is also subdivided into smaller districts, each with its own mayor and councils.

Judicial System

The highest judicial court in Peru is the Supreme Court, members of which are appointed by the National Council of the Judiciary. Lower courts include the magistrate courts, which handle civil matters and minor infractions of the law, and courts of first instance, which handle criminal, labor, and family matters according to their territory and area of specialty. Appellate courts are located in regional centers and hear appeals cases from the lower courts.

Taxation

Peru levies income, corporate, value-added, and excise taxes.

Armed Forces

The Peruvian Armed Forces are comprised of an army, navy, and air force.

Foreign Policy

Since its emergence as an independent nation, Peru has been perceived as an important and leading voice for developing countries worldwide. Of particular importance to Peru are its economic and political relations with its Latin American neighbors and its good standing with the U.S. This relationship has been marked by controversy due to the prevalence of the illicit drug trade in Latin America. Peru remains a member of the United Nations (UN) since 1949, and is also a member of several international economic and trade groups, including Asia-Pacific Economic Cooperation (APEC), Free Trade Area of the Americas (FTAA), and the World Trade Organization (WTO).

One of the most important aspects of Peru's foreign policy is its border relations with immediate neighbors. Because of the difficult terrain in South America, and because of Latin America's relatively late independence from Spain, territorial disputes were common in the 19th century. Evidence of these disputes is still present in today's foreign relations.

Peru and Ecuador were involved in a long-lasting dispute over a small section of land which lasted from the early 1800s until 1998. The territory in question was mostly rainforest that is difficult to navigate. However, the land was rich in natural resources. The area was originally discovered and recognized as territory of Quito, which was a part of Gran Colombia in the early

19th century. When Gran Colombia was split up, Quito became a part of Ecuador. The disputed area, however, was separated from the rest of Ecuador by the Andes Mountains. Therefore, the area was primarily inhabited and settled by Peruvians from the south, who clearly expressed their desire to be a part of Peru.

A series of treaties failed to resolve the dispute, which resulted in several conflicts: the Ecuadorian-Peruvian War (1858–1859), the Ecuador-Peru War (1941), the Paquisha War (1981), and the Cenepa War (1995). In fact, former U.S. President Bill Clinton, once referred to the dispute as the longest running armed conflict in the Western Hemisphere. Eventually mediated by Brazil, Argentina, Chile, and the U.S., the two sides signed a lasting treaty to end the dispute on October 26, 1998.

Peru also fought a territorial war against Chile from 1879 to 1883. Peru and Bolivia fought together against Chile for control of the Atacama Desert. Chile handily defeated both countries and even occupied the Peruvian capital of Lima for a short time. Chile gained several concessions and Bolivia actually lost access to the Pacific Ocean in the resolution.

Peruvian foreign policy has also been often overshadowed by Sendero Luminoso, or Shining Path. The Shining Path is a guerilla army dedicated to overthrowing the government of Peru. It has been designated a terrorist organization by the United States, the European Union (EU) and Canada due to its participation in drug trafficking, extortion, and kidnapping, and its disregard for civilian casualties. It is believed that an estimated 18,000 people were killed in the civil war from 1980 to 1990. Some estimates of those killed to date are as high as 70,000. The Shining Path's socialist movement was never popular in Peru. However, it has survived on raising funds from drug trafficking and gaining recruits disgruntled with unequal economic conditions and little opportunity.

During President Alan Garcia's first term (1985–1990), the government took a confrontational stance against countries such as U.S. Peru refused to pay its debts and vocally supported socialist insurgencies such as the Sandinistas in Central America. While Alberto Fujimori's government (1990–2000) attempted to repair relations, most developed nations withheld aid and decried his authoritarian and heavy-handed rule. However, the end of the drug trade was important to the U.S., and relations were eventually normalized. Garcia was reelected to the presidency in 2006. During his second term he sought to repair relations with Venezuela and Chile, and signed a free trade deal with the U.S. Since his election in 2011, President Ollanta Humala has worked to better relations across the region making state visits to countries including Brazil, Bolivia, Venezuela, and the United States.

Human Rights Profile

International human rights law insists that states respect civil and political rights, and also promote an individual's economic, social and cultural rights. The United Nations Universal Declaration on Human Rights (UDHR) is recognized as the standard for international human rights. Its authors sought the counsel of the world's great thinkers, philosophers, and religious leaders, and were careful to create a document that reflects the core values shared by every world culture. To read this document or view the articles relating to cultural human rights, click here: http://www.udhr.org/UDHR/default.htm.

Since the escalation of internal conflict in Peru in the latter half of the 20th century, Peru has frequently been brought to task by numerous international monitoring agencies over the violation of human rights. According to Human Rights Watch, though the government's conflict with Shining Path ended in 2000, injustices during the war remain to be accounted. The Truth and Reconciliation Commission estimates almost 70,000 were killed in the insurgency—half by the terrorist group and a third by government organizations.

During this conflict, President Alberto Fujimori was widely criticized for human rights abuses and oppressive policies—often entailing massacres and kidnapping—in his efforts to defeat Shining Path. His policies were criticized as clear violations of Articles 2, 3, 5 and 10 of the UDHR. Fujimori fled Peru to Japan after resigning the presidency. He has since been extradited and is awaiting trial for the arbitrary execution of over 15 people. However, military officers and members of death squads are still sought by human rights activists in an attempt to bring them to justice for crimes committed during the war.

Additionally, the intimidation of journalists has been a human rights concern in Peru. This issue was highlighted by the murder of Miguel Perez Julca, a radio journalist reporting on police corruption, in March 2007. Torture, a violation of Article 5, is also a problem as police and military personnel have received accusations of beatings and other forms of torture. Accused persons are often beaten when they are detained, and abuse of recruits is reported to be widespread in the military. Furthermore, authorities responsible for such torture and abuse are rarely held accountable.

Some witnesses to human rights abuses have claimed to have been intimidated or threatened by police and military forces. Conditions in Peruvian prisons are particularly dire. Overcrowding, lack of sanitation and health care, abuse from guards and fellow inmates, and poor nutrition are the norm. In addition, prison guards have been routinely accused of abusing inmates.

Generally, Peru's constitution is sound, and aligned with the principals of the UDHR. Arbitrary arrest, search, or entering one's home by police is illegal, and free speech and freedom of the press are guaranteed. The constitution also guarantees freedom of assembly. In fact, protests are quite common in Peru and occur much more frequently than in the United States. There is freedom of religion, although some have criticized the government for giving favorable policies (via benefits and taxation) to the Catholic Church. Though Peru prohibits discrimination based on race, sex, language and social status, enforcement against discrimination has been criticized as questionable. All of these basic freedoms have been infringed upon to different extents in recent history. However, most experts see the basic rights situation as improving.

Migration

Peru's net migration rate in 2014 is −2.69 per 1,000.

ECONOMY

Overview of the Economy

As a result of increased foreign and domestic investment in several sectors, Peru's economy is considered one of the best-managed and robust in South America.

The gross domestic product (GDP) per capita was an estimated $11,100 USD in 2013. The labor force of Peru is estimated at 10.3 million, with a nationwide unemployment rate of just over 3.6 percent (2012 estimate).

Lima is a major port city, was well as a major business center. It is Peru's financial and industrial hub, accounting for two-thirds of the country's gross domestic product (GDP). Most of Lima's industry is centered in the Callao-Lima-Vitarte corridor, and includes shipbuilding, oil refining, food processing, and manufacturing. The city's major products are cement, chemicals, pharmaceuticals, plastics, textiles, clothing, and furniture. Another of the city's major exports is gold, although the supply of the precious metal is less now than it was in the colonial era.

Industry

Important industries in Peru include nonferrous metals and nonmetallic mineral mining (including copper, gold and silver), petroleum and natural gas, fishing (with anchovies being a significant part of the catch) and fish meal, textiles, and food and clothing manufacture. Peruvian exports include coffee, petroleum, minerals, plastics, and machinery.

Peru's major export partners include the United States, Great Britain, China, Switzerland and Chile. The mining and mineral sectors of the economy have grown in recent years, while the energy industries have been in decline since the 1980s.

Labor

Lima's job market has been struggling since the 1990s, when many of the traditionally state-run companies were sold to private entrepreneurs. A devastating recession that lasted from 1997 to 1999 left half the population living below the poverty line. Most of Peru's manufacturers are located in Lima, due to the abundance of available laborers, but they are unable to employ all the Limeños (residents of Lima) seeking work. Roughly 75 percent of Peruvians work in the service industry.

Energy/Power/Natural Resources

The main natural resources of Peru include copper, silver, iron ore, gold, zinc, petroleum, timber (including cedar and mahogany), fish, coal, phosphate, potash, hydropower and natural gas.

Areas of environmental concern include deforestation from logging in the tropical rainforests, overgrazing in the coastal and sierra regions, desertification and soil erosion, water and air pollution (particularly in urban and industrial centers, such as Lima), and over-fishing.

Fishing

Peru claims to provide 10 percent of the world's fish catch. It is also a major exporter of fishmeal and fish oil. Privatization in port industries has allowed for increased investment and the fishing industry is credited with bringing currency from exports into the country as well as creating much-needed jobs. The fishing industry in Peru is strongly affected by El Niño, a climate pattern that has an impact on nutrient rich waters and fish harvests.

Forestry

Peru boasts the fourth largest area of rainforests in the world. The country's deforestation can be attributed to subsistence farming and forests can be said to recover from that use. Illegal logging, commercial agriculture, mining and gas exploration, and development are threats to rainforests.

Mining/Metals

Alluvial gold mining is a growing industry and a growing environmental threat to Peru. According to the BBC in 2009, the Peruvian government had granted 1,500 jungle mining licenses to energy and mineral mining companies. Its mining sector is dependent on the export of copper, zinc, gold, iron, and petroleum.

Agriculture

The main agricultural products in Peru include coffee, seed cotton, potatoes, sugarcane, rice, corn, and wheat. The coca plant is also widely grown for its traditional, medicinal uses. Since the plant is also used in the manufacture of cocaine, coca cultivation has come under closer scrutiny in recent years.

Animal Husbandry

The most important livestock raised in Peru include cattle, goats, pigs, horses, mules, and chickens. Also important to Peruvian agriculture are the hides and wool of sheep, llamas and vicuñas, used to make clothing for export.

Tourism

The tourism industry, in terms of profitability, is the second most important in Peru, behind mining. In recent years, Peru has experienced a large increase in tourism, with visits from 2.3 million people in 2010. Increased investments, both foreign and domestic, promise to expand the tourist industry even more.

Popular tourist destinations in Peru include the former capital of the Inca, Cusco (also spelled Cuzco). Near Cusco is Machu Picchu, or the "lost city of the Incas," a remote site that was only "discovered" in 1911. Ecotourists may also visit sites in the Amazon basin region, high in the Andes, or travel to islands in the middle of Lake Titicaca.

Colin Post, Craig Belanger, Alex K. Rich

DO YOU KNOW?

- The Quechua language has given us the English words "condor," "guano," "gaucho," "jerky" and "potato."

- An earthquake in 1950 exposed ancient Inca ruins in the city of Cusco.

- The guinea pig, or cuy, is found not only on the Peruvian table, but in the country's art as well. Throughout Peru, depictions of the Last Supper show Christ and his disciples dining on this traditional dish.

- Lima is the capital of Peru, and its name comes from the Quechua word for "talker," although the city is often known by its nickname, El Pulpo ("The Octopus"), so called because of its sprawling landscape and cultural influence.

Bibliography

Drinot, Paulo. *The Allure of Labor: Workers, Race, and the Making of the Peruvian State.* Durham, NC: Duke University Press, 2011.

Fodor's. *Fodor's Peru.* New York: Fodor's 2013.

Gray, Andrew. *Indigenous Rights and Development: Self-determination in an Amazonian Community.* New York: Berghahn Books, 1997.

Hudson, Rex A. *Peru: A Country Study.* Washington: GPO for the Library of Congress, 1992.

Lonely Planet. *Peru.* London: Lonely Planet, 2013.

Saona, Margarita. *Memory Matters in Transitional Peru.* Houndmills, Basingstoke, Hampshire: Palgrave Macmillan, 2014.

Starn, Orin, et al. *The Peru Reader: History, Culture, Politics.* Durham, NC: Duke University Press, 2005.

Theidon, Kimberly. *Intimate Enemies: Violence and Reconciliation in Peru.* Philadelphia: University of Pennsylvania Press, 2013.

Works Cited

Chauvin, Lucien. "Helping Peru's 'Invisible' Women." 14 September 2005. BBC News. http://news.bbc.co.uk/2/hi/americas/4222402.stm

Collyns, Dan. "Machu Picchu ruin 'found earlier'." BBC News June 2008: 1. BBC News, Lima. http://news.bbc.co.uk/1/hi/world/americas/7439397.stm

Hudson, Rex. "Peru – Foreign Relations." Library of Congress. http://countrystudies.us/peru/96.htm

Hudson, Rex. "Peru – Shining Path and Its Impact." Library of Congress. http://countrystudies.us/peru/96.htm

"Mass Sterilisation Scandal Shocks Peru." 24 July 2002. BBC News. http://news.bbc.co.uk/2/hi/americas/2148793.stm

Parker, Emily. "Storyteller." June 23, 2007. The Wall Street Journal. http://opinionjournal.com/editorial/feature.html?id=110010248

"Peru." *CIA World Factbook.* Washington, DC: CIA, 2014. https://www.cia.gov/library/publications/the-world-factbook/

"Peru." *Nations of the World.* Amenia, NY: Grey House Publishing, 2015.

"Peru: Country Reports on Human Rights Practices." 25 February 2004. U.S. Department of State. http://www.state.gov/g/drl/rls/hrrpt/2003/27916.htm

"Peru Internet Usage and Market Report." Internet World Stats. http://www.internetworldstats.com/sa/pe.htm

Ramos, José. José Carlos Ramos. http://www.artistajosecarlosramos.com/

Simmons, Beth A. "Territorial Disputes and Their Resolution, The Case of Ecuador and Peru." April 1999. United States Institute of Peace. http://www.usip.org/pubs/peaceworks/pwks27/chap3_27.html

"The Pisco, Peru, Earthquake of August 15, 2007." October 2007. Earthquake Engineering Research Institute. http://www.eeri.org/lfe/pdf/peru_pisco_eeri_preliminary_reconnaissance.pdf

"World Report: Peru." Human Rights Watch. http://hrw.org/englishwr2k8/docs/2008/01/31/peru17774.htm

Zegarra Ciguero, Luis and Gladys Villa Garcia. "Affordable, Quake-proof Adobe Housing in Peru." International Development Research Centre. http://www.idrc.ca/en/ev-2689-201-1-DO_TOPIC.html

Children from Suriname/Stock Photo © BartCo

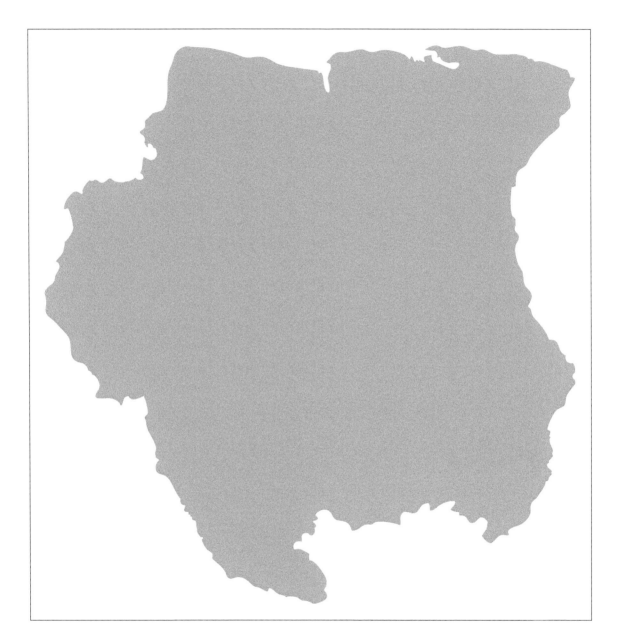

SURINAME

Introduction

Suriname, a former colony of the Netherlands called Dutch Guiana, is officially known as the Republic of Suriname ("Republiek Suriname"). It is one of the smallest South American countries, and is situated on the northeastern coast of South America.

The country is known for its vast rain forests, and for preserving and integrating African traditions in its culture. Historically, it has had a diverse ethnic and racial population and this racial segmentation permeates the country's culture and politics. The recent return to power of former despot Desi Bouterse has made some nervous about Suriname's prospects.

GENERAL INFORMATION

Official Language: Dutch
Population: 573,311 (2014 estimate)
Currency: Suriname Dollar
Coins: One hundred cents equal one Surinamese dollar. Coins are issued in denominations of 1, 5, 10, and 25 cents, as well as 1 and 2 ½ dollars.
Land Area: 156,000 square kilometers (60,231 square miles)
Water Area: 7,820 square kilometers (3,019 square miles)
National Anthem: "God zij met ons Suriname" ("God be with our Suriname")
Capital: Paramaribo
Time Zone: GMT -3

Flag Description: Suriname's flag features five horizontal stripes, a thicker red stripe in the center, flanked by thinner white stripes above and below, with wide green stripes on the top and bottom of the flag. A yellow star, symbolizing the country's ethnic groups, is centered on the red stripe. The red in the flag represents progress and love, the white stands for peace and justice, and the green stands for fertility and hope.

Population

Suriname's population is a mixture of ethnic groups, the largest of which are the Hindustani or East Indian group (37 percent) Creoles, and people of mixed race (31 percent). Other groups include the Javanese (15 percent), Maroons (10 percent), Amerindians (two percent), and Chinese (two percent). The country's mixed ethnic heritage reflects its history of plantation slavery.

Descendents of escaped African slaves in Suriname are known as Maroons. The Maroons

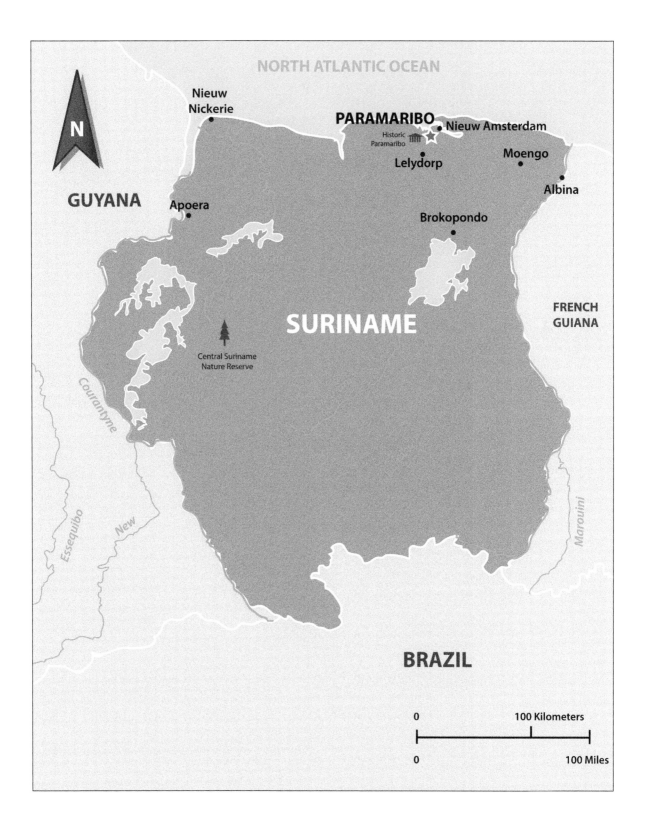

Principal Districts (with capital if applicable) by Population (2012):

- Paramaribo (246,132)
- Lelydorp (19,991)
- Nieuw-Nickerie (15,109)
- Moengo (8,252)
- Meerzog (7,381)
- Nieuw Amsterdam (5, 579)
- Marienburg (4,998)
- Wageningen (4,765)

may be divided into six subgroups: the Saramaka, Ndjuka, Matawai, Aluku (Boni), Paramaka, and Kwinti. The Maroon population continues to live in small communities in forested areas, relying on small-scale farming, hunting, and trading to survive. Maroons practice a religion called Winti, which derives from West African religions.

Most of Suriname's population lives in the north along the coast and in the urban center of the capital, Paramaribo.

Languages

While Dutch is the official language of Suriname, a number of languages are spoken there. Among these are English, Hindustani, Javanese, and Chinese or Hakka. Because of its ethnic diversity, there are also many Creole languages spoken in the country, including Sranan-Tongo or Surinamese, Paramakan, Ndjuka, Aluku, and Kwinti. Sranan-Tongo is a mixture of English, Dutch, Portuguese, and African.

Native People & Ethnic Groups

The earliest native people known to dwell in Suriname were an Amerindian people called the Surinas. Among other local tribes were the Arawak, Carib, and Warrau (Awarao) Indians, who called their land Guiana. The native people fought the early efforts of British explorers to establish colonies on their land.

British colonists finally succeeded in settling the land in 1650. They established sugar plantations there, and relied on African slaves to work the farms. Later, the Dutch Netherlands obtained

the region from Great Britain through the Treaty of Breda (1667). The Dutch became the primary European group and ruling class. They continued to import African slaves to work on the sugar plantations.

Creoles, or people of mixed race, were often descendents of slaves and slave owners. With the abolition of slavery in 1863, Chinese, Hindustanis, and Indonesians arrived as indentured servants to help support the agricultural industry.

Religions

Several different religions are practiced in Suriname, such as Hinduism, Islam, Judaism, and Roman Catholicism. African religious traditions are sometimes practiced along with Christianity among the Creole and Maroon people. Winti, a uniquely Afro-Surinamese religion, is practiced by the descendants of African slaves or Maroons.

Climate

Suriname has a tropical climate, with a rainforest climate along coast. The minor rainy season lasts from December to February, while the minor dry season extends from February to April. The major rainy season typically lasts from April to August, and the major dry season from August to December.

The warmest month in Suriname is September, while January is the coldest. However, the country's average temperature remains fairly constant at 27° Celsius (81° Fahrenheit). The temperature varies slightly, but Suriname does not see extreme high or low temperatures. The temperature generally falls several degrees at night, and fluctuates during the colder months. The country tends to have high humidity.

ENVIRONMENT & GEOGRAPHY

Topography

Suriname is bordered by the Atlantic Ocean to the north, by French Guiana to the east, and by Guyana to the west. Brazil lies to the south.

The northern part of Suriname is made up of sedimentary rock. The south tends to have higher elevations. There are a number of large rivers running from south to north, including the Marowyne, the Commewyne, the Suriname, the Sarramacca, and the Nickerie.

Suriname may be divided into three vegetative zones. The coastal plain in the north consists of sandbanks and mud banks, with few sandy beaches. This area is covered predominantly with salt marsh vegetation. The New Coastal Plain (17,000 square kilometers or 6,563 square miles), consists of clay, peat, marshes, and quartz sand ridges; it features the best agricultural land in the country. The Old Coastal Plain (4,000 square kilometers or 1,544 square miles), is a combination of swamps and dry ground, and also features valuable agricultural land. Most of Suriname's population lives in the New and Old Coastal Plains.

The second zone is composed of savannas and open land, while the third zone is mountainous and is located in the interior of the country. Much of the indigenous population still lives in the mountains and the forested interior. The highest mountain in the country is Juliana Peak at 1,280 meters/4,120 feet, located in the Wilhelmina Mountain range.

The sparsely populated south consists of savannas, tropical rainforest, and swamps. The Tumuc-Humac Mountain chain and the Sipalwani Plain, a savanna near the Brazilian border, are located there. Forests and jungles cover most of the country's land area.

Plants & Animals
Suriname's rainforests contain a high degree of biodiversity and are home to a number of animals, including howler monkeys, tarantulas, termites, crocodiles, and piranhas. The country's many snake species include anacondas and boa constrictors, which live in swampy habitats. There are four species of sea turtle that nest in Suriname, including the Oliver Ridley turtle.

Common plants include tropical trees such as pina palm, groenheart, ingipipa, letterhout/snakewood, cedar, and purpleheart. Various species of cactus, orchids, and fungi also grow in Suriname. Flowers that are found in Suriname include the Heisteria cauliflora, the Passiflora gladulosa,

and Ipomoea quamoclit. Because much of the interior remains unexplored, there are species of plant that have not yet been identified.

The country has set aside land for nature reserves, such as the Brownsberg Nature Park, the Central Suriname Wilderness Nature Reserve, and the Galibi Nature Reserve.

CUSTOMS & COURTESIES

Greetings
In Paramaribo and in river towns such as Albina and Nieuw-Nickerie, the handshake is considered the appropriate greeting. An accompanying "Hallo hoe gaat het?"("Hi, how is it going?") is the formal Surinamese greeting. Informally, many Surinamers use the Maroon street language, known as taki-taki, by greeting friends with "Fawaka?" ("How is it?"). When saying goodbye, Surinamers use the Dutch "Tot Ziens" ("See you soon"), while "Mo Syi" ("See you soon") is also widely used. Unlike other Latin American countries, males rarely kiss or embrace each other when greeting, while females customarily kiss each other three times, as is done in the Netherlands.

The interior of Suriname is dominated by rivers and walking paths which makes social interaction difficult. While a formal handshake is allowed, greetings are more distant, since most indigenous inlanders or Maroons tend to be naturally distrustful toward strangers. While more than 20 different languages are spoken in the interior, the Dutch phrase "Goedendag" ("Good day") is generally understood.

Gestures & Etiquette
The Surinamese have such ethnic diversity that it is difficult to isolate one gesture or identify common behaviors. However, the Surinamese enjoy joking about their differences and generally have a good sense of humor. Jokes about cultural differences between the Surinamese are quite common, and are rarely made with hostility. The Surinamese are also not very punctual with appointments or dates.

Punctuality is considered a trait carried over from colonial times and most Surinamese work according to their own private schedule. Sunday is considered a rest day for all ethnicities, though recent Chinese immigrants have their shops and restaurants open every day of the week.

Eating/Meals

Eating in Suriname is heavily influenced by the country's multicultural heritage. Breakfast, called "ontbijt" in Dutch, tends to be a light meal consisting of bread filled with curry-styled chicken and a cup of black coffee (blaka) or juice like fresh gembersap (ginger beer) or sinaasappelsap (orange juice).

Lunch is the principal meal of the day and, depending on socioeconomics, is commonly bought from vendors outside of the house or cooked by domestic servants. Traditionally, lunch was consumed at home and with the family. Due to the climate and noontime temperatures, a traditional midday nap would follow lunch. Dinner, called "avondeten" in Dutch, is typically a simple meal consumed sitting around a table during the work week, and may consist of leftovers from lunch or simple sandwiches.

Visiting

Visiting friends and family is regarded as a familial obligation for children living outside the family home. Most Surinamese pass their holidays and weekends at the family home. People who live in urban areas may only make it home on religious holidays such as Christmas, a voyage which can be an undertaking due to the terrain and poor infrastructure of the country. When invited to a Surinamese house, both rural and urban, it is common practice to bring an alcoholic beverage as a gift.

LIFESTYLE

Family

Traditionally, the Surinamese enjoy close familial ties across all ethnic groups. However, traditional family structures have undergone broad

changes due to the mass migrations since 1975 due to internal political conflict. In December 1982, 15 opponents of the military regime were murdered by troops, among them were lawyers, journalists, academics, businessmen, and military personnel. After many years of strife, the Decembermoorden (December killings) divided the country and many, including entire families, fled the country for the Netherlands. Even larger was the migration of young people to the Netherlands, which left elder Surinamese family members behind. While annual return visits to Suriname peak during Easter and Christmas, this emigration from Suriname has disrupted the more traditional family structures that previously existed in Suriname.

Within indigenous communities, mostly located in the tropical forest reserves, families are traditionally organized into a greater tribal family and live communally. While some younger indigenous people have moved to Paramaribo in recent years, the majority continue to live within their tribes and are closed off from the rest of Suriname. Similarly, the Maroon communities have large family ties that connect the individual to dozens of aunts, uncles, and cousins. This kinship between individuals makes for a broad definition of family. Generally, a family name with many members signifies a financially independent and successful family. Elders are treated respectfully and sought out for advice and guidance by the young.

Hindus, like their ancestors from northern India, have kept weekend traditions of large meal feasts with the extended families. They bring a similar approach to large public marriages and celebrations. In recent years, they have incorporated other cultural trends into their family lives and rituals. Women, for example, are no longer kept under tight social restrictions. However, this is mainly a trend in the capital area of Paramaribo.

Housing

Colonial history has added interesting value to much of Surinamese architecture. The historic inner city of Paramaribo consists of three-story wooden buildings, built in the 18th and 19th century. These are protected as a UNESCO World Heritage Site. A colony primarily built around plantations, Suriname today contains the dilapidated ruins of many large wooden plantation houses, a central part of the enormous tobacco, banana, and rice plantations that thrived there. Even today, most of Surinamese housing is constructed of wood.

Apartment complexes or high office buildings are seldom seen in Suriname. The inner city of Suriname is protected from renovation but areas outside the city center have allowed some small office parks to develop. The construction of the Jules Wijdenbosch Bridge (also known as the Suriname Bridge) over the Suriname River has led to some redevelopment on the outskirts of Paramaribo. This new redevelopment area has resulted in a healthier demographic composition. Longstanding, heavily overcrowded slums are being vacated as more people move to the outskirts for more room and better economic opportunity.

Food

Surinamese cuisine is a blend of various tastes and dishes that reflect the staples of Asian, Indian, American, and European culinary traditions. A major part of the Surinamese diet is rice, which provides a base for the meal. Moksi alesi ("mixed rice"), a quasi-national dish, is enjoyed by members of all different ethnicities in Suriname. It is flavored with rice, tomato paste, chilies, coconut milk, meat, fish and various beans and other legumes. Stewed in a pot for several hours, this spicy rice dish is an inexpensive lunch.

Both pom and pastei are believed to have been brought to Suriname by Jewish settlers in the 18th century. Pom is a type of potato dumpling made from either cassava or sweet potato. Boiled at first, the pom is then either deep-fried or baked until a crisp crust forms on the outside of the dumpling. Pastei is a chicken dish that is made by cooking the breast and drumsticks into a broth and then adding onions, peppers, and carrots. The chicken and vegetables are then molded into a pie and baked in an oven for several hours.

The Javanese of Suriname brought many of the tastes and flavors of Indonesia to the country. Two popular dishes often found in the Paramaribo are "nasi goring" and "bami goring." Nasi goring is Indonesian fried rice stuffed with seafood, meats, and various vegetables, while bami goreng is a similar dish served with a broad flat Indonesian rice noodle. Numerous Javanese warungs (food stalls) are found in city streets and typically serve both dishes.

Hindus in Suriname have added to Surinamese cuisine by introducing rotie, a special sort of thin pancake usually accompanied by a curry meat dish. Spicy and tasty, rotie comes filled with the Indian masala ingredient and is widely sold as rotie-kip kerrie (roti with curry flavoured chicken), rotie-warm vlees (roti with sour sweet pork, fried Chinese style), or rotie egg (roti with eggs and South Asian spices and herbs). In addition, Hindus have provided numerous curries to flavor rice and fish dishes.

Life's Milestones

In Suriname, many milestones are specific to certain ethnic groups. For example, a majority of Surinamese are Christian and observe baptism soon after a child is born. For Hindu Surinamese, a common celebration is the jatakarma, which is the Hindu birth ceremony. This is a two-week festival in which the child is named according to the horoscope, and the umbilical cord is ritually detached from the child's navel. Among the Muslims Javanese of Suriname, circumcision for males is generally undertaken at puberty, when the male turns 13 or 14.

CULTURAL HISTORY

Art

Suriname is a former colonial possession of the Netherlands. Originally inhabited by indigenous tribes, Suriname received periodic influxes of European, African, and Asian peoples to work on the agricultural plantations during the colonial period (1650–1975). As a result, post-independence Suriname is a blend of ethnic groups, a diversity which is reflected in Surinamese art and culture.

Visual arts in Suriname began with the native Caribbean tribes who settled along the coastal and interior waterways. Never very densely settled, Suriname retains little trace of these indigenous peoples. While artifacts are few and far between, a significant exception is found in the petroglyphs (incised rock images) and pictographs of the Corantijn River basin. Carved into the soft river rock of the basin, these patterns and humanoid forms are the first signs of human habitation in what is now Suriname.

The arrival of the Dutch and other European colonizers rapidly transformed Suriname into a plantation colony. Labor shortages brought large numbers of African slaves to Suriname. Harsh conditions on the plantations, however, caused many of these slaves to flee into the surrounding jungle, where they formed tribes that came to be known as Maroon communities. Isolated and remote, these Maroon communities resurrected the tribal forms and ways of life that were reminiscent of their African homeland. While little art existed in these communities, a type of folk art proliferated. Courtship rituals, for example, consisted of gift giving, where men selected a potential wife by giving a woman an elaborate woodcarving. These small wooden objects were decorated with various symbols and patterns.

Today, the native art of Suriname continues that tradition. It is typically made from natural materials, including wood and the fruit of the calabash tree (a hollow gourd). The woodcarvings of the Maroons are valued by both tourists and museums; these are often practical items like combs, trays, and canoe paddles that have been intricately engraved.

The duration of Dutch colonization introduced more European artistic traditions into Suriname. Today, independent Suriname has several initiatives to preserve and highlight Surinamese artists. The Federation of Visual Artists in Suriname (FVAS), established in 1998, brought international attention to numerous Surinamese visual artists such as Erwin de

Vries (1929–), Rudi Getrouw (1928–2002), and Paul Woei (1938–). All three of these painters received their formal training at art conservatories in the Netherlands, but returned to Suriname to paint and practice their craft. De Vries is the most prominent of the three artists, and his paintings and sculptures explore abstract human forms. His more historical and political works also comment on the legacy of African slavery within Suriname.

Architecture

Paramaribo center features elements of 16th and 17th century Dutch colonial architecture that has earned the designation of a UNESCO World Heritage site. According to UNESCO, the city center shows classical Dutch design with indigenous features constructed from local materials. The most basic of these homes are early wooden structures consisting of a square brick foundation with high gabled roofs. More public buildings that make up the city center are tall wooden buildings with impressive verandas and multistory, columned porches.

Drama

Dutch language productions are performed at the Suriname Cultural Center and the Ons Erf Cultural Center. Post-colonial playwrights, including Henk Tjon (1948-2009), have developed a vibrant Caribbean theater arts community as is evidenced by the Caribbean Festival of Arts (Carifesta), a regional arts festival held in a different Caribbean nation every two to four years. Tjon was also the founder and director of the National Theater of Suriname.

Music

Music in Suriname is as diverse as its people. One prominent musical style is kaseko, which is unique to Suriname and stems from the country's numerous Maroon communities. A fusion of Afro-Caribbean and Surinamese Creole music styles and sounds, the name kaseko is thought to be a corruption of the French phrase "casser le corps" ("break the body"), a type of slave dance practiced on the colonial plantations.

Traditional kaseko music starts with a call-and-response choral rhythm, African in origin, where the lead singer calls out a refrain which the choral accompaniment then repeats back to the singer. Harmonized to the vocals is a heavy instrumental beat performed by a percussion drum known as a skratji and a small separate snare drum. A wind section of horns, trumpets, trombones, and saxophones plays accompaniment. Kaseko is improvisational in nature and bands commonly hold impromptu parades through the streets during public holidays and festivities. In the years following World War II, kaseko was increasingly influenced by jazz, calypso, and rock and roll. Following increased Surinamese emigration to the Netherlands, kaseko has even enjoyed a popularity on mainland Europe.

Largely popular among the country's large Hindi population is another brand of music commonly known as chutney music. Chutney music developed among the various Indian communities of Guyana, Suriname, and Trinidad. Similar in origin to the religious folk music played on the Indian subcontinent, chutney music songs are romantic love ballads played to the accompaniment of native Indian instruments. These consist of the tabla, a small goatskin bass drum; the sitar, a gourd-shaped mandolin; dholak, a small handheld drum; harmonium, a type of pipe organ; and the dhantal, a long steel axle rod played by striking it with a horseshoe.

Chutney music experienced an explosion of popularity in Caribbean community during the 1960s and 1970s. The first popular Surinamese singer, Ramdew Chaitoe (1942–1994) was a harmonium musician. His 1967 *King of Suriname* album remains one of the highest-grossing chutney albums of all time. Another Surinamese chutney artists, was the female vocalist Dropati, whose 1968 chutney album *Let's Sing and Dance* earned Dropati the nickname "mother of chutney."

Literature

For much of Suriname's colonial history, the agricultural plantation life lent little opportunity to form a national literature. However, the drive for Surinamese independence that followed World War II revealed an increasingly educated and nationalistic literary class. These young professionals pushed for Surinamese independence and agitated for an end to Dutch colonialism in various poems, plays, and prose. Foremost among them was the essayist and poet Robin Ravales (1935–1983), better known by his pen name of Dobru, whose poem "Wan Bon" (One Tree) served as a symbol for a sovereign and diverse country.

Physician and novelist John de Bye (1942–), a more contemporary writer, gave a voice to the lost communities of Paramaribo through his historical works on the Jewish communities of Suriname. Ismene Krishnadath (1956–), a noted academic and writer, has published poetry and prose treating Suriname's Hindi community from a female perspective. The Surinamese government also supports Schrijvergroep 77 (Writer's Group 77), which is a public arts council dedicated to promoting literature and literacy within Suriname.

CULTURE

Arts & Entertainment

From independence onward, Suriname has experienced waves of political instability that have led to outbreaks of repression and violence. The political instability pauperized the country and forced a wide-scale exodus of the Surinamese middle class. In the ensuing unstable economic environment, it has been difficult for Suriname to foster and develop an artistic culture. However, increasing economic stability in recent years has allowed Suriname to begin hosting several festivals in order to further arts promotion.

A major milestone in Suriname occurred when the country was selected to host the eighth annual Caribbean Festival of Arts, known as Carifesta, in Paramaribo in 2003. Carifesta is a cultural festival designed to celebrate common culture of countries sharing the Caribbean coastline. Nearly 30 countries attended the two–week celebration and several delegations of Caribbean artists partook in the festivities. Surinamese artist groups, such as FVAC and Schrijvergroep 77, hosted conferences and symposiums that highlighted Surinamese culture and identity. The success of the festival led to an increased enthusiasm for arts festivals in Suriname and more groups were encouraged to develop arts festivals. Launched in 2002, the Suriname Jazz Festival is held in Paramaribo during the last weekend in October. By blending European and American jazz with native Surinamese musical traditions, the festival hopes to bring jazz music to a new generation of fans and listeners.

The development of the Back Lot, a 2002 arts organization established to promote films and filmmaking within Suriname, has also been important. Beginning in the 1990s, the last cinemas in Suriname shut their doors due to the worsening economy. However, several Surinamese filmmakers, then working in the Netherlands, created the Back Lot to foster filmmaking within Suriname. In conjunction with the International Documentary Festival of Amsterdam, the Back Lot annually hosts numerous film screenings in Suriname and receives international funding to help teach young Surinamese the principles of filmmaking.

Suriname's kaseko music has also been influenced by other music and dance styles, including reggae, calypso, and soca. Popular kaseko musicians include Lieve Hugo and Max Njiman. Aleke is a modern derivation of traditional music, and is popular among young people. Aleke songs often deal with important social issues such as AIDS and poverty. Well known aleke artists include Yakki Famirie.

Cultural Sites & Landmarks

Less urbanized, less populous, and less wealthy than many of its South American neighbors, Suriname has suffered serious economic difficulties in the decades following independence. However, these same economic difficulties have curtailed the widespread urbanization and overdevelopment common to Latin American cities. As a result, Suriname has preserved much of its colonial architecture and past. The capital of Paramaribo has been recognized as an United Nations Educational, Scientific and Cultural Organization (UNESCO) World Heritage Site since 2002.

Paramaribo is centered on the Onafhankelijkheidsplein (Independence Square), a rectangular square flanked on either side by the National Assembly and the Presidential Palace. Prior to independence, this square was called the Oranjeplein (Orange Square) in honor of the royal House of Orange, a European dynasty. It originally served as a parade ground for colonial troops stationed in Suriname. The Presidential Palace was originally built in 1730, and served as the main residence for the colonial governor. A recent multibillion dollar renovation paid for by the Dutch government helped preserve the building and convert it into the Presidential Palace, which now houses the living quarters for the Surinamese president. Whitewashed with a broad circling portico (porch structure), the palace resembles a typical Dutch plantation house. It is one of the few examples of 18th-century architecture in Suriname. Other examples of colonial architecture include the 18th-century residence of Susannah du Plessis, renowned for her cruelty toward slaves. The hallowed remains of Fort Zeelandia, originally constructed in 1640 and the main colonial headquarters for the Dutch military for three centuries, is another example.

Paramaribo also is home to several renowned churches, mosques, mandirs (Hindu temple), and synagogues. The largest church in the city is the Roman Catholic Petrus en Paulus Kathedraal (St. Peter and Paul Cathedral). Constructed between 1883 and 1885, the cathedral is the largest freestanding wooden structure in the Americas. Another fascinating building is the Neveh Shalom Synagogue. Built in 1716 on Keizerstraat (King Street), the synagogue was destroyed by fire in 1835 and was completely re-built. The existing synagogue served as the house of worship and meeting center for the small Jewish community that thrived in Paramaribo from the 18th to the 20th centuries. The stately two-story building is whitewashed and wrapped by a pillared portico. Like many other synagogues found in the Caribbean region, the floor of the synagogue is covered in sand. The sand recalls the ancient Jewish exodus from Egypt and the 40 years spent wandering in the wilderness after freedom from slavery in Egypt.

Paramaribo is also one of the few places in the world where a Jewish synagogue is located directly across the street from an Islamic mosque. The Ahmadiyya Anjuman Isha'at Islam Mosque was designed to serve as a worship center for the many Muslim Javanese and Hindu migrants who arrived to work the plantation fields of Suriname in the first decades of the 20th century. Construction on the mosque began in 1929 and lasted over a decade, since religious edicts stipulated that each phase of its construction be completed by hand. The four towering minarets (spiral towers) frame the distinctive dome of the mosque and help call the faithful to prayer five times daily. Both men and women worship in the mosque, but a separate woman's section is located on the second floor of the mosque.

In addition to the Historical Inner City of Paramaribo, Suriname is home to an additional World Heritage Site, the Central Suriname Nature Reserve. Included on the World Heritage List in 2000, the nature reserve is home to a tropical rainforest ecosystem that spans 16,000 square kilometers (6,177 square miles) and has a wide diversity of flora and fauna. Other natural sites that have spawned an increasing ecotourism business include Brokopondo Reservoir, one of the largest manmade lakes in the world, and the tribal villages and culture of the Maroons and the Amerindians, which are often located in remote Amazonian rainforest.

Libraries & Museums

The Suriname Museum, located at Fort Zeelandia, is a former fort constructed by the British and conquered by the Dutch in the 17th century. The museum houses historical and cultural artifacts, as well as an historical pharmacy and cobbler's shop. An open-air museum, the Openluchtmuseum, is located in Nieuw Amsterdam. Another museum and natural history museum are located in Paramaribo. The Library of Suriname at the Anton de Kom University has a central library and a medical library. Because there is no national library for the country, national artifacts are housed in local libraries, including at the university.

Holidays

In addition to commemorating their various religious holidays, the Surinamese celebrate the national holiday of Independence Day on November 25. At the end of each year, the Surinamese hold the Surifesta. This festival is popular with tourists; it includes street parties, cultural and artistic performances, and fireworks.

Youth Culture

Education in Suriname is free and compulsory from age six until 12, with instruction provided in Dutch. Secondary education consists of junior and senior levels, with the former typically lasting three–to–four years, and the latter lasting two–to–three years. This is followed by tertiary, or postsecondary, education, which is comprised of either university education or higher vocational education (elementary and home economic vocational studies are begun during the junior secondary level). At the turn of the century, half of all schools offering primary and secondary education had a religious affiliation. As of 2010, the country had an estimated 94.7 percent literacy rate.

Surinamese youth generally work from a young age to help contribute to family expenses. Like other Latin American cultures, football (soccer) is a passion for many young Surinamese boys. Many of the country's more talented athletes have earned places on Dutch European football clubs. Other popular sports and activities include basketball, volleyball, tennis, and the martial arts.

SOCIETY

Transportation

Public and private buses and taxis are common modes of transportation, but infrastructure problems make Suriname's waterways a cheaper and more efficient means of transportation within the country. Motorboats connect the interior of the country with the coast. Ports at Paramaribo and Wageningen are open to commercial shipping. Ferry service on the Marowijne River connects the Suriname town of Albina with Saint-Laurent-du-Maroni in French Guiana. A similar ferry exists in the west of Suriname between the towns of New Amsterdam, Suriname, and Rosignol, Guyana. A majority of people use motorboats or more maneuverable motorcycles for long–distance travel.

The Surinamese drive on the left-hand side of the road, and cars with wheels on the left-hand side are permitted. Seat belt use is required and cell phone usage in cars is restricted to hands-free operation.

Transportation Infrastructure

While Suriname established a well-developed infrastructure during its time as a Dutch colony, there has been little money to maintain this infrastructure since independence. In general, transportation within Suriname is difficult. For example, while there is an estimated 9,000 kilometers (5,592 miles) of roads in Suriname, only a fraction—an estimated 1,130 kilometers (702 miles) in 2003—are paved. The remainder is unpaved dirt roads that are frequently subjected to washouts, potholes, and a host of other maintenance issues. A railway line does exist in west Suriname between Brownsberg and Onverdacht, but the high cost of maintaining the rail line has caused service to be discontinued.

Long distance transportation within Suriname is heavily dependent on airports and waterways. There are about 50 airports in Suriname. The international airport of Suriname, Johan Adolf Pengel Airport, is located in Zanderij, south of Paramaribo. Daily and weekly flights connect Suriname with Brazil, the Caribbean, Miami (Florida), and Amsterdam. New Nickerie and Paramaribo also have paved runway airports. The remaining airports within Suriname are small.

Infrastructure loans from the Netherlands, the United States, and the World Bank have resulted in some concrete improvements. These include the Jules Wijdenbosch Bridge, which spans the Suriname River between Paramaribo and Meerzorg. At over 1,504 meters (4,900 feet) long, the bridge is designed to spur economic development in east Suriname. Between 2008 and 2013, the European Commission has committed €19.8 million.

Media & Communications

Suriname is home to numerous media outlets. Local and community newspapers, radio stations, and television channels can be found throughout the country. While some receive government subsidies, many of these outlets retain an independent voice. The Suriname constitution protects freedom of speech and most observers consider Suriname to have a free press. Reporters without Borders' 2014 Worldwide Press Freedom Index ranked Suriname 31st in the world for press freedom.

The only television stations in Suriname are both owned by the government and heavily subsidized. Algemene Televise Verzorging (ATV) broadcasts public interest shows in several languages along with American and European sitcoms. The Surinamese Televisie Stichting (STVS) produces most news content for the country. In 2007, STVS was involved in a controversy when government officials pressured STVS producers to stop broadcasting a program which examined the relationship between China and Taiwan. STVS producers complained, but the broadcast was cancelled and many accused the government of censorship. Others pointed out that heavy Chinese investment in Surinamese timber might have forced the cancellation.

The two leading newspapers of Suriname are *De Ware Tijd* ("The Real Time") and *De West* ("The West"), both of which are published daily and privately owned. Smaller newspapers printed in Hindi or Indonesian cater exclusively to those two ethnic groups. Newspapers were heavily involved in the independence movement and mobilizing opposition to oppressive military leader, and current president, Desi Bouterse (1945–). During the "December murders" of

1982, five of the executed victims were print journalists.

There are a great variety of radio stations in Suriname, both private and public. The leading stations are Radio Apintie, Radio Paramaribo, and Stichting Radio Omroep Suriname. Suriname has a very low rate of Internet usage accounting for only 34.7 percent of the population (2012 estimate).

SOCIAL DEVELOPMENT

Standard of Living

The country ranked one hundredth out of 187 countries on the 2014 United Nations Human Development Index, which measures quality of life indicators.

Water Consumption

Illegal mining has polluted many rivers and streams with both mercury and cyanide. The lack of sufficient wastewater treatment adds to this problem, as biological waste is also a problem. This has a direct result not only on drinking water but on water for agricultural irrigation. Urban populations, which rely on surface water, are under threat from both pollution and the over pumping of wells, which are threatened with salt–water intrusion. Because waste or sewer systems are under developed, particularly in the interior regions, this also poses a threat to water safety.

In 2012, 95.2 percent of the population had access to improved drinking sources, and only 80.3 percent had access to improved sanitation.

Education

Around 94.7 percent of Suriname's population can read and write (2010 estimate). The University of Suriname, which opened in 1968, is the country's only major university. It became an important center of resistance against the socialist military government during the 1980s.

Children between the ages of six and 12 must attend school in Suriname. Basic education consists of primary school and secondary school; vocational education is also available. Religious groups such as Muslims, Christians, and Hindus have set up their own schools, which have served to segregate education along religious lines. On average, female students in Suriname complete thirteen years of education while males complete 11 years.

Children are educated in the Dutch language, which makes learning more difficult for children who speak Dutch as a second language. Rural schools suffer more than schools in densely populated areas from a lack of qualified teachers. Much of the country's education system is financed by aid from the Netherlands, and by the European Development Fund.

According to UNESCO (United Nations Educational, Scientific and Cultural Organization), Suriname's educational system suffers from unmotivated teachers and staff, poorly trained teachers, a failing educational infrastructure, lack of instructional materials, high drop out and failure rates, and low student performance.

Women's Rights

The 1992 constitution guarantees equal rights to all citizens of Suriname and bars discrimination on the basis of gender or race. However, the government has not established any specific ministry nor enacted any special legislation to implement enforcement of the law. According to some critics, while women's rights are protected on paper in Suriname, the reality remains starkly different.

There are some signs of progress within the new legal framework. Women were granted the right to divorce and have sole legal custody of their children. However, civil codes inherited from the colonial era contradict the new divorce law and have yet to be overhauled. Abortion also remains illegal under civil code, but the law is infrequently enforced in practice and women have access to medically supervised abortions at health clinics. Equal employment rights for women are also guaranteed under the constitution. In reality, self-employment, and black market or informal labor remains the norm for most Surinamese, both male and female, rendering the enforcement of equal employment rights negligible.

The two issues most affecting women in Suriname are domestic violence and prostitution. No domestic violence law exists in Suriname and criminal prosecution for domestic violence is only brought to court if the victim files charges. According to the group Stiching Stop Geweld Tegen Vrowen (Stop Violence Against Women), legal structures in Suriname remain wholly inadequate for protecting women against domestic abuse. Threats and physical intimidation oftentimes prevent women from reporting domestic abuse cases. Police officials remain reluctant to intervene in what Surinamese society still considers to be a familial matter.

Prostitution is legal in Suriname, but only allowed in licensed brothels. However, street prostitution and human trafficking have become a huge problem in Suriname. Recent studies estimate that nearly 4,000 Brazilian and Dominican prostitutes work as street prostitutes in the country. No accurate estimate has been tallied of women trafficked through Suriname to work in brothels in the Netherlands and other parts of Europe. The human trafficking of women in Suriname is rapidly becoming the leading industry of the smuggling market, surpassing even the narcotics and arms trade.

Health Care

There are a number of tropical diseases that are prevalent in Suriname, including malaria, yellow fever, cholera, tetanus, and hepatitis A. The HIV/AIDS epidemic has also become a problem there. Poverty, contaminated water, and poor sanitation contribute to the spread of disease. Average life expectancy is 73–71 for men and 76 for women (2009 estimate).

During the political upheaval of the 1980s, much of Suriname's health infrastructure suffered. Many educated Surinamese, including nurses and physicians, emigrated to other countries. The country is seeking to update its health infrastructure through the cooperation of the Bureau of Public Health, the Regional Health Service, and the Medical Mission, which serves the remote regions of the country. The Ministry of Health subsidizes some health services for the

poor, the elderly, and children. Missionary workers and nonprofit organizations provide other health services.

GOVERNMENT

Structure

Suriname was a colony of the Netherlands from the late 17th century until 1975, when it was granted independence. Great Britain temporarily ruled Suriname from 1804 to 1816. Under British rule, Suriname ended the slave trade, although slavery was still legal in the country. It would not be abolished until 1863.

During the early 20th century, the Dutch government continued to support the colony financially and manage its political affairs. Local government and political power was severely restricted, with only two percent of the population able to vote for members of parliament. After World War II, there was an increase in the number of local political parties and political participation, and in 1954, Suriname was granted autonomy. Because of its mixture of ethnicities and races, a coalition government was necessary to represent the diverse population.

By the early 1970s, the country was preparing for independence. A number of Surinamese, particularly minority groups with little political power, feared that independence would mean the economic and political collapse of Suriname. Because of these fears, many immigrated to the Netherlands. During its early years of nationhood, Suriname did experience economic depression and political corruption.

The military seized power in 1980 in an effort to replace the democratic state with a socialist republic. While Suriname was under martial law, the nation was rocked by the 1982 December murders, where 15 opposition leaders, journalists, academics, and lawyers were executed. When the Maroon-backed Surinamese Liberation Army (SLA) opposed the government, soldiers raided Maroon villages and killed many of the people. Between 1980 and 1985, traditional political parties were banned by the government. The violence between the SLA and the government finally ended with a treaty in 1992, when the civil rights of Maroons were recognized and the country renewed the process of democratization.

Suriname is a constitutional democracy that ratified its first constitution on September 30, 1987. The government consists of three branches: the executive, including the president, vice-president (both elected by the National Assembly) and Council of Ministers; the legislative, which consists of the democratically elected National Assembly; and the judicial, which is headed by the Court of Justice. There are 10 administrative regions in Suriname. There is universal suffrage at age 18, and the government continues to be run by a coalition.

Political Parties

Today, Suriname has a number of political parties and as a parliamentary democracy, often sees the development of coalitions and alliances between parties. These alliances have a tendency to shift in terms of political platform and their alliance with other parties sharing common interests. Often, parliamentary systems are ruled by coalitions of two or more parties that unite to form a majority coalition. These coalitions differ in nature, with some coalitions having a lasting strength and others failing to govern at all. Additionally, it's not unusual for parties to dissolve because of personality conflicts within the organization.

In Suriname's 2010 legislative election, the coalition of former despotic leader, Desi Bouterse, Mega Combinatie, won a major victory returning Bouterse to power with 40 percent of the vote. The New Front for Democracy and Development represented the alliance of the National Party of Suriname, the Progressive Reform Party, the Democratic Alternative '91, and the Suriname Labour Party. This left-leaning group lost significant power over the previous election cycle with only 31 percent of the vote. The People's Alliance for Progress represented the Democratic National Platform 2000, Basic Party for Renewal and Democracy, and the Party

for National Unity and Solidarity, and gained almost 13 percent of the vote. Several other coalitions representing a large swath of political parties each received less than six percent of the vote.

Local Government

Suriname's 10 administrative districts are led by a commissioner, appointed by the president. Local councils are elected every five years.

Judicial System

The Court of Justice is the highest court in the country and judges are appointed for life. The Court of Justice hears appeals in civil and criminal cases. Cantonal courts hear civil and criminal cases and are presided over by a judge. Two lower courts preside over medical and military matters respectively. A constitutional court was created in the constitution, but as of 2014, one had never been seated. It would preside over constitutional matters. Under Suriname's system, the accused are entitled to representation and a trial.

Taxation

The government of Suriname levies an income tax, and a tax on pure revenue. Services, goods, and luxury items are taxed at different levels. Suriname's tariff system has been characterized as onerous by some critics.

Armed Forces

The National Leger (National Army) is made up of an army, navy, and air force and is largely comprised of Creoles. The Netherlands has provided military support when necessary, and the army has enlisted the assistance of the US military for training purposes. In recent years, the Chinese government has contributed to Suriname's military hardware needs.

Foreign Policy

As a former colonial possession of the Netherlands and a nation peopled by many diverse ethnicities, Suriname balances a complex system of foreign relations. Suriname is a member of several worldwide international organizations, including the United Nations (UN), the Organization of American States (OAS), and the International Monetary Fund (IMF). Locally, Suriname belongs to several regional organizations such as the Caribbean Community and Common Market (CARICOM) and the Association of Caribbean States (ACS). As a former Dutch colony, Suriname has strong associations with the European Union (EU) via the Lomé Convention trade agreement, as well as continuing security alliances with the Netherlands.

Suriname has ongoing territorial disputes with its neighbor to the west, Guyana. These clashes have a long history dating back to the time when the two countries were both colonial possessions. Neither the Netherlands nor Great Britain (which colonized Guyana) formally drew up internationally recognized boundaries between the two colonies. As a result, in the years following independence, both Suriname and Guyana have continued this conflict. At issue is the line of demarcation for Suriname's western border. Suriname claims that the whole of the Courantyne River is Surinamese territory, while Guyana lays claim to half of the river. As a result, from 1969 onward, Suriname and Guyana have had armed clashes over fishing rights and other uses of the river.

Recently, offshore oil rights have come to the forefront. In 2000, Surinamese naval boats expelled a Canadian company from drilling offshore. Guyana, the country which had authorized the drilling, protested and then filed suit against Suriname in an international admiralty court. Numerous committees between the two countries have attempted to resolve the matter. International arbitration has stressed the need for future cooperation between the two countries in order to further develop their natural resources. Nothing concrete has emerged from these negotiations. In the meantime, no new oil fields have been developed.

This lack of cooperation between Guyana and Suriname serves to impede improvements in other areas. Smuggling has become a major source of revenue in Suriname, an issue recently brought to light when former military strongman Dési Bouterse was convicted in a Dutch court for cocaine smuggling in 1999. His supporters in parliament passed laws forbidding the extradition of Bouterse, which led to a curtailment in Dutch foreign aid for the struggling country. After Bouterse was elected president of Suriname, relations became increasingly strained with both the EU, after the parliament passed a law granting amnesty to the newly elected cabinet, and the United States, after American authorities arrested Bouterse's son on drug and weapon trafficking charges. Today, the Dutch no longer maintain an embassy in Suriname and the international community is looking closely to the upcoming 2015 elections.

Human Rights Profile

International human rights law insists that states respect civil and political rights, and also promote an individual's economic, social, and cultural rights. The United Nations Universal Declaration on Human Rights (UDHR) is recognized as the standard for international human rights. Its authors sought the counsel of the world's great thinkers, philosophers, and religious leaders, and were careful to create a document that reflects the core values shared by every world culture. To read this document or view the articles relating to cultural human rights, click here: http://www.udhr.org/UDHR/default.htm.

Suriname has a mixed record on human rights. Shortly after gaining independence in 1975, the civilian government was overthrown in a military coup launched by Dési Bouterse. Appointed chairman of the National Military Council, Bouterse used his new position to enact martial law, banning most forms of free speech and political opposition to his government. This repression culminated with the "December murders" of 1982 in which 15 individuals, including trade union leaders, opposition politicians, journalists, and lawyers, were executed without trial in Fort Zeelandia. International condemnation followed and the UN, the US, and the Netherlands cut off foreign aid to Suriname. Following a civil war, Bouterse employed brutal methods to combat the insurgency. In 1986, Bouterse directed his forces in an attack on the Maroon village of Moiwana, where 36 unarmed civilians were killed. Investigations into the massacre were suppressed when the lead investigator was assassinated in Paramaribo in 1990.

This stranglehold on Surinamese political life was not eased until 2000, when Bouterse finally agreed to limited parliamentary elections. (In 1999, Bourterse was convicted of drug trafficking in absentia by the criminal court in the Netherlands.) With the inauguration of President Ronald Venetiaan (1936–) in 2000, calls for Bouterse to be brought to trial were renewed. As the leader of political opposition, however, Bouterse was able to fight off parliamentary attempts to bring him to trial. It was not until April 2008 that a military court martial began. After more than a year of litigation, however, Bouterse had yet to publicly testify on his own involvement in the killings (although he did admit to "political responsibility" for both the December killings and the Moiwana massacre). In 2013 the military court adjourned the trial, handing the matter over to the constitutional court, which has yet to be established. While the return of civilian government to Suriname had led the country to declare a renewed commitment to human rights, complaints still remained and the situation became increasingly complicated with Bouterse's return to power in 2010 followed immediately by the passage of an amnesty law in 2012. Police brutality remains common, but efforts by the Surinamese judiciary to reform the police have seen signs of progress. Additionally, human rights advocates have begun pressing for improvements within the country's prison system.

Human rights monitoring agencies also point to needed improvement in the Sipaliwini district and for the indigenous tribes there. Sipaliwini, the largest of Suriname's ten districts, has also been the least developed. Rich in timber and minerals (including gold), the area is populated by tribal Maroons and various other indigenous peoples. Desperate for revenue, the Surinamese government has granted numerous mining concessions and allowed miners and settlers from Brazil and French Guiana to settle in the Sipaliwini. There have been numerous reported clashes between these miners and the native indigenous. Moreover, concessions opened by Chinese lumber companies have caused widespread deforestation and environmental pollution. Lawsuits filed on behalf of the Surinamese indigenous have brought injunctions against the Surinamese government to halt further development of the area.

Migration

Suriname's net migration rate is .57 per 1,000 in 2014.

ECONOMY

Overview of the Economy

Beginning in the 17th century, Suriname exported many crops and natural resources important to the colonial economy of Britain, and later, the Netherlands. Today, the mineral bauxite is Suriname's most important export and natural resource. Bauxite can be processed to make aluminum.

Gold is also a valuable export, although it remains secondary to bauxite. Timber, fish, and shrimp are also widely exported from the country.

In 2013, the gross domestic product (GDP) of Suriname was an estimated $5.009 billion USD. The per capita GDP was $12,900 USD. The country has a high rate of unemployment (around 8.5 percent in 2013) and a high inflation rate. A large percentage of the population is employed by the government. Suriname's major trading partners are the United States and the Netherlands.

Industry

The major industry in Suriname is the extraction of bauxite, a mineral that is used in the manufacture of aluminum. The cement, footwear, tobacco, and beverage industries make up a large part of the manufacturing sector. In recent years, there has been an increase in oil production and in the creation of hydroelectric power.

Labor

Suriname's labor force numbers about 165,600. The majority of the workforce works in the service industry (78 percent), followed by 14 percent in the manufacturing sector and eight percent in agriculture. The unemployment rate in 2013 was 8.5 percent.

Energy/Power/Natural Resources

Suriname is the world's seventh-largest supplier of the mineral bauxite. It also manufactures and exports aluminum. Gold, nickel, diamonds, iron ore, copper, platinum, and manganese are also found there.

Fishing

Shrimp are a profitable resource within the country's fisheries.

Forestry

While nearly 80 percent of Suriname is covered in rain forest, it has been difficult to create an industry around the timber supply, in part because there are not enough roads into the country's interior.

Mining/Metals

Most bauxite mining occurs in the northeastern portion of the country, near Paranam and Moengo. Other mineral industries include the mining of gold and diamonds, although much of this mining activity is not regulated by the government.

Agriculture

A large portion of the Surinamese work force is employed in agriculture. The cultivation of rice is very important throughout the country; one of the largest rice farms in the world is found in Wageningen. Bananas are another important agricultural export for Suriname, which has also been developing its palm oil industry.

Animal Husbandry

The livestock industry in Suriname is gaining ground but is susceptible to disease. For that reason, the government has developed an animal disease monitoring and surveillance system. Suriname relies increasingly on imports in this area.

Tourism

Suriname has not developed a tourism infrastructure, and roads and transportation in the country tend to be poor. However, an international airport serves the capital of Paramaribo. The rainforests and nature reserves are attractive to ecotourists, and Paramaribo features several gardens and historical sites. However, crime tends to be high in the city, and robberies and muggings are common.

Jeffrey Bowman, Christina Healey

DO YOU KNOW?

- Suriname's Lake Brokopondo is one of the largest artificial lakes in the world, measuring 1,560 square kilometers (600 square miles).
- The first Jewish synagogue in the Western Hemisphere was constructed in Suriname in 1639.
- The jungles of Suriname are home to the blue poison dart frog, which is toxic to humans.

Bibliography

The Amazon: Brazil, Bolivia, Peru, Ecuador, Colombia, Venezuela and the Guianas. Berkeley: Lonely Planet Publishing, 2008.

Fey, Toon. *Surinam: Switi Sranan.* Amsterdam: KIT Publishers, 2003.

Hoefte, Rosemarijn. *Suriname in the Long Twentieth Century: Domination, Contestation, Globalization.* New York: Palgrave Macmillan, 2014.

Price, Richard. *Afro-American Arts of the Suriname Rain Forest.* Berkeley: University of California Press, 1980.

Westoll, Andrew. *The Riverbones: Stumbling after Eden in the Jungles of Suriname.* Toronto: Emblem Editions, 2009.

Williams, Colleen. *Discovering Suriname.* New York: Mason Crest Publishing, 2003.

Works Cited

http://www.centrelink.org/resurgence/suriname.htm

http://www.wrm.org.uy/countries/Surinam/logging.html

http://www.state.gov/g/drl/rls/hrrpt/2007/100654.htm

http://www.rsf.org/article.php3?id_article=6259

http://www.rsf.org/article.php3?id_article=22156

http://www.unhcr.org

http://www.rsf.org/article.php3?id_article=29032

http://www.internetworldstats.com/sa/sr.htm

http://news.bbc.co.uk/1/hi/world/americas/country_profiles/1211306.stm

http://world-gazetteer.com/wg.php?x=&men=gcis&lng=en&dat=32&geo=-199&srt=n2pn&col=ohq|

http://www.readytexartgallery.com/website/page.asp?menuid=14&site=arts

http://www.folklife.si.edu/resources/maroon/educational_guide/28.htm

http://books.google.com/books?id=sFCMaloGSTIC&pg=PA128&lpg=PA128&dq=maroon+art+suriname&source=bl&ots=3X9BuOSahx&sig=PiyJsqfdist89uk7-yIeBxqvhWs&hl=en&ei=DlacSauEGYH8tge-j0fDYBA&sa=X&oi=book_result&resnum=1&ct=result

https://www.cia.gov/library/publications/the-world-factbook/geos/ns.html

http://www.carifesta.net/viii/sub3-6.html

http://home.wxs.nl/~vrstg/guianas/suriname/suriname.htm

http://home.wanadoo.nl/javas/Vertellingen/Koesoebjono/JavaneseInSuriname.htm

http://www.newworldencyclopedia.org/entry/Petroglyph

http://worldmusiccentral.org/article.php?story=20030414202502213

http://mohabirrecords.us/index.php

http://www.telegraph.co.uk/travel/destinations/southamerica/2438329/Paramaribo-Suriname-Tropical-paradise.html

http://heritagesuriname.org/index.php?option=com_frontpage&Itemid=1

http://aaiil.org/suriname/books/misc/imdadiamemorialvolume/imdadiamemorialvolume.shtml

http://www.paramaribo.com/

http://www.travelblog.org/South-America/Suriname/Paramaribo/blog-179671.html

http://babakfakhamzadeh.com/site/index.php?c=12&i=1223

http://www.bh.org.il/Communities/Synagogue/Paramaribo.asp

http://www.virtualtourist.com/travel/South_America/Suriname/Distrikt_Paramaribo/Paramaribo-1623495/Things_To_Do-Paramaribo-BR-1.html

http://www.highbeam.com/doc/1P1-138466122.html

http://www.dominicantoday.com/dr/poverty/2008/5/11/27942/Nearly-4000-Dominican-women-are-prostitutes-in-Suriname

http://www.corpwatch.org/article.php?id=12478

Aerial view of Montevideo, Uruguay/Stock Photo © Rudimencial

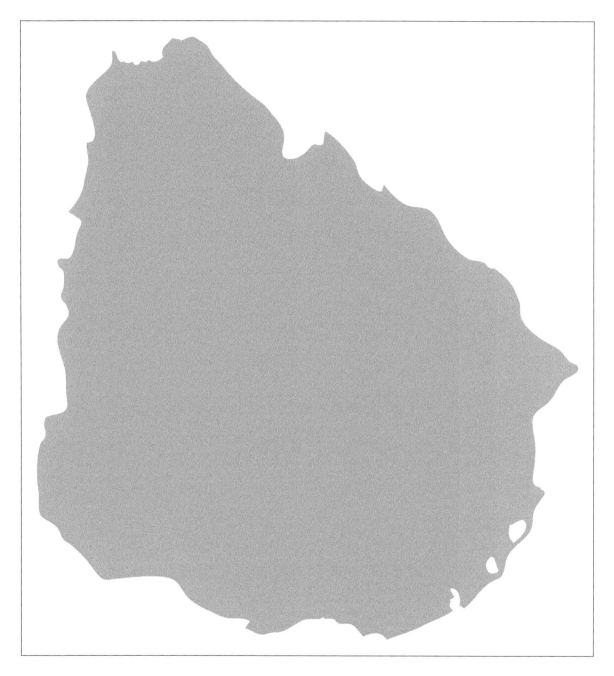

URUGUAY

Introduction

The República Oriental del Uruguay (Republic of Uruguay) is located in the southeastern part of South America. It borders Argentina to the west, northwest, and southwest, Brazil to the northeast, and the Atlantic Ocean to the southeast.

Uruguay is one of the most democratic countries in Latin America, and has one of the highest standards of living. Its extensive social welfare system includes free, high-quality education and health care. As of the early 21st century, Uruguay does not suffer from overpopulation or extreme poverty, nor is it experiencing environmental degradation.

Uruguay also has a high level of literacy and a long tradition of freedom of speech. This has resulted in a large number of authors and poets best known for their works with patriotic and rural themes. Young Uruguayans are also becoming more politically active and aware. According to a 2007 study, nearly half of the youth population view prioritized political matters as one of the primary topics that matter to them most.

Today Uruguay is leading the movement to legalize marijuana, becoming the first country in the world to regulate a marijuana national market. This has led to a marked increase in the overall GDP and has transformed the country into a sort of international pace-setter in this area.

GENERAL INFORMATION

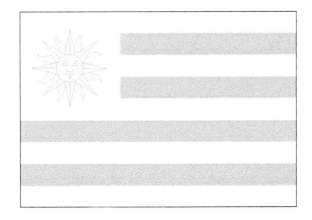

Official Language: Spanish
Population: 3,332,972 (2014 estimate)
Currency: Uruguayan peso
Coins: The Uruguayan peso is divided into 100 centésimos; coins in circulation, however, are in denominations of 1, 2, 5, and 10 pesos. The 50 centésimos coins were withdrawn from circulation in July 2010, and the 10 and 20 centésimos coins were removed from circulation earlier due to low value and inflation.
Land Area: 175,015 square kilometers (67,573 square miles)
Water Area: 1,200 square kilometers (463 square miles)
National Motto: "Libertad o Muerte" ("Liberty or Death")
National Anthem: "Orientales, la Patria o la Tumba!" ("Easterners, the Fatherland or Death!")
Capital: Montevideo
Time Zone: GMT -3

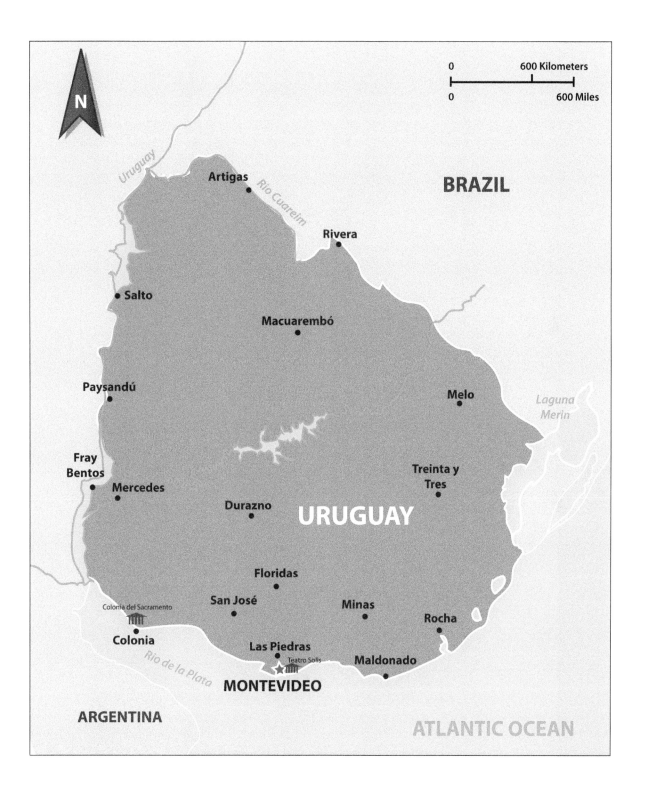

Principal Cities by Population (2012):

- Montevideo (1,300,000)
- Salto (108,197)
- Ciudad de la Costa (107,154)
- Las Piedras (80,052)
- Paysandú (78,868)
- Rivera (71,222)
- Maldonado (65,865)
- Tacuarembó (54,994)
- Melo (54,674)

Flag Description: The flag of Uruguay features a field (or background) composed of nine equal horizontal stripes alternating between white and blue. A square canton (in the upper left corner), five stripes in length, features the Sun of May symbol, a 16-rayed golden sun with a human face that represents the Inca sun god, Inti. The nine stripes represent Uruguay's nine original departments (there are now 19).

Population

Approximately eight percent of the Uruguayan population lives in rural areas, and an estimated 92 percent of Uruguayans reside in urban areas (2011 estimate). More than half of urban dwellers live in Montevideo, Uruguay's national capital and largest city, with a population of 1.3 million (and an unofficial 2012 metropolitan population of 1.8 million). In fact, Montevideo is likely home to over half of Uruguay's total population of 3.5 million, and its population had been doubling every 30 years since 1880. However, Montevideo itself has experienced an outflow of some of its best-educated citizens drawn by the higher salaries available in Buenos Aires and other nearby South American cities.

Uruguay's population growth is extremely stable, unlike that of other Latin American countries that suffer from severe overpopulation. The Uruguayan infant mortality rate is 8.97 deaths per 1,000 live births, and Uruguayans have an average life expectancy of 76 years (2014 estimate). The population growth rate was estimated at 0.26 percent in 2014.

Languages

Spanish is Uruguay's official language, but it has been influenced Uruguay's Portuguese-speaking neighbors. Near the border with Brazil, a combination of Spanish and Portuguese called Portuñal, or Brazilero, is spoken.

Native People & Ethnic Groups

The territory that would eventually become Uruguay was settled in 6000 BCE by stone tool-bearing hunter-gatherers who would, over the course of 6,000 years, branch into three tribes of indigenous people: the Chaná, the Guaraní, and the Charrúa.

The Chaná, the Guaraní, and the Charrúa were all well-established in the territory when the Spanish settled there in the 16th century, but were wiped out by mass extermination, disease, and assimilation over the next 300 years. The Chaná and the Guaraní disappeared in the 16th century, and the Charrúa endured until the 19th century. Few, if any, indigenous people remain in Uruguay, although the Guaraní still reside in other South American countries.

Today, the majority of Uruguayans (88 percent) are Caucasian. Most are descended from Spanish settlers who came to Uruguay between the 18th century and the beginning of the 20th century. Some are descended from Italian immigrants who came to Uruguay at the end of the 19th century. Minority groups include mestizos (people with mixed Spanish and indigenous heritage), who make up eight percent of the population. Blacks account for four percent of the population, and Amerindians make up less than one percent of the population. There are also small Portuguese, French, English, German, and African populations living in the country.

Religions

There is a marked separation of church and state in Uruguay, and although 66 percent of the population is Roman Catholic, many are not active practitioners, when compared to their Latin American neighbors. In Montevideo, the capital, a little less than two-thirds of the city's population identifies as Catholic; around 30 percent claim no religious affiliation. There are also very small Protestant and Jewish communities. Large numbers of Montevideo's Jews immigrated to Israel during the 1970s and 1980s.

Climate

Uruguay is located in the Southern Hemisphere, and as a result, its summer lasts from December to February, and winter lasts from June to August. During the summer, it is much hotter along the Río Uruguay than in the interior of the country. The average temperature in summer ranges from 17° to 28° Celsius (63° to 82° Fahrenheit), and the average winter temperature ranges from 6° to 14° Celsius (43° to 57° Fahrenheit).

Average yearly rainfall is 105 centimeters (41 inches). Rainfall is distributed relatively evenly, although summer months receive slightly less rain than winter months, and the south receives slightly less than the north. Strong winds whip through Uruguay in winter and spring, with no mountains on the landscape to block them.

Montevideo, the capital and largest city, enjoys a mild climate in which January (summertime) temperatures average between 17° Celsius (63° Fahrenheit) and 28° Celsius (82° Fahrenheit). July (winter) temperatures average between 6° Celsius (43° Fahrenheit) and 14° Celsius (57° Fahrenheit). The city is frequently subject to strong winds during the winter and spring. The cold winter wind known as the pampero, which frequently blows into Montevideo from the Argentine pampas, sometimes produces damaging effects on the capital's homes and buildings.

ENVIRONMENT & GEOGRAPHY

Topography

Low rolling hills and plains cover three-quarters of Uruguay's terrain. The remainder is mostly made up of level coastline along the Atlantic seaboard and level wetlands along the Río Uruguay and the Río de la Plata.

The Río Uruguay is the country's longest river at 435 kilometers (270 miles). The river acts as Uruguay's western border, separating Uruguay from Argentina. The Río Uruguay flows into the Río de la Plata in the southwest, an estuary that empties into the Atlantic Ocean.

As the national capital, Montevideo is located in southern Uruguay. The city sits on the northern bank of the Río de la Plata estuary on the Atlantic Ocean. It features miles of river shoreline, paralleled by the thoroughfare known as La Rambla, and a large, natural harbor that is one of the busiest in South America.

The hills of Uruguay do not rise over 1000 feet. Some hills are formed of granite, gneisses, marble, or schists deposits. The northern part of Uruguay has hills made out of sandstone or volcanic sills. Uruguay has no distinct geographical features with the exception of two ridges of low elevation: the Cuchilla de Haedo that extends from the north to central interior, and the Cuchilla Grande that extends from the northeast to the southeast. Uruguay's highest point is Cerro Catédral in the southeast, which has an elevation of 514 meters (1,686 feet) above sea level.

Plants & Animals

The bulk of Uruguay is blanketed by the Uruguayan savanna, a prairie consisting of over 400 species of annual and perennial grasses. Palm savannas are located near the Brazilian border and in the south near the coast, and small forests grow near Uruguay's rivers in the east.

Gallery forests contain hardwood and softwood trees and aromatic shrubs. Hardwood trees include algarobo, quebracho, coronilla, lapacho, guayabo, urunday, espinillo, lignum vitae, and nandubay. Softwood trees include acacia, eucalyptus (imported from Australia), ombú, alder, aloe, poplar, willow, mimosa, and ceibo.

Most large mammals are extinct in Uruguay, but small to medium-sized animals inhabit the forests and the higher elevations in the north. Rheas, five-foot tall flightless birds similar to ostriches, populate these areas as well.

Animals native to Uruguay include deer, otter, the small armadillo, the three-toed anteater, the coatimundi (mammal in the raccoon family), and large rodents such as the capybara and the nutria. Seals and sea lions can be found off Punta del Este, a resort area along the coast east of Montevideo.

Approximately 80 species of birds nest in the Uruguayan savannah. These include horneros (or oven birds), quail, crows, and partridge. In the wetlands along the rivers and the coast there are over 400 species of birds, including swans, royal ducks, and avestruz.

Freshwater fish such as golden salmon, pejerry, piranha, tararira, criolla, pompano, corvina, pacú, and surubí are abundant in Uruguay's rivers.

CUSTOMS & COURTESIES

Greetings

When Uruguayans meet someone for the first time, they will usually shake hands. Among friends and family, women give each other a kiss (un beso) on each cheek, while men often embrace (un abrazo). Men will also kiss women if they are close friends or relatives. Greetings generally depend on the time of day. The common phrase of "Hola" ("Hello") is appropriate anytime, but is also informal. The formal greeting used is "Buen dia" ("Good day"). In the morning and early afternoon, it is appropriate to say "Buenos dias" ("Good morning"), while "Buenas tardes" is used in the early evening. "Buenas noches" is used as both a salutation and farewell at night.

In the countryside, people tend to greet strangers that they pass in the street, though this is not common in urban areas. At social events, it is considered polite to greet every person in the group. In informal circles, like family, people refer to each other using their first names. In more formal circumstances people refer to each other by their last name, using honorific titles such as "Señor" ("Mr."), "Señora" ("Mrs.") and "Señorita" ("Ms."), or other professional titles.

Gestures & Etiquette

Uruguayans inherited many of their social customs from European traditions, and are serious, guarded and modest. It is important to take time to get to know someone before asking personal questions. For this reason, it's not appropriate to pry about personal topics, like family, if the person is a new acquaintance. Also, the country suffered a military dictatorship when some people's families were tortured or exiled, so this sensitive topic is often avoided. It is also important to use formal language with new friends by using the formal variation of "you," which is "usted."

Uruguayans tend to observe less personal space than America, but will give foreigners more space when having a conversation. They tend to maintain eye contact while conversing. There are several common hand gestures, like the thumbs up sign which means "OK." Doubt is expressed by touching four fingers to the thumb on the right hand. It is impolite to sit on anything but a chair, like ledges or the floor, and it is also impolite to put one's feet up on a table. Yawning should also be avoided, since it signals the end to a social engagement or a meeting. Public displays of affection are common. When eating, people keep their hands above the table, and when they are finished with their food, they might use a piece of bread to clean the plate.

Eating/Meals

In Uruguay, people usually eat a small breakfast consisting of a croissant (media luna) and coffee with milk (café con leche) or maté, a strong tea. Many people also take a mid-morning break. Lunch is the main meal of the day, eaten at noon or in the mid-afternoon. It generally consists of a soup or a salad, a main course of meat with vegetables, and dessert. Dinner is usually eaten late and is generally a smaller meal than lunch, but with some sort of meat, bread, and potatoes.

Restaurants, some of which serve foreign food, are popular in urban areas. Italian restaurants are common, but the most popular kind of restaurant is the parrillada, a restaurant that specializes in charcoal-grilled meat. A typical parrillada is the gaucho restaurant, decorated with cowboy memorabilia and photos of the countryside. Parrilladas serve asado (grilled meat), one of Uruguay's most popular dishes. Cervezerias (beer gardens) are also popular for socializing.

Maté (pronounced Mah-tay) is a strong tea and the national drink. It is an integral part of the Uruguayan diet and is consumed during and in-between meals. In fact, Uruguayans drink more mate than any other nationality. Also known as yerba maté, this plant is dried and ground, as it was by the indigenous peoples of the region. The powdery mixture is then placed into a special mate cup, usually a carved-out gourd, and hot water is poured on top. People then drink the tea with a metal straw called a bombilla. It is common for Uruguayans to carry a thermos with hot water, a mate cup, and a bag of mate leaves so they can drink the tea throughout the day.

Visiting

On Sundays, close friends and family tradition-ally gather for an asado (barbecue), when they grill different cuts of meat. Many Uruguayan family activities take place outdoors in a back-yard to eat, converse, and play football (soccer), the country's most popular sport. When visiting someone or out with a group of people, mate is often passed around and shared, with many peo-ple using the same metal straw. Typically, a host will serve all of his guests before he takes a drink.

Uruguayans are very hospitable, but expect guests to show consideration and gratitude for such treatment. Guests are also expected to be respectful of the other person's home and not to inconvenience the host. It is generally considered polite to call before going to someone's house, and ill-mannered to drop in without warning, especially during mealtimes. It's appropriate to bring a gift, such as chocolates or flowers, when invited to a person's home. In a business setting, it is common to be asked over to a person's home for coffee or drinks, but it is not polite to stay late, especially on weekdays.

LIFESTYLE

Family

Family ties are very strong in Uruguay, not only in the nuclear family (consisting of a mother, father, and their children), but also in the extended family, where aunts, uncles, cousins, and grand-parents are all close. Typically, rural families are larger, while in cities the average family has two children. Children usually live with their parents until they get married. The family structure is traditionally patriarchal, and the women of the household are generally responsible for most domestic duties and child rearing.

An important family practice in Uruguay, especially in the countryside, is compadrazgo. This is when parents pick a godmother or god-father for their new baby. Though the godpar-ents are not necessarily related to each other or the couple, they are chosen based on the role they will play in the baby's life. When the baby is baptized, the godparents assume their respon-sibility of lifelong support for the baby. This includes helping the child with school, jobs, money, and any other necessities that arise. For this reason, parents frequently choose godparents who are wealthier than they are. In return for his godparents' support, the child is expected to help his godparents whenever he is asked and to do favors for them. Since godparents are often from a different socioeconomic class than their god-child, compadrazgo helps create interclass rela-tionships within Uruguayan society.

Housing

Unlike other Latin American countries, most Uruguayans have adequate housing, since it is guaranteed by the constitution and by the Ley de Vivienda (Housing Law). As such, housing is largely financed by the public sector, a bureau of the government called the Banco Hipotecario de Uruguay, or the Uruguay Mortgage Bank. This bank constructs homes for low-income families and pensioners. Most people live in homes made of stable materials (like bricks) and most have indoor plumbing. According to a government census in 2004, only 3 percent of the population lived in homes made from precarious materials. In cities, 99.6 percent of residents had electricity, while 98.7 percent had indoor plumbing.

However, there are still differences depend-ing on social class. In rural areas, homes are usually small with sparse furniture and ample outdoor space. People use wood fires or bottled gas to cook and use wells or pumps for fresh water. These rural areas also have estancias, which are large, lavish ranches run by wealthy families. In the cities, the middle and upper classes live in apartment complexes or in affluent suburban homes. Despite government support for the poor, some shantytowns (informal settlements) exist in larger cities, and generally consist of dwellings without electricity and sanitation made from discarded material, such as wood or cardboard.

Food

Uruguayans are among the world's largest beef consumers, due to the gaucho tradition. In the late 1800s, Uruguay was a major exporter of animal hides, but due to a lack of refrigeration, producers were left with large amounts of meat they couldn't sell abroad. Thus began a long tradition of meat consumption. Uruguayans prefer their meat grilled with charcoal, like bife de chorizo (rump steak), lomo (fillet steak), and barbecued pork. One of the most popular cuts is asado de tira (ribs). Chops and sausages are popular, and include chorizo (sausage) and morcilla dulce (blood sausage made with orange peel and nuts). Besides charcoal-grilled, Uruguayans also like their meat milanesa style, which is breaded and deep fried.

Due to the influence of Italian immigrants, Italian cuisine is common in Uruguay. Italian settlers introduced pasta, ham, cheese, bread, and other culinary tastes and traditions to the Uruguayan palate. It is customary to eat gnocchi, a type of potato pasta, on the 29th day of the month in the Italian tradition. The Spanish influence made seafood such as fish and shrimp popular in coastal areas. Mazamorra, ground corn with milk, comes from South American cuisine. In the countryside, rice and potatoes are staple foods, since they are inexpensive and filling.

Snack food is abundant, and much of it involves meat. The chivito, a steak sandwich made with lettuce, tomato, egg, cheese, bacon, and other toppings, is the most popular snack. Empanadas (meat pastries), olímpicos (club sandwiches), húngaros (spicy sausages), and ponchos (sausages on a bun) are also common. Soups are also a part of the Uruguayan diet, including puchero (soup made with beef, beans, sausage, bacon, and vegetables), estofado (meat stew), and cazuela (stew made with tripe).

Desserts typically derive from European influences. One popular dessert is dulce de leche, a thick, caramel-like custard also common in Argentina. Other common desserts include meringue, chajá (sponge cake filled with cream and jam), mossini (creamy sponge pastry), lemon pie, and Italian-style ice cream. Though Uruguayans consume mate (mah-tay) more than any other drink, Uruguay produces its own wine and beer, which are popular alcoholic beverages. Clericot is a drink made with a mixture of white wine and fruit juice. Juices and licuados (shakes) are also common.

Life's Milestones

Uruguay is widely considered the most secular Latin American nation, with less than half of the population identifying as Roman Catholic. Nonetheless, many Uruguayan milestones are firmly rooted in the Christian faith, namely baptism, marriage, and funerary practices. Other milestones, such as the quinceañera, are similar to those found in other Latin American cultures. As in many other Latin American countries, the Uruguayan quinceañera is a large celebration held to mark a girl's 15th birthday. The celebration marks the transition into adulthood, and traditionally consists of a religious ceremony followed by an elaborate party with family and friends. The quinceañera tradition also calls for the birthday girl to dance the waltz, often with boys her age.

Marriage is another important milestone in Uruguayan life. When a man wants to marry, he is expected to ask his girlfriend's parents for permission. Once he does, both families help plan the wedding, which helps create a bond between them. Typically, the ceremony is held in a church and a formal party is held afterward.

CULTURAL HISTORY

Art

As in other Latin American cultures, art in Uruguay fully emerged in the modern era during the country's postcolonial period. Uruguay's most celebrated artist is Joaquin Torres García (1874–1949), considered the founder of constructive universalism. This movement was a Latin American art form in which pre-Columbian art styles were merged with modern European movements such as cubism and surrealism to form a type of universal art. Torres García's abstract style combined symbols using materials like glass and wire. He created paintings as well as murals and sculptures, the most famous being the Cosmic Monument in Rodó Park in Montevideo, a pink granite wall with pre-Columbian style engravings.

Other famous Uruguayan artists include Juan Manuel Blanes (1830–1901) and Pedro Figari (1861–1938). Known as "el pintor de la Patria," ("the painter of the motherland"), Blanes followed the early naturalist tradition by painting lifelike figures in nature. His themes focus on the history of Uruguay, including scenes from the Río de la Plata region, folklore, and the gaucho (cowboy) tradition. Figari was also a lawyer, politician, scholar, journalist, and even vice president of the country before he began painting at 60 years of age. An early modernist, he focused on the materials used to create the painting rather than drawing a realistic image. His themes include landscapes, rural life, gauchos, and Afro-Uruguayan culture. His style is known for his emphasis on movement and light, particularly the unique light of sunset on the plains.

Though some of the most celebrated Uruguayan art was created prior to 1950, Uruguay's most famous modern artists include José Belloni (1882–1965), Carlos Gonzalez (1905–1993), and Carlos Páez Vilaró (1923–2014). The country's most renowned sculptor, Belloni was trained in Europe and is responsible for creating several monuments in Montevideo. These include *La Diligencia* ("Diligence"), a life-size stagecoach and horses, and *La Carreta* ("The Carriage"), an ox-drawn wagon in Battle y Ordóñez Park. Gonzalez created elaborate black and white prints using carved wood blocks. Using only a knife, he carved entire scenes on wood depicting gaucho culture and rural life. Páez Vilaró created one of the longest murals in the world in Washington, DC. He was also a painter, sculptor, and architect, who built several famous sandcastle-like buildings in Uruguay and Argentina. His own home, *Casapueblo* (Village Home), is also a hotel and museum in Punta Ballena, Uruguay

Drama

Theater, especially open-air theater, is a very popular tradition in Uruguay. Many universities and high schools have theater groups, and elaborate plays and musicals are put on during Uruguay's Carnival celebration and for several weeks afterward. Known as tabladas, these plays are organized by collecting money and choosing local amateurs to perform in the productions. Every year, drama groups compete to win the best tablada. These productions often mock politicians and celebrities. The National Comedy Repertory Company, founded in 1948, is one of the country's most popular theater groups. Based in Montevideo, this group performs both Uruguayan and foreign plays.

Uruguay has a number of accomplished playwrights, including Florencio Sánchez (1875–1910) and Mauricio Rosencof (1933–). Sánchez wrote twenty plays about the Rio de la Plata region with mostly working-class characters. Using slang and typical language, his plays show what life was like in Buenos Aires and Montevideo at the turn of the 20th century. Rosencof was a member of the Tupamaros, a radical leftist youth movement in the 1960s, which led to his subsequent arrest and torture by the military dictatorship. He spent 10 years in jail, where he began writing poetry. Released in 1985, he wrote several popular plays including *El hijo que espera* ("The waiting son") and *Las cartas que no llegaron* ("The letters that didn't arrive").

Music & Dance

Music and dance in Uruguay was heavily influenced by European immigrants who brought styles like the polka and the waltz to their new home. The national dance is the pericón, a traditional folk dance with six or more couples. Folk music, with lyrics discussing gaucho life, often accompanies similar types of dance. The payada de contrapunto is another folk music tradition in which two singers improvise lyrics in a musical competition.

Montevideo's cultural scene tended to reflect that of nearby Buenos Aires throughout its history. Consequently, tango developed in Uruguay during the late 1800s. Tango is a type of music using two bandoneones (a type of accordion), two violins, a piano, and a double bass. Typically, the lyrics discuss love, the life of the poor, and urban struggle. Tango is also a type of ballroom dance performed with two partners in close proximity with sharp, precise movements.

Geraldo Matos Rodríguez (1897–1948) and Carlos Gardel (1890–1935) were two of Uruguay's most famous tango musicians. Matos Rodríguez was a composer and also the conductor of a tango orchestra. He wrote "La Cumparasita," one of the most famous tango songs of all time. Gardel's birthplace is disputed, though it is believed he was born in Uruguay and grew up in Argentina. Known as the "King of Tango," he was a composer and singer who sold thousands of records, toured Europe and Latin America, and acted in several films. Some of his most famous tangos include "Mi Buenos Aires querido" ("My beloved Buenos Aires") and "Soledad" ("Loneliness").

In Uruguay, music has always served as a means of political discussion. While murgas usually focus on politicians or recent events, other forms of music also are used to discuss politics and international affairs. For example, tango songs often discuss poverty, immigration, and social ills. Another type of music, called canto popular, was created in the 1960s as a means of social commentary. It focused on societal problems, called for change, and criticized the government. Since this music developed during the military dictatorship, which suppressed the freedom of speech, it was a way for Uruguayans to make their voices heard.

Literature

Uruguay has a high level of literacy and a long tradition of freedom of speech. This has resulted in a large number of authors and poets best known for their works with patriotic and rural themes. Jose Enrique Rodó (1872–1917) was an essayist and philosopher and one of Uruguay's most important intellectuals. His essay *Ariel*, written in 1900, compared Latin American and North American cultures, urging Latin Americans to value their own voice and to reject materialism.

Juan Zorrilla de San Martin (1855–1931), is known as the "poet of the fatherland." A career diplomat, he served as an ambassador and wrote several famous poems, including "La leyenda patria" ("The Patriotic Legend") and "Tabaré," which is about the fight between the Spanish explorers and the Charrúas, a Uruguayan indigenous tribe. Juana Ibarbourou (1892–1979) is Uruguay's most famous female poet. Dubbed "Juana la América" ("Juana the American"), she was one of Uruguay's first feminists. She wrote poems using simple language about nature, love, and death.

One of the most popular themes in Uruguayan literature is the gaucho, the Uruguayan cowboy. Bartolomé Hidalgo (1788–1822) was a poet who idealized the gaucho life and wrote about gaucho folklore. Eduardo Acevedo Diaz (1851–1921) also wrote about gaucho life in his famous novel *Soledad* (1894). Javier de Viana (1868–1926), author of the acclaimed novel *Gaucha* (1899), wrote novels and short stories about poverty and the demise of the gauchos.

The Uruguayan literary tradition persisted with the rise of world-renowned writers who modernized Latin American literature. Juan Carlos Onetti (1909–1994) began as a journalist and short story author, and transitioned into writing novels. His first book, *El Pozo* ("The Pit," 1939), is considered by some as the first modern Spanish American novel. Onetti's central themes focused on the solitary, gloomy life in the city and its suffering inhabitants. Eduardo Galeano (1940–) is a journalist and a novelist best known for his diverse array of fiction and non-fiction works and his unique way of writing about Latin American history. His most famous works include *Las venas abiertas de América Latina* ("The Open Veins of Latin America," 1971) and the *Memoria del Fuego* ("Memory of Fire") trilogy, published between 1982 and 1986. These discuss the historical exploitation of Latin America, as well as the social movements and resistance against oppressors.

One of Uruguay's most famous and prolific modern authors is Mario Benedetti (1920–). He has written more than forty books translated into fourteen languages. He was also a member of the Generation of 45, a modern literary movement made up of Uruguayan writers (including Juan Carlos Onetti). A political activist, he helped create a leftist rebel group El Movimiento de Independientes 26 de Marzo (The March 26 Independents Movement) in the 1970s and was forced into exile by the military dictatorship. His most famous novel is *La Tregua* ("The Truce," 1960), and he was also well known for his poetry.

CULTURE

Arts & Entertainment

Though many Uruguayan arts forms are influenced by European traditions, Uruguay's most important festival celebrates its African heritage. Carnival is held each year on the Monday and Tuesday before Ash Wednesday, which marks the beginning of Lent, a period of fasting and penitence in the Catholic religion. Uruguayan Carnival began in the colonial era, when African slaves were only permitted to celebrate their culture during the Carnival season. Segregated from the white Uruguayans, they danced and sang outside of the city walls of Montevideo, while wealthy white families would watch them by peering over the wall. Candombe is the most famous musical form that developed, a mixture of African Bantú drumming with influences from European music and the tango. Candombe was banned in the early 1800s at the request of the elite, who felt it was a threat to society.

During Carnival, groups called comparsas compete against one another in Las llamadas (The Calls), a huge parade in Montevideo. Each group builds and decorates floats, and also creates elaborate costumes and masks for its performers. Each comparsa has dancers and between fifty and 100 drummers. Each drum section is known as a cuerda. The cuerdas use three types of drums, called tamboriles: the piano, chico, and repique. Since they are different sizes and timbres, the drums form a unique sound when played together. There are approximately ninety comparsa groups in the capital. Another Carnival tradition is the Teatro de Verano, or Summer Theater. Tabladas are groups of actors, writers, and musicians, band together to write plays and musicals and perform outdoors for free during the Carnival season. The performances include humorous songs called murgas, which poke fun at recent political and social events.

Classical music and opera are popular in Uruguay, and the country has produced several classical composers including Eduardo Fabini (1882–1950) and Hector Alberto Tosar Errecart (1923–2002). Both wrote classical music and they incorporated Uruguayan folk themes into the music. Tosar was also a pianist, lyricist, and an orchestra conductor.

There is strong public support for the performance, visual, and literary arts in Uruguay. Montevideo houses three famous theaters: the Solís Theater, in which the National Comedy Repertory Company performs plays by Latin American playwrights; the Odeon Theater, which stages plays by Shakespeare; and the Verdi Theater. Montevideo also has many notable art galleries that feature works by early and contemporary Uruguayan artists.

Literature is probably the most popular of all Uruguayan forms of artistic expression. There is a wealth of Uruguayan authors, poets, and playwrights dating back to the 19th century. Prominent modern writers include essayist José Enrique Rodó (1872–1917), and contemporary writers Mario Benedetti and Eduardo Galeano.

Songwriting has traditionally been a means of expressing social and political concerns in Uruguay, and the tradition has endured into modern times. Popular song forms include the murgas, the canto popular, and the tango.

The tango is Uruguay's most popular style of music and dance. It is an intimate and flowing partner dance that moves to the dramatic rhythms of two accordions, called bandoneons, two violins, a double bass, and a piano. Another favorite dance and music is the candombe, which incorporates the rhythms of African drums.

The largest festival celebrated in Uruguay is Carnival, a three-day party that precedes the Catholic season of Lent. During Carnival, musicians and dancers take to the streets, and neighborhood communities put on street plays called tabladas.

Fútbol (soccer) is Uruguay's national sport. Water sports such as sailing and swimming are also popular.

Cultural Sites & Landmarks

The vibrant capital of Montevideo is often considered the cultural hub of Uruguay. Founded as a military stronghold in the 18th century, the city has a rich architectural heritage and has been home to the country's most prominent artists, musicians, and writers. The city experienced widespread European immigration during the late 19th and early 20th centuries, adding to its diverse culture and history. Some of the more famous sites include the Teatro Solis, the most famous theater in Uruguay, and the Estadio Centenario, the national stadium.

Located in the historic center of Montevideo, the Teatro Solis is the center of Uruguayan performing arts. Though construction began in 1842, the theater wasn't finished until 1856 since the country's civil war interrupted building efforts. The theater underwent several name changes, including Teatro del Progreso (Progress Theater) and Teatro del Sol (Sun Theater). It was ultimately named after Spanish explorer Juan Díaz de Solis (1470–1516), the first European to explore the Río de la Plata basin. Inaugurated with an operatic performance, the theater has

since featured dance, theater, and musical productions from all over the world. A fire destroyed part of the theater in 1997 and it was closed for renovations until a grand reopening in 2004.

The Estadio Centenario, or Century Stadium, is the heart of Uruguayan soccer and one of the largest in the country. The International Federation of Association Football (FIFA) named it one of its "classic football stadiums," a monument to international soccer. It is best known for being the site of the first ever FIFA World Cup in 1930, which Uruguay won. It was also the location of five South American soccer championships and four Copa América championships. The stadium is the home of the Uruguayan national soccer team and hosts local matches. The Estadio Centenario was named for the 100th anniversary of the Uruguayan constitution. It was originally built to hold nearly 102,000 spectators, but it was later remodeled to hold about 70,000 people.

Uruguay is also home to one World Heritage Site, the Historic Quarter of the City of Colonia del Sacramento, as recognized by the United Nations Educational, Scientific and Cultural Organization (UNESCO). The city was founded by the Portuguese in 1680 due to its strategic location on the Río de la Plata near Argentina and Brazil. It remained under constant dispute between the Spanish and Portuguese until Uruguay's independence in 1828. As a result, the city includes a mixture of architectural styles and cultural influences. The historic center of Colonia features various important buildings, including several museums, churches, and the city gate. The oldest church in Uruguay is found in Colonia, the Iglesia Matriz, built in 1680. The city gate, called el Portón de Campo, was built by the Portuguese as the entrance to the city in 1745.

Libraries & Museums

Montevideo is home to a number of notable museums and galleries. The National History Museum's collections are distributed among four restored historic houses in the Old City. The Museum of Fine Arts showcases works of Uruguayan art from the country's earliest days to the present. The Casa Rivera, which dates to 1802, displays indigenous artifacts and colonial oil paintings, including a panoramic depiction of late 18th-century Montevideo. The Museo del Gaucho y de la Moneda is devoted to the history and culture of Uruguayan cowboys, as reflected in the museum's collections of traditional gaucho clothing, tools, and similar items, as well as ornately outfitted stuffed horses.

Two museums of note are the Museo Portugués, built in 1730 by the Portuguese featuring Portuguese artifacts, as well as the Museo Municipal, built in 1795 featuring documents and artifacts from the city's inhabitants.

The National Library of Uruguay is located in Montevideo and dates back to the early 19th century. It serves as the country's legal depository. As of 2003, the country was home to roughly 130 public libraries and over 80 university libraries.

Holidays

Official holidays unique to Uruguay are Return of the 33 Exiles (April 1), which commemorates the arrival of the "Immortal 33," a group of Montevideo exiles who helped Uruguay win the war for independence in 1825. The Battle of Las Piedras is commemorated on May 18, a celebration of the victory of national hero José Artigas, who expelled the Spanish governor from Montevideo in 1814. Artigas' Birthday is observed on June 19.

Constitution Day (July 18) commemorates the drafting and signing of the first Uruguayan constitution in 1830. Independence Day (August 25) involves festivities held in Independence Square in Montevideo.

Youth Culture

The youth culture of Uruguay is similar to that of other Latin American countries. Football (soccer) is the dominant sport and pastime, and recreational activities include watching television, socializing, and other leisurely pursuits that transcend cultural boundaries. Music is also integral to Uruguayan youth culture, with Westernized genres such as ska and punk becoming increasingly popular.

Uruguayan youth are also becoming more technologically-savvy, and cell phone use is high among youth in Uruguay. In October 2009, while participating in the One Laptop Per Child (OLPC) program, Uruguay reportedly became the first country in which every primary school child received a free laptop computer.

Young Uruguayans are also becoming more politically active and aware. According to a 2007 study, many young Uruguayans have a renewed interest in politics. The study also revealed that nearly half of the youth population view prioritized political matters as one of the primary topics that matter to them most. Religion also remains prevalent among Uruguayan youth, and with the growth of the evangelical movement, church youth groups have become popular among teenagers.

SOCIETY

Transportation

In cities, buses remain the most popular mode of public transportation and generally offer extensive routes and relatively inexpensive prices. There are also sleeper buses which travel within the country and to neighboring Argentina and Brazil, as well as a ferry system to Argentina. In 1999, the city of Montevideo began plans to construct a metro system, including three underground lines and one above ground line. Today that system is operational, with several aboveground lines and two underground lines in operation. Traffic moves on the right-hand side of the road in Uruguay.

Transportation Infrastructure

Uruguay has one of the most extensive highway systems in South America. Three bridges connect to neighboring Argentina, and highways link the country of Brazil. There is also a large railway system, which connects to Argentina and Brazil, though this is principally used to transport goods. Montevideo maintains an important harbor, the only free port on South America's Atlantic coast (it is a customs–exclusive zone). There are 60 airports, several of which are international. The country is serviced by 10 international airlines. In 2010, the government announced an investment of more than $90 million (USD) into Uruguay's transportation infrastructure beginning in 2011, focusing mainly on river and marine infrastructure.

Media & Communications

Due to high literacy rates, newspapers and magazines are popular in Uruguay, and over 100 daily and weekly newspapers are published. Some newspapers are linked to certain political parties and represent their interests. The most popular morning newspapers are *El País* and *La República*, while the most popular evening newspapers are *El Diario* and *Últimas Notícias*. One of the most acclaimed weekly newspapers is *Búsqueda*.

Uruguay began broadcasting on its own television stations in 1956 and there are now over 60 stations. Novelas (soap operas) are very popular, as well as sporting events, especially football (soccer).

Telecommunications are very important in Uruguay. In 1999, the country had the most phone lines per capita in South America, with 350,000 lines. In 2007, that number had more than doubled, with over 965,000 lines in the country. Cell phone usage has also dramatically increased, going from 34.8 subscriptions per 100 people in 2005 to 147.3 in 2012. The Internet has also become popular, with an estimated 55.1 percent of users in 2012.

SOCIAL DEVELOPMENT

Standard of Living

Uruguay ranked 50th out of 187 countries on the 2014 United Nations Human Development Index, which compiles quality of life and standard of living indicators.

Water Consumption

According to 2013 statistics released by the World Health Organization, Uruguay meets the international standards for potable water, and has nearly universal coverage for its citizens in both access to improved drinking water and sanitation. In June 2010, the country received a $6.85 million grant to expand and improve water and sanitation in rural areas and schools. Agricultural activities are the primary source of water consumption in the country.

Education

Uruguay's educational system is one of the best in Latin America, which accounts for the country's literacy rate of 98.1 percent. Uruguayan children attend primary school for six years, from age six to 11, then secondary school from ages 12 to 18. Secondary school is divided into two three-year sections. Education is compulsory for children up to 14 years of age, and it is very rare for a Uruguayan child not to attend classes. Public education is free, but private schools charge tuition.

The two largest universities in Uruguay are both located in Montevideo. They are the University of the Republic, a free public institution, and the Catholic University, a private institution that charges tuition.

In the 2014 Gender Gap Index, which is published by the World Economic Forum and measures gender equity regarding economic, political, and educational participation, Uruguay ranked 82nd of the 142 countries analyzed.

Women's Rights

Uruguayan women have made considerable headway in gaining their rights as citizens. Until the early 20th century, women had few rights. They were not allowed to vote or file for divorce and were required to surrender any assets or land they had acquired to their husbands. Few women worked, and those who did earned far less than their male counterparts. Change began in the early 20th century when Paulina Luisi (1875–1950), Uruguay's first woman to earn a medical degree and to serve in the government, began the feminist movement, one of the first and most successful in Latin America.

Luisi promoted women's equality, sex education in schools, and women's suffrage. She helped found two feminist organizations, the Uruguay National Women's Council and the Uruguay Women's Suffrage Alliance, as well as the feminist magazine *Acción Femenina*. The feminist movement managed to integrate women of the elite as well as working-class women, which helped add to its success. This movement also helped inspire feminists in other countries and Luisi worked closely with women's groups abroad, especially in Argentina. Feminist groups are still active in Uruguay, and include Las Decidoras, La Casa de la Mujer de la Unión, and Cotidiano Mujer. These organizations continue Luisi's work by promoting women's reproductive, educational, and occupational rights. There is even a national holiday for women, Women's Day, celebrated every year on March 8.

Women finally did win the right to vote in 1932, and the first divorce law was established in 1907. In 1946, a law was passed guaranteeing women equal civil rights for men and women. In the 1960s, middle-class women began working outside the home, able to pay working-class women to take care of their children. However, machismo, a culturally embedded concept of exaggerated masculinity, is still prevalent in Uruguay. As a result, many men believe it is their responsibility to earn the family's income and for women to oversee domestic duties and child rearing. Though many girls receive an education, poor families, especially in the countryside, tend to favor male children if they cannot afford to send all their children to school. As a result, women in rural areas are less likely to receive an education, and some end up moving to the cities to work as domestic servants.

Despite some progress, Uruguayan women still earn less than Uruguayan men. In 2002, the average female salary was over 70 percent less than the average male salary, for the same job type. In 2014, it had grown to 53 percent. In 2014, a woman's average pay was $13,407 (USD) annually, while the average for men was roughly $23,497 (USD). Jobs tend to divide along gender lines—construction work is almost entirely dominated by men, whereas most teachers are women. Though many women receive a college education, few manage to enter male-dominated careers like engineering.

Rape and domestic violence are still problems, despite laws passed in the 1990s meant to protect women from violence. In 2002, feminist groups lobbied the Uruguayan congress to pass a law decriminalizing abortion, but the president overturned the bill. Though the practice is still against the law, thousands of abortions are performed each year. In addition, prostitution is legal for those over the age of 18, and the trafficking of women for prostitution remains a concern.

Health Care

Because over 90 percent of Uruguayans have health care coverage, and medical care is easily accessible and of high quality with an emphasis on preventative medicine, the overall health of Uruguayans is good.

Uruguay's health care system includes both private and public health care, with private care being slightly superior to government-subsidized public care. But while public health care is free, only 40 percent of Uruguayans take advantage of it. Most use the services of private, for-profit providers.

GOVERNMENT

Structure

Uruguay is a constitutional republic. The country became an independent state in 1928, under the terms of the Treaty of Montevideo.

The executive branch is comprised of the president, who is both the chief of state and the head of government, the vice-president, and a cabinet called the Council of Ministers. The president and vice president are elected by popular vote to five-year terms. The Council of Ministers is selected by the president.

The legislative branch is the General Assembly, a bicameral body comprised of the Chamber of Senators and the Chamber of

Representatives. The Chamber of Senators has 30 seats, while the Chamber of Representatives has 99 seats.

Political Parties

There are three major political parties in Uruguay. The Blancos, or the National Party, represents the conservatives and tend to be the minority party. The Colorado Party represents the liberal urban class, and has traditionally been the majority party in the General Assembly. The Broad Front coalition is a left-wing political body that is comprised of 11 parties. Following the 2014 parliamentary elections, Broad Front had 50 seats in the Chamber of Deputies and 15 seats in the Senate; the National Party had 32 seats in the chamber, and 10 in the Senate; and the Colorado Party had 13 seats in the chamber, and only four seats in the Senate. The Independent Party secured three seats in the Chamber of Deputies. Minor parties without representation include the Civic Union, a Christian democratic party, and Partido del Sol (Party of the Sun), a green party.

Local Government

Uruguay has 19 administrative divisions, or departments. An administrator is appointed to oversee each department. There is limited local self-government.

Judicial System

The judicial branch is based on the Spanish civil law system and consists of the Supreme Court, courts of appeal, and criminal and civil courts. Other courts include electorate and administrative courts, and a judicial system for the military. The constitution provides for separation of powers between the judicial branch and other branches of government, meaning that the president, vice president, cabinet, or General Assembly cannot control decisions made by the courts.

Taxation

Uruguay's tax rates are relatively moderate, with a top corporate and income tax rate of 30 percent. Other taxes levied include a value-added tax (or VAT, similar to a consumption tax)—taxed at a basic rate of 22 percent as of 2014—a wealth tax, and a capital gains tax. Local taxes include a property tax and a tax payable by building owners.

Armed Forces

The Armed Forces of Uruguay consist of three service branches—the National Army, the National Navy, and the Uruguayan Air Force. Conscription is legalized (for emergency purposes), and the ages for voluntary military service are between 18 and 30. The country has participated in 12 United Nations peacekeeping missions; to support these operations, the country purchased over 100 armed transport vehicles from Canada in 2010. The number of military personnel is considered high for the country's population.

Foreign Policy

Uruguayan foreign policy has typically prioritized regional stability and relation, multilateralism, and respect for international law and national sovereignty. Dubbed the "Switzerland of Latin America," Uruguay is a neutral country with a strong diplomatic tradition. Its strategic role in regional affairs is affected by its geographic location wedged between Argentina and Brazil. It is a member of nearly 60 international organizations, including Mercosur, the Asociación Latinoamericana de Integración (Latin American Integration Association, or LAIA), and the Rio Group.

Mercosur, also known as the Mercado Común del Sul (Southern Common Market), is a trade agreement among a group of South American nations. Uruguay was a founding member, along with Argentina, Brazil, and Paraguay in 1991. Later, Bolivia, Ecuador, Chile, Colombia, and Peru joined as associate members, meaning they are eligible for the benefits of membership except for customs agreements. The idea of the agreement is to allow for the free flow of goods, people, and services among the member countries. The resulting trade bloc accounts for around 75 percent of South American commerce. Mercosur is headquartered in Montevideo. The

Latin American Integration Association is an earlier and larger trade agreement, also known as the Montevideo Treaty. Signed in 1980, it includes 12 Latin American nations and seeks to lower tariffs and ease trade between the members. Its headquarters is also based in Uruguay's capital.

The Río Group was founded in Río de Janeiro, Brazil, in 1986. It is an international body intended to forge regional cooperation on matters of security, conflict, development, democracy, human rights, and drug trafficking. It consists of 23 member nations from South America, Central America, Mexico, and the Caribbean. A meeting with the member nations' presidents is held annually to discuss regional issues and encourage diplomatic ties in Latin America. The third annual Rio Group summit was held in Montevideo.

Despite Uruguay's history of diplomatic leadership, it did experience a major international conflict in 2005. Two European companies, Metsa-Botnia from Finland and Encc from Spain, began construction on two paper mill plants in Fray Bentos, located on the Uruguay River. The $1.7 billion (USD) project was the largest capital investment in Uruguayan history, and would provide jobs right after a major economic crisis in the country. However, Argentina was strongly opposed to the plant construction, staging mass protests, threatening to cut off gas supply lines, and appealing to the World Bank to stop the project. They believed that the plants would create pollution, harm the environment, and hurt tourism in Argentina. In 2006, the two countries went to the International Court of Justice (ICJ) to resolve the conflict, with the court ruling in favor of Uruguay in January 2007. Construction on the plants continued, despite ongoing complaints from Argentina.

Recent moves to legalize marijuana and establish an international market for its sale and trade, has led many nations to observe Uruguay more closely in the coming years.

Human Rights Profile

International human rights law insists that states respect civil and political rights, and also promote an individual's economic, social and cultural rights. The United Nations Universal Declaration on Human Rights is recognized as the standard for international human rights. Its authors sought the counsel of the world's great thinkers, philosophers, and religious leaders, and were careful to create a document that reflects the core values shared by every world culture. To read this document or view the articles relating to cultural human rights, click here: http://www.udhr.org/UDHR/default.htm.

Though Uruguay has relatively few contemporary human rights violations, it has struggled to confront those of the past, specifically those committed by the military dictatorship between 1973 and 1985. Members of the government from this period were responsible for the imprisonment, torture, disappearance, and murder of thousands of Uruguayans. Other prevalent human rights abuses during this period included arbitrary arrest and detention, forced exile, and the repression of freedom of speech. To exacerbate matters, the Expiry Law was passed in 1986, guaranteeing military leaders immunity from the crimes they perpetrated during the dictatorship. However, nearly 50 cases were excluded from the law beginning in 2005, allowing the judicial system to investigate and try military leaders accused of human rights abuses. In July 2011, a presidential decree allowed for investigations and prosecutions of an estimated 80 cases of human rights violations committed from 1973-1985.

There are also several current human rights violations Uruguay must confront. Prisons are overcrowded with a lack of food and medical care, and some prisons have seen abuse and excessive force used by the guards. There have also been complaints about the treatment of female prisoners and incarcerated adolescents being discriminated against, abused by guards, and receiving little health care. In many cases, some adolescents were held in precarious conditions, often confined to a cell for up to 23 hours per day, sometimes without beds. Domestic violence against women remains and is significantly further hindered by cultural traditions and social stigma. An estimated 17 women died at the hands of domestic violence between 2006 and 2007. There have also been human rights abuses by the judicial system. In 2008, over 60 percent of prison inmates had not received a sentence by the courts, violating their right to a fair trial and the appropriate penalty applicable to the crime.

ECONOMY

Uruguay's economy is service-based. In 2010, 73 percent of Uruguay's labor force worked in the service sector, which constituted 71 percent of the gross domestic product (GDP). Agriculture contributed 7.5 percent of the GDP, and industry accounted for 21.5 percent. In 2013, the gross domestic product (GDP) was estimated at $57.11 billion USD. Per capita GDP was $16,600. The unemployment rate was 6.5 percent in 2013. From 2005 through 2013, Uruguay had one of the fastest growing economies of South America.

Montevideo's economy revolves around its ocean port, through which an enormous volume of cargo—including dairy products, grains, wool, wine, cement, and refined petroleum products—passes en route primarily to destinations in North America and Europe. A substantial portion of the southern Atlantic fishing fleet is based out of Montevideo, which counts frozen and canned seafood as one of its chief exports.

Industry

Major industries include meat processing and the manufacture of transportation equipment, electrical machinery, petroleum products, chemicals, beverages, cement, and textiles such as leather and cloth. The country's most important exports are meat and other animal products. In 1999, agricultural products accounted for half of all exports. These include leather, wool, dairy products, and fish. Uruguay imports crude petroleum, machinery, vehicles, and chemicals.

Montevideo's manufacturing sector consists of oil refineries and factories that turn out

railway equipment. The production of leather and woolen goods is another major component of this sector. The meatpacking and processing industry also plays a key role in the local economy; frozen, canned, and packaged meat products represent one of Montevideo's leading exports.

Labor

In 2004, 70 percent of Uruguay's labor force worked in the service sector, which constituted 65 percent of the gross domestic product (GDP). The rest of Uruguay's 1.5 million-strong labor force was divided between agriculture and industry. In 2013, the national work force was estimated at 1.7 million, with the service sector accounting for approximately 73 percent of the labor force by occupation. The unemployment rate was recorded as 6.5 percent in 2013.

Energy/Power/Natural Resources

With the exception of small deposits of minerals, Uruguay has no natural resources, save the country's extensive fertile farmland. Most of the country's economy depends on the processing of animal products from the country's extensive livestock operations. The country has the potential to be a significant producer of hydroelectric power due to its waterways, though environmental degradation remains a concern.

Fishing

Uruguay's domestic fishing fleet is a mix of commercial, modernized vessels that export their catch, and artisanal fishermen who sell their catch for domestic consumption. Commercial species caught include shrimp, octopus, mussels, tuna, hake, and anchovy. The country's exclusive economic zone (EEZ) measures 11,930 square kilometers (4,606 square miles).

Forestry

Forestry is a major industry for Uruguay, and produces timber for pulp mills and for export as lumber. To stimulate the industry, the government had previously allowed tax breaks to land owners who transitioned their pastures for the production of wood. As of 2009, the country was home to 1 million hectares of plantation forests. As of 2010, Uruguay is poised to become a global supplier of furniture and construction-related materials, as the forestry industry is expected to expand due to foreign investment and natural growth. Working conditions for forestry workers and environmental protection remain concerns as the industry experiences swift growth in the early 21st century.

Mining/Metals

Uruguay does not possess significant deposits of mineral resources. The country's primary mineral industries are iron and steel, cement, and petroleum derivatives or products.

Agriculture

Rice is the most abundant crop cultivated in Uruguay. In 1999, more than 1 million tons were produced. Grains and cereals such as wheat, barley, sorghum, and oats are grown in the east, and fruits and vegetables such as corn, apples, and peaches in the south, mostly on small farms. Just over seven percent of the land is used to grow crops, while 77 percent is used for ranching. In recent years moves have been made to increase marijuana growing, as national demand is outpacing supply.

Animal Husbandry

Uruguay has a total area of 72,172 square miles of pastureland used for ranching. The animals on most of the land are cattle and sheep. Uruguayan sheep and cattle are raised on natural grasses, are known to be among the best livestock produced in Latin America. The exportation of wool and meat has helped bolster the Uruguayan economy.

Large ranches of more than 1,000 hectares (2,500 acres) are found in the northern part of Uruguay. Ranchers, who take advantage of Uruguay's natural grasslands, raised more than 12 million sheep and more than 10 million head of cattle in 2001. Meat production from livestock generates more revenue than crops. Meat production earns approximately $300 million (USD) annually.

Tourism

Uruguay attracts tourists from all over the world, bringing in hundreds of millions of dollars. In 2014, tourism in the country generated approximated $4.3 billion (USD) in export revenue, with a growth rate of 2.6 percent. One of Uruguay's most popular tourist destinations is Punta del Este, a coastal resort area east of Montevideo. Punta del Este boasts over 40 kilometers (25 miles) of beach and numerous luxury resorts, many of which are government-owned.

Montevideo is also a tourist hot-spot, offering a wide variety of attractions. Tourists flock to its theaters, art galleries, museums, and restaurants. Ciudad Vieja is an area of Montevideo that has restored neoclassical buildings from the 19th century.

Tourism, and the services sector that supports it, is an important and growing facet of Montevideo's economy. The city's historic landmarks attract many visitors, particularly Argentines and Brazilians, as do the city's river shore beaches. The water quality at the capital's beaches, however, is generally not as healthy as that found along the ocean coastline, so many tourists spend time in Montevideo as a starting point before setting out for nearby resort destinations.

A growing segment of the Uruguayan tourism sector is agritourism, or estancia (ranch) tourism, which is centered on the country's gaucho culture and ranching history and its associated folklore and agricultural traditions. This niche was largely born from the difficult economy experienced by the agricultural and livestock sector during the 1980s as a way to supplement farm income. As of 2010, an estimated 500 Uruguayan ranches are open to tourists.

By Rachel Glickhouse, Jamie Aronson,
Beverly Ballaro

DO YOU KNOW?

- Uruguay was the first Latin American country to grant women the right to vote.

- Because of the separation between church and state in Uruguay, some religious holidays also have secular names. For instance, Christmas is often called "Family Day."

- There are several hypotheses concerning the origins of the national capital's name. According to one legend, Montevideo is rooted in the exclamation of a Portuguese sailor who declared, after sighting the bluff on which the capital now sits, "Monte vide eu" ("I saw the hill"). Another account suggests that the name is an abbreviated form of the moniker given to the area by Spanish cartographers: "Monte Vi de Este a Oest" ("The sixth mountain from east to west").

- February 2 is the day when thousands of Montevideo citizens of African-Brazilian heritage celebrate the annual Festival of Iemanja. Crowds of the devoted, clad in white or pale blue, gather on the capital's Playa Ramirez beach to seek the blessings and protection of the sea goddess Iemanja. They make offerings of candles, flowers, fruit, music, and sometimes launch small boats carrying votive figurines of the goddess.

Bibliography

Andrews, George Reid. *Blackness in the White Nation: A History of Afro-Uruguay.* Chapel Hill, NC: University of North Carolina Press, 2010.

Churchill, Lindsey Blake. *Becoming the Tupamaros: Solidarity and Transnational Revolutionaries in Uruguay and the United States.* Nashville, TN: Vanderbilt University Press, 2014.

Dobler, Lavinia G. *The Land and People of Uruguay.* Philadelphia: Lippincott, 1965.

Empson, Christopher. *The Far Horizons: Thirty Years Among The Gauchos Of Uruguay.* Amsterdam: Purdue University Press, 2002.

Galeano, Eduardo H. *Days and nights of love and war.* New York: Monthly Review Press, 2000.

Knarr, James C. *Uruguay and the United States, 1903-1929.* Kent, Ohio: Kent State University Press, 2012.

Murray, J.H. *Travels in Uruguay, South America.* Kessinger Publishing, 2007.

Pendle, George. *Uruguay.* Greenwood Press Reprint, 1986.

Remedi, Gustavo. *Carnival Theater: Uruguay's popular performers and national culture.* Minneapolis: University of Minnesota Press, 2004.

Rosencof, Mauricio. *The Letters that Never Came.* Albuquerque: University of New Mexico Press, 2004.

Rough Guides. *Uruguay.* London: Rough Guides, 2014.

Salgado, Susana. *The Teatro Solís: 150 years of opera, concert, and ballet in Montevideo.* Middletown: Wesleyan University Press, 2003.

USA, Ibp. *Uruguay Country Study Guide.* Washington, DC: International Business Publications, 2009.

Works Cited

"Actividades durante el 2002-2003." Jovenes. Iglesia Evangelica Metodista en el Uruguay. <http://www.gbgm-umc.org/iemu/jovenes.htm>.

Agul, Jose Pedro. "Juan Manuel Blanes." 1966. Red Academica Uruguaya. <http://www.rau.edu.uy/uruguay/cultura/blanes2.htm>.

"Biografia." Carlos Páez Vilaró. <http://www.carlospaezvilaro.com/index2.htm>.

"Biografia: Mario Benedetti." El Mundo Libro. 2002. <http://www.elmundo.es/elmundolibro/2001/05/17/anticuario/990103416.html>.

"Carlos González." Artistas. Nov. 2004. Museu Nacional de Artes Visuales. <http://www.mnav.gub.uy/gonzalez.htm>.

Clark, Gregor. "Custom Guide: Uruguay." London: Lonely Planet, 2008.

"Classic Football: Centenario." FIFA.com. <http://www.fifa.com/classicfootball/stadiums/stadium=34866/detail.html>.

"Colonia del Sacramento: Patrimonio Historico de la Humanidad." Guia Colonia. <http://www.guiacolonia.com.uy/Turismo/Colonia/Patrimonio.htm>.

"Customs of Uruguay." Encarta Interactive World Atlas. <http://encarta.msn.com/sidebar_631522275/customs_of_uruguay.html>.

Di Candia, Cesar. "Estadio Centenario." El Pais [Montevideo] 5 May 2001. El Pais. 20 Jan. 2009 <http://www.uc.org.uy/pm0501.htm>.

DNI Americas. "El comité de los Derechos de Niño del Uruguay exige el cierre de dos centros de detención para adolescentes en Uruguay." Press release. 15 Oct. 2007.

"Defensa de niñas y niños Internacional." <http://www.dniamericas.org/index.php/20080825126/Noticias/El-comite-de-los-Derechos-de-Nino-del-Uruguay-exige-el-cierre-de-dos-centros-de-detencion-para-adole.dni>.

"Eduardo Fabini." La Escuela Digital. <http://www.escueladigital.com.uy/biografias/e_fabini.htm>.

Ehrick, Christine. "Madrinas and Missionaries: Uruguay and the Pan-American Women's Movement." Gender & History 10 (1998): 406-24.

"El Estadio Centenario." Red de Enlace Didactico. Consejo de Educacion Primaria. <http://www.cep.edu.uy/TizayPizarron/RevMtros103/estadio.htm>.

"El Mate." Red Academica Uruguaya. Jan. 2000. <http://www.rau.edu.uy/uruguay/cultura/mate.htm>.

"El Mercosur." MERCOSUR - Portal Oficial. Mercosur. <http://www.mercosur.int/msweb/portal%20intermediario/es/index.htm>.

"El Teatro Solis: un centro cultural para la ciudad y su gente." Area de Desarrollo Institucional, Departamento de Educacion (2008). Teatro Solis. <http://www.teatrosolis.org.uy/imgnoticias/19578.pdf>.

"El termo y el mate." Lo bueno de Uruguay. Dec. 2004. <http://www.lobuenodeuruguay.com/Internas/termomate.html>.

Ferrer, Horacio. "Geraldo Matos Rodriguez." Todo Tango. 1980. <http://www.todotango.com/spanish/creadores/gmrodriguez.asp>.

"Florencio Sánchez." Bibliotecas Virtuales. <http://www.bibliotecasvirtuales.com/biblioteca/literaturalatinoamericana/FSanchez/index.asp>.

Foster, Dean. The Global Etiquette Guide to Mexico and Latin America. New York: John Wiley & Sons, Inc, 2002.

Gago, Verónica. "Dangerous Liaisons: Latin American Feminists and the Left." NACLA Report on the Americas 40 (2007): 17-19.

Garcia, Adriana. "Uruguay paper mill to benefit environment-company." Reuters 28 Feb. 2007.

Hernandez, Marcelo. "Uruguay Women's Day." Associated Press 8 Mar. 2004.

"Historia." Por siempre...Gardel. Universidad Nacional de San Luis. <http://gardel.unsl.edu.ar/historia.htm>.

"Historia." Teatro Solis. <http://www.teatrosolis.org.uy/hncategoriasj12.cgi?30,31,0,,1>.

"Historic Quarter of the City of Colonia de Sacramento." UNESCO. <http://whc.unesco.org/en/list/747/>.

"Increase in Real Household Income." Uruguay Daily News 9 Oct. 2008. <http://www.uruguaydailynews.com/news.php?viewStory=2543>.

Jermyn, Leslie. "Cultures of the World: Uruguay." New York: Marshall Cavendish Corporation, 1999.

"Joaquin Torres Garcia Biography." Art Museum of the Americas. Organization of American States. <http://www.museum.oas.org/permanent/constructivism/torres_garcia/bio.html>.

"Jose Belloni." Nov. 1997. Red Academica Uruguaya. <http://www.rau.edu.uy/uruguay/cultura/belloni.htm>.

"Jóvenes e Internet: Encuesta de D'Alessio Irol en Latinoamerica." Zona Pediatrica. <http://www.zonapediatrica.com/varios/jovenes-e-internet.html>.

"Juan Manuel Blanes." Artistas. 4 Sept. 2003. Museu Nacional de Artes Visuales. <http://www.mnav.gub.uy/blanes.htm>.

"La jueza dispuso excarcelación de los hermanos Peirano Basso." La Republica 30 May 2007. <http://www.larepublica.com.uy/politica/259976-la-jueza-dispuso-excarcelacion-de-los-hermanos-peirano-basso>.

"La pagina de Eduardo Galeano." Patria Grande. 4 Oct. 2007. <http://www.patriagrande.net/uruguay/eduardo.galeano/index.htm>.

"La poblacion uruguaya." Kalipedia. <http://uy.kalipedia.com/geografia-uruguay/tema/ciudades-pobladas-uruguay.html?x1=20080731klpgeogur_32.Kes&x=20080731klpgeogur_34.Kes>.

"Los jóvenes uruguayos y la política." Espectador.com 13 Nov. 2007. <http://www.espectador.com/1v4_contenido.php?id=109104&sts=1>.

"Mision y Vision." Banco Hipotecario del Uruguay. <http://www.bhu.com.uy/Institucional/mision.html>.

"Movement: Joaquín Torres-García." 2002. Coleccion Cisneros. <http://www.coleccioncisneros.org/aw_move.asp?ID_Movement=11>.

"Museo Portugues." Guia Colonia. <http://guiacolonia.com.uy/Turismo/Colonia/MPortuges.htm>.

"Musica - Uruguay - Hector Tosar." Escuela de Ciencias y Humanidades. 28 Sept. 2006. Universidad EAFIT. <http://www.eafit.edu.co/EafitCn/CienciasYHumanidades/Pregrados/Musica/musicosLatinoamericanos/Paises/Uruguay/hectorTosar.htm>.

Nwanna, Gladson I. Do's and Don'ts Around the World: A Country Guide to Cultural and Social Taboos and Etiquette: South America. Baltimore: Frontline, Inc, 1998.

"Paseos recomendados en Colonia del Sacramento." Viajar a Colonia. <http://www.viajaracolonia.com.ar/Paseos.htm>.

"Patrimonio Historico de la Humanidad: Museos." Colonia Net. <http://www.colonianet.com/paseos.htm#museos>.

"Pedro Figari: Americanism." Art Museum of the Americas. The Organization of American States. <http://www.museum.oas.org/permanent/americanism/figari/writings_about.html#traditions>.

Pierri, Raul. "Uruguay: Puccini vive y lucha." Noticias en Español 18 Aug. 2005.

"Población en el País, según departamento." "Censos de Población años 2004 (Fase 1), 1996, 1985, 1975, 1963, 1908, 1860 y 1852." 2005. POBLACION, HOGARES Y VIVIENDAS. Instituto Nacional de Estadistica de Uruguay. <http://www.ine.gub.uy/socio-demograficos/pobhogyviv2008.asp>

"Profile: Mercosur - Common Market of the South." BBC News Americas. 18 Sept. 2008. BBC. <http://news.bbc.co.uk/2/hi/americas/5195834.stm>.

"Quienes Somos." ALADI. Asociacion Latinoamericano de Integracion. <http://www.aladi.org/>.

Rank, Anna. "Torres Garcias and the Pre-Columbian Art." Arte Mercosur. <http://www.artemercosur.org.uy/artistas/torres/pre.html>.

Reel, Monte. "An Economic Boon In Uruguay Becomes A Bane to Argentina." The Washington Post 13 Nov. 2005.

"The Río Group." The Brazilian Ministry of External Relations. <http://www.mre.gov.br/index.php?option=com_content&task=view&id=1511&Itemid=1259>.

"Rosencof, Mauricio." Dramaturgia Uruguaya. Ministerio de Educacion y Cultura. <http://www.dramaturgiauruguaya.gub.uy/obras/autores/mauricio-rosencof/>.

Shields, Charles J. Uruguay. Philadelphia: Mason Crest Publishers, 2004.

Situación de la vivienda en el Uruguay Informe de Divulgación. Rep. 2006. Instituto Nacional de Estadistica del Uruguay. <http://www.ine.gub.uy/enha2006/ENHA_Vivienda_%20Final_Corr.pdf>.

Terri, Morrison, Conway A. Wayne, and George A. Borden. Kiss, Bow, Or Shake Hands: How to Do Business in Sixty Countries. Avon, MA: Adams Media, 1994.

"Trabajo y Ingresos." Rep. 2006. Instituto Nacional de Estadistica del Uruguay. <http://www.ine.gub.uy/biblioteca/genero/CAP%204%20-%20TRABAJO%20E%20INGRESOS02.pdf>.

"Traditions from Around the World: Birthday Celebrations in Uruguay." Birthday Celebrations.net. <http://www.birthdaycelebrations.net/uruguayianbirthdays.htm>.

"Uruguay 2007-2008." Diplomacy in Action. July 2008. U.S. Department of State. <http://www.state.gov/r/pa/ei/bgn/2091.htm>."Uruguay 2007-2008." Diplomacy in Action. July 2008. U.S. Department of State. <http://www.state.gov/r/pa/ei/bgn/2091.htm>.

"Uruguay - Amnesty International Report 2008." Amnesty International. <http://www.amnesty.org/en/region/uruguay/report-2008>.

"Uruguay - Amnesty International Report 2007." Amnesty International. <http://www.amnesty.org/en/region/uruguay/report-2007>.

"Uruguay: City Population." City Population. 18 Mar. 2007. <http://www.citypopulation.de/Uruguay.html>.

"Uruguay: Women and Human Rights." Women's International Network News 19 (1993): 25.

"Uruguay." The World Factbook. CIA. <https://www.cia.gov/library/publications/the-world-factbook/geos/uy.html>.

"What is Candombe?" Candombe.com. <http://www.candombe.com/spanish.html>.

Witmer, Scott. "Writers Without Borders." In These Times 14 July 2006. <http://www.inthesetimes.com/article/2699/>.

VENEZUELA

Introduction

Venezuela is officially named the Bolivarian Republic of Venezuela. It is situated in the northern portion of South America, along the Caribbean coast. Venezuela achieved independence from Spain in 1811, along with Colombia, Panama and Ecuador. It has become an important economic and political leader among its Latin American and Caribbean neighbors.

The arts in Venezuela also keep traditional culture and practices alive, and have served as a thread of continuity connecting past traditions to modern day. In particular, festivals such as Carnival have created cultural and historical continuity, alive in times of great social, political, and economic change, and feature traditional instruments, songs, dances, stories, rituals and costumes, across Venezuelan society. Venezuelan artistry, society and history are united in the pageantry and symbolism of festivals.

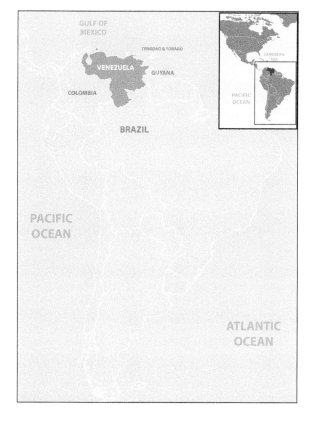

GENERAL INFORMATION

Official Language: Spanish
Population: 28,868,486 (2014 estimate)
Currency: Venezuelan fuerte (replaced the bolivar in January 2008)
Coins: Coins are available in denominations of 1, 5, 10, 12.5, 25, and 50 céntimos, and 1 fuerte (a fuerte is subdivided into 100 céntimos).
Land Area: 882,050 square kilometers (350,561 square miles)

Water Area: 30,000 square kilometers (11,583 square miles)
National Motto: "Dios y Federación" (Spanish, "God and Federation")
National Anthem: "Gloria al Bravo Pueblo" (Spanish, "Glory to the Brave People")
Capital: Caracas
Time Zone: GMT -4:30
Flag Description: Venezuela's flag is tricolored and consists of three equal horizontal bands: yellow (on top), blue, and then red. On the hoist (left side) of the yellow band is the Venezuelan coat of arms, while eight arching stars are centered in the middle blue band. Seven of the stars represent the seven provinces, while the eighth star, introduced in 2006, honors Simón Bolívar, the country's former political leader during independence.

Population

The majority of Venezuelans are mestizo, an ethnic mixture of Amerindian and European

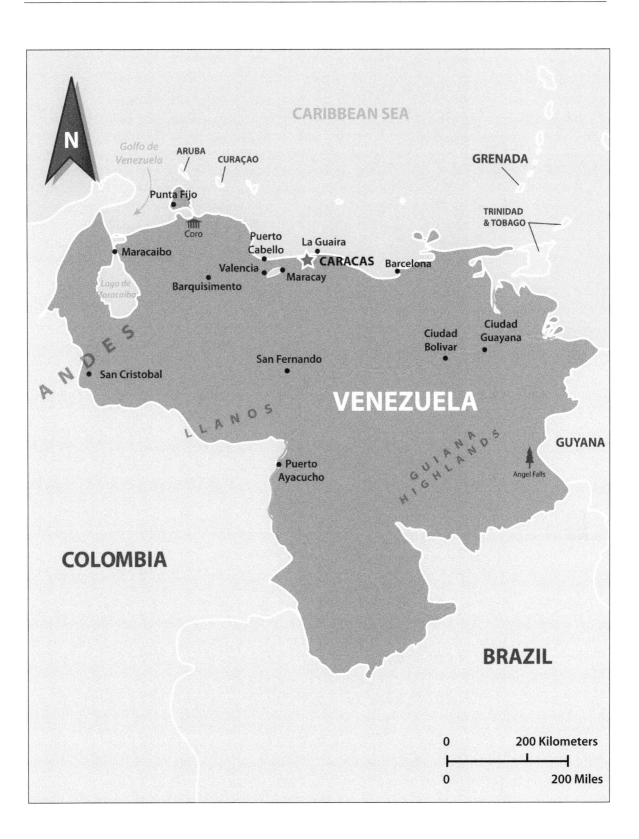

Principal Cities by Population (2012):

- Maracaibo (2,400,000)
- Caracas (2,000,000)
- Valencia (1,700,000)
- Barquisimeto (1,100,000)
- Ciudad Guayana (884,657)
- Maracay (637,372)
- Maturín (506,382)
- Barcelona (479,387)
- Ciudad Bolívar (440,018)
- Turmero (395,000)

ancestry that comprises around 67 percent of the population. White people of European descent make up 21 percent of the population. Other ethnicities found in Venezuela include Portuguese, Arab, German, African, and several indigenous populations.

The capital of Venezuela is Caracas, a city whose metropolitan area most likely exceeds six million people. In addition to Caracas, the largest cities in Venezuela are Maracaibo, Valencia, Barquisimeto and Ciudad Guayana. Venezuela is one of Latin America's most urbanized nations.

Most of the population of Venezuela (between 85 and 88 percent) lives in urban areas in the northern coastal portions of the country. The oil boom of the 20th century drove many rural Venezuelans into the cities, in part because a succession of governments focused spending on urban areas rather than rural ones. Only a very small proportion of the population (five percent) lives in the southern half of the country below the Orinoco River. As in many other countries in Latin America, the disparity between wealthy and poor in Venezuela is great.

Languages
The majority of Venezuelans speak Spanish, the national language, but the country itself features approximately 40 spoken languages. The most widely spoken indigenous languages, or Indo-Spanish languages, include Wayuu, Warao, Piaroa, Yanomami, Manduhuaca, Pemón, and

Guahibo. Italian, along with English, is one of the most highly represented foreign languages in Venezuela.

Native People & Ethnic Groups
The approximately 27 indigenous populations of Venezuela include the Wayuu, or Guajiro (220,000), who live near the Colombian border; the Yanomami (18,000), who can be found along the Amazon and Orinoco rivers; the Piaroa (17,000), also concentrated along the Orinoco and its tributaries; the Pemón (26,000); and the Warao (37,000). Some of these people remain isolated from the rest of Venezuelan society, and this fact affects their socio-political standing in the country.

Many of these peoples have struggled against encroachments on their native territories by industrialization, and suffer from high levels of disease and poverty. Since the late 1990s, the government of Venezuela has made some advances toward greater constitutional rights and privileges for indigenous peoples.

As of 2009, there are also large numbers of Italians (368,000), Portuguese (113,000), Colombians (198,000), and Lebanese Arabs (130,000) residing in Venezuela. Native Venezuelans represent 26,696,000 of the population.

Religions
The majority religion in Venezuela, as in most of Latin America, is Roman Catholicism; approximately 96 percent of the population is Catholic. The remainder of the population professes several Protestant faiths, which are rapidly converting Roman Catholics to their ranks throughout Latin America.

Climate
Overall, the climate of Venezuela is subtropical, but it varies from region to region. The Llanos are tropical while the mountainous areas are temperate. The coastal regions are both tropical and humid.

Average temperatures in winter are 15° to 26° Celsius (59° to 78° Fahrenheit) in Caracas, located in the north central region, and 23° to 32°

Celsius (73° to 90° Fahrenheit) in Maracaibo, located in the northwest, above Lago de Maracaibo. Average temperatures in summer range between 17° and 26° Celsius (63° to 80° Fahrenheit) in Caracas and 24° and 34° Celsius (76° to 94° Fahrenheit) in Maracaibo.

Seasons in Venezuela are either wet or dry with moderate temperature fluctuation. Average rainfall in the lowlands varies between 43 and 100 centimeters (16 and 40 inches); Caracas receives 75 centimeters (30 inches) a year.

ENVIRONMENT & GEOGRAPHY

Topography
Venezuela is situated in the northern portion of South America, along the Caribbean coast. Its neighbors are Colombia to the west, Brazil to the south and southeast, and Guyana to the east. The island nations of Aruba and Trinidad and Tobago lie off the Venezuelan coast, as do several other small Caribbean island nations and states.

Venezuela is comprised of the Guiana Highlands in the southern region, which contain hilly or mountainous areas with plateaus; the large Orinoco Plains, known as Llanos; tropical grasslands in the center of the country; the flat Maracaibo Lowlands in the northwest; and a mountainous region which forms the border with Colombia and stretches along the Caribbean coast.

The northern mountains contain the northeastern-most point of the Andes mountain chain. The coastal area is high and rugged in the east, while the west has large areas of lowlands, some of which are swampy.

The highest point in Venezuela is at Pico Bolivar (5,007 meters, or 16,427 feet), in the Cordillera de Merida range, south of Lago de Maracaibo in the northwest. The world's highest waterfall is Angel Falls (895 meters, or 2,937 feet) in the Guiana Highlands.

The Orinoco River traverses Venezuela and empties into the Atlantic Ocean. There are also two gulfs in Venezuela: the Gulf of Paria, near the mouth of the Orinoco, and the Gulf of Venezuela, in the far northwest. The tepuis, or high flat-topped mountains of the Guiana Highlands, are a distinct feature of the Venezuelan terrain.

Plants & Animals
Venezuela is ranked as one of the top countries in the world for biodiversity, boasting over 21,000 species of plants, and hundreds of species of amphibians, reptiles, and mammals.

Venezuelan flora includes large forests of palm, coral, mango, and brazilwood trees; carnivorous pitcher plants, some of which are endangered; long grass in the Llanos; and mangrove swamps in the Orinoco delta region. Bromeliads, fern, and orchids are also common.

Animals commonly found in Venezuela include spider monkeys, jaguars and ocelots, crocodiles, anacondas and boa constrictors, sloths, anteaters, and armadillos. Birds such as flamingos, herons, ibis, and oilbirds (or guacharos) are also common. Marine animals include sperm whales, dolphins, and manatees. Endangered animals in Venezuela include the giant otter and the giant armadillo, two species of mouse opossum, the variegated spider monkey, and the Venezuelan fish-eating rat.

CUSTOMS & COURTESIES

Greetings
In Venezuela, family and friends commonly greet each other with an abrazo (embrace). Male family and friends also typically greet each other with an embrace, sometimes accompanied by a pat on the back. However, embraces between men are exchanged only between men of the same economic or class status, and men of different economic or class statuses will not exchange physical greetings. Female family and friends greet each other with an abrazo and a kiss on the cheek.

Strangers, acquaintances and business relations typically greet each other with handshakes. Common polite verbal greeting shared by Venezuelans include "Hola" ("Hello"), "Buenos dias" ("Good morning"), "Buenas tardes" ("Good afternoon") and "Buenas noches" ("Good evening"). Religious blessing, such as "Vaya con Dios" ("Go with God") or "Adíos" ("Goodbye"), are also common. Polite greetings often include an inquiry into the health of the person and their family.

Eye contact is also important, as is a willingness to stand close to people in conversation. Venezuelans consider the act of moving back to regain personal space to be rude.

Polite conversation may cover topics such as sports, travel, or weather, and controversial subjects, such as politics and immigration, are generally avoided between acquaintances or business associates.

Gestures & Etiquette

Gesturing is a common form of communication in Venezuela, and it tends to be culturally specific as Venezuelan culture is a mix of Latin American, European, and Caribbean influences, Generally, Venezuelans convey non-verbal agreement by nodding their head forward or making a thumbs-up sign. However, Venezuelans have subtle variations to their gesturing. For example, polite and proper etiquette allows people engaged in conversation to stand quite close, typically with a half arm's length between bodies.

Venezuelans also tend to be very physically expressive. In particular, facial expressions are used to convey nuanced messages, and eye contact is maintained during conversation as an expression of interest and trust. Unfriendly and taboo gestures (gestures that are not socially acceptable) include placing an open palm on top of a closed fist, turning one's back on someone during conversation, and crossing the arms (which may convey that someone is inapproachable or upset).

In large groups, introductions begin with the elderly, and end with the youngest individuals. Visitors are not expected to extend a formal greeting to children. Formal speech and surnames are expected in most situations until informality has been mutually agreed upon. Venezuelans tend to dress in a formal manner in the business, social, and domestic settings, and cleanliness is prized.

Eating/Meals

Venezuelans typically have three meals a day, consisting of a hearty breakfast, a substantial mid-day meal traditionally shared with family, and a small evening super commonly eaten around eight o'clock. In Venezuela, dinner parties tend to begin later than specified, and dinner guests are not expected to arrive punctually. In fact, lateness is culturally acceptable and, in some instances, desirable, and a guest who arrives early or on time to a dinner party may be construed as overly eager. Additionally, dinner guests are typically expected to accept offers of coffee or food. Meals will often end with a cafecito (heavily sweetened coffee served in little cups).

In Venezuela, table manners follow continental rules, which specify that the left hand holds the fork and the right hand holds the knife. Food is almost always eaten with utensils rather than hands. Hands should be kept visible throughout the meal. The host or head of the family signals that it is time to eat by saying "buen provecho" which means "have a good meal." "¡Salud!" ("health") is a common drinking toast.

Visiting

In Venezuela, hospitality is highly valued and appreciated. When visiting someone's home in Venezuela, guests will generally be offered food and drink. In particular, cafecito is offered to visitors. Visitors are expected to stay 30 or more minutes after eating a meal for conversation and digestion. In addition, guests often bring small gifts—food, alcohol, and flowers are common. As the home is generally considered the domain of close friends and family, meetings, with acquaintances and business associates are typically held in restaurants.

National holidays and celebrations upon which families and friends visit include New Year's Eve, New Year's Day, Carnival, Ash Wednesday, Easter, Declaration of Independence Day, Simón Bolívar's birthday, Battle of Carabobo Day, Columbus Day, and Christmas Eve and Christmas Day. In Venezuela, Carnival, celebrated in February 40 days before Easter, is the biggest family celebration. Families and friends travel, often long distances, to celebrate with one another. In addition to national and regional celebrations associated with visiting, common informal social visiting events in Venezuela include birthdays, after the birth of a baby, in case of a death, around religious events and celebrations, and Sundays after mass.

LIFESTYLE

Family

Venezuelan families serve as social networks and tend to include a wide range of relatives. In some cases, these networks may also influence work, educational or political opportunities. While machismo (extensive displays of masculinity) is common, women, particularly grandmothers, receive great respect and decision-making power within families. Elders, in general, serve as advisors and caretakers for the young.

The family structure and experience of Venezuelan families is influenced by religion, climate and economy. Opportunities for family gatherings include festivals and church going. The majority of Venezuelans (96 percent) are Roman Catholic. Shared family Mass and prayer vigils are common family events. Children generally live with their parent's household until the adult children marry.

Venezuela's climate influences family relationships. The cooler temperatures in the Andean highlands require close living quarters and indoor activities, while the warm tropical climate throughout most of Venezuela promotes an outdoors lifestyle. Venezuela's economy has also influenced family structures and relationships. For example, in the late 20th century large numbers of individuals and families relocated throughout Venezuela for oil industry jobs.

Housing

Venezuela's climate, geography, and history are reflected in the country's housing. In particular, the climate—tropical and hot in the lowlands, and moderate in the highlands—has historically influenced the types of dwellings appropriate for life in Venezuela. Italian explorer Amerigo Vespucci (1454–1512) named the country Venezuela, which means "little Venice," because the country's stilt houses, common along Venezuelan lakes and rivers, reminded the explorer of similar structures built in Venice, Italy.

In modern Venezuela, architectural forms range from traditional stilt houses in the coastal countryside, and colonial-era buildings, to skyscrapers, such as the 56-story Central Park Office Towers in Caracas, built for business and urban living. The majority of Venezuelans—approximately 75 percent of the population—live in cities and towns, and the need for housing has created a building boom in Venezuela in recent years.

Food

The Venezuelan diet includes the staple agricultural products of the country, such as corn, sorghum, sugarcane, rice, bananas, vegetables, coffee, as well as beef, pork, and fish. Venezuelan cuisine is influenced by African, native Indian and European cuisines. Common Venezuelan flavors include garlic, onion, sweet pepper and coriander. The tropical climate produces fruits such as mango, papaya, avocado, bananas, coconut, melon, pineapple, and guava. Popular meat dishes include pernil (roasted pork), asado (roasted beef), bistec a caballo (steak with fried egg), and pork chops.

Typically Venezuelan dishes include arepas, empanadas, tequeños, and chicha. While these foods are eaten in other Latin American and Caribbean countries, Venezuela has a unique version of each, incorporating regional ingredients, tastes and flavors. Arepas (fried, baked, grilled, or poached corn pancakes) are eaten in place of bread, and are considered to be a national dish. Arepas may be small or large, and with filling (such as ham and cheese) or plain. They can also serve as a snack, side dish or a meal. Venezuelans often buy arepas from food stands or street vendors. Arepas are made with masa harina (a Venezuelan corn flour) which may be purchased pre-ground or made from dried corn kernels.

Empanadas are deep-fried pastries most often filled with savory ingredients such as cheese, pork, or chicken. Tequeños, named for the city of Los Teques, are long rolls stuffed with hot cheese or chocolate. Chicha is a drink associated with llaneros, or the Venezuelan cowboys. Chicha is made from ground rice, salt, condensed milk, sugar, vanilla, and ice.

Life's Milestones

In Venezuela, life's milestones correspond to Roman Catholic traditions and sacraments (activities that promote spiritual progress and growth). Religious and secular (non-religious) elements are often combined in Venezuelan life. Common Venezuelan milestones include baptism, confirmation, first communion and marriage.

In the Roman Catholic tradition, baptism is a sacrament performed to admit someone, usually an infant, into the Catholic Church. The ritual involves a formal pronouncement by a priest, the verbal support of godparents, the sign of the cross made on the forehead of the baptized person, and the pouring of holy water on the head of the baptized person.

Confirmation and First Communion are initiation rituals in the Catholic Church that mark the growing importance of faith and church in the young person's life.

In Venezuela, weddings are also usually held in a Catholic Church. The wedding includes a religious mass and a celebratory reception that traditionally features food and music. Marriage is associated with maturity and adulthood, and it is common for adult children to live in their parents' household until marriage. In addition to the religious milestones, Venezuelans celebrate the quinceañera, a girl's 15th birthday, as an important Venezuelan right of passage. Formal parties or balls and gifts of gold jewelry are common.

CULTURAL HISTORY

Art

Venezuela's fine arts reflect the country's Hispanic, indigenous and African roots. Common forms of visual art in Venezuela include drawings,

painting, sculpture, collage, mixed media and murals. Examples of indigenous art include cave art, basket weaving, masks and pottery.

Art in Venezuela has a long history of official support and patronage. Most recently, the period from the mid-1970s to the mid-1990s—a time of great oil wealth in Venezuela—saw great financial support for the arts, including the establishment of museums and other cultural organizations and institutions. Several aesthetic movements that have gained national prominence include the figurative movement, conceptualism and abstractionism, all of which reflect the social experiences and political tensions of life in Venezuela.

Venezuela's appreciation of visual art and architecture are united and reflected in the National Gallery of Art. The National Gallery of Art, located in Caracas, houses a permanent collection of art by Venezuelan artists of the past four centuries. Prominent collections include aboriginal art, colonial art, 19th-century master works, early 19th-century Círculo de Bellas Artes (a rebellious art movement called Circle of Fine Arts), and contemporary art.

Architecture

Venezuelan architecture includes modern design (as represented by the asymmetrical, mid 20th-century design of Central University of Caracas), colonial design (as represented by the 1873 National Congress Building), and indigenous or native design (as represented by coastal stilt houses).

The National Gallery of Art, located in Caracas, was designed by Venezuelan architect Carlos Raul Villanueva (1900–1975), and reflects an eclectic architectural sensibility borrowing façades (exterior of a building), porticos (roofed porch structure), and sculptural relief from many international architectural styles.

Drama

Venezuelan drama and dance are united in the pageantry and symbolism of national dances and festivals. There are Venezuelan dances, most notably the joropo, that are performed throughout the year in multiple types of venues and settings. In contrast, there are ritualistic dances and dramatic productions, such as the Diablos Danzantes de Yare ("Red Devils of Yare"), which are performed only in certain regions and during certain celebrations.

The Diablos Danzantes del Yare is a dramatic folktale and dance performed on Corpus Christi day (nine Thursdays after Holy Thursday). The dramatic performance is performed annually in a valley town called San Francisco de Yare, outside Caracas. The ritual dance or performance dates to the 18th century and involves masked dancers. The multi-day event involves the performance of fulias (native music), decimas (a native form of poetry often sung consisting of 10 stanzas), corrios (a form of musical poem) and dancing devils, dressed in red costumes and masks, moving through the streets. At the end of the event, the devils surrender and kneel in front of the church, symbolizing the triumph of righteousness over evil.

Parties and festivals throughout Venezuela often include or showcase joropo music and dance. The joropo, a dance for couples, has 36 different variations. The joropo is often performed to the song "Alma Llanera" (a song considered by many Venezuelans to be their unofficial national anthem). In addition to traditional folk forms of drama and dance, Venezuelans enjoy dancing in pop, salsa, calypso and meringue styles.

Music

The many ethnic groups found in Venezuela, including Spanish, Italian, Portuguese, Arab, German, African and indigenous, influence the sounds of Venezuelan music. In particular, Venezuelan national identity is strongly tied to the joropo (Spanish for "party"). Joropo, which is both a Venezuelan musical style and a dance, is a musical hybrid combining indigenous instruments, African slave melodies, and European or colonial waltz steps and timing. Dating back to the 18th century, the song and dance is performed in a wide range of venues, including orchestra concerts, popular radio, and at regional festivals. Other popular types of native Venezuelan musical styles include the gaita, precio, pasajes,

Various ethnic groups found in Venezuela influence the sounds of Venezuelan music and dance.

golpes and contrapuntos. Venezuelan musicians have also received international recognition for performance of non-native musical styles such as salsa, meringue, calypso, and jazz.

Popular Venezuelan instruments include the cuatro (a four-string guitar), the harp, the maracas and the drum. Venezuelan music is often associated with different lifestyles and geographic regions. For instance, the common Venezuelan instruments of the cuatro, the harp, and the maracas remind Venezuelans of ilaneros (Venezuelan cowboys) who live on the plains or grasslands of western Venezuela. Venezuelan drumming is associated with coastal regions and African influences. In addition to popular indigenous folk and popular music, Venezuela is the home of celebrated classical orchestras, operas and music schools, including the Symphonic Orchestra of Venezuela, Orchestra Simón Bolívar and the National Philharmonic Orchestra.

Literature

Early Venezuelan literature was comprised of the written documents created under Spanish rule, such as letters and chronicles. Contemporary Venezuelan literature is best known for fiction and poetry, and prominent themes include the natural world, colonization, globalization and childhood and adolescence.

Well-known Venezuelan poets include Eugenio Montejo (1938–2008), Hanni Ossott (1946–2002) and Rafael Arráiz Lucca (1959–). Well-known Venezuelan fiction writers include Rómulo Gallegos (1884–1969), Antonia Palacios (1916–2001), Teresa de la Parra (1889–1936), Arturo Uslar Pietri (1906–2001), Guillermo Meneses (1911–1978), José Balza (1939–) and Salvador Garmendia (1928–2001). Venezuelan writers, including the most celebrated writers such as Rómulo Gallegos and Arturo Uslar Pietri, tend to be more popular at home than abroad.

In addition to the classics of Venezuelan literature, there is a folk style and tradition of oral storytelling that influences and informs Venezuelan literature, as well as enriches Venezuelan life and society. Decimas and corrios are part of the tradition of oral story telling in Venezuela and Latin America. Decimas may be written, spoken, or sung. Oral storytelling, traditionally the domain of the illiterate, enriches festivals and ensures that traditional stories and histories are remembered.

CULTURE

Arts & Entertainment

In Venezuela, the arts reflect the country's willingness to embrace change, as well as remain connected to its past history and culture. Venezuela's collective identity and culture is in transition due to the oil boom at the end of the 20th century, and the drafting and development of Venezuela's first national constitution in 1999. The arts, particularly literature, architecture and visual arts, have reflected the changes and turmoil in society. For instance, the Venezuelan architect Carlos Raúl Villanueva's design of the City University of Caracas (built between 1940 and 1960) reflects Venezuela's increased internationalism and engagement with global styles. The Venezuelan writer Adriano González León (1931–2008) won the Premio Biblioteca Breve in 1968 (a literary award sponsored by Spain's Seix Barral) for his novel *País portátil*. Leon's work explores how a city can evolve into a mad and brutal place as a result of economic development and political change. He juxtaposes images of rural Venezuela with urban Caracas to highlight the problems of pollution and inhumane living conditions caused by poverty and immorality.

The arts in Venezuela also keep traditional culture and practices alive, and have served as a thread of continuity connecting past traditions to modern day. In particular, festivals such as Carnival, have created cultural and historical continuity across Venezuelan society. Venezuelan artistry, society and history are united in the pageantry and symbolism of festivals.

Venezuela's many festivals are held at different times throughout the year, and are based in specific towns and cities. Traditional Venezuelan festivals include Carnival, La Cruz de Mayo, Los Tambores de Barlovento, La Paradura del Niño and Semana Santa. Perhaps the most popular is the Venezuelan festival of Carnival, which dates back to the colonial era, and is celebrated each year in February. Venezuela's largest Carnival celebration occurs in the town of Callao, a location with a strong international and multicultural history. Callao's Carnival is a time in which music and dance matter more than social standing and race. Common costumes include devil masks, queens and court jesters.

Other Venezuelan festivals included the festival of La Cruz de Mayo, named after the Holy Cross, and celebrated annually on May 3; the festival of Los Tambores de Barlovento (which means The Drums of Barlovento), celebrated annually in March in the city of Barlovento, and is associated with African drum music; the festival of La Paradura del Niño, which occurs each year in early January in the Andean highlands, and which celebrates the child Jesus; the festival of Semana Santa (known in English as Easter), celebrated 40 days after Carnival. Ultimately, Venezuelan festivals, which vary in their dramatic themes and costumes, enact the social themes, religious imagery and historical narratives important to the Venezuelan people.

Folk music is popular among Venezuelans, particularly the llanera style, which has been assimilated into popular music. Venezuela is also home to a type of calypso music (calipso).

While football (soccer), boxing, wrestling and swimming are all popular sports, baseball remains the most popular sport in Venezuela. In fact, more than 50 Venezuelan baseball players participated in Major League Baseball's (MLB) spring training prior to the 2010 season.

Cultural Sites & Landmarks

Venezuela's cultural sites and landmarks are spread throughout the country's lowland cities and rural highlands. The United Nations Educational, Scientific and Cultural Organization (UNESCO) recognizes three sites in Venezuela as requiring international recognition and preservation efforts: the Ciudad Universitaria de Caracas (City University of Caracas); the town of Coro; and Canaima National Park.

Venezuelan architect Carlos Raúl Villanueva built the Ciudad Universitaria de Caracas between 1940 and 1960. The building, with its asymmetrical design and extensive use of provocative murals and sculpture, is an example of mid-20th century modern architecture. Areas of note within the university include Aula Magna (auditorium) with the "Clouds" sculpture of famed American sculptor Alexander Calder (1898–1976), the Olympic Stadium and the Covered Plaza.

The town of Coro, established in 1527, was Venezuela's first colonial town. Coro has 602 buildings, many of which are examples of Caribbean construction techniques (built of earth), Spanish mudéjar (a 12th- to 17th-century architectural sensibility) design and Dutch architectural styles. In 1993, the town and its port was recognized as a World Heritage Site, but was added to the list of endangered sites in 2005.

Canaima National Park is the seventh largest area of protected land in the world. The landscape is dominated by flat mountain tops, or mesas, and extensive systems of rivers, lagoons and waterfalls. The national park is perhaps best-known as the location of Angel Falls. Measured to be 15 to 17 times higher than Niagara Falls, Angel Falls is the world's highest waterfall— it has a drop of 807 meters (2,647 feet). The falls received world recognition and popularity when a North American pilot, Jimmy Angel (1899–1956), flew over the falls in 1933. Angel would later crash atop the falls, and his plane would remain there for 33 years. (The plane is now located in the Aviation Museum in the Venezuelan city of Maracay.)

Venezuelan cultural and natural sites under consideration for placement on UNESCO's World Heritage List include the city of La Guiara, Hacienda Chuao, and Ciudad Bolívar near the Orinoco River. Other important cultural sites in Venezuela include the Panteon National, the National Congress Building and the Caracas Museum of Fine Arts. The Panteon National, which houses the body of Venezuelan hero Simón Bolívar (1783–1830), an instrumental figure in Latin America's fight for independence, details Venezuela's struggle for independence from Spain. The National Congress Building, built in 1873, showcases a mural of the Venezuelan military, and the Caracas Museum of Fine Arts reflects and represents Venezuela's internationalism. Founded in 1917, the Caracas Museum of Fine Arts was also Venezuela's first art museum, and remains Venezuela's only location for art restoration.

Libraries & Museums

Many old cathedrals in Caracas serve as historical or art museums, the most notable of these being the Catedral Metropolitana and the Panteón Nacional (National Pantheon). La Galeria de Arte Nacional (The National Art Gallery) contains a collection of most Venezuelan artists, including the arts and crafts made by pre-Columbian native tribes. As the birthplace of South American revolutionary Simón Bolívar, Caracas hosts the Museo Bolívar, a museum located in the childhood home of the man Venezuelans refer to as "The Liberator."

The National Library of Venezuela (Biblioteca Nacional de Venezuela) was founded in 1833 in Caracas. It has more than an estimated 7.1 million volumes. Overall, as of 2005, there were 743 public libraries in the National Public Libraries System.

Holidays

Holidays in Venezuela include Labor Day (May 1); Carabobo's Battle (June 24), a commemoration of one of the country's most important military victories over Spain; Independence Day (July 5), which celebrates Venezuela's independence from Spain in 1816; the birthday of Simon Bolivar (July 24); and Dia de la Raza (or "Day of the Race," October 12), which is the Latin American equivalent of Columbus Day.

Youth Culture

Venezuela has a relatively young population; the median age is roughly 27, and as of 2014, 28 percent of the population was under the age of 14. In general, Venezuelan youth—following larger cultural trends and messages—are very fashion conscious, and teens of all economic classes tend to wear branded clothing. Dancing and cinema are popular youth activities, and beauty pageants remain a relevant social institution. In fact, Venezuela is known for its culture of beauty, and beauty schools, often held in a military-style fashion, have become a lucrative business in recent years. In addition, the crowning of Miss Venezuela is annually considered the most-watched TV program. Salsa and meringue are popular musical styles.

Economic class influences the social and educational opportunities available to youths. For instance, teens from wealthy backgrounds are often educated abroad, and wealthy Venezuelan teens are increasingly engaging in plastic surgery (particularly breast enhancement surgery) to improve their appearances. In fact, it has become

common for teenage girls to receive plastic surgery as a gift for their 15 birthday. This issue has heightened in recent years to the point that Venezuelan President Hugo Chávez has condemned the practice of plastic surgery undertaken by teens.

In contrast, youth from lower economic classes are challenged by a lack of educational opportunities, unemployment, violence and drugs. However, Venezuela's indigenous youth are increasingly engaging in identity-building projects such as youth radio. For example, teens from the Wayuu tribe, one of the largest indigenous groups in Venezuela, founded Radio Fe y Alegría in an effort to preserve and promote their cultural identities.

SOCIETY

Transportation

In Venezuela, common modes of local and regional transportation include cars, buses, trains, boats or planes. Despite large distances and sometimes slow transportation systems, travel in Venezuela is made relatively easy by extensive transportation linkages, and car rental and ownership is common. Additionally, Venezuela, an oil producing country, has consistently maintained low gas prices. However, extensive traffic in Venezuela's major cities and related pollution are growing concerns. Traffic is particularly congested during the afternoon when Venezuelans leave work for a long lunch at home.

Venezuelans drive on the right-hand side of the road.

Transportation Infrastructure

Travel by bus in Venezuela is common and inexpensive (the low price of gas in Venezuela keeps fare prices low). There are bus terminals and stops in most Venezuelan cities and towns, and buses are generally considered clean and safe. Additionally, two Venezuelan cities, Caracas and Los Teques, have underground commuter train systems. Venezuela also has a large railroad system which connects with Brazil, Guyana, and Colombia. Venezuela has approximately 390 airports, 128 of which had paved runways as of 2007. The Simón Bolívar International Airport of Maiquetia, outside of Caracas, is the hub of the country's many international airports.

Venezuela has extensive navigable waterways, with the Orinoco River and Lake de Maracaibo navigable by ocean vessels. Venezuela's main ports and maritime terminals include La Guaira, Maracaibo, Puerto Cabello and Punta Cardon. According to the International Maritime Bureau (IMB), Venezuela's coastal waters, particularly the Caribbean Sea, have been subject to maritime piracy.

Media & Communications

Mass media has grown in importance over the past 200 years since Venezuela's first newspaper, *Gaceta de Caracas*, went to press in 1808. There are a large number of daily papers, including *Últimas Noticias, Meridiano, El Mundo, El Nacional, Diario, El Universal, Panorama,* and *The Daily Journal*. The majority of contemporary mass media outlets are privately owned. Venezuela's radio system is large (approximately 11 million radios in 1997) and a particularly important source of news and entertainment for rural and poor sectors. Television, which began locally in 1953, is popular in Venezuela. There were approximately four million televisions in 1997. Stations include commercial, government, and religious content. Television ownership represents a status achievement for the urban poor of Venezuela.

As of 2012, Venezuela had approximately 7.65 million telephone lines and 30 million mobile cellular lines, and the communication system is characterized as expanding. The Venezuelan telephone system has a domestic satellite system with three earth bases. The Venezuelan government and business sector is committed to improving telephone service in rural regions, as well the development of a national fiber-optic networks to facilitate digital multimedia. In 2009, there were approximately nine million Internet users.

After President Hugo Chávez assumed office in 1998, and continuing under his successor, Nicolas Maduro, extensive media restrictions have been imposed in the country. For instance, the government controls media access to official events, and often denies access and information to private media outlets. Further, only government radio and television stations are granted permission to report from the presidential palace, and inaccurate media reporting (particularly reports that lead to social protests) carries a two-to-five year prison sentence. Additionally, Venezuelan law requires journalists to have a journalism degree, and those practicing journalism illegally face imprisonment.

SOCIAL DEVELOPMENT

Standard of Living

The Human Development Index ranked Venezuela 67th out of 187 countries in 2014. According to the United Nations, life expectancy for males is 71 years, and 77 years for women. Generally, Venezuela's standard of living is among the highest in South America.

Water Consumption

According to 2010 government estimates, 95 percent of the population has access to safe water, while sanitation or sewage collection extends to 85 percent of the population. Furthermore, the government states that approximately $600 million USD has been invested annually in the early 21st century—more specifically, during the presidency of Hugo Chavez—to improve drinking water and the wastewater treatment infrastructure. In 2010, the Inter-American Development Bank allocated a $50 million USD loan to help improve drinking water service and quality, with the government providing $25 million USD in counterpart funds.

Due to a severe drought that depleted Venezuela's reservoirs and threatened the nation's power grid—the Guri hydroelectric dam supplies roughly 70 percent of Venezuela's electricity—the government announced in February 2010 that it would punish excessive water usage. Consumers whose water rates exceeded allowable levels (40,000 liters or 10,567 gallons of water per month) would be subject to higher rates or a loss of service altogether.

Education

Venezuelans enjoy a free education, which is compulsory through the ninth grade. Only about half the population attends school beyond this level, and less than 10 percent attend college. The government spends about 20 percent of its national budget on education, which helps contribute to the country's high literacy rate, which is over 95 percent.

In the late 1970s, the Venezuelan government appointed a Minister for the Development of Human Intelligence to teach and study thinking skills; the result has been increased proficiency among students at all grade levels.

Among the major universities in Venezuela are the Universidad Simon Bolivar in Caracas, the Universidad de Los Andes, Central University of Venezuela, Andres Bello Catholic University in Caracas, Carabobo University in Valencia and the Polytechnical Institute in Barquisimeto. Since the late 1990s, efforts have been underway to centralize the country's universities into a system that is based on the system found in Cuba.

According to UNESCO's Education for All Global Monitoring Report released in 2010, education in Venezuela has seen significant improvements in recent years. In particular, primary school enrollment had increased from 87 percent in 1999 to 93 percent in 2007. (However, according to the report, an estimated 195,000 children are not enrolled in primary school.) Furthermore, enrollment in high school increased from 1.4 million in 1999 to 2.2 million in 2007, with approximately 26 percent attending private school.

In addition, the report stated that between 2000 and 2007, the literacy rate for Venezuelans over the age of fifteen was 95 percent, an increase of five percent from the period between 1985 and 1994.

Women's Rights

The role and treatment of women in Venezuelan society is changing as a result of increased education, opportunities and legal protections. In Venezuela, women enjoy comprehensive legal protections against domestic violence, rape, and discrimination, as well as equal rights in marriage. Legal protections against domestic violence include prison sentences for domestic abusers and the requirement that police and hospitals report domestic violence cases. Additionally, individuals found guilty of rape typically receive prison sentences of eight to 14 years, with sexual harassment also punishable by prison.

The Venezuelan government is also working to educate and embolden domestic abuse victims through a public awareness campaign and a national abuse hotline program. In terms of the workforce and political representation, Venezuelan law states that employers must not discriminate against women in pay or working conditions, and requires political parties to include equal numbers of male and female candidates.

In an effort to break the cycle of female poverty and raise the economic prospects of women in Venezuela, the National Institute for Women (Inamujer), a government-funded agency, provides small or micro loans to women of all ages and economic classes to start businesses. The banking program, referred to as Banco de la Mujer or Banmujer (the Women's Development Bank), began in 2001, and average loans range from $260 to $520 (USD). In addition to loans, Banmujer also provides non-banking services such as health education and business training to Venezuelan women.

While the Venezuelan constitution is largely non-sexist and considered to be a progressive, gender-neutral legal document, Venezuelan society, however, does not treat men and women equally. Despite legal protections, domestic violence is considered to be a national problem, and victims often refrain from reporting abuse due to social stigma. In addition, rape remains common and prostitution, though legal, is considered to be a serious social problem associated with abuse and disease. Sexual harassment also remains commonplace in workplaces and is usually dealt with as a private, rather than legal or criminal matter. Women also typically earn 30 percent less than men for the same jobs.

Human trafficking is one particularly large area of international concern in terms of women's rights in Venezuela. Human trafficking, which refers to the forced or coerced transport of people for the purpose of slavery and forced labor, has human rights, health, and security implications. In Venezuela, women and girls are typically moved throughout the country for purposes of sexual exploitation. In some instances, girls are forced into child prostitution circuits, and women and girls are forcibly sent to other countries for commercial sexual exploitation. The Venezuelan government works to combat human trafficking through prevention rather than criminal prosecution. However, victims-assistance programs for women and girls who have experienced human trafficking situations are few.

Health Care

The health care system in Venezuela was reformed in the late 1990s; as a result, universal health care is now a constitutional right of all Venezuelans. Since reforms were enacted, the level of health care participation among poorer communities has risen noticeably from earlier decades.

While the life expectancy of Venezuelans was around 45 years in the mid-20th century, it has reached an average of 74 years; 71 for men and 77 for women (2014 estimate). Venezuela has a decentralized health care system, which may help explain marked improvements in health care statistics for rural and urban populations alike.

GOVERNMENT

Structure

Unlike many other Latin American nations, Venezuela, a federal republic, has remained free of dictatorships since the mid-20th century.

Since then, the most powerful political parties have included the Accíon Democratica and the Comite de Organizacion Politica Electoral Independiente. The Movimiento Quinta Republica (Movement for the Fifth Republic) was founded by President Hugo Chavez, a popular but extremely controversial political figure, who proved able to withstand international and domestic pressures at the turn of the 21st century. Before his death, Chavez has instituted what he called a "socialist revolution" in Venezuela. He increased government control over various industries and continued to stoke his supporters with his anti-American rhetoric. It has been reported that Chavez had even moved to prepare his military for what he saw as a potential invasion of Venezuela by U.S. forces. His hand-picked successor, Nicolas Maduro, has continued along much the same path.

Since 1999, the government of Venezuela is comprised of the executive, legislative and judicial branches, but it also maintains a citizen's branch. The president is elected to six-year terms, and may be re-elected once. The legislative branch is the National Assembly, a unicameral body consisting of the Chamber of Deputies who are elected to five-year terms and may be re-elected twice. The Supreme Tribunal of Justice leads the judiciary. The unique citizen's branch consists of a prosecutor general, an ombudsman and a comptroller general, all of whom are appointed by the National Assembly to seven-year terms.

Venezuela is divided into 23 political districts, one federal district, and one federal dependency.

Political Parties

Venezuela has a multi-party system, but the country has essentially been a one-party dominant state in the early 21st century, since the election of President Hugo Chavez, the country's 53rd president. In December 2006, Chavez dissolved his left-wing Fifth Republic Movement party to create the United Socialist Party of Venezuela (PSUV), a consolidated left-wing party that unites the other pro-Chavez parties in Venezuela. While some parties did not conform and remain outside of the PSUV, Chavez's party represents the majority in the National Assembly. Opposition parties include the Democratic Action (AD), which staged an electoral boycott in 2005; PODEMOS, which is the only opposition voice in the National Assembly as of 2009; and the centrist Justice First Movement. In the April 2013 elections, following the death of Hugo Chavez, the PSUV claimed a 50.61 percent victory, with Maduro barely overcoming a challenge from opponent Henrique Radonski of Justice First, who won 49.1 percent of the vote.

Local Government

In terms of governance, Venezuela is divided into a capital district (Metropolitan District of Caracas), 23 states, and 335 municipalities, which are further subdivided into nearly 1,100 civil parishes. (The country's federal dependencies, which are islands scattered throughout the Caribbean, are overseen by the mayor of Caracas.) Municipalities are governed by an elected mayor and council. Under the new constitution, framed in 1999, Local Councils of Public Planning (CLPPs) are being implemented to promote broader participatory democracy amongst the citizenship.

Judicial System

The Supreme Tribunal of Justice is the highest court in Venezuela and is the court of last appeal. It is composed of 32 justices who serve a 12-year term. The court is subdivided into six chambers: constitutional, political administrative, electoral, civil appeals, criminal appeals, and social issues appeals. The lower court system consists of district and municipal courts and trial and appeal courts that hear criminal and civil matters. On a more complex level, these lower courts often have special jurisdiction (such as in tax or juvenile matters), and are subdivided as parish courts, district courts, courts of first instance, and appeals or superior courts. Venezuela has seen significant strides in terms of judicial reform in the early 21st century.

Taxation

Personal taxation in Venezuela is levied at a progressive rate, between six and 34 percent. As of July 2009, both the corporate income and capital gains tax rate are progressive up to 28 percent. The standard value-added tax (VAT) rate is 12 percent. Inheritance taxes are progressive up to 55 percent, and property taxes are levied at the municipal level. There is no stamp duty, capital acquisitions tax, or net wealth tax.

Armed Forces

The armed forces of Venezuela are officially known as the National Bolivarian Armed Forces, or Fuerza Armada Nacional Bolivariana (it was renamed in 2008). They consist of the Army, Air Force, Navy, the National Guard, and the National Militia, which serves in an auxiliary capacity. In 2006, the number of personnel in the armed forces was estimated at 82,000, though the militia, which Chavez had built up in recent years, is said to number about one million. Chavez, in fact, has reformed the armed forces significantly since taking power, which critics allege is merely an effort to further solidify his control, particularly after he put down an army-backed uprising in 2002. Between 2005 and 2008, the country reportedly purchased $4 billion worth of military equipment, including warplanes and assault rifles, from Russia, and those arms exports could surpass $5 billion in 2010.

Foreign Policy

Venezuela, officially called the Bolivarian Republic of Venezuela, is located at the northern edge of South America, sharing borders with Colombia, Brazil, and Guyana. The country's extensive northern coastline permits extensive trade and maritime access to the Caribbean Sea. Following the election of President Hugo Chávez in 1998, Venezuela became a politically controversial country. Chávez's development of a national constitution in 1999 received near unanimous international support. In contrast, Chávez's extensive and aggressive land claims angered neighboring countries. The same foreign policy, albeit a markedly less aggressive one, is being pursued by current president, Nicolas Maduro.

Venezuela has numerous international disputes. The border dispute between Venezuela and Guyana has a long history beginning in the 1800s, and Venezuela has exerted its claim to all land west of the Essequibo River in Guyana. In 1999, Venezuela claimed that the Essequibo area (a 56,000-square-mile region home to one-fifth of Guyana's population and rich with uranium, gold, diamonds and timber) was unfairly taken from Venezuela in a treaty signed in 1899. Venezuela made this territorial claim in part to prevent negotiation of a maritime boundary between Venezuela and Guyana. Guyana disputes the claim and plans to petition the United Nations Convention on the Law of the Sea (UNCLOS). Guyana also claims that Trinidad and Tobago's maritime boundary with Venezuela extends into Guyana waters.

Venezuela also has border and political disputes with Colombia. In 1999, Venezuela proposed a national charter to re-establish national boundaries as they were originally drawn under Spanish rule in 1810. This new national charter would be extremely advantageous for Venezuela, and Guyana and Colombia strongly opposed the redrawing of borders. Despite border disputes, Venezuela grants asylum to tens of thousands of Colombians each year fleeing narcotics and paramilitary activities.

Venezuela also claims ownership of a continental shelf extending over a large area of the Caribbean Sea. Neighboring nations, including Dominica, Saint Kitts and Nevis, Saint Lucia, and Saint Vincent and the Grenadines, dispute Venezuela's claim. However, foreign countries that support this claim include the United States, France, and the Netherlands. In addition to land disputes, Venezuela has been involved in numerous paramilitary disputes and actions. In March 2008, Colombia, Ecuador, and Venezuela ended a long-standing political feud. During the feud, Colombian military attacked interests in Ecuador prompting Ecuador and its ally Venezuela, to dispatch troops at Colombian

borders. The political relations of these three countries are expected to remain in a cautionary state.

Venezuela's international political relationships were increasingly strained under President Chávez's tenure. In particular, Venezuela and the U.S. have a strained political relationship, and in recent years Venezuela has strengthened it ties to Latin American and Middle Eastern countries not allied with the U.S. In 2014, Venezuela expelled several American diplomats on charges that they were promoting violence. However, the two countries remain strong economic partners. In fact, the U.S. is Venezuela's largest trading partner, and in 2012, American imports totaled 31.7 percent while exports to the U.S. totaled 39.1 percent. Other important trading partners include Colombia, Brazil, China, Mexico, Panama and the Netherlands Antilles.

Ultimately, Venezuela's economic and political volatility will likely remain as long as the nation is dependent on oil revenues to finance the running of the country. In 2007, oil revenues resulting from 90 percent of export earnings contributed 50 percent of the federal budget, and 30 percent of the gross domestic product (GDP).

Human Rights Profile

International human rights law insists that states respect civil and political rights, and also promote an individual's economic, social and cultural rights. The United Nations Universal Declaration on Human Rights (UDHR) is recognized as the standard for international human rights. Its authors sought the counsel of the world's great thinkers, philosophers, and religious leaders, and were careful to create a document that reflects the core values shared by every world culture. To read this document or view the articles relating to cultural human rights, click here: http://www. udhr.org/UDHR/default.htm.

In Venezuela, human rights guarantees have weakened under former President Hugo Chávez and current President, Nicolas Maduro. For instance, Article 2 of the UDHR is supported by the Venezuelan constitution, but not always in the actions of the government. While

Venezuelan law prohibits discrimination, a substantial number of Venezuelan citizens, most notably persons with disabilities, children and women and indigenous peoples, experience discrimination. Laws requiring universal physical access to public buildings and transportation for persons with disabilities are generally not enforced. As a result, persons with disabilities have limited physical access to transportation and public institutions.

The Venezuelan government is working to improve the rights and welfare of children, but the process is slow due to poverty and social stigmas. Children of indigenous and African origin have little access to schooling. An estimated 15,000 street children face detainment in juvenile detention centers on charges of curfew violations, rather than receiving medical and social aid. Lastly, the Venezuelan government largely ignores the indigenous peoples of Venezuela, with only few exceptions (such as literacy campaigns). In particular, indigenous peoples—numbering over 300,000 throughout 27 different ethnic groups—typically lack access to Venezuela's modern educational and medical facilities.

Article 16 of the Universal Declaration of Human Rights states that men and women of any race, nationality, or religion have the right to marry, and to found a family. Venezuela's constitution and society support this. Venezuelans, out of social custom, generally marry from within their ethic and economic group. While divorce is legal in Venezuela, the Roman Catholic Church disapproves of divorce and works to protect the sacrament of marriage. As a result, the country's divorce rates are low.

Venezuelan law supports Article 18 of the UDHR, which supports the right to freedom of thought, conscience, and religion, so long as the practice of religion does not violate public morality, decency, or the public order. While the Venezuelan government largely supports the freedom of religion, the government does limit and control the influence of religion in some instances. For example, the Venezuelan government requires foreign missionaries to apply for a special visa before entering the country. Religious groups have also been expelled from Venezuela on charges of interference and damage to indigenous peoples.

The Venezuelan government is increasingly lessening its commitment to Article 19, which guarantees the right to freedom of opinion and expression. Under President Chavez's rule, freedom of speech and press suffered. While the Venezuelan law has historically protected freedom of speech and of the press, free speech in Venezuela has been recently limited by new laws concerning libel and media content, legal attacks and physical intimidation. For instance, anyone found guilty of insulting the president, or other government officials, faces a sentencing of between six-to-30 months in prison.

Public contempt is also punishable by lengthy prison sentences. Under President Maduro things have gotten worse, with government clamping down on both the national and international press.

The Venezuelan government does not allow dissenting views or criticism. For instance, in 2008 President Chavez expelled the Human Rights Watch, an independent human rights watchdog organization, after the group released a report detailing the ways in which President Chavez's administration weakened public institutions and human rights. The Venezuelan government charged the group with anti-state activities, seized their cell phones, and denied the group contact with their national embassies, before escorting the group out of the country. More troubling is President Maduro's increased use of the military in quelling domestic troubles.

ECONOMY

Overview of the Economy

Venezuela's per capita gross domestic product (GDP) was estimated at $13,600 USD in 2013. Its labor force is around 14 million people (one-quarter of whom belong to labor unions), with an unemployment rate of 7.9 percent in 2013. The largest employment sector is services, followed by industry and agriculture. Despite its vital importance to the economy—petroleum accounts for nearly one-third of the South American country's GDP and over half of government revenue—the petroleum industry employs relatively few Venezuelans.

Industry

The world petroleum market is one of the most important factors affecting the economy of Venezuela. Because Venezuela contains some of the largest proven oil reserves in the world (the only countries with larger reserves are Saudi Arabia, Iran, Iraq, Kuwait, the United Arab Emirates and Russia), its most important industry is the petroleum industry. Venezuela exports over two million barrels of oil a day, making it the seventh largest exporter in the world.

Other major industries include steel and iron ore, cement and other construction materials, textiles, food and beverages, tires, and paper. Venezuela also assembles cars for its own automobile market, and for some outside markets.

Among its main exports are petroleum, bauxite aluminum, and steel. Venezuela's main trading partners are the Netherlands Antilles, Colombia, Brazil, Mexico, and the United States. (In fact, exports of consumer-oriented products from the U.S. to Venezuela ballooned from $35 million USD in 2003 to $150 million in 2008.)

Labor

Venezuela's labor force is around 14 million people (one-quarter of whom belong to labor unions), with an unemployment rate of 7.9 percent in 2013, up from 7.8 percent in 2012.

Energy/Power/Natural Resources

By far, petroleum is the most important natural resource for Venezuela, representing around 80 percent of the country's exports. Other valuable resources include natural gas, iron ore, gold, steel, coal, bauxite, timber, hydropower, and diamonds.

Land protection is of utmost concern in Venezuela; more than one-third of the country is protected. Other environmental concerns are waste control in Lago de Valencia, deforestation, soil degradation in the Llanos, and industrial pollution, such as mining-related environmental degradation and oil spills.

Fishing

Venezuela has a robust fishing industry, and small-scale fishermen provide an estimated 70 percent of fish in the country. The country is a significant producer of tuna, and shrimp remains Venezuela's most marketable catch. Other commercial catches include sardine, dogfish, squid, red snapper, and bass, and trout breeding has been introduced in some states.

In March 2009, the Venezuelan government banned trawl fishing, a drag method of commercial fishing that, locally, mostly collects shrimp off the Venezuelan coast. Venezuela's status as one of the largest global producers of natural gas and oil continues to be detrimental to the fishing industry, as oil pollution remains a primary threat to the local environment.

Forestry

Venezuela is heavily forested, but deforestation has been an issue in recent decades, primarily through development, illegal logging, and environmental degradation related to the energy and mining industries. In fact, an estimated 8.3 percent of the county's forest cover—approximately 4,313,000 hectares (10,657,655 acres)—was lost between 1990 and 2005. The government has implemented more sustainable practices in managing and protecting its forest resources in recent years, and plantation forestry (Caribbean pines) is now meeting most domestic industrial needs. Forestry now accounts for less than 0.5 percent of Venezuela's GDP.

Mining/Metals

Valuable resources include iron ore, gold, nickel, coal, bauxite, and diamonds. In recent years, the government has strengthened its role in the mining industry by creating new state mining companies and revoking certain mining concessions given to foreign companies.

Agriculture

Venezuela expends enormous resources on its petroleum and mineral markets, but very little on agriculture. Agriculture employs only a small part of the Venezuelan workforce. Among the country's most important crops are coffee, cocoa, corn, sorghum, sugarcane, fruits such as bananas and plantains, cassava, and rice. Beef and fish are also valuable agricultural products.

Since the shift from an agriculture-based economy to one that is reliant on oil, the government has had little success with agricultural reform programs. Such efforts have included limits on land ownership. One of the reasons for Venezuela's stunted agricultural activity is the vast amount of privately-owned land that lies fallow. This creates a source of trouble between wealthy landowners reformist politicians, regarding the redistribution of government-owned land. The country now imports a significant amount of agricultural products, with imports totaling approximately $7.5 million USD in 2008.

Animal Husbandry

Dairy and beef cattle have historically represented the bulk of Venezuela's livestock industry. The country recently entered into a commercial agreement with Argentina to develop the Venezuelan livestock industry, particularly the improvement of its beef supply. Argentina, a global leader in beef production, is known for its "all-natural" beef.

Tourism

Venezuela attracts about 615,000 tourists each year. Tourism has decreased during periods of economic and political instability, especially during the late 1990s and early 21st century. Popular destinations in Venezuela include the waterfalls and tepuis of Gran Sabana, beaches along the coastal north, the Andes region, and the Llanos. Overall, the tourism industry in Venezuela remains somewhat underdeveloped.

Simone Flynn, Craig Belanger,
Jeffrey Bowman

DO YOU KNOW?

- Venezuela has a higher percentage of protected land than any other nation in the Western Hemisphere.

- Six Venezuelan women have been named Miss Universe since 1979.

- After the 1812 earthquake destroyed much of Caracas, some Venezuelans believed that the natural disaster was divine punishment for rebelling against the Spanish crown.

Bibliography

Baker, Geoffrey. El Sistema: Orchestrating Venezuela's Youth. New York: Oxford University Press, 2014.

Brading, Ryan. Populism in Venezuela. New York: Routledge, 2013.

Braveboy-Wagner, Jacqueline Anne. The Venezuela-Guyana Border Dispute: Britain's

Colonial Legacy in Latin America. Boulder, Colorado: Westview Press, 1984.

Carroll, Rory. Commandante: Hugo Chávez's Venezuela. New York: Penguin Press, 2013.

Coronil, Fernando. The Magical State: Nature, Money, and Modernity in Venezuela.

Chicago: University Of Chicago Press, 1997.

Corrales, Javier. Dragon in the Tropics: Hugo Chávez and the Political Economy of Revolution in Venezuela. Washington, DC: Brookings Institution Press, 2011.

"Lonely Planet. Venezuela." Footscray, Victoria: Lonely Planet, 2010.

Maslin, Jaime. Socialist Dreams and Beauty Queens: A Couchsurfer's Memoir of Venezuela. New York: Skyhorse Publishing, 2011.

Salas, Miguel Tinker. Venezuela: What Everyone Needs to Know. New York: Oxford University Press, 2015.

Tarver, H. Michael, and Julia C. Frederick. The History of Venezuela. New York: Palgrave Macmillan, 2006.

Works Cited

"Background Note: Venezuela U.S. Department of State." Bureau of Western Hemisphere Affairs. <http://www.state.gov/r/pa/ei/bgn/35766.htm>.

Central Intelligence Agency. "CIA - The World Factbook — Venezuela." CIA World Fact Book: 244–244. History "Reference Center." EBSCO. <http://search.ebscohost.com/login.aspx?direct=true&db=khh&AN=24575900&site=ehost-live>.

"A Country Study: Venezuela." Library of Congress (2005). <http://lcweb2.loc.gov/frd/cs/vetoc.html>.

"Decima Poem Lesson." American Collection Educator's Site (n.d.). <http://www.ncteamericancollection.org/aaw_decima_poetry.htm>.

"Focus On Venezuela." AFS Intercultural Programs (n.d.). <http://www.afs.org/afs_or/focus_on/high_school/88>.

"Folklore and Traditions." U.S. Embassy to Venezuela (n.d.). <http://www.embavenez-us.org/kids.venezuela/folklore.traditions.htm>.

Johnson, Tim. "Tensions rising in Venezuela-Guyana territorial dispute." The Miami Herald (Nov. 1999). <http://www.latinamericanstudies.org/venezuela/dispute.htm>.

"Latest News." Embassy of the Bolivarian Republic of Venezuela in the United States. <http://www.embavenez-us.org/>.

Li, Kun. "Youth radio keeps indigenous culture alive in Venezuela." UNICEF for Children. <http://www.unicef.org/infobycountry/venezuela_38034.html>.

Romoero, A. "A Legend from the Venezuelan Plains." World Music Central (April 2008). <http://worldmusiccentral.org/article.php/vidal_colmenares_otro_llano>.

Tompkins, Cynthia. "Teen Life in Latin America and the Caribbean." Westport, CT: Greenwood Publishing Group, 2004.

"Universal Declaration of Human Rights." United Nations (1948). <http://www.udhr.org/UDHR/default.htm>.

"Venezuela." UNESCO World Heritage List. http://whc.unesco.org/en/statesparties/ve.

"Venezuela." Cooking by Country. <http://www.recipes4us.co.uk/Cooking%20by%20Country/Venezuela.htm>.

"Venezuela: Communication Styles." Center for Intercultural Learning (2006). <http://www.intercultures.ca/cil-cai/intercultural_issues-en.asp?lvl=8&ISO=VE&SubjectID=2>.

"Venezuela: Country Reports on Human Rights Practices." U.S. Department of State. <http://www.state.gov/g/drl/rls/hrrpt/2005/61745.htm>.

"Venezuela: Human Rights Watch Delegation Expelled." Human Rights News (Sep. 2008). < http://hrw.org/english/docs/2008/09/19/vcnczu19853.htm>.

Walker, Kristen. "Venezuela." UNESCO World Heritage List. <http://whc.unesco.org/en/list>.

"Welcome to Venezuela." Embassy of the Bolivarian Republic of Venezuela in Canada (n.d.). <http://www.misionvenezuela.org/ingles/index.htm>.

"Women's Development Bank In Venezuela: Caring." Scoop (July 2008). http://www.scoop.co.nz/stories/WO0807/S00361.htm.

Appendix One:
World Governments

Commonwealth

Guiding Premise

A commonwealth is an organization or alliance of nations connected for the purposes of satisfying a common interest. The participating states may retain their own governments, some of which are often considerably different from one another. Although commonwealth members tend to retain their own sovereign government institutions, they collaborate with other members to create mutually agreeable policies that meet their collective interests. Some nations join commonwealths to enhance their visibility and political power on the international stage. Others join commonwealths for security or economic reasons. Commonwealth members frequently engage in trade agreements, security pacts, and other programs. Some commonwealths are regional, while others are global.

Typical Structure

A commonwealth's structure depends largely on the nature of the organization and the interests it serves. Some commonwealths are relatively informal in nature, with members meeting on a periodic basis and participating voluntarily. This informality does not undermine the effectiveness of the organization, however—members still enjoy a closer relationship than that which exists among unaffiliated states. Commonwealths typically have a president, secretary general, or, in the case of the Commonwealth of Nations (a commonwealth that developed out of the British Empire), a monarch acting as the leader of the organization. Members appoint delegates to serve at summits, committee meetings, and other commonwealth events and programs.

Other commonwealths are more formal in structure and procedures. They operate based on mission statements with very specific goals and member participation requirements. These organizations have legislative bodies that meet regularly. There are even joint security operations involving members. The African Union, for example, operates according to a constitution and collectively addresses issues facing the entire African continent, such as HIV/AIDS, regional security, environmental protection, and economic cooperation.

One of the best-known commonwealths in modern history was the Soviet Union. This collective of communist states was similar to other commonwealths, but the members of the Soviet Union, although they retained their own sovereign government institutions, largely deferred to the organization's central leadership in Moscow, which in turn deferred to the Communist Party leadership. After the collapse of the Soviet Union, a dozen former Soviet states, including Russia, reconnected as the Commonwealth of Independent States. This organization features a central council in Minsk, Belarus. This council consists of the heads of state and heads of government for each member nation, along with their cabinet ministers for defense and foreign affairs.

Commonwealth structures and agendas vary. Some focus on trade and economic development, as well as using their respective members' collective power to address human rights, global climate change, and other issues. Others are focused on regional stability and mutual defense, including prevention of nuclear weapons proliferation. The diversity of issues for which commonwealths are formed contributes to the frequency of member meetings as well as the actions carried out by the organization.

Role of the Citizen

Most commonwealths are voluntary in nature, which means that the member states must choose to join with the approval of their respective governments. A nation with a democratic government, therefore, would need the sanction of its popularly elected legislative and executive bodies in order to proceed. Thus, the role of the private citizen with regard to a commonwealth is indirect—the people may have the power to vote for or against a legislative or executive candidate based on his or her position concerning membership in a commonwealth.

Some members of commonwealths, however, do not feature a democratic government, or their respective governmental infrastructures are not yet in place. Rwanda, for instance, is a developing nation whose 2009 decision to join the Commonwealth of Nations likely came from the political leadership with very little input from its citizens, as Rwandans have very limited political freedom.

While citizens may not directly influence the actions of a commonwealth, they may work closely with its representatives. Many volunteer nonprofit organizations—having direct experience with, for example, HIV/AIDS, certain minority groups, or environmental issues—work in partnership with the various branches of a commonwealth's central council. In fact, such organizations are frequently called upon in this regard to implement the policies of a commonwealth, receiving financial and logistical support

when working in impoverished and/or war-torn regions. Those working for such organizations may therefore prove invaluable to the effectiveness of a commonwealth's programs.

Michael Auerbach
Marblehead, Massachusetts

Examples

African Union
Commonwealth of Independent States
Commonwealth of Nations
Northern Mariana Islands (and the United States)
Puerto Rico (and the United States)

Bibliography

"About Commonwealth of Independent States." *Commonwealth of Independent States*. CIS, n.d. Web. 17 Jan. 2013.

"AU in a Nutshell." *African Union*. African Union Commission, n.d. Web. 17 Jan. 2013.

"The Commonwealth." *Commonwealth of Nations.* Nexus Strategic Partnerships Limited, 2013. Web. 17 Jan. 2013.

Communist

Guiding Premise

Communism is a political and economic system that seeks to eliminate private property and spread the benefits of labor equally throughout the populace. Communism is generally considered an outgrowth of socialism, a political and economic philosophy that advocates "socialized" or centralized ownership of the economy and the means of production.

Communism developed largely from the theories of Karl Marx (1818–83), who believed that a revolution led by the working class must occur before the state could achieve the even distribution of wealth and property and eliminate the class-based socioeconomic system of capitalist society. Marx believed that a truly equitable society required centralized control of credit, transportation, education, communication, agriculture, and industry, along with eliminating the rights of individuals to inherit or to own land.

Russia (formerly the Soviet Union) and China are the two largest countries to have been led by communist governments during the twentieth and twenty-first centuries. In both cases, the attempt to bring about a communist government came by way of violent revolutions in which members of the former government and ruling party were executed. Under Russian leader Vladimir Lenin (1870–1924) and Chinese leader Mao Zedong (1893–1976), strict dictatorships were instituted, curtailing individual rights in favor of state control. Lenin sought to expand communism into developing nations to counter the global spread of capitalism. Mao, in his form of communism, considered ongoing revolution within China a necessary aspect of communism. Both gave their names to their respective versions of communism, but neither Leninism nor Maoism managed to achieve the idealized utopia envisioned by Marx and other communist philosophers.

The primary difference between modern socialism and communism is that communist groups believe that a social revolution is necessary to create the idealized state without class structure, where socialists believe that the inequities of class structure can be addressed and eliminated through gradual change.

Typical Structure

Most modern communist governments define themselves as "socialist," though a national communist party exerts control over all branches of government. The designation of a "communist state" is primarily an external definition for a situation in which a communist party controls the government.

Among the examples of modern socialist states operating under the communist model are the People's Republic of China, the Republic of Cuba, and the Socialist Republic of Vietnam. However, each of these governments in fact operates through a mixed system of socialist and capitalist economic policies, allowing private ownership in some situations and sharply enforcing state control in others.

Typically, a communist state is led by the national communist party, a political group with voluntary membership and members in all sectors of the populace. While many individuals may join the communist party, the leadership of the party is generally selected by a smaller number of respected or venerated leaders from within the party. These leaders select a ruling committee that develops the political initiatives of the party, which are thereafter distributed throughout the government.

In China, the Communist Party elects both a chairperson, who serves as executive of the party, and a politburo, a standing committee that makes executive decisions on behalf of the party. In Cuba, the Communist Party selects individuals who sit for election to the National Assembly of People's Power, which then serves directly as the state's sole legislative body.

In the cases of China, Cuba, and Vietnam, the committees and leaders chosen by the communist party then participate directly in electing leaders to serve in the state judiciary. In addition, the central committees typically appoint individuals to serve as heads of the military and to lower-level, provincial, or municipal government positions. In China, the populace elects individuals to local, regional, and provincial councils that in turn elect representatives to sit on a legislative body known as the National People's Congress (NPC), though the NPC is generally considered a largely ceremonial institution without any substantial power to enact independent legislation.

In effect, most modern communist states are controlled by the leadership of the national communist party, though this leadership is achieved by direct and indirect control of lesser legislative, executive, and judicial bodies. In some cases, ceremonial and symbolic offices created under the communist party can evolve to take a larger role in state politics. In China, for instance, the NPC has come to play a more important role in developing legislation in the twenty-first century.

Role of the Citizen

In modern communist societies, citizens have little voice in selecting the leadership of the government. In many communist states, popular elections are held at local and national levels, but candidates are chosen by communist party leadership and citizens are not given the option to vote for representatives of opposing political parties.

In most cases, the state adopts policies that give the appearance of popular control over the government, while in actuality, governmental policies are influenced by a small number of leaders chosen from within the upper echelons of the party. Popularly elected leaders who oppose party policy are generally removed from office.

All existing communist states have been criticized for human rights violations in terms of curtailing the freedoms available to citizens and of enacting dictatorial and authoritarian policies. Cuba, Vietnam, and China, for instance, all have laws preventing citizens from opposing party policy or supporting a political movement that opposes the communist party. Communist governments have also been accused of using propaganda and misinformation to control the opinion of the populace regarding party leadership and therefore reducing the potential for popular resistance to communist policies.

Micah Issitt
Philadelphia, Pennsylvania

Examples
China
Cuba
Laos
North Korea
Vietnam

Bibliography
Caramani, Daniele. *Comparative Politics*. New York: Oxford UP, 2008. Print.
Priestland, David. *The Red Flag: A History of Communism.* New York: Grove, 2009. Print.
Service, Robert. *Comrades! A History of World Communism*. Cambridge: Harvard UP, 2007. Print.

Confederation/Confederacy

Guiding Premise

A confederation or confederacy is a loose alliance between political units, such as states or cantons, within a broader federal government. Confederations allow a central, federal government to create laws and regulations of broad national interest, but the sovereign units are granted the ultimate authority to carry out those laws and to create, implement, and enforce their own laws as well. Confederate governments are built on the notion that a single, central government should not have ultimate authority over sovereign states and populations. Some confederate governments were born due to the rise of European monarchies and empires that threatened to govern states from afar. Others were created out of respect for the diverse ideologies, cultures, and ideals of their respective regions. Confederations and confederacies may be hybrids, giving comparatively more power to a federal government while retaining respect for the sovereignty of their members. True confederate governments are rare in the twenty-first century.

Typical Structure

Confederate governments are typically characterized by the presence of both a central government and a set of regional, similarly organized, and sovereign (independent) governments. For example, a confederate government might have as its central government structure a system that features executive, legislative, and judicial branches. Each region that serves as members of the confederation would have in place a similar system, enabling the efficient flow of lawmaking and government services.

In some confederations, the executive branch of the central government is headed by a president or prime minister, who serves as the government's chief administrative officer, overseeing the military and other government operations. Meanwhile, at the regional level, another chief executive, such as a governor, is charged with the administration of that government's operations.

Legislative branches are also similarly designed. Confederations use parliaments or congresses that, in most cases, have two distinct chambers. One chamber consists of legislators who each represent an entire state, canton, or region. The other chamber consists of legislators representing certain populations of voters within that region. Legislatures at the regional level not only have the power to create and enforce their own laws, but also have the power to refuse to enact or enforce any laws handed down by the national government.

A confederation's judiciary is charged with ensuring that federal and regional laws are applied uniformly and within the limits of the confederation's constitutional framework. Central and regional governments both have such judicial institutions, with the latter addressing those legal matters administered in the state or canton and the former addressing legal issues of interest to the entire country.

Political parties also typically play a role in a confederate government. Political leadership is achieved by a party's majority status in either the executive or the legislative branches. Parties also play a role in forging a compromise on certain matters at both the regional and national levels. Some confederations take the diversity of political parties and their ideologies seriously enough to create coalition governments that can help avoid political stalemates.

Role of the Citizen

The political role of the citizen within a confederate political system depends largely on the constitution of the country. In some confederacies, for example, the people directly elect their legislative and executive leaders by popular vote. Some legislators are elected to open terms—they may technically be reelected, but this election is merely a formality, as they are allowed to stay in office until they decide to leave or they die—while others may be subject to term limits or other reelection rules. Popularly elected legislators and executives in turn draft, file, and pass new laws and regulations that ideally are favorable to the voters. Some confederate systems give popularly elected legislators the ability to elect a party leader to serve as prime minister or president.

Confederations are designed to empower the regional government and avoid the dominance of a distant national government. In this manner, citizens of a confederate government, in some cases, may enjoy the ability to put forth new legislative initiatives. Although the lawmaking process is expected to be administered by the legislators and executives, in such cases the people are allowed and even encouraged to connect and interact with their political representatives to ensure that the government remains open and accessible.

Michael Auerbach
Marblehead, Massachusetts

Examples

European Union

Switzerland

United States under the Articles of Confederation (1781–89)

Bibliography

"Government Type." *The World Factbook*. Central Intelligence Agency, n.d. Web. 17 Jan. 2013.

"Swiss Politics." *SwissWorld.org*. Federal Department of Foreign Affairs Presence Switzerland, n.d. Web. 17 Jan. 2013.

Constitutional Monarchy

Guiding Premise

A constitutional monarchy is a form of government in which the head of state is a monarch (a king or queen) with limited powers. The monarch has official duties, but those responsibilities are defined in the nation's constitution and not by the monarch. Meanwhile, the power to create and rescind laws is given to a legislative body. Constitutional monarchies retain the ceremony and traditions associated with nations that have long operated under a king or queen. However, the constitution prevents the monarch from becoming a tyrant. Additionally, the monarchy, which is typically a lifetime position, preserves a sense of stability and continuity in the government, as the legislative body undergoes periodic change associated with the election cycle.

Typical Structure

The structure of a constitutional monarchy varies from nation to nation. In some countries, the monarchy is predominantly ceremonial. In such cases, the monarch provides a largely symbolic role, reminding the people of their heritage and giving them comfort in times of difficulty. Such is the case in Japan, for example; the emperor of that country was stripped of any significant power after World War II but was allowed to continue his legacy in the interest of ensuring that the Japanese people would remain peaceful. Today, that nation still holds its monarchical family in the highest regard, but the government is controlled by the Diet (the legislature), with the prime minister serving in the executive role.

In other countries, the sovereign plays a more significant role. In the United Kingdom, the king or queen does have some power, including the powers to appoint the prime minister, to open or dissolve Parliament, to approve bills that have been passed by Parliament, and to declare war and make peace. However, the monarch largely defers to the government on these acts. In Bahrain, the king (or, until 2002, emir or hereditary ruler) was far more involved in government in the late twentieth and early twenty-first centuries than many other constitutional monarchs. In 1975, the emir of Bahrain dissolved the parliament, supposedly to run the government more effectively. His son would later implement a number of significant constitutional reforms that made the government more democratic in nature.

The key to the structure of this type of political system is the constitution. As is the case in the United States (a federal republic), a constitutional monarchy is carefully defined by the government's founding document. In Canada, for example, the king or queen of England is still recognized as the head of state, but that country's constitution gives the monarch no power other than ceremonial responsibilities. India, South Africa, and many other members of the Commonwealth of Nations (the English monarch's sphere of influence, spanning most of the former British colonies) have, since gaining their independence, created constitutions that grant no power to the English monarch; instead, they give all powers to their respective government institutions and, in some cases, recognize their own monarchs.

A defining feature of a constitutional monarchy is the fact that the monarch gives full respect to the limitations set forth by the constitution (and rarely seeks to alter such a document in his or her favor). Even in the United Kingdom itself—which does not have a written constitution, but rather a series of foundational documents—the king or queen does not step beyond the bounds set by customary rules. One interesting exception is in Bahrain, where Hamad bin Isa Al-Khalifa assumed the throne in 1999 and immediately implemented a series of reforms to the constitution in order to give greater definition to that country's democratic institutions, including resuming parliamentary elections in 2001. During the 2011 Arab Spring uprisings, Bahraini protesters called for further democratic reforms to be enacted, and tensions between the ruler and his opposition continue.

Role of the Citizen

In the past, monarchies ruled nations with absolute power; the only power the people had was the ability to unify and overthrow the ruling sovereign. Although the notion of an absolute monarchy has largely disappeared from the modern political landscape, many nations have retained their respective kings, queens, emperors, and other monarchs for the sake of ceremony and cultural heritage. In the modern constitutional monarchy, the people are empowered by their nation's foundational documents, which not only define the rights of the people but the limitations of their governments and sovereign as well. The people, through their legislators and through the democratic voting process, can modify their constitutions to expand or shrink the political involvement of the monarchy.

For example, the individual members of the Commonwealth of Nations, including Canada and Australia, have different constitutional parameters for the king or queen of England. In England, the monarch holds a number of powers, while in Canada, he or she is merely a ceremonial head of state (with all government power centered in the capital of Ottawa). In fact, in 1999, Australia held a referendum (a general vote) on whether to abolish its constitutional monarchy altogether and replace it with a presidential republic. In that case, the people voted to retain the monarchy, but the proposal was only narrowly defeated. These examples demonstrate the tremendous power the citizens of a constitutional monarchy may possess through the legislative process and the vote under the constitution.

Michael Auerbach
Marblehead, Massachusetts

Examples

Bahrain
Cambodia
Denmark
Japan
Lesotho
Malaysia
Morocco
Netherlands
Norway
Spain
Sweden
Thailand
United Kingdom

Bibliography

Bowman, John. "Constitutional Monarchies." *CBC News.* CBC, 4 Oct. 2002. Web. 17 Jan. 2013.
"The Role of the Monarchy." *Royal.gov.uk.* Royal Household, n.d. Web. 17 Jan. 2013.

Constitutional Republic

Guiding Premise

A constitutional republic is a governmental system in which citizens are involved in electing or appointing leaders who serve according to rules formulated in an official state constitution. In essence, the constitutional republic combines the political structure of a republic or republican governmental system with constitutional principles.

A republic is a government in which the head of state is empowered to hold office through law, not inheritance (as in a monarchy). A constitutional republic is a type of republic based on a constitution, a written body of fundamental precedents and principles from which the laws of the nation are developed.

Most constitutional republics in the modern world use a universal suffrage system, in which all citizens of the nation are empowered to vote for or against individuals who attempt to achieve public office. Universal suffrage is not required for a nation to qualify as a constitutional republic, and some nations may only allow certain categories of citizens to vote for elected leaders.

A constitutional republic differs from other forms of democratic systems in the roles assigned to both the leaders and the citizenry. In a pure democratic system, the government is formed by pure majority rule, and this system therefore ignores the opinions of any minority group. A republic, by contrast, is a form of government in which the government's role is limited by a written constitution aimed at promoting the welfare of all individuals, whether members of the majority or a minority.

Typical Structure

To qualify as a constitutional republic, a nation must choose a head of state (most often a president) through elections, according to constitutional law. In some nations, an elected president may serve alongside an appointed or elected individual who serves as leader of the legislature,

such as a prime minister, often called the "head of government." When the president also serves as head of government, the republic is said to operate under a presidential system.

Typically, the executive branch consists of the head of state and the executive offices, which are responsible for enforcing the laws and overseeing relations with other nations. The legislative branch makes laws and has overlapping duties with the executive office in terms of economic and military developments. The judicial branch, consisting of the courts, interprets the law and the constitution and enforces adherence to the law.

In a constitutional republic, the constitution describes the powers allotted to each branch of government and the means by which the governmental bodies are to be established. The constitution also describes the ways in which governmental branches interact in creating, interpreting, and enforcing laws. For instance, in the United States, the executive and legislative branches both have roles in determining the budget for the nation, and neither body is free to make budgetary legislation without the approval of the other branch.

Role of the Citizen

In a constitutional republic, the citizens have the power to control the evolution of the nation through the choice of representatives who serve on the government. These representatives can, generally through complicated means, create or abolish laws and even change the constitution itself through reinterpretations of constitutional principles or direct amendments.

Citizens in a republic are empowered, but generally not required, to play a role in electing leaders. In the United States, both state governments and the federal government function according to a republican system, and citizens are therefore allowed to take part in the election of leaders to both local and national offices. In addition, constitutional systems generally allow individuals to join political interest groups to further common political goals.

In a constitutional democratic republic such as Guatemala and Honduras, the president, who serves as chief of state and head of government, is elected directly by popular vote. In the United States, a constitutional federal republic, the president is elected by the Electoral College, whose members are selected according to the popular vote within each district. The Electoral College is intended to provide more weight to smaller states, thereby balancing the disproportionate voting power of states with larger populations. In all constitutional republics, the citizens elect leaders either directly or indirectly through other representatives chosen by popular vote. Therefore, the power to control the government is granted to the citizens of the constitutional republic.

Micah Issitt
Philadelphia, Pennsylvania

Examples
Guatemala
Honduras
Iceland
Paraguay
Peru
United States
Uruguay

Bibliography

Baylis, John, Steve Smith, and Patricia Owens. *The Globalization of World Politics: An Introduction to International Relations*. New York: Oxford UP, 2010. Print.

Caramani, Daniele. *Comparative Politics*. New York: Oxford UP, 2008. Print.

Garner, Robert, Peter Ferdinand, and Stephanie Lawson. *Introduction to Politics*. 2nd ed. Oxford: Oxford UP, 2009. Print.

Hague, Rod, and Martin Harrop. *Comparative Government and Politics: An Introduction*. New York: Palgrave, 2007. Print.

Democracy

Guiding Premise

Democracy is a political system based on majority rule, in which all citizens are guaranteed participatory rights to influence the evolution of government. There are many different types of democracy, based on the degree to which citizens participate in the formation and operation of the government. In a direct democratic system, citizens vote directly on proposed changes to law and public policy. In a representative democracy, individuals vote to elect representatives who then serve to create and negotiate public policy.

The democratic system of government first developed in Ancient Greece and has existed in many forms throughout history. While democratic systems always involve some type of majority rule component, most modern democracies have systems in place designed to equalize representation for minority groups or to promote the development of governmental policies that prevent oppression of minorities by members of the majority.

In modern democracies, one of the central principles is the idea that citizens must be allowed to participate in free elections to select leaders who serve in the government. In addition, voters in democratic systems elect political leaders for a limited period of time, thus ensuring that the leadership of the political system can change along with the changing views of the populace. Political theorists have defined democracy as a system in which the people are sovereign and the political power flows upward from the people to their elected leaders.

Typical Structure

In a typical democracy, the government is usually divided into executive, legislative, and judicial branches. Citizens participate in electing individuals to serve in one or more of these branches, and elected leaders appoint additional leaders to serve in other political offices. The democratic system, therefore, involves a combination of elected and appointed leadership.

Democratic systems may follow a presidential model, as in the United States, where citizens elect a president to serve as both head of state and head of government. In a presidential model, citizens may also participate in elections to fill other governmental bodies, including the legislature and judicial branch. In a parliamentary democracy, citizens elect individuals to a parliament, whose members in turn form a committee to appoint a leader, often called the prime minister, who serves as head of government.

In most democratic systems, the executive and legislative branches cooperate in the formation of laws, while the judicial branch enforces and interprets the laws produced by the government. Most democratic systems have developed a system of checks and balances designed to prevent any single branch of government from exerting a dominant influence over the development of governmental policy. These checks and balances may be instituted in a variety of ways, including the ability to block governmental initiatives and the ability to appoint members to various governmental agencies.

Democratic governments generally operate on the principle of political parties, which are organizations formed to influence political development. Candidates for office have the option of joining a political party, which can provide funding and other campaign assistance. In some democratic systems—called dominant party or one-party dominant systems—there is effectively a single political party. Dominant party systems allow for competition in democratic elections, but existing power structures often prevent opposing parties from competing successfully. In multiparty democratic systems, there are two or more political parties with the ability to compete for office, and citizens are able to choose among political parties during elections. Some countries only allow political parties to be active at the national level, while other countries allow political parties to play a role in local and regional elections.

Role of the Citizen

The citizens in a democratic society are seen as the ultimate source of political authority. Members of the government, by contrast, are seen as servants of the people, and are selected and elected to serve the people's interests. Democratic systems developed to protect and enhance the freedom of the people; however, for the system to function properly, citizens must engage in a number of civic duties.

In democratic nations, voting is a right that comes with citizenship. Though some democracies—Australia, for example—require citizens to vote by law, compulsory participation in elections is not common in democratic societies. Citizens are nonetheless encouraged to fulfill their voting rights and to stay informed regarding political issues. In addition, individuals are responsible for contributing to the well-being of society as a whole, usually through a system of taxation whereby part of an individual's earnings is used to pay for governmental services.

In many cases, complex governmental and legal issues must be simplified to ease understanding among the citizenry. This goal is partially met by having citizens elect leaders who must then explain to their constituents how they are shaping legislation and other government initiatives to reflect constituents' wants and needs. In the United States, citizens may participate in the election of local leaders within individual cities or counties, and also in the election of leaders who serve in the national legislature and executive offices.

Citizens in democratic societies are also empowered with the right to join political interest groups and political parties in an effort to further a broader political agenda. However, democratic societies oppose making group membership a requirement and have laws forbidding forcing an individual to join any group. Freedom of choice, especially with regard to political affiliation and preference, is one of the cornerstones of all democratic systems.

Micah Issitt
Philadelphia, Pennsylvania

Examples

Denmark
Sweden
Spain
Japan
Australia
Costa Rica
Uruguay
United States

Bibliography

Barington, Lowell. *Comparative Politics*: *Structures and Choices*. Boston: Wadsworth, 2012. Print.

Caramani, Daniele. *Comparative Politics*. New York: Oxford UP, 2008. Print.

Przeworski, Adam. *Democracy and the Limits of Self Government*, New York: Cambridge UP, 2010. Print.

Dictatorship/Military Dictatorship

Guiding Premise

Dictatorships and military dictatorships are political systems in which absolute power is held by an individual or military organization. Dictatorships are led by a single individual, under whom all political control is consolidated. Military dictatorships are similar in purpose, but place the system under the control of a military organization comprised of a single senior officer, or small group of officers. Often, dictatorships and military dictatorships are imposed as the result of a coup d'état in which the regime in question directly removes the incumbent regime, or after a power vacuum creates chaos in the nation. In both situations, the consolidation of absolute power is designed to establish a state of strict law and order.

Typical Structure

Dictatorships and military dictatorships vary in structure and nature. Some come about through the overthrow of other regimes, while others are installed through the democratic process, and then become a dictatorship as democratic rights are withdrawn. Still others are installed following a complete breakdown of government, often with the promise of establishing order.

Many examples of dictatorships can be found in the twentieth century, including Nazi Germany, Joseph Stalin's Soviet Union, and China under Mao Tse-tung. A number of dictatorships existed in Africa, such as the regimes of Idi Amin in Uganda, Charles Taylor in Liberia, and Mu'ammar Gadhafi in Libya. Dictatorships such as these consolidated power in the hands of an individual leader. A dictator serves as the sole decision-maker in the government, frequently using the military, secret police, or other security agencies to enforce the leader's will. Dictators also have control over state institutions like legislatures. A legislature may have the ability to develop and pass laws, but if its actions run counter to the dictator's will, the latter can—and

frequently does—dissolve the body, replacing its members with those more loyal to the dictator's agenda.

Military dictatorships consolidate power not in the hands of a civilian but in an individual or small group of military officers—the latter of which are often called "juntas." Because military dictatorships are frequently installed following a period of civil war and/or a coup d'état, the primary focus of the dictatorship is to achieve strict order through the application of military force. Military dictatorships are often installed with the promise of an eventual return to civilian and/or democratic control once the nation has regained stability. In the case of North Korea, one-party communist rule turned into a communist military dictatorship as its leader, Kim Il-Sung, assumed control of the military and brought its leadership into the government.

In the late twentieth and early twenty-first centuries, dictatorships and military dictatorships are most commonly found in developing nations, where poverty rates are high and regional stability is tenuous at best. Many are former European colonies, where charismatic leaders who boast of their national heritage have stepped in to replace colonial governments. National resources are typically directed toward military and security organizations in an attempt to ensure security and internal stability, keeping the regime in power and containing rivals. Human rights records in such political systems are typically heavily criticized by the international community.

Role of the Citizen

Dictatorships and military dictatorships are frequently installed because of the absence of viable democratic governments. There is often a disconnect, therefore, between the people and their leaders in a dictatorship. Of course, many dictatorships are identified as such by external entities and not by their own people. For example, the government of Zimbabwe is technically identified as a parliamentary democracy, with Robert Mugabe—who has been the elected leader of the country since 1980—as its president. However, the international community has long complained that Mugabe "won" his positions through political corruption, including alleged ballot stuffing. In 2008, Mugabe lost his first reelection campaign, but demanded a recount. While the recount continued, his supporters attacked opposition voters, utilizing violence and intimidation until his opponent, Morgan Tsvangirai, withdrew his candidacy, and Mugabe was restored as president.

By definition, citizens do not have a role in changing the course of a dictatorship's agenda. The people are usually called upon to join the military in support of the regime, or cast their vote consistently in favor of the ruling regime. Freedom of speech, the press, and assembly are virtually nonexistent, as those who speak out against the ruling regime are commonly jailed, tortured, or killed.

Michael Auerbach
Marblehead, Massachusetts

Examples

Belarus (dictatorship)
Fiji (military dictatorship)
North Korea (military dictatorship)
Zimbabwe (dictatorship)

Bibliography

Clayton, Jonathan. "China Aims to Bring Peace through Deals with Dictators and Warlords." *Times* [London]. Times Newspapers, 31 Jan. 2007. Web. 6 Feb. 2013.

"Robert Mugabe—Biography." *Biography.com.* A+E Television Networks, 2013. Web. 6 Feb. 2013.

Ecclesiastical

Guiding Premise

An ecclesiastical government is one in which the laws of the state are guided by and derived from religious law. Ecclesiastical governments can take a variety of forms and can be based on many different types of religious traditions. In some traditions, a deity or group of deities are considered to take a direct role in the formation of government, while other traditions utilize religious laws or principles indirectly to craft laws used to manage the state.

In many cultures, religious laws and tenets play a major role in determining the formation of national laws. Historically, the moral and ethical principles derived from Judeo-Christian tradition inspired many laws in Europe and North America. Few modern governments operate according to an ecclesiastical system, but Vatican City, which is commonly classified as a city-state, utilizes a modernized version of the ecclesiastical government model. All states utilizing an ecclesiastical or semi-ecclesiastical system have adopted a single state religion that is officially recognized by the government.

In some predominantly Islamic nations, including the Sudan, Oman, Iran, and Nigeria, Islamic law, known as sharia, is the basis for most national laws, and government leaders often must obtain approval by the leaders of the religious community before being allowed to serve in office. Most modern ecclesiastical or semi-ecclesiastical governments have adopted a mixed theocratic republic system in which individuals approved by religious authorities are elected by citizens to hold public office.

Typical Structure

In an ecclesiastical government, the church or recognized religious authority is the source of all state law. In a theocracy, which is one of the most common types of ecclesiastical governments, a deity or group of deities occupies a symbolic position as head of state, while representatives are chosen to lead the government based on their approval by the prevailing religious authority. In other types of ecclesiastical governments, the chief of state may be the leading figure in the church, such as in Vatican City, where the Catholic Pope is also considered the chief of state.

There are no modern nations that operate on a purely ecclesiastical system, though some Islamic countries, like Iran, have adopted a semi-ecclesiastical form of republican government. In Iran, the popularly elected Assembly of Experts—comprised of Islamic scholars called mujtahids—appoints an individual to serve as supreme leader of the nation for life, and this individual has veto power over all other governmental offices. Iranian religious leaders also approve other individuals to run as candidates for positions in the state legislature. In many cases, the citizens will elect an individual to serve as head of government, though this individual must conform to religious laws.

In an ecclesiastical government, those eligible to serve in the state legislature are generally members of the church hierarchy or have been approved for office by church leaders. In Tibet, which functioned as an ecclesiastical government until the Chinese takeover of 1951, executive and legislative duties were consolidated under a few religious leaders, called lamas, and influential citizens who maintained the country under a theocratic system. Most modern nations separate governmental functions between distinct but interrelated executive, legislative, and judicial branches.

Many modern semi-ecclesiastical nations have adopted a set of state principles in the form of a constitution to guide the operation of government and the establishment of laws. In mixed constitutional/theocratic systems, the constitution may be used to legitimize religious authority by codifying a set of laws and procedures that have been developed from religious scripture.

In addition, the existence of a constitution facilitates the process of altering laws and governmental procedures as religious authorities reinterpret religious scriptures and texts.

Role of the Citizen

Citizens in modern ecclesiastical and semi-ecclesiastical governments play a role in formulating the government though national and local elections. In some cases, religious authorities may approve more than one candidate for a certain position and citizens are then able to exercise legitimate choice in the electoral process. In other cases, popular support for one or more candidates may influence religious authorities when it comes time to nominate or appoint an individual to office.

In ecclesiastical governments, the freedoms and rights afforded to citizens may depend on their religious affiliation. Christians living in a Christian ecclesiastical government, for instance, may be allowed to run for and hold government office, while representatives of other religions may be denied this right. In addition, ecclesiastical governments may not recognize religious rights and rituals of other traditions and may not offer protection for those practicing religions other than the official state religion.

Though religious authority dominates politics and legislative development, popular influence is still an important part of the ecclesiastical system. Popular support for or against certain laws may convince the government to alter official policies. In addition, the populace may join local and regional religious bodies that can significantly affect national political developments. As local and regional religious groups grow in numbers and influence, they may promote candidates to political office, thereby helping to influence the evolution of government.

Micah Issitt
Philadelphia, Pennsylvania

Examples

Afghanistan
Iran
Nigeria
Oman
Vatican City

Bibliography

Barrington, Lowell. *Comparative Politics*: *Structures and Choices*. Boston: Wadsworth, 2012. Print.

Hallaq, Wael B. *An Introduction to Islamic Law*. New York: Cambridge UP, 2009. Print.

Hirschl, Ran. *Constitutional Theocracy*. Cambridge, MA: Harvard UP, 2010. Print.

Failed State

Guiding Premise

A failed state is a political unit that at one point had a stable government that provided basic services and security to its citizens, but then entered a period marked by devastating conflict, extreme poverty, overwhelming political corruption, and/or unlivable environmental conditions. Often, a group takes hold of a failed state's government through military means, staving off rivals to fill in a power vacuum. The nominal leadership of a failed state frequently uses its power to combat rival factions, implement extreme religious law, or protect and advance illicit activities (such as drug production or piracy). Failed states frequently retain their external borders, but within those borders are regions that may be dominated by a particular faction, effectively carving the state into disparate subunits, with some areas even attaining relative stability and security—a kind of de facto independence.

Typical Structure

Failed states vary in appearance based on a number of factors. One such factor is the type of government that existed prior to the state's collapse. For example, a failed state might have originally existed as a parliamentary democracy, with an active legislature and executive system that developed a functioning legal code and administered to the needs of the people. However, that state may not have adequately addressed the needs of certain groups, fostering a violent backlash and hastening the country's destabilization. An ineffectual legislature might have been dissolved by the executive (a prime minister or president), and in the absence of leadership, the government as a whole ceased to operate effectively.

Another major factor is demographics. Many states are comprised of two or more distinct ethnic, social, or religious groups. When the ruling party fails to effectively govern and/or serve the interests of a certain segment of the population, it may be ousted or simply ignored by the marginalized faction within the state. If the government falls, it creates a power vacuum that rival groups compete to fill. If one faction gains power, it must remain in a constant state of vigilance against its rivals, focusing more on keeping enemies in check than on rebuilding crippled government infrastructure. Some also seek to create theocracies based on extreme interpretations of a particular religious doctrine. Frequently, these regimes are themselves ousted by rivals within a few years, leaving no lasting government and keeping the state in chaos.

Failed states are also characterized by extreme poverty and a lack of modern technology. Potable water, electricity, food, and medicine are scarce among average citizens. In some cases, these conditions are worsened by natural events. Haiti, for example, was a failed state for many years before the devastating 2010 earthquake that razed the capitol city of Port au Prince, deepening the country's poverty and instability. Afghanistan and Ethiopia—with their harsh, arid climates—are also examples of failed states whose physical environments and lack of resources exacerbated an already extreme state of impoverishment.

Most failed states' conditions are also worsened by the presence of foreigners. Because their governments are either unable or unwilling to repel terrorists, for example, failed states frequently become havens for international terrorism. Somalia, Afghanistan, and Iraq are all examples of states that failed, enabling terrorist organizations to set up camp within their borders. As such groups pose a threat to other nations, those nations often send troops and weapons into the failed states to engage the terrorists. In recent years, NATO, the United Nations, and the African Union have all entered failed states to both combat terrorists and help rebuild government.

Role of the Citizen

Citizens of a failed state have very little say in the direction of their country. In most cases, when a faction assumes control over the government, it installs strict controls that limit the rights of citizens, particularly such rights as freedom of speech, freedom of assembly, and freedom of religion. Some regimes allow for "democratic" elections, but a continued lack of infrastructure and widespread corruption often negates the legitimacy of these elections.

Citizens of failed states are often called upon by the ruling regime (or a regional faction) to serve in its militia, helping it combat other factions within the state. In fact, many militias within failed states are comprised of people who were forced to join (under penalty of death) at a young age. Those who do not join militias are often drawn into criminal activity such as piracy and the drug trade.

Some citizens are able to make a difference by joining interest groups. Many citizens are able to achieve a limited amount of success sharing information about women's rights, HIV/AIDS and other issues. In some situations, these groups are able to gain international assistance from organizations that were unable to work with the failed government.

Michael Auerbach
Marblehead, Massachusetts

Examples
Chad
Democratic Republic of the Congo
Somalia
Sudan
Zimbabwe

Bibliography
"Failed States: Fixing a Broken World." *Economist*, 29 Jan. 2009. Web. 6 Feb. 2012.
"Failed States." Global Policy Forum, 2013. Web. 6 Feb. 2012.
"Somalia Tops Failed States Index for Fifth Year." *CNN.com*. Turner Broadcasting System, 18 June 2012. Web. 6 Feb. 2012.
Thürer, Daniel. (1999). "The 'Failed State' and International Law." *International Review of the Red Cross*. International Committee of the Red Cross, 31 Dec. 1999. Web. 6 Feb. 2012.

Federal Republic

Guiding Premise

A federal republic is a political system that features a central government as well as a set of regional subunits such as states or provinces. Federal republics are designed to limit the power of the central government, paring its focus to only matters of national interest. Typically, a greater degree of power is granted to the regional governments, which retain the ability to create their own laws of local relevance. The degree to which the federal and regional governments each enjoy authority varies from nation to nation, based on the country's interpretation of this republican form of government. By distributing authority to these separate but connected government institutions, federal republics give the greatest power to the people themselves, who typically vote directly for both their regional and national political representation.

Typical Structure

A federal republic's structure varies from nation to nation. However, most federal republics feature two distinct governing entities. The first is a central, federal government, usually based in the nation's capital city. The federal government's task is to address issues of national importance. These issues include defense and foreign relations, but also encompass matters of domestic interest that must be addressed in uniform fashion, such as social assistance programs, infrastructure, and certain taxes.

A federal republic is comprised of executive, legislative, and judicial branches. The executive is typically a president or prime minister—the former selected by popular vote, the latter selected by members of the legislature—and is charged with the administration of the federal government's programs and regulations. The legislature—such as the US Congress, the Austrian Parliament, or the German Bundestag—is charged with developing laws and managing government spending. The judiciary is charged

with ensuring that federal and state laws are enforced and that they are consistent with the country's constitution.

The federal government is limited in terms of its ability to assert authority over the regions. Instead, federal republics grant a degree of sovereignty to the different states, provinces, or regions that comprise the entire nation. These regions have their own governments, similar in structure and procedure to those of the federal government. They too have executives, legislatures, and judiciaries whose foci are limited to the regional government's respective jurisdictions.

The federal and regional segments of a republic are not completely independent of one another, however. Although the systems are intended to distribute power evenly, federal and regional governments are closely linked. This connectivity ensures the efficient collection of taxes, the regional distribution of federal funds, and a rapid response to issues of national importance. A federal republic's greatest strength, therefore, is the series of connections it maintains between the federal, regional, and local governments it contains.

Role of the Citizen

A federal republic is distinguished by the limitations of power it places on the national government. The primary goal of such a design was to place the power of government in the hands of the people. One of the ways the citizens' power is demonstrated is by participating in the electoral process. In a federal republic, the people elect their legislators. In some republics, the legislators in turn elect a prime minister, while in others, the people directly elect a president. The electoral process is an important way for citizens to influence the course of their government, both at the regional and federal levels. They do so by placing people who truly represent their diverse interests in the federal government.

The citizen is also empowered by participating in government as opposed to being subjected to it. In addition to taking part in the electoral process, the people are free to join and become active in a political party. A political party serves as a proxy for its members, representing their viewpoint and interests on a local and national level. In federal republics like Germany, a wide range of political parties are active in the legislature, advancing the political agendas of those they represent.

Michael Auerbach
Marblehead, Massachusetts

Examples

Austria
Brazil
Germany
India
Mexico
Nigeria
United States

Bibliography

"The Federal Principle." *Republik Österreich Parlament.* Republik Österreich Parlament, 8 Oct. 2010. Web. 6 Feb. 2013.

"The Federal Republic of Germany." *Deutscher Bundestag.* German Bundestag, 2013. Web. 6 Feb. 2013.

Collin, Nicholas. "An Essay on the Means of Promoting Federal Sentiments in the United States." *Friends of the Constitution: Writings of the "Other" Federalists, 1787–1788.* Ed. Colleen A. Sheehan and Gary L. McDowell. Online Library of Liberty, 2013. Web. 6 Feb. 2013.

Federation

Guiding Premise

A federation is a nation formed from the unification of smaller political entities. Federations feature federal governments that oversee nationwide issues. However, they also grant a degree of autonomy to the regional, state, or other local governments within the system. Federations are often formed because a collective of diverse regions find a common interest in unification. While the federal government is installed to address those needs, regions with their own distinct ethnic, socioeconomic, or political characteristics remain intact. This "separate but united" structure allows federations to avoid conflict and instability among their regions.

Typical Structure

The primary goal of a federation is to unify a country's political subunits within a national framework. The federal government, therefore, features institutions comprised of representatives from the states or regions. The representatives are typically elected by the residents of these regions, and some federal systems give the power to elect certain national leaders to these representatives. The regions themselves can vary considerably in size. The Russian Federation, for example, includes forty-six geographically large provinces as well as two more-concentrated cities as part of its eighty-three constituent federation members.

There are two institutions in which individuals from the constituent parts of a federation serve. The first institution is the legislature. Legislatures vary in appearance from nation to nation. For example, the US Congress is comprised of two chambers—the House of Representatives and the Senate—whose directly elected members act on behalf of their respective states. The German Parliament, on the other hand, consists of the directly elected Bundestag—which is tasked with electing the German federal chancellor, among other things—and the state-appointed Bundesrat, which works on behalf of the country's sixteen states.

The second institution is the executive. Here, the affairs of the nation are administered by a president or similar leader. Again, the structure and powers of a federal government's executive institutions varies from nation to nation according to their constitutional framework. Federal executive institutions are charged with management of state affairs, including oversight of the military, foreign relations, health care, and education. Similarly diverse is the power of the executive in relation to the legislative branch. Some prime ministers, for example, enjoy considerably greater power than the president. In fact, some presidents share power with other leaders, or councils thereof within the executive branch, serving as the diplomatic face of the nation but not playing a major role in lawmaking. In India, for example, the president is the chief executive of the federal government, but shares power with the prime minister and the Council of Ministers, headed by the prime minister.

In order to promote continuity between the federal government and the states, regions, or other political subunits in the federation, those subunits typically feature governments that largely mirror that of the central government. Some of these regional governments are modified according to their respective constitutions. For example, whereas the bicameral US Congress consists of the Senate and House of Representatives, Nebraska's state legislature only has one chamber. Such distinctive characteristics of state/regional governments reflect the geographic and cultural interests of the region in question. It also underscores the degree of autonomy given to such states under a federation government system.

Role of the Citizen

Federations vary in terms of both structure and distribution of power within government institutions. However, federal systems are typically democratic in nature, relying heavily on the participation of the electorate for installing representatives in those institutions. At the regional level, the people vote for their respective legislators and executives either directly or through political parties. The executive in turn appoints cabinet officials, while the legislators select a chamber leader. In US state governments, for example, such a leader might be a Senate president or speaker of the House of Representatives.

The people also play an important role in federal government. As residents of a given state or region, registered voters—again, through either a direct vote or through political parties—choose their legislators and national executives. In federations that utilize a parliamentary system, however, prime ministers are typically selected by the legislators and/or their political parties and not through a direct, national vote. Many constitutions limit the length of political leaders' respective terms of service and/or the number of times they may seek reelection, fostering an environment in which the democratic voting process is a frequent occurrence.

Michael Auerbach
Marblehead, Massachusetts

Examples

Australia
Germany
India
Mexico
Russia
United States

Bibliography

"Federal System of India." *Maps of India*. MapsOfIndia. com, 22 Sep. 2011. Web. 7 Feb. 2013.

"Political System." *Facts about Germany*. Frankfurter Societäts-Medien, 2011. Web. 7 Feb. 2013.

"Russia." *CIA World Factbook*. Central Intelligence Agency, 5 Feb. 2013. Web. 7 Feb. 2013.

Monarchy

Guiding Premise

A monarchy is a political system based on the sovereignty of a single individual who holds actual or symbolic authority over all governmental functions. The monarchy is one of the oldest forms of government in human history and was the most common type of government until the nineteenth century. In a monarchy, authority is inherited, usually through primogeniture, or inheritance by the eldest son.

In an absolute monarchy, the monarch holds authority over the government and functions as both head of state and head of government. In a constitutional monarchy, the role of the monarch is codified in the state constitution, and the powers afforded to the monarch are limited by constitutional law. Constitutional monarchies generally blend the inherited authority of the monarchy with popular control in the form of democratic elections. The monarch may continue to hold significant power over some aspects of government or may be relegated to a largely ceremonial or symbolic role.

In most ancient monarchies, the monarch was generally believed to have been chosen for his or her role by divine authority, and many monarchs in history have claimed to represent the will of a god or gods in their ascendancy to the position. In constitutional monarchies, the monarch may be seen as representing spiritual authority or may represent a link to the country's national heritage.

Typical Structure

In an absolute monarchy, a single monarch is empowered to head the government, including the formulation of all laws and leadership of the nation's armed forces. Oman is one example of a type of absolute monarchy called a sultanate, in which a family of leaders, called "sultans," inherits authority and leads the nation under an authoritarian system. Power in the Omani sultanate remains within the royal family. In the event

of the sultan's death or incapacitation, the Royal Family Council selects a successor by consensus from within the family line. Beneath the sultan is a council of ministers, appointed by the sultan, to create and disseminate official government policy. The sultan's council serves alongside an elected body of leaders who enforce and represent Islamic law and work with the sultan's ministers to create national laws.

In Japan, which is a constitutional monarchy, the Japanese emperor serves as the chief of state and symbolic representative of Japan's culture and history. The emperor officiates national ceremonies, meets with world leaders for diplomatic purposes, and symbolically appoints leaders to certain governmental posts. Governmental authority in Japan rests with the Diet, a legislative body of elected officials who serve limited terms of office and are elected through popular vote. A prime minister is also chosen to lead the Diet, and the prime minister is considered the official head of government.

The Kingdom of Norway is another example of a constitutional monarchy wherein the monarch serves a role that has been codified in the state constitution. The king of Norway is designated as the country's chief of state, serving as head of the nation's executive branch. Unlike Japan, where the monarch's role is largely symbolic, the monarch of Norway has considerable authority under the constitution, including the ability to veto and approve all laws and the power to declare war. Norway utilizes a parliamentary system, with a prime minister, chosen from individuals elected to the state parliament, serving as head of government. Though the monarch has authority over the executive functions of government, the legislature and prime minister are permitted the ability to override monarchical decisions with sufficient support, thereby providing a system of control to prevent the monarch from exerting a dominant influence over the government.

Role of the Citizen

The role of the citizen in a monarchy varies depending on whether the government is a constitutional or absolute monarchy. In an absolute monarchy, citizens have only those rights given to them by the monarch, and the monarch has the power to extend and retract freedoms and rights at will. In ancient monarchies, citizens accepted the authoritarian role of the monarch, because it was widely believed that the monarch's powers were derived from divine authority. In addition, in many absolute monarchies, the monarch has the power to arrest, detain, and imprison individuals without due process, thereby providing a strong disincentive for citizens to oppose the monarchy.

In a constitutional monarchy, citizens are generally given greater freedom to participate in the development of governmental policies. In Japan, Belgium, and Spain, for instance, citizens elect governmental leaders, and the elected legislature largely controls the creation and enforcement of laws. In some countries, like the Kingdom of Norway, the monarch may exert significant authority, but this authority is balanced by that of the legislature, which represents the sovereignty of the citizens and is chosen to promote and protect the interests of the public.

The absolute monarchies of medieval Europe, Asia, and Africa held power for centuries, but many eventually collapsed due to popular uprisings as citizens demanded representation within the government. The development of constitutional monarchies may be seen as a balanced system in which the citizens retain significant control over the development of their government while the history and traditions of the nation are represented by the continuation of the monarch's lineage. In the United Kingdom, the governments of Great Britain and Northern Ireland are entirely controlled by elected individuals, but the continuation of the monarchy is seen by many as an important link to the nation's historic identity.

Micah Issitt
Philadelphia, Pennsylvania

Examples

Belgium
Bhutan
Japan
Norway
Oman
United Kingdom

Bibliography

Barrington, Lowell. *Comparative Politics*: *Structures and Choices*. Boston: Wadsworth, 2012. Print.

Dresch, Paul, and James Piscatori, eds. *Monarchies and Nations: Globalisation and Identity in the Arab States of the Gulf.* London: Tauris, 2005. Print.

Kesselman, Mark, et al. *European Politics in Transition.* New York: Houghton, 2009. Print.

Parliamentary Monarchy

Guiding Premise

A parliamentary monarchy is a political system in which leadership of the government is shared between a monarchy, such as a king or queen, and the members of a democratically elected legislative body. In such governments, the monarch's role as head of state is limited by the country's constitution or other founding document, preventing the monarch from assuming too much control over the nation. As head of state, the monarch may provide input during the lawmaking process and other operations of government. Furthermore, the monarch, whose role is generally lifelong, acts as a stabilizing element for the government, while the legislative body is subject to the periodic changes that occur with each election cycle.

Typical Structure

Parliamentary monarchies vary in structure and distribution of power from nation to nation, based on the parameters established by each respective country's constitution or other founding document. In general, however, parliamentary monarchies feature a king, queen, or other sovereign who acts as head of state. In that capacity, the monarch's responsibilities may be little more than ceremonial in nature, allowing him or her to offer input during the lawmaking process, to approve the installation of government officials, and to act as the country's international representative. However, these responsibilities may be subject to the approval of the country's legislative body. For example, the king of Spain approves laws and regulations that have already been passed by the legislative branch; formally appoints the prime minister; and approves other ministers appointed by the prime minister. Yet, the king's responsibilities in those capacities are subject to the approval of the Cortes Generales, Spain's parliament.

In general, parliamentary monarchies help a country preserve its cultural heritage through their respective royal families, but grant the majority of government management and lawmaking responsibilities to the country's legislative branch and its various administrative ministries, such as education and defense. In most parliamentary monarchies, the ministers of government are appointed by the legislative body and usually by the prime minister. Although government ministries have the authority to carry out the country's laws and programs, they are also subject to criticism and removal by the legislative body if they fail to perform to expectations.

The legislative body itself consists of members elected through a democratic, constitutionally defined process. Term length, term limit, and the manner by which legislators may be elected are usually outlined in the country's founding documents. For example, in the Dutch parliament, members of the House of Representatives are elected every four years through a direct vote, while the members of the Senate are elected by provincial government councils every four years. By contrast, three-quarters of the members of Thailand's House of Representatives are elected in single-seat constituencies (smaller districts), while the remaining members are elected in larger, proportional representation districts; all members of the House are elected for four-year terms. A bare majority of Thailand's senators are elected by direct vote, with the remainder appointed by other members of the government.

Role of the Citizen

While the kings and queens of parliamentary monarchies are the nominal heads of state, these political systems are designed to be democratic governments. As such, they rely heavily on the input and involvement of the citizens. Participating in legislative elections is one of the most direct ways in which the citizen is empowered. Because the governments of such systems are subject to legislative oversight, the people—through their respective votes for members of parliament—have influence over their government.

Political parties and organizations such as local and municipal councils also play an important role in parliamentary monarchies. Citizens' participation in those organizations can help shape parliamentary agendas and build links between government and the public. In Norway, for example, nearly 70 percent of citizens are involved in at least one such organization, and consequently Norway's Storting (parliament) has a number of committees that are tied to those organizations at the regional and local levels. Thus, through voting and active political involvement at the local level, the citizens of a parliamentary monarchy help direct the political course of their nation.

Michael Auerbach
Marblehead, Massachusetts

Examples

Netherlands
Norway
Spain
Sweden
Thailand
United Kingdom

Bibliography

"Form of Government." *Norway.org*. Norway–The Official Site in the United States, n.d. Web. 17 Jan. 2013.

"Issues: Parliament." *Governmentl.nl*. Government of the Netherlands, n.d. Web. 17 Jan. 2013.

"King, Prime Minister, and Council of Ministers." *Country Studies: Spain*. Lib. of Congress, 2012. Web. 17 Jan. 2013.

"Thailand." *International Foundation for Electoral Systems*. IFES, 2013. Web. 17 Jan. 2013.

Parliamentary Republic

Guiding Premise

A parliamentary republic is a system wherein both executive and legislative powers are centralized in the legislature. In such a system, voters elect their national representatives to the parliamentary body, which in turn appoints the executive. In such an environment, legislation is passed more quickly than in a presidential system, which requires a consensus between the executive and legislature. It also enables the legislature to remove the executive in the event the latter does not perform to the satisfaction of the people. Parliamentary republics can also prevent the consolidation of power in a single leader, as even a prime minister must defer some authority to fellow legislative leaders.

Typical Structure

Parliamentary republics vary in structure from nation to nation, according to the respective country's constitution or other governing document. In general, such a system entails the merger of the legislature and head of state such as a president or other executive. The state may retain the executive, however. However, the executive's role may be largely ceremonial, as is the case in Greece, where the president has very little political authority. This "outsider" status has in fact enabled the Greek president to act as a diplomatic intermediary among sparring parliamentary leaders.

While many countries with such a system operate with an executive—who may or may not be directly elected, and who typically has limited powers—the bulk of a parliamentary republic's political authority rests with the legislature. The national government is comprised of democratically elected legislators and their appointees. The length of these representatives' respective terms, as well as the manner by which the legislators are elected, depend on the frameworks established by each individual nation. Some parliamentary republics utilize a constitution for this purpose, while others use a set of common laws or other legal precepts. In South Africa, members of the parliament's two chambers, the National Assembly and the National Council of Provinces, are elected differently. The former's members are elected directly by the citizens in each province, while the latter's members are installed by the provincial legislatures.

Once elected to parliament, legislators are often charged with more than just lawmaking. In many cases, members of parliament oversee the administration of state affairs as well. Legislative bodies in parliamentary republics are responsible for nominating an executive—typically a prime minister—to manage the government's various administrative responsibilities. Should the executive not adequately perform its duties, parliament has the power to remove the executive from office. In Ireland, for example, the Dail Eireann (the House of Representatives) is charged with forming the country's executive branch by nominating the Taoiseach (prime minister) and approving the prime minister's cabinet selections.

Role of the Citizen

A parliamentary republic is a democratic political system that relies on the involvement of an active electorate. This civic engagement includes a direct or indirect vote for representatives to parliament. While the people do not vote for an executive as well, by way of their vote for parliament, the citizenry indirectly influences the selection of the chief executive and the policies he or she follows. In many countries, the people also indirectly influence the national government by their votes in provincial government. As noted earlier, some countries' parliaments include chambers whose members are appointed by provincial leaders.

Citizens may also influence the political system through involvement in political parties. Such organizations help shape the platforms of parliamentary majorities as well as selecting candidates for prime minister and other government positions. The significance of political parties varies from nation to nation, but such organizations require the input and involvement of citizens.

Michael Auerbach
Marblehead, Massachusetts

Examples
Austria
Greece
Iceland
Ireland
Poland
South Africa

Bibliography
"About the Oireachtas." *Oireachtas.ie*. Houses of the Oireachtas, n.d. Web. 7 Feb. 2013.

"Our Parliament." *Parliament.gov*. Parliament of the Republic of South Africa, n.d. Web. 7 Feb. 2013.

Tagaris, Karolina, and Ingrid Melander. "Greek President Makes Last Push to Avert Elections." *Reuters*. Thomson Reuters, 12 May 2012. Web. 7 Feb. 2013.

Presidential

Guiding Premise

A presidential system is a type of democratic government in which the populace elects a single leader—a president—to serve as both head of state and the head of government. The presidential system developed from the monarchic governments of medieval and early modern Europe, in which a royal monarch, holder of an inherited office, served as both head of state and government. In the presidential system, the president does not inherit the office, but is chosen by either direct or indirect popular vote.

Presidential systems differ from parliamentary systems in that the president is both the chief executive and head of state, whereas in a parliamentary system another individual, usually called the "prime minister," serves as head of government and leader of the legislature. The presidential system evolved out of an effort to create an executive office that balances the influence of the legislature and the judiciary. The United States is the most prominent example of a democratic presidential system.

Some governments have adopted a semi-presidential system, which blends elements of the presidential system with the parliamentary system, and generally features a president who serves only as head of state. In constitutional governments, like the United States, Mexico, and Honduras, the role of the president is described in the nation's constitution, which also provides for the president's powers in relation to the other branches of government.

Typical Structure

In most modern presidential governments, power to create and enforce laws and international agreements is divided among three branches: the executive, legislative, and judicial. The executive office consists of the president and a number of presidential advisers—often called the cabinet—who typically serve at the president's discretion and are not elected to office. The terms of office for the president are codified in the state constitution and, in most cases, the president may serve a limited number of terms before he or she becomes ineligible for reelection.

The president serves as head of state and is therefore charged with negotiating and administering international treaties and agreements. In addition, the president serves as head of government and is therefore charged with overseeing the function of the government as a whole. The president is also empowered, in most presidential governments, with the ability to deploy the nation's armed forces. In some governments, including the United States, the approval of the legislature is needed for the country to officially declare war.

The legislative branch of the government proposes new laws, in the form of bills, but must cooperate with the executive office to pass these bills into law. The legislature and the executive branch also cooperate in determining the government budget. Unlike prime ministers under the parliamentary system, the president is not considered a member of the legislature and therefore acts independently as the chief executive, though a variety of governmental functions require action from both branches of government. A unique feature of the presidential system is that the election of the president is separate from the election of the legislature.

In presidential systems, members of the legislature are often less likely to vote according to the goals of their political party and may support legislation that is not supported by their chosen political party. In parliamentary systems, like the government of Great Britain, legislators are more likely to vote according to party policy. Presidential systems are also often marked by a relatively small number of political parties, which often allows one party to achieve a majority in the legislature. If this majority coincides with the election of a president from the same party, that party's platform or agenda becomes dominant until the next election cycle.

The judicial branch in a presidential system serves to enforce the laws among the populace. In most modern presidential democracies, the president appoints judges to federal posts, though in some governments, the legislature appoints judges. In some cases, the president may need the approval of the legislature to make judicial appointments.

Role of the Citizen

In a democratic presidential system, citizens are empowered with the ability to vote for president and therefore have ultimate control over who serves as head of government and head of state. Some presidential governments elect individuals to the presidency based on the result of a popular vote, while other governments use an indirect system, in which citizens vote for a party or for individuals who then serve as their representatives in electing the president. The United States utilizes an indirect system called the Electoral College.

Citizens in presidential systems are also typically allowed, though not required, to join political parties in an effort to promote a political agenda. Some governmental systems that are modeled on the presidential system allow the president to exert a dominant influence over the legislature and other branches of the government. In some cases, this can lead to a presidential dictatorship, in which the president may curtail the political rights of citizens. In most presidential systems, however, the roles and powers of the legislative and executive branches are balanced to protect the rights of the people to influence their government.

In a presidential system, citizens are permitted to vote for a president representing one political party, while simultaneously voting for legislators from other political parties. In this way, the presidential system allows citizens to determine the degree to which any single political party is permitted to have influence on political development.

Micah Issitt
Philadelphia, Pennsylvania

Examples
Benin
Costa Rica
Dominican Republic
Guatemala
Honduras
Mexico
United States
Venezuela

Bibliography

Barington, Lowell. *Comparative Politics*: *Structures and Choices*. Boston: Wadsworth, 2012. Print.

Caramani, Daniele. *Comparative Politics*. New York: Oxford UP, 2008. Print.

Garner, Robert, Peter Ferdinand, and Stephanie Lawson. *Introduction to Politics*. 2nd ed. Oxford: Oxford UP, 2009. Print.

Republic

Guiding Premise

A republic is a type of government based on the idea of popular or public sovereignty. The word "republic" is derived from Latin terms meaning "matters" and "the public." In essence, a republic is a government in which leaders are chosen by the public rather than by inheritance or by force. The republic or republican governmental system emerged in response to absolute monarchy, in which hereditary leaders retained all the power. In contrast, the republican system is intended to create a government that is responsive to the people's will.

Most modern republics operate based on a democratic system in which citizens elect leaders by popular vote. The United States and Mexico are examples of countries that use a democratic republican system to appoint leaders to office. However, universal suffrage (voting for all) is not required for a government to qualify as a republic, and it is possible for a country to have a republican government in which only certain categories of citizens, such as the wealthy, are allowed to vote in elections.

In addition to popular vote, most modern republics are further classified as constitutional republics, because the laws and rules for appointing leaders have been codified in a set of principles and guidelines known as a "constitution." When combined with universal suffrage and constitutional law, the republican system is intended to form a government that is based on the will of the majority while protecting the rights of minority groups.

Typical Structure

Republican governments are typically led by an elected head of state, generally a president. In cases where the president also serves as the head of government, the government is called a "presidential republic." In some republics, the head of state serves alongside an appointed or elected head of government, usually a prime minister.

This mixed form of government blends elements of the republic system with the parliamentary system found in countries such as the United Kingdom or India.

The president is part of the executive branch of government, which represents the country internationally and heads efforts to make and amend international agreements and treaties. The laws of a nation are typically created by the legislative branch, which may also be composed of elected leaders. Typically, the legislative and executive branches must cooperate on key initiatives, such as determining the national budget.

In addition to legislative and executive functions, most republics have a judiciary charged with enforcing and interpreting laws. The judicial branch may be composed of elected leaders, but in many cases, judicial officers are appointed by the president and/or the legislature. In the United States (a federal republic), the president, who leads the executive branch, appoints members to the federal judiciary, but these choices must be approved by the legislature before they take effect.

The duties and powers allotted to each branch of the republican government are interconnected with those of the other branches in a system of checks and balances. For instance, in Mexico (a federal republic), the legislature is empowered to create new tax guidelines for the public, but before legislative tax bills become law, they must first achieve majority support within the two branches of the Mexican legislature and receive the approval of the president. By creating a system of separate but balanced powers, the republican system seeks to prevent any one branch from exerting a dominant influence over the government.

Role of the Citizen

The role of the citizen in a republic depends largely on the type of republican system that the country has adopted. In democratic republics, popular elections and constitutional law give the public significant influence over governmental development and establish the people as the primary source of political power. Citizens in democratic republics are empowered to join political groups and to influence the development of laws and policies through the election of public leaders.

In many republican nations, a powerful political party or other political group can dominate the government, preventing competition from opposing political groups and curtailing the public's role in selecting and approving leaders. For instance, in the late twentieth century, a dominant political party maintained control of the Gambian presidency and legislature for more than thirty years, thereby significantly limiting the role of the citizenry in influencing the development of government policy.

In general, the republican system was intended to reverse the power structure typical of the monarchy system, in which inherited leaders possess all of the political power. In the republican system, leaders are chosen to represent the people's interests with terms of office created in such a way that new leaders must be chosen at regular intervals, thereby preventing a single leader or political entity from dominating the populace. In practice, popular power in a republic depends on preventing a political monopoly from becoming powerful enough to alter the laws of the country to suit the needs of a certain group rather than the whole.

Micah Issitt
Philadelphia, Pennsylvania

Examples

Algeria
Argentina
Armenia
France
Gambia
Mexico
San Marino
South Sudan
Tanzania
United States

Bibliography

Caramani, Daniele. *Comparative Politics*. New York: Oxford UP, 2008. Print.

Przeworski, Adam. *Democracy and the Limits of Self-Government*. New York: Cambridge UP, 2010. Print.

Socialist

Guiding Premise

Socialism is a political and economic system that seeks to elevate the common good of the citizenry by allowing the government to own all property and means of production. In the most basic model, citizens cooperatively elect members to government, and the government then acts on behalf of the people to manage the state's property, industry, production, and services.

In a socialist system, communal or government ownership of property and industry is intended to eliminate the formation of economic classes and to ensure an even distribution of wealth. Most modern socialists also believe that basic services, including medical and legal care, should be provided at the same level to all citizens and not depend on the individual citizen's ability to pay for better services. The origins of socialism can be traced to theorists such as Thomas More (1478–1535), who believed that private wealth and ownership led to the formation of a wealthy elite class that protected its own wealth while oppressing members of lower classes.

There are many different forms of socialist philosophy, some of which focus on economic systems, while others extend socialist ideas to other aspects of society. Communism may be considered a form of socialism, based on the idea that a working-class revolution is needed to initiate the ideal socialist society.

Typical Structure

Socialism exists in many forms around the world, and many governments use a socialist model for the distribution of key services, most often medical and legal aid. A socialist state is a government whose constitution explicitly gives the government powers to facilitate the creation of a socialist society.

The idealized model of the socialist state is one in which the populace elects leaders to head the government, and the government then oversees the distribution of wealth and goods among the populace, enforces the laws, and provides for the well-being of citizens. Many modern socialist governments follow a communist model, in which a national communist political party has ultimate control over governmental legislation and appointments.

There are many different models of socialist states, integrating elements of democratic or parliamentary systems. In these cases, democratic elections may be held to elect the head of state and the body of legislators. The primary difference between a socialist democracy and a capitalist democracy can be found in the state's role in the ownership of key industries. Most modern noncommunist socialist states provide state regulation and control over key industries but allow some free-market competition as well.

In a socialist system, government officials appoint leaders to oversee various industries and to regulate prices based on public welfare. For instance, if the government retains sole ownership over agricultural production, the government must appoint individuals to manage and oversee that industry, organize agricultural labor, and oversee the distribution of food products among the populace. Some countries, such as Sweden, have adopted a mixed model in which socialist industry management is blended with free-market competition.

Role of the Citizen

All citizens in a socialist system are considered workers, and thus all exist in the same economic class. While some citizens may receive higher pay than others—those who work in supervisory roles, for instance—limited ownership of private property and standardized access to services places all individuals on a level field with regard to basic welfare and economic prosperity.

The degree to which personal liberties are curtailed within a socialist system depends upon the type of socialist philosophy adopted and the degree to which corruption and authoritarianism play a role in government. In most modern communist governments, for instance, individuals are often prohibited from engaging in any activity seen as contrary to the overall goals of the state or to the policies of the dominant political party. While regulations of this kind are common in communist societies, social control over citizens is not necessary for a government to follow a socialist model.

Under democratic socialism, individuals are also expected to play a role in the formation of their government by electing leaders to serve in key positions. In Sri Lanka, for instance, citizens elect members to serve in the parliament and a president to serve as head of the executive branch. In Portugal, citizens vote in multiparty elections to elect a president who serves as head of state, and the president appoints a prime minister to serve as head of government. In both Portugal and Sri Lanka, the government is constitutionally bound to promote a socialist society, though both governments allow private ownership and control of certain industries.

Citizens in a socialist society are also expected to provide for one another by contributing to labor and by forfeiting some ownership rights to provide for the greater good. In the Kingdom of Sweden, a mixed parliamentary system, all citizens pay a higher tax rate to contribute to funds that provide for national health care, child care, education, and worker support systems. Citizens who have no children and require only minimal health care benefits pay the same tax rate as those who have greater need for the nation's socialized benefits.

Micah Issitt
Philadelphia, Pennsylvania

Examples

China
Cuba
Portugal
Sri Lanka
Venezuela
Zambia

Bibliography

Caramani, Daniele. *Comparative Politics*. New York: Oxford UP, 2008. Print.

Heilbroner, Robert. "Socialism." *Library of Economics and Liberty*. Liberty Fund, 2008. Web. 17 Jan. 2013.

Howard, Michael Wayne. *Socialism*. Amherst, NY: Humanity, 2001. Print.

Sultanate/Emirate

Guiding Premise

A sultanate or emirate form of government is a political system in which a hereditary ruler—a monarch, chieftain, or military leader—acts as the head of state. Emirates and sultanates are most commonly found in Islamic nations in the Middle East, although others are found in Southeast Asia as well. Sultans and emirs frequently assume titles such as president or prime minister in addition to their royal designations, meshing the traditional ideal of a monarch with the administrative capacities of a constitutional political system.

Typical Structure

A sultanate or emirate combines the administrative duties of the executive with the powers of a monarch. The emir or sultan acts as the head of government, appointing all cabinet ministers and officials. In Brunei, a sultanate, the government was established according to the constitution (set up after the country declared autonomy from Britain in 1959). The sultan did assemble a legislative council in order to facilitate the lawmaking process, but this council has consistently remained subject to the authority of the sultan and not to a democratic process. In 2004, there was some movement toward the election of at least some of the members of this council. In the meantime, the sultan maintains a ministerial system by appointment and also serves as the nation's chief religious leader.

In some cases, an emirate or sultanate appears similar to a federal system. In the United Arab Emirates (UAE), for example, the nation consists of not one but seven emirates. This system came into being after the seven small regions achieved independence from Great Britain. Each emirate developed its own government system under the leadership of an emir. However, in 1971, the individual emirates agreed to join as a federation, drafting a constitution that identified the areas of common interest to the entire group of emirates. Like Brunei, the UAE's initial government structure focused on the authority of the emirs and the various councils and ministries formed at the UAE's capital of Abu Dhabi. However, beginning in the early twenty-first century, the UAE's legislative body, the Federal National Council, has been elected by electoral colleges from the seven emirates, thus further engaging various local areas and reflecting their interests.

Sultanates and emirates are at times part of a larger nation, with the sultans or emirs answering to the authority of another government. This is the case in Malaysia, where the country is governed by a constitutional monarchy. However, most of Malaysia's western political units are governed by sultans, who act as regional governors and, in many cases, religious leaders, but remain subject to the king's authority in Malaysia's capital of Kuala Lumpur.

Role of the Citizen

Sultanates and emirates are traditionally non-democratic governments. Like those of other monarchs, the seats of emirs and sultans are hereditary. Any votes for these leaders to serve as prime minister or other head of government are cast by ministers selected by the emirs and sultans. Political parties may exist in these countries as well, but these parties are strictly managed by the sultan or emir; opposition parties are virtually nonexistent in such systems, and some emirates have no political parties at all.

As shown in the UAE and Malaysia, however, there are signs that the traditional sultanate or emirate is increasingly willing to engage their respective citizens. For example, the UAE, between 2006 and 2013, launched a series of reforms designed to strengthen the role of local governments and relations with the people they serve. Malaysia may allow sultans to continue their regional controls, but at the same time, the country continues to evolve its federal system, facilitating multiparty democratic elections for its national legislature.

Michael Auerbach
Marblehead, Massachusetts

Examples

Brunei
Kuwait
Malaysia
Qatar
United Arab Emirates

Bibliography

"Brunei." *The World Factbook*. Central Intelligence Agency, 2 Jan. 2013. Web. 17 Jan. 2013.

"Malaysia." *The World Factbook*. Central Intelligence Agency, 7 Jan. 2013. Web. 17 Jan. 2013.

"Political System." *UAE Interact*. UAE National Media Council, n.d. Web. 17 Jan. 2013.

Prime Minister's Office, Brunei Darussalam. Prime Minister's Office, Brunei Darussalam, 2013. Web. 17 Jan. 2013.

Theocratic Republic

Guiding Premise

A theocratic republic is a type of government blending popular and religious influence to determine the laws and governmental principles. A republic is a governmental system based on the concept of popular rule and takes its name from the Latin words for "public matter." The defining characteristic of a republic is that civic leaders hold elected, rather than inherited, offices. A theocracy is a governmental system in which a supreme deity is considered the ultimate authority guiding civil matters.

No modern nations can be classified as pure theocratic republics, but some nations, such as Iran, maintain a political system largely dominated by religious law. The Buddhist nation of Tibet operated under a theocratic system until it was taken over by Communist China in the early 1950s.

In general, a theocratic republic forms in a nation or other governmental system dominated by a single religious group. The laws of the government are formed in reference to a set of religious laws, either taken directly from sacred texts or formulated by religious scholars and authority figures. Most theocratic governments depend on a body of religious scholars who interpret religious scripture, advise all branches of government, and oversee the electoral process.

Typical Structure

In a typical republic, the government is divided into executive, legislative, and judicial branches, and citizens vote to elect leaders to one or more of the branches of government. In most modern republics, voters elect a head of state, usually a president, to lead the executive branch. In many republics, voters also elect individuals to serve as legislators. Members of the judiciary may be elected by voters or may be appointed to office by other elected leaders. In nontheocratic republics, the citizens are considered the ultimate source of authority in the government.

In a theocratic republic, however, one or more deities are considered to represent the ultimate governmental authority. In some cases, the government may designate a deity as the ultimate head of state. Typically, any individual serving as the functional head of state is believed to have been chosen by that deity, and candidates for the position must be approved by the prevailing religious authority.

In some cases, the religious authority supports popular elections to fill certain governmental posts. In Iran, for instance, citizens vote to elect members to the national parliament and a single individual to serve as president. The Iranian government is ultimately led by a supreme leader, who is appointed to office by the Assembly of Experts, the leaders of the country's Islamic community. Though the populace chooses the president and leaders to serve in the legislature, the supreme leader of Iran can overrule decisions made in any other branch of the government.

In a theocratic republic, the power to propose new laws may be given to the legislature, which works on legislation in conjunction with the executive branch. However, all laws must conform to religious law, and any legislation produced within the government is likely to be abolished if it is deemed by the religious authorities to violate religious principles. In addition, religious leaders typically decide which candidates are qualified to run for specific offices, thereby ensuring that the citizens will not elect individuals who are likely to oppose religious doctrine.

In addition, many modern nations that operate on a partially theocratic system may adopt a set of governmental principles in the form of a constitution, blended with religious law. This mixed constitutional theocratic system has been adopted by an increasing number of Islamic nations, including Iraq, Afghanistan, Mauritania, and some parts of Nigeria.

Role of the Citizen

Citizens in a theocratic republic are expected to play a role in forming the government through elections, but they are constrained in their choices by the prevailing religious authority. Citizens are also guaranteed certain freedoms, typically codified in a constitution, that have been formulated with reference to religious law. All citizens must adhere to religious laws, regardless of their personal religious beliefs or membership within any existing religious group.

In many Middle Eastern and African nations that operate on the basis of an Islamic theocracy, citizens elect leaders from groups of candidates chosen by the prevailing religious authority. While the choices presented to the citizens are more limited than in a democratic, multiparty republic, the citizens nevertheless play a role in determining the evolution of the government through their voting choices.

The freedoms and rights afforded to citizens in a theocratic republic may depend, in part, on the individual's religious affiliation. For instance, Muslims living in Islamic theocracies may be permitted to hold political office or to aspire to other influential political positions, while members of minority religious groups may find their rights and freedoms limited. Religious minorities living in Islamic republics may not be permitted to run for certain offices, such as president, and must follow laws that adhere to Islamic principles but may violate their own religious principles. Depending on the country and the adherents' religion, the practice of their faith may itself be considered criminal.

Micah Issitt
Philadelphia, Pennsylvania

Examples

Afghanistan
Iran
Iraq
Pakistan
Mauritania
Nigeria

Bibliography

Cooper, William W., and Piyu Yue. *Challenges of the Muslim World: Present, Future and Past*. Boston: Elsevier, 2008. Print.

Hirschl, Ran. *Constitutional Theocracy*. Cambridge: Harvard UP, 2010. Print.

Totalitarian

Guiding Premise

A totalitarian government is one in which a single political party maintains absolute control over the state and is responsible for creating all legislation without popular referendum. In general, totalitarianism is considered a type of authoritarian government where the laws and principles used to govern the country are based on the authority of the leading political group or dictator. Citizens under totalitarian regimes have limited freedoms and are subject to social controls dictated by the state.

The concept of totalitarianism evolved in fascist Italy in the 1920s, and was first used to describe the Italian government under dictator Benito Mussolini. The term became popular among critics of the authoritarian governments of Fascist Italy and Nazi Germany in the 1930s. Supporters of the totalitarian philosophy believed that a strong central government, with absolute control over all aspects of society, could achieve progress by avoiding political debate and power struggles between interest groups.

In theory, totalitarian regimes—like that of Nazi Germany and modern North Korea—can more effectively mobilize resources and direct a nation toward a set of overarching goals. Adolf Hitler was able to achieve vast increases in military power during a short period of time by controlling all procedural steps involved in promoting military development. In practice, however, pure totalitarianism has never been achieved, as citizens and political groups generally find ways to subvert complete government control.

Totalitarianism differs from authoritarianism in that a totalitarian government is based on the idea that the highest leader takes total control in order to create a flourishing society for the benefit of the people. By contrast, authoritarian regimes are based on the authority of a single, charismatic individual who develops policies designed to maintain personal power, rather than promote public interest.

Typical Structure

In a fully realized totalitarian system, a single leader or group of leaders controls all governmental functions, appointing individuals to serve in various posts to facilitate the development of legislation and oversee the enforcement of laws. In Nazi Germany, for instance, Adolf Hitler created a small group of executives to oversee the operation of the government. Governmental authority was then further disseminated through a complex network of departments, called ministries, with leaders appointed directly by Hitler.

Some totalitarian nations may adopt a state constitution in an effort to create the appearance of democratic popular control. In North Korea, the country officially operates under a multiparty democratic system, with citizens guaranteed the right to elect leaders to both the executive and legislative branches of government. In practice, the Workers' Party of North Korea is the only viable political party, as it actively controls competing parties and suppresses any attempt to mount political opposition. Under Supreme Leader Kim Il-sung, the Workers' Party amended the constitution to allow Kim to serve as the sole executive leader for life, without the possibility of being removed from office by any governmental action.

In some cases, totalitarian regimes may favor a presidential system, with the dictator serving officially as president, while other totalitarian governments may adopt a parliamentary system, with a prime minister as head of government. Though a single dictator generally heads the nation with widespread powers over a variety of governmental functions, a cabinet or group of high-ranking ministers may also play a prominent role in disseminating power throughout the various branches of government.

Role of the Citizen

Citizens in totalitarian regimes are often subject to strict social controls exerted by the leading political party. In many cases, totalitarian governments restrict the freedom of the press, expression, and speech in an effort to limit opposition to the government. In addition, totalitarian governments may use the threat of police or military action to prevent protest movements against the leading party. Totalitarian governments maintain absolute control over the courts and any security agency, and the legal/judicial system therefore exists only as an extension of the leading political party.

Totalitarian governments like North Korea also attempt to restrict citizens' access to information considered subversive. For instance, North Korean citizens are not allowed to freely utilize the Internet or any other informational source, but are instead only allowed access to government-approved websites and publications. In many cases, the attempt to control access to information creates a black market for publications and other forms of information banned by government policy.

In some cases, government propaganda and restricted access to information creates a situation in which citizens actively support the ruling regime. Citizens may honestly believe that the social and political restrictions imposed by the ruling party are necessary for the advancement of society. In other cases, citizens may accept governmental control to avoid reprisal from the military and police forces. Most totalitarian regimes have established severe penalties, including imprisonment, corporal punishment, and death, for criticizing the government or refusing to adhere to government policy.

Micah Issitt
Philadelphia, Pennsylvania

Examples

Fascist Italy (1922–1943)
Nazi Germany (1933–1945)
North Korea
Stalinist Russia (1924–1953)

Bibliography

Barrington, Lowell. *Comparative Politics*: *Structures and Choices*. Boston: Wadsworth, 2012. Print.

Gleason, Abbot. *Totalitarianism: The Inner History of the Cold War*. New York: Oxford UP, 1995. Print.

McEachern, Patrick. *Inside the Red Box: North Korea's Post-Totalitarian Regime*. New York: Columbia UP, 2010. Print.

Treaty System

Guiding Premise

A treaty system is a framework within which participating governments agree to collect and share scientific information gathered in a certain geographic region, or otherwise establish mutually agreeable standards for the use of that region. The participants establish rules and parameters by which researchers may establish research facilities and travel throughout the region, ensuring that there are no conflicts, that the environment is protected, and that the region is not used for illicit purposes. This system is particularly useful when the region in question is undeveloped and unpopulated, but could serve a number of strategic and scientific purposes.

Typical Structure

A treaty system of government is an agreement between certain governments that share a common interest in the use of a certain region to which no state or country has yet laid internationally recognized claim. Participating parties negotiate treaty systems that, upon agreement, form a framework by which the system will operate. Should the involved parties be United Nations member states, the treaty is then submitted to the UN Secretariat for registration and publication.

The agreement's founding ideals generally characterize the framework of a treaty. For example, the most prominent treaty system in operation today is the Antarctic Treaty System, which currently includes fifty nations whose scientists are studying Antarctica. This system, which entered into force in 1961, focuses on several topics, including environmental protection, tourism, scientific operations, and the peaceful use of that region. Within these topics, the treaty system enables participants to meet, cooperate, and share data on a wide range of subjects. Such cooperative activities include regional meetings, seminars, and large-scale conferences.

A treaty system is not a political institution in the same manner as state governments. Rather, it is an agreement administered by delegates from the involved entities. Scientists seeking to perform their research in Antarctica, for example, must apply through the scientific and/or government institutions of their respective nations. In the case of the United States, scientists may apply for grants from the National Science Foundation. These institutions then examine the study in question for its relevance to the treaty's ideals.

Central to the treaty system is the organization's governing body. In the case of the Antarctic Treaty, that body is the Antarctic Treaty Secretariat, which is based in Buenos Aires, Argentina. The Secretariat oversees all activities taking place under the treaty, welcomes new members, and addresses any conflicts or issues between participants. It also reviews any activities to ensure that they are in line with the parameters of the treaty. A treaty system is not a sovereign organization, however. Each participating government retains autonomy, facilitating its own scientific expeditions, sending delegates to the treaty system's main governing body, and reviewing the treaty to ensure that it coincides with its national interests.

Role of the Citizen

Although treaty systems are not sovereign government institutions, private citizens can and frequently do play an important role in their function and success. For example, the Antarctic Treaty System frequently conducts large-scale planning conferences, to which each participating government sends delegates. These teams are comprised of qualified scientists who are nominated and supported by their peers during the government's review process. In the United States, for example, the State Department oversees American participation in the Antarctic

Treaty System's events and programs, including delegate appointments.

Another area in which citizens are involved in a treaty system is in the ratification process. Every nation's government—usually through its legislative branch—must formally approve any treaty before the country can honor the agreement. This ratification is necessary for new treaties as well as treaties that must be reapproved every few years. Citizens, through their elected officials, may voice their support or disapproval of a new or updated treaty.

While participating governments administer treaty systems and their secretariats, those who conduct research or otherwise take part in activities in the region in question are not usually government employees. In Antarctica, for example, university professors, engineers, and other private professionals—supported by a combination of private and government funding—operate research stations.

Michael Auerbach
Marblehead, Massachusetts

Example
Antarctic Treaty System

Bibliography
"Antarctic." *Ocean and Polar Affairs.* US Department of State, 22 Mar. 2007. Web. 8 Feb. 2013.

"About Us." *Antarctic Treaty System.* Secretariat of the Antarctic Treaty, n.d. Web. 8 Feb. 2013.

"United Nations Treaty Series." *United Nations Treaty Collection.* United Nations, 2013. Web. 8 Feb. 2013.

"Educational Opportunities and Resources." *United States Antarctic Program.* National Science Foundation, 2013. Web. 8 Feb. 2013.

Appendix Two:
World Religions

African Religious Traditions

General Description

The religious traditions of Africa can be studied both religiously and ethnographically. Animism, or the belief that everything has a soul, is practiced in most tribal societies, including the Dogon (people of the cliffs), an ethnic group living primarily in Mali's central plateau region and in Burkina Faso. Many traditional faiths have extensive mythologies, rites, and histories, such as the Yoruba religion practiced by the Yoruba, an ethnic group of West Africa. In South Africa, the traditional religion of the Zulu people is based on a creator god, ancestor worship, and the existence of sorcerers and witches. Lastly, the Ethiopian or Abyssinian Church (formally the Ethiopian Orthodox Union Church) is a branch of Christianity unique to the east African nations of Ethiopia and Eritrea.

Number of Adherents Worldwide

Some 63 million Africans adhere to traditional religions such as animism. One of the largest groups practicing animism is the Dogon, who number about six hundred thousand. However, it is impossible to know how many practice traditional religion. In fact, many people practice animism alongside other religions, particularly Islam. Other religions have spread their adherence and influence through the African diaspora. In Africa, the Yoruba number between thirty-five and forty million and are located primarily in Benin, Togo and southwest Nigeria. The Zulu, the largest ethnic group in South Africa, total over eleven million. Like Islam, Christianity has affected the number of people who still hold traditional beliefs, making accurate predictions virtually impossible. The Ethiopian or Abyssinian Church has over thirty-nine million adherents in Ethiopia alone.

Basic Tenets

Animism holds that many spiritual beings have the power to help or hurt humans. The traditional faith is thus more concerned with appropriate rituals rather than worship of a deity, and focuses on day-to-day practicalities such as food, water supplies, and disease. Ancestors, particularly those most recently dead, are invoked for their aid. Those who practice animism believe in life after death; some adherents may attempt to contact the spirits of the dead. Animists acknowledge the existence of tribal gods. (However, African people traditionally do not make images of God, who is thought of as Spirit.)

The Dogon divide into two caste-like groups: the inneomo (pure) and innepuru (impure). The hogon leads the inneomo, who may not sacrifice animals and whose leaders are forbidden to hunt. The inneomo also cannot prepare or bury the dead. While the innepuru can do all of the above tasks, they cannot take part in the rituals for agricultural fertility. Selected young males called the olubaru lead the innepuru. The status of "pure" or "impure" is inherited. The Dogon have many gods. The chief god is called Amma, a creator god who is responsible for creating other gods and the earth.

The Dogon have a three-part concept of death. First the soul is sent to the realm of the dead to join the ancestors. Rites are then performed to remove any ritual polluting. Finally, when several members of the village have died, a rite known as dama occurs. In the ritual, a sacrifice is made to the Great Mask (which depicts a large wooden serpent and which is never actually worn) and dancers perform on the housetops where someone has died to scare off any lingering souls. Often, figures of Nommo (a worshipped ancestral spirit) are put near funeral pottery on the family shrine.

The Yoruba believe in predestination. Before birth, the ori (soul) kneels before Olorun, the wisest and most powerful deity, and selects a destiny. Rituals may assist the person in achieving his or her destiny, but it cannot be altered. The Yoruba, therefore, acknowledge a need for ritual and sacrifice, properly done according to the oracles.

Among the Yoruba, the shaman is known as the babalawo. He or she is able to communicate with ancestors, spirits and deities. Training for this work, which may include responsibility as a doctor, often requires three years. The shaman is consulted before major life decisions. During these consultations, the shaman dictates the right rituals and sacrifices, and to which gods they are to be offered for maximum benefit. In addition, the Yoruba poetry covers right conduct. Good character is at the heart of Yoruba ethics.

The Yoruba are polytheistic. The major god is Olorun, the sky god, considered all-powerful and holy, and a father to 401 children, also gods. He gave the task of creating human beings to the deity Obatala (though Olorun breathed life into them). Olorun also determines the destiny of each person. Onlie, the Great Mother Goddess, is in some ways the opposite of Olorun. Olorun is the one who judges a soul following death. For example, if the soul is accounted worthy, it will be reincarnated, while the unworthy go to the place of punishment. Ogun, the god of hunters, iron, and war, is another important god. He is also the patron of blacksmiths. The Yoruba have some 1,700 gods, collectively known as the Orisa.

The Yoruba believe in an afterlife. There are two heavens: one is a hot, dry place with potsherds, reserved for those who have done evil, while the other is a pleasant heaven for persons who have led a good life. There the ori (soul) may choose to "turn to be a child" on the earth once more.

In the Zulu tradition, the king was responsible for rainmaking and magic for the benefit of the nation. Rainmakers were also known as "shepherds of heaven." They performed rites during times of famine, drought or war, as well as during planting season, invoking royal ancestors for aid. Storms were considered a manifestation of God.

The Zulu are also polytheistic. They refer to a wise creator god who lives in heaven. This Supreme Being has complete control of everything in the universe, and is known as Unkulunkulu, the Great Oldest One. The Queen of heaven is a virgin who taught women useful arts; light surrounds her, and her glory is seen in rain, mist, and rainbows.

The Ethiopian Church incorporates not only Orthodox Christian beliefs, but also aspects of Judaism. The adherents distinguish between clean and unclean meats, practice circumcision, and observe the seventh-day Sabbath. The Ethiopian (or Abyssinian) Church is monotheistic and believes in the Christian God.

Sacred Text

Traditional religions such as animism generally have no written sacred texts. Instead, creation stories and other tales are passed down orally. The Yoruba do have some sacred poetry, in 256 chapters, known as odus. The text covers both right action in worship and ethical conduct. The Ethiopian Church has scriptures written in the ancient Ge'ez language, which is no longer used, except in church liturgy.

Major Figures

A spiritual leader, or hogon, oversees each district among the Dogon. There is a supreme hogon for the entire country. Among the Yoruba, the king, or oba, rules each town. He is also considered sacred and is responsible for performing rituals. Isaiah Shembe is a prophet or messiah among the Zulu. He founded the Nazareth Baptist Church (also called the amaNazaretha Church or Shembe Church), an independent Zulu Christian denomination. His son, Johannes Shembe, took the title Shembe II. In the Ethiopian Church, now fully independent, the head of the church is the Patriarch. Saint Frumentius, the first bishop of Axum in northern Ethiopia, is credited with beginning the Christian tradition during the fourth century. King Lalibela, noted for authorizing construction of monolithic churches carved underground, was a major figure in the twelfth century.

Major Holy Sites

Every spot in nature is sacred in animistic thinking. There is no division between sacred and profane—all of life is sacred, and Earth is Mother. Sky and mountains are often regarded as sacred space.

For the Yoruba of West Africa, Osogbo in Nigeria is a forest shrine. The main goddess is Oshun, goddess of the river. Until she arrived, the work done by male gods was not succeeding. People seeking to be protected from illness and women wishing to become pregnant seek Osun's help. Ilé-Ifè, an ancient Yoruba city in Nigeria, is another important site, and considered the spiritual hub of the Yoruba. According to the Yoruba creation myth, Olorun, god of the sky, set down Odudua, the founder of the Yoruba, in Ilé-Ifè. Shrines within the city include one to Ogun. The shrine is made of stones and wooden stumps.

Mount Nhlangakazi (Holy Mountain) is considered sacred to the Zulu Nazareth Baptist Church (amaNazaretha). There Isaiah Shembe built a High Place to serve as his headquarters. It is a twice-yearly site of pilgrimage for amaNazarites.

Sacred sites of the Ethiopian Church include the Church of St. Mary of Zion in Axum, considered the most sacred Ethiopian shrine. According to legend, the church stands adjacent to a guarded chapel which purportedly houses the Ark of the Covenant, a powerful biblical relic. The Ethiopian Church also considers sacred the eleven monolithic (rock-hewn) churches, still places of pilgrimage and devotion, that were recognized as a collective World Heritage Site by the United Nations Educational, Scientific and Cultural Organization.

Major Rites & Celebrations

Most African religions involve some sacrifice to appease or please the gods. Among the Yoruba, for example, dogs, which are helpful in both hunting and war, are sacrificed to Ogun. In many tribes, including the Yoruba, rites of passage for youth exist. The typical pattern is three-fold: removal from the tribe, instruction, and return to the tribe ready to assume adult responsibilities. In this initiation, the person may be marked bodily through scarification or circumcision. The Yoruba also have a yearly festival re-enacting

the story of Obatala and Oduduwa (generally perceived as the ancestor of the Yorubas). A second festival, which resembles a passion play, re-enacts the conflict between the grandsons of these two legendary figures. A third festival celebrates the heroine Moremi, who led the Yoruba to victory over the enemy Igbo, an ethnicity from southeastern Nigeria, and who ultimately reconciled the two tribes.

Yoruba death rites include a masked dancer who comes to the family following a death, assuring them of the ancestor's ongoing care for the family. If the person was important in the village, a mask will be carved and named for them. In yearly festivals, the deceased individual will then appear with other ancestors.

Masks are also used in a Dogon funeral ritual, the dama ceremony, which is led by the Awa, a secret society comprised of all adult Dogon males of the innepuru group. During ceremonial times, the hogon relinquishes control and the Awa control the community. At the end of the mourning period the dama ceremony begins when the Awa leave the village and return with both the front and back of their heads masked. Through rituals and dances, they lead the spirit of the deceased to the next world. Control of the village reverts to the hogon at that point. The Wagem rites govern contact with the ancestors. Following the dama ceremony, the eldest male descendant, called the ginna bana, adds a vessel to the family shrine in the name of the deceased. The spirit of the ancestor is persuaded to return to the descendents through magic and sacrificial offerings, creating a link from the living to the first ancestors.

Ethiopian Christians observe and mark most typical Christian rites, though some occur on different dates because of the difference in the Ethiopian and Western calendars. For example, Christmas in Ethiopia is celebrated on January 7.

ORIGINS

History & Geography

The Dogon live along the Bandiagara Cliffs, a rocky and mountainous region. (The Cliffs of Bandiagara, also called the Bandiagara Escarpment, were recognized as a UNESCO World Heritage Site due to the cultural landscape, including the ancient traditions of the Dogon and their architecture.) This area is south of the Sahara in a region called the Sahel, another region prone to drought (though not a desert). The population of the villages in the region is typically a thousand people or less. The cliffs of the Bandiagara have kept the Dogon separate from other people.

Myths of origin regarding the Dogon differ. One suggestion is that the Dogon came from Egypt, and then lived in Libya before entering the the region of what is now Burkina Faso, Mauritania, or Guinea. Near the close of the fifteenth century, they arrived in Mali.

Among the Yoruba, multiple myths regarding their origin exist. One traces their beginnings to Uruk in Mesopotamia or to Babylon, the site of present-day Iraq. Another story has the Yoruba in West Africa by 10,000 BCE.

After the death of the Zulu messiah Isaiah Shembe in 1935, his son Johannes became the leader of the Nazareth Baptist Church. He lacked the charisma of his father, but did hold the church together. His brother, Amos, became regent in 1976 when Johannes died. Johannes's son Londa split the church in 1979 when Amos refused to give up power. Tangled in South African politics, Londa was killed in 1989.

The Ethiopian Orthodox Church is the nation's official church. A legend states that Menelik, supposed to have been the son of the Queen of Sheba and King Solomon, founded the royal line. When Jesuits arrived in the seventeenth century, they failed to change the church, and the nation closed to missionary efforts for several hundred years. By retaining independence theologically and not being conquered politically, Ethiopia is sometimes considered a model for the new religious movements in Africa.

Founder or Major Prophet

The origins of most African traditional religions or faiths are accounted for through the actions of deities in creation stories rather than a particular founder. One exception, however, is Isaiah Shembe, who founded the Nazareth Baptist Church, also known as the Shembe Church or amaNazarite Church, in 1910 after receiving a number of revelations during a thunderstorm. Shembe was an itinerant Zulu preacher and healer. Through his influence and leadership, amaNazarites follow more Old Testament regulations than most Christians, including celebrating the Sabbath on Saturday rather than Sunday. They also refer to God as Jehovah, the Hebrew name for God. Shembe was regarded as the new Jesus Christ for his people, adapting Christianity to Zulu practice. He adopted the title Nkosi, which means king or chief.

The Ethiopian Orthodox church was founded, according to legend, by preaching from one of two New Testament figures—the disciple Matthew or the unnamed eunuch mentioned in Acts 8. According to historical evidence, the church began when Frumentius arrived at the royal court. Athanasius of Alexandria later consecrated Frumentius as patriarch of the church, linking it to the Christian church in Egypt.

Creation Stories

The Dogon believe that Amma, the sky god, was also the creator of the universe. Amma created two sets of twins, male and female. One of the males rebelled. To restore order, Amma sacrificed the other male, Nommo, strangling and scattering him to the four directions, then restoring him to life after five days. Nommo then became ruler of the universe and the children of his spirits became the Dogon. Thus the world continually moves between chaos and order, and the task of the Dogon is to keep the world in balance through rituals. In a five-year cycle, the aspects of this creation myth are re-enacted at altars throughout the Dogon land.

According to the Yoruba, after one botched attempt at creating the world, Olorun sent his son Obatala to create earth upon the waters. Obatala tossed some soil on the water and released a five-toed hen to spread it out. Next, Olorun told Obatala to make people from clay. Obatala grew bored with the work and drank too much wine. Thereafter, the people he made were misshapen or defective (handicapped). In anger, Olorun relieved him of the job and gave it to Odudua to complete. It was Odudua who made the Yoruba and founded a kingdom at Ilé-Ifè.

The word *Zulu* means "heaven or sky." The Zulu people believe they originated in heaven. They also believe in phansi, the place where spirits live and which is below the earth's surface.

Holy Places

Osun-Osogbo is a forest shrine in Nigeria dedicated to the Yoruba river goddess, Osun. It may be the last such sacred grove remaining among the Yoruba. Shrines, art, sculpture, and sanctuaries are part of the grove, which became a UNESCO World Heritage site in 2005.

Ilé-Ifè, regarded as the equivalent of Eden, is thought to be the site where the first Yoruba was placed. It was probably named for Ifa, the god associated with divination. The palace (Afin) of the spiritual head of the Yoruba, the oni, is located there. The oni has the responsibility to care for the staff of Oranmiyan, a Benin king. The staff, which is eighteen feet tall, is made of granite and shaped like an elephant's tusk.

Axum, the seat of the Ethiopian Christian Church, is a sacred site. The eleven rock-hewn churches of King Lalibela, especially that of Saint George, are a pilgrimage site. According to tradition, angels helped to carve the churches. More than 50,000 pilgrims come to the town of Lalibela at Christmas. After the Muslims captured Jerusalem in 1187, King Lalibela proclaimed his city the "New Jerusalem" because Christians could no longer go on pilgrimage to the Holy Land.

AFRICAN RELIGIONS IN DEPTH

Sacred Symbols

Because all of life is infused with religious meaning, any object or location may be considered or become sacred in traditional African religions. Masks, in particular, have special meaning and

may be worn during ceremonies. The mask often represents a god, whose power is passed to the one wearing the mask.

Sacred Practices & Gestures

The Yoruba practice divination in a form that is originally Arabic. There are sixteen basic figures—combined, they deliver a prophecy that the diviner is not to interpret. Instead, he or she recites verses from a classic source. Images may be made to prevent or cure illness. For example, the Yoruba have a smallpox spirit god that can be prayed to for healing. Daily prayer, both morning and evening, is part of life for most Yoruba.

In the amaNazarite Church, which Zulu Isaiah Shembe founded, singing is a key part of the faith. Shembe himself was a gifted composer of hymns. This sacred music was combined with dancing, during which the Zulu wear their traditional dress.

Rites, Celebrations & Services

The Dogon have three major cults. The Awa are associated with dances, featuring ornately carved masks, at funerals and on the anniversaries of deaths. The cult of the Earth god, Lebe, concerns itself with the agricultural cycles and fertility of the land; the hogon of the village guards the soil's purity and presides at ceremonies related to farming. The third cult, the Binu, is involved with communication with spirits, ancestor worship, and sacrifices. Binu shrines are in many locations. The Binu priest makes sacrifices of porridge made from millet and blood at planting time and also when the help of an ancestor is needed. Each clan within the Dogon community has a totem animal spirit—an ancestor spirit wishing to communicate with descendents may do so by taking the form of the animal.

The Dogon also have a celebration every fifty years at the appearing of the star Sirius B between two mountains. (Sirius is often the brightest star in the nighttime sky.) Young males leaving for three months prior to the sigui, as it is called, for a time of seclusion and speaking in private language. This celebration is rooted in the Dogon belief that amphibious creatures, the Nommo, visited their land about three thousand years ago.

The Yoruba offer Esu, the trickster god, palm wine and animal sacrifices. Because he is a trickster, he is considered a cheater, and being on his good side is important. The priests in Yoruba traditional religion are responsible for installing tribal chiefs and kings.

Among the Zulu, families determine the lobola, or bride price. They believe that a groom will respect his wife more if he must pay for her. Further gifts are then exchanged, and the bride's family traditionally gives the groom a goat or sheep to signify their acceptance of him. The groom's family provides meat for the wedding feast, slaughtering a cow on the morning of the wedding. The families assemble in a circle and the men, in costume, dance. The bride gives presents, usually mats or blankets, to members of her new family, who dance or sing their thanks. The final gift, to the groom, is a blanket, which is tossed over his head. Friends of the bride playfully beat him, demonstrating how they will respond if he mistreats his new wife. After the two families eat together, the couple is considered one.

In the traditional Zulu religion, ancestors three generations back are regarded as not yet settled in the afterlife. To help them settle, offerings of goats or other animals are made and rituals to help them settle into the community of ancestors are performed.

Christmas is a major celebration in Ethiopian Christianity. Priests rattle an instrument derived from biblical times, called the sistra, and chant to begin the mass. The festivities include drumming and a dance known as King David's dance.

Judy A. Johnson, MTS

Bibliography

A, Oladosu Olusegun. "Ethics and Judgement: A Panacea for Human Transformation in Yoruba Multireligious Society." *Asia Journal of Theology* 26.1 (2012): 88–104. Print.

Barnes, Trevor. *The Kingfisher Book of Religions*. New York: Kingfisher, 1999. Print.

Dawson, Allan Charles, ed. *Shrines in Africa: history, politics, and society*. Calgary: U of Calgary P, 2009. Print.

Doumbia, Adama, and Naomi Doumbia. *The Way of the Elders: West African Spirituality*. St. Paul: Llewellyn, 2004. Print.

Douny, Laurence. "The Role of Earth Shrines in the Socio-Symbolic Construction of the Dogon Territory: Towards a Philosophy of Containment." *Anthropology & Medicine* 18.2 (2011): 167–79. Print.

Friedenthal, Lora, and Dorothy Kavanaugh. *Religions of Africa*. Philadelphia: Mason Crest, 2007. Print.

Hayes, Stephen. "Orthodox Ecclesiology in Africa: A Study of the 'Ethiopian' Churches of South Africa." *International Journal for the Study of the Christian Church* 8.4 (2008): 337–54. Print.

Lugira, Aloysius M. *African Religion*. New York: Facts on File, 2004. Print.

Mbiti, John S. *African Religions and Philosophy*. 2nd ed. Oxford: Heinemann, 1991. Print.

Monteiro-Ferreira, Ana Maria. "Reevaluating Zulu Religion." *Journal of Black Studies* 35.3 (2005): 347–63. Print.

Peel, J. D. Y. "Yoruba Religion as a Global Phenomenon." *Journal of African History* 5.1 (2010): 107–8. Print.

Ray, Benjamin C. *African Religions*. 2nd ed. Upper Saddle River: Prentice, 2000. Print.

Thomas, Douglas E. *African Traditional Religion in the Modern World*. Jefferson: McFarland, 2005. Print.

Bahá'í Faith

General Description

The Bahá'í faith is the youngest of the world's religions. It began in the mid-nineteenth century, offering scholars the opportunity to observe a religion in the making. While some of the acts of religious founders such as Buddha or Jesus cannot be substantiated, the modern founders of Bahá'í were more contemporary figures.

Number of Adherents Worldwide

An estimated 5 to 7 million people follow the Bahá'í faith. Although strong in Middle Eastern nations such as Iran, where the faith originated, Bahá'í has reached people in many countries, particularly the United States and Canada.

Basic Tenets

The Bahá'í faith has three major doctrines. The first doctrine is that there is one transcendent God, and all religions worship that God, regardless of the name given to the deity. Adherents believe that religious figures such as Jesus Christ, the Buddha, and the Prophet Muhammad were different revelations of God unique to their time and place. The second doctrine is that there is only one religion, though each world faith is valid and was founded by a ""manifestation of God" who is part of a divine plan for educating humanity. The third doctrine is a belief in the unity of all humankind. In light of this underlying unity, those of the Bahá'í faith work for social justice. They believe that seeking consensus among various groups diffuses typical power struggles and to this end, they employ a method called consultation, which is a nonadversarial decision-making process.

The Bahá'í believe that the human soul is immortal, and that after death the soul moves nearer or farther away from God. The idea of an afterlife comprised of a literal "heaven" or "hell" is not part of the faith.

Sacred Text

The Most Holy Book, or the Tablets, written by Baha'u'llah, form the basis of Bahá'í teachings. Though not considered binding, scriptures from other faiths are regarded as "Divine Revelation."

Major Figures

The Bab (The Gate of God) Siyyad 'Ali Mohammad (1819–50), founder of the Bábí movement that broke from Islam, spoke of a coming new messenger of God. Mirza Hoseyn 'Ali Nuri (1817–92), who realized that he was that prophet, was given the title Baha'u'llah (Glory of God). From a member of Persia's landed gentry, he was part of the ruling class, and is considered the founder of the Bahá'í faith. His son, 'Abdu'l-Bahá (Servant of the Glory of God), who lived from 1844 until 1921, became the leader of the group after his father's death in 1892. The oldest son of his eldest daughter, Shogi Effendi Rabbani (1899–1957), oversaw a rapid expansion, visiting Egypt, America, and nations in Europe. Tahirih (the Pure One) was a woman poet who challenged stereotypes by appearing unveiled at meetings.

Major Holy Sites

The Bahá'í World Center is located near Haifa, Israel. The burial shrine of the Bab, a pilgrimage site, is there. The Shrine of Baha'u'llah near Acre, Israel, is another pilgrimage site. The American headquarters are in Wilmette, Illinois. Carmel in Israel is regarded as the world center of the faith.

Major Rites & Celebrations

Each year, the Bahá'í celebrate Ridvan Festival, a twelve-day feast from sunset on April 20 to sunset on May 2. The festival marks Baha'u'llah's declaration of prophethood, as prophesized by the Bab, at a Baghdad garden. (Ridvan means Paradise.) The holy days within that feast are the first (Baha'u'llah's garden arrival), ninth (the arrival of his family), and twelfth (his departure from Ridvan Garden)—on these days, the Bahá'í do not work. During this feast, people attend social events and meet for devotions. Baha'u'llah referred to it as the King of Festivals and Most Great Festival. The Bahá'í celebrate several other events, including World Religion Day and Race Unity Day, both founded by Bahá'í, as well as days connected with significant events in the life of the founder. Elections to the Spiritual Assemblies, and the national and local administrations; international elections are held every five years.

ORIGINS

History & Geography

Siyyad 'Ali Muhammad was born into a merchant family of Shiraz in 1819. Both his parents were descendents of the Prophet Muhammad, Islam's central figure. Like the Prophet, the man who became the Bab lost his father at an early age and was raised by an uncle. A devout child, he entered his uncle's business by age fifteen. After visiting Muslim holy cities, he returned to Shiraz, where he married a distant relative named Khadijih.

While on pilgrimage in 1844 to the black stone of Ka'bah, a sacred site in Islam, the Bab stood with his hand on that holy object and declared that he was the prophet for whom they had been waiting. The Sunni did not give credence to these claims. The Bab went to Persia, where the Shia sect was the majority. However, because Muhammad had been regarded as the "Seal of the Prophets," and the one who spoke the final revelation, Shia clergy viewed his claims as threatening, As such, nothing further would be revealed until the Day of Judgment. The authority of the clergy was in danger from this new movement.

The Bab was placed under house arrest, and then confined to a fortress on the Russian frontier. That move to a more remote area only increased the number of converts, as did a subsequent move to another Kurdish fortress. He

was eventually taken to Tabriz in Iran and tried before the Muslim clergy in 1848. Condemned, he was caned on the soles of his feet and treated by a British doctor who was impressed by him.

Despite his treatment and the persecution of his followers—many of the Bab's eighteen disciples, termed the "Letters of the Living," were persistently tortured and executed—the Bab refused to articulate a doctrine of jihad. The Babis could defend themselves, but were forbidden to use holy war as a means of religious conquest. In three major confrontations sparked by the Shia clergy, Babis were defeated. The Bab was sentenced as a heretic and shot by a firing squad in 1850. Lacking leadership and grief-stricken, in 1852 two young Babis fired on the shah in 1852, unleashing greater persecutions and cruelty against those of the Bahá'í faith.

A follower of the Bab, Mirza Hoseyn 'Ali Nuri, announced in 1863 that he was the one who was to come (the twelfth imam of Islam), the "Glory of God," or Baha'u'llah. Considered the founder of the Bahá'í Faith, he was a tireless writer who anointed his son, 'Abdu'l-Bahá, as the next leader. Despite deprivations and imprisonments, Baha'u'llah lived to be seventy-five years old, relinquishing control of the organization to 'Abdu'l-Bahá before the time of his death.

'Abdu'l-Bahá, whom his father had called "the Master," expanded the faith to the nations of Europe and North America. In 1893, at the Parliament of Religions at the Chicago World's Fair, the faith was first mentioned in the United States. Within a few years, communities of faith were established in Chicago and Wisconsin. In 1911, 'Abdu'l-Bahá began a twenty-eight month tour of Europe and North America to promote the Bahá'í faith. Administratively, he established the spiritual assemblies that were the forerunner of the Houses of Justice that his father had envisioned.

During World War I, 'Abdu'l-Bahá engaged in humanitarian work among the Palestinians in the Holy Land, where he lived. In recognition of his efforts, he was granted knighthood by the British government. Thousands of people, including many political and religious dignitaries, attended his funeral in 1921.

'Abdu'l-Bahá conferred the role of Guardian, or sole interpreter of Bahá'í teaching, to his eldest grandson, Shoghi Effendi Rabbani. To him, all questions regarding the faith were to be addressed. Shoghi Effendi Rabbani was a descendent of Baha'u'llah through both parents. He headed the Bahá'í faith from 1921 to 1963, achieving four major projects: he oversaw the physical development of the World Centre and expanded the administrative order; he carried out the plan his father had set in motion; and he provided for the translating and interpreting of Bahá'í teachings, as the writings of both the Bab and those of Baha'u'llah and 'Abdu'l-Bahá have been translated and published in more than eight hundred languages.

Beginning in 1937, Shoghi Effendi Rabbani began a series of specific plans with goals tied to deadlines. In 1953, during the second seven-year plan, the house of worship in Wilmette, Illinois, was completed and dedicated.

Although the beliefs originated in Shi'ite Islam, the Bahá'í Faith has been declared a new religion without connections to Islam. To followers of Islam, it is a heretical sect. During the reign of the Ayatollah Khomeini, a time when Iran was especially noted as intolerant of diverse views, the Bahá'í faced widespread persecution.

Founder or Major Prophet

Mirza Husayn Ali Nuri, known as Baha'u'llah, was born into privilege in 1817 in what was then Persia, now present-day Iran. At twenty-two, he declined a government post offered at his father's death. Although a member of a politically prestigious family, he did not follow the career path of several generations of his ancestors. Instead, he managed the family estates and devoted himself to charities, earning the title "Father of the Poor."

At twenty-seven, he followed the Babis's movement within Shia Islam, corresponding with the Bab and traveling to further the faith. He also provided financial support. In 1848, he organized and helped to direct a conference that explained the Bab's teaching. At the conference, he gave

symbolic names to the eighty-one followers who had attended, based on the spiritual qualities he had observed.

Although he managed to escape death during the persecutions before and after the Bab's death, a fact largely attributed to his upbringing, Baha'u'llah was imprisoned several times. During a four-month stay in an underground dungeon in Tehran, he realized from a dream that he was the one of whom the Bab had prophesied. After being released, he was banished from Persia and had his property confiscated by the shah. He went to Baghdad, refusing the offer of refuge that had come from Russia. Over the following three years a small band of followers joined him, including members of his family. When his younger brother attempted to take over the leadership of the Babis, Baha'u'llah spent two years in a self-imposed exile in the Kurdistan wilderness. In 1856, with the community near anarchy as a result of his brother's failure of leadership, Baha'u'llah returned to the community and restored its position over the next seven years.

Concerned by the growing popularity of the new faith, the shah demanded that the Babis move further away from Persia. They went to Constantinople where, in 1863, Baha'u'llah revealed to the whole group that he was "He Whom God Will Make Manifest." From there the Bahá'í were sent to Adrianople in Turkey, and at last, in 1868, to the town of Acre in the Holy Land. Baha'u'llah was imprisoned in Acre and survived severe prison conditions. In 1877, he moved from prison to a country estate, then to a mansion. He died in 1892 after a fever.

Philosophical Basis

The thinking of Shia Muslims contributed to the development of Bahá'í. The writings incorporate language and concepts from the Qur'an (Islam's holy book). Like Muslims, the Bahá'í believe that God is one. God sends messengers, the Manifestations of God, to instruct people and benefit society. These have included Jesus Christ, the Buddha, the Prophet Muhammad, Krishna, and the Bab. Bahá'í also goes further than Islam in accepting all religions—not just Judaism, Christianity, and Islam—as being part of a divinely inspired plan.

Shia Muslims believe that Muhammad's descendents should lead the faithful community. The leaders, known as imams, were considered infallible. The Sunni Muslims believed that following the way (sunna) of Muhammad was sufficient qualification for leadership. Sunni dynasties regarded the imams as a threat and executed them, starting with two of Muhammad's grandsons, who became Shia martyrs.

In Persia, a state with a long tradition of divinely appointed rulers, the Shia sect was strong. When the Safavids, a Shia dynasty, came to power in the sixteenth century, the custom of the imamate was victorious. One tradition states that in 873, the last appointed imam, who was still a child, went into hiding to avoid being killed. For the following sixty-nine years, this twelfth imam communicated through his deputies to the faithful. Each of the deputies was called bab, or gate, because they led to the "Hidden Imam." Four babs existed through 941, and the last one died without naming the next bab. The Hidden Imam is thought to emerge at the end of time to bring in a worldwide reign of justice. From this tradition came the expectation of a Mahdi (Guided One) to lead the people.

During the early nineteenth century, many followers of both the Christian and Islamic faiths expected their respective messiahs to return. Shia teachers believed that the return of the Mahdi imam was near. In 1843, one teacher, Siyyid Kázim, noted that the Hidden Imam had disappeared one thousand lunar years earlier. He urged the faithful to look for the Mahdi imam.

The following year in Shiraz, Siyyad 'Ali Mohammad announced that he was the Mahdi. (*Siyyad* is a term meaning descended from Muhammad.) He referred to himself as the Bab, though he expanded the term's meaning. Eighteen men, impressed with his ability to expound the Qur'an, believed him. They became the Letters of the Living, and were sent throughout Persia (present-day Iran) to announce the dawning of the Day of God.

In 1853, Mirza Husayn Ali Nuri experienced a revelation that he was "He Whom God Shall Make Manifest," the one of whom the Bab prophesied. Accepted as such, he began writing the words that became the Bahá'í scriptures. Much of what is known of the early days of the faith comes from a Cambridge academic, Edward Granville Browne, who first visited Baha'u'llah in the 1890. Browne wrote of his meeting, introducing this faith to the West.

The emphasis of the Bahá'í faith is on personal development and the breaking down of barriers between people. Service to humanity is important and encouraged. Marriage, with a belief in the equality of both men and women, is also encouraged. Consent of both sets of parents is required prior to marrying.

Holy Places

The shrine of the Bab near Haifa and that of Baha'u'llah near Acre, in Israel, are the two most revered sites for those of the Bahá'í faith. In 2008, the United Nations Educational, Scientific, and Cultural Organization (UNESCO) recognized both as World Heritage Sites. They are the first such sites from a modern religious tradition to be added to the list of sites. Both sites are appreciated for the formal gardens surrounding them that blend design elements from different cultures. For the Bahá'í, Baha'u'llah's shrine is the focus of prayer, comparable to the significance given to the Ka'bah in Mecca for Muslims or to the Western Wall for Jews.

As of 2013, there are seven Bahá'í temples in the world; an eighth temple is under construction in Chile. All temples are built with a center dome and nine sides, symbolizing both diversity and world unity. The North American temple is located in Wilmette, Illinois. There, daily prayer services take place as well as a Sunday service.

THE BAHÁ'Í FAITH IN DEPTH

Governance

Elected members of lay councils at international, national, and local levels administer the work of the faith. The Universal House of Justice in Haifa, Israel, is the location of the international nine-member body. Elections for all of these lay councils are by secret ballot, and do not include nominating, candidates, or campaigns. Those twenty-one and older are permitted to vote. The councils make decisions according to a process of collective decision-making called consultation. They strive to serve as a model for governing a united global society.

Personal Conduct

In addition to private prayer and acts of social justice, those of the Bahá'í faith are encouraged to have a profession, craft, or trade. They are also asked to shun and refrain from slander and partisan politics. Homosexuality and sexual activity outside marriage are forbidden, as is gambling.

The Bahá'í faith does not have professional clergy, nor does it engage in missionary work. However, Bahá'í may share their faith with others and may move to another country as a "pioneer." Pioneers are unlike traditional missionaries, and are expected to support themselves through a career and as a member of the community.

Avenues of Service

Those of the Bahá'í Faith place a high value on service to humanity, considering it an act of worship. This can be done through caring for one's own family or through one's choice of vocation. Within the local community, people may teach classes for children, mentor youth groups, host devotional programs, or teach adult study circles. Many are engaged in economic or social development programs as well. Although not mandated, a year or two of service is often undertaken following high school or during college.

United Nations Involvement

Beginning in 1947, just one year after the United Nations (UN) first met, the Bahá'í Faith was represented at that body. In 1948, the Bahá'í International Community was accredited by the UN as an international nongovernmental organization (NGO). In 1970, the faith received special consultative status with the UN Economic

and Social Council (ECOSOC). Following World War I, a Bahá'í office opened in Geneva, Switzerland, where the League of Nations was headquartered. Thus the Bahá'í Faith has a long tradition of supporting global institutions.

Money Matters

The International Bahá'í Fund exists to develop and support the growth of the faith, and the Universal House of Justice oversees the distribution of the money. Contributions are also used to maintain the Bahá'í World Center. No money is accepted from non-Bahá'í sources. National and local funds, administered by National or Local Spiritual Assemblies, are used in supporting service projects, publishing endeavors, schools, and Bahá'í centers. For the Bahá'í, the size of the donation is less important than regular contributions and the spirit of sacrifice behind them.

Food Restrictions

Bahá'í between fifteen and seventy years of age **fast** nineteen days a year, abstaining from food and drink from sunrise to sunset. Fasting occurs the first day of each month of the Bahá'í calendar, which divides the year into nineteen months of nineteen days each. The Bahá'í faithful do not drink alcohol or use narcotics, because these will deaden the mind with repeated use.

Rites, Celebrations & Services

Daily prayer and meditation is recommended in the Bahá'í faith. During services there are mediations and prayers, along with the reading of Bahá'í scriptures and other world faith traditions. There is no set ritual, no offerings, and no sermons. Unaccompanied by musical instruments, choirs also sing. Light refreshments may be served afterwards.

Bahá'í place great stress on marriage, the only state in which sex is permitted. Referred to as "a fortress for well-being and salvation," a monogamous, heterosexual marriage is the ideal. To express the oneness of humanity, interracial marriages are encouraged. After obtaining the consent of their parents, the couple takes the following vow: "We will all, verily, abide by the will of God." The remainder of the service may be individually crafted and may also include dance, music, feasting, and ceremony. Should a couple choose to end a marriage, they must first complete a year of living apart while trying to reconcile differences. Divorce is discouraged, but permitted after that initial year.

Judy A. Johnson, MTS

Bibliography

Albertson, Lorelei. *All about Bahá'í Faith*. University Pub., 2012. E-book.

Bowers, Kenneth E. *God Speaks Again: an Introduction to the Bahá'í Faith*. Wilmette: Bahá'í, 2004. Print.

Buck, Christopher. "The Interracial 'Bahá'í Movement' and the Black Intelligentsia: The Case of W. E. B. Du Bois." *Journal of Religious History* 36.4 (2012): 542–62. Print.

Cederquist, Druzelle. *The Story of Baha'u'llah*. Wilmette: Bahá'í, 2005. Print.

Echevarria, L. *Life Stories of Bahá'í Women in Canada: Constructing Religious Identity in the Twentieth Century*. Lang, 2011. E-book.

Garlington, William. *The Bahá'í Faith in America*. Lanham: Rowman, 2008. Print.

Hartz, Paula R. *Bahá'í Faith*. New York: Facts on File, 2006. Print.

Hatcher, William S. and J. Douglas Martin. *The Bahá'í Faith: The Emerging Global Religion*. Wilmette: Bahá'í, 2002. Print.

Karlberg, Michael. "Constructive Resilience: The Bahá'í Response to Oppression." *Peace & Change* 35.2 (2010): 222–57. Print.

Lee, Anthony A. *The Bahá'í Faith in Africa: Establishing a New Religious Movement, 1952–1962*. Brill NV, E-book.

Momen, Moojan. "Bahá'í Religious History." *Journal of Religious History* 36.4 (2012): 463–70. Print.

Momen, Moojan. *The Bahá'í Faith: A Beginner's Guide*. Oxford: Oneworld, 2007. Print.

Smith, Peter. *The Bahá'í Faith*. Cambridge: Cambridge UP, 2008. Print.

Wilkinson, Philip. *Religions*. New York: DK, 2008. Print.

Buddhism

General Description

Buddhism has three main branches: Theravada (Way of the Elders), also referred to as Hinayana (Lesser Vehicle); Mahayana (Greater Vehicle); and Vajrayana (Diamond Vehicle), also referred to as Tantric Buddhism. Vajrayana is sometimes thought of as an extension of Mahayana Buddhism. These can be further divided into many sects and schools, many of which are geographically based. In Buddhism, these different divisions or schools are regarded as alternative paths to enlightenment (Wilkinson 2008).

Number of Adherents Worldwide

An estimated 474 million people around the world are Buddhists. Of the major sects, Theravada Buddhism is the oldest, developed in the sixth century BCE. Its adherents include those of the Theravada Forest Tradition. From Mahayana Buddhism, which developed in the third to second centuries BCE, came several offshoots based on location. In what is now China, Pure Land Buddhism and Tibetan Buddhism developed in the seventh century. In Japan, Zen Buddhism developed in the twelfth century, Nichiren Buddhism developed a century later, and Soka Gakkai was founded in 1937. In California during the 1970s, the Serene Reflection Meditation began as a subset of Sōtō Zen. In Buddhism, these different divisions or schools are regarded as alternative paths to enlightenment.

Basic Tenets

Buddhists hold to the Three Universal Truths: impermanence, the lack of self, and suffering. These truths encompass the ideas that everything is impermanent and changing and that life is not satisfying because of its impermanence and the temporary nature of all things, including contentment. Buddhism also teaches the Four Noble Truths: All life is suffering (Dukkha). Desire and attachment cause suffering (Samudaya). Ceasing to desire or crave conceptual attachment ends suffering and leads to release (Nirodha). This release comes through following the Noble Eightfold Path—right understanding (or view), right intention, right speech, right conduct, right occupation, right effort, right mindfulness, and right concentration (Magga).

Although Buddhists do not believe in an afterlife as such, the soul undergoes a cycle of death and rebirth. Following the Noble Eightfold Path leads to the accumulation of good karma, allowing one to be reborn at a higher level. Karma is the Buddhist belief in cause-effect relationships; actions taken in one life have consequences in the next. Ultimately, many refer to the cessation or elimination of suffering as the primary goal of Buddhism.

Buddhists do not believe in gods. Salvation is to be found in following the teachings of Buddha, which are called the Dharma (law or truth). Buddhism does have saint-like bodhisattvas (enlightened beings) who reject ultimate enlightenment (Nirvana) for themselves to aid others.

Sacred Text

Buddhism has nothing comparable to the Qur'an (Islam's holy book) or the Bible. For Theravada Buddhists, an important text is the Pāli Canon, the collection of Buddha's teachings. Mahayana Buddhists recorded their version of these as sutras, many of them in verse. The Lotus Sutra is among the most important. The Buddhist scriptures are written in two languages of ancient India, Pali and Sanskrit, depending on the tradition in which they were developed. Some of these words, such as karma, have been transliterated into English and gained common usage.

Major Figures

Siddhartha Gautama (ca. 563 to 483 BCE) is the founder of Buddhism and regarded as the Buddha or Supreme Buddha. He is the most highly regarded historical figure in Buddhism.

He had two principle disciples: Sariputta and Mahamoggallana (or Maudgalyayana). In contemporary Buddhism, the fourteenth Dalai Lama, Tenzin Gyatso, is a significant person. Both he and Aung San Suu Kyi, a Buddhist of Myanmar who was held as a political prisoner for her stand against the oppressive regime of that nation, have been awarded the Nobel Peace Prize.

Major Holy Sites

Buddhist holy sites are located in several places in Asia. All of those directly related to the life of Siddhartha Gautama are located in the northern part of India near Nepal. Lumbini Grove is noted as the birthplace of the Buddha. He received enlightenment at Bodh Gaya and first began to teach in Sarnath. Kusinara is the city where he died.

In other Asian nations, some holy sites were once dedicated to other religions. Angkor Wat in Cambodia, for example, was constructed for the Hindu god Vishnu in the twelfth century CE. It became a Buddhist temple three hundred years later. It was once the largest religious monument in the world and still attracts visitors. In Java's central highlands sits Borobudur, the world's largest Buddhist shrine. The name means "Temple of Countless Buddhas." Its five terraces represent what must be overcome to reach enlightenment: worldly desires, evil intent, malicious joy, laziness, and doubt. It was built in the eighth and ninth centuries CE, only to fall into neglect at about the turn of the millennium; it was rediscovered in 1815. The complex has three miles of carvings illustrating the life and teachings of the Buddha. In Sri Lanka, the Temple of the Tooth, which houses what is believed to be one of the Buddha's teeth, is a popular pilgrimage site.

Some of the holy sites incorporate gifts of nature. China has four sacred Buddhist mountains, symbolizing the four corners of the universe. These mountains—Wǔtái Shān, Éméi Shān, Jiǔhuá Shān, and Pǔtuó Shān—are believed to be the homes of bodhisattvas. In central India outside Fardapur, there are twenty-nine caves carved into the granite, most of them with frescoes based on the Buddha's life. Ajanta, as the site is known, was created between 200 BCE and the fifth century CE. Five of the caves house temples.

The Buddha's birthday, his day of death, and the day of his enlightenment are all celebrated, either as one day or several. Different traditions and countries have their own additional celebrations, including Sri Lanka's Festival of the Tooth. Buddhists have a lunar calendar, and four days of each month are regarded as holy days.

ORIGINS

History & Geography

Buddhism began in what is now southern Nepal and northern India with the enlightenment of the Buddha. Following his death, members of the sangha, or community, spread the teachings across northern India. The First Buddhist Council took place in 486 BCE at Rajagaha. This council settled the Buddhist canon, the Tipitaka. In 386 BCE, a little more than a century after the Buddha died, a second Buddhist Council was held at Vesali. It was at this meeting that the two major schools of Buddhist thought—Theravada and Mahayana—began to differ.

Emperor Asoka, who ruled most of the Indian subcontinent from around 268 to 232 BCE, converted to Buddhism. He sent missionaries across India and into central parts of Asia. He also set up pillars with Buddhist messages in his own efforts to establish "true dharma" in the kingdom, although he did not create a state church. His desire for his subjects to live contently in this life led to promoting trade, maintaining canals and reservoirs, and the founding a system of medical care for both humans and animals. Asoka's son Mahinda went to southern Indian and to Sri Lanka with the message of Buddhism.

Asoka's empire fell shortly after his death. Under the following dynasties, evidence suggests Buddhists in India experienced persecution. The religion continued to grow, however, and during the first centuries CE, monasteries and monuments were constructed with support from local rulers. Some additional support came from women within the royal courts. Monastic centers also grew in number. By the fourth century CE, Buddhism had become one of the chief religious traditions in India.

During the Gupta dynasty, which lasted from about 320 to 600 CE, Buddhists and Hindus began enriching each other's traditions. Some Hindus felt that the Buddha was an incarnation of Vishnu, a Hindu god. Some Buddhists showed respect for Hindu deities.

Also during this era, Mahavihara, the concept of the "Great Monastery," came to be. These institutions served as universities for the study and development of Buddhist thinking. Some of them also included cultural and scientific study in the curriculum.

Traders and missionaries took the ideas of Buddhism to China. By the first century CE, Buddhism was established in that country. The religion died out or was absorbed into Hinduism in India. By the seventh century, a visiting Chinese monk found that Huns had invaded India from Central Asia and destroyed many Buddhist monasteries. The religion revived and flourished in the northeast part of India for several centuries.

Muslim invaders reached India in the twelfth and thirteenth centuries. They sacked the monasteries, some of which had grown very wealthy. Some even paid workers to care for both the land they owned and the monks, while some had indentured slaves. Because Buddhism become monastic rather than a religion of the laity, there was no groundswell for renewal following the Muslim invasion.

Prominent in eastern and Southeast Asia, Buddhism is the national religion in some countries. For example, in Thailand, everyone learns about Buddhism in school. Buddhism did not begin to reach Western culture until the nineteenth century, when the Lotus Sutra was translated into German. The first Buddhist temple in the United States was built in 1853 in San Francisco's Chinatown.

Chinese Communists took control of Tibet in 1950. Nine years later, the fourteenth Dalai Lama left for India, fearing persecution. The Dalai Lama is considered a living teacher (lama) who is to instruct others. (The term *dalai* means "great as the ocean.") In 1989, he received the Nobel Peace Prize.

Buddhism experienced a revival in India during the twentieth century. Although some of this new beginning was due in part to Tibetan immigrants seeking safety, a mass conversion in 1956 was the major factor. The year was chosen to honor the 2,500th anniversary of the Buddha's death year. Buddhism was chosen as an alternative to the strict caste structure of Hinduism, and hundreds of thousands of people of the Dalit caste, once known as untouchables, converted in a ceremony held in Nagpur.

Founder or Major Prophet
Siddhartha Gautama, who became known as the "Enlightened One," or Buddha, was a prince in what is now southern Nepal, but was then northern India during the sixth century BCE. The name Siddhartha means "he who achieves his aim." He was a member of the Sakya tribe of Nepal, belonging to the warrior caste. Many legends have grown around his birth and early childhood. One states that he was born in a grove in the woods, emerging from his mother's side able to walk and completely clean.

During Siddhartha's childhood, a Brahmin, or wise man, prophesied that he would grow to be a prince or a religious teacher who would help others overcome suffering. Because the life of a sage involved itinerant begging, the king did not want this life for his child. He kept Siddhartha in the palace and provided him with all the luxuries of his position, including a wife, Yashodhara. They had a son, Rahula.

Escaping from the palace at about the age of thirty, Gautama first encountered suffering in the form of an old man with a walking stick. The following day, he saw a man who was ill. On the third day, he witnessed a funeral procession. Finally he met a monk, who had nothing, but who radiated happiness. He determined to leave his privileged life, an act called the Great Renunciation. Because hair was a sign of vanity in his time, he shaved his head. He looked for enlightenment via an ascetic life of little food or sleep. He followed this path for six years, nearly starving to death. Eventually, he determined on a Middle Way, a path neither luxurious as he had known in the palace, nor ascetic as he had attempted.

After three days and nights of meditating under a tree at Bodh Gaya, Siddhartha achieved his goal of enlightenment, or Nirvana. He escaped fear of suffering and death.

The Buddha began his preaching career, which spanned some forty years, following his enlightenment. He gave his first sermon in northeast India at Sarnath in a deer park. The first five followers became the first community, or sangha. Buddha died around age eighty, in 483 BCE after he had eaten poisoned food. After warning his followers not to eat the food, he meditated until he died.

Buddhists believe in many enlightened ones. Siddhartha is in one tradition regarded as the fourth buddha, while other traditions hold him to have been the seventh or twenty-fifth buddha.

His disciples, who took the ideas throughout India, repeated his teachings. When the later Buddhists determined to write down the teachings of the Buddha, they met to discuss the ideas and agreed that a second meeting should occur in a century. At the third council, which was held at Pataliputta, divisions occurred. The two major divisions—Theravada and Mahayana—differ over the texts to be used and the interpretation of the teachings. Theravada can be translated as "the Teachings of the Elders," while Mahayana means "Great Vehicle."

Theravada Buddhists believe that only monks can achieve enlightenment through the teachings of another buddha, or enlightened being. Thus they try to spend some part of their lives in a monastery. Buddhists in the Mahayana tradition, on the other hand, feel that all people can achieve enlightenment, without being in a monastery. Mahayanans also regard some as bodhisattvas, people who have achieved the enlightened state but renounce Nirvana to help others achieve it.

Philosophical Basis

During Siddhartha's lifetime, Hinduism was the predominant religion in India. Many people, especially in northern India, were dissatisfied with the rituals and sacrifices of that religion. In addition, as many small kingdoms expanded and the unity of the tribes began to break down, many people were in religious turmoil and doubt. A number of sects within Hinduism developed.

The Hindu belief in the cycle of death and rebirth led some people to despair because they could not escape from suffering in their lives. Siddhartha was trying to resolve the suffering he saw in the world, but many of his ideas came from the Brahmin sect of Hinduism, although he reinterpreted them. Reincarnation, dharma, and reverence for cows are three of the ideas that carried over into Buddhism.

In northeast India at Bodh Gaya, he rested under a bodhi tree, sometimes called a bo tree. He meditated there until he achieved Nirvana, or complete enlightenment, derived from the freedom of fear that attached to suffering and death. As a result of his being enlightened, he was known as Buddha, a Sanskrit word meaning "awakened one." Wanting to help others, he began teaching his Four Noble Truths, along with the Noble Eightfold Path that would lead people to freedom from desire and suffering. He encouraged his followers to take Triple Refuge in the Three Precious Jewels: the Buddha, the teachings, and the sangha, or monastic community. Although at first Buddha was uncertain about including women in a sangha, his mother-in-law begged for the privilege.

Greed, hatred, and ignorance were three traits that Buddha felt people needed to conquer. All three create craving, the root of suffering. Greed and ignorance lead to a desire for things that are not needed, while hatred leads to a craving to destroy the hated object or person.

To the Four Noble Truths and Eightfold Path, early devotees of Buddhism added the Five Moral Precepts. These are to avoid taking drugs and alcohol, engaging in sexual misconduct, harming others, stealing, and lying.

The precepts of the Buddha were not written down for centuries. The first text did not appear for more than 350 years after the precepts were first spoken. One collection from Sri Lanka written in Pāli during the first century BCE is known as Three Baskets, or Tipitaka. The three baskets include Buddha's teaching (the Basket of Discourse), commentary on the sayings (the Basket of Special Doctrine), and the rules for monks to follow (the Basket of Discipline). The name Three Baskets refers to the fact that the sayings were first written on leaves from a palm tree that were then collected in baskets.

Holy Places

Buddhists make pilgrimages to places that relate to important events in Siddhartha's life. While Lumbini Grove, the place of Siddhartha's birth, is a prominent pilgrimage site, the primary site for pilgrimage is Bodh Gaya, the location where Buddha received enlightenment. Other pilgrimage sites include Sarnath, the deer park located in what is now Varanasi (Benares) where the Buddha first began to teach, and Kusinara, the city where he died. All of these are in the northern part of India near Nepal.

Other sites in Asia that honor various bodhisattvas have also become pilgrimage destinations. Mountains are often chosen; there are four in China, each with monasteries and temples built on them. In Japan, the Shikoku pilgrimage covers more than 700 miles and involves visits to eighty-eight temples along the route.

BUDDHISM IN DEPTH

Sacred Symbols

Many stylized statue poses of the Buddha exist, each with a different significance. One, in which the Buddha has both hands raised, palms facing outward, commemorates the calming of an elephant about to attack the Buddha. If only the right hand is raised, the hand symbolizes friendship and being unafraid. The teaching gesture is that of a hand with the thumb and first finger touching.

In Tibetan Buddhism, the teachings of Buddha regarding the cycle of rebirth are symbolized in the six-spoke wheel of life. One may be reborn into any of the six realms of life: hell, hungry spirits, warlike demons called Asuras, animals, humans, or gods. Another version of the wheel has eight spokes rather than six, to represent the Noble Eightfold Path. Still another wheel has twelve spokes, signifying both the Four Noble Truths and the Noble Eightfold Path.

Tibetan Buddhists have prayer beads similar to a rosary, with 108 beads representing the number of desires to be overcome prior to reaching enlightenment. The worshipper repeats the Triple Refuge—Buddha, dharma, and sangha—or a mantra.

The prayer wheel is another device that Tibetan Buddhists use. Inside the wheel is a roll of paper on which the sacred mantra—Hail to the jewel in the lotus—is written many times. The lotus is a symbol of growing spiritually; it grows in muddied waters, but with the stems and flowers, it reaches toward the sun. By turning the wheel and spinning the mantra, the practitioner spreads blessings. Bells may be rung to wake the hearer out of ignorance.

In Tantric Buddhism, the mandala, or circle, serves as a map of the entire cosmos. Mandalas may be made of colored grains of sand, carved or painted. They are used to help in meditation and are thought to have a spiritual energy.

Buddhism recognizes Eight Auspicious Symbols, including the banner, conch shell, fish, knot, lotus, treasure vase, umbrella, and wheel. Each has a particular significance. A conch shell, for example, is often blown to call worshippers to meetings. Because its sound travels far, it signifies the voice of Buddha traveling throughout the world. Fish are fertility symbols because they have thousands of offspring. In Buddhist imagery, they are often in facing pairs and fashioned of gold. The lotus represents spiritual growth, rooted in muddy water but flowering toward the sun. The umbrella symbolizes protection, because servants once used them to protect royalty from both sun and rain.

Sacred Practices & Gestures

Two major practices characterize Buddhism: gift-giving and showing respect to images and relics of the Buddha. The first is the transaction between laity and monks in which laypersons present sacrificial offerings to the monks, who in return share their higher state of spiritual being with the laity. Although Buddhist monks are permitted to own very little, they each have a begging bowl, which is often filled with rice.

Buddhists venerate statues of the Buddha, bodhisattvas, and saints; they also show respect to his relics, housed in stupas. When in the presence of a statue of the Buddha, worshippers have a series of movements they repeat three times, thus dedicating their movements to the Triple Refuge. It begins with a dedicated body: placing hands together with the palms cupped slightly and fingers touching, the devotee raises the hands to the forehead. The second step symbolizes right speech by lowering the hands to just below the mouth. In the third movement, the hands are lowered to the front of the chest, indicating that heart—and by extension, mind—are also dedicated to the Triple Refuge. The final movement is prostration. The devotee first gets on all fours, then lowers either the entire body to the floor or lowers the head, so that there are five points of contact with the floor.

Statues of the Buddha give a clue to the gestures held important to his followers. The gesture of turning the hand towards the ground indicates that one is observing Earth. Devotees assume a lotus position, with legs crossed, when in meditation.

Allowing the left hand to rest in the lap and the right hand to point down to Earth is a gesture used in meditation. Another common gesture is to touch thumb and fingertips together while the palms of both hands face up, thus forming a flat triangular shape. The triangle signifies the Three Jewels of Buddhism.

Food Restrictions

Buddhism does not require one to be a vegetarian. Many followers do not eat meat, however, because to do so involves killing other creatures. Both monks and laypersons may choose not to eat after noontime during the holy days of each month.

Rites, Celebrations, & Services

Ancient Buddhism recognized four holy days each month, known as *uposatha*. These days included the full moon and new moon days of each lunar month, as well as the eighth day after each of these moons appeared. Both monks and members of the laity have special religious duties during these four days. A special service takes place in which flowers are offered to images of the Buddha, precepts are repeated, and a sermon is preached. On these four days, an additional three precepts may be undertaken along with the five regularly observed. The three extra duties are to refrain from sleeping on a luxurious bed, eating any food after noon, and adorning the body or going to entertainments.

In Theravada nations, three major life events of the Buddha—birth, enlightenment, and entering nirvana—are celebrated on Vesak, or Buddha Day. In temples, statues of Buddha as a child are ceremonially cleaned. Worshippers may offer incense and flowers. To symbolize the Buddha's enlightenment, lights may be illuminated in trees and temples. Because it is a day of special kindness, some people in Thailand refrain from farm work that could harm living creatures. They may also seek special merit by freeing captive animals.

Other Buddhist nations that follow Mahayana Buddhism commemorate these events on three different days. In Japan, Hana Matsuri is the celebration of Buddha's birth. On that day, people create paper flower gardens to recall the gardens of Lumbini, Siddhartha's birthplace. Worshippers also pour perfumed tea over statues of Buddha; this is because, according to tradition, the gods provided scented water for Siddhartha's first bath.

Poson is celebrated in Sri Lanka to honor the coming of Buddhism during the reign of Emperor Asoka. Other holy persons are also celebrated in the countries where they had the greatest influence. In Tibet, for instance, the arrival of

Padmasambhava, who brought Buddhism to that nation, is observed.

Buddhists also integrate their own special celebrations into regular harvest festivals and New Year activities. These festivities may include a performance of an event in the life of any buddha or bodhisattva. For example, troupes of actors in Tibet specialize in enacting Buddhist legends. The festival of the Sacred Tooth is held in Kandy, Sri Lanka. According to one legend, a tooth of Buddha has been recovered, and it is paraded through the streets on this day. The tooth has been placed in a miniature stupa, or sealed mound, which is carried on an elephant's back.

Protection rituals have been common in Buddhism from earliest days. They may be public rituals meant to avoid a collective danger, such as those held in Sri Lanka and other Southeast Asia nations. Or they may be designed for private use. The role of these rituals is greater in Mahayana tradition, especially in Tibet. Mantras are chanted for this reason.

Customs surrounding death and burial differ between traditions and nations. A common factor, however, is the belief that the thoughts of a person at death are significant. This period may be extended for three days following death, due to a belief in consciousness for that amount of time after death. To prepare the mind of the dying, another person may read sacred texts aloud.

Judy A. Johnson, MTS

Bibliography

Armstrong, Karen. *Buddha*. New York: Penguin, 2001. Print.

Barnes, Trevor. *The Kingfisher Book of Religions*. New York: Kingfisher, 1999. Print.

Chodron, Thubten. *Buddhism for Beginners*. Ithaca: Snow Lion, 2001. Print.

Eckel, Malcolm David. *Buddhism*. Oxford: Oxford UP, 2002. Print.

Epstein, Ron. "Application of Buddhist Teachings in Modern Life." *Religion East & West* Oct. 2012: 52–61. Print.

Harding, John S. *Studying Buddhism in Practice*. Routledge, 2012. E-book. Studying Religions in Practice.

Harvey, Peter. *An Introduction to Buddhism: Teachings, History and Practices*. 2nd ed. Cambridge UP, 2013. E-book.

Heirman, Ann. "Buddhist Nuns: Between Past and Present." *International Review for the History of Religions* 58.5/6 (2011): 603–31. Print.

Langley, Myrtle. *Religion*. New York: Knopf, 1996. Print.

Low, Kim Cheng Patrick. "Three Treasures of Buddhism & Leadership Insights." *Culture & Religion Review Journal* 2012.3 (2012): 66–72. Print.

Low, Patrick Kim Cheng. "Leading Change, the Buddhist Perspective." *Culture & Religion Review Journal* 2012.1 (2012): 127–45. Print.

McMahan, David L. *Buddhism in the Modern World*. Routledge, 2012. E-book.

Meredith, Susan. *The Usborne Book of World Religions*. London: Usborne, 1995. Print.

Morgan, Diane. *Essential Buddhism: A Comprehensive Guide to Belief and Practice*. Praeger, 2010. E-book.

Wilkinson, Philip. *Buddhism*. New York: DK, 2003. Print.

Wilkinson, Philip. *Religions*. New York: DK, 2008. Print.

Christianity

General Description

Christianity is one of the world's major religions. It is based on the life and teachings of Jesus of Nazareth, called the Christ, or anointed one. It is believed that there are over thirty thousand denominations or sects of Christianity worldwide. Generally, most of these sects fall under the denominational families of Catholicism, Protestant, and Orthodox. (Anglican and Oriental Orthodox are sometimes added as separate branches.) Most denominations have developed since the seventeenth-century Protestant Reformation.

Number of Adherents Worldwide

Over 2.3 billion people around the world claim allegiance to Christianity in one of its many forms. The three major divisions are Roman Catholicism, Eastern Orthodox, and Protestant. Within each group are multiple denominations. Roman Catholics number more than 1.1 billion followers, while the Eastern Orthodox Church has between 260 and 278 million adherents. An estimated 800 million adherents follow one of the various Protestant denominations, including Anglican, Baptist, Lutheran, Presbyterian, and Methodist. Approximately 1 percent of Christians, or 28 million adherents, do not belong to one of the three major divisions

There are a number of other groups, such as the Amish, with an estimated 249,000 members, and the Quakers, numbering approximately 377,000. Both of these churches—along with Mennonites, who number 1.7 million—are in the peace tradition (their members are conscientious objectors). Pentecostals have 600 million adherents worldwide. Other groups that are not always considered Christian by more conservative groups include Jehovah's Witnesses (7.6 million) and Mormons (13 million) (Wilkinson, p. 104-121).

Basic Tenets

The summaries of the Christian faith are found in the Apostles Creed and Nicene Creed.

In addition, some churches have developed their own confessions of faith, such as Lutheranism's Augsburg Confession. Christianity is a monotheistic tradition, although most Christians believe in the Trinity, defined as one God in three separate but equal persons—Father, Son, and Holy Spirit. More modern, gender-neutral versions of the Trinitarian formula may refer to Creator, Redeemer, and Sanctifier. Many believe in the doctrine of original sin, which means that the disobedience of Adam and Eve in the Garden of Eden has been passed down through all people; because of this sin, humankind is in need of redemption. Jesus Christ was born, lived a sinless life, and then was crucified and resurrected as a substitute for humankind. Those who accept this sacrifice for sin will receive eternal life in a place of bliss after death. Many Christians believe that a Second Coming of Jesus will inaugurate a millennial kingdom and a final judgment (in which people will be judged according to their deeds and their eternal souls consigned to heaven or hell), as well as a resurrected physical body.

Sacred Text

The Bible is the sacred text of Christianity, which places more stress on the New Testament. The canon of the twenty-six books of the New Testament was finally determined in the latter half of the fourth century CE.

Major Figures

Christianity is based on the life and teachings of Jesus of Nazareth. His mother, Mary, is especially revered in Roman Catholicism and the Eastern Orthodox tradition, where she is known as Theotokos (God-bearer). Jesus spread his teachings through the twelve apostles, or disciples, who he himself chose and named. Paul (Saint Paul or Paul the Apostle), who became the first missionary to the Gentiles—and whose writings comprise a bulk of the New Testament—is a key figure for the theological treatises embedded in his letters to early churches. His conversion occurred after Jesus' crucifixion. All of these figures are biblically represented.

Under the Emperor Constantine, Christianity went from a persecuted religion to the state religion. Constantine also convened the Council of Nicea in 325 CE, which expressed the formula defining Jesus as fully God and fully human. Saint Augustine (354–430) was a key thinker of the early church who became the Bishop of Hippo in North Africa. He outlined the principles of just war and expressed the ideas of original sin. He also suggested what later became the Catholic doctrine of purgatory.

In the sixth century, Saint Benedict inscribed a rule for monks that became a basis for monastic life. Martin Luther, the monk who stood against the excesses of the Roman Catholic Church, ignited the seventeenth-century Protestant Reformation. He proclaimed that salvation came by grace alone, not through works. In the twentieth century, Pope John XXIII convened the Vatican II Council, or Second Vatican Council, which made sweeping changes to the liturgy and daily practice for Roman Catholics.

Major Holy Sites

The key events in the life of Jesus Christ occurred in the region of Palestine. Bethlehem is honored as the site of Jesus's birth; Jerusalem is especially revered as the site of Jesus's crucifixion. The capital of the empire, Rome, also became the center of Christianity until the Emperor Constantine shifted the focus to Constantinople. Rome today is the seat of the Vatican, an independent city-state that houses the government of the Roman Catholic Church. Canterbury, the site of the martyrdom of Saint Thomas Becket and seat of the archbishop of the Anglican Communion, is a pilgrimage site for Anglicans. There are also many pilgrimage sites, such as Compostela and Lourdes, for other branches of Christianity. In Ethiopia, Lalibela is the site of eleven churches carved from stone during the twelfth century. The site serves as a profound testimony to the vibrancy of the Christian faith in Africa.

Major Rites & Celebrations

The first rite of the church is baptism, a water-related ritual that is traditionally administered to infants or adults alike through some variant of sprinkling or immersion. Marriage is another rite of the church. Confession is a major part of life for Roman Catholics, although the idea is also present in other branches of Christianity.

The celebration of the Eucharist, or Holy Communion, is a key part of weekly worship for the liturgical churches such as those in the Roman Catholic or Anglican traditions. Nearly all Christians worship weekly on Sunday; services include readings of scripture, a sermon, singing of hymns, and may include Eucharist. Christians honor the birth of Jesus at Christmas and his death and resurrection at Easter. Easter is often considered the most significant liturgical feast, particularly in Orthodox branches.

Many Christians follow a calendar of liturgical seasons. Of these seasons, perhaps the best known is Lent, which is immediately preceded by Shrove Tuesday, also known as Mardi Gras. Lent is traditionally a time of fasting and self-examination in preparation for the Easter feast. Historically, Christians gave up rich foods. The day before Lent was a time for pancakes—to use up the butter and eggs—from which the term Mardi Gras (Fat Tuesday) derives. Lent begins with Ash Wednesday, when Christians are marked with the sign of the cross on their foreheads using ashes, a reminder that they are dust and will return to dust.

ORIGINS

History & Geography

Christianity was shaped in the desert and mountainous landscapes of Palestine, known as the Holy Land. Jesus was driven into the wilderness following his baptism, where he remained for forty days of fasting and temptation. The Gospels record that he often went to the mountains for solitude and prayer. The geography of the deserts and mountains also shaped early Christian spirituality, as men and women went into solitude to pray, eventually founding small communities of the so-called desert fathers and mothers.

Christianity at first was regarded as a sect within Judaism, though it differentiated itself early in the first century CE by breaking with the code of laws that defined Judaism, including the need for circumcision and ritual purity. Early Christianity then grew through the missionary work of the apostles, particularly Paul the Apostle, who traveled throughout the Mediterranean world and beyond the Roman Empire to preach the gospel (good news) of Jesus. (This is often called the Apostolic Age.)

Persecution under various Roman emperors only served to strengthen the emerging religion. In the early fourth century, the Emperor Constantine (ca. 272-337) made Christianity the official religion of the Roman Empire. He also convened the Council of Nicea in 325 CE to quell the religious controversies threatening the Pax Romana (Roman Peace), a time of stability and peace throughout the empire in the first and second centuries.

In 1054 the Great Schism, which involved differences over theology and practice, split the church into Eastern Orthodox and Roman Catholic branches. As Islam grew stronger, the Roman Catholic nations of Europe entered a period of Crusades—there were six Crusades in approximately 175 years, from 1095-1271—that attempted to take the Holy Land out of Muslim control.

A number of theologians became unhappy with the excesses of the Roman church and papal authority during the fifteenth and sixteenth centuries. The Protestant Reformation, originally an attempt to purify the church, was led by several men, most notably Martin Luther (1483-1546), whose ninety-five theses against the Catholic Church sparked the Reformation movement. Other leaders of the Protestant Reformation include John Knox (ca. 1510-1572), attributed as the founder of the Presbyterian denomination, John Calvin (1509-1564), a principle early developer of Calvinism, and Ulrich Zwingli (1484-1531), who initially spurred the Reformation in Switzerland. This period of

turmoil resulted in the founding of a number of church denominations: Lutherans, Presbyterians, and Anglicans. These groups were later joined by the Methodists and the Religious Society of Friends (Quakers).

During the sixteenth and seventeenth centuries, the Roman Catholic Church attempted to stem this wave of protest and schism with the Counter-Reformation. Concurrently, the Inquisition, an effort to root out heresy and control the rebellion, took place. There were various inquisitions, including the Spanish Inquisition, which was led by Ferdinand II of Aragon and Isabella I of Castile in mid-fifteenth century and sought to "guard" the orthodoxy of Catholicism in Spain. There was also the Portuguese Inquisition, which began in 1536 in Portugal under King John III, and the Roman Inquisition, which took place in the late fifteenth century in Rome under the Holy See.

During the modern age, some groups became concerned with the perceived conflicts between history (revealed through recent archaeological findings) and the sciences (as described by Charles Darwin and Sigmund Freud) and the literal interpretation of some biblical texts. Fundamentalist Christianity began at an 1895 meeting in Niagara Falls, New York, with an attempt to define the basics (fundamentals) of Christianity. These were given as the inerrant nature of the Bible, the divine nature of Jesus, his literal virgin birth, his substitutionary death and literal physical resurrection, and his soon return. Liberal Christians, on the other hand, focused more on what became known as the Social Gospel, an attempt to relieve human misery.

Controversies in the twenty-first century throughout Christendom focused on issues such as abortion, homosexuality, the ordination of women and gays, and the authority of the scriptures. An additional feature is the growth of Christianity in the Southern Hemisphere. In Africa, for example, the number of Christians grew from 10 million in 1900 to over 506 million a century later. Initially the result of empire-building and colonialism, the conversions in these nations have resulted in a unique blend of native religions and Christianity. Latin America has won renown for its liberation theology, which was first articulated in 1968 as God's call for justice and God's preference for the poor, demonstrated in the ministry and teachings of Jesus Christ. Africa, Asia, and South America are regions that are considered more morally and theologically conservative. Some suggest that by 2050, non-Latino white persons will comprise only 20 percent of Christians.

Founder or Major Prophet

Jesus of Nazareth was born into a peasant family. The date of his birth, determined by accounts in the Gospels of Matthew and Luke, could be as early as 4 or 5 BCE or as late as 6 CE. Mary, his mother, was regarded as a virgin; thus, Jesus' birth was a miracle, engendered by the Holy Spirit. His earthly father, Joseph, was a carpenter.

At about age thirty, Jesus began an itinerant ministry of preaching and healing following his baptism in the Jordan River by his cousin, John the Baptist. He selected twelve followers, known as apostles (sent-ones), and a larger circle of disciples (followers). Within a short time, Jesus' ministry and popularity attracted the negative attention of both the Jewish and Roman rulers. He offended the Jewish leaders with his emphasis on personal relationship with God rather than obedience to rules, as well as his claim to be coequal with God the Father.

For a period of one to three years (Gospel accounts vary in the chronology), Jesus taught and worked miracles, as recorded in the first four books of the New Testament, the Gospels of Matthew, Mark, Luke, and John. On what has become known as Palm Sunday, he rode triumphantly into Jerusalem on the back of a donkey while crowds threw palm branches at his feet. Knowing that his end was near, at a final meal with his disciples, known now to Christians as the Last Supper, Jesus gave final instructions to his followers.

He was subsequently captured, having been betrayed by Judas Iscariot, one of his own twelve apostles. A trial before the Jewish legislative body, the Sanhedrin, led to his being condemned for blasphemy. However, under Roman law, the Jews did not have the power to put anyone to death. A later trial under the Roman governor, Pontius Pilate, resulted in Jesus being crucified, although Pilate tried to prevent this action, declaring Jesus innocent.

According to Christian doctrine, following the crucifixion, Jesus rose from the dead three days later. He appeared before many over a span of forty days and instructed the remaining eleven apostles to continue spreading his teachings. He then ascended into heaven. Ultimately, his followers believed that he was the Messiah, the savior who was to come to the Jewish people and deliver them. Rather than offering political salvation, however, Jesus offered spiritual liberty.

Philosophical Basis

Jesus was a Jew who observed the rituals and festivals of his religion. The Gospels reveal that he attended synagogue worship and went to Jerusalem for celebrations such as Passover. His teachings both grew out of and challenged the religion of his birth.

The Jews of Jesus' time, ruled by the Roman Empire, hoped for a return to political power. This power would be concentrated in a Messiah, whose coming had been prophesied centuries before. There were frequent insurrections in Judea, led in Jesus' time by a group called the Zealots. Indeed, it is believed that one of the twelve apostles was part of this movement. Jesus, with his message of a kingdom of heaven, was viewed as perhaps the one who would usher in a return to political ascendancy.

When challenged to name the greatest commandment, Jesus answered that it was to love God with all the heart, soul, mind, and strength. He added that the second was to love one's neighbor as one's self, saying that these two commands summarized all the laws that the Jewish religion outlined.

Jewish society was concerned with ritual purity and with following the law. Jesus repeatedly flouted those laws by eating with prostitutes and tax collectors, by touching those deemed unclean, such as lepers, and by including

Gentiles in his mission. Women were part of his ministry, with some of them providing for him and his disciples from their own purses, others offering him a home and a meal, and still others among those listening to him teach.

Jesus's most famous sermon is called the Sermon on the Mount. In it, he offers blessings on those on the outskirts of power, such as the poor, the meek, and those who hunger and thirst for righteousness. While not abolishing the law that the Jews followed, he pointed out its inadequacies and the folly of parading one's faith publicly. Embedded in the sermon is what has become known as the Lord's Prayer, the repetition of which is often part of regular Sunday worship. Much of Jesus' teaching was offered in the form of parables, or short stories involving vignettes of everyday life: a woman adding yeast to dough or a farmer planting seeds. Many of these parables were attempts to explain the kingdom of heaven, a quality of life that was both present and to come.

Holy Places

The Christian church has many pilgrimage sites, some of them dating back to the Middle Ages. Saint James is thought to have been buried in Compostela, Spain, which was a destination for those who could not make the trip to the Holy Land. Lourdes, France, is one of the spots associated with healing miracles. Celtic Christians revere places such as the small Scottish isle of Iona, an early Christian mission. Assisi, Italy, is a destination for those who are attracted to Saint Francis (1181-1226), founder of the Franciscans. The Chartres Cathedral in France is another pilgrimage destination from the medieval period.

Jerusalem, Rome, and Canterbury are considered holy for their associations with the early church and Catholicism, as well as with Anglicanism. Within the Old City of Jerusalem is the Church of the Holy Sepulchre, an important pilgrimage site believed to house the burial place of Jesus. Another important pilgrimage site is the Church of the Nativity in Bethlehem. It is built on a cave believed to be the birthplace of Jesus, and is one of the oldest operating churches in existence.

CHRISTIANITY IN DEPTH

Sacred Symbols

The central symbol of Christianity is the cross, of which there are many variant designs. Some of them, such as Celtic crosses, are related to regions of the world. Others, such as the Crusader's cross, honor historic events. The dove is the symbol for the Holy Spirit, which descended in that shape on the gathered disciples at Pentecost after Jesus's ascension.

Various symbols represent Jesus. Candles allude to his reference to himself as the Light of the World, while the lamb stands for his being the perfect sacrifice, the Lamb of God. The fish symbol that is associated with Christianity has a number of meanings, both historic and symbolic. A fish shape stands for the Greek letters beginning the words Jesus Christ, Son of God, Savior; these letters form the word *ichthus*, the Greek word for "fish." Fish also featured prominently in the scriptures, and the early apostles were known as "fishers of man." The crucifixion symbol is also a popular Catholic Christian symbol.

All of these symbols may be expressed in stained glass. Used in medieval times, stained glass often depicted stories from the Bible as an aid to those who were illiterate.

Sacred Practices & Gestures

Roman Catholics honor seven sacraments, defined as outward signs of inward grace. These include the Eucharist, baptism, confirmation, marriage, ordination of priests, anointing the sick or dying with oil, and penance. The Eastern Orthodox Church refers to these seven as mysteries rather than sacraments.

Priests in the Roman Catholic Church must remain unmarried. In the Eastern Orthodox, Anglican, and Protestant denominations, they may marry. Both Roman Catholic and Eastern Orthodox refuse to ordain women to the priesthood.

The Orthodox Church practices a rite known as chrismation, anointing a child with oil following its baptism. The "oil of gladness," as it is known, is placed on the infant's head, eyes, ears, and mouth. This is similar to the practice of confirmation in some other denominations. Many Christian denominations practice anointing the sick or dying with oil, as well as using the oil to seal those who have been baptized.

Many Christians, especially Roman Catholics, use a rosary, or prayer beads, when praying. Orthodox believers may have icons, such as small paintings of God, saints or biblical events, as part of their worship. There may be a font of water that has been blessed as one enters some churches, which the worshippers use to make the sign of the cross, touching fingers to their forehead, heart, right chest, and left chest. Some Christians make the sign of the cross on the forehead, mouth, and heart to signify their desire for God to be in their minds, on their lips, and in their hearts.

Christians may genuflect, or kneel, as they enter or leave a pew in church. In some churches, particularly the Catholic and Orthodox, incense is burned during the service as a sweet smell to God.

In some traditions, praying to or for the dead is encouraged. The rationale for this is known as the communion of saints—the recognition that those who are gone are still a part of the community of faith.

Catholic, Orthodox, and some branches of other churches have monastic orders for both men and women. Monks and nuns may live in a cloister or be engaged in work in the wider world. They generally commit to a rule of life and to the work of prayer. Even those Christians who are not part of religious orders sometimes go on retreats, seeking quiet and perhaps some spiritual guidance from those associated with the monastery or convent.

Food Restrictions

Historically, Christians fasted during Lent as preparation for the Easter celebration. Prior to the Second Vatican Council in 1962,

Roman Catholics did not eat meat on Fridays. Conservative Christians in the Evangelical tradition tend to eliminate the use of alcohol, tobacco, and drugs.

Rites, Celebrations & Services

For churches in the liturgical tradition, the weekly celebration of the Eucharist is paramount. While many churches celebrate this ritual feast with wine and a wafer, many Protestant churches prefer to use grape juice and crackers or bread.

Church services vary widely. Quakers sit silently waiting for a word from God, while in many African American churches, hymns are sung for perhaps an hour before the lengthy sermon is delivered. Some churches have a prescribed order of worship that varies little from week to week. Most services, however, include prayer, a sermon, and singing, with or without musical accompaniment.

A church's architecture often gives clues as to the type of worship one will experience. A church with the pulpit in the center at the front generally is a Protestant church with an emphasis on the Word of God being preached. If the center of the front area is an altar, the worship's focus will be on the Eucharist.

Christmas and Easter are the two major Christian celebrations. In liturgical churches, Christmas is preceded by Advent, a time of preparation and quiet to ready the heart for the coming of Christ. Christmas has twelve days, from the birth date of December 25 to the Epiphany on January 6. Epiphany (to show) is the celebration of the arrival of the Magi (wise men) from the East who came to worship the young Jesus after having seen his star. Their arrival is believed to have been foretold by the Old Testament prophet Isaiah, who said "And the Gentiles shall come to thy light, and kings to the brightness of thy rising" (Isaiah 60:3). Epiphany is the revealing of the Messiah to the Gentiles.

In the early church, Easter was preceded by a solemn period of fasting and examination, especially for candidates for baptism and penitent sinners wishing to be reconciled. In Western churches, Lent begins with Ash Wednesday, which is six and half weeks prior to Easter. By excluding Sundays from the fast, Lent thus gives a forty-day fast, imitating that of Jesus in the wilderness. Historically forbidden foods during the fast included eggs, butter, meat, and fish. In the Eastern Church, dairy products, oil, and wine are also forbidden.

The week before Easter is known as Holy Week. It may include extra services such as Maundy Thursday, a time to remember Jesus's new commandment (*maundy* is etymologically related to *mandate*) to love one another. In some Catholic areas, the crucifixion is reenacted in a Passion play (depicting the passion—trial, suffering, and death—of Christ). Some churches will have an Easter vigil the Saturday night before or a sunrise service on Easter morning.

Judy A. Johnson, MTS

Bibliography

Bakker, Janel Kragt. "The Sister Church Phenomenon: A Case Study of the Restructuring of American Christianity against the Backdrop of Globalization." *International Bulletin of Missionary Research* 36.3 (2012): 129–34. Print.

Bandak, Andreas and Jonas Adelin Jørgensen. "Foregrounds and Backgrounds—Ventures in the Anthropology of Christianity." *Ethos: Journal of Anthropology* 77.4 (2012): 447–58. Print.

Barnes, Trevor. *The Kingfisher Book of Religions*. New York: Kingfisher, 1999. Print.

Chandler, Daniel Ross. "Christianity in Cross-Cultural Perspective: A Review of Recent Literature." *Asia Journal of Theology* 26.2 (2012): 44–57. Print.

Daughrity, Dyron B. "Christianity Is Moving from North to South—So What about the East?" *International Bulletin of Missionary Research* 35.1 (2011): 18–22. Print.

Kaatz, Kevin. *Voices of Early Christianity: Documents from the Origins of Christianity*. Santa Barbara: Greenwood, 2013. E-book.

Langley, Myrtle. *Religion*. New York: Alfred A. Knopf, 1996.

Lewis, Clive Staples. *Mere Christianity*. New York: Harper, 2001. Print.

McGrath, Alistair. *Christianity: An Introduction*. Hoboken, New Jersey: Wiley, 2006. Print.

Meredith, Susan. *The Usborne Book of World Religions*. London: Usborne, 1995. Print.

Ripley, Jennifer S. "Integration of Psychology and Christianity: 2022." *Journal of Psychology & Theology* 40.2 (2012): 150–54. Print.

Stefon, Matt. *Christianity: History, Belief, and Practice*. New York: Britannica Educational, 2012. E-book.

Wilkinson, Philip. *Christianity*. New York: DK, 2003. Print.

Wilkinson, Philip. *Religions*. New York: DK, 2008. Print.

Zoba, Wendy Murray. *The Beliefnet Guide to Evangelical Christianity*. New York: Three Leaves, 2005. Print.

East Asian Religions

General Description

East Asian religious and philosophical traditions include, among others, Confucianism, Taoism, and Shintoism. Confucianism is a philosophy introduced by the Chinese philosopher Confucius (Kongzi; 551–479 BCE) in the sixth century BCE, during the Zhou dynasty. Taoism, which centers on Tao, or "the way," is a religious and philosophical tradition that originated in China about two thousand years ago. Shinto, "the way of the spirits," is a Japanese tradition of devotion to spirits and rituals.

Number of Adherents Worldwide

Between 5 and 6 million people, the majority of them in China, practice Confucianism, once the state religion of China. About 20 million people identify as Taoists. Most of the Taoist practitioners are in China as well. In Japan, approximately 107 million people practice Shintoism, though many practitioners also practice Buddhism. Sects of Shinto include Tenrikyo (heavenly truth), founded in 1838, with nearly 2 million devotees. Shukyo Mahikari (divine light) is another, smaller sect founded in the 1960s. Like other sects, it is a blend of different religious traditions (Wilkinson 332–34).

Basic Tenets

Confucianism is a philosophy of life and does concerns itself not with theology but with life conduct. Chief among the aspects of life that must be tended are five key relationships, with particular focus on honoring ancestors and showing filial piety. Confucianism does not take a stand on the existence of God, though the founder, Confucius, referred to "heaven." Except for this reference, Confucianism does not address the question of life after death.

Taoists believe that Tao (the way or the flow) is in everything. Taoism teaches that qi, or life energy, needs to be balanced between yin and yang, which are the female and male principles of life, respectively. With its doctrine of the evil of violence, Taoism borders on pacifism, and it also preaches simplicity and naturalness. Taoists believe in five elements—wood, earth, air, fire and water—that need to be in harmony. The five elements lie at the heart of Chinese medicine, particularly acupuncture. In Taoism, it is believed that the soul returns to a state of nonbeing after death.

Shinto emphasizes nature and harmony, with a focus on lived experience rather than doctrine. Shinto, which means "the way of the gods," is a polytheistic religion; Amaterasu, the sun goddess, is the chief god. At one point in Japan's history, the emperor was believed to be a descendant of Amaterasu and therefore divine. In Tenrikyo Shinto, God is manifested most often as Oyakami, meaning "God the parent."

Shinto teaches that some souls can become kami, a spirit, following death. Each traditional home has a god-shelf, which honors family members believed to have become kami. An older family member tends to the god-shelf, placing a bit of food and some sake (rice wine) on the shelf. To do their work, kami must be nourished. The Tenrikyo sect includes concepts from Pure Land Buddhism, such as an afterlife and the idea of salvation.

Sacred Texts

Five classic texts are sacred to the Confucians. These include the I Ching, or Book of Changes; the Book of Odes; the Book of History; the Book of Rites; and the Annals of Spring and Autumn. The Analects, a collection of Confucius's sayings, is another revered classic. The Tao Te Ching (The Way of Power) is the most sacred book of the Taoists. Those who practice Shinto hold sacred two works: the Kojiki (Record of Ancient Matters) and the Nihon-gi (Chronicles of Japan). Both texts, which contain legends and creation myths, were written during the eighth century.

Major Figures

Confucius, who lived during the sixth century, was the first great philosopher of China. Mengzi (Meng-tzu; 371–289 BCE), known in the West as Mencius, developed Confucius's teachings about the higher power guiding human life. Another ancient Chinese philosopher, Laozi(or Lao-tzu), is the founder of Taoism. He is believed to have been a contemporary of Confucius's in the central region of China. Modern scholars are not certain he ever existed, though one account includes the story of Confucius visiting Laozi. Chuang Tzu wrote of Laozi and his ideas during the fourth and third centuries BCE. Shinto's major figures include Ō no Yasumaro (d. 723), the compiler of the Kokiji who acted under the orders of Empress Gemmei and consulted a bard known to have an infallible memory; the scholar Motoori Norinaga (1730–1800), whose work led to a revived interest in ancient Shinto texts; and Nakayama Miki (1798–1887), the farmer's wife who founded Tenrikyo.

Major Holy Sites

Most Confucian sacred places are located within private homes, where an ancestral shrine and an altar to gods and spirits are maintained. In China's Shandong Province is Qufu, the site of Confucius's family mansion, temple, and cemetery. The temple was built in 478 BCE, only a year after Confucius's death, and has been maintained and enlarged. In addition to its status as a holy site, the United Nations Educational, Scientific, and Cultural Organization (UNESCO) has placed it on their World Heritage List.

Taoists regard mountains as a way to communicate with Earth's primeval powers and with those who are immortal. Five of the nine sacred mountains in China are associated with Taoism: Hengshan in both the north and the south, Songshan in the south, Taishan in the east, and Huashan in the west. The holiest of the five is Taishan, which symbolizes stability, prevents natural disasters, and ensures fertility.

Shintoism has a high regard for natural beauty. As such, Shinto shrines are everywhere, particularly in mountains or near waterfalls.

Mountains in particular are regarded as homes of the gods. Mount Fuji is the holiest Shinto mountain, and climbing it to reach the shrine on its peak is an act of worship. More than forty thousand shrines are dedicated to Inari, the rice god.

Shinto was formalized during the Yamato period (the name for ancient Japan), and because the emperor of the imperial dynasty was from the Yamato area and was considered divine, the whole region is revered. At Ise, located near the coast in Mie Prefecture, southeast of Nara, the shrine has been rebuilt every twenty years for at least fourteen centuries. This rebuilding ensures that Toyouke-Ōmikami (the harvest goddess) and Amaterasu (the sun goddess) are renewed in vigor, which in turn invigorates both the rice crop and the imperial line. Those who have died in war are revered as kami in Japan. In Tokyo, a shrine called Yasukuni is dedicated to them. However, there is controversy surrounding the place because of its association with Japan's extreme nationalism prior to World War II.

Sacred Texts

Five classic texts are sacred to the Confucians. These include the I Ching, or Book of Changes; the Book of Odes; the Book of History; the Book of Rites; and the Annals of Spring and Autumn. The Analects, a collection of Confucius's sayings, is another revered classic. The Tao te Ching (The Way of Power) is the most sacred book of the Taoists. Those who practice Shinto hold sacred two works: the Kojiki (Record of Ancient Matters) and the Nihon-gi (Chronicles of Japan). Both texts, which contain legends and creation myths, were written during the eighth century.

Major Figures

Confucius, who lived during the sixth century, was the first great philosopher of China. Mengzi (Meng-tzu; 371–289 BCE), known in the West as Mencius, developed Confucius's teachings about the higher power guiding human life. Another ancient Chinese philosopher, Laozi,(or Lao-tzu) is the founder of Taoism. He is believed to have been a contemporary of Confucius in the central region of China. Modern scholars are not certain he ever existed, though one account includes the story of Confucius visiting Laozi. Chuang Tzu wrote of Laozi and his ideas during the fourth and third centuries BCE. Shinto's major figures include Ō no Yasumaro, the compiler of the Kokiji who acted under the orders of Empress Gemmei and consulted a bard known to have an infallible memory; the scholar Motoori Norinaga (1730–1800), whose work led to a revived interest in ancient Shinto texts; and Nakayama Miki (1798–1887), the farmer's wife who founded Tenrikyo.

Major Holy Sites

Most Confucian sacred places are located within private homes, where an ancestral shrine and an altar to gods and spirits are maintained. In China's Shandong Province is Qufu, the site of Confucius's family mansion, temple and cemetery. The temple was built in 478 BCE, only a year after Confucius's death, and has been maintained and enlarged. In addition to being a holy site, the United Nations Educational, Scientific, and Cultural Organization (UNESCO) has placed it on their World Heritage List.

Taoists consider mountains as a way to communicate with Earth's primeval powers and with those who are immortal. Five of the nine sacred mountains in China are associated with Taoism. They are Hengshan in both the north and south, Songshan in the south, Taishan in the east, and Huashan in the west. The holiest of the five is Taishan, which symbolizes stability, prevents natural disasters, and ensures fertility.

Shintoism has a high regard for natural beauty. As such, Shinto shrines are everywhere, particularly in mountains or near waterfalls. Mountains in particular are regarded as homes of the gods. Mount Fuji is the holiest Shinto mountain, and climbing it to reach the shrine on its peak is an act of worship. More than forty thousand shrines are dedicated to Inari, the rice god.

Shinto was formalized during the Yamato period (the name for ancient Japan), and because the emperor of the imperial dynasty is from the Yamato area, and was considered divine, the whole region is revered. At Ise, located near the coast in the Mie prefecture southeast of Nara, the shrine has been rebuilt every twenty years for at least fourteen centuries. This rebuilding ensures that Toyouke-Ōmikami (the harvest goddess) and Amaterasu (the sun goddess) are renewed in vigor, which in turn invigorates both the rice crop and the imperial line. Those who have died in war are revered as kami in Japan. In Tokyo, a shrine called Yasukuni is dedicated to them. However, there is controversy surrounding the place because of its association with Japan's extreme nationalism prior to World War II.

Major Rites & Celebrations

Confucian celebrations have to do with honoring people rather than gods. At Confucian temples, the philosopher's birthday is celebrated each September. In Taiwan, this day is called "Teacher's Day." Sacrifices, music and dance are part of the event.

Taoism has a jiao (offering) festival near the winter solstice. It celebrates the renewal of the yang force at this turning of the year. During the festival priests, who have been ritually purified, wear lavish clothing. The festival includes music and dancing, along with large effigies of the gods which are designed to frighten away the evil spirits. Yang's renewal is also the focus of New Year celebrations, which is a time for settling debts and cleaning house. Decorations in the yang warm colors of gold, orange and red abound.

Many of the Shinto festivals overlap with Buddhist ones. There are many local festivals and rituals, and each community has an annual festival at the shrine dedicated to the kami of the region. Japanese New Year, which is celebrated for three days, is a major feast. Since the sixteenth century, the Gion Festival has taken place in Kyoto, Japan. Decorated floats are part of the celebration of the shrine.

ORIGINS

History & Geography

During the Zhou dynasty (1050–256 BCE) in China, the idea of heaven as a force that controlled events came to the fore. Zhou rulers believed that they ruled as a result of the "Mandate of Heaven," viewing themselves as morally superior to those of the previous dynasty, the Shang dynasty (1600-1046 BCE). They linked virtue and power as the root of the state.

By the sixth century the Zhou rulers had lost much of their authority. Many schools of thought developed to restore harmony, and were collectively known as the "Hundred Schools." Confucius set forth his ideas within this historical context. He traveled China for thirteen years, urging rulers to put his ideas into practice and failing to achieve his goals. He returned home to teach for the rest of his life and his ideas were not adopted until the Han dynasty (206 BCE–220 CE). During the Han period, a university for the nation was established, as well as the bureaucratic civil service that continued until the twentieth century. When the Chinese Empire fell in 1911, the Confucian way became less important.

Confucianism had influenced not only early Chinese culture, but also the cultures of Japan, Korea, and Vietnam. The latter two nations also adopted the bureaucratic system. In Japan, Confucianism reached its height during the Tokugawa age (1600–1868 CE). Confucian scholars continue to interpret the philosophy for the modern period. Some regard the ideas of Confucius as key to the recent economic booms in the so-called "tiger" economies of East Asia (Hong Kong, Singapore, South Korea, Taiwan, and Thailand). Confucianism continues to be a major influence on East Asian nations and culture.

Taoism's power (te) manifests itself as a philosophy, a way of life, and a religion. Philosophically, Taoism is a sort of self-help regimen, concerned with expending power efficiently by avoiding conflicts and friction, rather than fighting against the flow of life. In China, it is known as School Taoism. As a way of life, Taoism is concerned with increasing the amount of qi available through what is eaten and through meditation, yoga, and tai chi (an ancient Chinese martial art form). Acupuncture and the use of medicinal herbs are outgrowths of this way of life. Church Taoism, influenced by Buddhism and Tao Chiao (religious Taoism), developed during the second century. This church looked for ways to use power for societal and individual benefit.

By the time of the Han dynasty (206–220 CE), Laozi had been elevated to the status of divine. Taoism found favor at court during the Tang dynasty (618–917 CE), during which the state underwrote temples. By adapting and encouraging people to study the writings of all three major faiths in China, Taoism remained relevant into the early twentieth century. During the 1960s and 1970s, Taoist books were burned and their temples were destroyed in the name of the Cultural Revolution (the Great Proletarian Cultural Revolution). Taoism remains popular and vital in Taiwan.

Shinto is an ancient religion, and some of its characteristics appeared during the Yayoi culture (ca. 300 BCE–300 CE). The focus was on local geographic features and the ancestry of local clan leaders. At first, women were permitted to be priests, but that equality was lost due to the influence of Confucian paternalism. The religion declined, but was revived in 1871 following the Meiji Restoration of the emperor. Shoguns (warlords) had ruled Japan for more than 250 years, and Shinto was the state religion until 1945. It was associated with the emperor cult and contributed to Japan's militarism. After the nation's defeat in World War II, the 1947 constitution forbade government involvement in any religion. In contemporary Shinto, women are permitted to become priests and girls, in some places, are allowed to carry the portable shrines during festivals.

Founder or Major Prophet

Confucius, or Kongzi ("Master Kong"), was a teacher whose early life may have included service in the government. He began traveling throughout the country around age fifty, attempting and failing to interest rulers in his ideas for creating a harmonious state. He returned to his home state after thirteen years, teaching a group of disciples who spread his ideas posthumously.

According to legend, Taoism's founder, Laozi, lived during the sixth century. Laozi may be translated as "Grand Old Master," and may be simply a term of endearment. He maintained the archives and lived simply in a western state of China. Weary of people who were uninterested in natural goodness and perhaps wanting greater solitude in his advanced years, he determined to leave China, heading for Tibet on a water buffalo. At the border, a gatekeeper wanted to persuade him to stay, but could not do so. He asked Laozi to leave behind his teachings. For three days Laozi transcribed his teachings, producing the five-thousand-word Tao Te Ching. He then rode off and was never heard of again. Unlike most founders of religions, he neither preached nor promoted his beliefs. Still, he was held with such regard that some emperors claimed descent from him.

No one is certain of the origin of Shinto, which did not have a founder or major prophet. Shinto—derived from two Chinese words, *shen* (spirit) and *dao* (way)—has been influenced by other religions, notably Confucianism and Buddhism.

Philosophical Basis

Confucianism sought to bring harmony to the state and society as a whole. This harmony was to be rooted in the Five Constant Relationships: between parents and children; husbands and wives; older and younger siblings; older and younger friends; and rulers and subjects. Each of these societal relationships existed to demonstrate mutual respect, service, honor, and love, resulting in a healthy society. The fact that three of the five relationships exist within the family highlights the importance of honoring family. Ritual maintains the li, or rightness, of everything, and is a way to guarantee that a person performed the correct action in any situation in life.

Taoism teaches that two basic components—yin and yang—are in all things, including health, the state, and relationships. Yin is the feminine principle, associated with soft, cold, dark, and moist things. Yang is the masculine principle, and is associated with hard, warm, light, and dry things. By keeping these two aspects of life balanced, harmony will be achieved. Another concept is that of wu-wei, action that is in harmony with nature, while qi is the life force in all beings. The Tao is always in harmony with the universe. Conflict is to be avoided, and soldiers are to go as if attending a funeral, solemnly and with compassion. Taoism also teaches the virtues of humility and selflessness.

Shinto is rooted in reverence for ancestors and for the spirits known as kami, which may be good or evil. By correctly worshipping the kami, Shintoists believe that they are assisting in purifying the world and aiding in its functioning.

Holy Places

Confucianism does not always distinguish between sacred and profane space. So much of nature is considered a holy place, as is each home's private shrine. In addition, some Confucian temples have decayed while others have been restored. Temples do not have statues or images. Instead, the names of Confucius and his noted followers are written on tablets. Like the emperor's palace, temples have the most important halls placed on the north-south axis of the building. Temples are also internally symmetrical, as might be expected of a system that honors order. In Beijing, the Temple of Heaven, just south of the emperor's palace, was one of the holiest places in imperial China.

Taoism's holy places are often in nature, particularly mountains. The holiest of the five sacred mountains in China is Taishan, located in the east. Taoism also reveres grottoes, which are caves thought to be illuminated by the light of heaven.

In the Shinto religion, nature is often the focus of holy sites. Mount Fuji is the most sacred mountain. Near Kyoto the largest shrine of Inari, the rice god, is located. The Grand Shrines at Ise are dedicated to two divinities, and for more than one thousand years, pilgrims have come to it. The Inner Shrine (Naiku) is dedicated to Amaterasu, the sun goddess, and is Shinto's most holy location. The Outer Shrine (Geku) is dedicated to

Toyouke, the goddess of the harvest. Every twenty years, Ise is torn down and rebuilt, thus renewing the gods. Shinto shrines all have torii, the sacred gateway. The most famous of these is built in the sea near the island of Miyajima. Those going to the shrine on this island go by boat through the torii.

EAST ASIAN RELIGIONS IN DEPTH

Sacred Symbols

Water is regarded as the source of life in Confucianism. The water symbol has thus become an unofficial symbol of Confucianism, represented by the Japanese ideogram or character for water, the Mizu, which somewhat resembles a stick figure with an extra leg. Other sacred symbols include the ancestor tablets in shrines of private homes, which are symbolic of the presence of the ancestor to whom offerings are made in hopes of aid.

While not a sacred symbol as the term is generally used, the black and white symbol of yin and yang is a common Taoist emblem. Peaches are also of a symbolic nature in Taoism, and often appear in Asian art. They are based on the four peaches that grew every three thousand years and which the mother of the fairies gave to the Han emperor Wu Ti (140–87 BCE). They are often symbolic of the Immortals.

The Shinto stylized sun, which appears on the Japanese flag, is associated with Amaterasu, the sun goddess. The torii, the gateway forming an entrance to sacred space, is another symbol associated with Shinto.

Sacred Practices & Gestures

Confucian rulers traditionally offered sacrifices honoring Confucius at the spring and autumnal equinoxes. Most of the Confucian practices take place at home shrines honoring the ancestors.

Taoists believe that one can reach Tao (the way) through physical movements, chanting, or meditation. Because mountains, caves, and springs are often regarded as sacred sites, pilgrimages are important to Taoists. At a Taoist

funeral, a paper fairy crane is part of the procession. After the funeral, the crane, which symbolizes a heavenly messenger, is burned. The soul of the deceased person is then thought to ride to heaven on the back of the crane.

Many Shinto shrines exist throughout Japan. Most of them have a sacred arch, known as a torii. At the shrine's entrance, worshippers rinse their mouths and wash their hands to be purified before entering the prayer hall. Before praying, a worshipper will clap twice and ring a bell to let the kami know they are there. Only priests may enter the inner hall, which is where the kami live. During a festival, however, the image of the kami is placed in a portable shrine and carried in a procession through town, so that all may receive a blessing.

Rites, Celebrations & Services

Early Confucianism had no priests, and bureaucrats performed any rituals that were necessary. When the Chinese Empire fell in 1911, imperial ceremonies ended as well. Rituals have become less important in modern times. In contemporary times the most important rite is marriage, the beginning of a new family for creating harmony. There is a correct protocol for each aspect of marriage, from the proposal and engagement to exchanging vows. During the ceremony, the groom takes the bride to his family's ancestor tablets to "introduce" her to them and receive a blessing. The couple bows to the ancestors during the ceremony.

After a death occurs, mourners wear coarse material and bring gifts of incense and money to help defray the costs. Added to the coffin holding are food offerings and significant possessions. A willow branch symbolizing the deceased's soul is carried with the coffin to the place of burial. After the burial, family members take the willow branch to their home altar and perform a ritual to add the deceased to the souls at the family's shrine.

Confucians and Taoists celebrate many of the same Chinese festivals, some of which originated before either Confucianism or Taoism began and reflect aspects of both traditions. While some festivals are not necessarily Taoist, they may be led by Taoist priests. During the Lantern Festival, which occurs on the first full moon of the New Year, offerings are made to the gods. Many of the festivals are tied to calendar events. Qingming (Clear and Bright) celebrates the coming of spring and is a time to remember the dead. During this time, families often go to the family gravesite for a picnic. The Double Fifth is the midsummer festival that occurs on the fifth day of the fifth month, and coincides with the peak of yang power. To protect themselves from too much of the male force, people don garments of the five colors—black, blue, red, white, and yellow—and with the five "poisons"—centipede, lizard, scorpion, snake, and toad—in the pattern of their clothes and on amulets. The gates of hell open at the Feast of the Hungry Ghosts. Priests have ceremonies that encourage the escaped evil spirits to repent or return to hell.

Marriage is an important rite in China, and thus in Taoism as well. Astrologers look at horoscopes to ensure that the bride and groom are well matched and to find the best day for the ceremony. The groom's family is always placed at the east (yang) and the bride's family to the west (yin) to bring harmony. When a person dies, the mourners again sit in the correct locations, while the head of the deceased points south. White is the color of mourning and of yin. At the home of the deceased, white cloths cover the family altar. Mourners may ease the soul's journey with symbolic artifacts or money. They may also go after the funeral to underground chambers beneath the temples to offer a sacrifice on behalf of the dead.

In the Shinto religion, rites exist for many life events. For example, pregnant women ask at a shrine for their children to be born safely, and the mother or grandmother brings a child who is thirty-two or thirty-three-days-old to a shrine for the first visit and blessing. A special festival also exists for children aged three, five or seven, who go to the shrine for purifying. In addition, a bride and groom are purified before the wedding, usually conducted by Shinto priests. Shinto priests may also offer blessings for a new car or building. The New Year and the Spring Festival are among the most important festivals, and shrine virgins, known as miko girls, may dance to celebrate life's renewal. Other festivals include the Feast of the Puppets, Boys' Day, the Water Kami Festival, the Star Feast, the Festival of the Dead, and the autumnal equinox.

Judy A. Johnson, MTS

Bibliography

Barnes, Trevor. *The Kingfisher Book of Religions*. New York: Kingfisher, 1999. Print.

Bell, Daniel A. "Reconciling Socialism and Confucianism? Reviving Tradition in China." *Dissent* 57.1 (2010): 91–99. Print.

Chang, Chung-yuan. *Creativity and Taoism: A Study of Chinese Philosophy, Art and Poetry*. London: Kingsley, 2011. E-book.

Coogan, Michael D., ed. *Eastern Religions*. New York: Oxford UP, 2005. Print.

Eliade, Mircea, and Ioan P. Couliano. *The Eliade Guide to World Religions*. New York: Harper, 1991. Print.

Lao Tzu. *Tao Te Ching*. Trans. Stephen Mitchell. New York: Harper, 1999. Print.

Li, Yingzhang. *Lao-tzu's Treatise on the Response of the Tao*. Trans. Eva Wong. New Haven: Yale UP, 2011. Print.

Littlejohn, Ronnie. *Confucianism: An Introduction*. New York: Tauris, 2011. E-book.

Littleton, C. Scott. *Shinto*. Oxford: Oxford UP, 2002. Print.

Mcvay, Kera. *All about Shinto*. Delhi: University, 2012. Ebook.

Merton, Thomas. *The Way of Chuang Tzu*. New York: New Directions, 1965. Print.

Oldstone-Moore, Jennifer. *Confucianism*. Oxford: Oxford UP, 2002. Print.

Poceski, Mario. *Chinese Religions: The EBook*. Providence, UT: Journal of Buddhist Ethics Online Books, 2009. E-book.

Van Norden, Bryan W. *Introduction to Classical Chinese Philosophy*. Indianapolis: Hackett, 2011. Print.

Wilkinson, Philip. *Religions*. New York: DK, 2008. Print.

Hinduism

General Description

Hinduism; modern Hinduism is comprised of the devotional sects of Vaishnavism, Shaivism, and Shaktism (though Smartism is sometimes listed as the fourth division). Hinduism is often used as umbrella term, since many point to Hinduism as a family of different religions.

Number of Adherents Worldwide

Between 13.8 and 15 percent of the world's population, or about one billion people, are adherents of Hinduism, making it the world's third largest religion after Christianity and Islam. The predominant sect is the Vaishnavite sect (Wilkinson, p. 333).

Basic Tenets

Hinduism is a way of life rather than a body of beliefs. Hindus believe in karma, the cosmic law of cause and effect that determines one's state in the next life. Additional beliefs include dharma, one's religious duty.

Hinduism has no true belief in an afterlife. Rather, it teaches a belief in reincarnation, known as samsara, and in moksha, the end of the cycle of rebirths. Different sects have different paths to moksha.

Hinduism is considered a polytheist religion. However, it is also accurate to say that Hinduism professes a belief in one God or Supreme Truth that is beyond comprehension (an absolute reality, called Brahman) and which manifests itself in many forms and names. These include Brahma, the creator; Vishnu, the protector; and Shiva, the re-creator or destroyer. Many sects are defined by their belief in multiple gods, but also by their worship of one ultimate manifestation. For example, Shaivism and Vaishnavism are based upon the recognition of Shiva and Vishnu, respectively, as the manifestation. In comparison, Shaktism recognizes the Divine Mother (Shakti) as the Supreme Being, while followers of Smartism worship a particular deity of their own choosing.

Major Deities

The Hindu trinity (Trimurti) is comprised of Brahma, the impersonal and absolute creator; Vishnu, the great preserver; and Shiva, the destroyer and re-creator. The goddesses corresponding to each god are Sarasvati, Lakshimi, and Parvati. Thousands of other gods (devas) and goddesses (devis) are worshipped, including Ganesha, Surya, and Kali. Each is believed to represent another aspect of the Supreme Being.

Sacred Texts

Hindus revere ancient texts such as the four Vedas, the 108 Upanishads, and others. No single text has the binding authority of the Qur'an (Islam's holy book) or Bible. Hindu literature is also defined by Sruti (revealed truth), which is heard, and Smriti (realized truth), which is remembered. The former is canonical, while the latter can be changing. For example, the Vedas and the Upanishads constitute Sruti texts, while epics, history, and law books constitute the latter. The Bhagavad Gita (The Song of God) is also considered a sacred scripture of Hinduism, and consists of a philosophical dialogue.

Major Figures

Major figures include: Shankara (788–820 CE), who defined the unity of the soul (atman) and absolute reality (Brahman); Ramanuja (1077–1157 CE), who emphasized bhakti, or love of God; Madhva (1199–1278 CE), scholar and writer, a proponent of dualism; Ramprahsad Sen (1718–1775 CE), composer of Hindu songs of devotion, poet, and mystic who influenced goddess worship in the; Raja Rammohun Roy (1772–1833 CE), abolished the custom of suttee, in which widows were burned on the funeral pyres of their dead husbands, and decried polygamy, rigid caste systems, and dowries; Rabindranath Tagore (1861–1941 CE), first Asian to win the Nobel Prize in Literature; Dr. Babasaheb R. Ambedkar (1891–1956 CE), writer of India's constitution and leader of a mass conversion to Buddhism; Mohandas K. Gandhi (1869–1948 CE), the "great soul" who left a legacy of effective use of nonviolence.

Major Holy Sites

The major holy sites of Hinduism are located within India. They include the Ganges River, in whose waters pilgrims come to bathe away their sins, as well as thousands of tirthas (places of pilgrimage), many of which are associated with particular deities. For example, the Char Dham pilgrimage centers, of which there are four—Badrinath (north), Puri (east), Dwarka (west) and Rameshwaram (south)—are considered the holy abodes or sacred temples of Vishnu. There are also seven ancient holy cities in India, including Ayodhya, believed to be the birthplace of Rama; Varanasi (Benares), known as the City of Light; Dwarka; Ujjian; Kanchipuram; Mathura; and Hardwar.

Major Rites & Celebrations

Diwali, the Festival of Lights, is a five-day festival that is considered a national holiday in India. Holi, the Festival of Colors, is the spring festival. Krishna Janmashtmi is Krishna's birthday. Shivaratri is Shiva's main festival. Navaratri, also known as the Durga festival or Dasserah, celebrates one of the stories of the gods and the victory of good over evil. Ganesh Chaturthi is the elephant-headed god Ganesha's birthday. Rathayatra, celebrated at Puri, India, is a festival for Jagannath, another word for Vishnu.

ORIGINS

History & Geography

Hinduism, which many people consider to be the oldest world religion, is unique in that it has no recorded origin or founder. Generally, it developed in the Indus Valley civilization several thousand years before the Common Era. The faith blends the Vedic traditions of the Indus Valley civilization and the invading nomadic tribes of the Aryans (prehistoric Indo-Europeans). Most of what is known of the Indus Valley civilization comes from archaeological excavations at Mohenjo-Daro (Mound of the Dead) and Harappa. (Because Harappa was a chief city of the period, the Indus Valley civilization is also referred to as the Harappan civilization.) The Vedas, a collection of ancient hymns, provides information about the Aryan culture.

The ancient Persian word *hind* means Indian, and for centuries, to be Indian was to be Hindu. Even now, about 80 percent of India's people consider themselves Hindu. The root word alludes to flowing, as a river flows. It is also etymologically related to the Indus River. At first, the term Hindu was used as an ethnic or cultural term, and travelers from Persia and Greece in the sixteenth century referred to those in the Indus Valley by that name. British writers coined the term *Hinduism* during the early part of the nineteenth century to describe the culture of India. The Hindus themselves often use the term Sanatana Dharma, meaning eternal law.

The Rigveda, a collection of hymns to various gods and goddesses written around 1500 BCE, is the first literary source for understanding Hinduism's history. The Vedas were chanted aloud for centuries before being written down around 1400 CE. The Rigveda is one of four major collections of Vedas, or wisdom: Rigveda, Yajurveda, Samaveda, and Atharvaveda. Together these four are called Samhitas.

Additionally, Hinduism relies on three other Vedic works: the Aranyakas, the Brahamans, and the Upanishads. The Upanishads is a philosophical work, possibly written down between 800 and 450 BCE, that attempts to answer life's big questions. Written in the form of a dialogue between a teacher (guru) and student (chela), the text's name means "to sit near," which describes the relationship between the two. Along with the Samhitas, these four are called Sruti (heard), a reference to their nature as revealed truth. The words in these texts cannot be altered.

Remaining works are called Smriti, meaning "remembered," to indicate that they were composed by human writers. The longer of the Smriti epics is the Mahabharata, the Great Story of the Bharatas. Written between 300 and 100 BCE, the epic is a classic tale of two rival, related families, including teaching as well as story. It is considered the longest single poem in existence, with about 200,000 lines. (A film made of it lasts for twelve hours.)

The Bhagavad Gita, or Song of the Lord, is the sixth section of the Mahabharata, but is often read as a stand-alone narrative of battle and acceptance of one's dharma. The Ramayana is the second, shorter epic of the Mahabharata, with about fifty thousand lines. Rama was the seventh incarnation, or avatar, of Vishnu. The narrative relates the abduction of his wife, Sita, and her rescue, accomplished with the help of the monkey god, Hanuman. Some have regarded the Mahabharata as an encyclopedia, and the Bhagavad Gita as the Bible within it.

Although many of the practices in the Vedas have been modified or discontinued, sections of it are memorized and repeated. Some of the hymns are recited at traditional ceremonies for the dead and at weddings.

Hinduism has affected American life and culture for many years. For example, the nineteenth-century transcendental writers Margaret Fuller and Ralph Waldo Emerson were both influenced by Hindu and Buddhist literature, while musician George Harrison, a member of the Beatles, adopted Hinduism and explored his new faith through his music, both with and without the Beatles. In 1965, the International Society for Krishna Consciousness (ISKCON), or the Hare Krishna movement, came to the Western world. In addition, many people have been drawn to yoga, which is associated with Hinduism's meditative practices.

Founder or Major Prophet

Hinduism has no founder or major prophet. It is a religion that has developed over many centuries and from many sources, many of which are unknown in their origins.

Philosophical Basis

Hinduism recognizes multiple ways to achieve salvation and escape the endless cycle of rebirth. The way of devotion is the most popular. Through worship of a single deity, the worshipper hopes to attain union with the divine. A second path is the way of knowledge, involving the use of meditation and reason. The third way is via action, or correctly performing religious observances in hope of receiving a blessing from the gods by accomplishing these duties.

Hinduism is considered the world's oldest religion, but Hindus maintain that it is also a way of living, not just a religion. There is great diversity as well as great tolerance in Hinduism. While Hinduism does not have a set of dogmatic formulations, it does blend the elements of devotion, doctrine, practice, society, and story as separate strands in a braid.

During the second century BCE, a sage named Patanjali outlined four life stages, and the fulfilled responsibilities inherent in each one placed one in harmony with dharma, or right conduct. Although these life stages are no longer observed strictly, their ideas still carry weight. Traditionally, these codes applied to men, and only to those in the Brahman caste; members of the warrior and merchant classes could follow them, but were not obligated. The Shudra and Dalit castes, along with women, were not part of the system. Historically, women were thought of as protected by fathers in their childhood, by husbands in their youth and adulthood, and by sons in old age. Only recently have women in India been educated beyond the skills of domestic responsibility and child rearing.

The earliest life stage is the student stage, or brahmacharya, a word that means "to conduct oneself in accord with Brahman." From ages twelve to twenty-four, young men were expected to undertake learning with a guru, or guide. During these twelve years of studying the Veda they were also expected to remain celibate.

The second stage, grihastha, is that of householder. A Hindu man married the bride that his parents had chosen, sired children, and created a livelihood on which the other three stages depended.

Vanaprastha is the third stage, involving retirement to solitude. Historically, this involved leaving the house and entering a forest dwelling.

A man's wife had the option to go with him or to remain. This stage also involved giving counsel to others and further study.

At the final stage of life, sannyasis, the Hindu renounces material goods, including a home of any sort. He may live in a forest or join an ashram, or community. He renounces even making a fire, and lives on fruit and roots that can be foraged. Many contemporary Hindus do not move to this stage, but remain at vanaprastha.

Yoga is another Hindu practice, more than three millennia old, which Patanjali codified. The four forms of yoga corresponded to the Hindu avenues of salvation. Hatha yoga is the posture yoga seeking union with god through action. Jnana yoga is the path to god through knowledge. Bhakti yoga is the way of love to god. Karma yoga is the method of finding god through work. By uniting the self, the practitioner unites with God. Yoga is related etymologically to the English word *yoke*—it attempts to yoke the individual with Brahman. All forms of yoga include meditation and the acceptance of other moral disciplines, such as self-discipline, truthfulness, nonviolence, and contentment.

Aryan society was stratified, and at the top of the social scale were the priests. This system was the basis for the caste system that had long dominated Hinduism. Caste, which was determined by birth, affected a person's occupation, diet, neighborhood, and marriage partner. Vedic hymns allude to four varnas, or occupations: Brahmins (priests), Kshatriyas (warriors), Vaishyas (merchants and common people), and Shudras (servants). A fifth class, the Untouchables, later known as Dalit (oppressed), referred to those who were regarded as a polluting force because they handled waste and dead bodies. The belief was that society would function properly if each group carried out its duties. These varnas later became wrongly blended with castes, or jatis, which were smaller groups also concerned with a person's place in society.

The practice of Hinduism concerns itself with ritual purity; even household chores can be done in a ritualistic way. Some traditions demand ritual purity before one can worship. Brahmin priests, for example, may not accept water or food from non-Brahmins. Refusal to do so is not viewed as classism, but an attempt to please the gods in maintaining ritual purity.

Mohandas Gandhi was one of those who refused to use the term *Untouchable*, using the term *harijan*(children of God), instead. Dr. Babasaheb R. Ambedkar, who wrote India's constitution, was a member of this class. Ambedkar and many of his supporters became Buddhists in an attempt to dispel the power of caste. In 1947, following India's independence from Britain, the caste system was officially banned, though it has continued to influence Indian society.

Ahimsa, or dynamic harmlessness, is another deeply rooted principle of Hinduism. It involves six pillars: refraining from eating all animal products; revering all of life; having integrity in thoughts, words, and deeds; exercising self-control; serving creation, nature, and humanity; and advancing truth and understanding.

Holy Places

In Hinduism, all water is considered holy, symbolizing the flow of life. For a Hindu, the Ganges River is perhaps the most holy of all bodies of water. It was named for the goddess of purification, Ganga. The waters of the Ganges are said to flow through Shiva's hair and have the ability to cleanse sin. Devout Hindus make pilgrimages to bathe in the Ganges. They may also visit fords in the rivers to symbolize the journey from one life to another.

Pilgrimages are also made to sites associated with the life of a god. For example, Lord Rama was said to have been born in Ayodhya, one of the seven holy cities in India. Other holy sites are Dwarka, Ujjian, Kanchipuram, Mathura, Hardwar, and Varanasi, the City of Light.

After leaving his mountain home, Lord Shiva was thought to have lived in Varanasi, or Benares, considered the holiest city. Before the sixth century, it became a center of education for Hindus. It has four miles of palaces and temples along the river. One of the many pilgrimage circuits covers thirty-five miles, lasts for five days, and includes prayer at 108 different shrines. Because of the river's sacred nature, Hindus come to bathe from its many stone steps, called ghats, and to drink the water. It is also the place where Hindus desire to be at their death or to have their ashes scattered. Because Varanasi is regarded as a place of crossing between earth and heaven, dying there is thought to free one from the cycle of rebirth.

The thirty-four Ellora Caves at Maharashtra, India, are known for their sculptures. Built between 600 and 1000 CE, they were cut into a tufa rock hillside on a curve shaped like a horseshoe, so that the caves go deeply into the rock face. Although the one-mile site includes temples for Buddhist, Jain, and Hindu faiths, the major figure of the caves is Shiva, and the largest temple is dedicated to Shiva.

Lastly, Hindu temples, or mandirs, are regarded as the gods' earthly homes. The buildings themselves are therefore holy, and Hindus remove their shoes before entering.

HINDUISM IN DEPTH

Sacred Symbols

The wheel of life represents samsara, the cycle of life, death and rebirth. Karma is what keeps the wheel spinning. Another circle is the hoop of flames in which Shiva, also known as the Lord of the Dance, or Natraja, is shown dancing creation into being. The flames signify the universe's energy and Shiva's power of both destruction and creation. Shiva balances on his right foot, which rests on a defeated demon that stands for ignorance.

The lotus is the symbol of creation, fertility, and purity. This flower is associated with Vishnu because as he slept, a lotus flower bloomed from his navel. From this lotus Brahma came forth to create the world. Yoga practitioners commonly assume the lotus position for meditation.

Murtis are the statues of gods that are found in both temples and private homes. They are often washed with milk and water, anointed with oil, dressed, and offered gifts of food or flowers. Incense may also be burned to make the air around the murti sweet and pure.

One of Krishna's symbols is the conch shell, a symbol of a demon he defeated. A conch shell is blown at temples to announce the beginning of the worship service. It is a visual reminder for followers of Krishna to overcome ignorance and evil in their lives.

For many years, the Hindus used the swastika as a holy symbol. (*Swastika* is a Sanskrit word for good fortune and well-being.) The four arms meet at a central point, demonstrating that the universe comes from one source. Each arm of the symbol represents a path to God and is bent to show that all paths are difficult. It is used at a time of new beginnings, such as at a wedding, where it is traditionally painted on a coconut using a red paste called kum kum. The symbol appears as a vertical gash across the horizontal layers on the southern face of Mount Kailas, one of the Himalayas's highest peaks, thought to have been the home of Shiva. The mountain is also near the source of the Ganges and the Indus Rivers. The use of the swastika as a symbol for Nazi Germany is abhorrent to Hindus.

Some Hindus use a mala, or rosary, of 108 wooden beads when they pray. As they worship, they repeat the names of God.

Sacred Practices & Gestures

Many homes have private altars or shrines to favorite gods. Statues or pictures of these deities are offered incense, flowers and food, as well as prayers. This daily devotion, known as puja, is generally the responsibility of women, many of whom are devoted to goddesses such as Kali or Sita. A rich family may devote an entire room of their house to the shrine.

Om, or Aum, a sacred syllable recorded first in the Upanishads, is made up of three Sanskrit letters. Writing the letter involves a symbol resembling the Arabic number three. Thus, it is a visual reminder of the Trimurti, the three major Hindu gods. The word is repeated at the beginning of all mantras or prayers.

Each day the Gayatri, which is perhaps the world's oldest recorded prayer, is chanted during the fire ritual. The prayer expresses gratitude to the sun for its shining and invokes blessings of prosperity on all. The ritual, typically done at large consecrated fire pits, may be done using burning candles instead.

Holy Hindu men are known as sadhus. They lead ascetic lives, wandering, begging, and living in caves in the mountains. Regarded as having greater spiritual power and wisdom, they are often consulted for advice.

Food Restrictions

Many Hindus are vegetarians because they embrace ahimsa (reverence for and protection of all life) and oppose killing. In fact, Hindus comprise about 70 percent of the world's vegetarians. They are generally lacto-vegetarians, meaning that they include dairy products in their diets. However, Hindus residing in the cold climate of Nepal and Tibet consume meat to increase their caloric intake.

Whether a culture practices vegetarianism or not, cows are thought to be sacred because Krishna acted as a cowherd as a young god. Thus cows are never eaten. Pigs are also forbidden, as are red foods, such as tomatoes or red lentils. In addition, garlic and onions are also not permitted. Alcohol is strictly forbidden.

Purity rituals before eating include cleaning the area where the food is to be eaten and reciting mantras or praying while sprinkling water around the food. Other rituals include Annaprasana, which celebrates a child's eating of solid food—traditionally rice—for the first time. In addition, at funerals departed souls are offered food, which Hindus believe will strengthen the soul for the journey to the ancestors' world.

Serving food to those in need also generates good karma. Food is offered during religious ceremonies and may later be shared with visiting devotees of the god.

To show their devotion to Shiva, many Hindus fast on Mondays. There is also a regular fast, known as agiaras, which occurs on the eleventh day of each two-week period. On that day, only one meal is eaten. During the month of Shravan, which many consider a holy month, people may eat only one meal, generally following sunset.

Rites, Celebrations & Services

Many Hindu celebrations are connected to the annual cycle of nature and can last for many days. In addition, celebrations that honor the gods are common. Shiva, one of the three major gods, is honored at Shivaratri in February or March. In August or September, Lord Krishna is honored at Krishnajanmashtmi. Prayer and fasting are part of this holiday.

During the spring equinox and just prior to the Hindu New Year, Holi is celebrated. It is a time to resolve disputes and forgive or pay debts. During this festival, people often have bonfires and throw objects that represent past impurity or disease into the fire.

Another festival occurs in July or August, marking the beginning of the agricultural year in northern India. Raksha Bandhan (the bond of protection) is a festival which celebrates sibling relationships. During the festivities, Hindus bind a bauble with silk thread to the wrists of family members and friends.

To reenact Rama's defeat of the demon Ravana, as narrated in the Ramayana, people make and burn effigies. This festival is called Navaratri in western India, also known as the Durgapuja in Bengal, and Dasserah in northern India. It occurs in September or October each year as a festival celebrating the victory of good over evil. September is also time to celebrate the elephant-headed god Ganesha's birthday at the festival of Ganesh Chaturthi.

Diwali, a five-day festival honoring Lakshmi (the goddess of good fortune and wealth), occurs in October or November. This Festival of Lights is the time when people light oil lamps and set off fireworks to help Rama find his way home after exile. Homes are cleaned in hopes that Lakshmi will come in the night to bless it. People may use colored rice flour to make patterns on their doorstep. Competitions for designs of these patterns, which are meant to welcome God to the house, frequently take place.

Jagannath, or Vishnu, is celebrated during the festival Rathayatra. A large image of Jagannath rides in a chariot pulled through the city of Puri.

The temple for Hindus is the home of the god. Only Brahmin priests may supervise worship there. The inner sanctuary of the building is called the garbhagriha, or womb-house; there the god resides. Worshippers must be ritually pure before the worship starts. The priest recites the mantras and reads sacred texts. Small lamps are lit, and everyone shares specially prepared and blessed food after the service ends.

Judy A. Johnson, MTS

Bibliography

Barnes, Trevor. *The Kingfisher Book of Religions*. New York: Kingfisher, 1999. Print.

Harley, Gail M. *Hindu and Sikh Faiths in America*. New York: Facts on File, 2003. Print.

Iyengar, B. K. S. and Noelle Perez-Christiaens. *Sparks of Divinity: The Teachings of B. K. S. Iyengar from 1959 to 1975*. Berkeley: Rodmell, 2012. E-book.

"The Joys of Hinduism." *Hinduism Today* Oct./Dec. 2006: 40–53. Print.

Langley, Myrtle. *Religion*. New York: Knopf, 1996. Print.

Meredith, Susan. *The Usborne Book of World Religions*. London: Usborne, 1995. Print.

Rajan, Rajewswari. "The Politics of Hindu 'Tolerance.'" *Boundary 2* 38.3 (2011): 67–86. Print.

Raman, Varadaraja V. "Hinduism and Science: Some Reflections." *Journal of Religion & Science* 47.3 (2012): 549–74. Print.

Renard, John. *Responses to 101 Questions on Hinduism*. Mahwah: Paulist, 1999. Print.

Siddhartha. "Open-Source Hinduism." *Religion & the Arts* 12.1–3 (2008): 34–41. Print.

Shouler, Kenneth and Susai Anthony. *The Everything Hinduism Book*. Avon: Adams, 2009. Print.

Soherwordi, Syed Hussain Shaheed. "'Hinduism'—A Western Construction or an Influence?" *South Asian Studies* 26.1 (2011): 203–14. Print.

Theodor, Ithamar. *Exploring the Bhagavad Gita: Philosophy, Structure, and Meaning*. Farnham and Burlington: Ashgate, 2010. E-book.

Whaling, Frank. *Understanding Hinduism*. Edinburgh: Dunedin, 2010. E-book.

Wilkinson, Philip. *Religions*. New York: DK, 2008. Print.

Islam

General Description

The word *Islam* derives from a word meaning "submission," particularly submission to the will of Allah. Muslims, those who practice Islam, fall into two major groups, Sunni and Shia (or Shi'i,) based on political rather than theological differences. Sunni Muslims follow the four Rightly Guided Caliphs, or Rashidun and believe that caliphs should be elected. Shia Muslims believe that the Prophet's nearest male relative, Ali ibn Abi Talib, should have ruled following Muhammad's death, and venerate the imams (prayer leaders) who are directly descended from Ali and the Prophet's daughter Fatima.

Number of Adherents Worldwide

Approximately 1.6 billion people, or 23 percent of the world's population, are Muslims. Of that total, between 87 and 90 percent of all Muslims are Sunni Muslims and between 10 and 13 percent of all Muslims are Shia. Followers of the Sufi sect, noted for its experiential, ecstatic focus, may be either Sunni or Shia.

Basic Tenets

Islam is a monotheistic faith; Muslims worship only one God, Allah. They also believe in an afterlife and that people are consigned to heaven or hell following the last judgment.

The Islamic faith rests on Five Pillars. The first pillar, Shahadah is the declaration of faith in the original Arabic, translated as: "I bear witness that there is no god but God and Muhammad is his Messenger." The second pillar, Salah, are prayers adherents say while facing Mecca five times daily at regular hours and also at the main service held each Friday at a mosque. Zakat, "the giving of a tax," is the third pillar and entails giving an income-based percentage of one's wealth to help the poor without attracting notice. The fourth pillar is fasting, or Sawm, during Ramadan, the ninth month of the Islamic calendar. Certain groups of people are excused from the fast, however. The final pillar is the Hajj, the pilgrimage to Mecca required of every able-bodied Muslim at least once in his or her lifetime.

Sacred Text

The Qur'an (Koran), meaning "recitation," is the holy book of Islam.

Major Figures

Muhammad, regarded as the Prophet to the Arabs—as Moses was to the Jews—is considered the exemplar of what it means to be a Muslim. His successors—Abu Bakr, Umar, Uthman, and Ali—were known as the four Rightly Guided Caliphs.

Major Holy Sites

Islam recognizes three major holy sites: Mecca, home of the Prophet; Medina, the city to which Muslims relocated when forced from Mecca due to persecution; and the Dome of the Rock in Jerusalem, believed to be the oldest Islamic building in existence. Muslims believe that in 621 CE Muhammad ascended to heaven (called the Night Journey) from a sacred stone upon which the Dome was constructed. Once in heaven, God instructed Muhammad concerning the need to pray at regular times daily...

There are also several mosques which are considered primary holy sites. These include the al-Aqsa Mosque in the Old City of Jerusalem, believed by many to be the third holiest site in Islam. The mosque, along with the Dome of the Rock, is located on Judaism's holiest site, the Temple Mount, where the Temple of Jerusalem is believed to have stood. Muslims also revere the Mosque of the Prophet (Al-Masjid al-Nabawi) in Medina, considered the resting place of the Prophet Muhammad and the second largest mosque in the world; and the Mosque of the Haram (Masjid al-Haram or the Sacred or Grand Mosque) in Mecca, thought to be the largest mosque in the world and site of the Ka'bah, "the sacred house," also known as "the Noble Cube," Islam's holiest structure.

Major Rites & Celebrations

Two major celebrations mark the Islamic calendar. 'Id al-Adha, the feast of sacrifice—including animal sacrifice—held communally at the close of the Hajj (annual pilgrimage), commemorates the account of God providing a ram instead of the son Abraham had been asked to sacrifice. The second festival, 'Id al-Fitr, denotes the end of Ramadan and is a time of feasting and gift giving.

ORIGINS

History & Geography

In 610 CE, a forty-year-old businessman from Mecca named Muhammad ibn Abdullah, from the powerful Arab tribe Quraysh, went to Mount Hira to meditate, as he regularly did for the month of Ramadan. During that month, an entire group of men, the hanif, retreated to caves. The pagan worship practiced in the region, as well as the cruelty and lack of care for the poor, distressed Muhammad. As the tribe to which he belonged had become wealthy through trade, it had begun disregarding traditions prescribed by the nomadic code.

The archangel Jibra'il (Gabriel) appeared in Muhammad's cave and commanded him to read the words of God contained in the scroll that the angel showed him. Like most people of his time, Muhammad was illiterate, but repeated the words Jibra'il said. Some followers of Islam believe that this cave at Jebel Nur, in what is now Saudi Arabia, is where Adam, the first human Allah created, lived.

A frightened Muhammad told only his wife, Khadija, about his experience. For two years, Muhammad received further revelations, sharing them only with family and close friends. Like other prophets, he was reluctant about his calling, fearing that he was—or would be accused of being—possessed by evil spirits or insane. At one point, he tried to commit suicide, but was stopped by the voice of Jibra'il affirming his status as God's messenger.

Muhammad recalled the words spoken to him, which were eventually written down. The Qur'an is noted for being a book of beautiful language, and Muhammad's message reached many. The Prophet thus broke the old pattern of allegiance to tribe and forged a new community based on shared practice.

Muhammad considered himself one who was to warn the others of a coming judgment. His call for social justice and denunciation of the wealthy disturbed the powerful Arab tribe members in Mecca. These men stood to lose the status and income derived from the annual festival to the Ka'bah. The Prophet and his followers were persecuted and were the subject of boycotts and death threats. In 622 CE, Muslim families began a migration (hijrah) to Yathrib, later known as Medina. Two years earlier, the city had sent envoys seeking Muhammad's leadership for their own troubled society. The hijrah marks the beginning of the Islamic calendar.

The persecutions eventually led to outright tribal warfare, linking Islam with political prowess through the victories of the faithful. The Muslims moved from being an oppressed minority to being a political force. In 630 CE, Muhammad and ten thousand of his followers marched to Mecca, taking the city without bloodshed. He destroyed the pagan idols that were housed and worshipped at the Ka'bah, instead associating the hajj with the story of Abraham sending his concubine Hagar and their son Ishmael (Ismail in Arabic) out into the wilderness. With this victory, Muhammad ended centuries of intertribal warfare.

Muhammad died in 632, without designating a successor. Some of the Muslims believed that his nearest male relative should rule, following the custom of the tribes. Ali ibn Abi Talib, although a pious Muslim, was still young. Therefore, Abu Bakr, the Prophet's father-in-law, took the title khalifah, or caliph, which means successor or deputy. Within two years Abu Bakr had stabilized Islam. He was followed by three additional men whom Muhammad had known. Collectively, the four are known as the Four Rightly Guided Caliphs, or the Rashidun. Their rule extended from 632 until 661. Each of the final three met a violent death.

Umar, the second caliph, increased the number of raids on adjacent lands during his ten-year rule, which began in 634. This not only increased wealth, but also gave Umar the authority he needed, since Arabs objected to the idea of a monarchy. Umar was known as the commander of the faithful. Under his leadership, the Islamic community marched into present-day Iraq, Syria, and Egypt and achieved victory over the Persians in 637.

Muslims elected Uthman ibn Affan as the third caliph after Umar was stabbed by a Persian prisoner of war. He extended Muslim conquests into North Africa as well as into Iran, Afghanistan, and parts of India. A group of soldiers mutinied in 656, assassinating Uthman.

Ali, Muhammad's son-in-law, was elected caliph of a greatly enlarged empire. Conflict developed between Ali and the ruler in Damascus whom Uthman had appointed governor of Syria. The fact that the governor came from a rival tribe led to further tensions. Increasingly, Damascus rather than Medina was viewed as the key Muslim locale. Ali was murdered in 661 during the internal struggles.

Within a century after Muhammad's death, Muslims had created an empire that stretched from Spain across Asia to India and facilitated the spread of Islam. The conquerors followed a policy of relative, though not perfect, tolerance toward adherents of other religions. Christians and Jews received special status as fellow "People of the Book," though they were still required to pay a special poll tax in exchange for military protection. Pagans, however, were required to convert to Islam or face death. Later, Hindus, Zoroastrians, and other peoples were also permitted to pay the tax rather than submit to conversion. Following the twelfth century, Sufi mystics made further converts in Central Asia, India, sub-Saharan Africa, and Turkey. Muslim traders also were responsible for the growth of Islam, particularly in China, Indonesia, and Malaya.

The Muslim empire continued to grow until it weakened in the fourteenth century, when it was replaced as a major world power by European states. The age of Muslim domination ended with the 1683 failure of the Ottoman Empire to capture Vienna, Austria.

Although lacking in political power until recent years, a majority of nations in Indonesia, the Middle East, and East and North Africa are predominately Islamic. The rise of Islamic fundamentalists who interpret the Qur'an literally and seek victory through acts of terrorism began in the late twentieth century. Such extremists do not represent the majority of the Muslim community, however.

Like Judaism and Christianity, Islam has been influenced by its development in a desert climate. Arabia, a region three times the size of France, is a land of steppe and desert whose unwelcoming climate kept it from being mapped with any precision until the 1950s. Because Yemen received monsoon rains, it could sustain agriculture and became a center for civilization as early as the second millennium BCE. In the seventh century CE, nomads roamed the area, guarding precious wells and oases. Raiding caravans and other tribes were common ways to obtain necessities.

Mecca was a pagan center of worship, but it was located not far from a Christian kingdom, Ethiopia, across the Red Sea. Further north, followers of both Judaism and Christianity had influenced members of Arab tribes. Jewish tribes inhabited Yathrib, the city later known as Medina. Neither Judaism nor Christianity was especially kind to those they considered pagans. According to an Arabian tradition, in 570 the Ethiopians attacked Yemen and attempted an attack on Mecca. Mecca was caught between two enemy empires—Christian Byzantine and Zoroastrian Persia—that fought a lengthy war during Muhammad's lifetime.

The contemporary clashes between Jews and Muslims are in part a result of the dispersion of Muslims who had lived in Palestine for centuries. More Jews began moving into the area under the British Mandate; in 1948, the state of Israel was proclaimed. Historically, Jews had been respected as a People of the Book.

Founder or Major Prophet

Muslims hold Allah to be the founder of their religion and Abraham to have been the first Muslim. Muhammad is God's prophet to the Arabs. The instructions that God gave Muhammad through the archangel Jibra'il and through direct revelation are the basis for the Islamic religion. These revelations were given over a period of twenty-one years. Because Muhammad and most of the Muslims were illiterate, the teachings were read publicly in chapters, or suras.

Muhammad did not believe he was founding a new religion. Rather, he was considered God's final Prophet, as Moses and Jesus had been prophets. His task was to call people to repent and to return to the straight path of God's law, called Sharia. God finally was sending a direct revelation to the Arab peoples, who had sometimes been taunted by the other civilizations as being left out of God's plan.

Muhammad, who had been orphaned by age six, was raised by an uncle. He became a successful businessman of an important tribe and married Khadija, for whom he worked. His integrity was such that he was known as al-Amin, the trusted one. He and Khadija had six children; four daughters survived. After Khadija's death, Muhammad married several women, as was the custom for a great chief. Several of the marriages were political in nature.

Muhammad is regarded as the living Qur'an. He is sometimes referred to as the perfect man, one who is an example of how a Muslim should live. He was ahead of his time in his attitudes toward women, listening to their counsel and granting them rights not enjoyed by women in other societies, including the right to inherit property and to divorce. (It should be noted that the Qur'an does not require the seclusion or veiling of all women.)

Islam has no religious leaders, especially those comparable to other religions. Each mosque has an imam to preach and preside over prayer at the Friday services. Although granted a moral authority, the imam is not a religious leader with a role comparable to that of rabbis or priests.

Philosophical Basis

Prior to Muhammad's receiving the Qur'an, the polytheistic tribes believed in Allah, "the god." Allah was far away and not part of worship rituals, although he had created the world and sustained it. He had three daughters who were goddesses.

Islam began pragmatically—the old tribal ways were not working—as a call for social justice, rooted in Muhammad's dissatisfaction with the increasing emphasis on accumulating wealth and an accompanying neglect of those in need. The struggle (jihad) to live according to God's desire for humans was to take place within the community, or the ummah. This effort was more important than dogmatic statements or beliefs about God. When the community prospered, this was a sign of God's blessing.

In addition, the revelation of the Qur'an gave Arab nations an official religion. The Persians around them had Zoroastrianism, the Romans and Byzantines had Christianity, and the Jews of the Diaspora had Judaism. With the establishment of Islam, Arabs finally could believe that they were part of God's plan for the world.

Four principles direct Islam's practice and doctrine. These include the Qur'an; the traditions, or sunnah; consensus, or ijma'; and individual thought, or ijtihad. The term sunnah, "well-trodden path," had been used by Arabs before Islam to refer to their tribal law.

A fifth important source for Islam is the Hadith, or report, a collection of the Prophet's words and actions, intended to serve as an example. Sunni Muslims refer to six collections made in the ninth century, while Shia Muslims have a separate Hadith of four collections.

Holy Places

Mecca was located just west of the Incense Road, a major trade route from southern Arabia to Palestine and Syria. Mecca was the Prophet's home and the site where he received his revelations. It is also the city where Islam's holiest structure, the Ka'bah, "the sacred house," was located. The Ka'bah was regarded as having been built by Abraham and his son Ishmael. This forty-three-foot gray stone cube was a center for pagan idols in the time of Muhammad. In 628 the Prophet removed 360 pagan idols—one for each day of the Arabic lunar year—from inside the Ka'bah.

When the followers of Muhammad experienced persecution for their beliefs, they fled to the city of Medina, formerly called Yathrib. When his uncle Abu Talib died, Muhammad lost the protection from persecution that his uncle had provided. He left for Ta'if in the mountains, but it was also a center for pagan cults, and he was driven out. After a group of men from Yathrib promised him protection, Muhammad sent seventy of his followers to the city, built around an oasis about 215 miles north. This migration, called the hijra, occurred in 622, the first year of the Muslim calendar. From this point on, Islam became an organized religion rather than a persecuted and minority cult. The Prophet was buried in Medina in 632, and his mosque in that city is deeply revered.

Islam's third holiest site is the Dome of the Rock in Jerusalem. Muslims believe that the Prophet Muhammad ascended to heaven in 621 from the rock located at the center of this mosque. During this so-called night journey, Allah gave him instructions about prayer. In the shrine at the Dome of the Rock is a strand of hair that Muslims believe was Muhammad's.

Shia Muslims also revere the place in present-day Iraq where Ali's son, Husayn, was martyred. They regard the burial place of Imam Ali ar-Rida in Meshed, Iran, as a site of pilgrimage as well.

ISLAM IN DEPTH

Sacred Symbols

Muslims revere the Black Stone, a possible meteorite that is considered a link to heaven. It is set inside the Ka'bah shrine's eastern corner. The Ka'bah is kept covered by the kiswa, a black velvet cloth decorated with embroidered calligraphy in gold. At the hajj, Muslims walk around it counterclockwise seven times as they recite prayers to Allah.

Muslim nations have long used the crescent moon and a star on their flags. The crescent moon, which the Ottomans first adopted as a symbol during the fifteenth century, is often placed on the dome of a mosque, pointing toward Mecca. For Muhammad, the waxing and waning of the moon signified the unchanging and eternal purpose of God. Upon seeing a new moon, the Prophet confessed his faith in God. Muslims rely on a lunar calendar and the Qur'an states that God created the stars to guide people to their destinations.

Islam forbids the making of graven images of animals or people, although not all Islamic cultures follow this rule strictly. The decorative arts of Islam have placed great emphasis on architecture and calligraphy to beautify mosques and other buildings. In addition, calligraphy, floral motifs, and geometric forms decorate some editions of the Qur'an's pages, much as Christian monks once decorated hand-copied scrolls of the Bible. These elaborate designs can also be seen on some prayer rugs, and are characteristic of Islamic art in general.

Sacred Practices & Gestures

When Muslims pray, they must do so facing Mecca, a decision Muhammad made in January 624 CE. Prior to that time, Jerusalem—a holy city for both Jews and Christians—had been the geographic focus. Prayer involves a series of movements that embody submission to Allah.

Muslims sometimes use a strand of prayer beads, known as subhah, to pray the names of God. The beads can be made of bone, precious stones, or wood. Strings may have twenty-five, thirty-three or 100 beads.

Food Restrictions

Those who are physically able to do so fast from both food and drink during the daylight hours of the month Ramadan. Although fasting is not required of the sick, the aged, menstruating or pregnant women, or children, some children attempt to fast, imitating their parents' devotion. Those who cannot fast are encouraged to do so the following Ramadan. This fast is intended to concentrate the mind on Allah. Muslims recite from the Qur'an during the month.

All meat must be prepared in a particular way so that it is halal, or permitted. While slaughtering the animal, the person must mention the name of Allah. Blood, considered unclean, must be allowed to drain. Because pigs were fed garbage, their meat was considered unclean. Thus Muslims eat no pork, even though in modern times, pigs are often raised on grain.

In three different revelations, Muslims are also forbidden to consume fermented beverages. Losing self-control because of drunkenness violates the Islamic desire for self-mastery.

Rites, Celebrations, and Services

The **mosque** is the spiritual center of the Muslim community. From the minaret (a tower outside the mosque), the call to worship occurs five times daily—at dawn, just past noon, at midafternoon, at sunset, and in the evening. In earliest times, a muezzin, the official responsible for this duty, gave the cry. In many modern countries, the call now comes over a speaker system. Also located outside are fountains to provide the necessary water for ritual washing before prayer. Muslims wash their face, hands, forearms, and feet, as well as remove their shoes before beginning their prayers. In the absence of water, ritual cleansing may occur using sand or a stone.

Praying involves a series of movements known as rak'ah. From a standing position, the worshipper recites the opening sura of the Qur'an, as well as a second sura. After bowing to demonstrate respect, the person again stands, then prostrates himself or herself to signal humility. Next, the person assumes a sitting posture in silent prayer before again prostrating. The last movement is a greeting of "Peace be with you and the mercy of Allah." The worshipper looks both left and right before saying these words, which are intended for all persons, present and not.

Although Muslims stop to pray during each day when the call is given, Friday is the time for communal prayer and worship at the mosque. The prayer hall is the largest space within the mosque. At one end is a niche known as the mihrab, indicating the direction of Mecca, toward which Muslims face when they pray. At first, Muhammad instructed his followers to pray facing Jerusalem, as the Jewish people did. This early orientation was also a way to renounce the pagan associations of Mecca. Some mosques serve as community centers, with additional rooms for study.

The hajj, an important annual celebration, was a custom before the founding of Islam. Pagan worship centered in Mecca at the Ka'bah, where devotees circled the cube and kissed the Black Stone that was embedded in it. All warfare was forbidden during the hajj, as was argument, speaking crossly, or killing even an insect.

Muslims celebrate the lives of saints and their death anniversaries, a time when the saints are thought to reach the height of their spiritual life. Mawlid an-Nabi refers to "the birth of the Prophet." Although it is cultural and not rooted in the Qur'an, in some Muslim countries this is a public holiday on which people recite the Burdah, a poem that praises Muhammad. Muslims also celebrate the night that the Prophet ascended to heaven, Lailat ul-Miraj. The Night of Power is held to be the night on which Allah decides the destiny of people individually and the world at large.

Like Jews, Muslims practice circumcision, a ceremony known as khitan. Unlike Jews, however, Muslims do not remove the foreskin when the male is a baby. This is often done when a boy is about seven, and must be done before the boy reaches the age of twelve.

Healthy adult Muslims fast between sunrise and sunset during the month of Ramadan. This commemorates the first of Muhammad's revelations. In some Muslim countries, cannons are fired before the beginning of the month, as well as at the beginning and end of each day of the month. Some Muslims read a portion of the Qur'an each day during the month.

Judy A. Johnson, MTS

Bibliography

Al-Saud, Laith, Scott W. Hibbard, and Aminah Beverly. *An Introduction to Islam in the 21st Century*. Wiley, 2013. E-book.

Armstrong, Lyall. "The Rise of Islam: Traditional and Revisionist Theories." *Theological Review* 33.2 (2012): 87–106. Print.

Armstrong, Karen. *Islam: A Short History*. New York: Mod. Lib., 2000. Print.

Aslan, Reza. *No god but God: The Origins, Evolution, and Future of Islam*. New York: Random, 2005. Print.

Badawi, Emran El-. "'For All Times and Places': A Humanistic Reception of the Qur'an." *English Language Notes* 50.2 (2012): 99–112. Print.

Barnes, Trevor. *The Kingfisher Book of Religions*. New York: Kingfisher, 1999. Print.

Ben Jelloun, Tahar. *Islam Explained*. Trans. Franklin Philip. New York: New, 2002. Print.

Esposito, John L. *Islam: the Straight Path*. New York: Oxford UP, 1988. Print.

Glady, Pearl. *Criticism of Islam*.Library, 2012. E-book.

Holland, Tom. "Where Mystery Meets History." *History Today* 62.5 (2012): 19–24. Print.

Langley, Myrtle. *Religion*. New York: Knopf, 1996. Print.

Lunde, Paul. *Islam: Faith, Culture, History*. London: DK, 2002. Print.

Nasr, Seyyed Hossein. *Islam: Religion, History, and Civilization*. New York: Harper, 2002. Print.

Pasha, Mustapha Kamal. "Islam and the Postsecular." *Review of International Studies* 38.5 (2012): 1041–56. Print.

Sayers, Destini and Simone Peebles. *Essence of Islam and Sufism*. College, 2012. E-book.

Schirmacher, Christine. "They Are Not All Martyrs: Islam on the Topics of Dying, Death, and Salvation in the Afterlife." *Evangelical Review of Theology* 36.3 (2012): 250–65. Print.

Wilkinson, Philip. *Islam*. New York: DK, 2002. Print.

Wilkinson, Philip. *Religions*. New York: DK, 2008. Print.

Jainism

General Description

Jainism is one of the major religions of India. The name of the religion itself is believed to be based on the Sanskrit word *ji*, which means "to conquer or triumph," or *jina*, which means "victor or conqueror." The earliest name of the group was Nirgrantha, meaning bondless, but it applied to monks and nuns only. There are two sects: the Svetambaras (the white clad), which are the more numerous and wear white clothing, and the Digambaras (the sky clad), the most stringent group; their holy men or monks do not wear clothing at all.

Number of Adherents Worldwide

Jainism has about five million adherents, most of them in India (in some estimates, the religion represents approximately 1 percent of India's population). Because the religion is demanding in nature, few beyond the Indian subcontinent have embraced it. Jainism has spread to Africa, the United States, and nations in the Commonwealth (nations once under British rule) by virtue of Indian migration to these countries.

Basic Tenets

The principle of nonviolence (ahimsa) is a defining feature of Jainism. This results in a pacifist religion that influenced Mohandas Gandhi's ideas on nonviolent resistance. Jains believe that because all living creatures have souls, harming any of those creatures is wrong. They therefore follow a strict vegetarian diet, and often wear masks so as to not inhale living organisms. The most important aspect of Jainism is perhaps the five abstinences: ahimsa, satya (truthfulness), asteya (refrain from stealing), brahmacarya (chaste living), and aparigraha (refrain from greed).

A religion without priests, Jainism emphasizes the importance of the adherents' actions. Like Buddhists and Hindus, Jainists believe in karma and reincarnation. Unlike the Buddhist and Hindu idea of karma, Jainists regard karma as tiny particles that cling to the soul as mud clings to shoes, gradually weighing down the soul. Good deeds wash away these particles. Jainists also believe in moksha, the possibility of being freed from the cycle of death and rebirth. Like many Indian religions, Jainism does not believe in an afterlife, but in a cycle of death and rebirth. Once freed from this cycle, the soul will remain in infinite bliss.

While Jains do not necessarily believe in and worship God or gods, they believe in divine beings. Those who have achieved moksha are often regarded by Jains in the same manner in which other religions regard deities. These include the twenty-four Tirthankaras (ford makers) or jinas (victors), those who have escaped the cycle of death and rebirth, and the Siddhas, the liberated souls without physical form. The idea of a judging, ruling, or creator God is not present in Jainism.

Jainists believe that happiness is not found in material possessions and seek to have few of them. They also stress the importance of environmentalism. Jainists follow the Three Jewels: Right Belief, Right Knowledge, and Right Conduct. To be completely achieved, these three must be practiced together. Jainists also agree to six daily obligations (avashyaka), which include confession, praising the twenty-four Tirthankaras (the spiritual leaders), and calm meditation.

Sacred Text

The words of Mahavira were passed down orally, but lost over a few centuries. During a famine in the mid-fourth century BCE, many monks died. The texts were finally written down, although the Jain sects do not agree as to whether they are Mahavira's actual words. There are forty-five sacred texts (Agamas), which make up the Agam Sutras, Jainism's canonical literature. They were probably written down no earlier than 300 BCE. Two of the primary texts are the Akaranga

Sutra, which outlines the rule of conduct for Jain monks, and the Kalpa Sutra, which contains biographies of the last two Tirthankara. The Digambaras, who believe that the Agamas were lost around 350 BCE, have two main texts and four compendia written between 100 and 800 CE by various scholars.

Major Figures

Jainism has no single founder. However, Mahavira (Great Hero) is one of the Tirthankaras or jinas (pathfinders). He is considered the most recent spiritual teacher in a line of twenty-four. Modern-day Jainism derives from Mahavira, and his words are the foundation of Jain scriptures. He was a contemporary of Siddhartha Gautama, who was revered as the Buddha. Both Mahavira and Rishabha (or Adinatha), the first of the twenty-four Tirthankaras, are attributed as the founder of Jainism, though each Tirthankara maintains founding attributes.

Major Holy Sites

The Jain temple at Ranakpur is located in the village of Rajasthan. Carved from amber stone with marble interiors, the temple was constructed in the fifteenth century CE. It is dedicated to the first Tirthankara. The temple has twenty-nine large halls and each of the temple's 1,444 columns has a unique design with carvings.

Sravanabegola in Karnataka state is the site of Gomateshwara, Lord Bahubali's fifty-seven-foot statue. It was constructed in 981 CE from a single chunk of gneiss. Bahubali is considered the son of the first Tirthankara. The Digambara sect believes him to have been the first human to be free from the world.

Other pilgrimage sites include the Palitana temples in Gujarat and the Dilwara temples in Rajasthan. Sometimes regarded as the most sacred of the many Jain temples, the Palitana temples include 863 marble-engraved temples. The Jain temples at Dilwara were constructed of marble during the eleventh and thirteenth centuries CE. These five temples are often considered the most beautiful Jain temples in existence.

Major Rites & Celebrations

Every twelve years, the festival of Mahamastakabhisheka (anointing of the head) occurs at a statue of one of Jain's holy men, Bahubali, the second son of the first Tirthankara. The statue is anointed with milk, curd, and ghee, a clarified butter. Nearly a million people attend this rite. Jainists also observe Diwali, the Hindu festival of lights, as it symbolizes Mahavira's enlightenment.

The solemn festival of Paryusana marks the end of the Jain year for the Svetambaras (also spelled Shvetambaras). During this eight-day festival, all Jains are asked to live as an ascetic (monk or nun) would for one day. Das Laxana, a ten-day festival similar to that of Paryusana, immediately follows for the Digambara sect. During these special religious holidays, worshippers are involved in praying, meditating, fasting, forgiveness, and acts of penance. These holy days are celebrated during August and September, which is monsoon season in India. During the monsoons, monks prefer to remain in one place so as to avoid killing the smallest insects that appear during the rainy season. The Kalpa Sutra, one of the Jain scriptures, is read in the morning during Paryusana.

The feast of Kartaki Purnima follows the four months of the rainy season. It is held in the first month (Kartik) according to one calendar, and marked by a pilgrimage to the Palitana temples. Doing so with a pure heart is said to remove all sins of both the present and past life. Those who do so are thought to receive the final salvation in the third or fifth birth.

ORIGINS

History & Geography

In the eastern basin of the Ganges River during the seventh century BCE, a teacher named Parshvanatha (or Parshva) gathered a community founded on abandoning earthly concerns. He is considered to be the twenty-third Tirthankara (ford-maker), the one who makes a path for salvation. During the following century, Vardhamana, called Mahavira (Great Hero), who was considered the twenty-fourth and final spiritual teacher of the age, formulated most Jain doctrine and practice. By the time of Mahavira's death, Jains numbered around 36,000 nuns and 14,000 monks.

A division occurred within Jainism during the fourth century CE. The most extreme ascetics, the Digambaras (the sky-clad), argued that even clothing showed too great an attachment to the world, and that laundering them in the river risked harming creatures. This argument applied only to men, as the Digambaras denied that a soul could be freed from a woman's body. The other group, the Svetambaras (the white-clad), believed that purity resided in the mind.

In 453 or 456 CE, a council of the Svetambara sect at Saurashtra in western India codified the canon still used. The split between the Digambaras, who did not take part in the meeting, and Svetambaras thus became permanent. Despite the split, Jainism's greatest flowering occurred during the early medieval age. After that time, Hindu sects devoted to the Hindu gods of Vishnu and Shiva flourished under the Gupta Empire (often referred to as India's golden age), slowing the spread of Jainism. Followers migrated to western and central India and the community became stronger.

The Digambaras were involved in politics through several medieval dynasties, and some Jain monks served as spiritual advisers. Royalty and high-ranking officials contributed to the building and maintenance of temples. Both branches of Jainism contributed a substantial literature. In the late medieval age, Jain monks ceased to live as ascetic wanders. They chose instead to don orange robes and to live at temples and other holy places.

The Muslims invaded India in the twelfth century. The Jains lost power and fractured over the next centuries into subgroups, some of which repudiated the worship of images. The poet and Digambara layman Banarsidas (1586-1643) played a significant role in a reform movement during the early 1600s. These reforms focused on the mystical side of Jainism, such as spiritual exploration of the inner self (meditation),

and denounced the formalized temple ritual. The movement, known as the Adhyatma movement, resulted in the Digambara Terapanth, a small Digambara sect.

The Jainists were well positioned in society following the departure of the British from India. Having long been associated with the artisan and merchant classes, they found new opportunities. As traditional Indian studies grew, spurred by Western interest, proponents of Jainism began to found publications and places of study (In fact, Jain libraries are believed to be the oldest in India.) The first Jain temple outside India was consecrated in Britain during the 1960s after Jains had gone there in the wake of political turmoil.

The Jains follow their typical profession as merchants. They publish English-language periodicals to spread their ideas on vegetarianism, environmentalism, and nonviolence (ahimsa). The ideas of ahimsa were formative for Mohandas Gandhi, born a Hindu. Gandhi used nonviolence as a wedge against the British Empire in India. Eventually, the British granted independence to India in 1947.

Virchand Gandhi (1864–1901) is believed to be the first Jain to arrive in America when he came over in 1893. He attended the first Parliament of World Religions, held in Chicago. Today North America has more than ninety Jain temples and centers. Jains in the West often follow professions such as banking and business to avoid destroying animal or plant life.

Founder or Major Prophet

Mahavira was born in India's Ganges Basin region. By tradition, he was born around 599 BCE, although some scholars think he may have lived a century later. His story bears a resemblance to that of the Buddha, with whom he was believed to have been a contemporary. His family was also of the Kshatriya (warrior) caste, and his father was a ruler of his clan. One tradition states that Mahavira's mother was of the Brahman (priestly) caste, although another places her in the Kshatriya.

Because he was not the eldest son, Mahavira was not in line for leadership of the clan.

He married a woman of his own caste and they had a daughter. Mahavira chose the life of a monk, with one garment. Later, he gave up wearing even that. He became a wandering ascetic around age thirty, with some legends stating that he tore out his hair before leaving home. He sought shelter in burial grounds and cremation sites, as well as at the base of trees. During the rainy season, however, he lived in towns and villages.

He followed a path of preaching and self-denial, after which he was enlightened (kevala). He spent the next thirty years teaching. Eleven disciples, all of whom were of the Brahman caste, gathered around him. At the end of his life, Mahavira committed Santhara, or ritual suicide through fasting.

Philosophical Basis

Like Buddhists and the Brahmin priests, the Jains believe in human incarnations of God, known as avatars. These avatars appear at the end of a time of decline to reinstate proper thinking and acting. Such a person was Mahavira. At the time of Mahavira's birth, India was experiencing great societal upheaval. Members of the warrior caste opposed the priestly caste, which exercised authority based on its supposed greater moral purity. Many people also opposed the slaughter of animals for the Vedic sacrifices.

Jainists share some beliefs with both Hinduism and Buddhism. The Hindu hero Rama, for example, is co-opted as a nonviolent Jain, while the deity Krishna is considered a cousin of Arishtanemi, the twenty-second Tirthankara. Like Buddhism, Jainism uses a wheel with twelve spokes; however, Jainism uses the wheel to explain time. The first half of the circle is the ascending stage, in which human happiness, prosperity, and life span increase. The latter half of the circle is the descending stage, involving a decrease of life span, prosperity, and happiness. The wheel of time is always in motion.

For Jainists, the universe is without beginning or ending, and contains layers of both heaven and hell. These layers include space beyond, which is without time, matter, or soul. The cosmos is depicted in art as a large human. The cloud layers surrounding the upper world are called universe space. Above them is the base, Nigoda, where lowest life forms live. The netherworld contains seven hells, each with a different stage of punishment and misery. The middle world contains the earth and remainder of the universe—mankind is located near the waist. There are thirty heavens in the upper world, where heavenly beings reside. In the supreme abode at the apex of the universe, liberated souls (siddha) live.

Jainism teaches that there are six universal entities. Only consciousness or soul is a living substance, while the remaining five are non-living. They include matter, medium of rest, medium of motion, time, and space. Jainism also does not believe in a God who can create, destroy, or protect. Worshipping goddesses and gods to achieve personal gain or material benefit is deemed useless.

Mahavira outlined five basic principles (often referred to as abstinences) for Jainist life, based on the teachings of the previous Tirthankara. They are detachment (aparigraha); the conduct of soul, primarily in sexual morality (brahmacharya); abstinence from stealing (asteya); abstinence from lying (satya); and nonviolence in every realm of the person (ahimsa).

Like other Indian religions, Jainism perceives life as four stages. The life of a student is brahmacharya-ashrama; the stage of family life is gruhasth-ashrama; in vanaprasth-ashrama, the Jainist concentrates on both family and aiding others through social services; and the final stage is sanyast-ashrama, a time of renouncing the world and becoming a monk.

Like many religions, Jainism has a bias toward males and toward the rigorous life of monks and nuns. A layperson cannot work off bad karma, but merely keeps new bad karma from accruing. By following a path of asceticism, however, monks and nuns can destroy karma. Even members of the laity follow eight rules of behavior and take twelve vows. Physical austerity is a key concept in Jainism, as a saint's highest ideal is to starve to death.

Holy Places

There are four major Jain pilgrimage sites: the Dilwara temples near Rajasthan; the Palitana temples; the Ranakpur temple; and Shravan Begola, the site of the statue of Lord Bahubali. In addition, Jains may make pilgrimages to the caves of Khandagiri and Udayagiri, which were cells for Jain monks carved from rock. The spaces carved are too short for a man to stand upright. They were essentially designed for prayer and meditation. Udayagiri has eighteen caves and Khandagiri has fifteen. The caves are decorated with elaborate carvings.

JAINISM IN DEPTH

Sacred Symbols

The open palm (Jain Hand) with a centered wheel, sometimes with the word *ahimsa* written on it, is a prominent Jain symbol. Seen as an icon of peace, the open palm symbol can be interpreted as a call to stop violence, and also means "assurance." It appears on the walls of Jain temples and in their publications. Jainism also employs a simple swastika symbol, considered to be the holiest symbol. It represents the four forms of worldly existence, and three dots above the swastika represent the Three Jewels. The Jain emblem, adopted in 1975, features both the Jain Hand (the open palm symbol with an inset wheel) and a swastika. This year was regarded as the 2,500th anniversary of Mahavira being enlightened.

Sacred Practices & Gestures

Jains may worship daily in their homes at private shrines. The Five Supreme Beings stand for stages in the path to enlightenment. Rising before daybreak, worshippers invoke these five. In addition, devout Jainists set aside forty-eight minutes daily to meditate.

To demonstrate faithfulness to the five vows that Jains undertake, there are four virtuous qualities that must be cultivated. They are compassion (karuna), respect and joy (pramoda), love and friendship (maitri), and indifference toward and noninvolvement with those who are arrogant

(madhyastha). Mahavira stressed that Jains must be friends to all living beings. Compassion goes beyond mere feeling; it involves offering both material and spiritual aid. Pramoda carries with it the idea of rejoicing enthusiastically over the virtues of others. There are contemplations associated with these virtues, and daily practice is suggested to attain mastery.

Some Jainists, both men and women, wear a dot on the forehead. This practice comes from Hinduism. During festivals, Jains may pray, chant, fast, or keep silent. These actions are seen as removing bad karma from the soul and moving the person toward ultimate happiness.

Food Restrictions

Jainists practice a strict vegetarian way of life (called Jain vegetarianism) to avoid harming any creature. They refuse to eat root vegetables, because by uprooting them, the entire plant dies. They prefer to wait for fruit to drop from trees rather than taking it from the branches. Starving to death, when ready, is seen as an ideal.

Rites, Celebrations & Services

Some festivals are held annually and their observances are based on a lunar calendar. Mahavir Jayanti is an example, as it celebrates Mahavira's birthday.

Jains may worship, bathe, and make offerings to images of the Tirthankaras in their home or in a temple. Svetambaras Jains also clothe and decorate the images. Because the Tirthankaras have been liberated, they cannot respond as a deity granting favors might. Although Jainism rejects belief in gods in favor of worshipping Tirthankaras, in actual practice, some Jainists pray to Hindu gods.

When Svetambara monks are initiated, they are given three pieces of clothing, including a small piece of white cloth to place over the mouth. The cloth, called a mukhavastrika, is designed to prevent the monk from accidentally eating insects.

Monks take great vows (mahavratas) at initiation. These include abstaining from lying, stealing, sexual activity, injury to any living thing, and personal possessions. Monks own a broom to sweep in front of where they are going to walk so that no small creatures are injured, along with an alms bowl and a robe. The Digambara monks practice a more stringent lifestyle, eating one meal a day, for which they beg.

Nuns in the Svetambaras are three times more common than are monks, even though they receive less honor, and are required to defer to the monks. In Digambara Jainism, the nuns wear robes and accept that they must be reborn as men before progressing upward.

The observance of Santhara, which is religious fasting until death, is a voluntary fasting undertaken with full knowledge. The ritual is also known as Sallekhana, and is not perceived as suicide by Jains, particularly as the prolonged nature of the ritual provides ample time for reflection. It is believed that at least one hundred people die every year from observing Santhara.

Judy A. Johnson, MTS

Bibliography

Aristarkhova, Irina. "Thou Shall Not Harm All Living Beings: Feminism, Jainism, and Animals." *Hypatia* 27.3 (2012): 636–50. Print.

Aukland, Knut. "Understanding Possession in Jainism: A Study of Oracular Possession in Nakoda." *Modern Asian Studies* 47.1 (2013): 103–34. Print.

Barnes, Trevor. *The Kingfisher Book of Religions*. New York: Kingfisher, 1999. Print.

Langley, Myrtle. *Religion*. New York: Knopf, 1996. Print.

Long, Jeffery. *Jainism: An Introduction*. London: I. B. Tauris, 2009. Print.

Long, Jeffrey. "Jainism: Key Themes." *Religion Compass* 5.9 (2011): 501–10. Print.

Rankin, Aidan. *The Jain Path*. Berkeley: O Books, 2006. Print.

Shah, Bharat S. *An Introduction to Jainism*. Great Neck: Setubandh, 2002. Print.

Titze, Kurt. *Jainism: A Pictorial Guide to the Religion of Non-Violence*. Delhi: Motilal Banarsidass, 2001. Print.

Tobias, Michael. *Life Force: the World of Jainism*. Berkeley:Asian Humanities, 1991. E-book, print.

Wiley, Kristi L. *The A to Z of Jainism*. Lanham: Scarecrow, 2009. Print.

Wiley, Kristi L. *Historical Dictionary of Jainism*. Lanham: Scarecrow, 2004. Print.

Wilkinson, Philip. *Religions*. New York: DK, 2008. Print.

Judaism

General Description

In modern Judaism, the main denominations (referred to as movements) are Orthodox Judaism (including Haredi and Hasidic Judaism); Conservative Judaism; Reform (Liberal) Judaism; Reconstructionist Judaism; and to a lesser extent, Humanistic Judaism. In addition, the Jewry of Ethiopia and Yemen are known for having distinct or alternative traditions. Classical Judaism is often organized by two branches: Ashkenazic (Northern Europe) and Sephardic Jews (Spain, Portugal, and North Africa).

Number of Adherents Worldwide

Judaism has an estimated 15 million adherents worldwide, with roughly 41 percent living in Israel and about 41 percent living in the United States. Ashkenazi Jews represent roughly 75 percent, while Sephardic Jews represent roughly 25 percent, with the remaining 5 percent split among alternative communities. Within the United States, a 2000-01 survey stated that 10 percent of American Jews identified as Orthodox (with that number increasing), 35 percent as Reform, 26 percent as Conservative, leaving the remainder with an alternative or no affiliation. [Source: Wilkinson, 2008]

Orthodox Judaism, which was founded around the thirteenth century BCE, has 3 million followers. Members of Reform Judaism, with roots in nineteenth-century Germany, wanted to live peacefully with non-Jews. Therefore, they left the laws that prevented this vision of peace and downplayed the idea of a Jewish state. Reform Judaism, also known as Progressive or Liberal Judaism, allows women rabbis and does not require its adherents to keep kosher. About 1.1 million Jews are Reform; they live primarily in the United States. When nonkosher food was served at the first graduation ceremony for Hebrew Union College, some felt that the Reform movement had gone too far. Thus the Conservative movement began in 1887. A group of rabbis founded the Jewish Theological Seminary in New York City, wanting to emphasize biblical authority above moral choice, as the Reform tradition stressed. Currently about 900,000 Jews practice this type of Judaism, which is theologically midway between Orthodox and Reform. The Hasidim, an ultra-conservative group, began in present-day Ukraine around 1740. There are 4.5 million Hasidic Jews.

Basic Tenets

Though there is no formal creed (statement of faith or belief), Jews value all life, social justice, education, generous giving, and the importance of living based on the principles and values espoused in the Torah (Jewish holy book). They believe in one all-powerful and creator God, Jehovah or Yaweh, a word derived from the Hebrew letters "YHWH," the unpronounceable name of God. The word is held to be sacred; copyists were required to bathe both before and after writing the word. Jews also believe in a coming Messiah who will initiate a Kingdom of Righteousness. They follow a complex law, composed of 613 commandments or mitzvot. Jews believe that they are God's Chosen People with a unique covenant relationship. They have a responsibility to practice hospitality and to improve the world.

The belief in the afterlife is a part of the Jewish faith. Similar to Christianity, this spiritual world is granted to those who abide by the Jewish faith and live a good life. Righteous Jews are rewarded in the afterlife by being able to discuss the Torah with Moses, who first received the law from God. Furthermore, certain Orthodox sects believe that wicked souls are destroyed or tormented after death.

Sacred Text

The complete Hebrew Bible is called the Tanakh. It includes the prophetic texts, called the Navi'im, the poetic writings, the Ketubim, and the Torah, meaning teaching, law, or guidance. Torah may refer to the entire body of Jewish law or to the first five books of the Hebrew Bible, known as the Pentateuch (it is the Old Testament in the Christian Bible). Also esteemed is the Talmud, made up of the Mishnah, a written collection of oral traditions, and Gemara, a commentary on the Mishnah. The Talmud covers many different subjects, such as law, stories and legends, medicine, and rituals.

Major Figures

The patriarchs are held to be the fathers of the faith. Abraham, the first patriarch, was called to leave his home in the Fertile Crescent for a land God would give him, and promised descendents as numerous as the stars. His son Isaac was followed by Jacob, whom God renamed Israel, and whose twelve sons became the heads of the twelve tribes of Israel. Moses was the man who, along with his brother Aaron, the founder of a priestly line, and their sister Miriam led the chosen people out of slavery in Egypt, where they had gone to escape famine. The Hebrew Bible also details the careers of a group of men and women known as judges, who were really tribal rulers, as well as of the prophets, who called the people to holy lives. Chief among the prophets was Elijah, who confronted wicked kings and performed many miracles. Several kings were key to the biblical narrative, among them David, who killed the giant Goliath, and Solomon, known for his wisdom and for the construction of a beautiful temple.

Major Holy Sites

Most of Judaism's holy sites are within Israel, the Holy Land, including Jerusalem, which was the capital of the United Kingdom of Israel under kings David and Solomon; David captured it from a Canaanite tribe around 1000 BCE. Within the Old City of Jerusalem is the Temple Mount (where the Temple of Jerusalem was built), often considered the religion's holiest site, the Foundation Stone (from which Judaism claims the world was created), and the Western (or Wailing) Wall. Other sites include Mount Sinai

in Egypt, the mountain upon which God gave Moses his laws.

Major Rites & Celebrations

The Jewish calendar recognizes several important holidays. Rosh Hashanah, literally "first of the year," is known as the Jewish New Year and inaugurates a season of self-examination and repentance that culminates in Yom Kippur, the Day of Atonement. Each spring, Passover commemorates the deliverance of the Hebrew people from Egypt. Shavuot celebrates the giving of the Torah to Moses, while Sukkot is the harvest festival. Festivals celebrating deliverance from enemies include Purim and Hanukkah. Young adolescents become members of the community at a bar or bat mitzvah, held near the twelfth or thirteenth birthday. The Sabbath, a cessation from work from Friday at sundown until Saturday when the first star appears, gives each week a rhythm.

ORIGINS

History & Geography

Called by God perhaps four thousand years ago, Abraham left from Ur of the Chaldees, or the Fertile Crescent in Mesopotamia in present-day Iraq, to go the eastern Mediterranean, the land of Canaan. Several generations later, the tribe went to Egypt to escape famine. They were later enslaved by a pharaoh, sometimes believed to have been Ramses II (ca. 1279–1213 BCE), who was noted for his many building projects. The Israelites returned to Canaan under Moses several hundred years after their arrival in Egypt. He was given the law, the Ten Commandments, plus the rest of the laws governing all aspects of life, on Mount Sinai about the thirteenth century BCE. This marked the beginning of a special covenant relationship between the new nation, known as Israel, and God.

Following a period of rule by judges, kings governed the nation. Major kings included David, son-in-law to the first king, Saul, and David's son, Solomon. The kingdom split at the beginning of the reign of Solomon's son

Rehoboam, who began ruling about 930 BCE. Rehoboam retained the ten northern tribes, while the two southern tribes followed a military commander rather than the Davidic line.

Rehoboam's kingdom was known as Israel, after the name Jehovah gave to Jacob. Judah was the name of the southern kingdom—one of Jacob's sons was named Judah. Prophets to both nations warned of coming judgment unless the people repented of mistreating the poor and other sins, such as idolatry. Unheeding, Israel was taken into captivity by the Assyrians in 722 BCE. and the Israelites assimilated into the nations around them.

The Babylonians captured Judah in 586 BCE. After Babylon had been captured in turn by Persians, the Jewish people were allowed to return to the land in 538 BCE. There they began reconstructing the temple and the walls of the city. In the second century BCE, Judas Maccabeus led a rebellion against the heavy taxes and oppression of the Greek conquerors, after they had levied high taxes and appointed priests who were not Jewish. Judas Maccabeus founded a new ruling dynasty, the Hasmoneans, which existed briefly before the region came under the control of Rome.

The Jewish people revolted against Roman rule in 70 CE, leading to the destruction of the second temple. The final destruction of Jerusalem occurred in 135 under the Roman Emperor Hadrian. He changed the city's name to Aelia Capitolina and the name of the country to Palaestina. With the cultic center of their religion gone, the religious leaders developed new methods of worship that centered in religious academies and in synagogues.

After Christianity became the official state religion of the Roman Empire in the early fourth century, Jews experienced persecution. They became known for their scholarship, trade, and banking over the next centuries, with periods of brutal persecution in Europe. Christians held Jews responsible for the death of Jesus, based on a passage in the New Testament. The Blood Libel, begun in England in 1144, falsely accused Jews of killing a Christian child to bake unleavened bread for Passover. This rumor persisted for centuries, and was repeated by Martin Luther during the Protestant Reformation. England expelled all Jews in 1290; they were not readmitted until 1656 under Oliver Cromwell, and not given citizenship until 1829. Jews were also held responsible for other catastrophes—namely poisoning wells and rivers to cause the Black Death in 1348—and were often made to wear special clothing, such as pointed hats, or badges with the Star of David or stone tablets on them.

The relationship between Muslims and Jews was more harmonious. During the Muslim Arab dominance, there was a "golden age" in Spain due to the contributions of Jews and Muslims, known as Moors in Spain. This ideal and harmonious period ended in 1492, when both Moors and Jews were expelled from Spain or forced to convert to Christianity.

Jews in Russia suffered as well. An estimated two million Jews fled the country to escape the pogroms (a Russian word meaning devastation) between 1881 and 1917. The twentieth-century Holocaust, in which an estimated six million Jews perished at the hands of Nazi Germany, was but the culmination of these centuries of persecution. The Nazis also destroyed more than six hundred synagogues.

The Holocaust gave impetus to the creation of the independent state of Israel. The Zionist movement, which called for the founding or reestablishment of a Jewish homeland, was started by Austrian Jew Theodor Herzl in the late nineteenth century, and succeeded in 1948. The British government, which had ruled the region under a mandate, left the area, and Israel was thus established. This ended the Diaspora, or dispersion, of the Jewish people that had begun nearly two millennia before when the Romans forced the Jews to leave their homeland.

Arab neighbors, some of whom had been removed forcibly from the land to create the nation of Israel, were displeased with the new political reality. Several wars have been fought, including the War of Independence in 1948, the Six-Day War in 1967, and the Yom Kippur War in 1973. In addition, tension between Israel and its neighboring Arab states is almost constant.

When the Jewish people were dispersed from Israel, two traditions began. The Ashkenazi Jews settled in Germany and central Europe. They spoke a mixture of the Hebrew dialect and German called Yiddish. Sephardic Jews lived in the Mediterranean countries, including Spain; their language, Ladino, mixed Hebrew and old Spanish.

Founder or Major Prophet

Judaism refers to three major patriarchs: Abraham, his son Isaac, and Isaac's son Jacob. Abraham is considered the first Jew and worshipper in Judaism, as the religion began through his covenant with God. As the forefather of the religion, he is often associated as the founder, though the founder technically is God, or Yahweh (YHWH). Additionally, the twelve sons of Jacob, who was also named Israel, became the founders of the twelve tribes of Israel.

Moses is regarded as a major prophet and as the Lawgiver. God revealed to Moses the complete law during the forty days that the Jewish leader spent on Mount Sinai during the wilderness journey from Egypt to Canaan. Thus, many attribute Moses as the founder of Judaism as a religion.

Philosophical Basis

Judaism began with Abraham's dissatisfaction with the polytheistic worship of his culture. Hearing the command of God to go to a land that would be shown to him, Abraham and his household obeyed. Abraham practiced circumcision and hospitality, cornerstones of the Jewish faith to this day. He and his descendents practiced a nomadic life, much like that of contemporary Bedouins. They migrated from one oasis or well to another, seeking pasture and water for the sheep and goats they herded.

The further development of Judaism came under the leadership of Moses. A Jewish child adopted by Pharaoh's daughter, he was raised and educated in the palace. As a man, he identified with the Jewish people, killing one of the Egyptians who was oppressing a Jew. He subsequently fled for his life, becoming a shepherd in the wilderness, where he remained for forty years. Called by God from a bush that burned but was not destroyed, he was commissioned to lead the people out of slavery in Egypt back to the Promised Land. That forty-year pilgrimage in the wilderness and desert of Arabia shaped the new nation.

Holy Places

The city of Jerusalem was first known as Salem. When King David overcame the Jebusites who lived there, the city, already some two thousand years old, became the capital of Israel. It is built on Mount Zion, which is still considered a sacred place. David's son Solomon built the First Temple in Jerusalem, centering the nation's spiritual as well as political life in the city. The Babylonians captured the city in 597 BCE and destroyed the Temple. For the next sixty years, the Jews remained in exile, until Cyrus the Persian conqueror of Babylon allowed them to return. They rebuilt the temple, but it was desecrated by Antiochus IV of Syria in 167 BCE. In 18 BCE, during a period of Roman occupation, Herod the Great began rebuilding and expanding the Temple. The Romans under the general Titus destroyed the Temple in 70 CE, just seven years after its completion.

The city eventually came under the rule of Persia, the Muslim Empire, and the Crusaders before coming under control of Britain. In 1948 an independent state of Israel was created. The following year, Jerusalem was divided between Israel, which made the western part the national capital, and Jordan, which ruled the eastern part of the city. The Western or Wailing Wall, a retaining wall built during Herod's time, is all that remains of the Second Temple. Devout Jews still come to the Wailing Wall to pray, sometimes placing their petitions on paper and folding the paper into the Wall's crevices. The Wall is known as a place where prayers are answered and a reminder of the perseverance of the Jewish people and faith. According to tradition, the Temple will be rebuilt when Messiah comes to inaugurate God's Kingdom.

The Temple Mount, located just outside Jerusalem on a natural acropolis, includes the Dome of the Rock. This shrine houses a rock held sacred by both Judaism and Islam. Jewish tradition states that it is the spot from which the world was created and the spot on which Abraham was asked to sacrifice his son Isaac. Muslims believe that from this rock Muhammad ascended for his night journey to heaven. Much of Jerusalem, including this holy site, has been and continues to be fought over by people of three faiths: Judaism, Islam, and Christianity.

Moses received the law from God on Mount Sinai. It is still regarded as a holy place.

JUDAISM IN DEPTH

Sacred Symbols

Observant Jewish men pray three times daily at home or in a synagogue, a center of worship, from the word meaning "meeting place." They wear a tallis, or a prayer shawl with tassles, during their morning prayer and on Yom Kippur, the Day of Atonement. They may also cover their heads as a sign of respect during prayer, wearing a skullcap known as a kippah or yarmulka. They find their prayers and blessings in a siddur, which literally means "order," because the prayers appear in the order in which they are recited for services. Jewish daily life also includes blessings for many things, including food.

Tefillin or phylacteries are the small black boxes made of leather from kosher animals that Jewish men wear on their foreheads and their left upper arms during prayer. They contain passages from the Torah. Placing the tefillin on the head reminds them to think about the Torah, while placing the box on the arm puts the Torah close to the heart.

The Law of Moses commands the people to remember the words of the law and to teach them to the children. A mezuzah helps to fulfill that command. A small box with some of the words of the law written on a scroll inside, a mezuzah is hung on the doorframes of every door in the house. Most often, the words of the Shema,

the Jewish recitation of faith, are written on the scroll. The Shema is repeated daily. "Hear, O Israel: the Lord your God, the Lord is one. . . . Love the Lord your God with all your heart, and with all your soul, and with all your might."

Jews adopted the Star of David, composed of two intersecting triangles, during the eighteenth century. There are several interpretations of the design. One is that it is the shape of King David's shield. Another idea is that it stands for daleth, the first letter of David's name. A third interpretation is that the six points refer to the days of the work week, and the inner, larger space represented the day of rest, the Sabbath, or Shabot. The Star of David appears on the flag of Israel. The flag itself is white, symbolizing peace and purity, and blue, symbolizing heaven and reminding all of God's activity.

The menorah is a seven-branch candlestick representing the light of the Torah. For Hanukkah, however, an eight-branched menorah is used. The extra candle is the servant candle, and is the one from which all others are lit.

Because the Torah is the crowning glory of life for Jewish people, a crown is sometimes used on coverings for the Torah. The scrolls of Torah are stored in a container, called an ark, which generally is covered with an ornate cloth called a mantle. The ark and mantle are often elaborately decorated with symbols, such as the lion of Judah. Because the Torah scroll, made of parchment from a kosher animal, is sacred and its pages are not to be touched, readers use a pointed stick called a yad. Even today, Torahs are written by hand in specially prepared ink and using a quill from a kosher bird. Scribes are trained for seven years.

A shofar is a ram's horn, blown as a call to repentance on Rosh Hashanah, the Jewish New Year. This holiday is the beginning of a ten-day preparation for the Day of Atonement, which is the most holy day in the Jewish calendar and a time of both fasting and repentance.

Sacred Practices & Gestures

Sacred practices can apply daily, weekly, annually, or over a lifetime's events. Reciting the Shema, the monotheistic creed taken from the

Torah, is a daily event. Keeping the Sabbath occurs weekly. Each year the festivals described above take place. Circumcision and bar or bat mitzvah are once-in-a-lifetime events. Each time someone dies, the mourners recite the Kaddish for seven days following death, and grieve for a year.

Food Restrictions

Kosher foods are those that can be eaten based on Jewish law. Animals that chew the cud and have cloven hooves, such as cows and lamb, and domestic poultry are considered kosher. Shellfish, pork, and birds of prey are forbidden. Keeping kosher also includes the method of preparing and storing the food. This includes animals which are slaughtered in a way to bring the least amount of pain and from which all blood is drained. In addition, dairy and meat products are to be kept separate, requiring separate refrigerators in the homes of the Orthodox.

Rites, Celebrations & Services

Sabbath is the weekly celebration honoring one of the Ten Commandments, which commands the people to honor the Sabbath by doing no work that day. The practice is rooted in the Genesis account that God rested on the seventh day after creating the world in six days. Because the Jewish day begins at sundown, the Sabbath lasts from Friday night to Saturday night. Special candles are lit and special food—included the braided egg bread called challah—for the evening meal is served. This day is filled with feasting, visiting, and worship.

Boys are circumcised at eight days of age. This rite, B'rit Milah, meaning "seal of the covenant," was first given to Abraham as a sign of the covenant. A trained circumciser, or mohel, may be a doctor or rabbi. The boy's name is officially announced at the ceremony. A girl's name is given at a special baby-naming ceremony or in the synagogue on the first Sabbath after she is born.

A boy becomes a "son of the commandment," or bar mitzvah, at age thirteen. At a special ceremony, the young man reads a portion of

Torah that he has prepared ahead of time. Most boys also give a speech at the service. Girls become bat mitzvah at age twelve. This ceremony developed in the twentieth century. Not all Orthodox communities will allow this rite. Girls may also read from the Torah and give a sermon in the synagogue, just as boys do.

When a Jewish person dies, mourners begin shiva, a seven-day mourning period. People usually gather at the home of the deceased, where mirrors are covered. In the home, the Kaddish, a collection of prayers that praise God and celebrate life, is recited. Traditionally, family members mourn for a full year, avoiding parties and festive occasions.

The Jewish calendar offers a series of feasts and festivals, beginning with Rosh Hashanah, the Jewish New Year. At this time, Jews recall the creation. They may also eat apples that have been dipped into honey and offer each other wishes for a sweet New Year. The next ten days are a time of reflection on the past year, preparing for Yom Kippur.

This Day of Atonement once included animal sacrifice at the Temple. Now it includes an all-day service at the synagogue and a twenty-five-hour fast. A ram's horn, called a shofar, is blown as a call to awaken to lead a holier life. The shofar reminds Jewish people of the ram that Abraham sacrificed in the place of his son, Isaac.

Passover, or Pesach, is the spring remembrance of God's deliverance of the people from slavery in Egypt. In the night that the Jewish people left Egypt, they were commanded to sacrifice a lamb for each household and sprinkle the blood on the lintels and doorposts. A destroying angel from God would "pass over" the homes with blood sprinkled. During the first two nights of Passover, a special meal is served known as a Seder, meaning order. The foods symbolize different aspects of the story of deliverance, which is told during the meal by the head of the family.

Shavuot has its origins as a harvest festival. This celebration of Moses receiving the Torah on Mount Sinai occurs fifty days after the second day of Passover. To welcome the first fruits of the season, the synagogue may be decorated with fruit and flowers. Traditionally, the Ten Commandments are read aloud in the synagogue.

Purim, which occurs in February or March, celebrates the deliverance of the Jews during their captivity in Persia in the fifth century BCE. The events of that experience are recorded in the Book of Esther in the Hebrew Bible (Tanakh). The book is read aloud during Purim.

Sukkot, the feast celebrating the end of the harvest, occurs in September or October. Jews recall God's provision for them in the wilderness when they left Egypt to return to Canaan. Traditionally, huts are made and decorated with flowers and fruits. The conclusion of Sukkot is marked by a synagogue service known as Simchat Torah, or Rejoicing in the Law. People sing and dance as the Torah scrolls are carried and passed from person to person.

Hanukkah, known as the Festival of Lights, takes place over eight days in December. It celebrates the rededicating of the Temple under the leader Judas Maccabeus, who led the people in recapturing the structure from Syria in 164 BCE. According to the story, the Jews had only enough oil in the Temple lamp to last one day, but the oil miraculously lasted for eight days, after which Judas Maccabeus re-dedicated the Temple. On each day of Hanukkah, one of the eight candles is lit until all are burning. The gift-giving custom associated with Hanukkah is relatively new, and may derive from traditional small gifts of candy or money. The practice may also have been encouraged among those integrated with communities that exchange gifts during the Christmas season.

Judy A. Johnson, MTS

Bibliography

Barnes, Trevor. *The Kingfisher Book of Religions*. New York: Kingfisher, 1999. Print.

"A Buffet to Suit All Tastes." *Economist* 28 Jul. 2012: Spec. section 4–6. Print.

Charing, Douglas. *Judaism*. London: DK, 2003. Print.

Coenen Snyder, Saskia. *Building a Public Judaism: Synagogues and Jewish Identity in Nineteenth-Century Europe*. Cambridge: Harvard UP, 2013. E-book.

Diamant, Anita. *Living a Jewish Life*. New York: Collins, 1996. Print.

Exler, Lisa and Rabbi Jill Jacobs. "A Judaism That Matters." *Journal of Jewish Communal Service* 87.1/2 (2012): 66–76. Print.

Gelernter, David Hillel. *Judaism: A Way of Being*. New Haven: Yale UP, 2009. E-book.

Kessler, Edward. *What Do Jews Believe?* New York: Walker, 2007. Print.

Krieger, Aliza Y. "The Role of Judaism in Family Relationships." *Journal of Multicultural Counseling & Development* 38.3 (2010): 154–65. Print.

Langley, Myrtle. *Religion*. New York: Knopf, 1996. Print.

Madsen, Catherine. "A Heart of Flesh: Beyond 'Creative Liturgy.'" *Cross Currents* 62.1 (2012): 11–20. Print.

Meredith, Susan. *The Usborne Book of World Religions*. London: Usborne, 1995. Print.

Schoen, Robert. *What I Wish My Christian Friends Knew About Judaism*. Chicago: Loyola, 2004. Print.

Stefnon, Matt. *Judaism: History, Belief, and Practice*. New York: Britannica Educational, 2012. E-book.

Wertheimer, Jack. "The Perplexities of Conservative Judaism." *Commentary* Sept. 2007: 38–44. Print.

Wilkinson, Philip. *Religions*. New York: DK, 2008. Print.

Sikhism

General Description

The youngest of the world religions, Sikhism has existed for only about five hundred years. Sikhism derives from the Sanskrit word *sishyas*, which means "disciple"; in the Punjabi language, it also means "disciple."

Number of Adherents Worldwide

An estimated 24.5 million people follow the Sikh religion. Most of the devotees live in Asia, particularly in the Punjab region of India (Wilkinson, p. 335).

Basic Tenets

Sikhism is a monotheistic religion. The deity is God, known as Nam, or Name. Other synonyms include the Divine, Ultimate, Ultimate Reality, Infinity, the Formless, Truth, and other attributes of God.

Sikhs adhere to three basic principles. These are hard work (kirt kao), worshipping the Divine Name (nam japo), and sharing what one has (vand cauko). Meditating on the Divine Name is seen as a method of moving toward a life totally devoted to God. In addition, Sikhs believe in karma, or moral cause and effect. They value hospitality to all, regardless of religion, and oppose caste distinctions. Sikhs delineate a series of five stages that move upward to gurmukh, total devotion to God. This service is called Seva. Sahaj, or tranquility, is practiced as a means of being united with God as well as of generating external good will. Sikhs are not in favor of external routines of religion; they may stop in their temple whenever it is convenient during the day.

Sikhism does not include a belief in the afterlife. Instead, the soul is believed to be reincarnated in successive lives and deaths, a belief borrowed from Hinduism. The goal is then to break this karmic cycle, and to merge the human spirit with that of God.

Sacred Text

The Guru Granth Sahib (also referred to as the Aad Guru Granth Sahib, or AGGS), composed of Adi Granth, meaning First Book, is the holy scripture of Sikhism. It is a collection of religious poetry that is meant to be sung. Called shabads, they were composed by the first five gurus, the ninth guru, and thirty-six additional holy men of northern India. Sikhs always show honor to the Guru Granth Sahib by carrying it above the head when in a procession.

A second major text is the Dasam Granth, or Tenth Book, created by followers of Guru Gobind Singh, the tenth guru. Much of it is devoted to retelling the Hindu stories of Krishna and Rama. Those who are allowed to read and care for the Granth Sahib are known as granthi. Granthi may also look after the gurdwara, or temple. In the gurdwara, the book rests on a throne with a wooden base and cushions covered in cloths placed in a prescribed order. If the book is not in use, it is covered with a cloth known as a rumala. When the book is read, a fan called a chauri is fanned over it as a sign of respect, just as followers of the gurus fanned them with chauris. At Amritsar, a city in northwestern India that houses the Golden Temple, the Guru Granth Sahib is carried on a palanquin (a covered, carried bed). If it is carried in the city, a kettle drum is struck and people welcome it by tossing rose petals.

Major Figures

Guru Nanak (1469–1539) is the founder of Sikhism. He was followed by nine other teachers, and collectively they are known as the Ten Gurus. Each of them was chosen by his predecessor and was thought to share the same spirit of that previous guru. Guru Arjan (1581–1606), the fifth guru, oversaw completion of the Golden Temple in Amritsar, India. Guru Gobind Singh (1675–1708) was the tenth and last human guru. He decreed that the True Guru henceforth would be the Granth Sahib, the scripture of the Sikhs. He also founded the Khalsa, originally a military order of male Sikhs willing to die for the faith; the term is now used to refer to all baptized Sikhs.

Major Holy Sites

Amritsar, India, is the holy city of Sikhism. Construction of the city began under Guru Ram Das (1574–1581), the fourth guru, during the 1570s. One legend says that the Muslim ruler, Emperor Akbar, gave the land to the third guru, Guru Amar Das (1552–74). Whether or not that is true, Amar Das did establish the location of Amritsar. He chose a site near a pool believed to hold healing water.

When construction of the Golden Temple began, only a small town existed. One legend says that a Muslim saint from Lahore, India, named Mian Mir laid the foundation stone of the first temple. It has been demolished and rebuilt three times. Although pilgrimage is not required of Sikhs, many come to see the shrines and the Golden Temple. They call it Harmandir Sahib, God's Temple, or Darbar Sahib, the Lord's Court. When the temple was completed during the tenure of the fifth guru, Arjan, he placed the first copy of the Guru Granth Sahib inside.

Every Sikh temple has a free kitchen attached to it, called a langar. After services, all people, regardless of caste or standing within the community, sit on the floor in a straight line and eat a simple vegetarian meal together. As a pilgrimage site, the langar serves 30,000–40,000 people daily, with more coming on Sundays and festival days. About forty volunteers work in the kitchen each day.

Major Rites & Celebrations

In addition to the community feasts at temple langars, Sikhs honor four rites of passage in a person's life: naming, marriage, initiation in Khalsa (pure) through the Amrit ceremony, and death.

There are eight major celebrations and several other minor ones in Sikhism. Half of them commemorate events in the lives of the ten gurus.

The others are Baisakhi, the new year festival; Diwali, the festival of light, which Hindus also celebrate; Hola Mahalla, which Gobind Singh created as an alternative to the Hindu festival of Holi, and which involves military parades; and the installing of the Guru Granth Sahib.

ORIGINS

History & Geography

The founder of Sikhism, Nanak, was born in 1469 CE in the Punjab region of northeast India, where both Hinduism and Islam were practiced. Both of these religions wanted control of the region. Nanak wanted the fighting between followers of these two traditions to end and looked for solutions to the violence.

Nanak blended elements of both religions and also combined the traditional apparel of both faiths to construct his clothing style. The Guru Granth Sahib further explains the division between Sikhs and the Islamic and Muslim faiths:

Nanak would become the first guru of the Sikh religion, known as Guru Nanak Dev. A Muslim musician named Bhai Mardana, considered the first follower, accompanied Nanak in his travels around India and Asia. Guru Nanak often sang, and singing remains an important part of worship for Sikhs. Before his death, Nanak renamed one of his disciples Angad, a word meaning "a part of his own self." He became Guru Angad Dev, the second guru, thus beginning the tradition of designating a successor and passing on the light to that person.

Guru Baba Ram Das, the fourth guru, who lived in the sixteenth century, began constructing Amritsar's Golden Temple. The structure was completed by his successor, Guru Arjan Dev, who also collected poems and songs written by the first four gurus and added his own. He included the work of Kabir and other Hindu and Muslim holy men as well. This became the Adi Granth, which he placed in the Golden Temple.

Guru Arjan was martyred in 1606 by Jehangir, the Muslim emperor. His son Hargobind became the sixth guru and introduced several important practices and changes. He wore two swords, representing both spiritual and worldly authority. Near the Golden Temple he had a building known as Akal Takht, or Throne of the Almighty, erected. In it was a court of justice as well as a group of administrators. Even today, orders and decisions enter the community from Akal Takht. Guru Hargobind was the last of the gurus with a direct link to Amritsar. Because of conflict with the Muslim rulers, he and all subsequent gurus moved from the city.

The tenth guru, Gobind Singh, created the Khalsa, the Community of the Pure, in 1699. The members of the Khalsa were to be known by five distinctive elements, all beginning with the letter *k*. These include kes, the refusal to cut the hair or trim the beard; kangha, the comb used to keep the long hair neatly combed in contrast to the Hindu ascetics who had matted hair; kaccha, shorts that would allow soldiers quick movement; kara, a thin steel bracelet worn to symbolize restraint; and kirpan, a short sword not to be used except in self-defense. Among other duties, members of this elite group were to defend the faith. Until the middle of the nineteenth century, when the British created an empire in India, the Khalsa remained largely undefeated.

In 1708, Guru Gobind Singh announced that he would be the final human guru. All subsequent leadership would come from the Guru Granth Sahib, now considered a living guru, the holy text Arjan had begun compiling more than a century earlier.

Muslim persecution under the Mughals led to the defeat of the Sikhs in 1716. The remaining Sikhs headed for the hills, re-emerging after decline of Mughal power. They were united under Ranjit Singh's kingdom from 1820 to 1839. They then came under the control of the British.

The British annexed the Punjab region, making it part of their Indian empire in 1849, and recruited Sikhs to serve in the army. The Sikhs remained loyal to the British during the Indian Mutiny of 1857–1858. As a result, they were given many privileges and land grants, and with

peace and prosperity, the first Singh Sabha was founded in 1873. This was an educational and religious reform movement.

During the early twentieth century, Sikhism was shaped in its more modern form. A group known as the Tat Khalsa, which was more progressive, became the dominant way of understanding the faith.

In 1897, a group of Sikh musicians within the British Army was invited to attend the Diamond Jubilee of Queen Victoria in England. They also traveled to Canada and were attracted by the nation's prairies, which were perfect for farming. The first group of Sikhs came to Canada soon after. By 1904, more than two hundred Sikhs had settled in British Columbia. Some of them later headed south to Washington, Oregon, and California in the United States. The first Sikh gurdwara in the United States was constructed in Stockton, California, in 1912. Sikhs became farmers, worked in lumber mills, and helped to construct the Western Pacific railroad. Yuba City, California, has one of the world's largest Sikh temples, built in 1968.

Sikh troops fought for Britain in World War I, achieving distinction. Following the war, in 1919, however, the British denied the Sikhs the right to gather for their New Year festival. When the Sikhs disobeyed, the British troops fired without warning on 10,000 Sikhs, 400 of whom were killed. This became known as the first Amritsar Massacre.

The British government in 1925 did give the Sikhs the right to help manage their own shrines. A fragile peace ensued between the British and the Sikhs, who again fought for the British Empire during World War II.

After the war ended, the Sikh hope for an independent state was dashed by the partition of India and Pakistan in 1947. Pakistan was in the Punjab region; thus, 2.5 million Sikhs lived in a Muslim country where they were not welcome. Many of them became part of the mass internal migration that followed Indian independence.

In 1966, a state with a Sikh majority came into existence after Punjab boundaries were redrawn. Strife continued throughout second half of twentieth century, however, as a result of continuing demands for Punjab autonomy. A second massacre at Amritsar occurred in 1984, resulting in the death of 450 Sikhs (though some estimates of the death toll are higher). Indian troops, under orders from Indian Prime Minister Indira Gandhi, fired on militant leaders of Sikhs, who had gone to the Golden Temple for refuge. This attack was considered a desecration of a sacred place, and the prime minister was later assassinated by her Sikh bodyguards in response. Restoration of the Akal Takht, the administrative headquarters, took fifteen years. The Sikh library was also burned, consuming ancient manuscripts.

In 1999, Sikhs celebrated the three-hundredth anniversary of the founding of Khalsa. There has been relative peace in India since that event. In the United States, however, Sikhs became the object of slander and physical attack following the acts of terrorism on September 11, 2001, as some Americans could not differentiate between Arab head coverings and Sikh turbans.

Founder or Major Prophet

Guru Nanak Dev was born into a Hindu family on April 15, 1469. His family belonged to the merchant caste, Khatri. His father worked as an accountant for a Muslim, who was also a local landlord. Nanak was educated in both the Hindu and Islamic traditions. According to legends, his teachers soon realized they had nothing further to teach him. After a direct revelation from Ultimate Reality that he received as a young man, Nanak proclaimed that there was neither Muslim nor Hindu. God had told Nanak "Rejoice in my Name," which became a central doctrine of Sikhism.

Nanak began to preach, leaving his wife and two sons behind. According to tradition, he traveled not only throughout India, but also eventually to Iraq, Saudi Arabia, and Mecca. This tradition and others were collected in a volume known as Janamsakhis. A Muslim servant of the family, Mardana, who also played a three-stringed musical instrument called the rebec, accompanied him, as did a Hindu poet, Bala Sandhu, who had been a friend from childhood

(though the extent of his importance or existence is often considered controversial).

Nanak traveled as an itinerant preacher for a quarter century and then founded a village, Kartarpur, on the bank of Punjab's Ravi River. Before his death he chose his successor, beginning a tradition that was followed until the tenth and final human guru.

Philosophical Basis

When Guru Nanak Dev, the first guru, began preaching in 1499 at about age thirty, he incorporated aspects of both Hinduism and Islam. From Hinduism, he took the ideas of karma and reincarnation. From Islam, he borrowed the Ultimate as the name of God. Some scholars see the influence of the religious reformer and poet Kabir, who lived from 1440 until 1518. Kabir merged the Bhakti (devotional) side of Hinduism with the Islamic Sufis, who were mystics.

Within the Hindu tradition in northern India was a branch called the Sants. The Sants believed that God was both with form and without form, unable to be represented concretely. Most of the Sants were illiterate and poor, but created poems that spoke of the divine being experienced in all things. This idea also rooted itself in Sikhism.

Guru Nanak Dev, who was raised as a Hindu, rejected the caste system in favor of equality of all persons. He also upheld the value of women, rejecting the burning of widows and female infanticide. When eating a communal meal, first begun as a protest against caste, everyone sits in a straight line and shares karah prasad (a pudding), which is provided by those of all castes. However, Sikhs are expected to marry within their caste. In some cases, especially in the United Kingdom, gurdwaras (places of worship) for a particular caste exist.

Holy Places

Amritsar, especially the Golden Temple, which was built in the sixteenth century under the supervision of the fifth guru, Guru Arjan, is the most sacred city.

Ram Das, the fourth guru, first began constructing a pool on the site in 1577. He called it

Amritsar, the pool of nectar. This sacred reflecting pool is a pilgrimage destination. Steps on the southern side of the pool allow visitors to gather water in bottles, to drink it, to bathe in it, or to sprinkle it on themselves.

SIKHISM IN DEPTH

Sacred Symbols

The khanda is the major symbol of Sikhism. It features a two-edged sword, representing justice and freedom, in the center. It is surrounded by a circle, a symbol of both balance and of the unity of God and humankind. A pair of curved swords (kirpans) surrounds the circle. One sword stands for religious concerns, the other for secular concerns. The khanda appears on Sikh flags, which are flown over every temple.

Members of the Khalsa have five symbols. They do not cut their hair, and men do not trim their beards. This symbol, kes, is to indicate a harmony with the ways of nature. To keep the long hair neat, a comb called a kangha is used. The third symbol is the kara, a bracelet usually made of steel to represent continuity and strength. When the Khalsa was first formed, soldiers wore loose-fitting shorts called kaccha. They were worn to symbolize moral restraint and purity. The final symbol is a short sword known as a kirpan, to be used only in self-defense. When bathing in sacred waters, the kirpan is tucked into the turban, which is worn to cover the long hair. The turban, which may be one of many colors, is wound from nearly five yards of cloth.

Sacred Practices & Gestures

Sikhs use Sat Sri Akal (truth is timeless) as a greeting, putting hands together and bowing toward the other person. To show respect, Sikhs keep their heads covered with a turban or veil. Before entering a temple, they remove their shoes. Some Sikhs may choose to wear a bindhi, the dot on the forehead usually associated with Hinduism.

When Guru Gobind Singh initiated the first men into the Khalsa, he put water in a steel bowl and added sugar, stirring the mixture with his sword and reciting verses from the Guru Granth as he did so. He thus created amrit (immortal), a holy water also used in baptism, or the Amrit ceremony. The water represents mental clarity, while sugar stands for sweetness. The sword invokes military courage, and the chanting of verses brings a poetic spirituality.

The Sikh ideal of bringing Ultimate Reality into every aspect of the day is expressed in prayers throughout the day. Daily morning prayer (Bani) consists of five different verses, most of them the work of one of the ten gurus; there are also two sets of evening prayers. Throughout the day, Sikhs repeat the Mul Mantra, "Ikk Oan Kar" (There is one Being). This is the first line of a brief creedal statement about Ultimate Reality.

Food Restrictions

Sikhs are not to eat halal meat, which is the Muslim equivalent of kosher. Both tobacco and alcohol are forbidden. Many Sikhs are vegetarians, although this is not commanded. Members of the Khalsa are not permitted to eat meat slaughtered according to Islamic or Hindu methods, because they believe these means cause pain to the animal.

Rites, Celebrations, & Services

The Sikhs observe four rite of passage rituals, with each emphasizing their distinction from the Hindu traditions. After a new mother is able to get up and bathe, the new baby is given a birth and naming ceremony in the gurdwara. The child is given a name based on the first letter of hymn from the Guru Granth Sahib at random. All males are additionally given the name Singh (lion); all females also receive the name Kaur (princess).

The marriage ceremony (anand karaj) is the second rite of passage. Rather than circle a sacred fire as the Hindus do, the Sikh couple walks four times around a copy of the Guru Granth Sahib, accompanied by singing. The bride often wears red, a traditional color for the Punjabi.

The amrit initiation into the Khalsa is considered the most important rite. It need not take place in a temple, but does require that five

Sikhs who are already Khalsa members conduct the ceremony. Amrit initiation may occur any time after a child is old enough to read the Guru Granth and understand the tenets of the faith. Some people, however, wait until their own children are grown before accepting this rite.

The funeral rite is the fourth and final rite of passage. A section of the Guru Granth is read. The body, dressed in the Five "K's," is cremated soon after death.

Initiation into the Khalsa is now open to both men and women. The earliest gurus opposed the Hindu custom of sati, which required a widow to be burned on her husband's funeral pyre. They were also against the Islamic custom of purdah, which required women to be veiled and covered in public. Women who are menstruating are not excluded from worship, as they are in some religions. Women as well as men can be leaders of the congregation and are permitted to read from the Guru Granth and recite sacred hymns.

The Sikh houses of worship are known as gurdwaras and include a langar, the communal dining area. People remove their shoes and cover their heads before entering. They touch their foreheads to the floor in front of the scripture to show respect. The service itself is in three parts. The first segment is Kirtan, singing hymns (kirtans) accompanied by musical instruments, which can last for several hours. It is followed by a set prayer called the Ardas, which has three parts. The first and final sections cannot be altered. In the first, the virtues of the gurus are extolled. In the last, the divine name is honored. In the center of the Ardas is a list of the Khalsa's troubles and victories, which a prayer leader recites in segments and to which the congregation responds with Vahiguru, considered a word for God. At the end of the service, members eat karah prasad, sacred food made of raw sugar, clarified butter, and coarse wheat flour. They then adjourn for a communal meal, Langar, the third section of worship.

Sikhism does not have a set day for worship similar to the Jewish Sabbath or Christian Sunday worship. However, the first day of the month on the Indian lunar calendar, sangrand, and the darkest night of the month, masia, are considered special days. Sangrand is a time for praying for the entire month. Masia is often considered an auspicious time for bathing in the holy pool at the temple.

Four of the major festivals that Sikhs observe surround important events in the lives of the gurus. These are known as gurpurabs, or anniversaries. Guru Nanak's birthday, Guru Gobind Singh's birthday, and the martyrdoms of the Gurus Arjan and Tegh Bahadur comprise the four main gurpurabs. Sikhs congregate in the gurudwaras to hear readings of the Guru Granth and lectures by Sikh scholars.

Baisakhi is the Indian New Year, the final day before the harvest begins. On this day in 1699, Guru Gobind Singh formed the first Khalsa, adding even more importance to the day for Sikhs. Each year, a new Sikh flag is placed at all temples.

Diwali, based on a word meaning string of lights, is a Hindu festival. For Sikhs, it is a time to remember the return of the sixth guru, Hargobind, to Amritsar after the emperor had imprisoned him. It is celebrated for three days at the Golden Temple. Sikhs paint and whitewash their houses and decorate them with candles and earthenware lamps.

Hola Mohalla, meaning attack and place of attack, is the Sikh spring festival, which corresponds to the Hindu festival Holi. It is also a three-day celebration and a time for training Sikhs as soldiers. Originally, it involved military exercises and mock battles, as well as competitions in archery, horsemanship, and wrestling. In contemporary times, the festival includes athletic contests, discussion, and singing.

Judy A. Johnson, MTS

Bibliography

Barnes, Trevor. *The Kingfisher Book of Religions.* New York: Kingfisher, 1999. Print.

Dhanjal, Beryl. *Amritsar.* New York: Dillon, 1993. Print.

Dhavan, Purnima. *When Sparrows Became Hawks: The Making of the Sikh Warrior Tradition, 1699–1799.* Oxford: Oxford UP, 2011. Print.

Eraly, Abraham, et. al. *India*. New York: DK, 2008. Print.

Harley, Gail M. *Hindu and Sikh Faiths in America*. New York: Facts on File, 2003. Print.

Jakobsh, Doris R. *Sikhism and Women: History, Texts, and Experience*. Oxford, New York: Oxford UP, 2010. Print.

Jhutti-Johal, Jagbir. *Sikhism Today*. London, New York: Continuum, 2011. Print.

Langley, Myrtle. *Religion*. New York: Knopf, 1996. Print.

Mann, Gurinder Singh. *Sikhism*. Upper Saddle River: Prentice, 2004. Print.

Meredith, Susan. *The Usborne Book of World Religions*. London: Usborne, 1995. Print.

Sidhu, Dawinder S. and Neha Singh Gohil. *Civil Rights in Wartime: The Post-9/11 Sikh Experience*. Ashgate, 2009. E-book.

Singh, Nikky-Guninder Kaur. *Sikhism*. New York: Facts on File, 1993. Print.

Singh, Nikky-Guninder Kaur. *Sikhism: An Introduction*. Tauris, 2011. E-book.

Singh, Surinder. *Introduction to Sikhism and Great Sikhs of the World*. Gurgaon: Shubhi, 2012. Print.

Wilkinson, Philip. *Religions*. New York: DK, 2008. Print.

Index